# Internet Marketing
## *Foundations and Applications*

**Carolyn Siegel**
EASTERN KENTUCKY UNIVERSITY

Houghton Mifflin Company
*Boston    New York*

*To Malcolm*

Editor-in-Chief: George T. Hoffman
Technology Manager/Development Editor: Damaris R. Curran
Assistant Editor: Julia Perez
Associate Project Editor: Kate Hartke
Editorial Assistant: May Jawdat
Senior Production/Design Coordinator: Sarah Ambrose
Senior Manufacturing Coordinator: Priscilla Bailey
Marketing Manager: Steven W. Mikels

Cover image: Jacey–Debut Art

Printed in the U.S.A.

Library of Congress Control Number: 2001133344

ISBN: 0-618-15043-9

123456789—DOC—07 06 05 04 03

# Contents

## Chapter 3   *Buyers and Online Behaviors*  50

## Chapter 4   *Sellers Marketing Online*  74

## Chapter 5   *Legal and Ethical Issues; Privacy and Security*  99

## Chapter 6   *The International Environment of Internet Marketing*  128

## MODULE II INFORMATION FOR COMPETITIVE MARKETING ADVANTAGE  157

## Chapter 7   *Internet Marketing Research*  158

## Chapter 12  *The Promotion Mix*  308

## MODULE IV  INTERNET MARKETING ACTION PLANS  341

## Chapter 13  *The Web Marketing Plan*  342

## Chapter 14    *Marketing Site Development: Content, Design, and Construction*  361

Within a remarkably short time, the Internet and World Wide Web have profoundly influenced the way we live, work, learn, and play. The pace of change has been exhilarating and, at times, unsettling. Marketing is leading the way in finding profitable applications for the Internet and Web—developing unique synergies, achieving operating efficiencies, serving existing customers more effectively, and searching out new online customers domestically and worldwide. Internet marketers are challenging traditional practices, models, and relationships. They are rewriting the book on how marketing can be practiced in the early 21st century.

## *Purpose of the Book*

There has never been a better time in the history of contemporary business to be teaching marketing. Yet at the same time, keeping up with the rapidly shifting environment makes teaching Internet marketing an intimidating task. That's why this textbook was written. It presents Internet marketing in a familiar pedagogical framework that is readily accessible to instructors and students. It fully integrates the streamlined printed book with comprehensive, interactive instructor and student web sites.

The book is targeted at college and university classes at the undergraduate level, but can be used in graduate classes or read by individuals curious about Internet marketing. It is appropriate for large lecture-size classes, as well as for small, hands-on applications-oriented sections. The format accommodates semester and quarter time frames, and can be used for online classes. The book and web site offer a large number of suggested activities and projects that can be assigned as homework or completed during class in computer classrooms. They include individual and team projects, debate topics, and case studies. Many take a short time to complete, others are longer and more complex, and some are term-long culminating activities.

## *Features of the Book*

The textbook introduces foundation Internet marketing concepts and applications and provides many examples of real world Internet marketing successes and failures. Textbook and web site materials are organized around a framework of four modules and associated chapters.

## TEXT CONTENT AND ORGANIZATION

*Chapter 1, The Internet: Past and Present,* defines Internet marketing and electronic commerce, and establishes similarities and differences with traditional marketing. It develops links from the Internet's past, showing how mankind's passion for communication, numeration, and industrialization led to innovations and discoveries that were essential to the Internet's creation. It establishes links to the Internet's present, explains how it was created and initially operated, and provides reasons why the release of the World Wide Web stimulated Internet commercialization. The chapter concludes by discussing effects of the Internet economy on business and society, and provides an initial look at how the Internet is changing society.

*Chapter 2, Internet Operations, Management, and Access,* begins with a brief explanation of how the Internet works and why it operates so smoothly, even though no single entity, government, or organization governs it. Attributes that make the World Wide Web so conducive to marketing activities are discussed. The chapter wraps up by introducing some important recent technologies and explaining how they are affecting the Internet and the consumers and enterprises that rely on it. They include Net-enabled automobiles, I-wired homes and appliances, web kiosks, wireless access, and mobile Internet marketing (m-marketing).

*Chapter 3, Buyers and Online Behaviors,* focuses on the types of buyers that are online and their distinguishing characteristics. It explores what buyers are doing online, which leads to a discussion of who's not online and why. Other types of behaviors that occur online, like anti-corporate activism, or behaviors that result from excessive Internet use, particularly social isolation and addictive behaviors, are presented within the context of why they concern Internet marketers.

*Chapter 4, Sellers Marketing Online,* explains how businesses are using the Internet and Web to market their products effectively. Next, the discussion widens to include other enterprises, particularly governments and non-profits, using online marketing to meet their goals. It presents examples of how individual sellers are using Internet marketing and describes external environmental factors that influence Internet marketing activities. These include the economic environment, technology, the social/cultural and natural environments, and government and legal factors.

*Chapter 5, Legal and Ethical Issues; Privacy and Security,* explains why Internet laws and jurisdiction are in such a state of flux and what remedies are being attempted. Internet marketers are confronted by important legal issues of jurisdiction, enforcement, taxation, privacy, and security. Ethical marketing behaviors are highlighted and the question of whether ethical marketing behaviors can be enforced on the Internet is debated. The chapter concludes with a discussion of online security problems and why they are of such pressing concern to buyers and sellers.

*Chapter 6, The International Environment of Internet Marketing,* discusses how international orientation affects Internet marketing strategy. It explains why marketing internationally is more complex than solely domestic Internet marketing. The current status of major international Internet markets are described. International issues that concern Internet marketers are identified and explained. This chapter is unique in that few Internet marketing textbooks examine the international environment at this depth, despite the fact that the majority of Internet users are from countries outside North America.

***Chapter 7, Internet Marketing Research,*** emphasizes the importance of information and data tools to Internet marketing, identifies applied Internet marketing research methods, and discusses what they can do for online marketers. Primary marketing research methods that are used online are described and contrasted with their offline equivalents, including online focus groups, surveys, simulations, and observation. The synergy between offline/online research is pointed out. Evidence is provided to support calling the Internet a marketing research secondary source *gold mine*. Issues that concern Internet marketing researchers are presented.

***Chapter 8, Operational Data Tools,*** emphasizes the growing importance of collaboration between Internet marketers and information technology professionals. It presents database basics and explains how they benefit Internet marketing and are becoming essential even to small and mid-size enterprises marketing online. It explores how databases, data warehouses, and data mining are operational marketing tools, describes privacy-sensitive techniques used to develop consumer profiles, and discusses the importance of the marketing intelligence process and how it is conducted online.

***Chapter 9, Products and Brands,*** begins the discussion of the Internet Marketing Mix. It explains how the characteristics of products affect how they are marketed online. It identifies consumer products best suited to online marketing and describes how enterprise products are sold and developed online. The chapter concludes with a discussion of why Internet branding is so important and presents examples of how it can be accomplished.

***Chapter 10, Price,*** identifies factors that affect how Internet prices are set. Internet price issues that concern consumers and enterprises are presented along with alternate Internet pricing models. Examples are given of the effects of online price transparency. It considers why some price strategies are successful online and others are not, and examines Internet payment alternatives for how buyers can pay for products online.

***Chapter 11, Place,*** classifies online distribution (place) activities and explains how they are influenced by the Internet environment. It identifies online place issues that concern Internet marketers and characterizes successful online consumer channel strategies and the reasons for their success. Disintermediation and reintermediation are presented. Customer Relationship Management (eCRM) is introduced with an explanation of how it can be used to meet buyer expectations and establish long term relationships, along with problems and cautions that highlight its shortcomings.

***Chapter 12, The Promotion Mix,*** identifies how marketing promotion is affected by the Internet and what online promotion issues concern Internet marketers and why. This includes spam (unsolicited commercial e-mail) and intrusive Web advertising such as persistent pop-ups and pop-unders (pop-behinds), and floating animation. The chapter deals at length with online advertising strategies and discusses why some are successful while others are not. Many examples are provided. The chapter concludes with an analysis of how sales promotions and permission marketing can be used effectively online.

***Chapter 13, The Web Marketing Plan,*** introduces web marketing planning and identifies what should be included in a plan and why. It emphasizes the value of marketing planning and writing a marketing plan. Web marketing plan implementation and control are discussed, along with the role of a web marketing budget. An example of web marketing planning in a small business is developed throughout the chapter.

*Chapter 14, Marketing Site Development: Content, Design, and Construction,* examines issues that must be considered prior to web site development, particularly as they focus on site content, design, and construction, including usability. It describes how web site content and design advance site goals, and explains the impact of construction issues on web site effectiveness.

## CHAPTER PEDAGOGY

- *Format:* Streamlined organization of modules and chapters follows a familiar pedagogical framework that is readily accessible to instructors and students.
- *Opening Vignette:* Each chapter begins with a brief scenario that illustrates major issues within the chapter.
- *Key Glossary Terms:* Important terms in each chapter are identified in bold and definitions are highlighted in the margin for easy reference.
- *Topic Updates:* Web icons found in each chapter direct students and instructors to updated information and expanded learning opportunities on the student web site.
- *Concept Check Questions:* Three concept check questions for each major topic in every chapter are useful tools for students to self-check their understanding of what they have read. Questions can be used for quizzes and to stimulate class discussion.
- *End-of-Chapter Review Questions:* Each chapter concludes with 15 self-test questions.
- *Chapter Summary Statements:* Summaries for each main chapter topic are helpful when students review for quizzes and exams.
- *Internet Marketing Application:* Each chapter has a hands-on Internet marketing application activity for students to use the Internet to illustrate key chapter concepts.
- *Web Site Links:* Web sites used in each chapter are identified by their web address (URL).
- *Concluding Case Study:* Each chapter has a closing case, followed by a student activity application (Check It Out) and an international component (A Global View).
- *International Orientation:* An international orientation is emphasized throughout the book, in addition to the international Internet marketing chapter. Many examples are used to reflect this emphasis.
- *Internet Marketing Ethics:* Ethical issues that confront Internet marketers are identified and discussed throughout the text.
- *Appendices:* Appendices, found only at the student web site, are extremely student-centered and include URL Citation Style Guides, Evaluating Online Sources, Online Information Search and Retrieval, Internet Marketing Careers, and Creating a Web Page.
- *PowerPoint Slides:* Slides were created for each chapter to emphasize key points and are found on the instructor web site.

# A Fully-Integrated Package

Given the rapid pace of change, teaching Internet marketing can become a full-time job. That is why the supporting materials are so important to this book. The instructor and student web sites, the Instructor's Resource Manual with Test Bank, and other supporting materials were developed by the author and tested by her undergraduate and MBA Internet marketing students. The web site is maintained by the author, who is committed to keeping it current, relevant, and useful.

## INSTRUCTOR WEB SITE

The instructor web site is closely integrated with the textbook and uses the same format of modules and chapters as the book. The site is easily accessed, logically organized, easy to use, and rich in information and additional materials that aid instructors in keeping their Internet marketing courses current and interesting. It includes such resources as Ask Dr. Siegel, an online instructor resource manual, and PowerPoint slides. This site is maintained and frequently updated by the author.

## STUDENT WEB SITE

The student web site is an extension of the textbook and, like the instructor web site, uses the same format of modules and chapters as the book and is maintained and frequently updated by the author. The student site includes the textbook appendices with hotlinks to web sites, the complete glossary and flashcards, web updates, web links, ready notes, chapter outlines, chapter abstracts and learning objectives, and a resource center.

## INSTRUCTOR'S RESOURCE MANUAL WITH TEST BANK

Available online as well as in print, the Instructor's Resource Manual with Test Bank includes a Sample Syllabus, Chapter Abstracts, Chapter Outlines, Teaching Notes, Internet Marketing Applications, Suggested Answers, Web Updates, Mini-Case Notes, and the Test Bank.

# Acknowledgments

Writing a textbook represents an enormous commitment. It's not the work of one person, although any shortcomings are the author's sole responsibility. The staff at Houghton Mifflin who worked so closely with me, particularly Editor-in-Chief George Hoffman, Technology Manager/Development Editor Damaris Curran, and Project Editor Kate Hartke, deserve great credit for their professionalism, understanding, and tireless efforts guiding this book from concept to reality. Words cannot express my appreciation for their support and expertise. Thanks are also due to an outstanding group of colleagues whose comments and advice were extremely helpful. They include Sridhar Balasubramanian, University of Texas; Charlene Barker, Spokane Falls Community College; Paul Dowling, University of Utah; Larry Goldstein, Iona College; Cheryl Gruse, DeVry College of Technology—Pomona; Linda Ferrell, University of Northern Colorado; Theresa B. Flaherty, Old Dominion University; J. Morgan Jones, University of North Carolina; Jay Lambe, Virginia Tech; Carla Meeske, University of Oregon; Mohan Menon, University of South Alabama;

George Milne, University of Massachusetts; Robert Moore, Mississippi State University; Deborah Moscardelli, Central Michigan University; Gillian Rice, Thunderbird College; Murph Sewall, University of Connecticut; Judith Spain and Norbert Elbert, Eastern Kentucky University; Fred Tennant, Webster University; and E. Sonny Butler, Georgia Southern University. I would also like to thank my students who inspired me to undertake this project. Over the past decade, they have tested the format of this book, its web site, and projects many times over. Their input was critical to keeping everything clear, accessible, and student-centered. Thank you, one and all.

Finally, while writing this book has been a joyous task in many respects, it has also been extraordinarily intense and time-consuming. It could never have been finished without the complete and unselfish encouragement of my husband, Malcolm. Your love has given me the confidence to undertake a project of this scope. Thanks also to Erik, Mark, and Stacey for making me a more patient, understanding person, and Taffy for being the best four-legged companion ever, particularly on those long nights when I worked and she dozed until dawn.

# Module I

# An Introduction to the Internet and the Environment of Internet Marketing

For most people, the Internet invaded their consciousness almost without warning. Before the early 1990s, few people other than scientists, researchers, academics, and the military were even aware of the Internet. The online world they used was black and white, with text and data transmitted in a noncommercial environment. The World Wide Web, the Internet's graphical service, was released in the winter of 1991–1992. Powerful user-friendly graphical browsers appeared in 1993 and quickly captured the public's imagination. Within five years, hundreds of millions of people worldwide, from toddlers to seniors, were online communicating with friends and family, searching for information, playing games, and shopping in an environment rich in pictures, animation, colors, and sounds. Commercialization brought marketers online and today, Internet marketing occurs around the world and is taught in a growing number of colleges and universities in the United States and abroad.

This book recognizes the breadth of Internet marketing and the importance of presenting it within the context of the greater Internet economy. In this economy, developments in electronic commerce and advances in information technology, as well as environmental factors beyond marketers' control, directly affect Internet marketing. It is also influenced by events in the past, which often have parallels in the present and sometimes provide insights into the future. Module I examines some of the important events and inventions that led to the Internet's creation, particularly in communication, numeracy, and industrialization. It explains how the Internet works and is managed, as well as which buyers and sellers are online and what they are doing. The final chapters in Module I examine environmental factors that affect the Internet and Internet marketing. Together, these chapters develop a foundation for the discussion of Internet marketing models and the effective use of the marketing mix.

## CHAPTER ONE

# The Internet: Past and Present

**LEARNING OBJECTIVES**

- To develop a marketing perspective in the Internet age, defining the activities of Internet marketing and electronic commerce, and comparing Internet and traditional marketing

- To examine links from the Internet's past, exploring how humans' passion for communication, numeration, and industrialization paved the way for the creation of the Internet

- To examine links to the Internet's present, exploring how it was created and initially operated, and how the World Wide Web stimulated Internet commercialization

- To identify current effects of the Internet economy on business and society, and glimpse how the Internet is changing the way we work, live, and play

## Sandy Goes Online

Sandy, a tax accountant, arrives home after a long day at the office to find a card in the mail from a college roommate announcing the birth of her first child. Sandy wants to send a special gift for the baby but knows she won't have time to go shopping until tax season ends. Then she remembers the beautiful baby quilt from Lands' End her sister received as a gift for her first child. Sandy turns on her personal computer, dials up her local Internet service provider (ISP), and logs onto the Internet's **World Wide Web (WWW, Web, W3)**. Once online, she clicks her **bookmark** for Lands' End and links to the company's web site (*http://www.landsend.com*). Sandy types "baby quilt" in the *Find a Product* box on the company's home page and clicks *enter*. A product page with an Infant Star Quilt and a Two by Two Crib Quilt appears on her computer screen. If she'd had problems or questions, she could have clicked on the *Lands' End Live* button to talk in real time to a salesperson. After examining pictures of both products, Sandy decides to purchase the Star Quilt. She copies the item number and the Lands' End toll-free telephone number, then logs off. Although Sandy frequently goes online to look for products, she still places her orders offline the old-fashioned way, by telephone.

**World Wide Web (WWW, Web, W3)**
Media-rich information system that operates on the Internet and where most commercialization is happening.

Sandy went **online** with her brand choice (Lands' End) and product type (baby crib quilt) already decided. Other people access the Internet with far less direction, for other reasons, to fill different needs. What they have in common is the *opportunity* to access the Internet, a *willingness* to go online, and the *ability* to work, play, and learn in a dynamic electronically mediated environment.

Sandy likes to window-shop on the Web, but she still has reservations about using a credit card for online purchases. Even so, Sandy increasingly uses the Internet to satisfy many of her needs. She sends email messages to family and friends, browses online stores, searches for information, downloads music, and when she has time, visits a chat room where women professionals have created a virtual community for networking and sharing business experiences.

What is the **Internet?** It is the world's largest network of interconnected (internetted) distributed computer networks. All computers and computer networks operating on the Internet must agree to use TCP/IP protocols. These communication standards allow seamless communication and data transmission across great distances in real time by computers and devices with different operating systems.

> Here and now begins a new era in the history of the world, and you can say you were there.
> *Johann Wolfgang von Goethe (1749–1832), German poet, novelist, dramatist, scientist.*[1]

Commercial activity is accelerating on the Internet and in businesses building out the Internet's physical infrastructure. Considering that Web commercialization began in 1993, the Internet's impact is remarkable. Many people believe a new revolutionary era in the human history of the world has begun; others dispute this view. If the Internet is *revolutionary*, it will trigger radical changes in how marketing and business are conducted. If it is *evolutionary*, then many current marketing and business practices will quickly adapt to this different but still familiar **marketing** environment.

Chapter 1 begins building the foundation for studying Internet marketing. It provides some key definitions and examines how linkages to milestone events and inventions in the past cumulatively paved the way for the Internet's development and future. It considers how the Internet was created and the contributions of people whose vision and determination made it happen. Chapter 1 concludes with a look at the Internet economy and its effects on business and society.

## *A Marketing Perspective in the Internet Age*

Millions of people like Sandy have already made the Internet and World Wide Web part of their daily lives. The Internet has had a major impact in North America, Western Europe, and other parts of the world. This distributed worldwide telecommunications network is affecting marketing, and marketing is affecting Internet commercialization.

### MARKETING DEFINED

People frequently talk about marketing but often without understanding it or by dismissing it as *just selling.* But marketing is much more than that, although selling is an important and highly visible marketing activity. Marketing is a collection of activities that bring buyers and sellers together to make exchanges that satisfy and give value to all parties. Marketing is a profession, process, and practice. It has been taught as an academic discipline for more than half a century. It began long before that, with the development of processes designed to clear product surpluses from markets and help balance supply and demand.

Practically anything can be marketed, from tangible goods to ideas, causes, places, groups, people, entertainment, information, and services. Marketing is performed by enterprises and individuals. In many enterprises, everyone from the CEO to office clerks is considered part of the marketing team. In others, marketers perform discrete tasks. Marketers are suppliers, manufacturers, brand and product managers, distributors, wholesalers, retailers, promotion managers, salespeople, and others. Marketers

### Bookmark
A Web address (URL) stored on the user's browser in a listing of favorite sites readily accessible for future linking.

### Online
When users connect to an Internet provider or other connector and enter a network, an intranet, an extranet, or the Internet.

### Internet
World's largest matrix of interconnected computer networks.

### Marketing
Activities that bring buyers and sellers together so they can make exchanges that deliver satisfaction and value to all parties.

initiate, plan, implement, and control processes that take products through their life cycle, from development to new product launch, management, and eventual discontinuation. They seek to facilitate exchange by establishing profitable, satisfying, long-term relationships with customers. Customers (buyers) are personal use consumers like Sandy and enterprises of all types—businesses, organizations, educational institutions, governments, health care providers, and groups.

Marketers communicate information about products, negotiate exchanges, and transport, store, inventory, display, and transfer products to buyers. They gather information about markets and competitors, perform marketing research, and use the results to improve product offers. They promote products, price and sell them, and assume risks associated with exchange.

Marketers use an array of tools to accomplish their goals and facilitate exchange. These tools or marketing variables are referred to collectively as the 4Ps—product, price, place (distribution), and promotion. All are more or less controllable and adjustable and can be used by marketers to customize market offers. Over the years successive attempts to replace the 4Ps with alternative concepts have failed to gain widespread acceptance. Because the 4Ps are enduring and still valuable organizing concepts, they are used as organizing concepts in this book.

## INTERNET MARKETING

**Internet marketing (emarketing)**

Marketing in electronic environments, primarily on the Internet, World Wide Web, intranets, and extranets.

**Internet marketing,** or emarketing, is marketing in electronic environments primarily on the Internet, on one or more of its services (WWW, email), or offline by enterprises that produce and sell Internet-related products. Like traditional marketing, the goal is still to facilitate exchange, build long-term customer relationships, and create utility, which is the benefit or value received from marketing exchange. The focus is on the synergy created when traditional marketing is performed in electronic environments that reduce or greatly eliminate time and space constraints, facilitate personalization and customization, and allow the interoperability of computers and other devices.

Internet marketing delivers time, place, possession, and form utility. The potential for *time utility* is far greater online than off because web storefronts never close, information is available nonstop, and searches can be conducted anytime the visitor is connected. The Internet is a 24/7/365 environment—twenty-four hours a day, seven days a week, 365 days a year. People with connectivity and the ability to search for the products or information they need or want online benefit from *place utility.* Place utility is provided by entertainment, news, weather, software, and other virtual products that can be delivered directly from the Internet to the visitor's computer or wireless device. Online visitors have worldwide access to stores and content. They also have seamless access to delivery services for tangible products purchased online. Buyers can take possession of purchased products with their credit card or online payment alternative, which creates *possession utility.* They benefit from *form utility* when products are customized or made available in the desired assortments or quantities. The Internet facilitates customization on a scale that cannot be approached offline.

Internet marketing is performed by enterprises that operate exclusively on the Internet (clicks only) and by others that have both an online and offline presence (bricks and clicks). Marketing is taking place in the infrastructure segment, where the Internet is being physically built out, and through ecommerce, where intermediaries sell products provided by other businesses and manufacturers sell their own products. It

**Intranet**

A proprietary computer network that operates like the Internet, using TCP/IP protocols, but is closed to outside users and typically restricted to employees.

**Extranet**

Proprietary network that links several intranets and users.

occurs on **intranets,** proprietary (private) computer networks walled off from outsiders, and **extranets,** networks that allow selected external enterprises intranet access. Internet marketing can be targeted to local domestic home-country, regional, national, or global markets. Virtually anything that is marketed offline is now sold online, from thoroughbred horses and copies of the U.S. Declaration of Independence, to sports trading cards, automotive parts, carbon steel, bath soap, and electric power.

Some marketing tactics must be changed or new tactics developed to suit the online environment; others can be applied directly from traditional offline marketing practices. For example, printed cents-off coupons are distributed in freestanding inserts (FSIs) in newspapers, as cutout coupons in magazines, through direct mail and door hangers, and now downloaded and printed from web sites like MyCoupons (*http://MyCoupons.com*) and DirectCoupons (*http://DirectCoupons.com*). Most local retailers accept the printed web version as readily as traditional offline coupons. Some traditional grocery stores deliver coupons weekly to customers who provide an email address.

The first attempts at Internet marketing on the Web in 1993 were by sites offering static electronic versions of printed marketing brochures. These sites were virtual billboards for companies testing the new environment. Business sites typically encouraged visitors to contact a company sales representative offline by telephone or fax. They offered information but were not interactive.

Next to appear were storefronts and malls that tried to re-create land-based retail stores in the virtual environment. Some were interactive and customers could send email to the company, comment on products, search online catalogs, even participate in online surveys, but not purchase products online. Today, most brochure sites and many malls have disappeared, often replaced by transaction sites that offer information, are interactive, and sell products. These sites take advantage of the Web's unique characteristics and offer dynamic, engaging, constantly changing content.

Amazon.com (*http://www.amazon.com*) began operations in 1995 and was quickly followed by a rush of **dot-com** businesses trying to figure out how to be profitable. A boom period continued from 1995 through 1999, when all sizes and types of enterprises went online. Old-line brick-and-mortar retailers like Wal-Mart (*http://www.walmart.com*) adopted dual distribution strategies, using their web sites as complements to retail store sales. Others, like Nordstrom (*http://www.nordstrom.com*) and JC Penney (*http://www2.jcpenney.com*), expanded into multichannel distribution using a web site to complement both catalogs and in-store sales. At the same time, the business-to-business (B2B) market expanded. Businesses began selling products to one another, forming strategic online alliances, sharing databases, creating buying groups and trading exchanges, hiring employees from web resumé sites, and using the Web for in-house and outsourced employee training.

By 2000–2001, a brutal retrenchment forced many dot-coms out of business, while others scrambled to create profitable business models and find financial backing. Between January 2000 and October 2001, an estimated seven hundred mostly consumer-oriented dot-coms shut down. Even though this period marked the end of the Internet bubble, a period of wild speculation and inflated expectations, some dot-coms managed to find financing and profit. This is not unprecedented, as it has happened before in U.S. business history. Procter & Gamble began operating in the middle of the 1837 economic panic; 3M, General Motors, IBM, Sun Microsystems, Microsoft, and General Electric all started business during recessions. A period of rapid economic expansion

**Dot-com**

Initially, any enterprise with an online business with a .com in its URL.

makes it easier to raise financing, even by companies lacking a sound business model. A period of economic downturn makes it imperative that a business manage its resources wisely, which can impose the discipline needed for sustainability.[2]

Terrorist attacks on September 11, 2001, in New York, Washington, D.C., and Pennsylvania dealt a blow to the U.S. economy and sounded a death knell for many already weakened dot-coms. Others gained customers who feared crowded malls and sought safe shopping online. In the weeks immediately following the attacks, online travel sites reported sharp revenue declines averaging 40 percent or more as fear of flying reduced both business and leisure travel. At the same time, traffic to news sites rose dramatically, often more than doubling or tripling preattack levels. The first deaths in more than a quarter century from anthrax, delivered in envelopes sent through the U.S. postal system, and fears of additional bioterrorism increased online bill paying over 20 percent from previous levels.[3] Flexible marketers responded quickly to the altered environment, changing advertising messages and market offers to accommodate badly shaken consumers and retrenching businesses.

Short-term disruptions, no matter how tragic or frightful, cannot stop the Internet's expansion and its increasing impact on business and society. In its short commercial history, people and enterprises have become dependent on the Internet's facilitation of communication, information, entertainment, community building, learning, and purchasing. The resilience and depth of the Internet economy, and increasing consumer and business dependence on it, underscore its essential role in contemporary life.

## ELECTRONIC COMMERCE

**ecommerce**
Business activities conducted on the Internet, Web, and other networked electronic systems. Also known as ebusiness, Web commerce, etailing, etc.

Electronic commerce existed before the Web through Electronic Data Interchange (EDI), the B2B exchange of data over *proprietary* computer networks, email, and fax. However, the Web is the driving force of Internet commercialization and where most consumer electronic commerce occurs. Electronic commerce has many names, including **ecommerce,** ebusiness, web commerce, and etailing (electronic retailing). It is business activities conducted on and for the Internet, its World Wide Web and other services such as email, and on intranets and extranets, by enterprises and consumers. It includes business transactions, information sharing, the maintenance of business relationships, and creation of online communities. Internet marketing is part of ecommerce and includes such activities as product procurement, product sales, online personal selling, customer service, order taking, order fulfillment, credit offers, publicity/public relations, advertising, and sales promotions.

### ✔ CONCEPT CHECK

1.  What is marketing and how does it provide value for buyers and sellers?
2.  How are Internet marketing and non-Internet marketing alike?
3.  What is ecommerce?

# *Links from the Past*

It is good advice to look to the future, yet learn from the past. Many events, inventions, and discoveries from the past contributed knowledge and processes essential to the creation of the Internet (figure 1-1). They happened slowly at first, thousands of

**Figure 1-1 Historical Triggers**

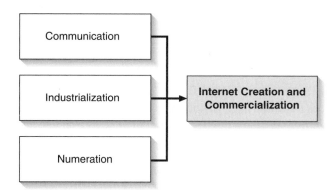

Human advances in communication, numeration, and industrialization triggered changes that created a need for marketing and the development of knowledge that led to the development of the Internet. People sought ways to communicate and share quantitative concepts, as well as to make work and life easier through mechanization.

years ago in isolated human communities. Later they spread across continents, triggering changes in how people lived and worked and how societies and economies functioned. They are associated with major economic transitions, from subsistence agriculture practiced by nonindustrial farming societies, to industrialization and modern manufacturing in the nineteenth century, service economies in the twentieth century, and information economies in the twenty-first. Parallels can be found between what happened historically, what is happening today, and what may happen in the future. They illustrate humankind's enduring need to communicate, numerate, and use machines to save labor and expand human potential. Historical events that triggered changes in business and society were responsible for the development of a need for marketing. If these changes had not occurred, marketing as we know it today wouldn't exist and there would be no need for Internet marketing courses.

## COMMUNICATION LINKS

Written communication is a fundamental human activity with a long history. Primitive people made cave drawings to depict incidents in their lives. The ancient Egyptians around 3,000 B.C. created hieroglyphics, symbols and pictographs scratched or carved on stone walls and tablets.[4] The Chinese compiled the earliest printed book around A.D. 868 but kept their invention secret for almost 900 years. Today, popular writers like Stephen King sell digital books on the Internet that readers pay for electronically, then download and store or print from their own computers.

The Egyptians developed papyrus rolls for writing in A.D. 800 to 900. These rolls became the primary writing materials for much of the known world, and the word *papyrus* eventually evolved into the English word *paper*.[5] Although some observers predicted that computers and the Internet would lead to a paperless world, that certainly has not happened thus far. Most people cling to the use of paper, preferring to print electronic files and web pages rather than read them online. Web retailers encourage customers to print order confirmations on paper, which acknowledges the still prevalent desire of customers for tangible proof of their purchase. Web content providers offer pages specially formatted for printing to accommodate those who dislike reading text directly from a computer screen.

## THE FIRST INFORMATION REVOLUTION

From the fourth through the fifteenth centuries, very few people other than clerics or nobles could read or write. Beautifully illustrated religious manuscripts were printed entirely by hand, laboriously copied letter by letter. The invention of the movable typeset printing press by Johann Gutenberg (c. 1398–1468) in Mainz, Germany, about A.D. 1445 triggered the first information revolution; the Internet triggered the second. Gutenberg's hand-powered press was modeled after a winepress, a clever adaptation of existing technology. Ink was rolled over the raised surfaces of handset letters, then pressed against a sheet of paper, parchment, or vellum.[6] The mechanical press allowed many copies of a manuscript to be printed relatively quickly, at a more affordable price. Once books were more widely available, it became popular and even fashionable for people to own them. This led to a dramatic increase in literacy rates and the creation of private and public libraries. Within thirty years, printed materials spread across Europe and the *divine art* of printing began transforming society. It was a driving force for the Renaissance, a period when learning, creativity, and artistry were valued and widely disseminated. Illiteracy was still common, but now ideas and information could be recorded and rapidly distributed among the growing literate population. The dissemination of ideas prompted challenges to established organizations, religions, thoughts, and practices. The pace of change in the sixteenth century was probably as breathtaking to scholars of that day as Internet-related changes are today.[7]

From the mid-1400s until the late 1800s, few improvements were made to the basic Gutenberg press. It wasn't until 1874 that the first commercial typewriter was manufactured. Typewriters were ubiquitous in most offices for more than a hundred years, when computers and printers began to replace them.

## INDUSTRIAL LINKS

Marketing wasn't needed in subsistence farming societies. Primitive marketing began when product surpluses became routine and had to be reduced or eliminated. Prior to the mid–eighteenth century, economies were based primarily on agriculture, commerce, or small-scale labor-intensive manufacturing. Inventions during two industrial revolutions led to large-scale, mechanized manufacturing and modern industries were born, along with modern marketing. Although British and U.S. inventions drove the revolutions, the effects were felt worldwide.

The first industrial revolution began in Britain in the early 1700s; the second in the United States after the Civil War, lasting until the early years of the twentieth century. They triggered great economic and social changes. Inventions revolutionized how products were made and how people worked and lived. Prices and costs dropped while output increased, and many unskilled laborers lost their jobs.

James Watt (1736–1819) developed a dependable, efficient steam engine that became the symbol of the first industrial revolution. It was as important to that revolution as the Internet is to the current information revolution.[8] Watt's engine allowed factories to become mobile, no longer tied to running water for powering water-wheels. Steam engines transformed textile manufacturing and dropped labor costs by half or more. Steam-powered railroads and ocean vessels carried people and products far and wide. The revolution was exported to France, Germany, Asia, and the United States, where more inventions quickly followed. Railroads were the greatest of the steam-powered machines, cheaply transporting vast quantities of freight long distances. They accelerated industrial and population expansions and led to the rise of the modern marketing society.

The second industrial revolution (1875–1903) was dominated by inventions made in the United States, particularly in electricity and chemicals. Inventions simplified communication across long distances and accelerated information dissemination among large numbers of people, much like the Internet today.

Not all aspects of industrialization were good. Factories needed cheap, unskilled labor. Because machines provided the power, women and children could work in factories and often they were exploited and forced to work under terribly harsh conditions. Most factory workers endured squalid living accommodations in overcrowded cities. Disease and poverty, pollution and lack of sanitation, were constant companions. Many lost their jobs to machines.

**Luddites**
Bands of laborers that protested industrialization.

**Luddites** were one group that tried to fight the rapid changes in society. They were named for a perhaps mythical textile worker, Ned Ludd, who reputedly dropped a hammer in a steam-powered textile machine to protest industrialization. For fifteen months from 1811 to 1812, these bands of English workers, fearful of losing their jobs and livelihoods, resisted the industrialization of the mills. Their revolt spread to the United States, where the execution of seventeen people in 1813 for violent protests essentially put an end to Luddite activities.[9] Like the Luddites, some people today fear the Internet, believing it to be a threat to society, human interaction and civility, and traditional values. They are sometimes referred to as neo-Luddites. Though their numbers are not large, their concerns should be considered.

## NUMERACY AND COMPUTER LINKS

Like written communication and industrialization, numeracy has a direct link to computers and the Internet. Numeracy, or counting, began as primitive people developed a capacity for thinking quantitatively and expressing the results in numeric form. The abacus, a simple hand-operated counting machine first introduced in Babylonia (present-day Iraq) between 3,000 and 2,000 B.C., was the earliest mechanical counting device and is still in use today. Almost 4,000 years passed before a reliable computing engine run by gears and wheels was proposed by Charles Babbage (1792–1871). Babbage is often called the father of modern computers for his model of a digital analytical engine designed to calculate Bernoulli numbers. This concept is considered the precursor to the modern digital computer. If Babbage's engine had been manufactured, it would have run on a plan written by Ada Byron, Countess of Lovelace (1815–1852), daughter of the poet Lord Byron. This was the first computer program and Ada Byron, the first computer programmer.[10] In 1979, a software language used on U.S. Department of Defense mainframe computers was named Ada in her honor.

Herman Hollerith (1860–1929) invented a system for recording and organizing data using a machine that sensed holes punched in cards.[11] His tabulation machine system, which later included card feeding, adding, and sorting processes, revolutionized statistical computation. Hollerith's device helped analyze 1880 U.S. census data and saved the government two years and US$5 million, a large sum in those days. Hollerith's Tabulating Machine Company evolved into the company that changed its name in 1924 to the International Business Machines Corporation (IBM).

The world's first practical large-scale digital computer was activated at the University of Pennsylvania in 1945. ENIAC (Electronic Numerical Integrator Analyzer and Computer) was originally designed to prepare firing and bombing tables for U.S. Army artillery in World War II. ENIAC was a monster. It had 19,000 vacuum tubes, thirty separate units, weighed over thirty tons, stood ten feet tall, and was 150 feet wide.[12] Despite its vast size, it had less computing power than today's personal computer. ENIAC was the first step in the development of the modern digital computing industry. Other important computer advances quickly followed.

## ✔ CONCEPT CHECK

1. What is the connection between developments in communication, numeracy, industrialization, and the Internet?
2. Why was the invention of the steam engine so important?
3. Why did some people fear industrialization? Why do some people today fear the Internet?

# Links to the Internet's Present

It has been over 550 years since Gutenberg invented the movable type printing press. Great changes have marked the intervening centuries, including a large increase in world population. The entire population of the known world in the 1400s was only one hundred million more than the population of the United States in the 1990s. By the 1700s, world population had doubled to around 680 million; by the mid-1800s, it had increased to approximately one billion. At the birth of the Internet in 1969, world population was around three billion. Today, it is over 6.1 billion.[13]

Another change is in the availability and use of more channels for mass and interpersonal communication. By the 1930s, large numbers of people in the United States and other industrialized nations could read and write, as well as listen to radio, talk on a telephone, teletype messages, and by 1939 in the United States, watch television. Today, people use the Internet as a multimedia communication channel to make telephone calls, listen to radio, watch television, video conference, fax messages, and email.

Innovations in the twenty-first century diffuse rapidly within countries and across the world, spread by mass communication and transportation. Diffusion is the process by which people adopt innovations, new products, and different ways of doing things. Inventions from the second industrial revolution diffused far faster than inventions from the first. At least a hundred and fifty to two hundred years passed before steam engines spread throughout Britain, France, Germany, the United States, and parts of Asia; the automobile took forty to fifty years to diffuse; vacuum tubes about twenty-five to thirty years; and the transistor only fifteen years.[14] The same is true with communication innovations. The second information (Internet) revolution is diffusing far faster than the first (table 1-1). Within five years after its release, the World Wide Web had spread around the world. People who were unaware of its release in 1991–1992, were using it five years later to shop, learn, play, communicate, and work.

| Table 1-1 Technology Diffusion Rates in the United States | |
| --- | --- |
| **Invention** | **Years to Reach Adoption by Fifty Million People** |
| Radio | 38 |
| Television | 13 |
| Personal Computer | 16 |
| Internet | 5[15] |

Another factor accelerating Internet adoption is Moore's Law. This law, as developed by Intel's Gordon Moore in 1965 and verified in the intervening years, states that computing power (the amount of information that can be stored on a chip) doubles every eighteen to twenty-four months. This means computers can steadily be made more powerful and cheaper, which increases the probability of commercializing new technologies such as artificial intelligence and virtual reality. Increased computational power lowers transistor and computer prices. Inexpensive computers and Internet-ready devices widen Internet accessibility and speed its worldwide adoption. It also lowers prices for handheld devices, DVD players, smart appliances, digital cameras, PlayStations, and a myriad of other products. Advances in computer storage, graphics, and networking are advancing even faster than Moore's Law.[16]

### THE COLD WAR

Initial funding to support research on Internet feasibility was a direct result of cold war fears. The cold war began at the end of World War II. A meeting between President Franklin D. Roosevelt, British Prime Minister Winston Churchill, and Secretary General of the Communist Party Josef Stalin at Yalta in 1945 is said to have marked its beginning. The three leaders signed agreements that many believe made overly generous concessions to the Soviet Union, in particular allowing the Soviets to extend political and economic control over Eastern Europe.[17] Growing mistrust between the United States and USSR led to a nuclear and conventional arms race, and a period of apprehension and verbal rancor that lasted until the fall of the Berlin Wall and breakup of the Soviet Union in 1991.

During the forty-six years the cold war lasted, both the United States and the Soviet Union (USSR) feared a nuclear attack by the other. The successful launch by the Soviets of the first Earth-orbiting artificial satellite, *Sputnik I*, on October 4, 1957, caught the United States off-guard. The USSR was assumed to have the technical capacity to hit U.S. targets with nuclear missiles. Responding to national fears, then Senator Lyndon Johnson warned that the Soviets had jumped ahead of the United States in the space race and stated, "Soon, they will be dropping bombs on us from space like kids dropping rocks onto cars from freeway overpasses!"[18]

**ARPA, ARPANet**
Advanced Research Projects Agency and Network, Internet precursor.

### ARPA AND DARPA

Most sources claim that the U.S. Department of Defense reacted to *Sputnik* by forming the Advanced Research Projects Agency (**ARPA**) in 1958 to create a national nuclear-proof communication network (**ARPANet**). A broader view is that ARPA's goal was for the military to fund research activities so the United States could regain the lead in science and technology from the Soviets.[19] This included finding a way for scientists to share scarce computer resources. ARPA initiated and funded a monumental research effort to develop a way for geographically separated computers to communicate over telephone lines using a common operating standard called the Network Control Protocol (NCP). The outcome was ARPANet, a wide-area, packet-switching, resource-sharing communication network.

By 1969, four peer computer nodes located at the University of California Los Angeles (UCLA), Stanford Research Institute (SRI), the University of California Santa Barbara (UCSB), and the University of Utah were ready to be linked. UCLA's computers were the first to initiate a host-to-host data exchange. When UCLA researchers attempted a login with the SRI computers, someone accidentally typed in *log win* rather than *login*, which crashed UCLA's computers.[20] Computer crashes continue to provoke users almost forty years later.

Within two years, a small network matrix of fifteen nodes connected twenty-three host computers at universities, the National Aeronautics and Space Administration (NASA), and research facilities around the United States. In 1972, ARPA was renamed the Defense Advanced Research Projects Agency (DARPA). The same year, the Internet went international with network connections through undersea Atlantic Ocean telephone cables linking the United States to University College of London, England, and the Royal Radar Establishment in Norway. The National Science Foundation (NSF) was also working on ways to connect supercomputers for academic research purposes through a reliable high-speed network **backbone.** NSF initiatives led to the development in 1986 of NSFNet, a major component of today's Internet.

The U.S. government funded many Internet-related inventions, including electronic mail (email). In late 1971, Ray Tomlinson, a computer engineer working for an ARPANet contractor, invented email, whose eventual importance even he failed to recognize. Email has been the single largest Internet service for more than a decade. Today, email permission marketing is one of the most profitable areas of online marketing.

## TCP/IP

Several other important events round out the 1970s. In 1974, Vinton Cerf at SRI and DARPA's Robert Kahn proposed the system for addressing and forwarding data packets (Internet Protocol, or IP), and the flow control system (Transmission Control Protocol, or TCP). **TCP/IP** protocols became the communication operating standard and rules for the Internet in 1983. Since January 1, 1983, all traffic and services operating on the Internet matrix must voluntarily agree to use TCP/IP communication protocols. Because all Internet-connected computers use TCP/IP, it means they can *talk* to one another, regardless of their operating system or computer type. The Internet's birth date is often officially stated as 1983, when the TCP/IP protocols and standardization were adopted. However, a strong case can be made that it should be the day in 1969 when the first four computer networks were linked.

Civilian interest in the Internet in the 1980s accelerated as the matrix of networked computers grew beyond the research community to include public and commercial activity. In 1986 NSF opened its previously restricted NSFNet backbone to all users. By 1987, the number of Internet hosts had grown to over ten thousand.[21] Traffic increasingly moved onto the NSFNet and in 1990, ARPANet ceased to exist.

**Backbone**
The Internet's largest transmission lines that handle its major traffic flows.

**TCP/IP**
The Transmission Control Protocol/Internet Protocol are standards for data packet transmission on the Internet.

## THE WORLD WIDE WEB

The Internet captured the public's imagination in the 1990s as its growth accelerated exponentially. Winter 1991–1992 was a key date in the Internet's commercial development. Tim Berners-Lee, an English researcher, was working at the European Particle Physics Laboratory (CERN) in Switzerland in the late 1980s. A need to find information quickly prompted him to write a program that linked key words to search for and retrieve information stored in computer files. His program, *Enquire*, was later expanded to handle finding and retrieving information in the CERN laboratory computers. This led to the design of a **hypertext** linked information retrieval system called the World Wide Web. In December 1991, CERN's newsletter announced the Web's creation. Although hypertext was an Apple Macintosh innovation, Tim Berners-Lee contributed the concept of an interconnected, user-friendly, global computer network accessible by anyone through a **browser** interface. He joined hypertext with the Internet's global matrix of networked computers. On June 30, 1993, CERN declared that WWW technology would be open (free to the public) and not proprietary.[22]

The Web is only one of many services that operate on the Internet matrix. It is the first global hypermedia sector (table 1-2) and where most Internet commercialization and marketing occurs. Users access the Web with a graphical browser (e.g., Netscape Navigator, Microsoft Explorer, or AOL), then enjoy an easy point and click interface that simplifies navigation. Once the Web was released, the pace of Internet adoption by businesses, organizations, governments, educational institutions, health care providers, and individuals increased dramatically, and many new milestones were reached.

**Hypertext**
Formatting language for creating web pages. Also known as HTML (Hyper-Text Markup Language).

**Browser**
Software that allows the user to view and retrieve WWW sites.

| Table 1-2  Advantages of Hypermedia | |
|---|---|
| Open | It allows data transfers to computer servers located across the hall or across the world in a matter of seconds, assuming no network delays, to computers with different operating system. |
| Interactive | It allows instant access to key words or topics within a document, on different pages, or different servers. |
| Dynamic | Changes can be made quickly on pages and sites. |
| Media rich | It allows the use of text, pictures, sound, and video on the same page. |

### ✔ CONCEPT CHECK

1. How does the Internet's rate of diffusion (acceptance and use) compare with the rates of diffusion for earlier inventions? Why is it different?
2. What was the cold war and how is it linked to the Internet's creation?
3. Who is Tim Berners-Lee? What contribution did he make to Internet commercialization?

# *Internet Indicators and the Future*

Internet commercialization has already had a significant impact on the United States, Canada, Europe, and parts of Asia and South America. It has affected business and society in countries with high Internet adoption rates and is beginning to influence countries where adoption is under way. The Internet economy is creating new jobs and transforming old ones. Internet use is changing how people communicate, shop, play, work, and learn.

## THE INTERNET ECONOMY

The Internet economy includes all activities related to the Internet that contribute to a nation's economy as measured in its gross domestic product (GDP). The Internet economy is large and varied, encompassing activities on the Internet and its infrastructure, as well as offline activities that serve the Internet. Business has been involved with the Internet since the days of ARPANet. Electronic Data Interchange (EDI) was occurring on private Internet-like networks as early as the 1970s; however, commercialization on the public Internet's World Wide Web is typically measured from the introduction of the first user-friendly graphical web browser (1993). The Web's enriched environment and open network standards have driven commercialization.

The Center for Research in Electronic Commerce, University of Texas at Austin (UT), has conducted Internet economic indicator studies commissioned by Cisco Systems since October 1999. The Year 2000 study reported that sales and marketing jobs generated more Internet-related employment than other jobs, including those in information technology. In 2000, the Internet economy directly supported over four million workers, up from two million in 1999. These jobs were either newly created by Internet activity or shifted to the Internet when companies recognized the benefits of online operations. Internet commerce is the single largest area of job growth in the Internet economy.[23] Although many jobs were lost because of the 2000–2001 economic downturn and immediately after 9/11/01, recovery will bring rehiring and new job growth, particularly as Internet use expands worldwide.

The Center identifies four segments of the U.S. Internet economy: Infrastructure, Network Applications Infrastructure, Intermediaries, and Internet Commerce. These segments grew 22.6 percent from Q2 1999 to Q2 2000. UT researchers projected over US$830 billion added to the US economy in 2000, a 58 percent increase over 1999. Since 1995 the Internet economy has contributed almost a third of U.S. economic growth. Despite the dramatic pullback in dot-com valuations in 2000–2001, it is projected that ecommerce will generate as much as $6.9 trillion in revenues by 2003.[24] The U.S. Department of Commerce estimates that by the year 2006, almost half the U.S. workforce will have jobs that are related either directly or indirectly to the Internet and information technology. Many of these jobs will be in currently unknown occupations.[25]

The Internet economy is based on low-cost communication networks using worldwide Internet technologies and standards. It includes human capital (employees) and the innovative applications they develop. The Internet allows electronic markets to interconnect so buyers and sellers can make exchanges online. Both producers and intermediaries provide goods and services that make markets function efficiently. The Internet system also includes policy and legal frameworks for conducting and regulating business over the networks. Revenue and jobs are created by the following.

**BUILDING OUT THE INTERNET INFRASTRUCTURE**    For example, selling personal computers, software, handheld devices, routers, servers, digital telephone lines, and equipment needed to expand and maintain the matrix as more people go online and more networks connect. Companies involved in the infrastructure include Dell Computer (*http://www.dell.com*) and Cisco Systems (*http://www.cisco.com*).

**ELECTRONIC COMMERCE**    Transactions conducted between businesses (B2B sales) include product sales and the formation of networks of suppliers and even competitors in joint ventures online designed to reduce costs and improve operating efficiencies. An example is ForestExpress (*http://timber.forestexpress.com*), a timber electronic marketplace that operates auctions for its members.

**RETAIL SALES**    Sales of tangible goods to consumers (business-to-consumer [B2C] sales) of such products as books, apparel, computers, automobiles, and flowers that must be delivered using traditional distribution intermediaries and software, music, tickets, and digital products that can be delivered directly through electronic channels. Examples include Amazon.com and Travelocity (*http://www.travelocity.com*).[26]

*WEB UPDATE*

*The Internet Economy*

## SEPTEMBER 11, 2001

The U.S. economy received a massive jolt on the morning of September 11, 2001, when two hijacked domestic airlines crashed into the World Trade Centers in New York, another struck the Pentagon outside Washington, D.C., and a fourth flew into the ground in Pennsylvania when passengers tried to wrest control of the plane from terrorists. Immediately after the attacks, U.S. stock exchange activity was halted, most television and Internet advertising was suspended, web news sites were overwhelmed by visitors, some businesses shut down, and the nation and much of the world viewed unfolding events amid rising anxiety, anger, and grief. The short-term economic effects were negative. An economy already in recession was further weakened. Unemployment rose, consumer confidence fell, and businesses struggled.

Despite the uncertainty and faltering economy, there were bright spots. Forrester Research (*http://www.forrester.com*) stuck by its estimate of an 11 percent increase in 2001 holiday spending online over 2000 spending. It forecast that many consumers would send gifts rather than travel over the holidays, and many gifts would be purchased online rather than in malls. Surprisingly, Forrester's online retail sales tracking service reported that even in a national emergency, people still shopped online. Between the time of the attacks on September 11 and the next evening, over US$96 million in online sales were recorded.[27]

President George W. Bush's declaration of war on terrorists, subsequent military action in Afghanistan, and anthrax attacks by mail further roiled the economy and raised anxiety among consumers. Despite these events, within a short time after September 11, consumers and enterprises began returning to online activities. Although growth forecasts were dampened, the survival of Internet commerce was never in doubt.

## BUSINESS IMPLICATIONS

It took over 550 years to get from Gutenberg to the Web but less than 10 years for the Internet economy to become an important economic factor in the United States and other countries. It is difficult to predict where the Internet is going, but it is triggering changes that are happening faster than any human invention in the past. Some of the greatest Internet-stimulated changes are being experienced in computing and electronics, telecommunications, financial services, retailing, energy, and travel.

The Internet provides opportunities for the development of new business models, companies, financing arrangements, corporate structures, and competitive relationships. First mover dot-coms (businesses first online in their product category) that initially had no offline presence include the following:

**TRAVEL**   Travelocity.com (*http://www.travelocity.com*) and Expedia.com (*http://www.expedia.com*) let consumers book their own airline tickets, cruises, and vacation packages, provide comprehensive travel information 24/7/365, and are crowding out many traditional single-service travel agents.

**BOOKS**   Amazon.com has pioneered online book purchases and led the way in personalization, customization, and building communities of readers with similar interests while taking business from established retail booksellers.

**SECURITIES**   e*Trade now E*TRADE Financial (*http://us.etrade.com/e/t/home*) is a pathsetter in online brokerages, offering stocks, options, IPOs, banking and savings, letting customers trade after hours and extending into mobile e-trades while forcing traditional financial retailers to go online and do the same.

**AUCTIONS**   eBay (*http://www.ebay.com*), which bills itself *as Your Personal Trading Company,* offers online auctions for almost any imaginable product, anytime, anywhere sold by consumers and enterprises, and although there are copies, no other auction business approaches its market share.

For established bricks-and-clicks businesses like Lands' End, the Internet opens a new channel of distribution, adding to its retail store and catalog sales, reaching buyers in other countries, and better serving its corporate clients. Many businesses have gone online to find new members of their channels of distribution—suppliers, buyers, warehouses, retailers, or transport companies. Others are using the Internet to create buying groups or communities of businesses in the same industry. Many of these relationships are unique and probably could not have occurred without the Internet or a comparable electronic environment. The Internet simplifies communication and allows enterprises to create multifunctional teams with employees physically distant from one another.

Do all businesses belong online? Certainly not, but businesses that fail to have an online presence risk losing out to competitors who aggressively exploit the Internet's advantages (table 1-3).

Are there disadvantages to being online? Absolutely. Many businesses that rushed to be the first online and were undercapitalized, had weak business models, were not committed to customer service, were poorly managed, or couldn't generate profits have been driven into bankruptcy, merged, or been acquired. Some businesses haven't figured out how to drive consumers to their web sites, convert them to customers, and retain them. Others have failed because they lacked an order fulfillment infrastructure to support online sales. Some have experienced costly security failures or failed to guarantee and protect consumer privacy.

## SOCIETAL IMPLICATIONS

The Internet was invented in the United States, yet this country's 286 million people are only a small fraction of the world's population. This can be an advantage if it

## Table 1-3  Business Advantages of Going Online

| | |
|---|---|
| Access | As more consumers go online, businesses with an Internet presence can enlarge their customer base. It is still early in the Internet's commercial history, and at least 5.7 billion people are *not* online. Most will not go online in the immediate future, but those who do should be desirable customers. Some first mover advantage can still be enjoyed by businesses that are established online before the majority of consumers hop aboard. |
| Worldwide Exposure | Once a business goes online it is an international business. This exposes customers worldwide to product offers. A business may choose not to engage in international marketing online, but for many it will be their best opportunity to attract international buyers. |
| Speed | Customers can find products quickly and their orders can be taken online; some products can be delivered online, others within twenty-four hours or less. This is a competitive advantage for Internet sellers and a disadvantage for those that are not. |
| Pricing Transparency | Comparison pricing can be conducted by the customer or a shopping site like MySimon.com (*http://www.mysimon.com/*) that can search the Web for products and retrieve pricing information. This means that pricing can become almost transparent since it is relatively easy to collect almost complete pricing information. This is an advantage for businesses shopping online for raw materials, supplies, and parts as well as for consumers. It is also a force that should keep prices competitive. |
| Reduced Inventory Costs | Online ordering in real time means that inventory holding costs can be reduced and in many product categories, products can be made to order and delivered just-in-time (JIT), which eliminates holding costs. Extranets can be used to signal suppliers electronically when reorders are needed, which reduces inventory holding costs for buyer and seller. |
| Reduced Intermediary Costs | The elimination of intermediaries (*disintermediation*) is impractical for any tangible products that must be transported from online seller to offline buyer. However, if customers buy directly online from a manufacturer, savings can result from the elimination of some intermediaries (wholesalers and retailers). |
| Reduced Supply Costs | Businesses can obtain supplies, materials, and parts faster online and often far cheaper than from traditional methods (see pricing transparency). Online businesses can join buying pools where demand is aggregated and group buying secures lower prices. |
| Customer Satisfaction | Products that were mass-merchandized in the past can be customized through one-to-one online relationships with customers. Mass customer support can be provided online. Businesses that satisfy their customers have a competitive advantage. |

means billions of possible future buyers who may purchase U.S. products online. It can be a disadvantage if American dominance of the Internet accelerates the export of U.S. goods and popular culture, increases nationalism and protectionism in other nations, and exacerbates anti-American feelings.[28] This is a worldwide environment, yet not all people embrace it equally nor will everyone enjoy its benefits.

The Internet will encourage freedom of expression and capitalism in nations that are not now democratic or capitalistic. Shutting off Internet access may prove difficult if not impossible, as some governments are learning. The free exchange of ideas online and exposure to goods and services unavailable in their home countries may encourage political and economic dissent, which some governments fear.[29]

Because the Internet is borderless, taxing online sales and regulating online activities are highly complicated. Jurisdiction and control are controversial issues that defy easy solutions. Considerable debate has already taken place over such online activities as gambling, visual pornography, marketing to children, and unregulated pharmaceutical sales that are allowed by some countries and banned by others.

The Internet is changing the way many professionals work. Telecommuting is facilitated through many Internet services, particularly email and web mail. Hotels and airports are catering to workers who must connect to the Internet even while traveling. The Internet is creating new jobs in occupations that didn't exist ten years ago, for example webmaster/webmistress (site administrator) and web site designer.

Learning is undergoing revolutionary changes because the global Internet never closes. Distance learning means new ways of attending classes and earning academic degrees. The number of ecommerce and Internet marketing classes and majors at U.S. universities is growing rapidly. The United States, with the most highly regarded university system in the world, will gain export revenues through university classes and degrees offered worldwide on the Web.[30]

It is unclear whether or not a *digital divide* actually exists, but concern is expressed that minority groups, the poor, and other vulnerable groups will be disenfranchised by lack of Internet access. This could lead to further polarization within and between societies and groups of people. An alternate view holds that, as prices fall for Internet devices and access, more people who might have been disenfranchised in a digital divide will go online. Survey data support this view, showing increasing numbers of African Americans, Hispanic Americans, and Asian Americans going online in the United States.[31]

Just as the first industrial revolution had its Luddites, contemporary neo-Luddites are raising moral and ethical arguments against the excesses of modern technology. They fear that the Internet and other technologies threaten our essential humanity and sense of community, and they urge great caution accepting them. Others censure the Internet for making visual pornography widely accessible, allowing selling to kids, encouraging gambling, providing a forum for hate groups, giving haven to terrorists, and letting people become so engrossed with the online world that they isolate themselves from offline social relationships.

## THE FUTURE

Making predictions about the Internet's future is very risky. However, some predictions are more plausible than others. For example, far from seeing the United States in decline, as some futurists predicted for the turn of the century, the United States is in an enviable position to continue to exploit the Internet and benefit from its promise. The United States will retain its advantage if domestic research and development continues to produce innovations that move the technology in new directions, and the government restrains from ill-conceived heavy-handed restrictions. Tomorrow's Internet will be different from today's, and some advances are already being anticipated. They include

**SPEED**    Faster and more stable Internet connections

**WIRELESS**    Widespread adoption of wireless handheld and other noncomputer Internet access devices

**SECURITY**    Software that greatly reduces security concerns

**SPEECH**    Speech commands replacing typed commands

**MULTITASKING**    Multiple concurrent web site access where sites are held on the screen all at the same time to allow easier comparison shopping

**VISUALIZATION**    Visualization, virtual reality, even holographic images so customers can "feel" products

**JOBS**    New types of jobs and occupations created by the expanding Internet economy

**BARRIER-FREE**    Easier Internet access for people with disabilities

Enterprises and consumers will continue to drive the Internet's growth; serving their needs more effectively and efficiently will drive its evolution. Businesses want the Internet to lower operating costs and increase revenues (and profits). Universities want the Internet to recruit students, encourage alumni giving, and disseminate positive information about their programs and faculty. Hospitals want it to market their services to consumers and medical practitioners, lower procurement costs, and deliver health information to patients and clinicians. Governments want the Internet to reduce procurement costs, provide convenient services to citizens, disseminate information and promote responsible citizen behaviors, and in a growing number of cases, lower voting costs through online registration and voting. Marketers want the Internet to provide access to new markets and new customer-pleasing products, creating exchanges in a win-win environment, where buyers and sellers both benefit.

### ✔ CONCEPT CHECK

1. How is the Internet economy contributing to the U.S. economy?
2. Do all businesses belong online? Why not?
3. Are all societal effects of the Internet beneficial?

## *Summary*

### *A Marketing Perspective in the Internet Age*

Internet marketing is marketing in electronic environments, primarily on the Internet, on one or more of its services (WWW, email), or in offline sectors involved with Internet-related activities. Both traditional and Internet marketing focus on exchange, relationship building, and providing value (utility). They perform the same functions and often, the same businesses are involved, off- and online. Ecommerce is business activities conducted in electronic environments, including online on the World Wide Web, but also on other Internet services, extranets and intranets. These activities include Internet marketing.

### *Links from the Past*

Developments in written communication began with cave drawings and continued with hieroglyphics and hand-printing methods. The first information revolution dates from the invention of the movable typeset printing press around A.D. 1445. The mechanical press allowed many copies of a manuscript to be printed in far less time than handwritten methods and at a price more people could afford. The industrial revolutions moved nations to large-scale machine-intensive manufacturing, and modern industries were born, along with modern marketing, to facilitate transactions and clear markets of excess products. Charles Babbage proposed a digital Analytical Engine, the precursor of the modern electronic computer that would have run on a plan written by Ada Byron. Herman Hollerith invented a system for recording and organizing data using cards with holes punched in them. ENIAC I was the world's first practical all electronic large-scale, general-purpose digital computer.

### Links to the Internet's Present

The Internet's initial development is linked to the cold war, which began at the end of World War II. ARPANet directly evolved into the Internet. In 1983, a date often used to mark the Internet's birth, the TCP/IP protocols were accepted as the communication operating standard for the Internet. Because all Internet-connected computers use TCP/IP, it means they can exchange data even if they use different operating systems. Tim Berners-Lee at CERN created the World Wide Web; CERN released it in the winter of 1991–1992. The Web and graphical browsers facilitated the development of Internet commercialization.

### Internet Indicators and the Future

The Internet is a global matrix of interlinked computer networks developed in the United States and now used worldwide. Any computer network can join the Internet but must agree to observe TCP/IP protocols. The Internet has many services (or sectors) that developed independently but operate as part of the global network and adhere to TCP/IP. The Internet economy includes all activities related to the Internet that contribute to a nation's economy, often measured in its GDP. The Internet economy is divided into four segments: Infrastructure, Network Applications, Intermediaries, and Commerce. Businesses can profit from being online, as well as suffer online problems. Effects of the Internet on society will be felt in such areas as trade, expansion of freedom of speech and business activities, problems with taxation and regulation, encouragement of portable professionals, revolutions in distance learning, creation of *digital divides,* and neo-Luddite concerns.

## Internet Marketing Application

The following statement was made early in this chapter: *Virtually anything that is marketed offline is now sold online, from thoroughbred horses and copies of the U.S. Declaration of Independence, to sports trading cards, automotive parts, carbon steel, bath soap, and electric power.* Test this proposition using a popular search engine like Google (*http://www.google.com*) to see if the items *really* are available for sale online. Search for each product by name with the phrase "for sale" after the product. For example, "thoroughbred horses for sale." Is the statement confirmed?

| Product | For Sale Online | Not For Sale Online |
|---|---|---|
| Thoroughbred horses | | |
| U.S. Declaration of Independence | | |
| Sports trading cards | | |
| Automotive parts | | |
| Carbon steel | | |
| Bath soap | | |
| Electric power | | |

# *Chapter Review Questions*

1. Why was Gutenberg's invention considered the trigger for the first information revolution?
2. Why did the earliest people in farming societies *not* need marketing?
3. What contribution did Ada Byron make to the computer revolution?
4. What might have happened to Internet development if CERN had made the WWW proprietary?
5. What roles do mass communication and transportation play in the diffusion of innovations?
6. Why did tiny *Sputnik I* cause such fear in the United States?
7. Why is it still important that all computers and devices connected to the Internet use TCP/IP?
8. What are the four sectors of the Internet economy? In which sector does Amazon.com operate?
9. What risks are associated with ecommerce?
10. What industry sectors are experiencing the greatest effects from Internet commerce?
11. Why is the Internet potentially a force for democracy and free markets?
12. Explain why events that happened hundreds and even thousands of years ago contributed to the eventual creation of the Internet.
13. How can the United States export higher education?
14. Why is the United States expected to continue to lead the Internet revolution?
15. Do you think the Internet is revolutionary or evolutionary? Explain your answer.

# Case Study

## Lands' End, Inc.

Sandy, from the beginning of the chapter, went online to purchase a baby crib quilt from Lands' End in Dodgeville, WI, USA. Lands' End was incorporated in 1963 as the Lands' End Yacht Stores. In those days, a good day meant receiving fifteen mail-order sales. Today, Lands' End is the fifteenth-largest mail-order company in the world, with annual sales of over US$1.3 billion.

This more than forty-year-old direct merchant has made a major commitment to Internet marketing and building its web presence. As a direct merchant, Lands' End acts as its own intermediary, working with mills and manufacturers to develop products, then distributing them directly to consumers and enterprises. Its products appeal to quality-conscious middle-age customers, a principal target market, and consumers who appreciate traditional casual apparel.

Lands' End is a multichannel merchant, selling products through catalogs, retail stores, and online. In FY 2001, the company distributed 269 million catalogs, including its general flagship catalog, *The Lands' End Catalog*, and specialty catalogs for men, women, kids, women wearing sizes 18W to 26W, school, home, and corporate sales. The company has sixteen outlet and inlet stores in the United States, two outlets in the United Kingdom (UK), and one in Japan. Management has made a commitment to expanding web sales worldwide.

Lands' End launched its U.S. web site in 1995. It was one of the first direct merchants to go online, at the time offering only one hundred products along with its popular stories and editorials. Today, nearly every product in its hard copy catalog is also sold online. The site's very popular *Overstocks* section offers first-quality merchandise at discounts up to 75 percent off the original price.

In FY 1998, the site generated revenue of only US$18 million. By FY 1999, however, it attracted fifteen million visitors and earned US$61 million in revenue. In the first two quarters of FY 2000, over fourteen million visitors came to the site. Online sales in FY2001 were US$218 million.

In addition to its U.S. web site, Lands' End also has sites in the United Kingdom, Japan, Germany, France, Ireland, and Italy as well as Corporate Sales web sites selling company apparel, awards, and gifts. Landsend.com is the world's largest (in business volume) apparel web site. It has also been a leader in developing new ways to enhance the shopping experience and to foster one-on-one relationships with its customers.

Lands' End has always been known for superb customer service, and their service online is no different. Shoppers can talk to a personal shopper and get advice on styles and fit through *Lands' End Live*. The Lands' End *My Personal Shopper* and a visitor can use collaborative surfing in a live chat or text option to visit the same web page and discuss products simultaneously. The personal shopper can push a page to the shopper's computer screen and recommend products. Other online services feature include style advice, a three-dimensional model for fitting clothes, flattering swimsuit fitting advice, a capacity for men to "build" the Oxford shirt they want by selecting options, and *Shop With a Friend*. Lands' End realizes that shopping is often a social event and the Internet can be isolating, so *Shop With a Friend* allows friends to be together online, on the same Lands' End page, and chat in real time.

Lands' End also has a large business customer base. Annual corporate sales exceed US$140 million for Lands' End products embroidered with corporate logos. They are even customizing web sites for corporate customers. The General Motors Saturn Division has its own Lands' End intranet site, where the company's more than eight thousand employees can shop. Cisco Systems is another intranet customer with its own web site.

Lands' End makes the most of its established infrastructure. Online orders are fulfilled through the same warehouse as its catalog orders. This warehouse is the size of sixteen football fields, and employees can sort ten thousand pieces per hour. In a busy day, they ship 150,000 orders. Product packaging is printed with the company's 1-800 number and web address.

Why is Lands' End so successful online? At Lands' End, the customer is always right. The company has always guaranteed every product it offers. Lands' End was the first cataloger to offer toll-free 1-800 numbers; its customer service lines are open 24/7/365. The same philosophy drives its web sites. Lands' End online is personalized, helpful, convenient, and one of the most successful examples of the convergence of Internet, catalog, personal service, and telephone. It uses the most advanced technology to create a flawless shopping experience. It is the epitome of a company operating on the customer-centric marketing concept philosophy, constantly striving to find new ways to use the electronic environment to improve customer service.

In May 2002, Sears Roebuck agreed to pay over $1.9 billion to purchase Lands' End. Sears and Lands' End are very customer-centered businesses. The purchase should eventually be beneficial to Sears's online and offline operations.[32]

## CHECK IT OUT

Visit landsend.com and examine how the front page provides clear instructions for visitors in an easily readable format. How easy is it to find *My Personal Shopper, Overstocks,* and *My Virtual Model*? What makes this giant direct merchant so customer-centered? What marketing strategies might Lands' End use in the future to make its web site even more appealing?

## A GLOBAL PERSPECTIVE

Lands' End is an international marketer with catalog operations and warehouses in the United Kingdom, Germany, and Japan. Catalogs in those countries are written in the local language and products are priced in the local currency—the pound, euro, and yen, respectively. Germany converted to the euro in January 2002.

At the landsend.com front page, click on *International Sites: Shop in Your Local Language.* How does Lands' End accommodate VAT, duties, and other taxes for international shoppers who purchase from the U.S. site? Should differences in prices be expected? Select a turtleneck from the U.S. site, noting its price and product number. Find the same product on one of the international sites. Using an online currency converter (Universal Currency Converter at *http://www.xe.com/ucc* or Yahoo! at *http://finance.yahoo.com/m3*) calculate the percent price difference. How much is it?

Carefully examine the front pages for Germany, France, United Kingdom, and Japan. Has the company maintained consistent design elements on the pages? In particular, evaluate colors, type, and product pictures. Are some of the same customer-centric approaches used on the international sites? How successful is Lands' End in projecting its image through its international web sites?

# CHAPTER TWO

# *Internet Operations, Management, and Access*

## LEARNING OBJECTIVES

- To understand how the Internet, the world's largest internetted network of computer networks, works

- To be able to explain why the Internet operates smoothly, even though it is not governed by any single entity, government, or organization

- To identify attributes of the World Wide Web that make it so conducive to marketing activities

- To learn about new technologies and how they are affecting the Internet and the consumers and enterprises that rely on it

## David Gets A Job Marketing Routers

David graduated in June with a bachelor's degree in marketing. He was hired almost immediately by a multinational corporation that manufactures routers for the Internet. Although David knows a little about routers from the Internet marketing class he took his senior year, he will have to undergo extensive on-the-job training to learn the company's product line. He will be working with trade shows, developing brochures and presentations, and helping staff the company's booth at Internet World Fall, the world's largest e-commerce and Internet technology conference. David knows he will learn a lot there. He will meet marketing representatives from other companies, see what exhibitors offer in their booths, hear speakers, and attend panels that will increase his knowledge of the Internet industry. For five days he will be able to experience technology on the cutting edge of Internet development.[1]

**Infrastructure**
The physical equipment and software (and protocols) that make up the Internet.

David's company manufactures and sells equipment that other businesses buy to operate and extend the Internet's physical **infrastructure**. These business buyers include service access providers, telecommunications companies, backbone carriers, and manufacturers of optical and high-speed networking equipment. Chapter 2 begins with operations and how the Internet works. It examines how order is maintained on this enormous voluntary network of networks, how the Web operates, and why it is attractive to marketers. The chapter concludes with a discussion of new technologies and other ways to access the Internet, including the mobile Internet and m-marketing.

# *How The Internet Works*

Understanding Internet marketing also requires understanding the basics of how the Internet and World Wide Web work. As defined in Chapter 1, the Internet is the largest matrix of interconnected distributed computer networks in the world. Its thousands of networks and millions of computers operate within a loose voluntary association, without a central governing authority. It is a dynamic open system, not closed (proprietary), and more networks link to it each day, bound together by a common agreement to run on the TCP/IP communication language standard or protocol.

## OPERATIONS AND SOFTWARE

**Email (Electronic Mail)**
Messages typed by a sender on one computer and sent electronically to one or more receiver computers.

**Internet service provider (ISP)**
A business that provides Internet access for consumers and enterprises.

To help visualize how the Internet operates on a physical level, consider the data transmission process for a single **email (electronic mail)** message sent from the United States to England (see figure 2-1). The same general process is used to send web pages and other files over the Internet, although each operates under its own protocols (operating rules) in addition to TCP/IP standards. A sender in the United States emails a friend in London. If the sender is at home, he or she typically will use a personal computer, modem, and standard telephone line to dial up (connect to) an **Internet service provider** (**ISP**), which provides access to the Internet. There are more than ten thousand ISPs in the United States and thousands more worldwide. They vary in size from small, local businesses with low-speed Internet access to huge international companies with high-speed access that are part of the backbone. The largest ten U.S. ISPs generate over 65 percent of Internet access revenues. They include WorldCom/UUNet, AT&T, PSINet, Cable & Wireless, Sprint, and Genuity.

**Figure 2-1  Routing an Email Message from the United States to England**

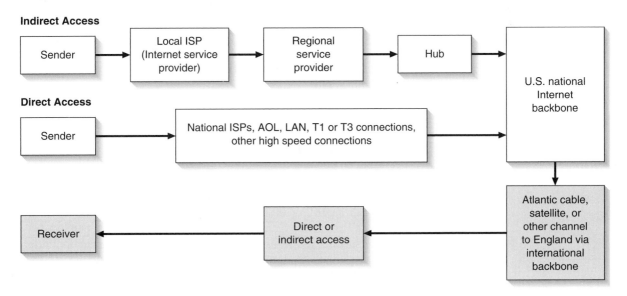

Routers send data packets on the "best" paths (routes) from sender to receiver.

Low-transmission-capacity ISPs do not connect directly to the Internet. They provide *indirect access* because small ISPs must connect to a larger service provider, usually a regional service provider (RSP), that connects to the backbone. National ISPs with high transmission capacity have *direct access* because they connect directly to the backbone. Larger ISPs typically offer several types of high-speed access in addition to low-speed dial-up service.

**Bandwidth** is transmission capacity, that is, how fast data (communication signal frequencies) flow per unit of time through a transmission line. A 57,600 bps (bits per second) dial-up modem has twice the speed of a 28,800 bps modem. A digital subscriber line (DSL) in a home or small office can transmit 6.1 megabits (millions of bits) per second. Bandwidth is often compared to a pipeline. Small local ISPs, which have very small data transmission pipelines, connect to RSPs with larger pipelines. Backbones have the largest pipelines of all and can transmit data far faster than smaller pipelines. Large text files and sound files, computer programs, streaming media, three-dimensional images, and virtual reality require far greater bandwidth than text-only files.

*Narrowband* is a term sometimes used to describe very small bandwidth, usually transmitting text only. **Broadband** means very large bandwidth with very high data transmission speed variously described as from 256 kbps (kilobits) to six MHz (Megahertz) wide. Both DSL and cable TV are broadband services. Many marketers regard broadband as essential to making their web sites more interactive, dynamic, and enticing to consumers. Consumers like it because they can go online with DSL or cable without tying up their home telephone. By 2000, more than two million DSL lines were in use in the United States, up 435 percent from the previous year, and almost four million high-speed cable connections existed, an increase of 153 percent over 1999.[2]

Most consumer Internet access in the United States is by dial-up modem on standard telephone lines. By 2003, over 77 percent of Internet-wired U.S. households will still use dial-up connections, with 11 percent using cable modems; 8 percent, DSL; and around 3 percent, satellite.[3] Although consumers are interested in speedier connects, they appear unwilling to pay for them. Most express their satisfaction with existing modem speed. It is also proving more difficult than expected to make faster connections available to everyone who wants them. This frustrates Internet marketers that want to take advantage of web enhancements to make sites more exciting and dynamic. Many enhanced features requiring high-speed connections are ill-advised for target markets still operating on slow dial-up modems. Streaming audio and video are extremely slow to download on dial-up modems and can cause computer crashes. This does not create goodwill for the sender.

Internet access from an office, school, or other organization often is through a local area network (LAN) connected to a cable. If the LAN is running on part or all of a very fast connection line, a T1 or T3, it connects directly to the national Internet backbone without routing through an ISP or other intermediate service provider. This is also called *direct access*. A T1 transmits data at 1.544 megabits (million bits) per second, a T3 at 45 megabits per second. Other users connect through online service providers (OSPs) such as America Online (AOL) or large telecommunications companies (AT&T, MCI, Verizon, the regional Bell operating companies or RBOCs) whose networks form part of the Internet matrix.

Without the sender knowing it, his or her email message is broken into small inde-

**Bandwidth**
The amount of data (communication signal frequencies) that can be transmitted through a particular communication line or channel per unit of time.

**Broadband**
Very large bandwidth with high-speed data transmission speed; DSL and cable TV are broadband services.

pendent digital units called *data packets*, each tagged with a unique identification number. Packets are routed along network transmission lines ranging from small-capacity lines leased by ISPs, through hubs (transfer points), to the major high-speed lines of national networks that interconnect to form the Internet's backbone. Many different routers (computers) in varying size networks must select the best paths for each packet to travel.

At some point, the data packets from the original email message leave the U.S. backbone (see figure 2-1). They may travel under the Atlantic Ocean on huge underseas cable transmission lines or be bounced from Earth-orbiting satellites to networks in England. Once the packets arrive, they will be reassembled into the original email message, which the receiver can download and read. This process usually happens so quickly and seamlessly that sender and receiver have no idea what's occurred or where the data packets have traveled. However, sometimes parts of networks or whole networks crash (stop operating), or are removed from service for repair or maintenance, and data packets can be delayed, garbled, or lost.

Because the Internet is a loosely distributed association where work (transmitting data) is shared by many computers and networks, networks can go offline without bringing down the entire matrix. The Internet was built for **redundancy,** multiple possible paths to any destination. In February 1999, an undersea Atlantic Ocean transatlantic cable was severed and its backup systems failed. This shut down Britain's largest network, the Joint Academic Network (Janet) and halted Internet communication with the United States for twenty-four hours. The rest of the Internet was unaffected, and other routes were found around the downed network.[4] Thus, the Internet is a robust system, a necessity for any marketer trying to conduct sustained business activities.

If the receiver in London replies, his or her email's data packets will not travel exactly the same return route as the original data packets sent from the United States. Because the Internet was designed for redundancy, there is no right way for data to get from a sender to a receiver. This means that each data packet usually takes a different route to its destination.

Routers and servers are essential to smooth Internet operations. **Routers** are sophisticated computers and the routing protocols embedded in the software that runs them. The Internet's millions of routers each connect two or more networks and direct traffic over those networks. Routers read each data packet's address to determine the packet's destination, then evaluate network traffic conditions on the networks to which they connect and decide the fastest and best route along which to forward the packet. Each Internet router can forward ten thousand to two hundred thousand or more data packets a second.

**Servers** serve data. They are computers and also the software that runs them. At one time servers were very large computers; today, they are often the same size as the typical personal computer and, indeed, could be that same computer. Servers offer one or many services on the Internet, LANs, intranets, and extranets. For example, a web server provides web services, and a mail server provides email services.

Routers, servers, and other devices run on software, which powers the Internet. Software includes programs, documents, and data that run one or millions of computers.[5] Applications software performs specific tasks for users and is familiar to anyone who uses Word, Excel, PowerPoint, or other programs. Systems software runs operating

**Redundancy**
The Internet is a distributed system where if one part slows down or stops, data packets can be directed to other parts.

**Router**
Sophisticated computers and the routing protocols embedded in the software that runs them.

**Server**
Computers, and the software that runs them, that serve data.

### Table 2-1 Software Running on the Internet and Its Services

| Software Category | Tasks |
| --- | --- |
| email | Run email servers, facilitates communication |
| Antivirus | Protect operating systems, files from unauthorized access |
| HTML editors | Create web pages and sites |
| Browsers | Access, read multimedia web pages |
| USENet readers | Post and read messages from lists |
| Firewalls | Protect from unwanted, unauthorized entry |

systems or support applications that manage the other programs in a computer or device, for example, UNIX, Windows, OS/2, Mac OS, or Linux. Internet software drives specific activities on the Internet or an Internet service such as the Web or email (see table 2-1). These examples represent a small sample of the enormous amount of software operating on the Internet and its networks.

## INTERNET SERVICES
The Internet hosts many services (also called systems or sectors) that developed independently but operate on the global matrix and adhere to TCP/IP protocols. Each service also has its own software protocols that direct a particular activity. Marketing activities occur on many of these services, in addition to the Web. The most popular include the following:

**ELECTRONIC MAIL (EMAIL)**    Used for the communication of messages and permission marketing activities. Typically operates on Simple Mail Transfer Protocol (SMTP) or Post Office Protocol (POP).

**USENET**    Newsgroups where users can post and respond to bulletin board messages; often used for online marketing research. Network News Transport Protocol (NMTP) facilitates USENet communication.

**FILE TRANSFER PROTOCOL (FTP)**    A service for sending, storing, and retrieving data files, moving files from one computer to another.

**TELNET**    A transfer service that allows a user to connect directly to other computer systems on the Internet and access stored files.

**CHAT OR INTERNET RELAY CHAT (IRC)**    A "real-time" communication service where users can "talk" either by text or voice can be used for marketing focus groups.

**CU-SeeMe**    Videoconferencing, where users send and receive sound and pictures, can be used for marketing research.

**WORLD WIDE WEB**    The hypermedia sector where most ecommerce and Internet marketing occur. HyperText Transfer Protocol (http) governs World Wide Web functions. Also runs web mail.

## INTRANETS AND EXTRANETS

Many enterprises have proprietary intranets (intraorganizational networks) and extranets (multiple intranets connected all or in part to other approved intranets). Intranets are private networks that run the same type of software and adhere to the same protocols as the Internet and, usually, the Web. Access is restricted to company employees and other approved users. Most intranets have public Internet and web access; some do not and are run solely within a company. Intranets are sealed off from the public Internet by **firewalls,** hardware and software designed to stop unauthorized access by external visitors. Firewalls, which protect databases and other proprietary information from unauthorized users, vary in cost and complexity, ranging from passwords or fairly simple IP address checks that filter out unauthorized users, to extremely sophisticated, expensive hardware and software systems that create multiple layers of protection.

**Firewall**
A combination of hardware and software that stops unauthorized access to an intranet by external parties usually coming from the Internet.

Because the Internet effectively facilitates communication over great distances, regardless of time or computer platform, employees can use a corporate intranet to share databases and information almost effortlessly. Teams can work collaboratively on projects despite geographical separation using email, chat, corporate web pages, and other Internet services. For example, Ford designers at plants around the world used a company intranet to collaborate on developing the 1996 Taurus.[6] Intranets can save time, eliminate physical face-to-face meetings that otherwise would require travel, reduce paperwork, facilitate scheduling by maintaining centralized calendars, provide employees with ready access to company data and documents, and generally speed information flow. They can facilitate workplace decentralization. Although there also are downsides (see table 2-2), a growing number of enterprises consider intranets essential to their operations.

Marc Andreessen, cofounder of Netscape, is credited with introducing the concept and term *extranet*.[7] An extranet is part of a company's private intranet opened selectively

---

### Table 2-2  Downsides to Intranets

| | |
|---|---|
| Expensive to Construct | Intranets can be costly, particularly if employees have old or incompatible computers and software that must be replaced. |
| Expensive to Maintain | Upkeep costs can be high, particularly as new technology makes equipment and software obsolete and forces its replacement. Firewalls are expensive to maintain and must be upgraded regularly for maximum protection. |
| Susceptible to Security Breaches | Poorly constructed and out-of-date firewalls can be breached, which leaves company databases, files, and records vulnerable to unauthorized access. |
| Impersonal | At the same time intranets are credited with cutting travel time and facilitating employee long-distance work teams, they are also criticized for eliminating or reducing the synergy that can develop in face-to-face interactions. |

to users from outside the company. Such users may be customers, suppliers, joint venture partners, or others approved for access. They can enter the extranet from the public Internet or from proprietary intranets. Like intranets, extranets also use Internet technology, which means they allow communication between computer platforms regardless of computer or program. Extranet firewalls are programmed to allow authorized visitors in and keep unauthorized visitors out.

Extranets can support marketing activities. As mentioned in chapter 1, Lands' End (*http://www.landsend.com*) custom-creates web sites specifically for a participating company, restricting access to employees and featuring products the company allows employees to buy, such as uniforms at reduced corporate rates and monogrammed with the company logo, or selected items that are gifts or rewards for designated work accomplishments. Company employees access the customized Lands' End site through their company's intranet. Lands' End has made custom web sites for General Motors' (GM) Saturn Division, RadioShack, Carolina Power & Light, Cisco Systems, and others. Lands' End's computers check each visitor's IP address to verify that it is authorized. This approach is very successful for both Lands' End and its cooperating company customers.[8]

United Parcel Service (UPS) opens its intranet to selected external visitors seeking package transit information. Any public Internet user can visit the UPS web site (*http://www.ups.com*), but only authorized customers presenting a bona fide tracking number can enter the package tracking system.

Companies or organizations that link their intranets can share information and work collaboratively to save time, effort, and money. For example, they can share training programs and news of common interest. Inventory holding costs can be reduced, reorder times shortened, and paperwork reduced or eliminated if suppliers can directly access company sales data and initiate automatic product repurchases (*rebuys*) in real time. Extranets can be used to service customers faster and provide personalized attention. Authorized customers can access product catalogs on a company's intranet, which reduces the costs of producing and distributing hardcopy catalogs, as shown in the Lands' End example.

Security is a top concern with extranets, as it is with intranets. The cost of implementing an extranet can be high, particularly if extensive security measures are required. Legal issues are another concern. Having an extranet can mean a significant increase in email and persistent electronic paper trails.

## BARRIERS

Since its inception the Internet has been regarded as an open environment where information is voluntarily shared. Vinton Cerf, one of the Internet's founders, stated this philosophy in a speech titled, "The Internet Is for Everyone: How Easy to Say—How Hard to Achieve."[9] He identified barriers to making the Internet accessible, including the following:

**AFFORDABILITY**   The Internet must be affordable so people worldwide can come online and share in its benefits.

**LACK OF OPEN ACCESS AND FREEDOM OF SPEECH**   Governments must not restrict access and censor content; people must be able to freely exchange ideas.

**UNDERCAPACITY**    The Internet's technology must continue to evolve so the Internet matrix can expand sufficiently to handle anticipated traffic growth. This requires flexibility and absence of overbearing governmental restrictions and excessive proprietary controls.

**COMPLEXITY**    Internet interfaces (connecting devices) must be simplified, made user-friendly so it will be easier to go online and benefit from being there.

**INCOMPATIBLE LAWS**    Legal restrictions must not hinder growth, but instead protect freedom of expression and copyrights.

**LACK OF PRIVACY**    Privacy and the confidentiality of transactions must be protected. Fear of lack of privacy is a serious concern that stops some people from going online.

**SECURITY**    Protected spaces must be created for young people.

**IRRESPONSIBLE USE**    Everyone must join in being responsible for the use of the Internet and share in its wealth.

Cerf calls for everyone to work with the Internet Society and others to achieve these goals. He believes the convergence of media—television, radio, telephony, and print—will become a reality on the Internet, particularly as broadband access spreads. Thus, he suggests that the Internet will advance democracy and extend voting franchises by opening access to these processes to more people. It will become the repository of "all we have accomplished as a society." And, Cerf predicts, the Internet will move off Earth with the NASA Mars mission, leading to a functioning Earth-Mars Internet link by 2008.

Cerf's vision is noble, but he realizes the difficulty of achieving most of the goals. Many governments do not support free speech and democracy offline, so they will attempt to exert online censorship, more or less successfully. Only in the United States is speech protected by the First Amendment guarantee of freedom of speech. The disparity in economic wealth worldwide means that fully industrialized countries with highly educated workforces already benefit from Internet adoption while others do not. Poor countries with poorly educated workforces already experience varying difficulty in getting a critical mass of enterprises and people connected. Some require significant outside help to do so.

Internet marketers need enterprises and consumers online that can purchase products. This suggests that having *everyone* online literally is not necessarily desirable from a marketing perspective. Evidence is mounting that countries and businesses are carving up the Internet and erecting access barriers. Legal and regulatory issues are becoming more complex and divisive rather than less so. Although privacy should be protected, Internet marketers must be allowed to collect sufficient, relevant information about customers so they can use the information to customize and personalize offers. U.S. marketers doing business in the European Union (EU) must comply with restrictive privacy policies that, if enforced, will undermine their ability to collect customer information. Protecting children online is another contentious issue. Despite these problems, the Internet will grow and evolve, perhaps not as purely as Vinton Cerf hopes, but in a form that supports commerce and still accomplishes some of the goals set for it to achieve. As for whether it *should* grow and evolve, having lived with Internet commercialization for over a decade, most consumers and enterprises would greatly mourn its loss should it cease to exist. It has become an inextricable part of our society and economy, and its benefits already far outweigh its costs.

## VULNERABILITY

The Internet is robust but not invulnerable. Concern about its vulnerability was growing prior to 9/11/01 although no imminent cyberterrorism threat was identified. Government officials, scientists, academics, and private industry groups had been talking for years about how to protect the Internet against wide-scale attacks. Since September 11, the talk has greater urgency.

**Cyberterrorism**
Terrorism against the Internet, its networks, or linked computers with the intent of disrupting Internet activities.

Cyberterrorism is terrorism against the Internet, its networks, or linked computers with the intent of disrupting Internet communications, spreading fear, causing economic chaos, corrupting or stealing information, or otherwise compromising the system. Cyberterrorism is violence designed to advance a political or social agenda and cause grave harm to its victims. Although some attacks on specific corporate web sites are called civil disobedience and other attacks are senseless vandalism, they are not true cyberterrorism, which has a far wider impact.

The complexity, size, and interdependencies of the networks and computers making up the Internet's infrastructure make it vulnerable. Small numbers of terrorists with knowledge and motivation can launch an attack remotely and anonymously. They can hijack computers and networks, then turn them against other computers and networks in coordinated distributed denial of service (DDoS) attacks that block legitimate traffic from reaching web sites. They can spread computer viruses that can quickly create havoc in infected systems. Terrorists also can use the Internet to communicate among themselves and launch and coordinate terrorist attacks offline.

Malicious individuals and groups pose an asymmetrical threat that is difficult to track down, intercept, and eliminate. Enterprises with Internet-connected computers are urged to strengthen system security to protect their data and avoid being hijacked and used in DDoS or other attacks. Because the Internet is borderless, prevention must extend to worldwide cooperation in the development and implementation of strategies designed to protect the matrix. Countries that do not cooperate could risk being disconnected. Unfortunately, regulations designed to protect Internet operations may also seriously restrict the free exchange of information for which it is known.

**WEB UPDATE**

Cyberterrorism

A widespread terrorist attack on the Internet would be devastating to its commercialization, at least short term, and cost millions if not billions of dollars in lost revenues and repairs. It would disrupt transactions, slow or halt transmissions, block access to web sites, compromise payment security, expose data, and undermine confidence in doing business online.[10] Lessons learned from the September 2001 terrorist attacks, the estimated cost of the attacks in excess of US$120 billion, and the vulnerability of the Internet are finally galvanizing governments in the principal Internet-using nations to take steps to harden and protect the global network.

## ✔ CONCEPT CHECK

1. Describe how data are transmitted over the Internet. Use email as an example.
2. Although an "Internet for Everyone" is a noble goal, is it one that also serves the best interests of Internet marketers?
3. Why should Internet marketers be concerned about cyberterrorism?

# *Internet Management*

Internet marketing occurs on a global electronic network shared by millions of computers and over a half billion users. Given its size and distributed structure, it would be easy to assume that a highly structured, powerful central management system maintains the stability of the matrix, avoids chaos, and gets all members to cooperate and coordinate their efforts. Instead, Internet management is just the opposite.

NSFNet's privatization marked the beginning of less U.S. government Internet oversight. The government didn't disappear from Internet management entirely, however, and it continues to fund the next-generation very high speed Internet for academic research (vBNS and Internet2).[11] Nevertheless, throughout the 1990s, private companies took on more tasks formerly the prerogative of U.S. government agencies.

Today, the Internet is run by no single entity, yet many individuals, organizations, and governments contribute to its management, growth, and continued stable operation. Governments are working together on many issues to develop uniform responses to thorny jurisdiction problems. For example, some U.S. government agencies are struggling with how to effectively regulate U.S. companies doing business online. The U.S. Federal Trade Commission (FTC) has taken a lead role on many business issues. Other agencies actively involved with online commercialization include the U.S. Federal Communication Commission (FCC), the National Science Foundation (NSF), and the National Telecommunications and Information Administration (NTIA). The Federal Bureau of Investigation (FBI), the National Security Agency (NSA), and other agencies focus on issues of individual, enterprise, and national Internet security.

Private companies, among them telecommunications companies, ISPs, national service providers, cable television companies, hardware and software manufacturers, domain name registrars, and others, also collaborate to help run the Internet. Self-regulation plays an important role in addressing significant problems of Internet use, including privacy and free speech, and reassuring consumers about the safety of doing business online. Also critical to the maintenance of order are voluntary professional committees, which decide technical standards, policy, and the Internet's future direction.

## THE INTERNET SOCIETY (ISOC)

First among the voluntary professional committees is the Internet Society (ISOC at *http://www.isoc.org*). Founded in 1992 and located in Reston, Virginia, USA, the ISOC is a nonprofit, nongovernmental, international organization that broadly considers Internet operating standards, public policy, education, and membership issues. Some have called it the conscience of the Internet for its concern about privacy, open access, Internet governance, and cybercrime. Members represent over a hundred nations and include more than 150 organizations and six thousand individuals. The ISOC is an umbrella organization and home for other committees responsible for infrastructure standards, including the Internet Engineering Task Force (IETF) and the Internet Architecture Board (IAB).

The IETF (*http://www.ietf.org*), an international volunteer committee of network designers, operators, vendors, and researchers concerned with the evolution of the

Internet architecture and its smooth operation, considers routing, data transport, and security. The IAB (*http://www.iab.org/iab*) is a technical advisory group of the ISOC that oversees the Internet's architecture and standards, protocols and procedures.

## OTHER COMMITTEES

Other voluntary committees contribute to maintaining order and standardization, and planning for the Internet's growth. The Internet Research Task Force (IRTF at *http://www.irtf.org*) promotes research to further the Internet's evolution. Its research groups focus on the future of Internet protocols, applications, architecture, and technology. The Internet Societal Task Force (ISTF at *http://www.istf.isoc.org*) is an open organization of people committed to advancing the mission of the ISOC. The ISTF works "To assure the open development, evolution and use of the Internet for the benefit of all people throughout the world." Concerns of the task force include accessibility and barriers to Internet use (social, economic, regulatory, physical); privacy and the protection of Internet users; education and school access to the Internet; economics and its influence on Internet penetration rates; regulation and its effect on Internet expansion; and problems associated with taxing the Internet. The Electronic Frontier Foundation (EFF at *http://www.istf.isoc.org*) is a nonprofit organization dedicated to protecting civil liberties, privacy, and freedom of expression on the Internet.

The World Wide Web Consortium (W3C at *http://www.w3.org/pub/WWW*), with over five hundred member organizations worldwide, is an industry-supported organization that develops standards for the World Wide Web, HTTP, HTML, and other web protocols. Created in October 1994, the W3C is dedicated to maintaining web interoperability and growth. It was established through the collaboration of CERN, DARPA, and the European Community (EU) and currently is heading efforts to create the Semantic Web, which will extend the current WWW to more effectively interconnect people and computers.

The Internet Corporation for Assigned Names and Numbers (ICANN at *http://www.icann.org*) is a nonprofit corporation responsible for allocating IP addresses and managing the domain name system. ICANN accredits companies that register domain names for business and organizations.

## SELF-REGULATION

Another mechanism for managing Internet activities is self-regulation, which frequently is undertaken to prevent the need for government regulation. TRUSTe (*http://www.truste.org*), an independent, nonprofit organization began operations on June 10, 1997. It offers assistance to businesses developing web site privacy statements, operates the online TRUSTe privacy seal program, and awards the TRUSTe hyperlink seal to sites with acceptable privacy practices. Its goals are to provide consumers with control over personal information collected online, web publishers with a process for obtaining a seal that reassures consumers their privacy is protected, and government regulators with evidence that business can successfully self-regulate. TRUSTe program sponsors include AOL, Excite, Intel, Intuit, Microsoft, Verizon, Novell, and Symantec.

Another form of Internet self-regulation is industry-specific. The Verified Internet Pharmacy Practice Sites (VIPPS) program was implemented in spring 1999 by the almost hundred-year-old National Association of Boards of Pharmacy (NABP). NABP is the only professional association representing pharmacy boards in all fifty states of the United States, the District of Columbia, Guam, Puerto Rico, the Virgin Islands, New Zealand, nine Canadian Provinces, and four Australian states (*http://www.nabp.net/ vipps/intro.asp*). The VIPPS online pharmacy certification process was developed by a task force of state and federal regulatory associations, professional associations, and consumer advocacy groups. The VIPPS seal indicates that an online pharmacy has complied with VIPPS and NABP certification requirements for such standards as patient privacy rights and authentication and security of prescription orders. VIPPS-certified online pharmacies include Walgreens.com (*http://www.walgreens.com*), Clickpharmacy.com (*Clickpharmacy.com*), iPrescription.net (*http://iPrescription.net*), and Drugstore.com (*http://www.drugstore.com*).

A final example is the Better Business Bureau (BBB, *http://www.bbbonline.org*), which provides a BBBOnLine Reliability seal program. The program verifies that authorized businesses meet BBB membership standards and have the right to display the reliability seal. Its goal is to promote trust and confidence in businesses displaying the reliability or BBB privacy seals. Its mission is "to help Web users find reliable, trustworthy businesses online, and to help reliable businesses identify themselves as such, all via voluntary self-regulatory programs that help avoid government regulation of the Internet."[12]

Seal programs can be very reassuring to consumers. A seal from a reputable organization is visual reassurance that a site is safe and reputable. Even a well-known retailer like Walgreens with more than 3,650 stores nationwide benefits from its VIPPS certification, as consumers who shop the offline stores may still need reassurance about shopping the Walgreens web site. The challenge for organizations issuing seals is to implement continuous member monitoring programs to avoid having a certified site undermine the seal's credibility by failing to maintain acceptable standards. The challenge for Internet marketers is to recognize that sites displaying seals have a competitive advantage over sites that do not. Prominently displayed seals on a site's home page work 24/7/365 to visually remind visitors that the site is concerned about their well-being.

### ✔ CONCEPT CHECK

1. What role do professional organizations play in managing the Internet?
2. What are ISOC and ICANN? What do they contribute to Internet management?
3. Why is self-regulation needed?

## *How The Web Works*

**HyperText Transfer Protocol (HTTP)**
The protocol or standards for transferring files including web pages, images, text, sound, video, graphics, and virtual reality.

The World Wide Web has captured the public's imagination and is where most Internet marketing occurs. It is bright, colorful, interesting, useful, informative, and entertaining. Like every system operating on the Internet matrix, the Web adheres to the TCP/IP protocol. However, it also requires a unique protocol, **HyperText Transfer Protocol** (**HTTP**), for transferring files, including web pages, images, text, sound, video, graphics, and virtual reality. Because so much Internet growth and marketing is on the Web, it is appropriate at this point to consider how it works and why it is an object of such intense marketing interest.

## WEB PAGES

A web page looks like a standard computer application page but is distinguished by the arrangement of its text, graphics, design, and multimedia elements, and hypertext links. Web pages can be made larger or smaller to fit a computer screen or the viewer's preferences. They can be scrolled down or sideways if the page doesn't fit on a screen. The viewer can move backward and forward between pages linked in a multipage web site, store pages for later use, print pages, and easily move from one web site to another. Most new computers have sufficient memory so that multiple web pages can be worked on or viewed concurrently.

Browsers make the Web user-friendly. Browser software locates, retrieves, and views web pages. The most popular browsers are graphical (Netscape, Microsoft Internet Explorer, and AOL), but some people still use text-only browsers such as Lynx or turn off the graphic capacity in Netscape or Explorer to speed download time. Text-only browsers download faster because they read text and ignore graphics or other multimedia-rich elements. Marketers should consider this when developing product pages and include text product descriptions where appropriate.

Web pages are written in a text-based format known as the HyperText Markup Language (HTML) that is the page's source code. The code tells a web browser where text and images should be placed on the page, what colors and backgrounds are used, and generally how the page is composed. HTML code is written with tags that indicate where page elements begin and end. An example of HTML coding for this paragraph is shown below.

Pages written in HTML usually contain links (hypertext connections or **hyperlinks**). Links are what make the Web so interesting and useful. A link is a connection from a

# *HTML Code*

```
‹HTML›
‹HEAD›
 ‹META NAME="GENERATOR" CONTENT="Adobe PageMill 3.0 Mac"›
 ‹META HTTP-EQUIV="Content-Type" CONTENT="text/html; charset=iso-8859-1"›
 ‹META NAME="Generator" CONTENT="Microsoft Word 73.1"›
 ‹TITLE›HTML Code‹/TITLE›
‹/HEAD›
‹BODY BGCOLOR="#ffffff"›


Web pages are written in a text-based format known as the HyperText Markup Language
(HTML) that is the page's source code. The code tells a web browser where text and images
should be placed on the page, what colors and backgrounds are used, and generally how the
page is composed. HTML code is written with tags that indicate where page elements begin
and end. If this paragraph were written in HTML, the source code would look like this
‹!—SELECTION—›‹!—/SELECTION—›
‹/BODY›
‹/HTML›
```

**Hyperlink**

Links in web documents written in hypertext that, if clicked on, instruct the browser to retrieve information from that link.

word, image, or object to another area within a page, to another page within a web site, or to a different web site. The highlighted word is the most common link, although images and animations are often linked. A link typically is highlighted, colored, and underlined. When a user clicks on a link, the browser initiates delivery of the linked item, page, or site. HTML editing programs (FrontPage, Netscape Composer, Dreamweaver) simplify web page construction.

Web site pages are stored on a web server running Mac, Windows, Apache, UNIX, or other operating system. Servers can run multiple software programs simultaneously. Some web servers, called *hosts*, store the web files being requested. *Client* servers are computers that request information.[13] To complicate matters, some servers can be both host and client.

**Applets**

Little application programs running on web servers that are widely used because they download quickly and require little bandwidth.

**Applets** are little application programs embedded in web pages that run on web servers, hence the diminutive *applet*. Applets add text scrolling, animated graphics, calculators, and other customized functions to web pages. They are widely used because they download quickly and require little bandwidth. Applets are written in Sun's Java programming language (*http://java.sun.com/applets/index.html*).

Many web pages and sites are successful, others far less so or not at all. Some are very slow downloading, often because they contain an excess of animated graphics or large sound files. Some sites are so complicated and poorly organized that it takes too long for a visitor to drill down to a destination page, so they click past the site. Content on some web pages is hard to understand or not informative. Other pages are on web sites that have moved without a forwarding address, have been abandoned, have links that do not work, or haven't been updated since 1993![14]

## WEB ADDRESSES

**Address**

Four types of addresses currently are in use: email addresses, IP or Internet addresses, hardware addresses, and URL addresses on the World Wide Web.

A web page **address** is an important marketing tool for building awareness and directing visitors to a site. Just as people have an address that identifies the location of their home or business, all locations on the Internet and Web have an address. Four types of addresses currently are in use: email addresses, IP or Internet addresses, hardware addresses, and URL addresses on the World Wide Web. Web pages are addressed using the Internet Protocol (IP) and a unique **Uniform Resource Locator** (**URL**) address that a browser reads. A typical URL looks like *http://business.college.hmco.com/students*. The anatomy of this address is explained in table 2-3. Computers actually read a named address in four groups of numbers (from 0 to 255) separated by periods, like 192.107.41.31. The numbered address tells a browser exactly where to locate the requested file in the domain and server.

**Uniform Resource Locator (URL)**

Address that a web browser reads.

Many addresses are dropping the *http://www* and using only hostname and file location in their visible address. For example, the Weather Channel can be reached at *weather.com*, which is faster than typing *http://www.weather.com*. The Weather Channel registered many forms of its address, including both long and short forms, so a visitor can type any of several address names and still get routed to the right place.

## DOMAINS AND NAMES

Until 1984, all Internet (IP) addresses were numeric, a ten-digit number. People can easily remember the seven digits of their local telephone number and their nine-digit social security number. However, they are far less likely to remember a solely numeric

| Table 2-3  Anatomy of a Web Address | |
| --- | --- |
| A web address | *http://business.college.hmco.com/students* is read by a web browser. The address provides the following information. |
| http://business.college.hmco.com | Protocol type (HyperText Transfer Protocol) Hostname: business.college.hmco.com domain name, file on Houghton Mifflin server |
| students | In the directory (default folder) for students The file for the student business front page for the Houghton Mifflin College division Written in HyperText Markup Language (HTML) |

Internet address unless it is for their own web site. Therefore, domain names were introduced to simplify Internet addressing by allowing the substitution of words for numbers, although each address has a corresponding number read by browsers.

The Domain Name System (DNS) established a hierarchical order for top and secondary level domains. The original top-level domains (TLDs) were .edu, .com, .net., .org, .gov, .mil, and the two-digit Country Codes (CC). In many countries, second-level domains appear directly before the Country Code, so an address registered in England might read *http://www.cgull.co.uk*, where the category, .com, comes before the Country Code.[15] The first registered domain was Symbolics.com (March 15, 1984); others followed quickly, including purdue.edu, ucla.edu, and mitre.org.[16]

In October 2000, the number of registered web sites passed 30 million and was forecast to exceed 60 million within 18 months.[17] Concern about dwindling numbers of the most desirable names, particularly dot-coms, led the ICANN to pass a resolution that agrees to "the introduction of new TLDs in a measured and responsible manner."[18] The ICANN's goal is to increase competition and reduce profiteering by entrepreneurs that buy domain names to exploit their trademark or proprietary value, then hold the name ransom for sale to the highest bidder. Eleven new names were added in November 2000 (see table 2-4). Although the new TLDs will ease the shortage of names, it adds to the expense of registering all possible variations of an address.

| Table 2-4  New TLDs | |
| --- | --- |
| **Domain** | **Type** |
| .info | General use |
| .biz | Business |
| .name | Individuals |
| .pro | Professionals |
| .museum | Museums |
| .coop | Business cooperatives |
| .aero | Aviation industry |

Registering a domain name once is not enough to secure the name. Over 249 different domain names are used worldwide. CBS owns its registration for CBS.com in only four places; in 46 other places, a different business uses CBS.com.[19] Each name can have closely worded descriptors as well as different domains. For example, to protect the name Cgull Systems would require paying for the four available TLDs (.com, .org, .net, and .biz), as well as similar-sounding names. Thus, it would mean registering and paying for Cgull.com, Cgull.org, Cgull.net, Cgull.biz as well as such variations on the name as Seagull.com, Seagull.org, Seagull.net, Seagull.biz, AboutCgull.com, About Cgull.net, and so on. Registering multiple names crowds out others who might try to infringe on the name, and aliases direct visitors to the site even if they type in a misspelled name.

Domain names are valuable property, and care should go into their construction and protection (see "Domain Naming" below). Many domain names have been bought by speculators who plan to sell them in the future to companies or famous individuals whose trademarks they have usurped. Companies frequently sue to recover domain names that are clearly trademark infringements. Hasbro, Inc. was forced to sue to be able to register candyland.com. They won their case by proving that the pornography site registered at the Candyland address diluted the company's forty-seven-year-old trademark for the popular children's board game.[20] Actress Julia Roberts appealed to the World Intellectual Property Organization (WIPO) for control of the Internet domain name juliaroberts.com that had been registered by an accused *cybersquatter* (someone who registers famous names in "bad faith," to sell for profit or exploit). A WIPO arbitration panel extended commercial protection to Ms. Roberts as a famous individual whose name is her trademark. It ruled against the cybersquatter who "had no legitimate interest in the domain name and used it in bad faith."[21] Of course, this didn't stop the hundreds of people who operate web sites devoted to the actress and use her name somewhere in their web address. The U.S. Anticybersquatting Consumer Protection Act of 1999 criminalizes the unauthorized use of trademark-protected names in Internet domain addresses, but it remains to be seen how effective this will be in stopping a worldwide names market.[22]

Domain names do not last forever. Domain contracts can run from one to ten years. If some people have their way, domain names eventually will become irrelevant. Directory services are beginning to appear that sort out requests for site addresses by full company name, which eliminates the need for domain names.

As web page and site numbers increase, it will become harder for marketers to penetrate the clutter and contact potential customers. Reaching existing customers is not as much a problem. Online marketers already capture customer email addresses in databases, then use the information to periodically contact them by email

## Domain Naming

What's in a name? Domain names must be carefully worded to be descriptive, clear, memorable, and legally protected. They can contain any letter from a to z; numerals 1 to 9; and hyphens and underlines, but not directly under words. Letters can be lowercased or capitalized. Length is an issue as the numbers, letters, hyphens, and underlines must not exceed sixty-seven characters. Domain names should be trademarked to protect them from legal challenge by others. However, before registering, the name should be checked to see whether or not it is already trademarked.[23] A catchy URL should be listed in as many locations as possible so search engines, spiders, indexes, and directories can push the address to buyers. Many businesses will do this for a company. TrafficBoost.com (*http://TrafficBoost.com*) will list a web site URL with over 500 directories and search engines worldwide for under US$100.

with reminders of the site and its offers. Because current customers are more involved with a site they've visited or bought from, they also are more likely to pay attention to television, radio, newspaper, magazine, or online advertisements that contain the site's URL. They may have bookmarked the site to facilitate an easy return visit.

Until 1999, domain names could be registered through only one company, Network Solutions Inc., which held a U.S. government-sanctioned monopoly on names ending in the domains .com, .net, and .org.[24] Now, more than eighty companies are accredited and qualified registrars of .com, .net, and .org domain names. Another seventy are accredited but not yet operational. Internationally accredited and qualified registrars are in Canada, France, the Republic of Korean, China, Germany, and Japan. Many more are accredited but not yet operational in Israel, New Zealand, Australia, Taiwan, and elsewhere.[25]

Registering domain names is a big business. Network Solutions, now a VeriSign company, registered only 13,000 domain names in 1993, 100,000 in 1995, and one million in 1997. Over 16 million names were registered in 2001. A web hosting company providing server space for web businesses can register a domain name for businesses purchasing its services. Most businesses, however, go directly to a DNS registration company. Registering a domain name can cost as little as US$15. Companies often charge from US$25 to US$50 to register a .com, .net, or .org.

## PORTALS

To portal or not is a key question for web marketers. **Portals** are ports of entry, gateways to the Web with links to web sites that are of general interest (*generic or horizontal portals*) or special interest to like-minded people (*niche or vertical portals*). Generic portals include Netscape's Netcenter (*http://www.netscape.com*), Yahoo! (*http://www.yahoo.com*), and AOL.com (*http://www.aol.com*). Niche portals are like targeted cable television networks, Lifetime (women), CNBC (stock pickers), and ESPN (sports fans), that schedule programming to suit their audience's interests. Portal revenues mostly come from selling onsite advertising space. AOL, however, also profits from its subscriber base.

The first portals were the original online services (AOL, Prodigy, CompuServe) that offered shopping malls, email, lists, search engines, and other services to subscribers. Netscape created one of the first portals at Netcenter. Today, many search engines have transformed themselves into portals in order to retain and grow their customer bases.

Netscape's portal (*http://netscape.com*) has many of the same features as other generic gateways. It offers links for general web searches as well as a weather search. The latest news is highlighted, with links to stories behind the headlines. It has a shopping center, web tools for booking airline flights, business information with a stock ticker, channels for special interest links, a web calendar that can be personalized, and sports news. These features are designed to highlight "deals" for the consumer and push them toward favored sites. Encouraging consumers to personalize a web default page, making it their start page, is a savvy marketing tactic. Personalization is practically no-cost for the web host, a Netcenter or Yahoo! It builds a ready audience for content pushed from the host. It also pressures hosts to add new features and fresh content so the start-up page doesn't become stale. If it does, there is always another host eager to capture bored consumers looking for a more enticing personalized start-up page.

Business as well as consumer portals are springing up all over the Web; many are public and others are proprietary. Business intranet portals are niche gateways with content and links that serve a select group of people, the company's employees. General business portals are niche portals with business links. The public business portal Business.com (*http://www.business.com*) has a search engine that links to more than twenty-five thousand different business topics. This portal had to purchase its domain name for US$7.5 million from an entrepreneur who speculated someone would be willing to pay that high a price for this highly descriptive URL.

Portals exist for kids (Alfy, The Web Portal for Kids at *http://www.alfy.com*), cowboys (the eCowboy Network for rodeo, country music at *http://www.ecowboy.com*), equine sites (clipclop at *http://www.clipclop.com*), health (Florida's e-Health portal at *http://www.floridahealthstat.com*), and just about any known interest. Must a marketer link his or her web site to a portal? It will become hard to avoid them if the Web continues to favor portal development. As the Web expands, interest-oriented portals may become essential entry points for consumers and enterprises overwhelmed by the choices facing them. On the other hand, portals have a tendency to get extremely cluttered, which can frustrate consumers trying to use them. They also pose a contradiction, for most marketers want customers to stay on their sites (stick), while portals direct consumers to other sites. Finally, individuals will soon be able to purchase software that allows them to create personalized portals. If this happens, commercial portals may find their strongest competition comes from consumers who portal.

## ✔ CONCEPT CHECK

1. What makes the Web so attractive to marketers?
2. Why do web sites need multiple domain names?
3. Why would a marketer place an advertisement for a web site on a *niche* portal?

# New Applications and Access Alternatives

Marketers must understand their customers in order to develop irresistible market offers. This understanding is called *customer insight*. When it comes to the Internet and the Web, it means learning where, how, why, and when target markets go online to use the Internet and the Web, and what they do once they are there. For example, the United States has more home Internet users than any other country, although Hong Kong has the highest rate of growth of users going online from home. Over 160 million people in the United States have home Internet access, compared with 14.6 million in Germany, and 15 million in the United Kingdom. Almost 60 percent of Americans go online from home, an increase from 52 percent in 2000 and only 39 percent in 1999. This compares with 41 million who go online in the office.[26] What does it mean to marketers that more Internet users go online from home? One key implication is that web marketing sites must avoid loading their pages with high-bandwidth streaming audio and video, because home users are far less likely to have broadband than office users.

Marketers must also understand and track the adoption of new Internet-based technologies and access alternatives as they appear for home use, at work, and play. In particular, this means wireless, a highly popular access alternative in Asia and Europe that is also making inroads into the U.S. market. Widespread adoption of wireless will cause many web sites to offer alternative streamlined pages specially configured for the far smaller wireless screens.

## AT HOME

The newest thing in residential construction is high-speed Internet access wired into a home while it is being built. Whole house wiring or *domestic digitization* lets homeowners create smart digital in-home networks where all the owner's computers and digital applications can go online. Home networking is also penetrating the existing home market. This includes adding home networking hardware and software, firewalls, home servers, and home gateway and automatic products. By 2006, the connected home market is expected to grow to US$9.2 billion globally, up from US$1.4 billion in 2001.[27] This market is ripe for broadband services. Picture the I-wired homeowner downloading music, movies-on-demand, or virtual reality while relaxing in his or her La-Z-Boy Explorer ecliner (*http://www.lazyboy.com*) with a wireless keyboard and WebTV Plus connection in the armrest. Even though this is an exciting vision, it won't be something the majority of Americans will experience for a long time, if ever. Rather than completely rewiring homes for networked services, it is more likely that a far cheaper alternative will be adopted. Apple Computer is moving in this direction with the concept of its iMac as the center of the home entertainment and communication network, some of which is wireless.

Another aspect of home connectedness is the convergence of television, computers, and the Internet through WebTV or I-TV. Microsoft's MSNTV (*http://www.msntv.com*) thus far has only generated lukewarm enthusiasm among consumers. A black box sitting on a television set lets viewers surf the Internet and check email. Consumers must purchase the box and pay a monthly Internet access fee. Most WebTV owners do not own a PC. Microsoft's WebTV has about one million subscribers after over five years of selling the product. Apparently, game players prefer play stations, email users want small screen privacy, web surfers want faster access and more than just one screen at a time, and TV watchers are not buying into the concept of web-enhanced television programs. Cost is another factor, particularly since PC prices continue to fall, and low cost Internet access is still available.

AOLTV (*http://www.aoltv.com*) may succeed where others have failed because it uses the same features as AOL online services and has access to the vast entertainment resources of Time Warner (*http://www.aoltimewarner.com*) and its 13 million subscribers to Time Warner cable television. AOL bought Time Warner for US$165 billion in 2000. AOLTV may attract AOL customers from its over 33 million subscriber base. AOLTV lets AOL subscribers access their AOL email and buddy list, chat, and message, as well as surf the Net and watch television.[28] Fees for accessing the Internet by AOLTV are lower for AOL members.

If consumers do not feel like clicking their way to the Internet, they will soon be issuing voice commands. They can already speak live to an online customer service representative at Lands' End. Yahoo! and Excite@Home offer verbal chats for their users, and Net2Phone (*http://www.net2phone.com*) routes cellular phone calls over the Internet. Voice-over-the-Net technology is just beginning to have an impact and will grow in popularity, particularly among those people who have never mastered typing.[29]

Think of a home air conditioner that can be turned on in response to an email message sent from a car phone and refrigerators that send distress calls via the Internet to a factory service representative when they malfunction. Home appliances will monitor themselves and signal for help when it is needed, without their owner's knowledge until it comes time for the repairperson to schedule a house call. Cisco Systems and Whirlpool Corp. are developing a line of Internet-ready appliances designed to increase operating efficiency. The question is whether they can be made affordable and attractive to consumers.[30]

In Japan, Toyota's Crown Athlete luxury sedan has an Internet navigation system called Monet that tracks the car's location using wireless communication and the Global (Satellite) Positioning System (GPS). It can read email messages aloud to the driver and accepts verbal commands to give a weather report or provide other information downloaded from the Internet. Monet also displays real-time video displays of traffic at major intersections. "The car is the next big frontier on the Net."[31] Although this sounds exciting, there are downsides. Drivers are already distracted by cell phones, imagine what may happen when they have a full array of Internet-connected devices on their dashboards. Internet-connected PCs are beginning to appear in the backseat area of selected minivan models. In addition to surfing the Net, playing online games, and downloading email, the PCs can play DVD movies. Long trips with small children will be far quieter in these vans.

Apparently it is not enough for consumers to access the Internet at home, in the office, and cars. Now people can ride web-enabled elevators in buildings in four U.S. cities or see an Internet news scroll while accessing their ATM at San Francisco's Wells Fargo banks. News, weather, sports, and stock market updates are displayed on ten-inch monitors mounted on elevators in Chicago, New York, and Boston. Each screen is displayed for ten seconds, with thirty different screens in each complete rotation.[32] Internet elevator broadcasts are prime sites for marketing promotions. They can also be a source of extreme irritation for people riding elevators with malfunctioning Internet screens that broadcast only static. Another recent innovation is the appearance of high-speed Internet kiosks, which are popping up in many locations, including malls, airports, subway stations, restaurants, and offline retail stores. For example, visitors to Universal Studios Theme Park in Orlando, Florida, USA, can access AOL email from computer terminal kiosks located throughout the park. Some observers expect that public pay phones will evolve into Internet-enabled devices.[33] Clearly, the Internet and the Web are ubiquitous in contemporary life.

**WEB UPDATE**

Internet and Web Technologies at Home and in the Workplace

## AT WORK

Businesses displaced by the September 11, 2001, New York World Trade Centers attacks had to immediately find new office space. An estimated ten thousand jobs left New York City in the days following the disaster. Many businesses also began considering whether or not they should return to high-visibility workplaces. As a Lehman Brothers spokesperson said, "It doesn't really matter where we work. You're a computer terminal and a phone line away from Wall Street."[34]

Decentralized workplaces were becoming more common even before 9/11. Mobile professionals can connect to their offices and customers by wireless phone, net appliance, and various other devices that can be used on the ground or in the air. Most large and medium-sized airports have telecomport facilities for mobile users. Hotels catering to business travelers have Internet access in rooms. Moreover, many hotels have on-site technicians able to make even the trickiest net connections for visitors. They market this service to business travelers, and it is a competitive marketing advantage for them, differentiating them from the competition.

Many workers telecommute from home over the Internet to their company's intranet. This reduces the office space needed for them and saves transportation expenses. However, telecommuters often complain that they work much longer hours when based at home because the demarcation between home and office is less distinct.

Intranets allow company employees to collaborate in real time by text, voice, and visual display regardless of their physical location. This increased communication ease has many advantages, but it also has drawbacks. Electronic messages can pile up in email boxes faster than paper memos in an in box. Rather than freeing workers from mountains of paper, Internet technology is burying some of them in a glut of paper and electronic files.

Mobile professionals include marketers and those targeted by marketers. An immediate concern when interacting with mobile professionals is the physical size of the screen they are reading and the keypad they are using to type messages. Both are more limiting than standard computer screens and keyboards. This requires a significant adjustment in message content size and display.

## WIRELESS AND M-MARKETING

The United States is the most PC-centric industrialized nation in the world, yet by 2005 an estimated eighty-five million people in the United States are expected to use wireless, up from less than five million in 2000. By 2005, that number should increase to over ninety-six million. Business wireless use will lead the way, as mobile employees are more likely to need high-speed wireless Internet access, which their employers will provide. Consumers want wireless from their phones or personal data assistants (PDAs).[35]

Wireless net access worldwide is expected to increase from 39 million in 2000 to 729 million by 2005. Increased adoption of wireless in the United States does not mean PCs are being abandoned, just that there is a growing market for wireless devices out-of-home. By 2005, 74 percent of U.S. households but only 43 percent of European households are still expected to use PCs to go online.[36] Europeans prefer wireless interactive devices, particularly wireless telephone headsets and personal digital assistants (PDAs), that are smaller, cheaper, and less complex than PCs. By the end of 2001, wireless was far more popular in Europe and Japan than in the United States. China, with a population over 1.3 billion, has been promoting wireless phones for accessing the Internet because the vast majority of Chinese lack wired phone connections, which would be prohibitively expensive to provide.

In Japan, wireless handsets are the rage among teens and young adults because it is a fun, fast, fashionable, and relatively cheap means of communication. Nippon Telegraph and Telephone's (NTT) DoCoMo (*http://www.nttdocomo.co.jp*) markets wireless handsets (i-mode) that allow users to press one button and go online through the company's wireless portal and stay online as long as they wish. DoCoMo has captured over 70 percent of Japan's local wireless market with 29 million subscribers, and it is expanding globally (*http://www.nttdocomo.co.jp/corporate/gb/eg/index.html*). Do-

CoMo's subscribers can talk, send email, chat, and download content from more than twenty thousand mini-web sites created solely for the i-mode technology that runs the handsets. They can conduct financial transactions, order tickets, and make restaurant reservations. Handsets have color screens for displaying text and graphics. The product suits the Japanese market, which is low on PC penetration. Although DoCoMo is entering the U.S. market (*http://www.docomo-usa.com*), its i-mode platform is currently incompatible with the U.S. telecommunication system. DoCoMo is also marketing its headsets and services in Europe and Brazil.[37]

Consumers worldwide use wireless handsets and PDAs for keeping in touch with family and friends, downloading information, making purchases, trading stocks, and in some countries, making vending machine purchases. Personal information management devices, wireless handheld computers, are useful because they organize information and retrieve it, as well as share it with home computers and other people's computers. Salespeople use wireless devices to access their company's intranet and check inventories in real time, place orders, receive sales updates, and check databases. Sony is using wireless in merchandising, where field salespeople check in-store PlayStation inventories and adjust their marketing tactics accordingly. UPS has been using customized order taking and tracking wireless handsets for years.[38]

Some U.S. consumers and enterprise users are going wireless with wireless laptops, standard PCs hooked to wireless LANs, and satellite delivery systems. Others use wireless devices like the BlackBerry email pager that alerts users when corporate email is received and allows an easy read-and-respond interface. Palm Pilot devices are larger than pagers and have a far more visible visual display.[39] The Omnisky is based on the PalmV and supports web weather, traffic, and stock market reports. It can access any standard Internet mail account and browse any web site, including special small-sized sites for reduced screen devices.

Bluetooth (*http://www.bluetooth.com*), named for the tenth-century Viking king who unified Norway and Denmark, uses a different approach to wireless. It is radio signal based and allows the close proximity connectivity of Internet appliances. The short-range radio hookup is housed on a microchip, and products with a Bluetooth chip can communicate wirelessly. For example, a wireless computer with a Bluetooth chip inside can communicate wirelessly to a Bluetooth-equipped printer. The same general process is used in remote control automobile door locks and wireless personal computers operating off an airport. It is expected that Bluetooth will be in over 1.4 billion appliances by 2015.[40]

Some look at this wireless boom and m(for mobile)-marketing with expectations of great profits; all should realize, however, that there are problems marketing the current wireless products to U.S. consumers. Wireless handsets cannot download fat web pages, which means they cannot surf the web as PCs can. They also often experience slow connection speeds, dead zones due to limited roaming areas, blocked reception by obstacles like tall buildings, and security breaches because wireless is more susceptible to being overheard than wired access. In addition, bandwidth limitations slow download speed, often to narrowband text-only. Unlike Europe and Japan, there is no single wireless standard in the United States, which exacerbates the dead zone problem.[41] Another problem is that users may develop carpal tunnel syndrome from thumb typing on small keyboards and eye strain from the small monochrome screens. Some people are concerned about the fact that wireless devices can be equipped with a chip that links to the Global Positioning System (GPS) so users are identified geographically whenever they connect. This presents opportunities for further invasions of consumer privacy as they go online. The Federal Communication Commission is requiring that all U.S. wireless handsets have precise positioning for 911 calls.

Despite the preceding concerns, the market for wireless is very appealing. Young adults ten to twenty-four years of age are the most likely early adopters in the next several years. By 2004, half of all U.S. young adults are expected to own and regularly use such a device.[42]

Internet marketers recognize the potential in sales of the devices, access fees, and the potential to make offers via wireless. This is why so many web sites initially created for PC users now provide links to mobile web sites, leaner sites that can be quickly downloaded to mobile screens.

**WEB UPDATE**

Wireless and m-Marketing

One certainty about the Internet has been that human ingenuity finds solutions to problems and regularly advances the technology to new levels. Wireless may be the answer in countries where standard wired access is difficult if not impossible. Wireless will be popular among mobile professional and some consumers, particularly new technology early adopters. Wired and wireless will continue to coexist in North America, as many Internet users will wait for prices to come down and the devices to improve before going wireless. In the meantime, the next generation of wireless devices (G3) is moving toward fully net-enabled devices where wireless handsets will be a telephone, data terminal, music player, game board, and message center.

### ✔ CONCEPT CHECK

1. What value do net or i-appliances provide to their target markets?
2. Why do many consumers in other countries like wireless Internet access devices?
3. What are some problems facing wireless Internet device marketers in the United States?

## *Summary*

### *How the Internet Works*

Most consumers in the United States still use a modem and standard telephone line to connect to the Internet. Local area networks often connect users in businesses, schools, and organizations. Data (email, web pages, etc.) are broken into small independent digital packets routed along network transmission lines. When they arrive at their destination, they are reassembled into their original form. An important advantage of the Internet is its redundancy, which is a necessity for conducting online business activities because multiple routes for data transmission increase the probability that data will be delivered. Routers and servers are essential to smooth Internet operations and the transmission of data packets. Software includes programs, documents, and data that run one or millions of computers. The Internet hosts many services that developed independently but operate on the global matrix and adhere to the TCP/IP protocol. Many businesses and organizations have proprietary intranets and extranets, where marketing often takes place. Security is a top concern with the Internet, intranets, and extranets. Although the Internet has been promoted as an open environment where information is voluntarily shared, significant barriers exist to having everyone go online. Cyberterrorism is a growing concern and preventive measures are being taken by enterprises and governments in anticipation of future attacks against the Internet.

### Internet Management

The Internet is run by no single entity, yet many individuals, organizations, and governments contribute to its management, growth, and continued stable operation. The U.S. Federal Trade Commission has taken a lead role on many Internet business issues. Self-regulation plays an important role in addressing significant problems of Internet use. First among the voluntary committees is The Internet Society. The World Wide Web Consortium develops standards for the World Wide Web, HTTP, HTML, and other web protocols. The Internet Corporation for Assigned Names and Numbers allocates IP addresses and manages the domain name system. Self-regulation is often undertaken to prevent the need for government regulation. TRUSTe, VIPPS, and BBBOnline are examples of industry self-regulation.

### How the Web Works

Like every system operating on the Internet matrix, the Web adheres to the TCP/IP protocol suite. It also requires a unique protocol, HyperText Transfer Protocol (HTTP), for transferring files including web pages. Special browser software locates, retrieves, and views web pages. Text-only browsers download faster than graphical browsers. Many web pages and sites are successful; others far less so. Web page addresses are an important marketing tool. Many addresses are dropping the *http://www* and using only hostname and file location. Domain names were introduced to simplify Internet addressing by allowing the substitution of words for numbers. Many domain names have been bought by speculators who plan to sell them in the future for profit. As web page and site numbers increase, it will become harder for marketers to penetrate the clutter and reach potential customers. Portals are gateways to the Web with links to web sites that are generic or niche. Business as well as consumer portals are all over the Web. Portals pose a contradiction, for most marketers want customers to stay on their sites (stick), while portals direct visitors to other sites.

### New Applications and Access Alternatives

New Internet-based technologies and access alternatives are being introduced on a regular basis. High-speed Internet access is being wired into some new homes. Millions have been spent attempting to merge television, computers, and the Internet through the much hyped WebTV or I-TV. Consumers will soon be issuing voice commands online. Some new automobiles are becoming net enabled. Internet kiosks are showing up in many locations. Mobile professionals connect to their offices and customers by wireless phone and other mobile devices that can be used in the air or on the ground. Wireless Internet access is more popular in Europe and Japan than in the United States. In Japan, wireless handsets are the rage among teens and young adults. Some U.S. consumers and business users are going wireless with wireless laptops, standard PCs hooked to wireless LANs, and satellite delivery systems. Bluetooth is a radio-based system that allows the close proximity connectivity of Internet appliances.

## Internet Marketing Application

DoCoMo is just one of the companies vying for the vast U.S. market. Nokia (*http://www.nokiausa.com*), Motorola (*http://www.motorola.com*), and Sony (*http://www.sony.com*) are others. Compare their market offers and determine which company is using its web site to most effectively market company products. Visit each of the web sites and answer these questions.

1. How easy is it to locate a wireless Internet device from the web site front page? Count the number of clicks it takes.

2. Once the product is located, is the target market obvious? If so, describe their characteristics.
3. Are product attributes stated clearly? What are they?
4. Does the product appear easy to use? Why?
5. Are product prices clearly stated? If so, which product is most expensive?
6. Based on the web site evaluation, which product has a marketing advantage over the others? Why?

# Chapter Review Questions

1. What role do ISPs play in getting consumers online?
2. What is the benefit of Internet redundancy?
3. What role does each of the following play on the Internet? TCP/IP, POP, FTP, SMTP.
4. What is the marketing value of domain names?
5. Why are portals a contradiction to how marketers want consumers to behave?
6. What barriers limit access to the Internet?
7. What effects will the growing numbers of web pages have on advertisers?
8. Why has web-enabled television not been a great success?

9. What is TRUSTe? How does it help manage the Internet?
10. Does the WWW operate on TCP/IP? Explain.
11. What is the difference between HTTP and HTML?
12. What is a cybersquatter? Is this just good business or is it a serious threat to trademarks?
13. Identify four examples of TLDs.
14. Why do users like wireless?
15. Why might senior citizens prefer wireless to PCs?

# Case Study

## Cisco Systems

David, the router marketer from the opening vignette, does not work for Cisco Systems (*http://www.cisco.com*), but perhaps he wishes he did. Cisco is an undisputed power in the Internet economy, the Mercedes of network equipment vendors. Cisco controls more than two-thirds of the world market for networking products—routers, switches, access servers, concentrators, hubs, adapters, cards, and software solutions. Company revenues for the fiscal year ended July 31, 1999, were US$12.2 billion, up from US$8.5 billion the previous year. Its one-year sales grew 43.7 percent. However, along with other high-tech companies, Cisco took a beating in the 2000–2001 economic downturn as sales dropped 25 percent in Q2. Its stock price fell to less than a fifth of its previous year's high. For the first time in its history, the company laid off employees, more than eight thousand worldwide.

Cisco is facing growing competition from both established companies and start-ups. At the same time, it is forming alliances with other companies to develop software and standards for voice and data communication systems for businesses and other enterprises. Its joint offering with Oracle, the largest software provider for ebusiness, is aimed at providing integrated capabilities for communication—email, phone, web collaborating, web chat, and interactive voice response.

Cisco has a vast training network that works with businesses to develop Internet and communication solutions. Cisco and the U.S. Small Business Administration (SBA) are developing training programs on "Internet Essentials for Growing Business Online," six online sessions for small businesses. Cisco joined with other industry leaders to create the Mobile Wireless Internet Forum (MWIF). Its goal is to accelerate deployment of open standards for Internet mobile wireless networks operating on IP protocols, to provide a seamless interface between the wireless industry and the Internet.

Observers agree that Cisco listens carefully to its customers. It diligently collects customer feedback to make sure they are satisfied. Annual employee bonuses are tied to customer satisfaction ratings. Cisco employees have high productivity and a strong incentive to keep the company customer-centered. These factors will serve the company well as the U.S. economy recovers.

Cisco's customer-centered philosophy is also reflected in the company's response to September 11th. Some of its largest corporate clients were displaced or affected by the collapse of the World Trade Centers. Cisco immediately sent employees to help these clients restore their networks and get back online. Cisco's wireless office networks were used to restore phone and data service, protected by the company's security software and hardware. Some of its clients were back in business within twenty-four hours after the attacks.

Spending to rebuild and replace destroyed networks, routers, and servers in the New York area could exceed US$300 million, with Cisco positioned to receive a large portion. Cisco also stands to benefit from how well its wireless networks worked during the crisis, as companies evaluate whether they should return to hardwire networks or go wireless. As one big customer commented, "This puts Cisco as much in the catbird seat as anybody can be for the next five years." Although the company took a beating with the rest of the high-tech Internet-related companies, it has no debt and over US$18 billion in cash and equivalents, which gives it reserves to bridge the gap until recovery.[43]

## CHECK IT OUT

Visit Hoover's Online at *http://www.hoovers.com* and locate Cisco Systems. Find the company capsule view. What companies are Cisco's main competitors? Visit Cisco at *http://www.cisco.com* and look for marketing jobs. Even though Cisco laid employees off in 2001, are they hiring now? What kinds of marketing jobs are available and where are they located? What skills are needed? Is experience required? What would a student have to do to prepare for a job at Cisco?

## A GLOBAL PERSPECTIVE

How accommodating is Cisco to international visitors on its web home page? For the answer, visit *http://www.cisco.com/public/countries_languages. shtml*. How many countries and languages are listed for country contacts and document language translations? In what countries does Cisco maintain servers? Based on evidence from this page, what countries are Cisco's principal target markets? Visit several of the country web sites and although the language is not English, look for consistency of web design, content, and technology. Even though Cisco localizes its web sites with local languages and images, are these sites still clearly Cisco sites? Is there any marketing advantage to this consistency?

# CHAPTER THREE

# *Buyers and Online Behaviors*

**LEARNING OBJECTIVES**

- To identify the types of buyers who are online and their distinguishing characteristics
- To learn what buyers are doing online
- To identify who is not online and why
- To understand other types of behaviors that occur online and why they interest Internet marketers

## Charlie's Peace Rose

Charlie, a vigorous seventy-two-year-old, retired eight years ago after a successful career marketing medical imaging equipment to hospitals and clinics. Since then he's indulged his passion for roses by becoming a champion grower. His garden is ablaze with flowering floribundas, climbers, hybrid teas, and multifloras. Yesterday Charlie was talking across the backyard fence to his neighbor Frank. Charlie was showing off a beautiful Peace Rose in bud stage when Frank asked Charlie how the Peace Rose got its name. Charlie had to admit he really didn't know but was sure he'd find the answer on the Web. Frank, a lifelong friend, feigned shock that an "old guy" like Charlie even knew how to get on the Internet. Charlie chuckled, then explained he had been surfing the Web since the release of the first graphical browser in 1993. There was not much he *couldn't* find there. To prove his point, Charlie invited Frank into his house, booted his computer, and at Google (*http://www.google.com*) typed the key words *Peace Rose* in the search box. In 0.12 seconds, Google returned a list with more than 650,000 links. Charlie clicked on a link to a site sponsored by the American Rose Society and learned how in 1939 a famous rose-growing family in France bred the rose from a single seed. During World War II, before the fall of France, propagating stock (budwood) was smuggled out of the country in the last diplomatic pouches to leave Paris. To ensure the rose's survival, budwood was sent to family friends in the United States, Germany, and Italy. It thrived in all three countries and was introduced to the market by the names *Peace* in the United States, *Gloria Dei* in Germany, *Gioia* in Italy, and *Mme. A. Meilland* (to honor the grower's mother) in France. The rose was christened *Peace* to commemorate the end of the war and hope for the future. Formally introduced on the day Berlin fell to Allied troops (April 29, 1945), today it is the most famous rose in the world and the most popular rose ever bred. When the United Nations was founded in 1945 in San Francisco, the Pacific Rose Society presented each country's delegate with a single Peace bloom. Today, *Peace* remains a symbol of humankind's enduring quest for peace.[1]

**Segment**
A relatively homogeneous collection of consumers or enterprises with similar characteristics and buying behaviors.

Charlie is a member of a rapidly growing Internet **segment,** Americans born before 1964. Senior Internet users (those who are fifty or older) doubled between 1996 and 1999 and by 2003 will include at least 27 percent of all Americans over age fifty-five. Like Charlie, older consumers are multipurpose, multitask users. They access the Internet primarily from home where they avidly use email and search the Web for information about their hobbies, travel, health, finances, and other topics.[2] Like younger Internet users, they often do more than one task at a time, such as reading email while listening to web radio or downloading text in one browser window while using a second window to look at real-time local weather radar or a stock ticker. This illustrates why Internet marketers cannot assume they have their visitors' undivided attention.

**Marketing dyad**
A buyer and seller interacting in pursuit of an exchange.

Many types of buyers go online to connect with sellers offering an amazing array of products. Buyers are half of the **marketing dyad,** that is, the parties to a marketing exchange. This chapter identifies the types of buyers who are online and examines what they are doing. It also looks at who is not online and why, and other online behaviors that interest marketers. Sellers, the other half of the marketing dyad, are examined in Chapter 4, the companion to this chapter.

## *Online Buyer Types*

The Internet has the potential to bring buyers and sellers together in the biggest, most dynamically competitive marketplace the world has ever known. Before the Internet's commercialization, most marketers were not greatly interested in it, but interest is now widespread because many believe a presence on the Internet and particularly the World Wide Web has many benefits. On the Web, marketers can reach large numbers of buyers who were previously inaccessible, make offers 24/7/365, sell more products, reduce their operating costs, and save transaction time and expense. But first they must determine what and how many buyers are online, what they want/need, and what they are doing. Marketers have always had an abiding interest in buyers, studying their characteristics and behaviors, then putting this information to work creating attractive market offers.

**Buyer**
A consumer or enterprise engaging in an exchange with a seller to obtain something of value.

**Buyers** are personal use consumers and enterprises purchasing products in a marketplace. They are typically classified separately, although the distinctions sometimes blur. **Enterprise buyers** are owners or employees making purchases for their businesses or other entities. Enterprise buyers may use their work Internet connection to make personal purchases and when they go online from home, they may be doing so for work reasons.

**Enterprise buyers**
Businesses, governments, hospitals and clinics, organizations, and other groups making purchases in a marketplace.

Consumers are people who buy products for their own use, or that of family, friends, or others, but not on a regular basis for commercial purposes. Consumers outnumber enterprises online and off. Consumer spending contributes two-thirds of the U.S. gross domestic product (GDP) and drives enterprise production, buying, and selling decisions. Business, government, and other enterprise buyers make costlier purchases in greater volumes than consumers. Exchanges are what marketers seek to facilitate online and offline. Business-to-business exchanges are abbreviated **B2B,** business-to-consumer exchanges are **B2C,** consumer-to-consumer exchanges are **C2C,** and business-to-public sector exchanges are **B2P.**

**B2B**

Business-to-business marketing exchanges where businesses sell to other businesses online or offline.

**B2C**

Business-to-consumer marketing exchanges where businesses sell to consumers online or offline.

**C2C**

Consumer-to-consumer marketing exchanges where individuals sell to other individuals particularly on online auctions.

**B2P**

Business-to-public sector marketing exchanges where businesses sell to government and public sector enterprises.

## BUSINESSES

A business is a legally incorporated entity whose activities are conducted to make a profit. The terms *business, firm,* and *company* are used interchangeably. *Enterprise* is a broader term that includes businesses as well as governments, educational institutions, profit and nonprofit health care organizations, museums, religious groups, and others. More than twenty-five million nonfarm entities filed U.S. business income tax returns in 2000. This undercounts the total number of U.S. businesses since it does not include the hidden or underground economy of businesses that evade taxes. It does include self-employed sole proprietorships with no employees or payroll other than the owner-operator, part-time employees, nannies, and over one million individuals in direct sales ventures like Herbal Life (*http://www.herbalife.com*) and Avon (*http://www.avon.com*).

Almost six million nonfarm firms report annual revenues from less than US$1 million to more than US$100 million.[3] Over 83 percent of all U.S. businesses are small companies with revenues less than US$1 million. The largest companies, with annual revenues over US$100 million, represent less than 1 percent of all U.S. businesses, yet account for over 40 percent of all employment and more than 60 percent of total business revenue. Midsize businesses make up the remainder.[4]

**SMALL BUSINESSES**   A small business is independently owned and operated and not dominant in its operational area; its number of employees and annual income fit criteria set for a small business by the U.S. Small Business Administration (SBA) or state law. Many small businesses are home-based; others are small retailers, services, manufacturers, distributors, and professionals or others working out of offices, factories, stores, or similar facilities. The definition of small business varies greatly by industry and definition source. Small in manufacturing might be five hundred or fewer employees, while a service business like a dry cleaner or specialty retailer may have fewer than ten employees.

The small business market is extremely diverse and segmented. It is difficult to know the exact number of small businesses because of the underground economy and the ease with which small businesses start up and disappear. Dun & Bradstreet (*http://www.dnb.com*) has a U.S. database with about eleven million small businesses; other sources estimate over twenty-five million.

What is most important about U.S. small businesses is their growing presence online as buyers and sellers. According to Dun & Bradstreet's "20th Annual Survey of Small Businesses," approximately two-thirds of all small businesses have Internet access, and over 50 percent have web sites. Sixty percent of the small businesses online intend to increase their use of the Web in the near future. A growing number of small businesses are using wireless to go online for email and document exchanges. More than one hundred thousand went wireless in 2001, up from only forty-four thousand in 2000.[5] The Inc. 500 (*http://www2.inc.com/inc500*) list of superstar small companies is online, as is the Forbes 200 (*http://www.forbes.com/200best*) list of best small companies. Small businesses are finding new customers online, cutting procurement costs, driving customers to their offline stores, and learning how to operate more efficiently. Some are using the Internet to internationalize.

At least fifty large corporations offer services to small companies that are designed to help them develop a web presence. Online do-it-yourself tools and U.S. Small Business Development Centers (SBDCs) throughout the country help small businesses go online. In addition, many large businesses target online small businesses with self-help and product information. Office Depot (*http://www.officedepot.com*) offers a comprehensive *Small Business Handbook* to its small business customers. Dell Computer (*http://www.dell.com*) has Small Business Systems web pages. Dun & Bradstreet has web pages that target commercial credit services to small businesses. They and many others recognize the aggregate value of small business buyers and the power of the Internet to reach millions of them easily, quickly, and inexpensively.

**LARGE BUSINESSES** Most large businesses have one or more public web sites, along with intranets and extranets. Over 90 percent of large and midsize U.S. businesses are online; 98 percent are expected to be online by 2002–2003.[6] The Fortune 500 and Global 500 (*http://www.fortune.com*) have web sites, as do the Forbes (*http://www.forbes.com*) 500 Leading Companies and Platinum 400. Fortune's E-50 identify the most powerful online superstars along with companies that operate in the Internet infrastructure sector.

eMarketer (*http://www.emarketer.com*) estimates that almost 7 million midsize to large U.S. businesses will have Internet access by 2003, up from 4.5 million in 2000.[7] Among new web sites registered in 2000, 44 percent served consumer markets, 38 percent were B2Bs, and the rest were media, information, and web services. More than one-third of B2B web sites are actively trying to generate sales from their sites. Over 40 percent of midsize businesses already are making purchases online.[8]

All but a very small minority of U.S. businesses will likely be online by 2003. Latecomers, small and midsize, will be motivated to become Internet users because they fear losing customers to competitors that are online, want to reduce their costs, and increase revenues. They will be helped by continued downward pressures on the costs of computer systems, Internet access, and web construction and maintenance. B2B Internet marketers will have millions of additional small businesses to target. Competition will intensify. Well-known branded businesses will have a clear awareness advantage with newcomers. Small niche businesses will carve out special markets while many midsize businesses could be left scrambling to reach buyers.

### CONSUMERS

**Consumers**
Personal or end-use buyers making purchases for themselves, family, friends.

**Consumers** are individuals, groups, families, households, and others who make exchanges on their own behalf or for others, but not for businesses or other enterprises on a regular basis. They are often called *personal use* consumers to differentiate their buying goals from enterprise buyers. The U.S. population of over 286 million is only 4.6 percent of the total world population of over 6.2 billion, yet it is the most desirable consumer market in the world because of its size, high median income, relative homogeneity (including almost universal use of the English language), and eagerness to spend. Data from the 2000 census confirm that the U.S. population is aging and has become more ethnically diverse, with more nontraditional households than traditional ones. Traditional households are composed of a mom and dad, and one or more children. In the 1960 census they represented 45 percent of the population; in 2000 they were only 23.5 percent. The 76.5 percent of nontraditional U.S. households are singles, single parents, divorcees, empty nesters, people of the opposite sex living together, and gays. The baby-boom cohort is moving inexorably toward retirement while their children are entering the prime buying years. There are fewer young adults ages twenty to thirty-four, the prime years for building brand loyalty. The number of kids under five is shrinking as a percentage of the total population. Large numbers of immigrants from China, Mexico, and India have entered the country. Marketers offline and online will be forced to adjust to many of these changes in order to remain competitive. Such adjustments are already showing up in consumer product advertisements that feature nontraditional households.[9]

Early U.S. Internet users generally were highly educated (college and postgraduate) white males employed in professional, technical, or managerial jobs with higher than average incomes. U.S. Internet users today more closely mirror the general population, but not exactly. Over 64 percent of the U.S. population is online and includes more women than men (52.18 percent to 47.28 percent) and more minorities than ever before. Internet users are still more highly educated; at least 32 percent have a college or postgraduate degree, compared with 22 percent of the general U.S. population. Higher-income consumers are far more likely to be online than lower-income consumers, and they spend more time online than other groups. Over 80 percent of people in households with more than US$75,000 annual incomes are online compared with 38 percent of people in households with less than US$30,000. Younger consumers are more likely to be online than retirees. Over 76 percent of people ages eighteen to forty-nine are online; only 15 percent of those aged sixty-five or older are online.[10]

By 2004, the U.S. online population is expected to be over 210 million, and the demographics of those online are clearly shifting. For example, many new users will be older, less affluent, and less highly educated than earlier Internet adopters, and they will have different reasons for going online. Newer users are less interested in browsing, more interested in familiar brands, and more likely to use generic portals. These changes present opportunities and challenges for Internet marketers. For some marketers, the demographic changes will be meaningful only if they affect the narrowly defined consumer markets they are currently targeting. Because the consumer market is highly segmented, general demographics will be meaningless to many Internet marketers.

Several factors make it difficult to construct a useful profile of the *average* Internet consumer. Research that counts a single Internet-connected computer in a multiperson household may not capture how many people use it, how frequently they connect, or what they do online. If the household is the measurement unit, then user numbers may be seriously undercounted and variation in use undocumented. Research organizations use different parameters to describe groups under study. Some count online populations as people two years old and older; others count users eighteen years and older. Moreover, definitions of *young* and *old* vary. Online demographic research is occurring within a highly dynamic environment where changes occur rapidly and often unexpectedly. New users go online easily and others go offline. This volatility complicates user counts. These and other measurement problems have led to disparities in reported Internet demographics. Even so, trends clearly indicate that growing numbers of consumers of all ages throughout the world are becoming Internet users and, therefore, potential Internet marketing targets.[11]

**AGES**  Although adults dominated the Internet in its earliest days, today younger people are going online in growing numbers, as are seniors. The majority of U.S. Internet users are thirty-five to fifty-four years old,. However, individuals eighteen to forty-nine (63 percent of the U.S. population) represent 76 percent of the online population. People over sixty-five are the least likely to become Internet users.

**Baby boom**
People born between 1946 and 1964.

**ADULTS**  People over fifty years old are 37 percent of the population, but they represent only 24 percent of those online. As the seventy-five million **baby-boom** cohort (people born between 1946 and 1964) ages, the number of online seniors will grow proportionally, but many of these people are already online, so they will not be counted as new users. Baby boomers are approximately 27 percent of the U.S. population.[12]

Older adult Internet users are more likely to be married, better educated, and living on relatively high retirement incomes. In addition, they are more likely to go online only from home (over 80 percent). They typically spend more time online than most other users, seeking information, shopping, and playing games in addition to sending email. More older men than older women are online, despite women outnumbering men in the offline age cohort. Retirement appears to be a significant factor predicting higher Internet use.[13]

**CHILDREN, TEENS, AND TWEENS**  By late 2000, 45 percent of U.S. children under age eighteen, over 30 million, had Internet access. More than 73 percent of kids twelve to seventeen (teens or tweens) are online; 29 percent of children under twelve are online. Teens are the most rapidly growing age online cohort. By 2010, teens will be 33.9 million strong, the largest number of that age cohort this country has ever known. Although girls and boys are online in equal numbers, teen girls are a rapidly growing segment. More than 4.4 million girls (twelve to seventeen years old) were online by May 2000, up 126 percent from the previous year.[14] This market is heavily segmented with many subgroups that follow their own fashions. Teens are frequent communicators and great fans of instant messaging and wireless.

Children are big Internet users, but their ability to purchase is limited by whether they can use a parent's credit card or other convenient payment option. Some web sites have site-specific web debit cards, where parents purchase an account and the child can make debit purchases up to the amount deposited in the account. Rocket-Cash.com (*http://RocketCash.com*) offers digital wallets that allow kids to make purchases at sites that accept them, but only up to the amount deposited in the wallet by a parent or guardian.[15]

**STUDENTS**  U.S. college students are a highly wired group; 87 percent were Internet users by 1999, nearly 100 percent by 2001. They are PC-oriented, with 92 percent owning their own computer, and over 30 percent of college students say they are *Internet dependent*. This is an encouraging sign for marketers, because it suggests that this group will be comfortable shopping the Internet when they reach their prime buying years.

Many students live in wired university dormitories or connect from their own apartments or parents' homes. Since an estimated 70 percent of college students have credit cards, buying online presents few problems for them other than maxing out their credit limits. Soon most college students will regard the Internet in the same class of necessities as the telephone, television, and stereo, and they will not remember a world without the Internet.

Public school students are similarly wired. In the European Union, 90 percent of schools have Internet access. The U.S. rate is 98+ percent, inching toward total Internet access.[16] However, these numbers must be viewed cautiously. Having Internet access in a school does not mean that every student has an equal opportunity to become Internet-proficient. Nor does it mean they are likely to become high Internet users. College attendance is a better predictor of significant Internet use.

**GENDER** Very few women were Internet users in its earliest years. Women represented only 24 percent of the U.S. online population in 1995. By 2000, women were 50.6 percent of the online population and by 2001, 52.18 percent. Sixty percent of all new users going online in 1999 were women. The average U.S. female Internet user works fulltime, has children, and accounts for around 70 percent of online sales. This is not surprising since offline, U.S. women make 80 to 85 percent of all retail decisions. Like male users, women tend to be more highly educated, with higher incomes than their offline counterparts, and they are younger.

Men are slightly less than half the U.S. Internet-using population, but male users dominate in the rest of the world. Outside the United States, men make two-thirds of all online purchases. This reversal from the U.S. pattern is a function of disparities in educational attainment in many countries, particularly newly industrializing nations where education and work opportunities are denied or restricted for many women and men exercise greater control over financial decisions. It also may indicate that men are using the Internet at work, that homes lack PCs or other access devices, and/or that Internet access fees at home, where women are more likely to log on, are prohibitive.

Germany has the most males online, 63 percent of all German Internet users. France is not far behind at 61.9 percent, followed by Italy (60.9 percent), Spain (60.9 percent), and Belgium (60.6 percent). Those nearing the U.S. gender distribution are Canada (49 percent male), Australia (51.6 percent), and New Zealand (52.5 percent).[17]

**ETHNICITY** African Americans are almost 13 percent of the U.S. population and 8 percent of the online population. Almost 8.2 million African Americans are online, which is about 26 percent of the African-American population. They are spending more time online than in the past and viewing more web pages. They are also more likely to go online using wireless. Cheaper Internet access and lower costs for access devices (PCs and wireless) are fueling the growth in African-American and Hispanic Internet use.

Nearly half (49 percent) of all U.S. Hispanics are online. However, fewer go online at home (54 percent) than at work (63 percent), a reversal of the norm for other groups. More Hispanic women, youth, and lower-income people are going online than in the past. The number of Hispanic Internet users is growing more rapidly than any group except Asian Americans.

Although U.S. whites outnumber minority group members online, proportionally more Asian Americans use the Internet. Sixty-nine percent of Asian-American households are online. Their high Internet adoption rate is related to their higher income and education levels, and positive orientation toward technology.[18]

Marketers are aware of the advantages of reaching online members of ethnic minorities since they represent markets with money to spend and they are comfortable using electronic technology. The eighty-plus million U.S. African Americans, Hispanics, and Asian Americans have annual spending power of over US$1 trillion. Ethnic portals can be an effective way of targeting some minority group members. However, ethnic group members have highly diverse interests and buying behaviors, which means most Internet marketing offers must be tailored more or less to these differences. Examples of ethnic portals include Afronet (*http://www.afronet.com*), an African-American portal; Todo Latino (*http://www.todolatino.com*), a Latino/Hispanic-American portal for professionals; and AsianAvenue (*http://www.AsianAvenue.com*), a portal for Asian Americans.

Some web sites and portals target ethnic markets. *Source: Reprinted by permission of Afronet, Inc. http://www.afronet.com.*

**GEOGRAPHICS** U.S. consumers connect mostly from home (almost 70 percent), with 44 percent hooked up for at least one or more hours daily. These online users live in city suburbs (49 percent), within a city (37 percent), or in rural areas (14 percent). Cities with the highest proportion of Internet-using households are Portland (Oregon), Seattle, San Francisco, Boston, San Diego, Washington, Denver, Orlando, Hartford/New Haven (Connecticut), and Kansas City (Missouri). Over 70 percent of the homes in Portland and Seattle have Internet access. The top twenty-five U.S. cities with Internet access all exceed 50 percent penetration rates.[19]

**Internet adoption**
Consumers and enterprises adopting use of the Internet.

**INTERNATIONAL CONSUMERS** The highest growth rate of **Internet adoption** by consumers is happening outside North America (United States and Canada). This was expected since more than half the U.S. population (the innovators, early adopters, and early majority) are already online and the last half (late majority and laggards) will be slower to join them. Some nonadopters will never go online (see figure 3-1). The United States has a large lead in absolute numbers of Internet users that it will maintain until around 2003, when the Asia-Pacific region will have more people online than North America or Europe.[20]

Non-English-speaking consumers began using the commercial Internet around 1995. Adoption has occurred most rapidly in industrialized countries with high incomes and education levels. It has been slower in countries with low average incomes and education levels. In 1999, 15 countries out of 190 countries online were responsible for 82 percent of all web traffic. An estimated 513.41 million consumers worldwide

**Figure 3-1 Internet Adoption**

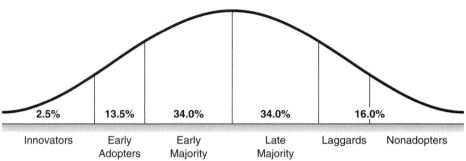

| 2.5% | 13.5% | 34.0% | 34.0% | 16.0% |
|---|---|---|---|---|
| Innovators | Early Adopters | Early Majority | Late Majority | Laggards    Nonadopters |

Consumers' adoption of new technologies varies according to how ready they are to try new products and processes. Readiness to use the Internet can be seen as a function of individual characteristics (aptitude, knowledge, risk response) and opportunity (time, money, information, equipment). Innovators are the first online and represent about 2 percent of a typical market. Next are the early adopters (13.5 percent), early majority (34 percent), late majority (34 percent), and finally the laggards (16 percent). Some consumers will never use the Internet and are nonadopters.

were Internet users by November 2001, which increased to more than 550 million by mid-2002. North Americans (United States and Canada) dominated Internet and web usage in the Web's first decade. Countries with over 50 percent of their population online include the United States, Canada, Australia, Denmark, Norway, Sweden, and the United Kingdom. More will be said about international markets in Chapter 6.

The breadth of buyer types and their enthusiasm for the virtual environment implies that marketers have many opportunities for creating profitable exchanges with both **mass markets** and **niche markets**. Growth will continue worldwide, which emphasizes the potential for reaching more consumer markets, particularly outside North America. At the same time that more consumers are using the Internet, so are more marketers. This hints at how crowded the selling space will become as adoption spreads. It presents a conundrum, for as much as marketers may want the potential revenues represented by having more consumers online, they will have to work harder to reach and keep them. Many U.S. marketers will also be forced to confront their domestic myopia.

**Mass markets**
Markets that are not differentiated into groups.

**Niche markets**
Relatively homogeneous parts (subsegments) of a market.

## OTHER ENTERPRISES

Other enterprises online run the gamut from the U.S. government, the largest single buyer, seller, and employer in the country, to colleges; clinics; hospitals; professionals like dentists, lawyers, and accountants; museums; religious groups; charities; private nonprofit agencies; and others. How and why they use the Internet and the Web vary greatly.

From the beginning of Internet commercialization, the federal government has been a proponent of its use as well as one of its largest users. Popularized as *The Digital Superhighway*, the Internet was highly promoted by the Clinton administration for use by governments, schools, businesses, and citizens. It was viewed as a means for the federal government to achieve significant savings in purchasing (eprocurement). The Federal Acquisition Streamlining Act (FASA) of 1994 was signed into law by President William Clinton on October 13, 1994. FASA mandates that the federal government use eprocurement to reduce paperwork, speed transaction times, and streamline purchasing procedures (see the Purchasing section on p. 63 for more discussion of eprocurement).

All fifty state governments are online; many engage in eprocurement, and some report significant savings. The State of Nebraska Department of Roads only accepts electronically submitted contractor's bids; handwritten or typed bids are no longer used. The Commonwealth of Kentucky's Personnel Cabinet (*http://www.state.ky.us/ agencies/personnel/jobspage.htm*) posts job vacancies online, and its Ecommerce Directory (*http://ky-purchases.com*) lists bid opportunities and other information for vendors interested in selling to the state. e-Texas (*http://www.e-texas.org*) is an ambitious effort by the State of Texas to construct a comprehensive state portal for all the state's business. As the Texas comptroller states on the e-Texas home page, "My goal is to see that Texans are online rather than in line."

Large city governments and many midsize ones are online. Small cities are more likely to be part of a regional web site than have independent sites. Most regional administrative bodies have Internet connections, along with public utilities, airports, and similar facilities.

Most two- and four- year colleges and universities are on the Web. The University of Texas at Austin (*http:// www.utexas.edu/world/univ*) maintains a linked list of regionally accredited four-year state universities that currently includes around fifteen hundred schools.

Most hospitals and many medical clinics, doctors, dentists, and medical practices are online. Many are buying products and recruiting staff. Hospital-Hub.com (*http://www.hospitalhub.com*) is a recruiting center for professional

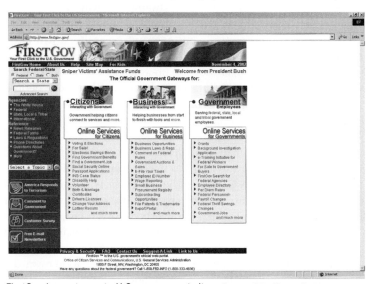

FirstGov is a gateway to U.S. government sites. *Source: http://www.firstgov.gov.*

staff; HospitalNetwork.com (*http://www.hospitalnetwork.com*) is a portal for hospital buyers. Behavioral health and mental retardation centers use the Internet, as do nontraditional medical workers.

Large numbers of churches and religious organizations are online, including synagogues and mosques, Bahá'í Communities, the Society of Friends, religious schools, and university student religious groups. Charities large and small use the Internet, and environmental activists are online, as are human rights observers, and other groups. In short, it would be easier to list the types of enterprises *not* online than to catalog those that are Internet users.

✔ **CONCEPT CHECK**

1. What distinguishes enterprise from consumer buyers?
2. What are some differences between the earliest Internet consumer adopters and consumers going online now?
3. What is the marketing significance that more than a half billion people are online and only about 160 million live in the United States?

# What Buyers Are Doing Online

Once online, enterprise and consumer buyers engage in many of the same activities, although with some differences. Top online consumer activities are sending email (93 percent), seeking information (80 percent), and purchasing (52 percent). Buyers seek information about hobbies (79 percent), products (73 percent), travel (68 percent), leisure activities (65 percent), weather (64 percent), and news (63 percent). They also visit government web sites (51 percent).[21] Nondirected web surfing is one thing U.S. consumers are doing less of, preferring instead to go straight to favored sites. This pressures marketers to ensure site visibility and accessibility so buyers can find it and sticky content that is interesting, informative, and relevant so visitors will *stick around*, make a purchase, and bookmark the site for a return visit. In the United States, the decrease in nondirected surfing is showing up as a slight reduction in the amount of time buyers spend online, which is interpreted to mean that more people know where they want to go and do not waste as much time searching.

## COMMUNICATING

The urge to communicate has been a dominant human characteristic since prehistoric times as cave drawings demonstrate. The Internet has made communication far easier and faster than ever before in human history. Although email is the single most used Internet service, interpersonal communication also takes place in online bulletin boards, instant messaging, and chat rooms. Email is popular because it is fast, geographically unbounded, cheap, and reliable. U.S. web users use email extensively while Canadians (41 percent) use more voice chat than their southern neighbors. The convergence of telephone, Internet, fax, and wireless is moving communication toward a new form that creates a seamless integration of voice, text, and image.

**WEB UPDATE**

*Buyers and What They are Doing Online*

After the terrorist attacks on September 11, 2001, many Internet users went online searching for news while others used email to communicate with friends and colleagues, particularly in parts of New York where telephone lines were inoperable or jammed. The Internet's redundancy (distributed data transmission) was needed to route email messages around areas that had been reduced to rubble. Many people in the United States and sympathetic countries used message and discussion boards, chat rooms, and listservs to express their feelings and share in a sense of community with others experiencing the same emotions. Around 25 percent of Internet users were multitasking, listening to the radio or television while also posting messages online.[22]

Businesses and other enterprises used email extensively before the terrorist attacks. When many mailrooms in New York and the Washington, D.C., area were closed because of anthrax contamination in October–November 2001, dependence on email increased.

Paper, telephone, and fax still play an important role in work-related communication, but email use is increasing far faster than older methods. Its success also emphasizes a significant problem: Email is so easy to send that its use is abused. It is not unusual to hear of a salesperson or manager receiving hundreds of emails each day or taking hours to sort through batches of email messages. Marketing promotions sent by email clog boxes that are not effectively protected and sometimes crash computers when large batches are received simultaneously at a company's email servers. However, ask most people to give up email and they would probably refuse. It is a ubiquitous part of work and everyday life in the United States and many other countries.

Consumers are hooked on email. A Carnegie Mellon University study, *The Home-Net Project*, reported that email is the driving force getting many consumers to first use the Internet. Heavy email use is also a predictor of whether or not people continue Internet use. The authors conclude that email is a self-reinforcing activity; the more consumers do it, the more likely they are to continue using it. Thus, email becomes a social obligation and one that women respond to more than men because of their partiality for creating and nurturing social networks. Senior citizens are highly motivated to use email to connect with children and grandchildren. Often, this is their primary reason for going and staying online. These results suggest the value of email as a marketing tool for nurturing customer relationships and brand building.[23] They also can be viewed as a warning that as email volume increases, marketers will find it more challenging to effectively cut through the clutter with meaningful, enticing marketing messages.

College students are heavy email users, with 89 percent saying it is their most common web activity. Teens also use the Internet for email (83 percent), with 44 percent saying it is their primary reason for going online. Although email is used by all ages, chat rooms are most heavily used by teens and young adults (those under age twenty-five). This means chat rooms are a good place to monitor teen trends, as well as keep an eye on how this market views products and competitors. Both chat rooms and email are popular marketing tools for religious groups, which use them to reach and recruit members.[24] Instant messaging is the rage among many teens, who can spend hours communicating with multiple friends simultaneously.

## SEEKING INFORMATION

The Internet is a vast public library literally available at the click of a mouse. Although businesses and consumers use it extensively for gathering information and research, they show a deep reluctance to pay for it. The marketing challenge is to convince users that content and/or service are worth the cost of a subscription or onetime charge. The economic slowdown and dot-com meltdown (2000–2002) forced many sites to begin charging for information that formerly was free. This did not sit well with some buyers while others quickly adapted to the new reality. Whether or not buyers will pay for information depends on the value of the information and its timeliness, the reasonableness of the price, and whether or not the information is available free elsewhere.

Online information seekers pose both an opportunity and threat to traditional hard-copy newspapers. More consumers are reading newspapers online. Online news is timely and updated more frequently than hardcopy, can be personalized to the consumer's interests, and is available 24/7/365. Initial fears that virtual papers would mean the end of traditional ones appear to be unfounded. The reality is that many traditional newspapers have migrated to the Internet, where they are developing a strong following. Some marketers that advertise in hard-copy newspapers have followed the papers online, embedding special interest advertisements in personalized papers delivered to the reader's computer. Many newspapers are marketing information by offering free published articles within a week of their publication date. After that, buyers must pay for archived information.

Business and consumer buyers seek travel information online, researching destinations and airfares. About 35 percent of buyers book flights online.[25] Far more research travel information online, then go offline to finalize reservations, frequently using the online price to bargain for offline discounts. Thus, travel agents are feeling the pressure of increased use of online bookings. Online sites rebounded from the effects of the September 11 terrorist attacks more rapidly than airline or agent sales, which indicates that buyers responded to online incentives, including lots of fare discounts.[26] In an effort to cut costs, some airlines have shifted completely to electronic tickets, charging a penalty for printing paper versions.

Almost as many consumers seek financial information online as read weather reports or news. Approximately 26 percent of U.S. online consumers track stocks. Of investors with Internet access, almost 40 percent have tracked stocks or mutual funds, 30 percent have checked their bank account balances, 15 percent have bought or sold stocks, and close to 10 percent have bought or sold mutual funds. These consumers are not all adults; many younger people also are using financial web sites. Online broker accounts for funds and stocks are expected to top US$1.5 trillion by 2003. A financial site that is repositioning itself as a financial portal, The Motley Fool (*http://www.fool.com*), combines offline newspaper columns with its widening online presence.[27]

College students regularly search the Web for information, browsing for topics of interest (67 percent), conducting academic research (62 percent), looking at news (41 percent), researching and making travel plans (31 percent), and reading magazines (19 percent). Teens use the Web for research and information (69 percent), with 19 percent saying it is their primary reason for going online.[28]

Buyers' thirst for information presents an opportunity to attract and keep them on a web site or a permission email list. Offering content that buyers value and refreshing it on a regular basis can strengthen a relationship and increase sales. Content is king online, and information is the type of content that most buyers value. The downside is that too much content, the wrong content, or stale content drives users away from a site. Feedback from desirable users can be extremely helpful in determining the type and amount of content, and how frequently it should be changed. Even better, if web marketers can get users to identify the content they want on a site, a home page can be personalized with content they value. This increases the value of the site and the probability of establishing a long-term relationship with the user. Content personalization is often found on ISPs, portals, and online news sources.

## GAMING AND OTHER ENTERTAINMENT

Almost all age groups play games on the Internet, including about 30 percent of all Internet users, 62 percent of young adults, and 41 percent of consumers over fifty. Women are 46 percent of online gamers. The convergence of play stations and the Internet is attracting more users to online gaming. Young men are still the most loyal and largest group of gamers, but a growing number of young women are joining them. Males prefer football and outer space games; women prefer business simulations and classic arcade games. The next step will be wireless gaming, which may give another boost to the business.[29] Popular entertainment sites are Neopets.com (*http://Neopets.com*) and Pogo.com (*http://www.pogo.com*).

Younger U.S. consumers (early twenties and younger) are the most likely to listen to music online. This is a case where age clearly defines a market dominated by young people in the United States. In other parts of the world, consumers of all ages listen to music online in roughly equal numbers. Napster (*http://www.napster.com*) was the most popular music site, with more than twenty million users, until legal problems forced it offline and eventually into bankruptcy. Jupiter Media Metrix, an online research firm, estimates music sales on the Internet of US$5.4 billion by 2005. However, almost seven million Internet users swapped music files in August 2001 with non-Napster applications. Users strongly support free music file sharing online, to the consternation of the music industry.[30] Peer-to-peer music sharing, which does not involve downloads from commercial web sites, may undermine the profitability of commercial music sites. Users spoiled by Napster and similar free play offers are unlikely to warmly embrace pay-for-play sites, particularly if they are highly restrictive and limit sharing and replays.

## PURCHASING

The Boston Consulting Group estimates that U.S. B2B transactions will grow from US$1.2 trillion in 2000 to US$4.8 trillion in 2004. B2B online purchases will represent 40 percent of *all* B2B procurement by 2004. ActiveMedia Research (*http://www.activmediaresearch.com*) reports that across all types of web businesses, at least 50 percent currently purchase products online for their company. Many businesses will purchase only from online suppliers in order to cut transaction costs.[31] This does not mean the end of one-to-one electronic data interchange (EDI) proprietary systems or web sites that only provide information about their products and rely on personal selling to complete a deal. By comparison, online consumer buying is expected to reach US$86.3 billion in 2003, up from US$17.3 billion in 1999.[32]

**Eprocurement**
Business B2B buying online.

Business buying online is called **eprocurement** to distinguish it from offline traditional paper-based procurement. Advantages of eprocurement are faster order times, reduction or elimination of paperwork, time savings, access to a wider range of products, and cost reductions. Businesses purchase raw materials, supplies, parts, and/or finished products for their own production processes, operations, or for resale. They also buy services, information, knowledge, and expertise from others, and recruit personnel. A business does not have to be online with its own web site in order to purchase from another business that is online. Businesses also use intranets and extranets for purchasing.

**B2B web exchange**
A web site that facilitates B2B online buying and selling.

A **B2B web exchange** is where many businesses are buying and selling to one another. An exchange is a web site designed to let businesses realize transaction cost savings and greater efficiencies from online buying. Often small businesses pool their orders (demand aggregation) to increase their buying clout. Intercompany online trade is expected to increase from US$406 billion in 2000 to US$5.2 trillion in 2004, about 38 percent of all B2B sales. Some businesses are using electronic purchasing to find cheaper suppliers, better manage their supply chains, and reduce inventory holding costs through tighter inventory control. Online buying is expected to replace some proprietary EDI networks. The initial promise of eprocurement has not yet been realized, and many businesses still don't know how to use it effectively.[33] This will change, however, as word of eprocurement savings circulate within industries.

Agribusiness is using web B2B to make farmers more efficient. XSAg.com (*http://www.xsag.com/Chem/Buyers.Asp*) helps farmers buy herbicides, insecticides, machine parts, and other products online. Chemicals can be purchased from auctions or by fixed price. The nation's 2.1 million farmers spend almost US$200 billion annually on farm products, and about 60 percent of the largest U.S. farmers (380,000) are connected to the Internet. Farms.com (*http://www.farms.com*), Directag.com (*http://www.directag.com*), and others are vying for the valuable agribusiness market.[34]

Training is another product businesses are buying online. The U.S. market for web-based corporate training will increase from US$1.1 billion in 1999 to $11.4 billion by 2003. Businesses like web-based training because employees can train at their own desks without incurring costly travel time. It also avoids the cost of paying a trainer to come to the company.[35]

One more type of B2B online buyer, the dot-com liquidator, deserves mention in light of the dot-com pullback and economic downturn. Liquidators look for dot-com failures and buy unsold inventories and equipment at the lowest possible price, often 30 to 50 percent of wholesale cost. Liquidated products are sold online to enterprise or consumer buyers, below the original retailer's cost. Overstock.com (*http://www.overstock.com*) and SmartBargains.com (*http://www.smartbargains.com*) are dot-com liquidators.[36] They sell everything from stereo speakers to high-fashion apparel and jewelry. Liquidators also purchase excess and out-of-season inventory for resale. Selling these products online vastly increases the size of the potential buyer market.

FedBizOpps (*http://www2.eps.gov/epsgeneralinfo.html*), the governmentwide portal for online purchasing, is designed to provide one-stop identification of government business opportunities for sellers. The U.S. government buys everything from sophisticated and hugely expensive defense weaponry to over US$14 billion spent annually by the Department of Defense for equipment ranging from shoes, boots, fuel, and tools to medical supplies. The government also recruits military personnel online (*http://goarmy.com*) and is a partner with AllMeetings.com, now part of GetThere, Inc. (*http://www.getthere.com*), to provide travel and meeting planning training for government administrative assistants and secretaries.

The PurchaseNet Exchange (*http://www.PurchaseNet.com*) is specifically designed for higher education buyers. It manages bid requests and price quotes for purchases of products from light fixtures to office supplies. The Global Education Network (*http://www.gen.com*) is recruiting faculty for its online university courses. A growing number of universities use the Internet to market classes and programs in ecommerce, Internet marketing, and information technology, hot specialties that attract students. They also recruit online for students and faculty.

Consumer purchasing is more profitable and sizable with each passing year. However, lots of window-shopping is still going on, where buyers look at and research what is offered online, then make their purchase offline. This reflects continued consumer concern about security and privacy, which is discussed in Chapter 5.

Wealthy consumers with assets more than US$1 million are spending more online and are more likely to view stock quotes (63 percent) than less affluent users (25 percent). Popular sites targeting wealthy Internet consumer buyers are HomePortfolio.com (*http://HomePortfolio.com*) and Rolex.com (*http://www.Rolex.com*).[37] Like other consumers, the wealthy also buy airline tickets, make hotel reservations, and purchase computer software.

College students are purchasing online, which is both bad and good. It is bad from the standpoint that students are notoriously low on discretionary funds and are prone to overextending their credit; it is good that they are comfortable making online purchases and should continue doing so after graduation. At least 81 percent have made purchases on the Internet. Most popular purchase categories are books, compact music discs, and clothing. College students are called the *leading edge* of online shoppers. They access the Internet from multiple sites, most often with high-speed connections (T1, T3) through school.[38] They are not rushing to purchase textbooks online, however, preferring the convenience of the campus bookstore.

Teens are also purchasing more online. European and U.S. teens spent US$1.3 billion online in 2001; by 2005 they are expected to spend more than US$10.6 billion. The availability of prepaid credit and debit cards are getting teens to spend more online. Top categories for teen online purchases are CDs/cassette tapes, clothing, books, computer software, and toys. This is not that different from their parents, whose top purchase categories are books, CDs, cassette tapes, computer software, toys, and clothing. Teens are harder to reach than other buyers. They are attracted to popular brands and are among the most brand loyal customers. However, their loyalty can change quickly as fashions change. They are targeted online by companies like Gap (*http://www.gap.com*) and teen portals ALLOY.com (*http://alloy.com/index.html*) and Snowball.com (*http://www.snowball.com*), which bills itself as "The on-line network for the Internet generation."[39]

Women are emerging as bigtime buyers online. Smart marketers recognize differences in shopping preferences and practices of men and women. For example, women as well as men purchase consumer electronics. However, women want usability, recommendations about what to buy, and attractive packaging. Men prefer having specs (specifications), lots of jargon, and big black box packaging. Recognizing this, hifi.com has launched a site specifically for women, herhifi.com (*http://www.herhifi.com*), that shows a marked difference in approach from the main site. This includes having an in-house expert, Kate, who answers questions in "plain English."[40]

Women are price and quality sensitive, but they also value the convenience of shopping online and online service speed. They want to be treated with respect and have their privacy guaranteed. Although they value their privacy, they also want to receive personal attention and customized offers. This presents a challenge for marketers to collect the information needed to personalize and customize without offending buyers.

## ✔ CONCEPT CHECK

1. What activities do buyers engage in on the Internet?
2. Knowing that buyers want information online, what can marketers do to increase the appeal of their web sites?
3. Why are teens and tweens such attractive marketing targets?

# *Who Is Not Online*

The concept of an Internet for everyone is far from being realized and may never be achieved, even in the United States. Some enterprises and consumers are not online by choice. Others face barriers to becoming Internet users. It's the latter group that particularly concerns Internet marketers, as they represent lost potential customers.

### DIGITAL DIVIDES

**Digital divide**
A real or presumed gap or barrier that hinders Internet use by consumers and/or enterprises.

It is highly debated whether or not there is a **digital divide,** a widening gap between Internet users and consumers and enterprises that are not online. Several types of digital divides have been identified. One digital divide is between richer and poorer countries, for example, North America and Europe (richer and fully industrialized) and many countries in South America or most of Africa (poorer and less industrialized). The question is whether the richer, more industrialized nations will help poorer nations become Internet users so they can take advantage of what the technology can do for their countries and people. Of course, this also will result in developing markets for Western products online.

Digital divides also occur within Europe between northern and southern regions. Internet use is highest in northern Europe and lowest in southern. This is the result of wage disparities and liberal telecommunications policies in the more affluent north. Education and in-school access are believed to be keys to solving the problem.[41]

Another divide is between segments of the U.S. population, which are mainly separated by income and education. This digital divide, however, appears to be closing rapidly. For example, the United States has almost universal Internet access in its public schools. Rapidly falling computer prices are another factor closing the gap. Families can buy computers for under US$500, and many schools have grant programs for low-income students. Some schools also allow students free Internet access after regular school hours. Internet access is available in public libraries, Internet cafes, and through some service organizations.

A third divide exists between younger and older consumers. The very elderly are significantly underrepresented online. This can be explained by their techno- and/or computer phobia, fear of a loss of privacy or security threat online, insufficient funds to purchase a PC or ISP, disability, and/or lack of interest. Consumers over sixty-five express the least interest in going online. This divide will resolve itself with time, as the more techno-savvy baby boomers grow older and become the Internet-using elderly.

A fourth divide exists between the general U.S. population online and Native Americans. Only 1 percent of Native Americans are online, fewer than five hundred thousand. This is explained generally by low incomes and educational attainment. Native American access may be among the more intractable divides facing those who want access equality. It will take a disciplined effort by the U.S. government and corporations working with Native American leaders to make Internet access a priority and reality.

A divide also exists between urban and rural areas. Population concentrations in cities and densely populated suburban areas lead to better ISP service and the availability of DSL and cable, whereas in some rural areas users can connect only through costly long distance hookups or satellite. Although this is becoming less of a problem in the United States, it remains a considerable barrier in other parts of the world where rural areas lack any telephone access.

**WEB UPDATE**

Digital Divides

## OFFLINE BY CHOICE

Thousands of businesses and millions of U.S. consumers may never use the Internet. Some businesses will not go online or create a web site because they see little benefit and too many costs. Consumer nonadopters may not connect for many of the same reasons that the very elderly will not go online; that is, some consumers believe the Internet poses a security threat or fear it can become an obsession and control their lives. Others simply prefer to live an unconnected life. Neo-Luddites harbor deep suspicion of the technology and what they perceive as a threat to societal and individual values. Some consumers have shopped online, had a bad experience, and disconnected citing privacy or security concerns and dissatisfaction with online retailing. Many consumers simply prefer shopping in a conventional store. For them shopping is a social experience that cannot be duplicated on the Internet, at least not yet. Whatever nonadopters' reasons, marketers can reach them with conventional offline marketing tactics.

## CONSUMERS WITH DISABILITIES

Consumers in the United States who have physical impairments (disabilities) spend more than US$175 billion annually. This includes 1.1 million blind Americans who need an audible translation of text embedded on web pages if they are to use the Internet. At least 8 percent of Internet users have a physical or learning disability; 4 percent are blind. For the blind, the Internet has the potential to deliver tremendous communication advantages. To facilitate their Internet use, the National Foundation for the Blind is asking web site owners to include text descriptors of all graphics so screen reading software can translate the text. The colorblind have difficulty understanding navigation icons that are colored graphics without text. U.S. government agencies are making their web sites accessible to the disabled, primarily by adding text for describing graphics, at a cost from US$85 million to US$691 million. Barriers that have kept many disabled off the Internet are beginning to fall, but very slowly.[42]

## ✔ CONCEPT CHECK

1. What are digital divides and why should marketers be concerned with them?
2. Why would anyone *not* want to use the Internet?
3. Why should marketers support initiatives to remove Internet access barriers for the disabled?

# Other Behaviors

Ours is not a utopian world, online or off. Businesses and consumers can behave badly or have negative experiences in either environment. Some problems associated with Internet use affect marketing, directly and/or indirectly. For example, social isolation can negatively affect exchange behaviors. In addition, complaints about business behaviors online certainly require a marketing response. Anticorporate web sites can reach millions of people and reduce revenues and undermine marketing efforts through negative word-of-mouth about a business. Marketers can respond to some but not all of these behaviors.

## SOCIAL ISOLATION

Two recent studies point to problems associated with extended Internet use. The HomeNet Project from Carnegie Mellon University found that greater use of the Internet is associated with statistically significant declines in social interactions with family and friends, and higher levels of loneliness and depression. The Stanford Institute for the Quantitative Study of Society (SIQSS) study confirms these results and adds that high wired adults have less time for shopping in stores, reading newspapers, or interacting with family and friends. They attend fewer social events, and 59 percent watched less television.[43]

These studies are disturbing for both societal and marketing reasons. From a societal perspective, dysfunctional effects directly related to Internet use could have a dampening effect on Internet adoption and lend weight to latent antitechnology biases. From a marketing perspective, dysfunctional effects could undermine marketing efforts aimed at getting consumers to use the Internet for commercial purposes. Study results appear to contradict a key benefit of Internet use, maintaining communication contact with family and friends. However, communicating by email is not the same as going on a family picnic or sharing an evening hanging out with friends. The reduction in shopping has obvious negative implications for marketing exchanges. Watching less television means consumers will be exposed to fewer advertising messages, which could impede their receiving information about products and web sites.

## ADDICTIVE AND IMPULSE-CONTROL BEHAVIORS

Although Internet addiction has been mentioned in the press, at this time it has no official diagnostic medical category. Difficulty controlling Internet use can mask symptoms of serious underlying mental conditions. Studies on compulsive Internet use found that participants exhibiting such behaviors often also exhibit well-known clinically recognized disorders. It is likely that extended Internet use can exacerbate symptoms of already existing problems, particularly related to obsessive compulsive disorders (OCD).[44] Behaviors often identified as addictive include excessive engagement with cybersex sites, overinvolvement with chat room socializing while avoiding face-to-face interactions, and obsessive online gaming or gambling to the extent that these behaviors dominate daily life. These behaviors can ruin lives when they become extreme.

The extent to which the Internet may be affecting people who are already prone to impulse control problems is unknown. If it emerges as a significant problem that involves large numbers of people, it could slow Internet adoption rates and affect marketing efforts. At this point, not enough evidence exists to indicate this is happening, and rushing to respond could have unintended consequences.

## COMPLAINTS AND ANTICORPORATE ACTIVISM

Most reputable businesses work hard to ensure that buyers are satisfied with their purchases, yet buyers can still experience postpurchase regret (dissonance) or be seriously discontented with goods, service, and the purchasing experience. Thus, web sites have sprung up to channel consumer complaints to the offending source. Ecomplaints.com (*http://www.ecomplaints.com*) and Complaints.com (*http://www.complaints.com*) are sites that forward consumer complaints directly to companies free of charge. Some sites survey discontented consumers about their product preferences and sell this information to interested companies. Most sites keep complaints private; others post them for all to see. Businesses with the most complaints against them are airlines, ISPs, and long distance telephone service. Consumer complaints are a protected form of free speech, as long as the complainer is not knowingly trying to harm a business.[45] Complaints to these sites can be about off- or online experiences.

Anticorporate activism is far more hostile than consumer complaints, because anticorporate web sites give highly frustrated buyers an opportunity to vent their hostility against a corporate offender with the possibility of having their complaints read by millions of people worldwide. Angry customers provide only one side of a story, and companies often have difficulty dealing with the comments. Some have sued anticorporate web site owners for trademark infringement. Other owners have been bought off by the company they are shaming. Sometimes a company will make amends in an effort to get an anticorporate web site owner to shut down or moderate complaint intensity. For example, Fujifilm responded to an anti-Fuji site by offering a public apology to offended buyers for poor after-sale service. The company also severed ties with the offending agent responsible for the poor service. Anticorporate web protests are particularly effective because of the ease of creating a site and the speed of dissemination of negative comments.[46] Disgruntled employees often use anticorporate web sites to anonymously vent their hostility toward their employers. Their comments combined with those of angry buyers can be extremely damaging.

## COMMUNITY BUILDING

**Consumer community**
A group of people with a common purpose or interest that interacts online to share information, support, and concern.

**Business communities**
Associations of businesses whose members show a willingness and ability to help one another or facilitate B2B activities.

***WEB UPDATE***

Communities

A **consumer community** is a group of people with a common purpose or interest who interact online to share information, support, and concern. People often form highly personal commitments to online communities. Some communities are maintained on business web sites, but the business must be very careful not to intrude. Community members typically resent blatant marketing messages intruding on their space. Amazon.com (*http://www.amazon.com*) has created a community with its book buying customers, soliciting their book reviews and involving them in recommendations. Kraft Food's Interactive Kitchen (*http://www.kraft.com*) is a cooking web site where consumers share recipes and email their *Wisdom of Moms* consumer comments for posting on the site. Kraft encourages consumer information sharing while promoting company products in a low-key setting.

**Business communities** are associations of businesses whose members show a willingness and ability to help one another or facilitate B2B activities. General Electric has established a community through its Trading Process Network (TPN) where it has transacted US$1 billion in purchases with more than 1,400 suppliers worldwide. The network gives suppliers greater exposure with GE, standardizes transactions, and provides a more orderly exchange process.[47]

## ✔ CONCEPT CHECK

1. Explain how the same environment that encourages communication also can create social isolation.
2. What is the difference between anticorporate web sites and online consumer complaint sites?
3. How can marketers benefit from community building on the Web without offending the visitors who form the communities?

# Summary

## Online Buyer Types

Buyers are enterprises or consumers. Enterprises are businesses and other entities like schools, governments, and hospitals. Businesses large and small are using the Internet and the Web to buy products they need for production and operations or to resell. Many large businesses offer support to small businesses that want to become interactive. Consumers purchase products for their own use or for family, friends, or related purposes, but not regularly for commercial use. Consumer demographics are shifting in the general population as well as online. Internet-using consumers in the United States are beginning to mirror the characteristics of the general population, but some differences still exist. Online users have higher incomes, more advanced education, and are younger. They mostly connect from home and live in city suburbs, within a city, or in rural areas. Women slightly outnumber men online in the United States but not in other parts of the world. Children are big Internet users, but their ability to purchase is limited by whether or not they can use their parents' credit cards or other convenient payment options. Most college students are online. Seniors are another category of online consumers whose Internet use is increasing. While U.S. whites outnumber minority group members online in numbers, there are proportionally more Asian Americans using the Internet. Marketers are well aware of the advantages of reaching online members of ethnic minorities since they represent markets with money to spend and they are comfortable using electronic technology.

## What Buyers Are Doing Online

Once buyers get online, they engage in many activities that are similar to what they do offline. Top online activities include communication, information seeking, entertainment (by consumers), and purchasing. Although email is the single most used Internet service, interpersonal communication also takes place in online bulletin boards, through instant messaging, and in chat rooms. Email, which is popular because it is fast, geographically unbounded, cheap, and reliable, is the driving force getting many consumers to use the Internet. College students and teens are highly involved with sending and receiving email. Teens also heavily use instant messaging and chat rooms. Businesses and consumers use the Internet extensively for gathering information, but they show a deep reluctance to pay for it. Business and consumer buyers seek travel information online, researching destinations and airfares. Many buyers research travel information online, then go offline to finalize reservations, frequently using the online price to bargain for offline discounts. Almost as many consumers seek financial information online as read weather reports or news. College students regularly search the Web for information, as do teens. Almost all age groups play games on the Internet. Younger U.S. consumers are the most likely to listen to music online. A B2B web exchange is where businesses buy and sell to one another. Exchanges are designed to let businesses realize transaction cost savings and greater efficiencies from online buying. Small business buyers also participate in online B2B. Agribusiness is using web B2B to make farmers more efficient. Businesses are buying training online. Dot-com liquidators look for dot-com failures and buy unsold inventories and equipment at the lowest possible price for resale online. Wealthy consumers are spending more online and are more likely to view stock quotes than less affluent users.

## Who Is Not Online

The concept of an Internet for everyone is not yet realized. One digital divide is between richer and poorer countries. Another is between segments of the U.S. population, mainly divided by income and education. A third divide exists between younger and older consumers. A fourth divide exists between the general U.S. population online and Native Americans. A divide also exists in Europe, between the north and south. In addition, a rural-urban divide exists. Thousands of businesses and millions of U.S. consumers may never use the Internet. Some businesses will not incur the costs of creating a web site and going online because they see no advantage to it. Consumer nonadopters often believe the Internet poses a security threat or fear it can become an obsession and control their lives, whereas others simply prefer to live an unconnected life. Neo-Luddites harbor deep suspicion of the technology and what they perceive as a threat to society. Some consumers have shopped online, had a bad experience, and disconnected. Other consumers simply prefer shopping in a conventional store. Physically impaired (disabled) consumers experience barriers to using the Internet.

### Other Behaviors

Excessive use of the Internet is associated with statistically significant declines in social interactions with family and friends, and higher levels of loneliness and depression. High wired adults have less time for shopping in stores or interacting with family and friends. They attend fewer social events and watch less television. From a societal perspective, dysfunctional effects directly related to Internet use could have a dampening effect on Internet adoption and lend weight to any latent antitechnology bias. Dysfunctional effects could undermine marketing efforts directed at getting consumers to use the Internet for commercial purposes. Although Internet addiction has been mentioned in the press, at this time it has no official diagnostic category. Web sites have sprung up to channel consumer complaints to the offending source. The most complained about businesses are airlines, ISPs, and long distance telephone service. Anticorporate activism is more hostile than complaints, because anticorporate web sites give highly frustrated buyers an opportunity to vent their hostility against a corporate offender with the possibility of having their complaints read by millions of people worldwide. Communities are springing up all over the Web. They are associations of businesses or consumers whose members share an interest and show a willingness and ability to help one another.

# Internet Marketing Application

One of the Web's most appealing qualities is the way it facilitates interpersonal communication among people in online communities. Communities are places where people with shared interests can communicate, expressing their thoughts, support, and concerns. Some businesses provide space for communities on their Web sites. It is their way of reaching out to consumers. Kraft Foods has its *Wisdom of Moms* interactive site where moms can share their recipes and feelings about holidays and food-related events. Campbell's Soup calls their web site *Campbell's Community*. Ragu has *Mama's Cucina*, with a picture of Mama greeting each web site visitor.

Visit each site, study their community, then answer the following questions.

1. Why are food sites particularly well suited to community building?
2. Which of these businesses has most effectively captured the spirit of community on its web site?
3. Do the sites keep their community areas free of promotional messages?
4. Why do these sites want to build communities?

Sites to visit:
Kraft Foods at *http://www.kraftfoods.com/html/ xchange/index.html*
Campbell's Soup at *http://www.campbellsoup.com*
Ragu at *http://www.eat.com*

# Chapter Review Questions

1. Why are baby boomers such a valuable target market?
2. What is a marketing dyad?
3. How does eprocurement differ from offline conventional procurement?
4. What are consumers doing online?
5. Are Internet adoption laggards the same as nonadopters? Explain.
6. Why is the U.S. government so eager to promote eprocurement?
7. Are newspapers facing extinction because of the Internet?
8. What makes communication such an important factor drawing users online?
9. Should richer nations help poorer nations go online?
10. What is Internet-induced social isolation?
11. Is Internet addiction a serious problem?
12. Should anticorporate web sites be banned?
13. Are consumer web complaint sites a good thing for businesses? Explain.
14. What is community building on the Internet?
15. Do digital divides really exist?

# Case Study

## A Community Known as GE

If Charlie, from the beginning of the chapter, had not retired, he might be marketing General Electric (GE) medical imaging equipment online. GE is one of the world's most successful multibusiness corporations and number one or two in every market in which the company competes. In 2000, GE developed a new three-part business strategy—Make, Buy, Sell—in recognition of how the Internet is changing the way businesses operate. Part of the effort involved assigning a *Destroy Your Business (DYB)* group to each GE business. The DYB group analyzed how a dot-com could threaten the business, then developed a response designed to allow it to maintain its market dominance.

One DYB group developed customer web centers to build supplier loyalty and cut support expenses. Customers of GE Plastics and GE Power Systems use a central portal to mix polymers or get specifications for turbine performance. The GE Appliances DYB created Internet kiosks at Home Depots that allow customers to order GE appliances and schedule delivery times. This system clears inventory faster and speeds restocking. GE is increasing procurement efficiency through its Global Supplier Network (GSN).

The company is using the Internet and its ebusiness strategies to improve its sourcing operations and purchasing. The company closed the year 2000 with more than US$6 billion worth of goods and services auctioned online. The eprocurement target for 2001 was 30 percent, with projected savings of 7 to 10 percent. GE regularly holds web auctions where prequalified suppliers can bid for over US$15 billion of its business. GE buys maintenance repair equipment, supplies and office furniture, screwdrivers and hammers, light bulbs, fax machines, and copiers online. By combining orders from its many companies worldwide, GE uses auctions to drive down costs. GE conducts more than four million transactions a year. If all were moved to the Web, GE executives say the cost of transactions would fall to US$5 from the current rate of US$50 to US$100 for each transaction made.

In June 1999, Jack Welch, GE's chairman at the time, had this to say about the Internet, "The Internet makes old, young. Makes big, small. Makes slow, fast. It is truly the elixir that big companies need. It just doesn't get much better than this." At the GE Annual Share Owners Meeting in April 2000, Welch added, "Any company, old or new, that does not see this technology literally as important as breathing, could be on its last breath. But for those of us, including GE, who are capturing it, energized by it and see it as the greatest opportunity in our history, the excitement is like nothing we've ever experienced." And in December 2000, "The Internet is allowing us to make quantum changes, real breakthroughs. You can't think incrementally, you have to think transformationally. We're still seeing just the tip of the iceberg."[48]

On September 7, 2001, Jeffrey R. Immelt was appointed chairman of the board and CEO of GE, succeeding Jack Welch. Immelt's vision for the company includes continuing the digital transformation of backroom operations and globalization.

## CHECK IT OUT

General Electric is a vast corporation with many independent business units. They include aircraft engines, appliances, capital services, medical systems, NBC, research and development, and transportation systems, among others. The company has highly developed training and career management systems in place to help employees develop their skills and advance within or across GE business units. Check out the GE career pages beginning at *http://www.gecareers.com*. Look for reasons to work for GE at *http://www.gecareers.com/WorkingForGE/index.cfm*. Go to the Career Search page (*http://www.gecareers.com/search.cfm*) and see what jobs are currently available. A recent search found jobs for marketing majors available in the following areas. Do any of the currently listed GE jobs involve online marketing?

- Communications Leadership Development Program
- Distribution and Sales Program
- GE Capital CEF-Leadership Development Program
- Leadership Development Program
- Management Development Program
- Professional Management Development Program
- Technical Sales Leadership Program

## A GLOBAL PERSPECTIVE

General Electric is a global competitor, as shown in its listing of country links on its front page. Visit GE in Europe (*http://www.ge.com/europe*) and follow the links to learn about GE's history in Europe and its future there. Go to *http://www.ge.com/europe/e-bus.html* and read about GE's four strategic growth initiatives that will drive company growth—digitization, six sigma, product services, and globalization. What is *e-sell*? What is GE doing to achieve it? What is *e-make*? How will digitization give GE a sustainable competitive advantage?

## CHAPTER FOUR

# Sellers Marketing Online

## Marketing an MBA Program

Rick is a professional staff member in a university that enrolls more than twenty-five thousand students at the undergraduate, master's, and doctoral levels. He is responsible for marketing the university's Master of Business of Administration (MBA) program to prospective students. He plans, implements, and manages marketing activities designed to raise awareness of the program among prime target markets and increase enrollment. Several times a year he recruits students at Graduate Management Admission Council (GMAC) MBA forums (*http://www.gmac.com*), specialized non-profit trade shows that attract more than eighteen thousand participants annually to shows held in major U.S. cities and Tokyo, Seoul, Shanghai, Hong Kong, and Singapore. Prospective students at each forum meet with program representatives and participate in workshops on such topics as

"Selecting the Right Business School and Getting the Right School to Select You." Rick likes to attend forums because they allow him to speak face-to-face with large numbers of prospects. He also interacts with prospective students on his program's web site. Rick is responsible for making the site informative, timely, and interactive. Most MBA programs are online; more than five hundred programs worldwide are linked from GMAC's web site. Rick has learned that prospective students, particularly those planning to enroll full-time, often shop for a school online using a school's web site as a window into the program. That is why he spends so much time keeping the site current and answering email. Prompt personal contact by email makes a positive impression on prospective students, so he is committed to ensuring that their email is answered within twenty-four hours of its time stamp.[1]

Higher education marketing is big business in the United States, and colleges and universities have found that online marketing is a highly effective way to recruit students. Higher education institutions were identified as buyers in Chapter 3; their role

**Figure 4-1  Goals and Tasks in the Reciprocal Marketing Exchange Relationship**

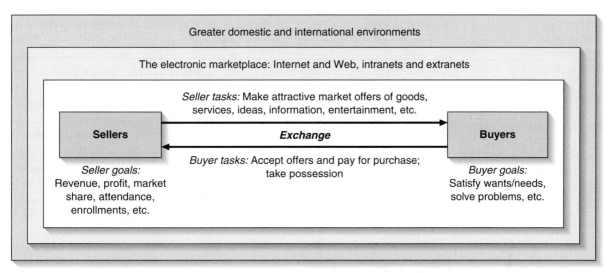

Marketing exchange involves sellers and buyers in a reciprocal interdependent relationship. Without buyers, sellers' offers cannot accomplish organizational goals for revenue and market share. Without sellers, buyers' needs/wants go unsatisfied, and their problems go unsolved. Often dyadic roles reverse. Although General Electric (*http://www.ge.com*) is a massive global corporation best known for its sales to businesses, consumers, governments, and other enterprises, it is also a huge buyer. The exchange relationship is affected by what is happening online, particularly where it concerns privacy and transaction security. The electronic marketplace does not exist in a vacuum; it is affected by events and policies in both the domestic U.S. and international environments. The Internet also affects these environments.

as sellers is examined in this chapter. This discussion illustrates how the same enterprises and individuals that are buyers in one situation may be sellers in others.

The marketing dyad of buyers and sellers participates in a reciprocal marketing exchange relationship where both parties have goals and tasks (see figure 4-1). Dyad members interact in highly volatile electronic markets where sellers are under considerable pressure to manage the exchange relationship and buyers, particularly consumers, are sometimes erratic. Buyers and sellers can be enterprises and/or consumers.

Chapter 4 identifies the types of sellers using the Internet and World Wide Web and examines how they are using marketing to achieve their goals. The Internet marketing efforts of governments, nonprofit organizations (NPOs), nongovernmental organizations (NGOs), and other enterprises are included because they contribute so much to the economy and are effectively using the Internet and the Web to market their products. The chapter concludes by considering external environment factors that influence sellers and Internet marketing success.

# *Business Sellers*

**Clicks only**
Businesses that market their products solely online on the Internet, World Wide Web, and/or intranets and extranets.

**Bricks and clicks**
Businesses that market their products online (clicks) and offline (bricks) using a dual or multidistribution channel strategy.

Businesses that went online when Internet commercialization began were **clicks only,** which operated only on the Internet, and **bricks and clicks,** which had both offline (bricks) and online (clicks) operations. It was widely predicted that clicks-only businesses would miraculously reinvent marketing, eliminate distributors, reshape buyer-seller relations, make pricing transparent, reduce transaction and inventory costs, and attract hundreds of millions of new customers worldwide to the virtual environment. Amazon.com (*http://www.amazon.com*) was a model for the digital revolution. As commercialization progressed through the late 1990s, several thousand U.S. clicks-only dot-coms went online, investors often indiscriminately showered them with extravagant amounts of investment capital, share prices skyrocketed, the stock market became overvalued, and the press helped create an almost manic enthusiasm for all things web. It was a period of *irrational exuberance* according to Federal Reserve chair Alan Greenspan. His comment described the U.S. stock market, including overvalued technology and dot-com stocks.

The bubble was bound to burst and it did. Much has been written and said about the dramatic shakeout that began in mid-2000 and resulted in the shuttering of many businesses during the 2001–2002 economic downturn. A shakeout had been widely predicted and when it arrived, the landscape quickly became littered with failed dot-coms. They included trendy United Kingdom apparel retailer Boo.com (which later resurfaced under new management at *http://www.boo.com*), toy seller Toysmart.com, price comparison site Brandwise.com, and online charity Hugging Hands International, among an estimated seven hundred to one thousand others. Most failed dot-coms never produced a profit, and investors grew tired of waiting for them to materialize. Others burned through their cash before they could reach their targeted profit date. Some never made it to their scheduled initial public offerings (IPOs). Internet retailers (etailers) were particularly hard hit.

The shakeout was brutal, but not unprecedented. Consider what happened to the U.S. automobile industry in its infancy. In the first hundred years of U.S. automobile production, thousands of manufacturers turned out handmade and later mass-produced cars. Today, two major U.S. auto makers are left—Ford and General Motors. The first car to be produced in the United States was the Duryea. Other pioneer automobiles were the Haynes, Packard, Hudson, Nash, Maxwell, Willys-Overland, Kaiser, Frazer, and Studebaker. Most people have never heard of them.[2] Soon the same will be true of the recently deceased dot-coms.

The great majority of original automobile pioneers simply closed their doors, others were bought out, and consolidation drastically reduced the number of competitors. Although obvious differences exist between manufacturing automobiles and operating profitable dot-coms, the similarity lies in the nature of American capitalism and free market competition. Entrepreneurs are drawn to new industries whose early years tend to be highly speculative, volatile, and risky. Just as there was a shakeout in automobile manufacturing, there also was a shakeout in the early years of biotechnology and personal computers in the 1980s.

Large numbers of first- and second-wave dot-coms will fail, but several factors argue against the same drastic consolidation that led to only two surviving major U.S. automobile manufacturers. First, the cost of entry for a start-up dot-com is far lower than for an automaker in an industry that requires massive capital outlays. Second, an increasing number of dot-coms are bricks-and-clicks offspring of already profitable and well-established branded offline companies, so they benefit from their parent company's expertise, established channels, recognizable brand names, financial stability, and loyal customers. Third, a growing number (over half) of remaining dot-coms are profitable and more are on the verge of profitability, so these survivors have a higher probability of long-term success. Their success will attract a new wave of web entrants that should be more web savvy, risk averse, and better positioned to compete and profit.

Businesses go online for a variety of reasons. About 95 percent use the Internet to promote and sell products.[3] Internet marketing takes place on *Web storefronts* where products are sold directly to enterprises and/or consumers. It also happens at *Web auctions* and *exchanges* on the Internet, intranets, and extranets as well as on *push sites* that provide product information online that pushes consumers toward purchases at traditional offline retail stores or enterprise buyers toward contacting an offline sales force.

**WEB UPDATE**

Dot-coms

## WEB STOREFRONTS

Most early commercial web sites were static information-only sites with no email options or other interactive functions. They displayed electronic catalogs, brochures, annual reports, and other printed materials that were digitized and stored in files on servers accessible to anyone with a computer, browser, ISP, and the patience to endure slow download times and text only. These pioneer information-only sites did not have email or sell online, and the information they provided was available offline in traditional form. Many were online with no clear idea of how to strategically use the new environment. They went online to stake a claim in the new environment or because they were keeping up with competitors that were probably equally ill prepared.

Most but not all information-only sites soon realized they were missing out on the Web's unique interactivity, so they added email. The next step for many was to become *transactive*. Transaction sites sell products directly from highly visible web storefronts closely watched by the general public, the press, government regulators, and investors. They also sell products on intranets and extranets. Large, small, and midsize businesses are transacting business online. They may be clicks-only or bricks-and-clicks. Targets can be other businesses, other enterprises, consumers, or a mixture of the three. They sell a wide variety of products—tangibles, intangibles, and services. A simple way to classify storefronts is by three key criteria: *place, buyers*, and *products*.

**PLACE** Place or distribution is where marketing takes place and how buyers take possession of the products they have purchased. Online storefronts may be clicks-only or bricks-and-clicks enterprises. Amazon.com was one of the first and most widely known *clicks-only* storefronts with a business that operated solely on the Internet. It had no offline stores, catalogs, or other distribution channels. Wal-Mart.com (*http://www.walmart.com*), the world's largest retailer, is an example of a *bricks-and-clicks* retailer that operates two (dual) or more (multi-) distribution channels, one or more online and at least one other channel offline. Wal-Mart markets its products from its web storefront and more than thirty-five hundred traditional Wal-Mart stores in the United States and eleven hundred more stores worldwide (see figure 4-2).

**Figure 4-2  Place**

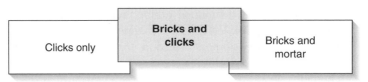

**Clicks Only**  Business has a web storefront, no offline selling; one distribution channel
**Bricks and Clicks**  Business has both an online web storefront and offline selling site(s) and/or catalog sales, at least two (dual) distribution channels and possibly more than two (multichannel)
**Bricks and Mortar**  Business has no web storefront and sells only through offline stores and/or catalogs, single or dual distribution, none online

**Bricks and mortar**
Businesses that market their products only offline in traditional stores and/or offices.

A **bricks-and-mortar** business is offline only and may never go online. However, that does not preclude its selling to or buying from clicks-only or bricks-and-clicks businesses. Many local small businesses, particularly those in services like car detailing, dry cleaning, or child care may never go online because they perceive the costs of doing so are greater than the benefits. However, other small local businesses will conclude that *not* being online puts them at a competitive disadvantage, so they will create an online presence, often information-only or interactive but not necessarily a transaction site.

It is difficult to determine exactly how many businesses fit each category—clicks only, bricks and clicks, or bricks and mortar. The following four factors suggest that bricks and clicks already outnumber clicks only online:

1. High failure rate of existing dot-com clicks only
2. High entry costs for any new clicks only that must create high brand awareness to survive
3. Number of clicks only that are setting up offline selling channels and becoming bricks and clicks
4. Number of bricks and mortars going online for their first, second, or sometimes third try at Internet marketing

It is clear that with time, bricks and clicks with dual and multiple channels of distribution will dominate Internet marketing. The web will be an essential channel of distribution for them, with unique characteristics that will create synergy with their offline channels. Large and midsize businesses and other enterprises that already have high brand awareness among their target markets will be able to use that recognition to help secure an audience for their online ventures. Small, niche businesses will also find it profitable to serve existing customers online.

**Place, Clicks Only**  Amazon.com opened its virtual doors in July 1995 and today boasts "The Earth's Biggest Selection," referring to its expanding product assortment achieved largely through acquisitions and partnerships with other businesses. Amazon has evolved from a books-only storefront to an online department store selling books, videos, music, magazine subscriptions, wireless phones, health and beauty supplies, kitchen equipment, tools and hardware, automobiles, toys, cameras, and other products in more than 220 countries. Although Amazon has offline distribution centers, it still has no traditional retail stores, although they are rumored to be in Amazon's future. The company mailed its first hard-copy catalog in 2001. Amazon has partnerships with bricks-and-clicks retailers Target (*http://www.target.com*) and Circuit City (*http://www.circuitcity.com*), which also maintain their own independent web sites, and Toys "R" Us and Babies "R" Us, which do not. Amazon, which has followed a rapid growth and aggressive brand-building strategy, is often called a **first mover** because it was the first business of its kind to set up shop on the Web in the first wave of commercialization. At one time being a first mover was considered an advantage. Now its downsides are recognized, mainly in the high front-end marketing costs associated with building a brand name and the delay of profits as available resources are used to rapidly expand the business. It is more likely that any true advantage will be enjoyed by the second, third, and possibly subsequent waves of enterprises that arrive after the first movers and learn from their predecessors' mistakes.

eZiba.com (*http://www.eziba.com*; *ziba* is the Persian word for *beautiful*) was launched in November 1999 as a pure Internet premier product marketer with no offline retail stores. It is far smaller than Amazon and rather than follow the Amazonian mass marketing strategy, eZiba is a *niche* marketer targeting select buyers that value handmade products from exotic parts of the world. eZiba's web site, a global ebazaar, markets handcrafted jewelry, pottery, apparel, and art work created by artisans worldwide. Unlike Amazon, eZiba claims very low marketing expenditures were needed to build its brand name. Online sales have exceeded expectations. Not surprisingly, Amazon.com has invested US$17.5 million in eZiba.[4] In 2001, eZiba began mailing hard-copy catalogs to its online buyers and prospects.

E*TRADE, now E*TRADE Financial (*http://us.etrade.com/e/t/home*), was one of the first solely online financial brokers and a favorite of day traders who spent their days in front of computer screens making massive numbers of small stock trades. Through the acquisition of online bank Telebanc, E*TRADE Financial now has an onsite bank, E*TRADE Bank. The company is **test marketing** E-Trade Zones, offline storefronts located in SuperTarget stores. If they are successful in drawing customers to open E*TRADE.com accounts and use its bank and automatic teller machines (ATMs), E*TRADE Zones will be rolled out nationwide as part of the company's strategy to establish a national offline presence. E*TRADE Financial illustrates two trends, that of clicks only moving offline and that of businesses moving toward blending online and offline in a **oneline marketing** model with a seamless flow between what happens online in a web storefront and offline in a bricks-and-mortar store. E*TRADE Financial is using its E*TRADE Zone and E*TRADE ATMs to create a seamless flow of customer service. E*TRADE Zones operate from 9:00 A.M. until 9:00 P.M., seven days a week, coming close to the 24/7/365 approach of E*TRADE.com. Ironically, E*TRADE spent a considerable portion of its 1999 marketing budget of US$390 million on advertisements that taunted its stodgy bricks-and-mortar competitors for being solely offline businesses.[5]

**Place, Bricks and Clicks**  According to the National Retail Federation, Lands' End (*http://www.landsend.com*) is the largest seller of apparel online and the world's

**First mover**
A dot-com business that went online in the first wave of Internet commercialization.

**Test marketing**
Testing a new product or concept by introducing it to a small subset of a market.

**Oneline marketing**
Integration of online and offline activities to develop synergy between the two, where the effect of the whole (online plus offline) is greater than the sum of the parts.

second-largest mail-order apparel merchant. Lands' End, which opened its online store-front in 1995, is a mixed marketer, a bricks and clicks with a significant web storefront, catalog sales, and its own traditional retail stores. It has forty years of experience as a direct merchant with a massive backend order **fulfillment** infrastructure. This infra-structure allowed the company to serve as many as fifteen thousand online customers each hour during the peak 2000 holiday season and get their orders delivered cor-rectly and on time. In FY 2000, Lands' End had twenty-eight million site visitors. It has more than thirty-one million individual names on its mailing list.[6]

Lands' End was purchased by Sears, Roebuck and Company in 2002 and its prod-ucts began appearing in a limited number of Sears's over 850 stores in Fall 2002. Lands' End gives Sears a high-quality apparel line and considerable Internet marketing ex-pertise. Sears gives Lands' End offline retail store exposure and access to in-store re-turns, which many customers prefer. It should be a beneficial match for both companies.

Wal-Mart.com, founded in January 2000, initially was independent from parent Wal-Mart Stores, Inc. In 2001 Wal-Mart, Inc. bought out Accel Partners, part owner of the original Wal-Mart web site. Wal-Mart.com now is a separate business unit within Wal-Mart, Inc. The move to integrate the web site fully with the offline operation il-lustrates the parent company's vision of a seamless online-offline, or *oneline*, experi-ence. The company vows to create a "compelling experience for consumers" where they can purchase from Wal-Mart online, offline, or in a web kiosk within retail stores. Marketing supports the integration, particularly through a return policy that allows complete refunds of online purchases in Wal-Mart stores or by mail with a prepaid United States Postal Service return label. The concept for Wal-Mart.com is a virtual neighborhood Wal-Mart with a great selection, friendly service, and "Every Day Low Prices." Wal-Mart.com offers more than six hundred thousand **stock keeping units (SKUs)** on its web site. Like the retail stores, Wal-Mart.com has a merchandise assort-ment selected for its customers. The site does not sell firearms or much apparel.[7]

Trying to classify web sites by the place criteria can get fairly complicated. Eventu-ally, place will no longer be a key criteria. Instead, integrated online/offline *oneline* mar-keting will be the norm for most businesses, as illustrated by the second wave of traditional bricks-and-clicks businesses that have become serious about using their web site as another channel of distribution. They include Charles Schwab (*http://www.charlesschwab.com*), Kmart (*http://www.bluelight.com* or *http://www.kmart.com*), Kroger (*http://www.kroger.com*), and Prudential (*http://www.Prudential.com*).

**BUYERS**   A second way to classify storefronts is by their customers. To a great extent, buyers determine what products are sold, their prices, where they are sold (place), and how. Many businesses sell to a combination of buyers and thus have mixed target markets. Dell Computer (*http://www.dell.com*) has consumer, business, health care, and government buyers, who may purchase the same products. Some etailers, like Silly Goose Toy Store (*http://sillygoosetoys.com*), sell only to consumers.

**Buyers, B2B**   Business-to-business (B2B) is an extremely active sector of online com-mercial activity with revenues that may exceed the B2C sector's. Many operate on proprietary extranets, so their activities are not as visible to the public and press as B2C transactions. FinancialMachine.com (*http://www.ecx.com/partners/fm*) is an ex-ample. It is a B2B that offers credit products to online vendors, particularly small

**Fulfillment**
The back end of the order; activities needed to deliver purchased prod-ucts to the buyer.

**Stock keeping units (SKUs)**
Identifying numbers used in inventory control; each product stocked by a business has its own SKU.

businesses with little experience in the electronic environment. Small businesses can purchase bank-approved merchant accounts that let them accept online credit card purchases and web-based payment transaction software that sets up shopping carts on a vendor's site. Penpro (*http://www.penpro.com*) is another B2B, a promotional advertising company selling promotional products to businesses.

**Buyers, B2C**  Progressive Auto Insurance Co. (*http://www.progressive.com*) is a B2C that uses its storefront to sell insurance online or connect consumers to the more than thirty thousand independent insurance agents nationwide that sell its products. It offers automobile, motorcycle, homeowners, and other types of insurance online 24/7/365. B2Cs are more highly scrutinized than B2Bs and serve a greater number of buyers. Most people are far more familiar with a B2C like Amazon.com than any B2B.

**Buyers, B2P**  Some businesses sell only to nonbusiness enterprises. Tally's (*http://www.jvtally.com*), a 122-year-old church supply house, is a B2P business that sells to church clergy and laity. Bagwell Promotions (*http://www.churchmax.com*) is another example. It is a church advertising and promotion business with more than a hundred and twenty thousand church promotion products from armbands and badges to Yo-Yos. ElectionSupply.com (*http://www.electionsupply.com*) markets reconditioned election equipment, vote recorders, ballot boxes, and voting booths for government buyers. e-CityHall.com sells OurTown software, which helps cities manage their online information systems and control interactive components of the Electronic City Hall web site. OurTown also lets citizens conduct business with their city government, obtain information, report potholes, and submit applications for permits and licenses.

**Buyers, Mixed**  Mixed sellers make offers to some combination of businesses, consumers, governments, and organizations, in other words, a mixed group of buyers. Larger companies are more likely to have mixed buyer markets. Smaller businesses are more likely to concentrate their marketing resources on one customer type or niche. Dell Computer, like other hardware manufacturers, sells computers B2B, B2C, and B2P. Its web storefront is particularly user-friendly, with a tutorial on how to order online, reasons why ordering online makes sense, and for state government buyers it provides an interactive state map that links to personalized government pages.

**PRODUCTS**  The third classification category is the *product* being marketed. Classifying the types of products marketed online is difficult at best, given their vast numbers and types. Products are everything from music to military equipment, apples to apparel. With few exceptions, almost any product sold offline can be sold online. Products may be tangible goods (books, automobiles, apparel), services (training, learning), pure **digital products** (online games, software, music, information, tickets), or a mixture of a core product with associated services or digitals.

**Digital product**
A product that is electronic; for example, music downloaded to a buyer's computer.

**Products, Digital**  Digital products illustrate why the Internet promised such radical changes in marketing. These products are purchased online and delivered electronically, directly to the buyer's or another recipient's computer. Net Detective (*http://www.unlovedcrimes.com/netdet*) offers a purely digital product. Buyers can download Net Detective software or have it delivered by email. A buyer can even test a demonstration copy before paying for the fully enabled version. Obviously, the company is confident that product knowledge will lead to sales. Another example is free ecards from Blue Mountain (*http://free.bluemountain.com*) or another site that can be sent to a recipient to celebrate a birthday, anniversary, or other occasion.

Advertising is a digital product sold extensively online. It is hard to avoid online banner and pop-up advertisements and sponsorships. Many highly visible web businesses rely on advertising revenue. For example, Yahoo! (*http://www.yahoo.com*) and AOL (*http://www.aol.com*) sell advertising space on their web pages to other businesses. DoubleClick (*http://doubleclick.com*) is an advertising solutions business that markets online advertising campaigns to business clients worldwide.

Many web storefronts sell information in digital form. One of the more successful multitier subscription content sites is the online *Wall Street Journal* (*http://www.wsj.com*), which offers some content free but charges for access to most current and all archived articles. The *Journal* is sold offline through vending machines, newsstands, and by home, school, or office delivery. Other newspapers also offer the current day's news free but charge for archived articles delivered by fax, email, or on screen. The *New York Times* (*http://www.nytimes.com*) lets visitors search for an article, then view the first few lines free. The full article can be charged to any major credit card, then printed or saved to the buyer's hard drive. Advantages of online newspapers are their timeliness, since they can be updated at any time; content search capacity; and convenience. However, they are not particularly profitable yet, since readers are not rushing to trade in their print copies for digital. Many potential buyers resist reading lengthy articles online. They also do not want to pay to access archived articles, particularly since many archived articles can be retrieved from free sources.

Expedia.com (*http://www.expedia.com*), Travelocity.com (*http://www.travelocity.com*), and Orbitz (*http://www.orbitz.com*) are travel portals selling digital airline tickets that may or may not be printed as traditional hard-copy tickets at the airport. Some airlines only use electronic ticketing that completely eliminates paper copies. Forrester Research predicts that by 2003, twenty-six million households will use digital ticketing. Buyers appreciate the convenience, speed, price, and choice offered on these web sites. Airlines save money by avoiding paper tickets and travel agent fees. These storefronts are expanding their offers with more hotels, cruises, vacation packages, and other products designed to cross-sell and up-sell buyers. For example, vacation packages may include:

- Airfare
- Hotel
- Rental car
- Ski lift tickets
- Ski rentals
- Snorkeling
- River rafting
- Sightseeing tours

**Products, Goods** Tangible goods are products that must be delivered through traditional delivery services, principally United Parcel Service (UPS at *http://www.ups.com*), Federal Express (FedEx at *http:// www. fedex.com*), the United States Postal Service (USPS at *http://www.usps.com*), or other carrier, or picked up from a traditional store. Some buyers do not want to wait for products to be delivered several days or weeks after purchase. Same-day delivery is a desirable goal but difficult to achieve. Barnes & Noble (*http://www.barnesandnoble.com*) offers it Monday through Friday in Manhattan, New York, for select items. Starbucks (*http://www.starbucks.com*) entered into an alliance with New York City delivery service Kozmo to deliver coffee beans, grinders, and other products that Starbucks sells online. Kozmo, which had been delivering in Manhattan since 1998, claimed delivery time within its service area of under one hour by bicycle, scooter, or motorbike, but the geographic area served was limited. Kozmo even planned to eventually deliver hot Starbucks coffee.[8] Kozmo's orange-jacketed runners were a welcome addition to urban life but the company could not sustain the delivery model and shut down in early 2001. Starbucks still sells its goods online, but only with standard shipping.

College textbook company Follet has an online storefront, efollett (*http://www.efollett.com*), that directly targets students from its over one thousand affiliated epartner campuses. The site also serves students from campuses without Follett stores. Students can sell "gently used" textbooks to efollett epartners, at no shipping cost to the seller. The site also sells ebooks, purely digital products. Students are not drawn to online textbook purchases. They prefer the convenience of their college or university bookstore and do not yet see sufficient reason to switch.

**WEB UPDATE**

Ebooks

**Products, Services**  A service, unlike a good, typically is created and consumed almost simultaneously. Seller and buyer typically are in close proximity and the services produced cannot be inventoried or stored. Perhaps the thought of going online to find one's perfect mate is not everyone's ideal, but matchmaking is a service marketed on such web storefronts as Single Search Global (*http://www.singlesearch.com*). The service has a graduated pricing scale, starting at a prepaid US$10 for the first match. Although online psychological counseling is not endorsed by any major psychological professional organization, it is extremely easy to find psychologists marketing their services online. Financial services sites, including Charles Schwab, e*TRADE FINANCIAL, Primerica (*http://www.primerica.com*), and others, vie for buyers. Other services available online include insurance (Geico Direct at *http://www.geico.com*), ISP connections (IGLOU Internet Services, Inc. at *http://www.iglou.com*), enterprise software (BroadVision at *http://www.BroadVision.com*), and training and development solutions (Employee Development Systems, Inc. at *http://www.edsiusa.com*) among many others.

Many services are well suited to online marketing with its interactivity and direct buyer-seller interface. Others, like hair cutting, cannot be delivered online; however, salons can schedule appointments from a web site. Dry cleaners can provide cleaning information online, but not the service itself. Thus, services are a mixed bag with some far better suited than others to online marketing.

**Products, Mixed**  Apple, Inc. (*http://www.apple.com*) markets a mixture of products online. It sells its computers and peripherals, as well as service through the Apple-Care Protection Plan (*http://www.apple.com/support/products/proplan.htm*), which extends the original one-year warranty on its computers to three years. Epson (*http://*

*www.epson.com*) sells its printers online and also offers printer drivers that can be downloaded directly from its web site.

## AUCTIONS AND WEB EXCHANGES

Rather than sell directly from a web storefront, some businesses act as managers for others' exchanges. eBay (*http://www.ebay.com*), founded in September 1995, is the best-known example of an exchange manager. It facilitates auctions for consumers as well as businesses and other enterprises, with more than five million products for sale on the main site, sixty local sites in the United States, or twelve country-specific sites worldwide. eBay has more than 46.1 million registered users and operates several levels of auctions, including eBay Premier auctions of fine art. Beginning in early 2001, eBay allied with iCollector.com (*http://www.iCollector.com*) to offer Premier Auctions anywhere in the world through iCollector's three hundred auction house partners. eBay sells onsite advertising and charges two seller fees, a variable rate insertion fee (rate depends on opening bid price) and a final value sale price fee, generally 1.25 to 5 percent of the final sale price.

Auctions are extremely popular with consumers selling products C2C, consumer-to-consumer. eBay is a massive online C2C garage sale that engages consumers in an exciting buying environment vastly larger than any offline equivalent. For some consumers, it is an opportunity to empty closets, basements, attics, and garages of junk that others will treasure. Many consumers experience the thrill of the chase, as they hunt down and bid for a coveted item.

FreeMarkets Asset Auctions (*http://assetauctions.freemarkets.com*) is an enterprise market maker, a service that attracts sellers and buyers of surplus assets including equipment, machine tools, aircraft, and industrial products. It hosts traditional auctions, private auctions, and an open trading marketplace. The company claimed US$2.7 billion in customer savings for the first half of 2000 from sales in over 165 goods and services categories, with more than a hundred fifty thousand suppliers participating worldwide.

A variety of marketing activities occur on B2B web exchanges. Exchanges are specialized businesses that use their software and management expertise to bring business, industrial, government, or nonprofit buyers and sellers together to negotiate sales, schedule payments, arrange deliveries, and provide after-sale service. Many of the eight hundred to fourteen hundred online B2B exchanges are not expected to survive as consolidation takes its toll. They are particularly vulnerable to takeover because of high start-up and marketing costs associated with entering the market and establishing their brand name.[9] Private exchanges have a greater probability of success because they can control participants better than public exchanges. This extends to inviting selected buyers and sellers to participate, excluding buyers or sellers that are not known to the industry, and verifying buyer and seller credentials before they can make exchanges.

Most B2B buying exchanges specialize in one industry. MedAssets.com (*MedAssets Exchange at http://www.medassets.com*) is a B2B for the health care industry. It hosts a web exchange where more than ten thousand members nationwide can purchase medical equipment and supplies. The company serves small clinics as well as large medical campuses.

WorldWide Retail Exchange (*http://www.worldwideretailexchange.org/*) is an Internet common marketplace with sixty-one retail industry leader members worldwide. Its goal is to connect buyers and sellers in the retail industry through an online exchange. Founding members include Target Corp., Kmart Corp., Safeway Inc., Walgreen's Inc., Royal Ahold NV in the Netherlands, and Marks & Spencer in the United Kingdom. Members expect to lower costs through electronic auctions for operating supplies (paper, computers, office equipment) and later, by standardizing purchase orders, inventory tracking, and requests for quotes. More savings will come from eliminating telephone and fax expenses, as well as paper transactions. It claims to have saved members over US$ 471 million through use of its online auctions and negotiations.

Many enterprises have not figured out how to effectively use auctions or web exchanges, so the early promise of cost reductions at many of these sites has failed to materialize. For other enterprises, web technologies are improving productivity and saving money. They saved businesses an estimated US$155 billion from 1998 to 2000. By 2005, the savings should reach US$500 billion.[10]

## PUSH SITES

Not all businesses with web sites sell online or manage auctions or exchanges. Instead, they use their sites to provide information about their products and/or business activities. The goal is to push buyers to telephone, fax, or visit them offline; send for a hard-copy catalog; or contact a member of their traditional sales force. Some businesses use **push sites** because their products are not appropriate for storefront selling. Others do so because they want to avoid problems or responsibilities associated with online selling, or they do not have the resources or revenue stream to maintain a storefront.

**Push sites**

Web sites that do not sell directly to buyers but instead provide information that pushes buyers offline to complete the sale.

DCN International (*http://www.dcnintl.com*) is a B2P that manufactures naval platforms, aircraft carriers, frigates, submarines, combat systems, and other military vessels for government buyers. It is highly unlikely that any business selling such specialized, expensive, and customized products could do so from a web storefront. The site provides product pictures and specifications, along with contact information designed to push potential customers to make contact offline with DCN's professional sales force.

Procter & Gamble (*http://www.pg.com/*), the giant consumer goods company, has a push site of a different kind. Rather than directly selling its more than three hundred brands online at its corporate web site, it drives consumers to stores that do. Its web site offers tips and tools on using P&G products to make life healthier and more enjoyable, and it gives visitors an opportunity to help the company improve its existing brands and create new ones. It will even send visitors free samples. Many of P&G's products can be bought online at other storefronts. For example, Wal-Mart.com, Drugstore.com (*http://www.drugstore.com*), and other online pharmacies sell the consumer version of Crest Whitestrips. In addition, the P&G site has a *dentist finder* that lets visitors search by zip code for local dentists who use professional-strength Crest Whitestrips for teeth whitening.

Subway (*http://www.subway.com*) has 16,581 restaurants in seventy-three countries. It does not sell its sandwiches online, but its web site does tell visitors where

Subway's restaurants are located through its *Find a Restaurant* search. For health-conscious consumers, the site gives nutritional information on Subway products, which might be enough to push them toward a restaurant and product purchase. Subway is well positioned to let buyers order sandwiches online for local delivery in select areas. This is the logical next step in developing oneline Internet marketing.

## ✔ CONCEPT CHECK

1. What is a web storefront and why have one?
2. How do web exchanges facilitate online marketing?
3. Explain the marketing strategy behind web push sites.

# Government and Other Enterprise Sellers

Chapter 3 examined governments and other enterprises that are online buyers. Many of the same entities are also online sellers.

### THE PUBLIC SECTOR

While the U.S. government is the largest single buyer in the United States, it is also a big online seller. In fiscal 2000, the U.S. government registered US$3.6 billion in online sales from its 164 web sites. It sold Amtrak tickets, repossessed houses, stamps, reservations at national parks, and access to federal case and docket data.[11] The General Services Administration (*http://www.gsaauctions.gov*), the business side of the U.S. government, was a pioneer in using its web site to sell excess and surplus federal assets. The general public can register at the site and bid electronically on office equipment, furniture, scientific instruments, heavy machinery, aviation equipment, naval vessels, and vehicles.

The Department of Housing and Urban Development (HUD) sells HUD homes (*http://www.hud.gov/offices/hsg/sfh/reo/homes.cfm*) to real estate brokers and the public. HUD also uses electronic auctions to sell surplus properties. The Central Intelligence Agency (*http://www.odci.gov/cia/publications/factbook/docs/purchase.htm*) sells its *World Factbook* online and the Department of Commerce (*http://www.census.gov/statab/www*) markets *The Statistical Abstract of the United States*.

State governments are getting into the business of selling licenses online. For example, the State of Hawaii (*http://www.hawaii.gov*) sells fishing and hunting licenses from its web site, and New Mexico (*http://www.state.nm.us*) has online vehicle registrations. Many states list surplus property to be auctioned on their web sites.

Governments are enthusiastic sellers online because of the Internet's convenience, which eliminates the need for buyers to travel to government offices; almost universal reach; savings from reduced printing and distribution costs; and the potential for downsizing as more services are offered online. Web interactivity and almost universal access in public libraries and schools brings government closer to its constituents.

### UNIVERSITIES AND ELEARNING

Before the Internet, universities marketed themselves to students primarily through printed materials, on-campus visits, and for the more sought-after students, personal telephone calls. Today, the Internet is a prime marketing tool selling schools to Internet-savvy traditional and nontraditional students. American University's Kogod School of Business receives over 95 percent of its student applications online through its web site (*http://www.kogod.american.edu*). The site was launched in 1999; since then it has recorded well over thirty-six thousand unique visits. Kogod uses databases to manage its contacts with prospective students and follows up contacts with emails, telephone calls, and mailed brochures. Its web site uses the latest technology to provide an interactive home page for prospective students and corporate recruiters that links them to needed information.[12]

Virtual college tours are replacing traditional campus visits for many students. Virtual tours save time and money, as well as help students narrow their college choice. They allow universities to market their programs using text, graphics, animation, and interactivity. For example, Duke University offers prospective students Duke 360 (*http://www.duke.edu/web/duketour*), a panoramic tour of the campus using low- or high-bandwidth versions. A 1998 survey of college-bound high school seniors by a Baltimore higher education marketing firm reported 78 percent visited college web sites, up from 4 percent in 1996.[13]

Like many national athletics programs, the Duke University Blue Devils (*http://goduke.fansonly.com*) are online at their official site. They market Duke football, soccer, conditioning, baseball, and basketball camps. The Duke store sells a broad assortment of products, from apparel to watches. Customers can order online or by telephone. Successful national athletics programs often host elaborate web sites that are informative and encourage interactions and transactions. They are a productive way to maintain ties with sometimes elusive alumni.

Colleges and universities are reporting excellent results from their online marketing efforts including more admissions from previously untapped geographical areas. Thus, many schools are paying marketing consultants to redesign their web sites to make them more appealing, easier to use, and more student-friendly. Higher education institutions will increasingly turn to Internet marketing as the competition for paying students intensifies. Students like the convenience of shopping for a college or university online.[14] Convenience and reach also attracts corporate recruiters who frequently use some university web sites to prescreen job applicants.

There were only four hundred online corporate universities in 1988; by 2000 the number had grown to more than sixteen hundred. Corporate university elearning is a highly competitive and profitable industry. International Data Corp. (IDC) projects growth in the U.S. market for corporate classes from about US$1 billion in 1999 to more than US$11 billion in 2003, a compound annual growth rate of nearly 80 percent. Web-based instruction is highly cost-effective, saving as much as 40 to 60 percent annually from corporate training budgets. IBM reported saving US$200 million in one year by purchasing online learning programs so employees could train at their workplace computers.[15]

Online training and education have a number of important benefits. They can save time and money, as well as eliminate disruptions caused when employees attend off-site training sessions. They also make training programs cost-effective for small and midsize businesses. Public and private universities recognize the value of online training and corporate education profits. The marketing of these programs will become more aggressive as the numbers of competitors increase.

**WEB UPDATE**

Internet Marketing by Colleges and Universities

## ARTS AND CULTURE

The Metropolitan Museum of Art's Met Store (*http://www.metmuseum.org/store/index.asp*) offers an extensive line of books and art-based objects in an elegant multi-page online catalog. The site has the latest in shopping basket technology, and online sales benefit the buyer as well as the organization. Not to be outdone, online stores are operated by the Metropolitan Opera Guild (*http://www.metopera.org/guild*), Kennedy Center for the Performing Arts (*http://www.kennedy-center.org/giftshop*), San Francisco Opera (*http://www.sfopera.com*), and National Public Radio (NPR at *http://shop.npr.org*) among others. NPR has a growing product line of books, apparel, recordings, videos, and other products whose sales help support NPR and its local affiliates.

Internet marketing vastly extends the reach of arts and cultural organizations, particularly those with national and international reputations like the Metropolitan Opera. It can also be used by local arts organizations seeking more timely communication with their patrons and the reduction or elimination of costly hard-copy catalogs and newsletters. It allows umbrella arts organizations like the California Assembly of Local Arts Agencies (CALAA at *http://www.calaa.net*) to showcase member organizations and market the local arts concept. CALAA is a nonprofit membership organization representing California's 250 local community arts organizations (private) and arts-related local government agencies (public).

Arts patrons typically are highly educated, higher-income consumers who spend more time and money online. They are more likely than the general population to be regular Internet users with faster access. Arts organizations increasingly recognize the effectiveness of Internet marketing in reaching these target markets from web storefronts and by email. In addition to providing information online, which is what many visitors seek, organizations sell products from their gift shops and tickets for future performances, distribute digital newsletters and announcements, or provide online product catalogs that push visitors toward an offline purchase. Schoolchildren are another prime target market for many arts organizations whose goal is to develop future patrons. Arts organization web sites often include pages specially designed for young people, to market the arts and the concept of participation. The National Gallery of Art (*http://www.nga.gov/kids/kids.htm*) has highly engaging interactive kids' pages that raise awareness about visual art and the Gallery.

## RELIGIOUS GROUPS

The Pew Internet and American Life Project reports that in the United States, more people go online for religious than secular purposes, and large numbers of religious organizations use the Internet. Churches, synagogues, mosques, and other houses of worship use email to maintain contact with members and reach nonmembers. They email newsletters, bulletins, and sermons. The Pew survey revealed that 80 percent of the churches and synagogues that participated in the study had web sites at least one year old, and 83 percent say the sites are useful in getting visitors to attend services.[16] Religious marketing is an area that is often overlooked, yet its importance is growing in U.S. society where religious groups must compete with a wide variety of secular activities.

Not all religious groups go as far as the Fellowship Church in Grapevine, Texas, that changed its name to fellowshipchurch.com. Fellowship Church (*http://www.*

*fellowshipchurch.com*) may be the first church to dot-com itself to identify more intimately with the Internet and attract Internet-savvy members. The church, which actively uses online marketing to advance its mission of connecting with the culture and new technology, has positioned its web site much like the web portals Yahoo! and AOL. It provides secular services along with the more expected sermons, Bible games, Bible reference materials, and daily devotionals.[17] Visitors can order books, music, and videos from its online bookstore.

The United Methodist Publishing House (UMPH) is helping church web sites host online bookstores. UMPH also runs the seventy-five-store Cokesbury retail chain and Cokesbury Online (*http://www.cokesbury.com*), which serves a hundred fifty thousand North American congregations selling Bibles, curriculum, communion wafers, and other religious products from its online store. Participating church web sites display on their front page a bookstore button branded with the church's name but linked to Cokesbury Online. Since its launch in Fall 1998, Cokesbury Online has far exceeded initial expectations for online sales.[18]

## OTHER ENTERPRISES

Cause-related marketing benefits nonprofit organizations (NPOs) from private adoption agencies to community mental health/mental retardation boards, substance abuse programs, and Ronald McDonald Houses for families with seriously ill hospitalized children. Tax-exempt public charities that solicit funds from the public are classified as 501(c)(3) organizations. NPOs can market themselves and their causes in several ways. They use their web sites to attract volunteers, solicit donors, develop databases, increase the number of dues paying members, and promote their goals. Some use their sites for charity auctions. Online donations are a growth industry. In 2000 less than 2 percent of charitable donations were received online; that should grow to 40 percent by 2005.[19]

Nonprofits are finding that online retailing is highly profitable; among these nonprofits are such disparate organizations as the National Rifle Association (*http://www.mynra.com*) the American Civil Liberties Union (*http://forms.aclu.org/store/storemain.cfm*) and Save the Children (*http://www.savethechildren.org*). The consensus is that niche marketing on the Internet is even more profitable than traditional off-line direct marketing.[20]

Some NPOs turn to affiliate marketing or "Shop-for-a-Cause" programs at so-called charity malls. Charities that sign up for these programs receive a donation (usually 5 percent of the purchase) for each purchase by a registered consumer at the web site of an affiliated retailer. Portals such as GreaterGood.com (*http://www.greatergood.com*) and CharityMall.com (*http://www.charitymall.com*) direct consumers to affiliated retailers that forward a portion of each purchase to the consumer's charity of choice. These donations are not tax deductible for the consumer.[21] GreaterGood forwards donations to local and national charities, schools, and college scholarship funds. Affiliated retailers include Nordstrom (*http://store.nordstrom.com*), Lands' End (*http://www.landsend.com*), DisneyStore (*http://disney.store.go.com*), Wal-Mart, and JC Penney. Causes include Big Brothers Big Sisters, The Elizabeth Glaser Pediatric AIDS Foundation, and Make-A-Wish Foundation of America. At the Schoolpop web site (*http://www.schoolpop.com*) consumers can designate a school they want to receive up to 20 percent of any purchase from a list of more than three hundred affiliated online stores. Cooperating retailers include Amazon.com, Dell Computer, Office Max (*http://www.officemax.com*), and Barnes & Noble (*http://www.bn.com*).[22]

Unfortunately, while the Internet is attractive for marketing an NPO, it also facilitates deceptions and frauds in the name of charity. According to the U.S. Federal Trade Commission (*http://www.ftc.gov/bcp/conline/pubs/tmarkg/charity.htm*) NPOs raised US$143 billion in 1995 and fraudsters collected around US$1.43 billion.[23] Fraud was a problem even in the wake of fundraising for the September 11th terrorist attack victims and their families. Within days after 9/11, the National Fraud Information Center (NFIC at *http://www.fraud.org*) began receiving consumer complaints about phone calls and emails fraudulently soliciting money for rescue efforts, victims' families, and to hunt Al-Qaeda terrorist leader Osama bin Laden. Legitimate fundraising groups like the American Red Cross Liberty Disaster Relief Fund, United Way September 11 Fund, and Twin Towers Fund for aid of New York City workers killed in the rescue efforts lost millions of dollars in potential contributions. Individuals defrauded by cyber thieves lost their money. Others lost their identity when swindlers emailed them asking for personal information to replace records supposedly lost in the World Trade Center building collapse.[24]

### ✔ CONCEPT CHECK

1. How can taxpayers benefit from online sales of surplus government property?
2. Are museums, operas, and similar cultural organizations online niche or mass marketers? Explain.
3. How can religious groups effectively use Internet marketing to achieve their goals?

# *Individual Sellers*

Businesses, governments, and organizations are not the only online sellers. The low cost of setting up a web site and the potential for reaching a large domestic or international audience are enough to encourage individuals to go online, marketing their products and themselves. Individual sellers range from artists and athletes to lawyers and other professionals. Some do it all themselves; others seek the help of marketing consultants to design, construct, and maintain a web site.

### PROFESSIONALS

Lawyers, doctors, dentists, consultants, psychologists, and other professionals have invaded the Web, marketing their services either directly from a web storefront or from a push site. Professionals can be located through search engines and sites that provide directories and locate local practitioners. Lawyers.com (*http://www.lawyers.com*) is a lawyer-locating service, categorizing lawyers by specialty and geography. Search-Pointe's ConsumerInfoCentral (*http://www.consumerinfocentral.com*) offers a doctor and chiropractor locator for all fifty states. The American Dental Association (*http://www.ada.org/public/directory/index.html*) has a dentist locator service. Psychotherapist Search (*http://psychotherapistsearch.com*) is a national registry by state of psychotherapists, marriage counselors, family and child counselors, and various types of clinicians.

Although some professionals have marketed their services offline for years, it is still a controversial practice. Most professional organizations accept tasteful, low-key web marketing sites and online professional portals with links to practitioners by state or city. What most condemn are blatant web sites that make exaggerated claims and prey on vulnerable individuals in a time of personal crisis. Most professions self-regulate and can threaten decertification of members who use the online environment inappropriately. They have no direct control over non-members. Complaints against professionals can be made to professional organizations or appropriate federal government agencies.

## ARTISTS AND CRAFTSPEOPLE

The visual richness of the web makes it an exciting environment for selling art products by individuals, arts organizations, government economic development agencies, and businesses. ArtMartCraftFair (*http://artamerica.com/a6s/a-@0142.html*) has links to individual artists selling their work online. Kentucky Virtual (*http://www.kentuckyvirtual.com*) markets the finest products handmade by Kentucky artisans, craftspeople, furniture makers, and farmers. Products include apparel and accessories, paintings and prints, sculpture, crafts, fine gifts, food, furniture, and holiday items. Kentucky gift baskets stocked with Kentucky Derby glasses, chocolate Derby bars, caramels, and Blue Monday candies are particularly popular.

## UNEXPECTED SELLERS

Considering the vast number of web sites and pages, finding small business and individual sellers online would appear to be an insurmountable task. However, with a bit of product-specific digging, they can be found. Selling farm produce online should defy the limits of electronic technology. However, a proxy exists at the Farmer's Market Online (*http://www.farmersmarketonline.com*). Farmers rent virtual *booth space*, which are links to web pages where they sell directly to buyers. This is a small business version of a B2C or C2C web exchange.

Individual proprietor sites can be located through search engines by using product-specific keyword descriptors. A consumer searching for *handmade wooden toys* might find a link to Don (*http://boschkitchen.com/toys/index.html*), who has been making handmade wooden toys since 1945. Don has an online catalog on his web site and accepts orders. A search for *handmade baskets* finds Baskets by Bernie (*http://www.basketsbybernie.com*), who has been making unique baskets since 1978. Bernie (Bernadine) does not accept orders online at this time, but encourages interested visitors to contact her by email or telephone. Understandably, push sites are common among individual sellers who do not have the sales volume, expertise, or need to deal with the complexities of a storefront transaction site.

Sports legends also are launching personal web storefronts or joining sports malls. Sports memorabilia is a US$2 billion industry, so using web storefronts could be good for the sports stars, as well as for the sites that host them for a small percentage of sales. Clicks-only sports malls have undergone considerable consolidation and bricks-and-clicks sports retailers now clearly dominate the market.[25] Golf phenomenon Tiger Woods (*http://www.tigerwoods.com*) has an official web site sponsored by American Express, Asahi soft drinks, Buick PGA golf, Golf Digest, and others. It has information about Tiger's golfing activities as well as an online store with cobranded apparel linked to Nike (*http://www.nike.com*) and memorabilia whose sale benefits the Tiger Woods Foundation. The Foundation was established in 1996 to support programs designed to create positive environments for underprivileged youth.

## ✔ CONCEPT CHECK

1. Should professionals like lawyers and doctors market their services online?
2. Why is the Web an inviting environment for artists and craftspeople?
3. How can an individual seller effectively market his or her products online?

# *Environmental Influences on Internet Marketing*

Marketing never occurs in a vacuum. To the contrary, marketing activities and ultimately marketing success are affected by what happens inside and outside the business or other enterprise (see figure 4-3).

*Internal factors* exist within a business or enterprise. Factors like human resources, capital, and level of cooperation must be considered whenever Internet marketing decisions are made. These factors are more controllable than external factors, but that doesn't mean marketing has control over them. Successful Internet marketing requires the commitment of top management decision makers, as well as other key company members and teams. In larger businesses this includes decision makers in finance and accounting, human resources, production, research and development, and purchasing. In smaller and midsize businesses, it means anyone whose work could affect or be affected by Internet marketing. Internet marketing requires teamwork, particularly cooperation and collaboration between marketing and information technology professionals. Implementing, maintaining, and upgrading web marketing activities requires a resource commitment of people, money, equipment, and time. This can lead to turf wars unless a consensus is developed and maintained to support Internet marketing efforts.

Internet marketing requires skilled and committed people. Therefore, human resource departments must provide enough people with the required skills and support to plan, implement, and control Internet marketing activities. It also requires clearly articulated goals and objectives for what Internet marketing must contribute to busi-

**Figure 4-3  Environmental Influences on Marketing**

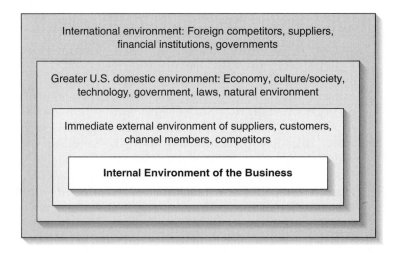

International environment: Foreign competitors, suppliers, financial institutions, governments

Greater U.S. domestic environment: Economy, culture/society, technology, government, laws, natural environment

Immediate external environment of suppliers, customers, channel members, competitors

**Internal Environment of the Business**

ness and marketing plans and production processes that produce products in sufficient quantity and quality to satisfy online buyers. Marketers cannot control many of these internal factors, but they can influence them, particularly by making a compelling case that cooperation increases revenues and profits.

*External factors* are far less controllable than those inside the business. The immediate external environment includes businesses and people that interact most closely and directly with the business. They are suppliers providing raw materials, parts, equipment, supplies, and finished products used in business operations and sales. They are marketing intermediaries that transport products and perform warehouse and inventory control functions. Buyers are part of this environment, as are competitors and stakeholders.

The greater U.S. domestic environment directly affects the business and its Internet marketing activities. Although the largest corporations may influence some factors within this environment, most companies cannot. External factors are economic, technological, societal, cultural, natural, governmental, and legal.

Every business whether or not it actively engages in the international Internet market is affected by the greater global environment. Each country's own domestic environment contributes to the global environment. Since any business that has a web site is an international marketer because of the borderless nature of the Internet, what happens in the global environment also affects each Internet marketer directly or indirectly. Some of these effects can be extreme. All environmental factors require constant monitoring to determine when factors are turning against the marketing effort or present opportunities. This is particularly true of Internet marketing, which occurs in a highly volatile environment of its own, as well as being vulnerable to what is happening around the world. Several key U.S. macroenvironmental factors are examined in the following sections.

## THE ECONOMIC ENVIRONMENT

Internet commercialization began during a period of great economic prosperity for the United States and many parts of the world. From 1993 until mid-2000, the stock market soared, productivity steadily increased, and consumer confidence was at an all-time record high. Internet commercial growth seemed destined to expand forever. At the same time, computing power continued to observe Moore's Law and computer prices fell steadily. ISPs and AOL in the United States converted to monthly access fees rather than charge by time used. Many services offered free email and/or Net access. For many marketers, a rosy economy meant comparatively easy work in securing financing and purchasing advertising and other promotions designed to get buyers to buy.

A contentious presidential election, impatience with unprofitable dot-coms, and a slowing economy thrust the U.S. economy into an economic downturn by late 2000 and a recession in mid-2001. An economic downturn has serious implications. For many Internet marketers, it was a knock-out punch. **Consumer confidence,** a key indicator and frequently used predictor of consumers' willingness to purchase, fell proportionally and suggested harder times to come.[26] It took a tailspin after the terrorist attacks, falling to its lowest levels since the early 1990s. Consumer pessimism can lead to delayed or avoided purchases. This negatively affects revenues online or off, creating a ripple effect that touches most sectors of the economy.

Marketers are particularly vulnerable to changes in the economic environment. This includes factors that influence consumer and business confidence, purchasing and

**Consumer confidence**
A measure of the confidence consumers have in their economic future and the nation's economy, often used as a predictor of future consumer buying.

spending patterns. Marketers can do little to affect consumer confidence as a whole. However, online marketers can reduce prices to stimulate short-term sales. For the Christmas 2001 buying season, many offered free shipping and handling for purchases over a minimal amount. Others used preseason clearance sales to boost site traffic. Online advertising expenditures, however, were not increased and in many cases, suffered serious reductions. Despite the slowing economy, Christmas 2001 online sales grew over the previous year, and 2002 began strong. B2C online sales of almost US$50 billion in 2001 were projected to grow to US$75 billion in 2002 and over US$155 billion by 2005.

## TECHNOLOGY

Advances in technology are what got the Internet and Internet marketing where they are today. However, technology is a double-edged sword. Keeping up with new technology is extremely expensive. In addition, technological advances can threaten established ways of doing business. If wireless handheld Internet devices become popular in the United States, it will challenge marketers to redesign or re-create web storefronts to accommodate the smaller screens. New technologies on the horizon that could make online shopping more engaging for consumers include 3-D imaging, where consumers experience products in three-dimensional space, and sensations transmitted through a specially constructed intelligent mouse. As the viewer moves the cursor over an object, such as a sweater, the *feel* of the object is transmitted to the mouse and the consumer experiences sensation. Like economic factors, technology requires constant monitoring.

## THE SOCIAL/CULTURAL ENVIRONMENT

The social/cultural environment involves people interacting within families, communities, groups, and nations. People influence purchase decisions and other consumer behaviors. Families and reference groups exert perhaps the most direct influence. Consumer fears about Internet safety and security can seriously slow commercialization. Consumer adoption of new technologies will determine whether or not the Internet becomes like the telephone or television, with near-universal access.

## THE NATURAL ENVIRONMENT

It may be difficult to visualize a link between the Internet and the natural world, yet they are inseparably bound. The Internet relies on physical connections such as wires, telephone lines, cables, satellites, and other equipment that can be damaged or destroyed when natural or man-made disasters occur. Increased use of computers and the Internet have been implicated in the natural gas and power shortage that struck California in early 2001. Widespread consumer and business Internet use added an estimated 10 percent to electricity demand. As demand grows, it will pressure natural gas reserves and power supplies.[27]

Internet marketing can be seriously hampered by power shortages, particularly in the United States where the majority of Internet users rely on computers and modems to access the Web. Although Internet marketers can do little to increase power supplies, they may have an opportunity to aggressively market handheld wireless devices that operate independently of electrical power other than when they are recharging. Persistent power supply problems and rolling brownouts are serious threats to web commercialization. Power disruptions stop consumers and businesses from reaching the electronic marketplace and restrict business activities.

Man-made disasters can be equally disruptive. When terrorist attacks collapsed the twin towers of the World Trade Center in Manhattan, high-speed switches and circuits in its basement and adjacent buildings were destroyed, along with computers and access lines throughout the stricken area. Financial firms at or near the Trade Center lost contact with customers and their own branches. Securities and data processing came to a halt for Bank of New York's (BoNY) headquarters and branches in the Trade Center area. Some Earthlink and AT&T WorldNet customers lost Internet access. As the crisis unfolded, the financial community joined to cover liquidity problems caused by losses at BoNY, Cantor Fitzgerald, and other firms. Internet companies offered free bandwidth to others so they could maintain operations. Internet traffic was routed around the destroyed equipment. Many companies relied on mirror sites far from Manhattan to restore files and customer service. While broadband and voice service in Washington, D.C., and New York City experienced delays, they continued to function despite extremely high traffic counts.[28]

## GOVERNMENT AND LEGAL FACTORS

All business, whether online or off, are controlled by government regulations and laws. These topics are considered at length in Chapter 5.

### ✔ CONCEPT CHECK

1. Why is it important that support for Internet marketing be developed and maintained within the business?
2. How can an economic downturn affect Internet marketing?
3. Explain how natural forces can threaten web marketing.

# *Summary*

### *Business Sellers*

The economic downturn and dot-com shakeout of 2000–2001 should not be interpreted as the end of Internet commercialization. Similar events have happened in U.S. commercial history—in automobiles, biotechnology, and personal computers. Most businesses go online to promote and sell their products. They are marketing online in a variety of ways through web storefronts (transaction sites), auctions and web exchanges, and push sites. Three criteria for classifying online storefront sellers are place, buyers, and products. Place refers to distribution and delivery channels. Some businesses are bricks and mortar with no online marketing. Others are clicks only or have dual or multi-distribution channels (online and off). Some bricks and mortars sell to businesses that are online. Amazon.com is perhaps the best-known clicks-only online seller. Bricks and clicks are the most prevalent type of business online. Oneline marketing is the seamless integration of online and offline marketing ac-

tivities. Buyers are B2B, B2C, B2P, or a combination (mixed). Products, the offer made to potential buyers, can be purely digital, tangible goods, intangible services, or a mixture. Auctions and web exchanges are other ways that buyers and sellers connect online. Various businesses host consumer, business, government, or industry auctions. Web exchanges can specialize in products that interest one industry or deal in products that many industries need to purchase. Push sites do not sell online; instead they push buyers offline where products can be purchased.

### *Government and Other Enterprise Sellers*

Governments sell products online to better serve constituents, streamline their operations, generate revenue, and reduce costs. The U.S. government auctions excess and surplus federal assets. The Department of Housing and Urban Development auctions surplus real estate. Government publications are sold online. State governments sell licenses online, along with surplus equipment. Universities are using the Web to reach and recruit students, and keep in touch with alumni. Virtual college tours are replacing college visits for many students. For-profit elearning is also growing. Arts and cultural organizations are selling products from their online gift shops as well as tickets. Religious groups go online to recruit members, advance their beliefs, reduce costs, and obtain donations and volunteers. Cause-related organizations are doing much the same. They are raising money, selling products, and using online charity malls to market their causes.

### Individual Sellers

Lawyers, doctors, dentists, marketing consultants, and others are using the Web to market their services. They are using web storefronts as well as push sites. Some are listed in professional malls, locator services with search engines that allow consumers to search for a practitioner in a particular specialty and location. Artists find the Web a rich visual environment for marketing their creative products. Some maintain independent web sites, others list with artists' malls.

Individuals and small businesses make up a large part of the millions of web pages that exist. They range from farmers' markets online that link consumers to individual farmers, to handmade toy makers.

### Environmental Influences on Internet Marketing

Marketing does not occur in a vacuum. Internet marketing is affected by environmental influences within and external to the company. Internally, management as well as people in other functional areas should be encouraged to cooperate, support, and sometimes participate in the Internet marketing effort. The immediate macroenvironment includes all the businesses and people with whom the business and marketer interact most frequently. The Internet effort is influenced by what happens in the greater U.S. macroenvironment, as well as the global environment. Marketers must monitor the economic environment, the technology environment, the social/cultural environment, the natural environment, and the government and legal environments.

## Internet Marketing Application

Marketing is more often associated with for-profit businesses than charities, yet both use similar marketing tools to achieve their goals. Like businesses, charities were not immune to the dot-com bust, and some, like Charities-on-the-Net (http://www.charity.ndirect.co.uk), shut down when additional funding did not materialize. Charities of all types are online, including religious charities and those that collect and distribute money for children's causes, the environment, animals, and the poor. Many charities mobilized after September 11 to help victims and their families. Many businesses online and offline support charities. PETsMART Charities (http://www.petsmart.com/charities/petsmart_charities/index.shtml) is a 501(c) 3 organization that works to save the lives of homeless, abandoned, and distressed pets. It has given more than US$15 million to animal welfare organizations. McDon-

ald's (http://www.rmhc.com) has Ronald McDonald House Charities. Goodwill Industries International (http://shopgoodwill.com) is composed of 182 local, autonomous member organizations in North America and 45 international associate members in thirty-four countries. Goodwill helps people become self-sufficient and employable.

Visit the following sites. Evaluate how they are marketing their charities to visitors. How are their approaches similar? How are they different? What, if any, incentives are offered for contributions? Which has the most unique approach to fundraising?

PETsMART Charities at http://www.petsmart.com/products/product_27404.shtml

Ronald McDonald House Charities at http://www.rmhc.com

Goodwill Industries at http://shopgoodwill.com

# *Chapter Review Questions*

1. Explain the roles of buyer and seller in the reciprocal marketing exchange relationship.
2. Did all dot-coms fail in 2000–2001? Explain.
3. What three key criteria are used to classify web selling sites?
4. Contrast the following: clicks only, bricks and clicks, bricks and mortar.
5. Is there really a first mover advantage?
6. What is test marketing? How is E*TRADE FINANCIAL using test marketing?
7. What is a digital product?
8. Why do buyers like electronic airline tickets?
9. What are some services sold online? How are they different from digital products and tangible goods?
10. How are universities using the Web to market their programs?
11. Why would consumers respond to the shop-for-a-cause strategy?
12. Should all artists market their work online?
13. What external factors influence Internet marketing?
14. Would an economic downturn affect all Internet marketing activities equally? Explain.
15. Why is technology a double-edged sword for Internet marketers?

## Can Wal-Mart.com Be the Wal-Mart of the Web?

# Case Study

Wal-Mart Stores, Inc. is the elephant of the retail world. The world's largest mass merchandise retailer is bigger than Sears, Kmart, and JC Penney combined, with 1.4 million employees worldwide and US$218 billion in annual sales (2002). Its 2001–2002 one-year sales growth was 14 percent. Wal-Mart has more than four thousand stores worldwide including Wal-Mart Stores, SAM'S Club Members Warehouse, Wal-Mart Supercenters, and international stores. It is also the number one retailer in Canada and Mexico. According to Wal-Mart Stores, Inc., more than a hundred million customers visit its stores each week.

The first Wal-Mart store opened in 1962. The first in-house web storefront was launched June 1995, relaunched July 1996, and again in Fall 1999. In January 2000 it spun off its in-house operations to a new independent company, Wal-Mart.com, of which Wal-Mart Stores, Inc. was majority owner. Other owners were its venture capital partner Accel Partners and Wal-Mart.com employees. In 2001, Wal-Mart, Inc. bought out Accel and integrated Walmart.com into the parent company.

The strategy for the Wal-Mart.com site is to "serve customers in a way they want to be served where they want to be served." Wal-Mart.com plans to be ecommerce for the masses by integrating the online storefront with offline stores. This includes a rollout of interactive in-store kiosks that give customers access to products not in the store and a gift registry. The web storefront is an attractive alternative for people who like Wal-Mart's low prices but hate shopping their stores.

Wal-Mart brings unmatched marketing clout to its web presence. It has an outstanding back-office system and strong vendor relationships. Its commitment to "Always low prices" is customer-pleasing. It's a highly experienced retailer with instant name recognition. The return policy for products bought from Wal-Mart.com at any Wal-Mart store is an advantage over clicks-only and most bricks-and-clicks retailers.

When Wal-Mart.com was independent from Wal-Mart Stores, Inc., it enjoyed a competitive price advantage because it was exempt from sales tax in all states except California, Utah, and Arkansas, where the company had a physical presence (nexus). When Walmart.com was integrated into Wal-Mart Stores, Inc., it lost the tax advantage because the parent company has a nexus in all fifty states.

Wal-Mart has a highly diverse product base that facilitates cross-selling. Its customers mirror the general U.S. population, so over 60 percent of them have computers for accessing Wal-Mart.com. If it adheres to the following advice of founder Sam Walton (1918–1992), it should be an online success:

> *"The secret of successful retailing is to give your customers what they want. And really, if you think about it from your point of view as a customer, you want everything: a wide assortment of good quality merchandise; the lowest possible prices; guaranteed satisfaction with what you buy; friendly, knowledgeable service; convenient hours; free parking; a pleasant shopping experience."*[29]

### CHECK IT OUT

Visit Wal-Mart.com (*http://www.walmart.com*) and evaluate the site using Sam Walton's advice. How well does it perform? Would Mr. Walton be satisfied? If not, what should the site do to bring itself more in line with Mr. Walton's philosophy. Is there another web storefront that does a better job satisfying Mr. Walton's requirements for successful retailing?

### A GLOBAL PERSPECTIVE

Wal-Mart has operating units in Argentina (11), Brazil (20), Canada (174), Germany (94), Korea (6), Mexico (572), Puerto Rico (15), the UK (241), and China (11).

Visit Wal-Mart México (*http://www.walmart-mexico.com.mx*).

- How many Wal-Mart stores are in Mexico?
- When did the first Wal-Mart open there?
- Where are most of the company's units located geographically?
- Is the Mexico web site information only, interactive, or transaction?
- Compare the design of the United States and Mexican web sites. How are they alike? How are they different?

## CHAPTER FIVE

# Legal and Ethical Issues; Privacy and Security

- To understand why Internet laws and jurisdiction are in a state of flux and what remedies are being attempted

- To learn what important legal issues confront Internet marketers

- To consider whether ethical marketing behaviors can be enforced on the Internet

- To understand why online security problems concern buyers and sellers

## Tomás Shops Thailand

Tomás has been trying to find the right birthday gift for his wife, an orchid collector who is anxious to add a *Dendrobium Mae Klong River* to her collection. No U.S. grower has one, but Tomás locates a web site in Thailand selling the plant. Without a moment's hesitation, Tomás drops the plant's icon in the virtual shopping basket and pays for it with his debit card. His initial pleasure fades when the orchid fails to arrive in time for his wife's birthday. He emails the orchid Web site asking about the purchase and is told the orchid was sent and if it has not arrived, it is the fault of the shipping company. Subsequent emails to the site go unanswered. The shipping company tells Tomás it has no record of the order and blames the seller. Neither the seller nor the shipping company will accept responsibility for the lost order. Tomás is frustrated and does not know what to believe or where to turn for help. The order was not insured and the purchase was debited to his account almost immediately. He has lost his money, his temper, and any interest in ever shopping online again at a web site in another country.

Tomás's sad story is illustrative of several problems. One problem is buyer negligence. In this case, the buyer (Tomás) did not take any safeguards before making the purchase. He could have used some smart web shopping tips (see "Tips for Smart Web Shopping" on p. 101)) from the U.S. Federal Trade Commission (FTC at *http://www.ftc.gov*), Visa (*http://www.visa.com*) and other credit card companies, or the National Consumers League (*http://www.nclnet.org*). These and other organizations are trying to educate consumers in order to encourage electronic transactions and discourage fraud. Unfortunately, most consumers are unaware the information exists or choose to ignore it.

The second problem is web sites that are not customer-centric. In Tomás's case, a customer-centered web site would have been more concerned about replacing the missing orchid than deflecting blame. Web shopping sites that adhere to the marketing concept do everything possible to satisfy their customers and maintain good relations with them. This includes providing essential information, clearly stating return and refund policies, and explaining how to track orders. It also means that a web storefront that is unprepared to accommodate international orders should not accept them.

A third problem is the lack of consensus on Internet law. Although the orchid purchase took place on the borderless Internet, it involved a buyer and seller from two different countries. It would be difficult if not impossible to get a refund from a web site in another country if the site's owner refused the refund request.

Finally, there is the problem of fraud. While Tomás acted in good faith, other buyers and sellers sometimes do not. Sellers defrauded by buyers absorb the loss, while consumers with zero liability for online credit card purchases typically do not.

Although there are great advantages to doing business online, there also are drawbacks. Some of the most vexing challenges facing Internet marketers involve legal and ethical issues, and online safety and security. Chapter 5 begins with a discussion of legal issues, then continues with ethical challenges facing Internet marketers and some responses. Privacy and security, the concluding topics, concern both buyers and sellers and have been identified as top reasons why some buyers swear they will never go online. Because the Internet's legal environment is dynamic and unpredictable, information presented here should not be taken as legal advice or opinion on any specific facts or circumstances.

# Laws and Jurisdiction

In the opening story, a U.S. citizen (the buyer) purchased an orchid plant from a Thai citizen (the seller) operating a web storefront (commercial establishment) from a server in Bangkok. It is about a twenty-hour airplane flight from the United States to Thailand; the online trip takes a mouse click. The U.S. buyer paid for the orchid plant by debit card, which has less protection against fraud than a credit card. Had he used a credit card, the card's zero online liability guarantee might have protected him. When the plant did not arrive, he could have stopped payment had he acted quickly enough. However, payment on the debit card had already been processed, so he had to decide whether it was worth the effort to try to get a refund. Buyers are more likely to seek restitution when their loss is significant and less likely to do so when their loss is small. If they think about it at all, most U.S. citizens probably assume U.S. laws will protect all their online transactions. That is a risky assumption.

## INTERNET LAW

The Internet is borderless, a worldwide network of internetted computer networks linking people and nations electronically. For a body of Internet law to be effective, first it must be accepted by all internetted nations and then enforced either by existing bodies such as the World Trade Organization (WTO) or United Nations (UN), or a new agency created specifically for the purpose. A patchwork of laws accepted by only some but not all connected nations will cause chaos and be unenforceable. It will also have a detrimental effect on Internet commercialization. Currently, there is no

# Tips for Smart Web Shopping

Governments and organizations are trying to educate buyers about safe shopping online to encourage electronic transactions and discourage fraud. Questions online buyers should ask before making a purchase include

## IS THE BUSINESS LEGITIMATE?

Is the business well known? Is it affiliated with trade groups or self-regulation associations? Does the web site have VeriSign (*http://www.verisign.com*), BBBOnline (*http://www.bbbonline.org*), TRUSTe (*http://www.truste.com*), or other reliability and security seals posted on the front page. Buyers should avoid businesses that do not provide information about themselves and their business practices, return policies, and commitment to customer satisfaction. Buyers should print the site's email and post office addresses, phone and fax numbers, and other store contact information for future reference.

## ARE PRICES AND CONDITIONS CLEARLY STATED?

Is sufficient information present about product prices and conditions? Buyers should print product prices and conditions in case a dispute arises. If sufficient information is not present, they should call or email the company to obtain the information before ordering, and check to make sure all conditions, refund information, and costs are clearly and completely stated.

## IS THE TRANSACTION CURRENCY CALCULATED?

Are transaction prices clearly stated in U.S. currency denominations? If prices on foreign web sites are not stated in U.S. dollars, the buyer should contact the seller and determine how exchange rates are calculated. Buyers need to know prices in domestic currency terms and exchange rates on the day of purchase even when their credit card company automatically makes the currency conversion.

## IS ORDERING SECURE?

Are security seals posted on the site? Before placing an order, buyers should look for the closed lock icon on the lower browser screen that signals ordering information is encrypted. They need to click the lock to learn the current security status of the site's server and print the completed order form with an itemized purchase list and order confirmation email.

## IS PRIVACY RESPECTED?

Does the site have a clear privacy statement? Is collected information sold to third parties? Is there an opt-out box to avoid future contacts? The buyer should click the opt-out box if future contact is not wanted and refuse the sale of personal information to third parties.

## IS THERE RECOURSE?

How strong is the company's commitment to customer satisfaction? How do they resolve complaints? The storefront should have a clear statement about paying return shipping if they make a mistake in the order. Does the company strongly state a desire to settle problems fairly, without extra charges?

## IS THE CREDIT CARD STATEMENT CORRECT?

Buyers should carefully review all monthly credit and debit card billing statements and ensure online purchases are accurately billed. They should look for unauthorized purchases or overcharges and report them to the credit issuing company, bank, and/or consumer fraud protection organizations.[1]

body of Internet law. In its absence, laws dealing with specific Internet activities are being formulated by legislatures, agencies, and courts in nations worldwide. Judges often rule on Internet disputes using historical precedent derived from non-Internet business law cases and codes. Sometimes contradictory Internet laws are passed by legislatures in different countries, which adds to the confusion about what is and is not legal, and where. New technologies, without direct existing equivalents, muddy the legal waters even further. An example is **peer-to-peer (P2P) computing**, where computer resources, information, and files are shared directly between peer computers. This is the Napster music-sharing model. Peer-to-peer computing makes it more difficult to enforce copyright and other laws since peer computers that are transmitting or sharing data could number in the tens or hundreds of millions.

**Peer-to-peer (P2P) computing**
Sharing computer resources, data, and information by direct exchange of data, computer-to-computer.

Why should anyone care that nations collaboratively develop a body of Internet law? As more consumers, businesses, and other enterprises become online buyers and sellers, maintaining order will be more difficult without an internationally agreed upon and enforced set of rules. Web marketers must know where they are liable for problems buyers have with their products, how they can resolve problems with buyers, or where they can obtain redress should problems arise with their own purchases. They must know where to report and resolve fraud claims and disputes about product offers, online promotions, site content pirating, trademark and copyright infringement, anticorporate sites, and hacker attacks. Most marketplace problems can be resolved without legal action. For those issues that require legal remedies, it becomes critical to know what laws will be used to evaluate a dispute, which courts have jurisdiction, and how difficult it will be to reach those courts in terms of time, money, distance, and convenience. The patchwork of laws and restrictions Internet marketers face today slows commercialization, adds to the cost of doing business online, makes many marketers reluctant to accept international orders, and compromises the Internet's ability to host a truly safe, frictionless global commercial community.

Laws are commands created and declared by legislatures, enforced with regulations promulgated by agencies, and interpreted by appropriate courts. They are the social cement that binds a nation together with uniform standards, expectations, and sanctions and that brings order to international trade. U.S. courts have the power to interpret U.S. laws and resolve disputes within U.S. borders and in some cases, abroad. Each state has rights granted by the U.S. Constitution to create, declare, and enforce laws within its borders. U.S. businesses must comply with *commercial laws*, the legal rules and principles that deal with businesses and commercial transactions; *civil laws* governing private rights; and *criminal laws* governing crime and its prosecution. In addition, certain federal quasi-judicial agencies can make authoritative rules or regulations that have the force of law. For example, FTC and Federal Communication Commission (FCC at *http://www.fcc.gov*) rules regulate business activities in the United States. The FTC also collects consumer complaints and may use consumer complaint information in its investigations of business activities, although it does not resolve individual disputes.

National legal systems vary, though most are built on either common or case law (U.S., UK), Roman or code law (France and former French colonies), or Islamic law (Iran). The world's most populous nation, the People's Republic of China (PRC), is a Communist state with a unique legal system that incorporates custom along with commercial, immigration, and criminal law. Despite these differences, a body of international business law has developed from mutually agreed upon rules and treaties that control the actions and rights of nations in areas where their interests intersect. This does not stop all disputes from occurring, but it stops most from escalating into trade wars or worse.

Nations and organizations are struggling to find ways to deal with Internet legal issues. The United Nations (UN) Commission on International Trade Law (UNCITRAL at *http://www.uncitral.org/en-index.htm*) meets regularly to develop strategies and guidelines to encourage nations to harmonize and integrate their trade laws. UNCITRAL's Working Group on Electronic Commerce (*http://www.uncitral.org*) has produced legislative guidelines for governments to use when drafting Internet commerce laws. The committee is attempting to encourage coordination, cooperation, and harmonization of Internet commerce laws.[2] Thus far, it is unclear if UNCITRAL has had much impact.

The American Bar Association (ABA at *http://www.abanet.org*) is a professional organization of lawyers and judges. Its Global Cyberspace Jurisdiction Project has issued a report, *Achieving Legal and Business Order in Cyberspace: A Report on Global Jurisdiction Issues Created by the Internet*, calling for a multinational jurisdiction commission to deal with Internet privacy, consumer protection, banking, taxation, gambling, and other issues.[3]

The World Trade Organization (WTO at *http://www.wto.org*) is the only international organization dealing directly with trade rules and disputes between nations. WTO agreements, negotiated and ratified by a majority of the world's trading nations, promote free trade, reduce tariffs, and settle trade disputes before they erupt into trade wars. Its members adopted a declaration on global electronic commerce in May 1998 encouraging the continued practice of no customs duties on products purchased online. A work group report in July 1999 concluded that most Internet purchases were services covered by the General Agreement on Trade in Services (GATS).[4] These initiatives are not binding on members, however, so they have not brought clarity to the status of online activities.

The Organization for Economic Cooperation and Development (OECD at *http://www.oecd.org*) has issued reports on Internet taxation, hosted international forums on the global Internet marketplace, and formulated new guidelines for voluntary codes of conduct for businesses involved in Internet commerce. The United States was one of twenty-nine countries that signed the OECD guidelines.[5]

Delegates from fifty-two nations to the Hague Convention on Jurisdiction and Foreign Judgments (*http://www.hcch.net/e/workprog/jdgm.html*) have been meeting since 1992 to negotiate common Internet business jurisdiction rules and to try to formulate common agreements on online copyrights, free speech, and ecommerce. They have been debating the very nature of the Internet, whether it is stores that buyers visit or traveling salespeople who visit buyers. Depending on the outcome, consumers could have the right to sue foreign web sites from the consumers' home jurisdictions, which would be a nightmare for U.S. web businesses.

If the treaty is ever finalized and ratified, it will require participants to enforce each other's laws even if the actions are contrary to local laws. All member states will agree to enforce so-called white listed laws, while black listed laws are issues that will be avoided, and the remaining most contentious (gray) areas are where judgments will be made case by case. If this treaty is enforced, it will mean that countries with the narrowest, most restrictive laws, a China or Morocco, will get other nations to enforce their laws. Free speech advocates, librarians, online stores, and global ISPs oppose the treaty. Global web businesses fear they will have to check each of their sites, which can number in the hundreds, to ensure they are not breaking the laws of any treaty member nation or violating copyrights. U.S. refusal to sign could seriously undermine the treaty because the majority of Internet-based businesses are based in the United States.[6]

Because the Internet is such a unique environment, some legal scholars recommend a separate jurisdiction for it modeled on those created for Antarctica, outer space, and the high seas.[7] Like the Internet, the high seas (oceans) are borderless and many countries share a strong interest in what happens to them. The United Nations "Convention on the Law of the Sea," an international agreement on the oceans, their preservation, and commercial disputes, was implemented in November 1994 after negotiations that lasted more than fourteen years. The 150 countries that developed the Convention agreed that problems of the oceans are interrelated and have to be dealt with as a whole. The Convention contains traditional rules and introduces new legal concepts and, perhaps most significantly, a framework for the future development of rules.[8]

The Convention has not eliminated all disputes, but it has brought a level of harmonization and cooperation to a highly volatile issue. While a convention may be exactly what the Internet needs, it is doubtful that nations, Internet marketers, consumers, and others can wait fourteen or more years for a framework to be developed, approved, and implemented.

## JURISDICTION

**Jurisdiction**

Determines which courts have the right to exercise authority in a dispute.

**Jurisdiction** determines which courts have the *right* to exercise authority, the *power* to decide outcomes in a controversy, and the *control* over issues and parties.[9] It determines where laws are applicable and can be enforced. Before the Internet's commercialization, jurisdiction was mainly contiguous with physical borders. Since the borderless Internet operates interstate and intercountry, what courts and laws have jurisdiction is far more difficult to ascertain. For buyers and sellers, a home-country court and its laws typically are more desirable, less expensive, and more convenient than those of another country or group of countries like the European Union (EU). Most businesses will understandably seek a home-country legal advantage.

The expansion of international business in the latter half of the twentieth century forced courts to face thorny cross-border jurisdictional questions. Sometimes they responded by extending their jurisdiction over defendants outside their own borders (extraterritorially), bringing cases back to their own home-country jurisdiction (forum) for consideration. On other occasions, they declined jurisdiction if it was determined that bringing a case back to their forum posed hardships on the parties or that courts in another forum were better suited to decide the case. Some courts have applied international jurisdiction case law to Internet jurisdiction disputes; others have tried to devise new jurisdiction tests.

**INTERACTIVE/PASSIVE RELATIONS TEST**  An emerging jurisdiction test frequently used by courts is whether a web site has interactive or passive business relations with visitors from its own or another state, province, country, or country group. A web storefront has **interactive business relations** when it actively sells to buyers, has two-way online communication as part of a business relationship, and/or uses activities directly designed to solicit business from a target market. A 1-800 toll-free or fax number to take orders meets the minimum contact standard of an interactive business site for many courts. A Web storefront has **passive business relations** when it does not directly sell or have interactions from the site. It may provide one-way information and even advertise, but it maintains a low level of business activity and does not have minimum contact with visitors. The more interactively commercial a site is with the citizens of a particular jurisdiction, the more likely the site will be liable within that jurisdiction, even if the site is housed on a server in a different jurisdiction. The case most often used as an example of this principle is *Zippo Manufacturing Co. v. Zippo Dot Com, Inc.*[10] The practice of awarding jurisdiction over a nonresident that repeatedly solicits business in a state (forum) is known as the long-arm statute.

If Tomás had purchased the orchid from a U.S. grower operating a web storefront from a U.S. server, jurisdiction would have been clear. Tomás could have sued for restitution in his state's civil courts because the grower was doing business with citizens of his state, thus the state probably had jurisdiction. In *Inset Systems, Inc. v. Instructions Set, Inc.*, the courts ruled the web site operator was under the state's jurisdiction because the web site offered a toll-free number that solicited business from the state's citizens; thus, it was an interactive site with *minimum contact*. In *Rannoch, Inc. v. Rannoch Corporation*, the state of Virginia was not given jurisdiction over an interactive web site whose server was operating in Virginia because it could not be proven that Virginia citizens had business dealings with the site; thus, it did not have *minimum contact*. Interactive web site accessibility was the controlling factor in determining jurisdiction. In a third case, a different Virginia court claimed jurisdiction because, although one of the parties had no ties to the state of Virginia, his ISP (America Online) was Virginia-based.[11] A state with jurisdiction can order an in-state web site removed from the server housing it for containing illegal or objectionable content.

**UPLOAD/DOWNLOAD STATUS TEST**  An interactive U.S. web storefront is considered to be doing business internationally unless it explicitly refuses to accept international orders. In the current climate, this means that if data from an interactive web storefront are accessed in another country, the site is doing business within that country's borders.[12] It gets more complicated if the business also has servers, mirror sites, or server farms in one or more other countries. Then jurisdiction is even less clear.

A second standard often used by courts is **upload status** or **download status**. The country where the site's server is located typically is held to have jurisdiction. U.S. jurisdiction prevails when a buyer from another country purchases from a U.S. site. If a U.S. consumer accesses a storefront in another country, jurisdiction is in the country where the site/server is located. By this standard, a nation (forum) clearly has jurisdiction over what its citizens upload and download from servers and ISPs within its borders.[13] However, a recent case in Japan shows its courts assuming jurisdiction over Japanese citizens using a web site hosted on a U.S. server. A Japanese citizen living in Japan posted and sent pornographic images from a U.S. server to other Japanese

---

**Interactive business relations**
Actively selling to buyers from a web storefront.

**Passive business relations**
Having minimum contact with site visitors, not selling or interacting.

**Upload status**
Jurisdiction determined by location of server and visitors.

**Download status**
Receiving data from a server, transmitting it to a different computer or server.

citizens in Japan. He claimed a server-is-elsewhere defense that he was exempt from Japanese law because the images originated from a U.S. server. The Japanese court claimed jurisdiction because he was a Japanese citizen living in Japan targeting buyers also in Japan. He was sent to jail for eighteen months.[14] A similar ruling in the United Kingdom claimed jurisdiction over a UK citizen who set up pornography web sites on a California server from his home in the UK. UK users gained access to his U.S. sites with credit cards. Because he uploaded material from his home in the UK to the U.S.-based sites, the British courts claimed jurisdiction; however, had prosecutors lost the case, they were willing to let the United States extradite and prosecute the accused.[15]

Some jurisdictional disputes can be resolved without going to court. In 1999, Amazon.com (*http://www.amazon.com*) was accused of selling hate literature in Germany despite that country's ban on selling manifestos like Hitler's *Mein Kampf*. The German Justice Ministry investigated the complaint. Amazon protested it was not violating German law because its German web storefront did not offer the materials in German to German buyers. However, German buyers were purchasing the books in English from Amazon's U.S. web storefront and having them mailed to Germany. An Amazon spokesperson ended the dispute by saying, "It's absolutely crystal clear that the German-language version is banned in Germany. It is not legally definitely clear to us what the status of the English version is. So to ensure that we're in compliance with the laws of a democratically run nation, we are not selling Mein Kampf into Germany from Amazon.com."[16] Amazon was smart to avoid a confrontation with the German courts, which it probably would have lost. However, in doing so Amazon also complied with Germany jurisdiction control.

Yahoo! had a somewhat similar problem with France, which tried to extend its jurisdiction to the United States. A French judge in May 2000 ruled that Yahoo! had to find a way to prevent French users from seeing hate-related materials on its U.S. Web portal. Nazi-oriented auction items and related Internet links are illegal under French law. Yahoo! responded that it couldn't block French users from accessing its site and to comply would mean removing all such items and links. In the end, a U.S. district court judge in November 2001 found that Yahoo! could ignore French law because if it complied, its right to free expression under the First Amendment of the U.S. Constitution would have been violated.[17] Thus, U.S. jurisdiction prevailed. In the three years from 1996 to 1999, about seventy U.S. Internet jurisdiction cases were heard.[18] The number will surely rise until jurisdiction requirements are clarified and harmonized. The enormous challenge of doing this in a borderless electronic environment suggests the issue will not be resolved easily. Too loose an interpretation means web storefront operators could be prosecuted in every forum where a buyer can access their site. If each nation assumes it can regulate the Internet because it has territorial standing, the Internet will be walled off into small fiefdoms, with laws and rules that make doing business online internationally a legal nightmare. Jurisdiction is more likely to be claimed if a web site has a nexus in a country. A *nexus* is a physical presence, a commercial relationship with a warehouse, retail store, office and employees, or intermediaries. Sites can limit their liability in a country by not having a nexus, maintaining their domain name and site in English, and not targeting the country's citizens.[19] This may become a common response to countries that enforce particularly punitive Internet laws and may isolate them from mainstream Internet commerce.

Despite the complexities of clarifying jurisdiction requirements, some progress is being made in building common Internet law against online (cyber) crime. The Convention on Cybercrime (*http://conventions.coe.int*), a thirty-country group composed of the United States, Canada, Japan, South Africa, and representatives of twenty-six Council of Europe member states, worked four years to develop the first international treaty on cybercrimes. The Convention covers crimes committed on the Internet and other computer networks, particularly copyright infringement, computer fraud, child pornography, and hacking. Its mission is to produce a common criminal policy designed to protect society through the adoption of legislation and heightened international cooperation among nations and businesses. The treaty also provides guidelines for how the Internet should be policed within the jurisdictions of the signatories. The treaty was signed in November 2001 and will be enforced when five countries, including three member nations of the Council of Europe, ratify it. It is open for all nations to sign. The European Union intends to use this treaty as a foundation for drafting its own cybercrime laws. Some civil rights groups and ISPs oppose the treaty for its vague language, lack of public comment, and the heavy burden it places on service providers.[20] It illustrates the potential for walling off the Internet, where activities that are legal on sites housed in some nations are criminal and subject to prosecution in others. The treaty will not have widespread legitimacy unless the majority of internetted nations ratify and enforce it.

## THE U.S. INTERNET POLICE?

Passage of antiterrorism legislation that could make the United States the world's Internet police is a direct result of the terrorist attacks on September 11, 2001. The USA Patriot Act of 2001 contains provisions that will greatly expand U.S. government monitoring of email, Internet, and cellular phone communications. The bill was signed into law by President George W. Bush on October 26, 2001. It has no equivalent in other nations. The law gives the U.S. government unprecedented access to electronic communication within the United States using its Carnivore and other surveillance technology. Since more than 80 percent of Internet access points in Asia, Africa, and South America are routed through hubs in Virginia or California, it means the United States can prosecute foreign hackers or others using these hubs even if what is being communicated is legal in the country of origin. This includes gambling and adult content communications. The extent of this massive extension of U.S. sovereignty is clear from the following example. An online seller housed on a server in China sends data to a buyer whose ISP is in China. Because the data travel from China to the Virginia hub then back to China, while it is in the U.S. traveling along U.S. phone lines it can be intercepted by U.S. government agents. If the data break U.S. laws, the sender can be prosecuted in U.S. courts. This Act greatly expands U.S. jurisdictional reach.[21]

The USA Patriot Act of 2001, designed to give the U.S. government access to terrorist email messages so that future attacks can be thwarted, takes advantage of the U.S. dominance over major Internet backbone transfer points. The law will have repercussions when and if it is enforced. Other countries are unlikely to be pleased with the intrusion of the FBI or other U.S. government agencies into its citizens' data exchanges, and U.S. prosecution of foreign web owners could have a chilling effect on Internet commercialization. The law could reinforce the image of a bullying United States trying to impose its values on the rest of the world.

## INCIDENCE VERSUS HYPERBOLE

How afraid should consumers and businesses be of the Internet? With more people and businesses going online, as many as one billion people by 2005, the incidence of personal, commercial, and criminal wrongdoing will certainly increase.[22] Some individuals and businesses will exploit the Internet's unique characteristics, particularly its almost instantaneous communication and relative anonymity, just as others exploit consumers and enterprises offline. Internet fraud and other crimes are legitimate concerns. However, the media often exaggerates their incidence, which fuels fear. Some businesses make similar extravagant claims in order to promote the need for their security products.

Not surprisingly, consumers are confused about the threat of doing business online. Marketing research has shown that their greatest fear is theft of a credit card number or other personal information while it is in transit to a web site. In reality, credit card theft in transit is almost nonexistent. If it occurs, it will be from a web site's own poorly protected computers. Shopping online carries virtually no risk for consumers if they use credit cards, because credit card companies have a US$50 liability limit. Most major bank credit cards have zero online liability.[23]

The National Consumers League's (NCL) Internet Fraud Watch (*http://www. nclnet.org*) received reports from consumers of losses totaling US$6.152 million in 2001. In all of 2000, reported losses were only US$3.387 million. This increase must be viewed cautiously because it may indicate that consumers are better informed about where they can report fraud rather than indicating a sharp increase in its incidence. Even so, a certain amount of consumer fraud goes unreported because people do not know where to report it, they are ashamed to do so, or the amount is not significant enough for them to take the trouble to seek restitution. Some consumers are more vulnerable than others to con artists who prey on their weaknesses, naiveté, or greed. Others become susceptible in a period of grief. That is what happened almost immediately after the September 11 terrorist attacks, when swindlers began fake fundraising by email and from web sites for families of the victims or to stop terrorism.[24] Normally cautious people were susceptible because their emotions overcame their good sense. Some businesses are more vulnerable to fraud or other crimes at least partly because they fail to take proper precautions against them. If they are victimized, they may not report it to prevent having their insurance or merchant credit charges increased. Other businesses are attractive targets because they are highly visible or in controversial industries like tobacco or pharmaceuticals.

Governments, law enforcement agencies, corporations, and industry organizations are all becoming more visible and aggressive in the fight against cybercrime. In addition, the courts are becoming more experienced in dealing with it, and consumers are becoming better educated about how to protect themselves online and where to report complaints. At the same time, individuals and enterprises are developing new and more sophisticated ways to perpetrate frauds and other crimes. It will require heightened vigilance, stricter enforcement, increased consumer and business education, better computer protection, and stronger commitment to ensure that the Internet will be a safer place in the future.

## ✔ CONCEPT CHECK

1. Why are internationally agreed upon Internet laws needed?
2. Is creating a separate jurisdiction for the Internet a good idea?
3. How legitimate are fears about doing business online?

# Legal Concerns

Legal issues trouble online consumers and enterprises alike. Space constraints limit the discussion of all legal issues, but that does not minimize their importance. Consumers are concerned about the safety of online transactions, fraud and scams, and loss of privacy. Businesses are concerned about fraud and crimes against their property, liability, contracts, taxation, and security and privacy. This section considers some prominent legal issues that currently concern Internet marketers.

## FRAUD

Fraud is a criminal act, the intentional exploitation of a person, group, or enterprise for gain. It is a perversion of the truth in order to convince the victim to surrender something of value or a legal right. Internet fraud is perpetrated through email, chat rooms, web sites, and news groups. Consumer fraud occurs when a purchase that is paid for is not received, a merchant deliberately overcharges for a purchase, a credit card number or identity is stolen, a product purchased at auction differs from its description or is never sent to the buyer, money is lost in get-rich-quick or work-at-home schemes, or insurance or loan costs are inflated. Enterprises are vulnerable to orders paid for by stolen credit cards as well as many of the same frauds committed against consumers.

Offline businesses have laws, traditions, and practices that guide and regulate their domestic as well as export and import activities, and established processes for seeking restitution. Online, they face a more volatile environment, where it is possible to face different interpretations of laws in every state and country in which a web storefront is active. It is easy to conclude that for some, the World Wide Web is still pretty wild.

The Internet Fraud Complaint Center, a joint venture of the FBI and the National White Collar Crime Center, collected 20,014 complaints about online fraud in its first six months of operation in 2000. These complaints represented a total reported dollar loss of US$4.6 million. Over 49,700 complaints were registered in 2001, representing US$17.8 million in losses. Most online consumer fraud reported in 1999 (87 percent), 2000 (64.1 percent), and 2001 (42.8 percent) was committed at online auction sites.[25] In addition to auction fraud, nondeliverable purchases and payments were 20.3 percent of the complaints, Nigerian letter fraud was 15.5 percent, and credit or debit card fraud 9/4 percent. Other complaints were for fraud involving investments, employment (get-rich-quick, work-at-home), loans, home improvements, multilevel marketing, credit cards, investments, and other crimes that have offline equivalents.[26]

The Center received far more C2C fraud complaints (76 percent in 2001 down from over 90 percent in 2000) than B2C (24 percent up from 7.9 percent in 2000). California, Florida, New York, and Texas were the leading states for individual perpetrators (those committing fraud); California and Pennsylvania were the top states for business perpetrators. By far most perpetrators came from the United States with

Canada and the U.K. trailing far behind. Solicitation methods typically involved multiple approaches. Most contact is initially made by email, followed by web sites.[27]

The industry-leading auction site eBay (*http://www.ebay.com*) recognizes that auction fraud puts its business model at risk. A classic auction house can be held liable if items sold on its site are not legitimate. If it is a marketplace, an independent intermediary, then its liability is dramatically reduced or eliminated. In 2001, the company survived a US$100 million class action lawsuit that alleged it was liable for the sale of phony sports memorabilia in its auctions because it was an auctioneer. Plantiffs argued that "eBay has facilitated, and continues to facilitate, a safe haven for the unscrupulous dealers perpetrating the forged collectibles scheme." The San Diego judge hearing the case dismissed it, finding that eBay was a marketplace, a venue where product sellers were responsible for authenticating their own product offers. eBay does restrict products auctioned and excludes drugs, alcohol, firearms, and body parts. Sometimes it also steps in to cancel auctions as it did with the proposed auction of the prison ID card of Kevin Mitnick, a notorious computer hacker.[28]

eBay is responding to the fraud threat in several ways. It has implemented an onsite self-monitoring program to reduce fraud and protect itself from liability for frauds perpetrated by those using its auctions. It is diversifying through joint ventures with other companies, acquiring new businesses, and expanding its fixed price site, Half.com (*http://www.half.com*) in an effort to become an ecommerce portal. It is aggressively barring wrongdoers from its auctions and now offers a Fraud Protection Program that protects purchases for up to US$200 minus a US$25 charge. eBay defines fraud as paying for an item and never receiving it or receiving an item that is less than what is described.

How much online fraud businesses experience is not known at least in part because many businesses do not want others to know how much they have lost. Average annual estimated losses for U.S. businesses total around 6 percent of sales or US$400 billion.[29] Estimates for 2000 online B2B revenues range from US$336 billion (Jupiter Communications) to US$1.2 trillion (Boston Consulting Group).[30] Using the 6 percent loss estimate, online B2B fraud might be in the range of US$20 to $72 billion, or more.

## *Safeguarding an Ecommerce Site*

Tips for online storefronts include:

- Check credit card authorizations in real time to make sure the card is not stolen or lost.
- Verify billing address with the issuing card company.
- Ask buyer for the nonembossed credit card number code on the card.
- Use detection software to see if transactions meet criteria for greater scrutiny.
- Check transactions against statistical profiles of fraudulent transaction.
- Hold orders that exceed a preset amount and check them for accuracy.
- Check suspect orders against an in-house or commercial database of past frauds.
- Check telephone numbers for authenticity.
- If an order is suspicious, call the customer to confirm it.
- Post cyber shoplifting notices on the site that fraud will be prosecuted.
- Track product deliveries.[31]

Online businesses are responding to fraud and other cybercrimes. The nonprofit Worldwide E-Commerce Fraud Prevention Network was formed in Fall 2000 with over 375 charter members, including American Express, Amazon.com, and Expedia.com. In January 2001, it launched a fraud prevention web site (*http://www. MerchantFraudSquad. com*) where online sellers can access advice (see "Safeguarding an Ecommerce Site" on p. 110) on safeguarding their web site against online credit card fraud and learn about new fraud preventing technologies.

## PROPERTY PROTECTION: COPYRIGHT, PATENTS, TRADEMARKS, AND DOMAIN NAMES

Fraud is not the only concern of Internet marketers. Crimes against property are also increasing. Property is something owned or possessed, for example a trademark or web site content.

**COPYRIGHT** A copyright protects published or unpublished original tangible intellectual property (not facts or ideas), such as a literary, musical, dramatic, artistic, or architectural work. Protection extends for the life of the creator plus fifty years. In the United States, copyright is covered in the Copyright Act of 1976, Title 17 of the U.S. Code. Copyrights can be registered with the U.S. Library of Congress (*http://lcweb. loc.gov/copyright*), but to be protected, new works do not have to be registered or even identified with a copyright notice. The Digital Millennium Copyright Act of 1998 (Public Law 105-304) amends Title 17 and ratifies the World Intellectual Property Organization (WIPO at *http://www.wipo.org/index.html.en*) Treaty. It is designed to strengthen copyright protection over digital products and the right of transmission; however, its complexity is adding confusion rather than reducing it. Copyright violations can be prosecuted as criminal acts.

Most copyright disputes are about content (images, sounds, data, programs, games, music) copied from web sites, text copied to bulletin boards, caching (storing pages or whole sites), and linking, primarily deep linking. *Deep linking* is a relatively new process that occurs when links to pages in a site bypass that site's front page so site ownership recognition is avoided.[32]

Entertainment companies like AOL-Time Warner (*http://www.aoltimewarner.com*) and newspapers like *The New York Times* (*http://www.nytimes.com*) argue that they need greater protection for content on their Web sites because content is so easy to copy. It is impossible for most small businesses or individuals to search millions of web pages looking for copyright infringement. It is even more difficult to determine if copyright-protected materials have been downloaded. An added complication is the doctrine of fair use that allows a limited amount of copying for such activities as news reporting, research, and education.

Copyright infringement is a serious problem for web marketers. To combat it, some trade associations aggressively search the Web for copyright theft. In early 2001, the Motion Picture Association of America (MPAA at *http://www.mpaa.org*) listened in on chat rooms and heard talk of DeCSS, software that descrambles (De) the Content Scrambling System (CSS) protecting Digital Video Disk (DVD) movies. The software, created by a fifteen-year-old Norwegian boy, allows any computer with a DVD drive to download and unscramble copyright-protected DVD movies, allowing them to be transmitted unscrambled anywhere on the Internet.[33] If DeCSS or comparable software becomes widely available, it could cost DVD copyright holders hundreds of millions of dollars or more in lost revenues.

**PATENTS** The U.S. Patent Act is in Title 35 of the U.S. Code. The U.S. Patent and Trademark Office (USPTO at *http://www.uspto.gov*) is part of the Department of Commerce. A patent is an official document that gives the owner exclusive right for a limited time to a unique product made by an invention, the invention process, or design. Many companies are disputing patent rights over Internet and web technologies, and some of these efforts threaten the adoption of the technologies and their improvement through widespread use. Akamai Technologies (*http://www.akamai.com*) is suing a competitor over content delivery patents and caching services. Amazon.com obtained patent rights for its one-click ordering technology, and the courts forced one of its competitor to switch to a two-click ordering process. This patent claim and threats to enforce it have angered those promoting a free web. Amazon.com has also been granted patent rights for its affiliate program, where a web site that links to Amazon receives payment if a customer takes the link and makes a purchase from Amazon. Granting patents for what seem like widely used and unoriginal processes has led to harsh criticism of the Patent Office for not keeping up with technology.[34] Negative publicity about Amazon's one-click and affiliate patents, and the threat of possible boycotts, caused Amazon to modify its stance and call for reform in the patenting process.

Liberal interpretation of patent laws by the USPTO has resulted in a surge in the number of patents issued for processes widely used by Internet storefronts. According to the USPTO, in 1991 only two Internet-related patents were granted. By 1999 that number rose to 200; 2,517 were issued in the first half of 2000.[35] It is doubtful if many enterprises will pay royalties for repeated use of patented Internet processes. Instead, these patents could constrict online business expansion and impede the spread of technologies needed to make commercialization more viable. Many are being challenged in court.

**TRADEMARKS** Trade and service marks are legal marks (words, phrases, symbols, product shapes, logos) used to identify owners of goods or services within a country. Trademark protection comes from the Lanham Trademark Act of 1946. The USPTO registers U.S. trademarks for products used in interstate commerce. Internationally, countries have different trademark rules, and because there is no global trademark registration process, a company must register its trademark in each country in which it does business if it wants to protect it. Trademark law was simplified in 1999 with passage of the Trademark Law Treaty Implementation Act (TLTIA, PL105-330, 112 Stat. 3064 [15 U.S.C. 1051]), designed to harmonize U.S. trademark laws with those of other countries also signing the treaty.[36]

Many businesses use trademark protection as grounds to force competitors to stop using similar sounding names. For example, trademark protection was claimed by Reel.com (*http://reel.com*) for the name *reel*. It forced two competitors to stop using the name in their domain names or license the name from Reel.com.[37]

**DOMAIN NAMES** A domain name is a form of trademark, an exclusive right to a unique address on the Internet's World Wide Web. Disputes typically arise over the second-level domain name, the name to the left of the top-level domain name (TLD), in most cases .com, .org, or .net. Both the American Marketing Association and the American

Medical Association might have used the second-level domain name *ama*. However, the American Marketing Association registered first and was awarded *http://www.ama.org*; the American Medical Association registered *http://www.ama-assn.org*. It does not take much thought to see which is the more user-friendly name. After several years the American Marketing Association decided its domain name was not sufficiently descriptive and changed it to MarketingPower.com (*http://www.marketingpower.com*).

The U.S. Anticybersquatting Consumer Protection Act (ACPA, PL106-113 [1999]) protects trademark holders from those that register domain names in bad faith for profit or to divert profits from the legal holder. The maximum penalty is US$100,000 per domain name. A federal judge in Pennsylvania recently ordered a cybersquatter to pay the maximum fine for infringing on a trademark held by another company.[38] Anheuser-Busch (*http://www.anheuser-busch.com*) went to court to retrieve the Michelobight.com domain name from a cybersquatter.[39] On the day *McCall's Magazine* (new title *ROSIE* at *http://www.rosiemagazine.com*) announced its venture *Rosie, the Magazine* with Rosie O'Donnell, a cybersquatter registered Rosiesmccalls.com. The dispute was heard by an arbitration panel of the World Intellectual Property Organization (WIPO). The arbitration system was started in October 1999 by the Internet Corporation for Assigned Names and Numbers (ICANN at *http://www.ICANN.org*) and is administered by WIPO. It avoids costly trials and promises decisions within two months.[40]

Cybersquatters are more than a nuisance; they can cost a trademark owner lost revenues and bad relations with customers, along with the expense of having to ransom the domain name. Cybersquatting generally forces businesses to register multiple domain names so visitors are not accidentally diverted to a site with a similar-sounding name. Registering sound-alikes is a favorite ploy of adult content (pornography) sites. Even the White House has been victimized this way and visitors that mistype the domain name immediately realize they are in the wrong place.

## LIABILITY

Liability is a duty, responsibility, or obligation. Product liability means being held responsible for knowingly selling a defective and/or dangerous product. Marketers have a professional obligation to promote products that are not defective or dangerous. Businesses can be held liable for many things, from environmental contamination to employee harassment. An ISP can be held liable for the behavior of its customers, for example, copyright infringement, *if* the ISP knows the behavior is happening and takes no action. Medical web sites' liability risk increases if they provide specific information about a visitor's medical condition. Since there is no Internet liability law, courts often rely on existing law, for example, medical malpractice law in the case of medical web sites, and try to make it fit the case.[41]

The FTC is the government watchdog agency that looks for online scams and frauds. Its Internet Coordinating Committee holds surf days when members search the Web for work-at-home, fix-your-credit, college scholarship, and travel scams. The FTC issues warnings to sites that are liable for prosecution; often the sites shut down before being investigated further. The Securities and Exchange Commission (SEC at *http://www.sec.gov*) monitors online investment offers.[42]

**Disclaimer**
A disavowal of liability.

A **disclaimer** is a disavowal of liability. Many web sites have disclaimers either on their front pages or linked to a separate disclaimer page within the site. There are few guidelines on what should be in a disclaimer, nor is it clear how effective they are in limiting liability, particularly in foreign jurisdictions. A web storefront might restrict

**WEB UPDATE**

Disclaimers

its liability with a disclaimer, but it must be carefully worded and placed because opinions differ on what is acceptable. A national domestic disclaimer placed on or linked from a web storefront page might state that the site accepts orders only from certain U.S. states. An international disclaimer might state that the site accepts orders only from U.S. citizens in the continental United States. Unfortunately, it is not always clear where a buyer is located, and sometimes buyers are not truthful about themselves or their locations. Thus, although disclaimers should be used, they cannot be relied on exclusively to effectively filter buyers and protect sellers.

## CONTRACTS AND DIGITAL SIGNATURES

A contract is a binding agreement between two or more parties that spells out their responsibilities in a particular situation. In the United States, a highly litigious society, legal contracts are the accepted way of defining a business arrangement. One difficulty in completing contracts online has been the inability to provide authenticated, unforgeable, and uncopyable signatures for the contract parties. This has been addressed by the Electronic Signatures in Global and National Commerce Act (ESIGN), which became effective October 1, 2000. The law allows **digital signatures** to have the same authority as traditional signatures on paper documents. Digital signatures are encrypted certificates, that is, code that verifies authenticity. Encryption software like Pretty Good Privacy (*http://www.pgp.com*) can create a digital signature (see "The 128-Bit Hash" below), technically a 128-bit hash or key combination of encrypted letters, numbers, and symbols that represent a signature. Two keys are needed to operate the system. The signature owner uses the private key to sign a document, and the key owner provides the public key to those who need to authenticate his or her signature. Signed documents are compared with the key to authenticate the signature.

Critics say the digital signature is more a seal than a real signature and that there is no guarantee the person sending the signature is the bona fide signer. At least one virus has surfaced that tries to steal digital signature hashes from computer files.[43]

**Digital signatures**
Encrypted certificates, code that verifies authenticity with the same authority as traditional signatures on paper documents.

## *The 128-Bit Hash*

A digital signature privacy program computes a new hash each time someone needs to use a digital signature. The hash is encrypted with the person's private key and placed at the end of the message. Anyone who has the public key can verify the signature. It looks something like the following.

This email message has been signed.

——Begin (name of encryption software) Signature——

ASdsadSADIWeuoqAsdCJL45sduwasdDASdladjs/ASD298348wsdadLASdjasdlknmclasd-nas34dliwulllSADAds45msd554dmasdpo63423qeisdasSDa8soijSdaoDSadamWemasds-dQomcsad/0a8sda9s8d2eacalb+as674s/SADmsdadsASd5456oSAdlcas2asd===0asdjclsd

——End (name of encryption software) Signature——

Fifteen U.S. states adopted digital signature ]
nally acted. ESIGN brings consistency beca'
standards if they intend to implement digital
ply to all documents; court orders, product
still exempt.[44] Given the present technolog'
able to signatures that are written or faxed

## SPEECH: CONSUMER COMPLAI'
## FREE SPEECH

Most marketers would prefer to receive no c
are justified, however, and can provide valuable feed..
either case, consumers will tell far more people about a bad c.,
one. Positive word-of-mouth (WOM) can increase sales; negative v,
them. The Internet has made it incredibly easy to create anticorporate *suck* s..
disseminate negative and sometimes defamatory statements to a worldwide audience
with relative impunity. Most complaints center on bad customer service, product dissatisfaction, or missing parts. Some are run by disgruntled employees or encourage
inflammatory comments from them. The consensus is that it is a big mistake for a web
storefront owner to do nothing about online complaints. Suck sites are growing in
number, scope, and popularity.[45] Companies have taken legal action against online
corporate bashing sites when their trademarks are linked to or stored on the sites.
Others have bought out the owners and shut the sites. Buying a domain name to shut
it down does not stop the site owner from opening another site unless the terms of sale
prohibit such activity, at least for a period of time post sale.

## TAXATION

The U.S. Constitution gives the federal government and the states the right to levy
taxes on citizens, businesses, and organizations. Taxes redistribute income and provide services for the common good, such as defense. Sales tax is a state taxing device.
The United States does not have a national sales tax or a value-added tax (VAT) like
that used in Europe. The Internet Tax Freedom Act of 1998 (PL105-277), which postponed any tax on Internet transactions until October 21, 2001, was based on the concepts that information should not be taxed and infant online businesses should not be
weakened by being taxed. Two relevant U.S. Supreme Court rulings in 1967 and 1992
found that state and local governments (forums) do not have the authority to collect
taxes on nonstate (remote) retailers without a physical presence or nexus within the
forum's borders. This presence can be a warehouse, retail outlet, or business office.
Most states and bricks-and-mortar retailers favor sales taxes. They argue that states
need the tax revenues, that nontaxing Internet sales discriminates against offline sellers that collect sales tax, and that it is unfair to the poor and others who are not online
since they must pay offline taxes without having access to tax-free online sales. Lost
state sales taxes on Internet transactions were an estimated US$13+ billion in 2001.[46]
Online retail sales were only slightly more than 1 percent of total retail sales. In 2001,
thirty-two states agreed to the Streamlined Sales Tax Project's simplified sales tax
model that harmonizes state tax codes on Internet sales. However, four major technology states, California, Massachusetts, Virginia, and Colorado, were reluctant to en-
dorse the project because taxes could slow online sales, weaken dot-coms, lose jobs,

and negatively affect their economies.[47] It is unclear where or how taxes, if approved, will be collected.

In November 2001 the U.S. Congress extended the tax moratorium an additional two years until November 1, 2003. President Bush signed the bill, although he would have preferred a longer extension. Bush predicted that 2001 holiday spending online would be around 15 percent of total holiday spending and vowed the bill will "keep access to ecommerce services affordable."[48]

Those seeking to encourage Internet commercialization argue for leaving the Internet tax-free. With tens of thousands of taxing authorities in the United States and countless international taxing authorities, it would be difficult and costly to collect and redistribute online sales taxes. Encouraging tax-free online transactions provides greater long-term benefit if it stimulates the growth of dot-com businesses that employ more people and pay more taxes in the process.

## GAMBLING AND VISUAL PORNOGRAPHY

Gambling is a popular activity offline in casinos, lotteries, horse and dog racing tracks, and sports betting. It is highly regulated, with controlling federal and state laws. Internet gambling attracted around 25 million customers in 2000, generating an estimated US$1.2 billion in revenues, an increase of 80 percent over 1999.[49] Revenues are forecast to exceed US$4.5 billion by 2002. Online gambling is aggressively marketed through advertisements on search engine sites, travel sites, and other web locations, and by email. Customers obviously are finding the sites; Uproar.com (*http://www.uproar.com*) had more than 4,500,000 unique visitors in 2000.

The 1961 Federal Interstate Wire Act (18 U.S.C.A. §1084), updated in 2002, prohibits the use of interstate telephone lines for transmitting gambling information except for horse racing. As a result, gambling sites targeting U.S. consumers are mostly offshore, operating from ISPs in gambling havens like Costa Rica and various Caribbean countries where online gambling is legal and welcomed for its jobs and contributions to local economies. Many of the estimated 250 to 1,400 gambling sites worldwide have established commercial operations in offshore host countries. U.S. casinos and other legal gambling operations oppose online gambling for the most part because they are losing customers to the sites. States are losing taxes. Social agencies criticize the ease with which gambling addicts can access online games. A new avenue of attack has opened against the sites as credit card companies are being pressured to stop allowing their customers to do business with online gambling sites. However, some U.S. gambling businesses realize if the Congress passes stringent anti-online gambling legislation, they could be locked out of a highly lucrative Internet business opportunity. Rivals in other countries report growing revenues, much of it from U.S. visitors. For example a virtual gaming site from the Australian Northern Territory had eighty-five thousand players from 210 countries in the first sixteen months of its operation. Revenues were US$77.5 million.[50]

Like online gambling, online adult content (visual pornography) is also under attack, particularly by those committed to making child pornography less accessible. It is difficult to determine total revenue from online adult content sites because many of them do not want to appear profitable. Offline pornography in the United States is estimated to be around a US$8 billion industry. According to Forrester Research, adult content sites generated more than US$800 million in 1998 and were expected to reach over US$1 billion by 2000. Like gambling, some major credit card companies are putting a stop to customer charges at adult content sites. They claim these sites encourage fraud and it is too costly to continue doing business with them.[51] However, unfiltered reports of what people search for at search engines like MetaCrawler's Metaspy (*http://www.metaspy.com*) and Kanoodle Search Spy (*http://www.kanoodle.com/spy*) clearly indicate the popularity of sex sites.

**Type-in consumers**
Consumers searching for pornography by typing in keywords at a search engine that they believe may lead them to adult content sites.

Domain names with naughty four-letter words draw in crowds of **type-in consumers** trolling for pornography by typing in keywords that they expect will link to adult content sites. Adult sites claim **conversion rates,** that is, visitors converted to subscribers, of one in thirty-six and higher. However, most of the estimated 200 to 300,000 adult content sites only post banner ads for other adult sites or are individual sites that generate little revenue. Several large privately held companies dominate the industry. About fifteen to twenty-five million U.S. consumers visit these sites monthly, and three of the sites claim annual gross incomes of US$100 to $150 million.[52]

**Conversion rates**
Number of visitors to a web site that are converted to subscribers or buyers.

Why are online pornography sites so popular? They offer convenience and anonymity, satisfy visitor curiosity, and provide entertainment for those who like erotic content. Sexual imagery draws consumers; technology and content get them to return. Although the United States still hosts the greatest number of pornography sites, sites in Europe and Asia also are booming. Playboy Online (*http://www.playboy.com*), a wholly owned subsidiary of publicly traded Playboy Enterprises, Inc., is one of the few branded adult sites and the number one lifestyle and entertainment destination for men. On the Web since 1994, its network of branded sites generated US$5.6 million in revenue in the first six months of 1999. Net revenues for the fiscal year ending December 31, 2001 for Playboy Online were US$27.5 million, a nine percent increase over the previous year. The site registers several million visitors each month. Playboy also has a members-only subscription site, Playboy CyberClub, where, for US$60 per year, its over 100,000 members can participate in online chats and exclusive events, and access Playboy's programming library.[53]

## ✔ CONCEPT CHECK

1. Why should a web site operator be concerned about copyright infringement?
2. What is the relationship between domain names and trademarks?
3. Why are digital signatures needed online?

# *Online Ethics and Privacy*

Ethics and privacy are often spoken of together, particularly when criticizing Internet marketing practices. Because marketing activities are highly visible and designed to blatantly promote products and encourage marketing exchanges, they are particularly vulnerable to criticism. Much of it is deserved, some is not.

## ONLINE ETHICS

Ethics is a system of moral principles, rules of conduct that a society develops over time. It is the right and wrong, good and bad, that parents teach their children and that adults enforce for others through sanctions on unethical social behaviors. Unethical behaviors are not always illegal; illegal behaviors are unethical. While societies share many ethical principles, what is ethical in one country is not necessarily so in another. Even within countries different subsegments can disagree on moral principles. This becomes even more complicated on the Internet where there is no code of *cyberethics*, ethical online social behaviors, and people from many different cultures interact without necessarily being identified by their country of origin.

The U.S. Department of Justice and the Information Technology Association of America (ITAA) has formed a Cybercitizen Partnership (*http://www.cybercitizenship.org*) to develop a curriculum to teach schoolchildren the ethical use of technology. In light of a recent survey of more than forty-seven thousand elementary and middle school students who revealed they do not consider hacking a crime, this effort is obviously needed. Internet ethics is not taught in schools, yet many schools are dealing with specific Internet ethical and legal situations, particularly copyright infringement and plagiarism, hacking, cyberpornography, and hate email. Some students perceive the Internet's anonymity as protection against their own online actions.[54]

The speed of Internet communication and its reach, relative anonymity, and low cost tempt some to engage in questionable behaviors. Areas of Internet marketing concern include conducting marketing research online, the marketing of professionals, marketing to children and other vulnerable groups, marketing restricted products, and unsolicited commercial email, or **spam**.

**Spam**
Unsolicited commercial bulk email.

**ONLINE CONSUMER RESEARCH** A vast amount of online consumer research is being conducted by marketers and others. The ease of collecting information online coupled with the large numbers of consumers in chat rooms makes the Internet an attractive place for sociologists, psychologists, anthropologists, and consumer behavior researchers. At this time, no commonly widely accepted guidelines for conducting online consumer research exist. Some key questions that Internet researchers are debating include

**INFORMATION STATUS** Is the information posted in online support groups public or private? If it is private, what is the obligation of the researcher to inform subjects that their postings are being used in a research study? Should researchers use postings and archives without informed consent?

**IDENTIFICATION** Should researchers make their presence known in chat rooms? If so, will this compromise the postings and change participants' responses and reactions?

**SCIENTIFIC SOUNDNESS** How scientifically sound are data collected from chat rooms where participants are anonymous and/or create new identities for themselves? Does the environment distort participants' behavior?

**INFORMATION USE** If a company sponsors a chat room in order to collect information, should the company warn participants that their comments are monitored? For example, do pharmaceutical companies hosting a support group chat room for patients with the condition the pharmaceutical is treating have an obligation to inform the chat room moderator or participants that the group is being studied?

Because so much research is being conducted online and more is expected, it has been suggested that a warning label be developed to alert public chat room participants that researchers are present. An ethical warning label would be required on any site where observations or other forms of online research take place. The Association of

Internet Researchers (*http://aoir.org*), an ʻ
from many disciplines and countries, i
Because Internet consumer research ʻ
should be part of these discussions
for online consumer research.

## MARKETING OF PROFESSIO

sionals market themselves ʻ
their professions. Profession..
adhere to or face sanctions. Lʻ
through web sites and email. Althoug.
false or misleading statements, exaggerau.
advertising is prohibited, and soliciting legal wʻ
inappropriate behavior.

The American Marketing Association has a Code oi
Internet. The statement reiterates AMA's commitment to etiʻ
in all aspects of marketing. It warns marketers to do no harm oʻ
rights of privacy, ownership, and access; and to adhere to all applicabʻ
ulations. If members fail to adhere to this code, the AMA vows to suspenʻ
their membership.[56] Chances are that any marketer violating these standards iʻ
ready be in far more serious trouble with his or her employer and possibly the laʻ

Other professional organizations have also issued Internet marketing guidelines.
The Electronic Retailing Association (*http://www.retailing.org*) has Online Marketing
Guidelines for online advertising and email. The guidelines encourage fair, ethical,
and responsible Internet marketing with the goal of promoting consumer confidence
in ecommerce. The Interactive Direct Marketing Association (*http://www.the-dma.org/
library/guidelines/onlineguidelines.shtml*) has Online Privacy Principles and Guidance
for email marketing and online data collection from children. These and other marketing organizations have a vested interest in promoting ethical behaviors by their
members. Otherwise, government may lay a heavy hand on their activities, using laws
and regulation to gain compliance. Although organization efforts are commendable,
they cannot control nonmembers, and the sanctions they apply to members often are
not sufficiently stringent to guarantee widespread compliance.

**MARKETING TO CHILDREN AND OTHER VULNERABLE GROUPS**  Online hard-sell
advertising to children and other vulnerable groups is unethical and in some cases, illegal. Children and impaired adults typically are unable to accurately judge differences
between advertising and entertainment, and they are vulnerable to high-pressure
personal data collection techniques. Children are more likely than adults to provide
personal information online, particularly when offered a free gift for the information.
The Children's Online Privacy Protection Act (COPPA) clearly defines rules web site
marketers must follow when targeting children under thirteen. The FTC enforces
COPPA and prosecutes violations.[57]

**MARKETING RESTRICTED PRODUCTS**  Critics complain that alcohol and tobacco
companies are using the Web to promote their products to children and youth. Their web
sites are designed to attract youthful visitors, who can enter the sites by lying about
their ages. The Center for Media Education (*http://www.rwjf.org/health/032436s.htm*)

ied research that tracked and analyzed online marketing of these products. The search revealed that alcohol companies are using online marketing tactics designed to appeal to teens and college age drinkers. Cigarette companies are less aggressive in establishing a web presence marketing to youth, but chat rooms and bulletin boards appeal to a prosmoking culture that glamorizes the products. Cigar sites target older consumers. Web sites are proliferating for all these products.

**UNSOLICITED COMMERCIAL EMAILS** Unsolicited commercial email, also called spam, is a growing problem for consumer and enterprise recipients. It is discussed in the next section.

### SPAM—NOT ILLEGAL, YET

Unsolicited commercial bulk email, or spam, is a problem, but not yet illegal nationally. Spam irritates consumers, overwhelms ISPs, and costs businesses by clogging employee email boxes and crashing servers under the volume of spammed email. Although spam is not illegal, it is sometimes used to commit fraud, which is illegal. Work-at-home scams are popular online, and they are often conducted by email. Two men recently received prison sentences for harvesting consumer email addresses and using them to spam offers of a job stuffing envelopes at home. More than twelve thousand people responded and paid a US$35 processing fee for information they never received.[58]

Courts have overturned several state antispam laws for restricting the constitutional right of free speech. The ethics of several large ISPs have been questioned for not self-regulating the problem on their own services. In some cases, ISPs provide havens for spammers, despite their protests that they are doing everything possible to protect their customers from unwanted emails.

### SELF-REGULATION

Self-regulation often is undertaken by professional organizations, businesses, and industries to avoid government regulation. It is also designed to provide ethical boundaries in ambiguous circumstances and, sometimes, to calm consumer fears. For example, to allay consumer fears about medical information privacy online, the American Medical Association "has developed principles to guide the development and posting of Web site content, govern acquisition and posting of online advertising and sponsorship, [also to] ensure site visitors' and patients' rights to privacy and confidentiality, and provide effective and secure means of e-commerce."[59] DoubleClick (*http://www.doubleclick.net*), the global Internet advertising company responsible for placing most online banner advertisements, formed an independent Consumer Privacy Advisory Board of consumer advocates, security experts, and online privacy authorities to advise the company on ways it can improve privacy procedures.[60] This is a wise move considering the highly negative public relations crisis the firm weathered over consumer privacy and implanting cookies on the computers of unknowing consumers who clicked on its banner advertisements. Although self-regulation can be effective, it is also often criticized as being a superficial self-serving response to serious marketplace problems that ultimately require government intervention. The U.S. government, for the most part, has maintained a hands-off approach to the Internet, preferring self-regulation over intervention, at least for now.

## PRIVACY OR PERSONALIZATION

How far should marketers go in collecting information about consumers in order to personalize an offer? Personalization is what the neighborhood shopkeeper practiced in the early 1900s because he knew what his customers wanted; he either stored the information in his memory or a card file database that recorded customers' past purchases and what they owed. This customer intimacy was possible because the storekeeper and his customers established long-term relationships. He tracked their wants and needs, and did everything possible to please them, which earned their loyalty.

**Personalization (one-to-one marketing)** online relies on information in consumer profiles collected from self-divulgence, cookies, monitoring chat room messages, sales transactions, email feedback, and onsite tracking. Online storefront operators use software to collect consumer data, organize it in databases, mine it to identify consumers with the highest probability of responding to specific marketing offers, then make offers personalized to these individuals or segments.

Many portals encourage consumers and businesses to customize their web page by selecting content that interests them. The personalized page becomes their default boot-up home page. Portals offer free email, instant messenger service, a personal calendar, and other customized features as enticements. At the same time, these personalized home pages are used to collect information about consumers' interests and online behaviors. These data are collected and analyzed, then used to personalize banner advertisements and targeted email. While consumers may dislike this in-depth penetration of their personal information space, businesses want the information that personalization offers. Marketers recognize the value of personalization but also must protect consumers' privacy in order to build customer loyalty. Good privacy practices can create an online competitive advantage.

Privacy is consumers' number one complaint and fear about the Internet. The most onerous practice involves collecting personal information from children. Public outcries about harmful marketing and data collection practices led Congress in 1998 to pass the Children's Online Privacy Protection Act (COPPA), which went into effect April 21, 2000. Web sites collecting information from children under the age of thirteen must comply with FTC regulations restricting the collection of personally identifiable information without a parent's consent. The FTC can levy civil penalties up to US$11,000 per violation. COPPA shouldn't be confused with the Child Online Protection Act (COPA) that was ruled an unconstitutional violation of First Amendment free-speech rights on June 22, 2000. COPA required web sites with commercial content to bar underage readers from any material that might be "harmful to minors." This exceedingly broad law would have required storefront operators to severely censor site content according to the most conservative standards in order to avoid criminal liability.[61]

Most web site marketers post privacy statements linked from the front page, but most visitors do not bother to read the statements carefully or at all.[62] This behavior appears to contradict consumers' stated concern about privacy. More likely it reflects the complexity of the statements and their length.

What are consumers worried about? There is a trust gap between what consumers fear businesses will do with their personal information and how businesses claim they will use it. Consumers do not want their personal information sold to third parties, and they want to access the information businesses collect about them. They are more

**Personalization (one-to-one marketing)**

Using software to learn about customers and their buying behaviors and preferences, and then using these data to customize offers.

willing to provide personal information to a web site that displays a privacy seal. Most do not have privacy-protecting software installed on their computers, however, despite their privacy fears. They have mixed feelings about personalization, doubting that it will provide benefits enough to justify providing personal information.[63]

Consumers have a right to worry. Businesses can change their privacy policies almost instantaneously. They can go from claiming they do not sell consumer information to third parties, to selling it. Some sell it even though they claim otherwise. Many bankrupt Internet businesses are finding that their only valuable asset is consumer information, which they are selling despite prior promises that they would not. Vast amounts of data are being collected and stored. These data warehouses are vulnerable to theft as well as tracking. Health sites collect confidential data on medical test results, etailers collect credit card information as well as addresses, and financial services sites collect social security numbers and account information. In the wrong hands these data can expose consumers to unwanted marketing solicitations as well as fraud. Despite the huge quantities of detailed information being collected, most businesses do not have the capacity to actually turn it into useful marketing information. They are wasting a valuable resource and scaring consumers at the same time. They are also creating more interest in Congress about regulating online privacy.[64]

Raised privacy concerns have led more than a hundred companies, including IBM, AT&T, and American Express, to create a new position of Chief Privacy Office (CPO). CPOs are responsible for ensuring compliance with privacy protection in many areas of the business, from human resources to marketing practices, online and off.[65] Creating this position may reflect the belief that privacy problems are difficult to solve on an ad hoc basis, and more stringent government regulation will demand compliance in the future.

Make no mistake, privacy is also a concern offline. Bar code cards are offered in grocery stores, video rental stores, health clubs, and at gas stations. These wands are high-tech information storage devices that track consumer purchases and create customer profiles. Millions have been issued.[66] Why are consumers more concerned about online privacy than offline key chain cards, which store masses of data on distant servers? Key chain cards are opt-in devices and an old technology akin to the credit card. Customers must sign up with the grocery store, gas station, or other vendor to obtain them. They are convenient and often deliver discounts, special offers, and other promotional incentives. Consumers self-divulge information willingly for the benefits they will receive. Key chain cards seem innocuous when compared with online information collection. Consumers fear online information thieves who could steal their identity or credit card numbers, or even stalk and harm them. Offline information collection by comparison appears to be just a nuisance.

## ✔ CONCEPT CHECK

1. What are ethics and why are they important online as well as off?
2. What is it about spam that makes it so irritating and often costly?
3. What should marketers do to reassure consumers about online privacy?

# *Security*

Security means protection against an attac
ing the safety of online banking and credit
web sites and databases, vaccinating con
stopping such cyberterrorism as denial-of-s

## HACKERS AND CRACKERS

Although they are usually identified as Inte
groups with an almost obsessive interest in
gramming problems. Typically, they do not
are often hired by companies to test their
vandals, that is, individuals and groups that
defenses, penetrate a site to change prices and content, steal credit card numbers or
data, do damage, and brag about their vandalism. Crackers have struck the *New York
Times* as well as Microsoft, where they took advantage of an employee's mistake to in-
filtrate the corporate site and penetrate protected source code. Crackers are particularly attracted to online banking software, web registration forms, and other sources
of consumer data. They attack applications software and force their way into corporate databases.

Losses are difficult to calculate because many attacks are never discovered, and
when they are, site operators often do not report them for fear of negative publicity.
Site attacks are becoming more organized, with gangs operating from the Ukraine and
Russia gaining access to consumer credit cards by exploiting vulnerabilities in server
software. Recently, the FBI and U.S. Secret Service reported the theft of over a million card numbers from more than forty victim sites. The attackers informed the sites
that card numbers were stolen, then tried to sell security services to the operator to
prevent future attacks. Some stolen numbers may have been sold to organized crime
members.[67] News of such activities seriously undermines confidence about doing
business online.

## CYBERTERRORISM AND DENIAL-OF-SERVICE (DOS) ATTACKS

**Denial-of-service (DOS attacks)** occur when vandals block legitimate users from accessing a web site by overloading it with traffic designed to tie up or crash its server(s).
The traffic can come from unsuspecting computers that have been taken over specifically to launch DOS attacks. In February 2000, massive DOS attacks were launched
against E*TRADE (*http://www.etrade.com*), Yahoo! (*http://www.yahoo.com*), Buy.com
(*http://www.buy.com*), CNN.com (*http://www.cnn.com*), and Amazon.com (*http://www.
amazon.com*). Legitimate traffic trying to access the sites got the equivalent of a busy
signal. Business losses were in the millions of dollars. These attacks sent a clear message to site operators that security is a growing concern and must be increased to
prevent future lost revenues and, more critically, lost consumer and business confidence. It was also a chilling warning that computers connected directly to the Internet can be used by cyberterrorists to launch a DOS attack, often without the owner's
knowledge.

Since 9/11 discussions about cyberterrorism have taken on a new urgency. A terrorist cell could launch a cyberattack designed to halt Internet traffic or worse. Attackers

## Hackers
Individuals and groups
with an almost obsessive
interest in using program-
mable systems to solve
programming problems.

## Crackers
Internet vandals, individuals and groups that attack
web sites.

## Denial-of-service
## (DOS) Attacks
Vandals block legitimate
users from accessing a
web site by overloading it
with traffic designed to tie
up or crash its server(s).

penetrate data warehouses and create havoc with credit card numbers or financial information. They could breach security systems that operate dams, power grids, and emergency services. The United States as a society and its economic system are dependent on electronic networks for communication and transactions. The Internet is its own worst enemy in that manuals and guidebooks are online that describe in detail how such attacks could be launched. Any war on terrorism must include cyberterrorists among its most critical targets.

## VIRUSES

Viruses, programs designed to penetrate and infect a host computer or network, are another security problem for individuals and networks and could be part of a cyberterrorist attack. Often launched from infected email, viruses have also been known to travel between documents in Excel and Word 97 documents.[68] Some viruses are merely nuisances; others can crash a hard drive or steal data. Some viruses reproduce by using the victim's address book to send infecting emails to unsuspecting recipients. Viruses are expected to be a continuing problem that requires monitoring and the use of up-to-date antivirus software to protect individual computers and networks.

## ✔ CONCEPT CHECK

1. Why is web security a growing concern?
2. What is a DOS attack and how can it hurt a web storefront?
3. What is cyberterrorism?

# *Summary*

### *Laws and Jurisdiction*

To be effective, a body of Internet law must be ratified by all internetted nations. Currently, there is no body of Internet law. In its absence, laws dealing with specific Internet activities are being formulated by legislatures, agencies, and courts around the world. These laws often are contradictory. Because of the growing numbers of consumers and enterprises going online, Internet laws are needed to maintain order. Many organizations are trying to deal with Internet legal issues. Some recommend a separate jurisdiction for the Internet like those created for Antarctica, outer space, and the high seas. Jurisdiction determines which courts have the right to exercise authority. One emerging jurisdiction test is whether the web site has interactive or passive business relations with visitors. A second test is upload or download status. Despite the relatively low incidence of online fraud against consumers, fear of fraud cost businesses lost online sales. Auction fraud, consumer-to-consumer, is the top complaint. Businesses also experience online fraud, but how much is not known at least in part because many businesses do not want others to know how much they have lost.

### *Legal Concerns*

Principal consumer concerns are about the safety of online transactions, unresponsive sellers, fraud and scams, and loss of privacy. For marketers, fraud, security, and privacy also are issues, along with protection of their property, liability, contracts, and taxation. Most copyright disputes are about content copied, text on bulletin boards, caching, and deep linking. Many companies are disputing patent rights over Internet and web technologies. Disputes typically arise over the second-level domain name if it is trademark protected. ISPs can be held liable for the behavior of customers, for example, copyright infringement, if the ISP knows the behavior is happening and takes no action. The Federal Trade Commission (FTC) looks for online scams and frauds. The Electronic Signatures in Global and National Commerce Act (ESIGN) gives digital signatures the same authority as traditional signatures on paper documents, with some exceptions. Companies have taken legal action against online corporate bashing sites if their trademarks are linked to or stored on the sites. The Internet Tax Freedom Act of 1998 postponed levying any tax on Internet transactions and was based on the concepts that information should not be taxed and infant online businesses should be protected. Most states and bricks-and-mortar retailers favor collecting sales taxes. Those seeking to encourage Internet commercialization argue for leaving the Internet tax-free. Online gambling is aggressively marketed through advertisements on search engine sites, travel sites, and other web locations, and by email. Some U.S. gambling businesses realize that if the Congress passes stringent anti-online gambling legislation, they could be locked out of a highly lucrative Internet business opportunity. Online adult content sites are also under attack, particularly by those concerned about child pornography.

## Online Ethics and Privacy

The speed of Internet communication and its reach, relative anonymity, and low cost of entry tempt some to engage in unethical behaviors. Problem areas are marketing research online, marketing of professionals, marketing to children and other vulnerable groups, marketing restricted products, and unsolicited commercial email. Unsolicited commercial bulk email (spam) is not yet illegal. Spam irritates consumers, overwhelm ISPs, and costs businesses by clogging employee email boxes and sometimes crashing servers. Self-regulation is undertaken by professional organizations, businesses, and industries often to avoid government regulation. It is also designed to provide ethical boundaries in ambiguous circumstances and, sometimes, to calm consumer fears. Internet ethics is not taught in schools, yet many schools are dealing with specific Internet ethical and legal situations, particularly copyright and plagiarism, hacking, and hate email. Personalization, or one-to-one marketing, builds individual consumer profiles. Marketers recognize the value of personalization but also must protect consumers' privacy in order to maintain customer loyalty. Good privacy practices can create an online competitive advantage. The most onerous practice involves collecting personal information from children. The Children's Online Privacy Protection Act (COPPA) requires sites collecting information from children under the age of thirteen to comply with FTC regulations restricting the collection of personally identifiable information without a parent's consent. Over one hundred companies, including IBM, AT&T, and American Express, have created a new position, Chief Privacy Office (CPO). Key chain cards seem innocuous when compared with online information collection. Consumers fear that online information thieves could steal their identity or their credit card numbers, or even stalk and harm them.

## Security

Online security means protecting the safety of online banking and credit card transactions, keeping hackers out of web sites and databases, vaccinating computers against virus-infected email, and stopping such cyberterrorism as denial-of-service (DOS) attacks. Crackers are Internet vandals, individuals and groups that attack web sites to breach their security defenses, penetrate the site, and change prices and content, steal credit card numbers or data, do damage, and brag about their vandalism. Losses are difficult to calculate since many attacks are never discovered, and when they are, site operators often do not report them for fear of negative publicity. DOS attacks occur when vandals block legitimate users from accessing a web site by overloading it with traffic designed to tie up or crash its server(s). Viruses are programs designed to penetrate and infect a host computer or network. Some viruses are nuisances; others can crash a hard drive or steal data. Viruses are expected to be a continuing problem that requires monitoring and the use of up-to-date antivirus software to protect individual computers and networks.

# Internet Marketing Application

Although consumers are very concerned about their privacy, they tend not to read web site privacy statements. Part of the reason has to be the length of the statements and the complexity of the language. Visit several high-traffic web sites and evaluate their privacy statements. Determine how consumer-friendly they are and how likely they will be read. Answer the following questions for each site.

1. Is the privacy statement link clearly visible on the web site front page?
2. Does the link work?

3. Evaluate the privacy statement for
   a. Length
   b. Language complexity
   c. Probability that it will be read by visitors

Create a checklist of the key points a good privacy statement should cover. Sites that might be visited include

America Online at *http://www.aol.com*
Yahoo! at *http://www.yahoo.com*
E*TRADE at *http://www.etrade.com*

# Chapter Review Questions

1. What should a web shopper check on a store-front before making a purchase?
2. On what three major systems are most national legal systems built?
3. What international organizations are working to develop Internet laws?
4. Why is jurisdiction an important Internet marketing issue?
5. Should consumers and businesses be afraid of making online transactions?
6. What should a web storefront do to guard against fraud?
7. What is copyright and how is it being violated online?

8. Why are patents for online processes potentially damaging to Internet commerce?
9. Is trademark infringement only a web problem?
10. Are disclaimers a foolproof way to escape liability? Explain.
11. How do digital signatures work?
12. Should Internet transactions be taxed?
13. Should consumers be allowed to gamble online?
14. Is spam unethical? Is it illegal?
15. What's the difference between a hacker and a cracker? Does the difference in names really matter?

## Napster, File-sharing, and Copyright Infringement

# Case Study

Napster was founded in January 1999. The site was quickly embraced by music lovers who downloaded the free Napster file-sharing software, then copied MP3 music files to their computer hard drives. The private use of downloaded music is legal; sharing music with others is piracy if the music is copyright protected. This is what many Napster users did, using peer-to-peer (P2P) computing that easily shared the music files they downloaded with others over the Internet.

By December 1999, Napster had been sued by the Recording Industry of America (RIAA) for copyright infringement. It quickly became the most celebrated online copyright case. RIAA claims that losses through music file-sharing costs the industry over US$300 million annually. In October 2000, Napster began developing a legal file-sharing system that would allow it to stay in business if the courts ruled against its free sharing system. On February 12, 2001, they did just that; the Ninth Circuit U.S. Court of Appeals ruled that Napster violated copyright laws and had to honor copyrights or close.

Napster was not the only file-sharing site online. Gnutella (*http://www.gnutella.wego.com*) is a fully distributed information-sharing site with a much broader network than just music. Unlike Napster, it is highly decentralized, so it is a more difficult target for regulators. One thing is certain: The digital distribution of music will be big business, with or without Napster. In defense of Napster, it is said the more music people hear, the more they are likely to buy. High school and college students are the biggest fans of the music-sharing sites; they are also the biggest buyers of music CDs.[69]

### CHECK IT OUT

Visit Napster at *http://www.napster.com* and see what is happening on the site. Is it an active web storefront selling music subscriptions? Have you visited Napster or one of the other music sites to download their software? Do you think these sites should be shut down? Can peer-to-peer file transfers be stopped? Is the shrink-wrapped music CD doomed? Would you subscribe to a pay-per-play music site?

### A GLOBAL PERSPECTIVE

MP3.com (*http://www.mp3.com*) offers free music of all types, from alternative to classical. It runs sites in France, Germany, Spain, the United Kingdom, and Japan. Products at each site are tailored to the target market, listing the top forty tunes in each market at the top of the play list. MP3 or MPEG Audio Layer 3 shrinks music into small digital units that can be downloaded and played on a personal computer. The files can be copied and shared. Hundreds of thousands of music files are stored in databases that consumers can easily access. MP3 in Australia (*http://www.mp3.com.au*) claims it is Australia's most popular music service. The Australian site (*http://www.mp3.com.au/musicuse.asp*) posts the following disclaimer. Is it enough to stop users from sharing MP3 files?

> *All material on MP3.com.au is protected by copyright law and by international treaties. You may download this material and make a reasonable number of copies of this material only for your own personal use. You may not otherwise reproduce, distribute, publicly perform, publicly display, or create derivative works of this material, unless authorized by the appropriate copyright owner(s).*[70]

Compare the top forty musical hits on the United States MP3 site with several other MP3 sites. How alike or dissimilar are consumer tastes in these markets? Are many U.S. hits also on international sites? Why is U.S. music popular internationally?

Sites to visit

MP3 France at *http://fr.mp3.com*
MP3 Germany at *http://de.mp3.com*
MP3 Spain at *http://es.mp3.com*
MP3 Australia at *http://www.mp3.com.au*
MP3 UK at *http://uk.mp3.com*

## CHAPTER SIX

# The International Environment of Internet Marketing

## LEARNING OBJECTIVES

- To learn how international orientation affects Internet marketing strategy
- To understand why marketing internationally is more complex than solely domestic Internet marketing
- To determine the current status of major international Internet markets
- To appreciate the importance of international issues that concern Internet marketers

## Selling Top-notch Saddles

Alex handcrafts cowboy saddles and sells them from his workshop store in Oklahoma, USA. Positive word of mouth and half-page ads in the top three U.S. horse and rider periodicals have kept him supplied with a comfortably steady stream of orders for more than twenty years. His customers are pleasure riders from the southwestern United States looking for fine-quality leatherwork, a comfortable centered seat, and attractive tack. Last year, Alex's college-age daughter got him interested in the Internet. The culminating project in her Internet Marketing class required designing and implementing a web storefront for a local small business client. Naturally, she chose her Dad's business, *Top-Notch Saddles*, and contracted with an ISP in Oklahoma City to host the completed web site. Almost immediately after going online, Alex began receiving orders through the site, which accepts payment by check or money order, no credit cards. One day Alex received an online order for his most expensive ready-to-ride chestnut leather saddle, lined in

sheepskin with double-buckle silver cheek adjustments. The list price was US$2,495 plus shipping and handling (S&H). Alex was startled by the customer's location—the Sicilian city of Palermo, Italy. Alex had never before received an international order for his saddles and was unsure how to fulfill it. The Italian customer emailed that she would send a *cheque* [*sic*] or bank transfer for the saddle, whichever was preferred. This international order was an eye opener for Alex. Suddenly, he realized the full implications of the *World Wide* Web. His daughter referred him to the local office of DHL Worldwide Express (*http://www.dhl-usa.com/index*), whose customer service representative explained how Alex could outsource his international shipping and custom clearance needs to DHL's Worldwide Priority Express service. With DHL's help and the cooperation of the Italian customer, two weeks later the saddle arrived in Palermo and Alex's daughter began considering how she could make her Dad's web site more inviting to international buyers.

For a small web storefront like Alex's, becoming an international marketer can be as simple as adding a statement on a web site home page that international customers are welcome, then creating a linked page for them with special purchasing instructions for their orders. **Outsourcing** (subcontracting) shipping and customs clearance to experts like DHL (*http://www.dhl-usa.com/index*), UPS (*http://www.ups.com*), or FedEx (*http://www.fedex.com/us/*) makes sense for Internet marketers like Alex who accept international orders if they are received but do not actively solicit them. At a minimum, an international page should contain pricing information for international orders, particularly how much to add to the U.S. list price for international shipping and handling; directions on where to send a bank draft, money order, or other payment form; and a link to an international shipper. It is doubtful that a very small Internet marketer could afford to create and maintain a multilingual, multicultural mirror site or would have sufficient numbers of international customers to justify doing so. Since Alex lives in the southwestern United States, he should consider adding a Spanish language page for Spanish-speaking U.S., Mexican, or South American customers. This is a low-cost option that could enhance his sales among a previously untapped group.

This chapter looks broadly at the international environment facing Internet marketers. It begins by examining international orientation and market selection strategies. The current status of key Internet markets is considered. The chapter continues by identifying issues that concern international Internet marketers.

## *International Orientation*

Some businesses have actively taken advantage of the Internet's unique global reach to initiate, expand, and/or maintain their international marketing activities almost from the beginning of commercialization. Others have avoided internationalizing their web sites or even considering international marketing opportunities.

**International Internet marketing** is international marketing in electronically mediated environments on the Internet and World Wide Web, intranets, and/or extranets making offers to and from more than just the marketer's domestic (home) market. An **international Internet market** is external to the marketer's home country of operations and may be consumers, enterprises, or both. Marketing mix variables are adjusted to serve the target market. The market must be reachable online and sufficiently large to make targeting it profitable. Buyers in the market must be affluent enough to make purchases, have the authority to do so, a mechanism to make payment (credit, check, money order, etc.), and a means for taking delivery. A market may be a country, segmented groups within a country, a region or group of countries, a mass or niche market of consumers, and/or enterprise buyers.

International Internet marketing occurs when . . .

A Canadian or Mexican citizen makes a purchase from a U.S. web storefront hosted by a U.S. ISP. Even though Canada and Mexico are members of the North American Free Trade Agreement (NAFTA) along with the United States, they are still international markets.

A buyer for a multinational company sets up a corporate account at Lands' End (*http://ocs.landsend.com/*) hosted on a U.S. server. Company employees can purchase logo'd

### Outsourcing
Subcontracting functions such as international shipping to other companies.

### International Internet marketing
Marketing via electronically mediated environments, particularly the Internet and World Wide Web to more than one country.

### International Internet market
An Internet market external to the marketer's home country.

[*sic*] work shirts online at Landsend.com from their company's offices in Amsterdam, the Netherlands and Moscow, Russia.

A U.S. citizen purchases a six-box video set of the television series *Brideshead Revisited* online from Amazon.com in England (*http://www.amazon.co.uk*) for £22.99 (pounds). The video is out of stock at Amazon.com (*http://www.amazon.com*) in the United States. The U.S. buyer is delighted to find the videos but will be unhappy to learn when they arrive that they are in PAL format, which is incompatible with U.S. VCRs.

A small business owner/operator in Katmandu, Nepal, purchases two dozen silk saris online from an Indian web storefront housed on a server in Delhi for US$42.05 each and has them delivered to his store by UPS.

A Brazilian downloads a *Greenhouse Effect* by *GAINGREEN* hip-hop rap netCD to her home computer from MP3.com for US$4.00 (http://genres.mp3.com/music/hip_hop_rap/).

Internationalization is not strategically appropriate for all bricks-and-mortar businesses or all web marketers. However, the borderless global nature of the Internet means that even solely domestic online marketers with no desire or intention to use the Internet internationally must address the issue of international access, if only to clearly state they do not accept international orders. Many of these businesses will never take advantage of the Internet's global reach; others are not doing so now but may in the future. All are exposed to the international Internet environment when they go online to do business.

### FACTORS AFFECTING INTERNATIONAL STRATEGY

At the beginning of Internet commercialization, internationalization was not an issue. The United States led the world in commercializing the Internet, and marketing to international buyers and sellers was not important because there were so few of them. In less than a decade, that picture had changed dramatically. Today, the Internet is truly international, and even small U.S. Internet marketers must decide whether or not it is in their best interests to interact with the rest of the world. Some will adopt an **exclusionary international Internet marketing strategy**—being on the Internet but staying solely domestic home-country oriented, excluding international buyers. Others will adopt an **inclusionary international Internet marketing strategy** attempting to target, reach, interact, and trade with some or all international buyers.

What determines international strategy? *Current strategy* is a key factor. International offline marketers are more likely to also be international online marketers, usually targeting key markets currently served and those that are in its expansion plans. Small and midsize solely domestic marketers may find internationalization beyond their capacities and needs, particularly if they have exclusively local home-country selling areas. IBM (*http://www.ibm.com*) is a prominent international marketer offline and online. A local computer repair shop that provides service within a single city market is not.

*Market offer* also influences international strategy. Culturally sensitive products are more complex and challenging to market internationally online and offline. Cultural differences will affect apparel color, placement of keys on a computer keyboard,

---

**Exclusionary international Internet marketing strategy**

Marketing on the Internet but marketing remains solely home-country domestic, excluding international buyers.

**Inclusionary international Internet marketing strategy**

Marketing to international as well as domestic buyers online.

the language of a word processing program, and how many golf balls go in a pack because certain numbers are bad luck in prime target markets. Some offers are clearly specific to one country market. For example, patriotic apparel and artifacts, pins, flags, and other tangible items were marketed heavily on U.S. web sites to U.S. buyers after September 11, 2001. They were appropriate for this market, far less so for international markets.

*Customer demand* is closely related to market offer. If demand is exclusively home-country local, then Internet marketing and web sites will be local. If demand is international, then Internet marketing and web sites most likely will be international. Sometimes a major customer drags its suppliers online, forcing them to become international Internet marketers. For example, General Electric's (*http://www.ge.com*) former chairman and CEO Jack Welch made it clear that he wanted GE suppliers to be online in order to do business with the huge conglomerate. This had a considerable impact on suppliers that had only one customer, GE. Most, however, were not ready to make the move, and GE had to back off this demand, at least in the short-term. GE's new ebusiness concept is *make-buy-sell*, and its goals are reduced procurement costs, increased productivity, and increased revenues through the *e-volution* of its operations. GE markets products in one hundred countries and has more than three hundred thousand employees worldwide. Its many domestic and international web sites receive over 200 million page views per month. GE clearly is an actively international Internet marketer, as are many of its suppliers.

*Management* is another significant influence, as proactive internationally oriented managers are more likely to promote inclusionary rather than exclusionary marketing strategies. Their commitment to international Internet marketing will cause resources to be allocated accordingly. An internationally oriented ebusiness manager with the clout of a Jack Welch is a major force moving a business toward international markets. On the other hand, small business owner/operators content with revenues from local home-country domestic markets are less likely to want to bother with or run the risks associated with internationalizing their Internet operations.

*Competitors* can spur Internet marketers to internationalize, because fear of being left behind by the competition is a potent motivator. So is waking up to offshore Internet marketers competing for one's local home-country customers.

*Domestic economic conditions*, particularly a domestic economic downturn, can encourage marketers to develop international revenue sources to hedge against losses. International marketers spread the risk by offsetting losses in one market against gains in others. *Government encouragement*, particularly through a tax moratorium or special financing opportunities, can stimulate online exporting.

Finally, *serendipity* is a factor. It was Alex's good fortune to receive that first international order because it motivated him to recognize that his bottom line could be enhanced with relatively little effort. This led Alex to consider strategies for marketing to other international buyers via his web site in a cost-effective way.

International Internet marketing is not risk free. Risk is the possibility that something may be lost or harm may occur. It is both a hazard and the probability that a loss may occur. Savvy Internet marketers identify risk factors and develop strategies to reduce their probability and effects. Risks associated with international Internet marketing include the following.

**OVEREXPANSION**     Entering too many international markets and/or creating and maintaining too many localized web sites too fast can result in large cash drains, insufficient human resources to maintain the expansion, and collapse. It can strain fulfillment and result in frustrated rather than satisfied buyers.

**BRAND DILUTION**     Some brand names, particularly luxury goods, risk diluting the value of their brand name through overexposure with too many web sites in too many markets. In this case, familiarity can tarnish brand equity.

**OVERESTIMATION**     Overly optimistic estimates of the potential benefits of Internet internationalizing can result in insufficient consideration of the costs of expansion. Estimates tend to be influenced by the degree of enthusiasm for internationalizing—greater enthusiasm often leads to greater overestimation of benefits and underestimation of costs.

**UNDERESTIMATION**     Underestimating the competition in international markets can be disastrous. The most desirable international Internet markets are also the most highly competitive, particularly in North America and Western Europe. This means greater numbers of competitive web marketing sites along with advertising clutter, greater expense in getting a top listing on local search engines, higher ISP charges, and related costs.

**REGULATION**     Every international target market is potentially unstable, some obviously more so than others. Some governments are more intrusive and their regulation of Internet commerce restricts Internet marketing activities as well as adds costs. Actively marketing to buyers in these markets results in exposure to their legal systems and courts when disputes arise.

Every Internet marketer considering going international should carefully assess the risks and costs, then weigh them against potential benefits. International risks along with contentment in being solely home-country domestic are enough to persuade many U.S. Internet marketers that going international at this time is not a strategically well timed decision. When costs are greater than potential benefits, the best action may be to maintain the status quo. However, because change is swift and inevitable, particularly online, risk assessments should be conducted regularly to ensure that potentially profitable international Internet opportunities are capitalized on when they appear, and losses are minimized.

## STAGES OF INTERNATIONAL INVOLVEMENT

The challenge for Internet marketers going international is fourfold, to effectively and profitably *target, reach, interact,* and *trade* with offshore buyers. Once the decision to go international is made, *target* markets must be selected and strategies developed to *reach* buyers in the key markets. This is getting more difficult as the Web gets cluttered with billions of pages, email spam increases, and more buyers go wireless, which necessitates web pages to accommodate smaller screens. Sites must *interact* with non-U.S., non-English-speaking buyers. This often requires localizing sites, which can be very costly. Finally, methods must be implemented to facilitate cross-border online *trade*. This includes solving logistics and shipping requirements for moving tangible goods into offshore markets and handling returns. It means finding satisfactory and secure payment mechanisms that protect both buyer and seller and

accommodate currency conversions, currency rate fluct...
cross-market price variations. It also means overcom...
barriers designed to protect online local home-count...
vantage over others.

Many and perhaps most U.S. Internet marketers ...
mentioned, Alex's first international order was unexp...
ber of the European Union (EU), roughly 5,716 mile...
lahoma, USA. Alex did not have international custo...
a web site for his business, and he did not promote his p...
any market outside the United States, not even to buyers in neighboring Mexico.
stead, a highly motivated buyer found him, perhaps by searching Yahoo! Italia (*http://
it.yahoo.com*) using key words *L' americano sella* (American saddles) or *il handmade
sella* (handmade saddles). The buyer clearly knew enough English to understand
Alex's English-only web site.

Alex is an example of a **passive international Internet marketer** (figure 6-1) accepting international orders only if they happen to reach his web site. Other than the
one international page his daughter created, Alex does not differentiate between international and domestic customers. He has a *one-site-serves-all* strategy. Perhaps if
he receives more international orders in the future he will eventually become an **active
international Internet marketer**. Active international Internet marketers are more
vigorous in developing, maintaining, and extending their international buyer base.
They decide where and how to target their offers. They make decisions about site design and maintenance, cultural and linguistic adaptations, currency and size conversions, product standards, ISP hosting, shipping, and how to comply with local legal
and regulatory restrictions. Multinational corporations often develop multicultural,
multilingual mirror sites hosted by U.S. ISPs or local sites created for and hosted in
each key international target market served. Their start-up and maintenance expenses
are greater than solely domestic home-country or passively international sites. They
recognize the need to serve existing international buyers and find new ones, and they
are poised to take advantage of increased non-U.S. web traffic (55 percent of total web
traffic in 2001) and growing non-U.S. revenue production (62 percent of total B2C
revenue by 2004).[1]

Businesses can evolve from being solely home-country domestic to going global by
marketing on the Internet. This is one of the most remarkable advantages of being online, having worldwide market exposure often at relatively little cost. Most Internet
start-ups and small businesses with web storefronts could never achieve equal international exposure offline.

## EXCLUSIONARY STRATEGIES

Exclusionary strategy markets vary. They may be national in scope, interstate or inter-
province, within several counties or parishes, or local in a single city or several adjacent
cities, restricting Internet marketing activities to those preselected home-country lo-
cales. What they are not is international.

Nordstrom (*http://store.nordstrom.com*), a respected department store, has 136
stores in twenty-six states, along with twenty-three international Façonnable boutiques primarily in Europe. Go to the company's web site and the virtual shopping
bag states "At this time, we are not able to send orders internationally. You may, however,

**Passive international
Internet marketer**
Accepts international
orders but does not
actively solicit them.

**Active international
Internet marketer**
Internet marketers that
are proactive about
developing, maintaining,
and extending their
international buyer base
and international Internet
marketing activities.

**Figure 6-1 International Internet Marketing Involvement**

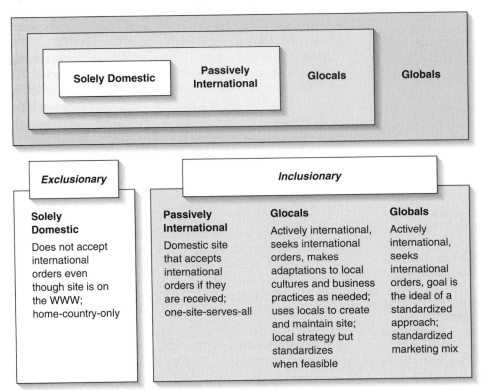

All marketers are not equally interested in, committed to, or involved with international Internet markets. Some will always be *solely domestic* with a home-country-only strategy. *Solely domestic* marketers should clearly identify their solely domestic operations to avoid misunderstandings. Some domestic sites are *passively international*. They have a one-site-fits-all strategy based on the home-country strategy. The most energetic international Internet marketers are *actively international*. Even among this group, approaches to internationalization vary. *Glocals* seek international buyers. Their strategy is to localize, that is, make site adaptations to appeal to local markets but standardize if and when feasible to do so. This strategy is also known as *Think Global, Act Local*. *Globals* actively seek international buyers. Their strategy is one of standardization, treating all markets alike with a more-or-less culture-neutral approach. Globalization is an ideal rather than a realistic strategy.

purchase from an international address and ship to a U.S. destination." Thus, Nordstrom has a national, solely U.S. Internet market. At some time in the future, it may decide that the benefits of accepting international orders are greater than the costs and risks of doing so. Alternately, Nordstrom may decide to localize sites in countries where it already has Façonnable boutiques and still not accept international orders from its U.S. site.

Other exclusionary Internet marketers are local. Mink's Nursery (*http://www.minksnursery.com*) has been selling plants and landscaping services in a four-county area around London, Kentucky, USA, since 1942. Its web site states that it "provides complete lawn and landscaping maintenance to many commercial and residential customers in the *Laurel, Whitley, Knox, and Clay* [italics added] county areas." Obviously, an international effort is neither needed nor a wise expenditure of time and money for Mink's. In this case, a local exclusionary strategy makes sense. Mink's bricks-and-mortar store is unlikely to sell its products to international customers unless they are visiting or temporarily living in the local served market. International Internet marketers are unlikely to target Mink's customers in the four-county region or exert competitive pressure for Mink's to internationalize its site. Mink's was wise to state its local service area on its web site to avoid potential misunderstandings.

## INCLUSIONARY STRATEGIES

Inclusionary strategies vary from accepting international orders if they occur to actively seeking them. Alex's web site is passively international; that is, he takes international orders if they are offered, but he does not actively seek them. Alex does not differentiate between domestic and international buyers or promote his site internationally. He places the responsibility for completing international orders on the buyer and outsources international shipping and customs clearance to other businesses. Passive international Internet marketing is often a first step toward a more active approach. Success with international orders and the extra revenue they add to the balance sheet can provide the needed incentive to begin targeting offshore online buyers.

Another approach excludes international sales online but uses web sites and email to inform international buyers, promote offers, and drive buyers toward bricks-and-mortar outlets, catalog sales, and/or a professional sales force. The latter approach is used by the Boeing Company (*http://www.boeing.com/defense-space/military/flash.html*), the world's largest military aircraft manufacturer. Its web site provides information about such products as the F-15E Eagle, the world's premier fighter-bomber. However, the plane cannot be purchased online. The site pushes domestic and international defense departments or governments to contact the company's offline professional sales force to discuss a potential purchase.

**Localized Internet marketing strategy**
Translating pages and making cultural and purchasing accommodations on web pages and email targeted to international markets.

A **localized Internet marketing strategy** adapts marketing offers to accommodate local preferences and customs. This is a customized approach consistent with a view of buyer groups as heterogeneous with many different needs, wants, and preferences. It requires adapting to local customs and constructing the marketing site and offer to appeal to local tastes. A localized strategy can be used for one or many markets. A **glocal strategy** is localization applied globally (worldwide).

**Glocal strategy**
Localization applied globally by adapting web sites to key target market local cultures but still trying to maintain some standardization.

Coca-Cola (*http://www2.Coca-Cola.com*), headquartered in Atlanta, Georgia, USA, is an example of a company with a glocal strategy. Founded in 1886, the company states, "we 'think local and act local,' because we need to listen to all the voices around the world asking for beverages that span the entire spectrum of tastes and occasions." Coca-Cola produces over 230 different product brands in more than two hundred countries, with strategic business units (SBUs) making localized decisions in the Americas, Asia, and Europe/Africa. Matching its local strategy, the company has web sites in over thirty countries (*http://www2.Coca-Cola.com/golocal/index.html*) adapted to each local market or market group. Localized web sites are in such countries as Argentina, Australia, Brazil, China, France, German, Great Britain, Hungary, Italy, Japan, Korea, New Zealand, Norway, Peru, Russia, South Africa, Spain, and the United States.

Although Coca-Cola maintains it is a local marketer, it also standardizes on its local web sites. Its trade-dress-protected bottle is displayed on most sites, and Coca-Cola red is either a prominent background or contrast color. *Trade dress* is the legally registered image of a product used in its marketing and includes nonfunctional design elements, packaging, colors, shapes, and/or symbols. Trade dress is protected in the United States under the Lanham Act of 1946. Coke sites offer English translations in Argentina and Colombia. Its Japanese and Korean sites integrate English with the domestic language, and the Singapore site is in English. European Coke sites are much edgier in their visual images, and the Belgian/Luxembourg site is far sexier than anything shown in the United States. All sites rely heavily on a youth orientation, music, and graphic intensity; most use flash technology. Coca-Cola has made a considerable effort at the SBU level to adapt web site look, sound, and content to local tastes.

**Global marketing**
Offering an undifferentiated marketing mix to perceived homogeneous markets worldwide.

**Global marketing** is offering an undifferentiated marketing mix to homogeneous markets worldwide. Although the terms international and global are often used interchangeably, they are different. For most marketers, global marketing is an unrealized ideal. Harvard Business Professor Emeritus Theodore Levitt was the first to propose that widespread access to communication, transport, and travel were driving buyers worldwide toward wanting and accepting the same product offers. Levitt believed this movement toward *converging commonalities* would allow marketers to standardize their offers rather than require them to adapt to local preferences. Benefits are obvious from economies of scale in production to distribution, promotion, and management.[2] Theoretically, a business using a global strategy can make one product offer to all markets. This approach is consistent with the view of *homogeneous* consumers. The Internet has undermined the globalization concept to a great extent, making it possible to effectively and efficiently mass customize offers and personalize customer contact. At the same time, it has also been extremely effective in spreading information about product offers available on web sites hosted in other countries. If Levitt had been able to predict the invention of the World Wide Web and its commercialization, he would have added the Internet to the forces driving converging commonalities.

## ✔ CONCEPT CHECK

1. Explain the concept of target, reach, interact, and trade.
2. What factors help determine an online marketer's international orientation?
3. Are some marketers strategically right to ignore the *World Wide* Web?

# Selecting International Markets

International markets obviously are quite different. Some contain a far higher concentration of prospective buyers and more fully developed electronic marketing infrastructures than others. Whether or not a market is a desirable Internet target depends on the match between a business's goals and resources and the market's potential and risks.

## SERENDIPITY MARKETS

Alex's interest in international Internet marketing was formed when he received his first international order. Now his marketing goals have expanded to include selling more saddles to international buyers with the least amount of effort and risk. Alex needs to identify international markets where horses are ridden Western-style and buyers can pay the price for his saddles, as well as conduct business in English. He needs a sufficient concentration of prospective buyers to make it profitable to target them, as well as the means to reach them electronically, a convertible currency that supports international transactions, and a legal environment that does not impede them. A dependable transportation infrastructure must exist so his saddles can be delivered or returned.

Alex must have more than one Italian customer to justify targeting Italy or even the EU. He can determine if other international visitors are visiting his site by having his ISP analyze his web server transfer (activity) logs that track user-site interactions. This analysis can identify the country of origin of site visitors and aggregate the data so Alex can identify potential offshore target markets. Once he knows which markets are promising, Alex should register his site URL with local search engines in each market. He can locate search engines through Search Engine Colossus (*http://www. searchenginecolossus.com*), which links to search engines in 165 countries. Registering with a local search engine is a low-cost method for gaining exposure in international markets. Alex can use AltaVista's translating service (*http://babelfish.altavista.com/tr*) to find key phrases to use with local search engines and include in metatags. Marketers go where the customers are and if Alex is serious about targeting international markets, that is exactly what he must do.

**Log file analysis**
A software program that collects information from visitors' browsers and facilitates a country-of-origin analysis.

Alex's **log file analysis** may reveal that very few international visitors are browsing his site. Given a low level of interest from international visitors, it is likely he will adopt a *wait-and-see* attitude about internationalizing. If he receives more international orders, it may stimulate his interest in actively seeking buyers from abroad. In any case, he should begin thinking about targeting Spanish-speakers in the United States and Mexico. Many initial international marketing efforts are directed toward North American Free Trade Agreement (NAFTA) partners Canada and Mexico. Canada is particularly desirable because its language and culture are more familiar to U.S. marketers. However, Mexico has a strong equestrian tradition and might be a more promising market for Alex's products.

## CURRENT BUYERS

Many businesses have no trouble identifying their international Internet target markets. They target their current buyers. For example, country-of-origin log file data and careful study of Internet demographics helped Yahoo! determine where it needed localized web sites. Localizing required translating web pages into the local language and making accommodations for cultural, purchasing, legal, and other differences specific to local markets. By 2002, Yahoo! supported nine European sites, nine sites in Asia-Pacific, and six in the Americas. However, each site was standardized in its technology and format.

Lands' End was mailing hard-copy catalogs to customers in England, France, Germany, and Japan before it constructed web storefronts and warehouses in those countries. Amazon.com, eBay, AOL (*http://www.aol.com*), and other Internet pure plays used a U.S.-extension strategy, starting in the United States where their buyers were concentrated, then targeting countries with large numbers of buyers rapidly going online. A pure play is another way of describing a clicks-only business.

B2B marketers are less concerned with cultural adaptation than B2C marketers. Their international target markets are more likely to be current offline target markets where they already have a significant operations with offices, plants, warehouses, and sales forces. Extranets also offer cross-border opportunities to market to offshore suppliers, customers, and partners.

### ECONOMIC FACTORS

Internet growth and market penetration has been greatest in the most affluent, industrialized nations. Currently there are slightly over two hundred countries in the world according to One World-Nations Online (*http://www.nationsonline.org/oneworld*). A precise count is surprisingly elusive since even major international organizations disagree on numbers of countries. The World Bank (*http://www.worldbank.org/data/dataquery.html*) counts 207 countries with populations more than or equal to thirty thousand, yet the United Nations (*http://www.un.org/Overview/growth.htm#90*) has only 189 member nations.[3] However many there are, the world's countries vary greatly on many key dimensions, from land mass to comparative measures of resources, labor and capital, technology, and entrepreneurship activities. Countries frequently are classified by national economic productivity. The World Bank's grouping of countries (see "World Bank Groups" below) by gross national product (GNP) per capita is widely used for macrolevel comparisons. These groupings fail to capture the distribution of economic resources, pockets of affluence, and education that exist within low-income and lower-middle-income countries, and the pockets of poverty and undereducation that exist within advanced economies. However, it would be a mistake to assume that no Internet marketing is occurring in countries even in the lowest-income group. Low-income-group countries often have solely domestic banking web sites for higher-income citizens and actively international tourism and travel sites. Most have web sites hosted by their central government and major businesses. Internet access is far too expensive for most enterprises and consumers but can be found in cybercafés, restaurants and bars where patrons pay to go online, or in public buildings like libraries and post offices.

## *World Bank Groups*

World Bank groups are defined by gross national product (GNP) per capita, a measure of the total production and consumption of goods and services per person (capita) in a nation. The world's poorest nations have annual GNPs or gross domestic products (GDPs) of less than US$755 per person (per capita).

| World Bank Group | GNP per cap (1999 est.) |
|---|---|
| Low Income | ≤US$755 |
| Lower Middle Income | US$756 to $2,995 |
| Upper Middle Income | US$2,996 to $9,265 |
| High Income | ≥US$9,266[4] |

Ethiopia, a landlocked country in Eastern Africa, is in the World Bank's low-income group. Roughly twice the size of Texas, it is one of the oldest countries in Africa and the world. Ethiopia's almost sixty-six million people have a per capita GDP of US$600 (2000 estimate). The economy is 45 percent agricultural, 12 percent industrial, and 43 percent service-based. In December 2000 the country had 84 ISPs and around ten thousand Internet users.[5]

Based on these data, Ethiopia would appear a highly unlikely place for Internet marketing. However, Ethiopia has a web storefront targeting high-income Ethiopians living abroad and in Addis Ababa, the capital city. EthioGift.com (*http://www.EthioGift.com*) offers secure online credit card ordering for flowers, traditional Ethiopian apparel and spices, food, and sheep. A minimum 25 kilogram (kg) sheep is US$58, a big sheep (30 kg) is US$73, and a *very big* sheep (35 kg) is US$97. Ethiopian newspapers are online along with trading companies, ISPs, and travel sites.[6]

Bangladesh, also one of the world's poorest nations, is a lower-middle-income-group country. It has a population of over 130 million and a very high birthrate. Most Internet activity is centered in the capital, Dhaka. Bangladesh has had email service since late 1993. The country has more than forty-five ISPs, most of which are in Dhaka. The number of Internet users is still small, however; in 1999, there were only thirty thousand. Yet Bangladesh has a growing number of businesses online from travel sites to the Online Yellow Pages of Bangladesh, Biman Bangladesh Airlines, the *Daily Star* newspaper, and ISPs. Some of these online businesses are marketing their products to international buyers. Others are buyers themselves or are seeking international partners.[7]

## INTERNET READINESS

**Internet readiness (IR)**

An indication of how prepared a country, region, or area is to effectively make Internet access and activities widely available.

**Internet readiness (IR)** is another macrolevel grouping method used to differentiate markets. It is an indication of how prepared a country, region, or area is to effectively use information and communication technologies, make Internet access widely available, and participate in Internet-related commercial and public sector activities. Internet readiness as an indicator of Internet marketing receptiveness and competitiveness is a more useful measure for Internet marketers to consider in seeking new markets, but it should not be the only indicator used.

Countries and country borders have always played an important role in determining legal status and trade targets. Cross-border trade has been going on since ancient times. It has flourished since the end of World War II, particularly among the world's major cross-border trading nations, as they looked to international markets for growth and expansion, and hedges against downturns in their own domestic economies. Today, while countries obviously remain important, the key to understanding Internet readiness worldwide often lies in evaluating regions and parts of countries. They can be sorted into three categories: the *least-Internet-ready areas (LIRAs)*, *Internet-ready areas (IRAs)*, and *Internet leaders (ILs)*. Although these categories resemble the historic Third World, Second World, and First World classification of nations by economic development level, industrialization alone is not necessarily a predictor of Internet-readiness, nor is GNP or GDP. Luxembourg, Bermuda, Monaco, and the Cayman Islands were among the world's top ten GDP per capita countries in 1999, but clearly they are not Internet leaders. Israel, Taiwan, and South Korea did not make the top twenty-five but are leaders.[8]

**LEAST-INTERNET-READY AREAS (LIRAS)** Approximately 35 percent of the world's population, around two billion people, live in the world's LIRAs (see "Least-Internet-Ready Areas of the World" on p. 140), where the majority of people have little if any awareness of the Internet. LIRAs, but not always the countries in which they are located, represent the world's lowest economic status areas. They are mostly poor, subsistence farming areas that lack the infrastructure needed to connect to the Internet using land-based telephone lines and sufficient numbers of educated, affluent people to purchase access and use it. LIRAs are at the wrong end of the international Internet

**Metered Internet access**
Internet access charges calculated per minute online.

**Flat rate Internet access pricing**
Users pay a flat monthly fee for Internet access irrespective of time actually spent online.

digital divide. The divide is the gap between *haves*, those with affordable, easy access to communication and information technologies, and *have-nots*. The lack of infrastructure construction and Internet access, and the cost of providing it, are key factors keeping the digital gap from narrowing. By contrast, Internet leaders like the United States have large and expanding communication and information infrastructures and relatively inexpensive, mostly unmetered, and reasonably taxed Internet access.[9] The United States had **metered Internet access** when graphical browsers were first introduced, with access charges calculated per minute online. The change to **flat rate Internet access pricing,** where users pay a flat monthly fee regardless of time online, accelerated U.S. Internet adoption and use, and set the stage for the initial explosive rate of commercialization.

Some governments are making an effort to provide Internet access to the poorest and/or most remote parts of their countries. For example, the Brazilian government announced a plan in 2001 to invest about US$400 million in extending Internet access to people in the rain forest and dry countryside. It includes launching a free public ISP that covers the entire country. The over 150 million Brazilians currently not online will have access through Internet terminals mainly at post offices. In a separate initiative, a nongovernmental agency (NGO), Viva Rio, launched a portal that extends Internet use to the Brazilian urban poor. Viva Favela (*http://www. vivafavela.com.br/english.asp*)

## Least-Internet-Ready Areas of the World (LIRAs)

These areas represent the least likely target markets for most, but not all, Internet marketers. However, that does not mean they are totally cut off from the Internet and/or Internet marketing activities. In some cases, governments are funding projects designed to get people in these areas online, often through public Internet connections available in public schools, libraries, and post offices, and through private sector Internet cafés.

Southern Mexico and pockets of tropical Central America
Andean countries
Most of tropical Brazil
Tropical sub-Saharan Africa
The former Soviet Union farthest from European and Asian markets
Landlocked parts of Asia, including the Ganges Valley states of India
Landlocked Laos and Cambodia
Deep-interior states of China[10]

was launched July 3, 2001, and targets Rio de Janeiro's low-income communities. It offers access to goods and services, as well as information and news.[11] Although the vast majority of Internet marketers will not target LIRAs, some will. These and similar initiatives will make products available to a large number of previously inaccessible potential buyers. However, access alone will not make them prime targets for most U.S. Internet marketers.

LIRAs were one of Vinton Cerf's concerns when he called for governments and organizations to ensure that someday the Internet would be for everyone (see Chapter 2). While the plight of Internet have-nots is attracting international attention, solutions are not always readily evident, simple, or cheap. LIRAs are not prime Internet marketing targets nor are they likely to produce Internet marketing competitors or innovations. However, infrastructure builders may find them attractive if and when funds materialize for the construction of communication and information infrastructures that support Internet activities.

**INTERNET-READY AREAS (IRAS)** The middle levels of countries and regions, about half the world's population (approximately three billion people), are far better off economically than LIRAs, and their populations are more likely to be aware of the Internet. They have communication and information infrastructures, although not always equally distributed, and are Internet ready, though not universally so. Many people in IRAs use information and communication technologies and can develop marketable applications from technological innovations. They benefit from Internet commercialization and are prime Internet marketing targets *and* competitors. IRAs are rapidly developing and building out local access (see "Internet-Ready Areas of the World" above). While some have relatively low GDPs, they represent areas where many Internet marketers will find profitable numbers of receptive buyers and possibly partners, business-to-business (B2B), business-to-consumer (B2C), and business-to-public sector (B2P).

## Internet-Ready Areas of the World (IRAs)

Internet-ready areas include:

Coastal India, particularly Bangalore, a center of computer activity
Nontropical south-central and coastal Brazil, São Paulo, Rio de Janeiro, Campinas
Northern Mexico and Mexico City
Costa Rica
Hungary
Estonia
Malaysia
Parts of the former Soviet Union nearest European and Asian markets
Parts of Thailand
Parts of China particularly Shanghai, Nanjing, Hangzhou, Hong Kong, and Shandong
   Province in coastal East China; coastal Shenzhen
Pretoria, Johannesburg, and Gauteng Province South Africa[12]

**IRAs Are Building Access**

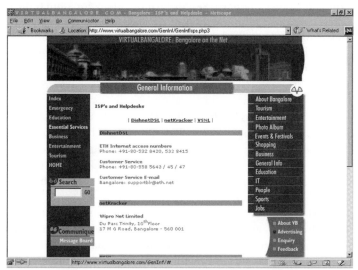

ISP activity is growing rapidly in IRAs. It is becoming easier and cheaper to find Internet access in these areas. *Source:* Reprinted by permission of Virtualbangalore.com. *http://www.virtualbangalore.com/GenInf/GenInfIsps.php3.*

**INTERNET LEADERS (ILS)** About 15 percent of the world's population, less than a billion people, are contributing innovations that are fueling Internet commercialization. People in these economically dominant countries are information technology innovators and entrepreneurs, with nearly universal awareness of the Internet. Leaders include the fully developed countries—the United States, Canada, Western Europe, Japan, Australia and New Zealand—along with Taiwan, South Korea, and Israel. According to the Economist Intelligence Unit, the five most Internet prepared countries in the world are the United States, Sweden, Finland, Norway, and the Netherlands, followed by the United Kingdom, Canada, Singapore, Hong Kong, and Switzerland.[13] These countries are rapidly building out the Internet's infrastructure and conducting research that will allow the Internet and the Web to evolve to the next level. ILs provide the innovations that IRAs use and adapt. Leaders are highly competitive and represent desirable target markets; however, even they have digital divides within their borders usually related to income, education, location (rural versus urban), and infrastructure access.

## ✔ CONCEPT CHECK

1. Explain what Alex's international opportunity had to do with serendipity.
2. Why should an Internet marketer target current international buyers?
3. Explain how economic factors and Internet readiness are alike yet also different.

# The International Internet Population

By 2005, the online population worldwide is forecast to be well over one billion, up from more than 544 million in 2002. Currently, the fifteen top Internet-using countries represent more than 80 percent of all users, but only about 15 percent of the world's offline population. The United States will continue to dominate in overall number of Internet users, but its share will drop as Internet use rises among the other top countries in the next five years. The United States may represent as little as 29 percent of all Internet users by 2005.[14]

**WEB UPDATE**

Top Internet Countries

Even though online populations clearly are shifting toward international markets, only about one-third of U.S. Internet businesses currently target them.[15] This is not surprising. It reflects the desirability of the affluent, Internet-savvy U.S. market where many marketers can find all the buyers they currently need or can handle. It also emphasizes how much easier and cheaper it is to market in one's home country backyard where language and culture are known, there is a single currency, deliveries and returns are relatively simple, and online and offline marketing are complementary. For many businesses, this justifies staying exclusively domestic today. For some, going international is not appropriate or advisable, now or in the future. For others, failing to internationalize soon could be a costly mistake.

## THE AMERICAS

Internet use in the Americas is dominated by the United States and Canada. U.S. consumers are world leaders in online buying, and the U.S. market is where the competition currently is most intense. Canada is an attractive though far smaller market than the United States and has the highest Internet penetration (over 60 percent) in the Americas and second highest in the world. Canada and Mexico are the number one and two trading partners of the United States.[16]

Many U.S. businesses first go international by exporting to Canada. Doing so online is a natural extension of this strategy. However, web sites or email promotions targeting Canadians must accommodate the country's French language requirement along with a different currency, culture, and even with NAFTA, cross-border logistics challenges. Nevertheless, Canada is an attractive market—wealthy, Internet-savvy, and close, which reduces shipping costs for tangible goods.

Canadians shop U.S. sites for the variety of products offered online, particularly those not offered on Canadian sites. In 2000, 90 percent of Canadian teens went on-line, leading the world in music downloads. Canadian B2C sales in 2000 were over US$2.76 billion, and more than 50 percent of online Canadians shop U.S. sites. Over 75 percent of Canadian small business are online; more than 40 percent are actively doing business electronically.[17]

Although Mexico is a vital U.S. trading partner, Internet use is catching on far more slowly there. By 2004, 6.4 million Mexicans (8.6 percent) are expected to be online, up from 1.5 million (2.2 percent) in 2001. Mexican online spending should reach US$1.5 billion by 2005. U.S. online retailers have an opportunity to capture more of the growing Mexican market. Mexican consumers like the convenience of online shopping, but local online retailers are not delivering good customer service, prices are high, and product choices are poor. U.S. marketers already targeting Mexican buyers should accommodate existing buyers online with localized pages.[18]

Internet use in Latin America overall is expected to grow from 15 million in 2000 to 75 million by 2005. However, low credit card use is slowing B2C revenues. America Online has been aggressively marketing in Brazil since 1999. Brazil, Mexico, and Argentina are the principal Latin American growth markets, representing about 66 percent of online activity. However, economic problems, particularly in Argentina, are slowing Internet expansion. Large U.S. online marketers already target Latin America, principally Mexico and Brazil. In comparing the world's major market areas, Latin America lags Western Europe and Asia/Oceania in Internet penetration, revenue production, and market potential.[19]

## EUROPE

European web marketing is being pushed by businesses, individuals, and government and it is growing rapidly. Europe currently represents over 31 percent of the world's online population. France, Germany, the Netherlands, Italy, Sweden and the United Kingdom are 80 percent of the European market. Targeting these countries means accommodating six languages, six legal systems, and three currencies.[20]

The European market is dominated by Western and Northern Europe, particularly Britain, Germany, France, Italy, and the Scandinavian countries. Although the European Union (EU) has harmonized currencies (the euro €) and many business regulations, they are still heterogeneous markets, each with distinct languages and culture, and some still with their own currency. Southern parts of Europe are going online at a slower rate, which also means they are less clogged with local online marketing competition.

About 70 percent of small and midsize European businesses are online, with 40 percent on their own web sites. Europe leads the United States in the use of mobile Internet access and digital interactive television. Free or low-cost online access and government encouragement are driving Internet growth in these areas.[21]

A major problem facing U.S. online marketers in Europe is relatively low credit card use. Many Germans are reluctant to use credit or debit cards for payments. While the number of credit cards per one thousand people is 2,793 in the United States, it is only 1,297 in Germany, and 567 in France. The United Kingdom is slightly higher at 1,527. Preferred payments are collect on delivery (COD) and bank drafts. By comparison, 75 percent of U.S. and Canadian shoppers use credit cards online; less than 50 percent use them outside North America.[22] This makes B2C cross-border transactions more difficult for U.S. marketers accustomed to credit card transactions. It slows verification, increases the risk of fraud, and delays shipments.

Significant differences persist in the major European markets. Britain has the highest number of interactive television users (23 percent of all online households) compared with WebTV's 7.5 percent share in the United States. Only 35 percent of the British use PCs to go online compared with over 60 percent in the United States. Teletext, one-way television messaging, is still popular in Europe. The role of Minitel, the French government proprietary text-only network operated by France Telecom, is diminishing in France while Internet use is growing.[23] Wireless Internet use is increasing more rapidly in Europe than in the United States, which means U.S. marketers targeting Europeans must adapt to a variant of existing web technology and create minisites that are less text and graphics intensive.

Europeans guard their privacy more closely than Americans, their governments are more restrictive about marketing promotions. Germany bans comparative advertisements and refused to allow Lands' End's 100 percent satisfaction guarantee to be used online because it placed smaller local retailers at a competitive disadvantage. When it comes to advertising copy online, buyers in the United Kingdom expect exaggerations; Germans want specific, exact, honest promotion messages. The flippant humor enjoyed by the British offends Germans.[24] Generally, it is wise to avoid online humor.

## ASIA AND OCEANIA

Asia and Oceania are dominated by Japanese users, but China will overtake the area because of the enormous Chinese population. Current estimates of numbers of Chinese online are misleading since many Chinese share the cost of Internet connections, and public Internet cafés are popular logon points. China has the largest population in the region and world, along with great obstacles to successfully targeting its buyers. It is already the second-largest market of at-home Internet users. Credit card use is low, and Chinese online B2B is more productive currently than B2C. The government promotes wireless access because of the lack of telephone lines and the high cost of installing them, particularly in the interior. Only parts of this vast country are Internet ready, and relatively few of its people can afford to purchase products online. However, China has a young, highly educated urban population that is relatively affluent and Internet-savvy. While China is moving toward a free market economy, government control remains strong and pervasive. It is also poses high risks for copyright and patent infringement, credit card theft, spammers, and hactivists (hackers or crackers using the Internet for political protests).

Japan is a leader in the use of i-mode wireless Internet technology. Miniaturization is the hallmark of wireless handsets and other Internet-ready devices. Web sites accessed by these devices must be simple, highly focused, and thin, unencumbered by excessive file size, animation, or graphics. Japan has an almost nonexistent rate of credit card use, because Japanese consumers prefer to order online, then pick up and pay for their purchase in *conbinis*, local convenience stores like 7-Eleven that dot the country. These stores now have Internet terminals on-site for shoppers' convenience. Because Japanese consumers want to deal personally with merchants, the massive numbers of mom-and-pop convenience stores create a distribution system that is both an opportunity and an impediment to online order fulfillment. Japanese culture is very different from the United States. Even eBay, whose Internet marketing model has been successfully exported to other parts of the world, failed to make revenue projections in Japan and was forced to withdraw from the market in early 2002. The company entered the market late, after Yahoo! auctions, and was unprepared for the strong preference Japanese buyers have for new, not used products.[25]

South Korea has an Internet usage rate of over 45 percent and along with Australia and New Zealand, is a high ecommerce growth area. All three have educated, literate consumers who are already purchasing online.[26] Australia and New Zealand are appealing English-speaking targets. However, they are far from the United States, and high shipping costs for tangible goods can escalate prices beyond what local consumers are willing to pay.

## OTHER REGIONS

Other markets contain some surprising pockets of Internet activity. Tiny Estonia, population around one and a half million, has 28 percent of its population online, and 90 percent of its public sector workers use computers. Although the country undoubtedly benefits from being adjacent to high-tech, highly wired Scandinavia countries, Internet use is encouraged by its government. The Estonian Parliament has passed a proposal to guarantee Internet access to every citizen.[27]

In Eastern Europe, Hungary has invested heavily in high-tech education and has a growing Internet usage rate. Russian Internet use is rising rapidly and is fifteenth in the world in the number of users; it was up fivefold in just two years. Russians use the Internet extensively in school and at work.

India has a population of more than one billion people, and some experts predict it will overtake China as the world's population leader within the next twenty years. It has an educated workforce with many English speakers and growing multinational investment. Its rapidly expanding information technology (IT) sector played a critical role in debugging code for Y2K. At the same time the country still endures regular power shortages and overwhelming government red tape. While urbanites are rushing online, vast stretches of the country are LIRAs.

### ✔ CONCEPT CHECK

1. What European countries are attractive Internet markets?
2. Canada and Mexico are top offline U.S. trading partners. Are they top trading partners online?
3. What makes China a good online marketing target? What makes it high risk?

# International Issues

The complexity, cost, and risks of going international should give pause to Internet marketers considering it. At the same time, international opportunities and profit potential should motivate them to seriously consider doing so. This section examines some key issues that should concern current and prospective international Internet marketers.

## LANGUAGE

Before the turn of the century, English was the Internet default language, with as many as 96 percent of all web sites written in English, despite it being the first language of only 6 percent of the world's population. The year 2000 marked a turning point when non-English-speaking Internet users for the first time outnumbered native English speakers. This is just the beginning of the proportional decline in the number of English-speaking Internet users and dominance of English-only web pages. Although English speakers still represent the largest single online language bloc, they are only 40.2 percent of the total world online population; non-English speakers combined were 59.8 percent of the online population in 2002. By 2003, it is expected that the majority of web page content will be in Chinese.[28]

Currently, Europeans are the second largest bloc of Internet users. Over 75 percent speak a second language, and English is spoken by 90 percent of multilingual Europeans. Even so, the importance of using local target market languages is emphasized by a Forrester Research report stating that visitors stay twice as long on sites written in their native language and adapted to their culture. Nine in ten non-English speakers prefer their own language on web sites even when English is their second language.[29]

Grouping by the same language may be intuitively appealing, but important variations exist even within what is seemingly the same language. Differences between American, British, Australian, South African, and other forms of English are well documented and include spelling (color or colour), meaning (car trunk or boot), and pronunciation, which could become a significant problem when voice recognition software becomes widely available. At the same time, English clearly is still the predominant business language worldwide, and using it on a web site is a relatively rational choice unless a site is targeted to a group for whom English is clearly not appropriate.

Putting an American spin on English can be detrimental. American slang and obviously U.S.-centric English should be avoided on offshore targeted web sites, as many international users are sensitive to perceived U.S. Internet dominance and the heavy-handed export of American culture. Nonetheless, the use of American English to describe technical specifications is preferred in non-English-speaking countries because it is authoritative and represents expert judgments.

Because British and American English are much more similar than English and European languages, Britain is often the first step for Internet marketers aiming toward the European market. This was a strategy used by eBay and Amazon that targeted London first, then Germany. Although Britain may be the path of least linguistic resistance, it is not necessarily the best approach to the continent given the considerable differences between marketing to the British and continentals.[30] After January 1, 2002, currency became one significant difference between England and other EU countries that adopted the euro as their common legal tender.

Spain and the U.S. Hispanic population are attractive target markets for Latin American web marketers. The U.S. Spanish-speaking Hispanic population has high credit card use and more buying power than other Spanish-speaking markets. It is unclear if U.S. Spanish-speakers will be drawn to Latin American sites unless the sites offer comparative prices, good service, and something these buyers cannot find on U.S. sites.[31]

Although almost any language can be written on a web page, Latin-based alphabets cause fewer browser errors because they require *single bytes* to represent a character. A byte is a unit of data composed of eight binary (0 or 1) digits. Cyrillic, Arabic, Chinese, Japanese, and Korean are *double-byte* languages that take two bytes to create each character. English-based browsers calibrated to read single bytes need software converters to read double-byte characters. As a result, single-byte browsers accessing double-byte languages often show question marks rather than decipherable characters. For example, Microsoft's Internet Explorer browser returns "????? ???? ?? ?? ??? ??? ?? ????" from the Korean web site of Lexmark, a popular U.S. company, not Korean language characters.[32] Conversion software is getting better at making the adjustment. U.S. web marketers targeting Chinese, Japanese, and Korean markets will benefit from voice recognition software, expected to become widely available around 2010. In the meantime, targeting double-byte-language countries and regions poses special problems and costs. Even if browsers are converted to read double-byte characters, back-end software may not be adaptable, which jeopardizes online order taking and being able to respond to information requests.

Some web marketers make a considerable effort to *lingualize* their sites offering translations in one or more other languages. The Salt Lake 2002 Winter Olympic Games (*http://www.saltlake2002.com*) offered one translation (bilingual) in French while the 2000 Summer Olympic Games in Sydney, Australia (*http://www.gamesinfo.com.au/default.asp*), offered translations in twelve languages (multilingual), several in double-byte characters. The archived Sydney Olympics site also offers a chart (*http://www.gamesinfo.com.au/mi/MIBR.html*) that helps visitors determine if their browser can display Arabic, Simple Chinese, Japanese, Korean, and Cyrillic characters. By contrast, 63 percent of Fortune 100 U.S. web sites are still English only.[33]

Canadian bilingualism extends to some but not all Canadian web sites. The Constitution of Canada recognizes English and French as the country's official languages with equality of status and equal rights and privileges in all institutions of the Parliament and government. All government sites are bilingual; for example, the Government of Canada site (*http://canada.gc.ca*) has both English and French mirror versions. The Province of Quebec has more stringent bilingual requirements enforced through the Office de la langue Française. French is the dominant language in the Province, where 81.9 percent of Quebecers speak it at home. Militant Francophones want French to

## Single- and Double-Byte Web Sites

Single-byte U.S. (Western) browsers accessing double-byte languages often show question marks or a series of boxes rather than readable characters unless they have special translating software installed.
*Copyright © by Houghton Mifflin Company. Reprinted with permission.*
*http://college.hmco.com/students/index.html.*

*Translation by http://babel.altavista.com/tr.*

be the dominant language of all web sites housed in Quebec. Thus, the Quebec Tourist Guide (*http://www.quebecweb.com*) is in French, although some English is available. Many Quebec web sites are in French, with no English translation.[34]

Language is the most obvious difference between domestic home-country and international markets. Translating pages and whole sites into other languages can help make offshore customers feel welcome, but the cost of translation can be high. It is not necessary to translate everything and marketers are well advised to streamline and edit before translating. Generally, the fewer words, the lower the cost. Size is also an issue in markets where wireless is popular. Small screens, often no larger than two inches square, discourage reading large amounts of text. Large text files are also a problem for markets where average download times are slow, particularly 28.8 bps. The cost of translating email is far less, as little as fifteen to eighteen U.S. cents per word, which is an incentive to marketers seeking a low-cost method for promoting online offers internationally via wireless.[35]

Translation takes place on multiple levels. It can be as superficial as translating one page for offshore visitors or as deep as offering a fully translated mirror site localized to each served market. To be effective, translation should include content text as well as frequently asked questions (FAQs), feedback forms, product specifications, privacy statements, security warnings, shopping cart instructions, contact information, and the like. It also requires registering with popular local search engines in target markets using local language keyword descriptors for metatags. In most cases, easily misunderstood colloquialisms, slang, buzzwords, and idioms must be avoided unless they have been adopted locally.

Web marketers lingualize using translation software, a linguistic translator, or native speaker, or by hiring a multilingual content management firm. These alternatives are costly and will be incomplete if they ignore cultural differences.

Another important aspect of language should be kept in mind and that is language as a product. Asians spend an estimated US$20 to $30 billion each year on English lessons. For many Asians, instruction via the Internet is much cheaper than private instruction or face-to-face classes. Most English elearning sites are 24/7/365 operations with human instructors available to interact with students as needed. This requires streaming audio and video technologies that are found in many Asian businesses but not homes.[36] Online English instruction represents a profitable marketing opportunity for U.S. universities.

## CULTURE

**Online culture**

An extension of offline culture; includes the look and feel of a web site, acceptable colors, measures, and even how much text or animation is acceptable on a page.

Culture is composed of behaviors, customs, beliefs, coping mechanisms, art, rituals, customs, language, and other factors that characterize a group of people and delineate it from other groups. **Online culture** is an extension of offline culture and includes the look and feel of a web site, acceptable colors, measurements and standards, use of body parts, politics, humor, history, children, animals, flags, women, acronyms, abbreviations, and even how much text or animation is acceptable on a web page. It also influences responses to email marketing, online promotions, and pricing strategies. Sites can be *culturally neutral*, avoiding cultural nuances and attempting to appeal to cultural universals; *culturally local*, targeting locals with specific cultural nuances; or *culturally U.S.-centric*, U.S. culture biased.

Businesses that target online international audiences yet ignore cultural differences risk offending international buyers. For example, in the United States and Western European countries, dogs are pets, often regarded as family members. In France, dogs can sit at the table with their masters in fine restaurants. Their images on web pages convey warm, friendly messages in these cultures. Putting a dog picture or icon on a web site targeted to Asia conveys a distinctly different impression, however, since in some parts of Asia dogs are food for humans.

Black is a popular background color commonly found on U.S. web sites, where it is regarded as a sophisticated web color, conveying a sense of style, mystery, or high fashion. But black is a sinister or unlucky color in Asia, Europe, and Latin America, and its use on a web site communicates a far different message than intended. Red is a good luck color in parts of China, yet overdoing red in web design can be insulting to the target audience if it is interpreted as patronizing. Red should not be used in on-screen text targeted to China as it is negatively associated with the Chinese Cultural Revolution, while black, white, and green are unlucky. Lucky colors in India are yellow, red, and green; white and black are unlucky. Germans, on the other hand, prefer cool colors, blues and grays with red accents.[37] Blue is the most culturally acceptable web color internationally.

Numbers likewise have different meanings. For example, web marketers targeting North America, Australia, and much of Western Europe should avoid the number thirteen, which is perceived as unlucky, as is 666. Japan's Nippon Airlines does not use seats numbered four, nine, or thirteen. Four has the same pronunciation as the Japanese word for death; nine sounds like agony or torture. Four is also unlucky in China because it is similar to the word for death; eight is lucky because it sounds like the word for wealth or riches.[38]

Answering email requests for information from internationals requires understanding how people expect to be addressed. Whereas Americans tend to be informal, often using first names, to reply to an email using a first name in Asia is insulting and incorrect. The use of family names and courtesy titles requires reformatting order boxes and other HTML forms created for Western-style names. In China, it is difficult or impossible to distinguish between male and female names, and married names may not be used. A married woman may use Madam or Mrs. with her maiden name.[39] This seriously complicates email marketing and personalization efforts, unless they are directed by local native speakers who understand local cultural nuances.

Measurements and numbers vary between markets. A woman's size nine medium shoe in the United States is a size 7.5 in the United Kingdom, a 41 in Europe, an 8.5 in Australia, and a 30 in Japan. Currencies vary, but online currency converters are easily linked to a web page, and major international credit card companies make conversions for charges to their cards. Dates and time are not reported consistently. What is the date 01/12/02? Is it the twelfth of January 2002 or the first of December 2002? It all depends on who is reading the date. In the United States, it is read as January; in other parts of the world, it is December. The ISO 8601:1988 International Date Format is year-month-day, so the January date would be written 2002-01-12. However, most web sites ignore this format and use the local one. In Mandarin Chinese, the same date is

二零零一年一月十二号[40]

Picturing body parts online is taboo in many markets. Naked foot bottoms are unacceptable screen images for Belgians. A pointing finger, a frequently used web icon, should not be used on sites targeted to Portugal because a finger is commonly used to beckon a prostitute. Women's arms, legs, or other body parts should be avoided on web pages targeted to Muslim countries.[41]

**Culturalization**
Localizing a web site to conform to cultural standards and preferences in targeted markets.

A fully internationalized web site requires **culturalization,** localizing the site to conform to cultural standards in the targeted markets. It is a costly process to create a localized site, maintain, and update it. Internet marketers that localize in several countries risk incurring costs that can rapidly drain cash reserves. This happened to the original Boo.com (*http://www.boo.com*) fashion apparel site that attempted to localize sites in fourteen countries simultaneously, burned through its cash reserves, and ended up declaring bankruptcy.[42]

Grouping by culture is a tricky business. French culture in Montreal, Canada, is quite different from French culture in Paris, France, or former French colonies in Africa. That is why so many web marketers still use countries as the level at which localization decisions are made and language as the first localization task.

## GOVERNMENTS

Although the Internet is described as borderless, it is inextricably bound to countries and their governments, legal systems, and regulatory controls. Any Internet marketer doing business internationally must be aware of the changing legal environment in each market targeted (see Chapter 5). This is an area where legal outsourcing, that is, engaging local legal experts to advise on marketing decisions, and constant monitoring are necessary. Ignorance of the law in international markets is not defensible and can be a costly mistake.

Governments administer local export laws, tariffs (taxes), and customs standards and set documentation requirements. Express delivery and freight forwarding companies can help marketers deal with these matters in the majority of the world's markets. Tangible goods exporters in particular need expert assistance and should consider outsourcing. Specialized software vendors can help by providing documentation and regulatory information for most markets.

Governments can prohibit the sale and distribution of certain products within their borders and sometimes try to do so in other countries. Consider the Yahoo! case in France (see Chapter 5), where a U.S. site was told by the French government that it had to install filtering software on its California, U.S. site to prevent French citizens from participating in online auctions of Nazi memorabilia. Germany also has similar lawsuits pending.[43] As mentioned earlier, German courts stopped Lands' End from offering its standard 100 percent satisfaction guarantee because it was ruled an unfair competitive advantage over small German retailers that could not afford to make a comparable offer. Lands' End had no choice but to remove the guarantee from its German site.

Governments can prohibit their nationals from doing business with other countries. The U.S. government enforces embargoes and sanctions that restrict or prohibit trade with such countries as Cuba, North Korea, Libya, Sudan, and Syria. These bans extend to online sales. Other areas in which government actions should be monitored include the following.

**PRIVACY** European Union (EU) privacy standards are far more rigorous than in the United States. U.S. marketers routinely collect personal consumer data electronically (see Chapter 7), share it with other companies, and use it to personalize online advertisements and offers, and for email permission marketing. The EU's 1998 Directive on Privacy Protection requires that everyone, regardless of nationality, doing business online or offline in the fifteen-member EU countries comply with the EU's strict privacy regulations or be prohibited from collecting and transferring data about EU buyers. The EU law requires anyone processing such data to permit consumers to see, change, and/or delete data about themselves.

In effect, the EU is attempting to extraterritorially force EU privacy restrictions on other countries, including the United States, mandating that other countries adhere to EU privacy laws in their own markets. This means a European consumer making a purchase on a U.S.-hosted web site is protected by the EU directive and theoretically, the U.S.-based host is liable in European courts for invasion of that consumer's privacy.

Some U.S. businesses have protection under voluntary *safe harbor* provisions; many do not. Safe harbor provisions, which were negotiated between the U.S. government and the EU, are agreements that allow U.S. businesses to self-regulate and declare they are abiding by the EU standards, thereby receiving protection from prosecution or litigation in Europe. By early 2002, around forty U.S. businesses had agreed to the terms, Microsoft (*http://www.microsoft.com*) among them. Alternately, a company can be approved by the TRUSTe EU Safe Harbor Web Privacy Program (*http://www.truste.com/programs/pub_harbor.html*). The EU directive sets a dangerous precedent of imposing Internet laws on other countries. It is not alone, as Canada and Argentina have passed similar laws.[44]

Encryption is another privacy concern. Encryption software secures data transfers, particularly shopping basket transactions. The Chinese government demands that all online businesses targeting China reveal what encryption software they are using so the government can monitor their sites. This has serious implications for privacy on the sites and hints at intellectual and property piracy risks.

**REGULATION**  While U.S. businesses fear government overregulation, Europeans are concerned about underregulation. Europe has a much greater level of government intervention than the United States, which sets the stage for conflict between the two. European countries are far more restrictive about promotions; for example, many will not allow advertising to children. Small businesses are aggressively protected from pricing, distribution, and product advantages enjoyed by large businesses. The EU has a Telecommunications Anti-spamming Act that permits email marketing as long as it is clearly identified as marketing material and companies get the recipient's permission to send it prior to doing so. This is an almost impossible requirement and one that could be devastating to email marketing if enforced.

The Chinese government also closely monitors and regulates business. It bans most online advertising and what is allowed must be licensed by the State Administration of Industry and Commerce (SAIC).[45] Although China promises great opportunities, it has a highly regulated, volatile, risky business environment.

**TAXATION**  The U.S. government gave Internet commercialization a boost by delaying taxes, which is a much more hands-off approach than that taken by the EU or other areas. Taxing authority is a government function, and many are collecting taxes on online purchases, including the value-added tax (VAT). Tariffs continue to impede cross-border trade. The sale of steel negotiated online through B2B exchanges can be taxed many times and in many countries.[46]

**CENSORSHIP**  The Chinese government monitors its citizens online and has been accused of launching cyberattacks against Falun Gong sites in Canada. Burma and North Korea are keeping Internet technology from their citizens. Censorship exists online more in Asia than other places. Singapore has been selective in blocking access to certain web sites. China uses the Internet to exert control, monitoring its citizens in chat rooms and on web sites, as well as using the Web to spread propaganda and denounce political activists. China blocks some Western periodicals and frequently will not let its citizens read *Time* or the *New York Times* online.[47] In its English chat room, Sohu.com, the leading Internet communication company in China whose investors include Intel, Dow Jones, IDG, Morningside, and Goldman Sachs, lists nine things prohibited by Chinese law. It warns visitors, "If you are a Chinese national and willingly choose to break these laws, SOHU.com is legally obliged to report you to the Public Security Bureau."

**FRAUD**  Get-rich-quick schemes are popping up everywhere. Internet con artists know no boundaries and because of the magnitude of the problem, an unprecedented international partnership was organized to sweep the Internet and gather information on sixteen hundred suspected sites. *GetRichQuick.com*, the popular name of the project, was conducted the week of February 28, 2000. It involved law enforcement officials in twenty-eight countries on five continents. This type of collaborative effort holds promise for reassuring buyers about the safety of being online. It targeted work-at-home schemes, illegal lotteries, pyramid schemes, and the like.[48]

## OTHER FACTORS

A number of additional international marketing factors are of concern, including the actions of direct and indirect competitors, both domestic and international. Their market offers and marketing actions, including copyright, patent, and web piracy activities, should be monitored. The Internet facilitates legal competitive intelligence gathering (see Chapter 7). Monitoring the competitive environment also can help identify future partners as smaller businesses join forces to share localization costs.

Buying behaviors change, and monitoring them can be a demanding undertaking. As Internet demographics shift and become more international, it will become even more important, and more challenging, to track the effects. Data on buyer behavior can be collected onsite or purchased from syndicated research businesses (see Chapter 7).

The United States is not adopting mobile commerce as rapidly as the Japanese and many Western Europeans. However, 3G technology and later generations will make m-commerce more attractive. As this happens, online U.S. marketers will have to create a new generation of web sites designed to accommodate wireless. This will happen in Europe more rapidly than in the United States, which is still heavily PC-oriented. However, as more attractive wireless devices are introduced, wireless penetration will accelerate.

✔ **CONCEPT CHECK**

1. Why should Internet marketers monitor what government is doing in served markets?
2. What is the *safe harbor* agreement and how does it protect U.S. Internet marketers?
3. Why is it important to monitor online competitors and technology changes?

# *Summary*

### *International Orientation*

Internet marketers differ in their international orientation. Some are highly active in marketing to international buyers; others are not and confine their Internet marketing to solely domestic home-country markets. International Internet marketing is not appropriate for all businesses. However, once they go online all businesses are exposed to the international environment. Many factors determine international orientation. Stages of international orientation range from solely domestic to global. Any Internet marketer considering going international should carefully weigh the risks, costs, and potential benefits. Exclusionary and inclusionary strategies are both evident online.

### *Selecting International Markets*

International Internet markets are selected in several ways. Some are the result of serendipity, a chance international order that stimulates interest in going international. Many businesses target their current offline international customers so their market selection decision is fairly clear-cut. Economic factors influence selection decisions. Far more Internet marketing is happening in upper-middle- and high-income countries than in low- and lower-middle-income countries. Even the lowest-income countries have email and some Internet activity, particularly in banking and tourism. Internet readiness is another grouping method that provides useful information for market selection decisions. Some Internet activity is happening even in the least-Internet-ready areas of the world.

### *The International Internet Population*

Although the United States will continue to have the greatest number of Internet users for the near future, its share will drop as Internet use penetrates more populous areas of the world. Regions of the world of most interest to Internet marketers are the Americas, Europe, and Asia-Oceania. The U.S. and Canadian markets dominate the Americas, although Internet use is accelerating in Mexico and Brazil. The European market is dominated by Western and Northern Europe, particularly the United Kingdom, Germany, France, Italy, and the Scandinavian countries. The Asia-Oceania region is dominated by Internet use in Japan and South Korea. China's Internet use is accelerating. Other areas of growing Internet use are India and Eastern Europe.

### *International Issues*

Language and culture are key issues that must be addressed by Internet marketers targeting international markets. English is no longer the default web language. Grouping markets by the same language is not as effective as it sounds. Single-byte languages are read by most browsers; far fewer can read double-byte languages. Language is the most obvious difference between domestic and international markets. Online culture is an extension of offline culture and another important influence on international Internet marketing. Cultural factors include colors, measurements and standards, use of body parts, humor, history, children, animals, flags and symbols, and other factors that define a society. Governments are a powerful influence on Internet marketers. Differences in privacy standards are becoming a contentious issue, particularly between the European Union and other countries. Other issues are regulations, taxation, censorship, and fraud. Direct and indirect competitors can affect marketing effectiveness. Buyer behaviors and changes in technology are additional issues that concern international Internet marketers.

# Internet Marketing Application

What services can an international shipping company provide an Internet marketer considering going international? Compare the international services offered by any two of the following companies. Based on your evaluations, which company should a small Internet marketer like Alex select for international shipping and customs clearance? Why?

- DHL Worldwide Express at *http://www.dhl-usa.com/ index*
- FedEx at *http://www.fedex.com*
- UPS at *http://www.ups.com*
- USPS at *http://usps.com*

### Do they . . .

Have a site search engine?

Offer customs clearance?

Use third-party vendors so shipments change hands?

Have express service for nondutiable shipments?

Have package tracking from anywhere on the WWW?

List area telephone country codes?

Link to a currency converter?

Have a shipment rate calculator?

Have cultural tips for doing business abroad?

State the number of countries served?

Have localized sites in key international markets?

Make it easy for small Internet businesses to find useful information on the site?

# Chapter Review Questions

1. What activities might a small international Internet marketer outsource?
2. Is it international marketing when a U.S. citizen in San Diego makes a purchase from a Mexican web storefront? Explain.
3. What types of businesses will probably always use their web sites for solely domestic marketing?
4. Explain the concept of Internet readiness groups. How can this information be useful to an Internet marketer considering internationalizing?
5. Is language really an issue for *all* Internet marketers?
6. Why is grouping by language similarity appealing yet risky?
7. Why is the U.S. Hispanic population attracting the attention of Latin American Internet marketers?
8. Explain the difference between single- and double-byte languages.
9. What are some compelling reasons not to use a black background on an international web site?

10. Are all Latin American countries equally good target markets?
11. Why should low credit card use in international markets be a problem to international Internet marketers in the United States?
12. Contrast local and glocal strategies.

13. What type of international Internet marketing strategy is Coca-Cola using?
14. Would U.S. online buyers benefit from EU-style privacy regulations?
15. What serious problems are associated with targeting China?

# Case Study

## Yahoo! Everywhere

Yahoo! began as an information directory, evolved into an Internet portal, and is now a communications, commerce, and media company. Its sites are drawing audiences worldwide and Yahoo! is the number one search directory in one hundred countries. It is the number three top visited site in France, number four in Germany, three in the United Kingdom, and one in Japan. The Santa Clara, California, U.S.-based company hosts sites in over twenty countries using the same marketing model, offering a free service and generating revenue mostly from advertising. It had over 210 million unique visitors in September 2001, up from 166 million at the same time in 2000, and served more than three thousand advertisers in Q3 2001, including 1,673 international clients. Yahoo! has learned through market research that word of mouth is one of the primary reasons people go to the site.

Yahoo! localizes its sites linguistically, although its basic search design is standardized as is the technology used on the sites. The company recently began its first television advertising campaign in China designed to raise consumer awareness and break into the competitive local market. Yahoo! China joins Yahoo! Hong Kong, Yahoo! South Korea, and Yahoo! Japan in spreading the brand across Asia. Worldwide, Yahoo! claims 145 million registered users. It reaches 42 percent of all U.S. wired households daily and is considered the top Internet brand in the world.

Yahoo!'s challenge in Asia is to inform consumers about its services, including email, shopping, auctions, community building, online file storage, and of course, Internet directory search. Yahoo! founder Jerry Yang promotes localization as the way for the brand to be accepted in Asia. It is essential to understand what the local audience wants, then provide it. Yahoo! has made some important strategic alliances, including a barter agreement with Pepsi-Cola, Co., where Pepsi put the portal's logo on 1.5 billion soda cans and Yahoo! promoted Pepsi's loyalty program. This program had consumers collect points from bottle caps, then purchase prizes from a cobranded Pepsi-Yahoo! web site. Three million consumers signed onto the site and registered to win. In the process, they surrendered detailed information about themselves that Pepsi used to refine its online promotion effort.[49]

### CHECK IT OUT

Company press releases are a source of valuable information. Yahoo!'s press releases (*http://docs.yahoo.com/info/pr/releases.html*) provide a window into the company's activities, its goals, accomplishments, and relationships with other companies. Check out Yahoo! by reading some of the company's recent releases. What companies are Yahoo!'s joint venture partners? What marketing programs are they initiating? What sponsors are undertaking marketing programs with Yahoo!? Is Yahoo! still the *Number One Global Destination*? Is Yahoo! cobranding? If so, with what brand? Is Yahoo! a global brand? What is the role of Yahoo!'s chief global marketing director?

## A GLOBAL PERSPECTIVE

Coca-Cola's strategy is clearly glocal. If a strategy is glocal, local adaptations will be obvious on home pages in key target markets. If it is global, sites will be standardized in their colors, content, interactivity, and features.

Print a screen shot of Yahoo!'s U.S. home page (*http://www.yahoo.com*), preferably in color, and compare it with screen shot prints of any three other country sites but not sites in double-byte language countries like China. The list of country sites is at the bottom of the front page. Select ten points of comparison on the U.S. home page that are key indicators of Yahoo!'s design, content, interactivity, or features. For example, a design element is blue print on a white background. A content element is listing search categories like *Arts & Humanities*. An interactivity element is a search box. A feature is *Personalize My Yahoo!* Based on this comparison, what is Yahoo!'s strategy—glocal, global, or something in between?

# Module II

# *Information for Competitive Marketing Advantage*

Information is the fuel of the new economy. It plays a key role in developing and maintaining a sustainable competitive marketing advantage. Collecting, evaluating, and applying information faster and better than the competition can be the defining edge in today's marketplace and the means for successfully managing customer relationships. The Internet's unique reach, speed, and interactivity make continuous data gathering feasible. At the same time, the massive collection of consumer data through marketing research and operational data tools is heightening the debate over the erosion of privacy online and scaring some buyers away from ever going online.

Data, the building blocks of the information age, are discrete numbers, text, images, and symbols that represent identities, actions, and preferences. Sophisticated software collects, compiles, organizes, and refines data to extract information that humans convert into knowledge. Marketing knowledge of customers and prospects, competitors, industries, and the environment improves decisions and, ultimately, profitability.

Marketing research and operational data tools are the subjects of Module II. Surveys, conjoint analysis, focus groups, brainstorming, consumer panels, and secondary research are all being conducted online via the Web and email with methods adapted from traditional offline marketing research. Online marketing research has gained acceptance within professional research communities as studies report high levels of validity, reliability, and projectability. Professional validation of Internet marketing research along with its lower costs, greater reach, and faster response times are compelling reasons why more marketing research activity will shift online in the near future.

Operation data tools are the companion side of the information equation. These tools compile data into databases and warehouses, facilitate data analysis and mining, allow marketing intelligence gathering and web profiling, and collect even more data from behavioral tracking devices like cookies and bugs. They are even more controversial than marketing research because they collect far more data and are operational 24/7/365.

# *Internet Marketing Research*

## LEARNING OBJECTIVES

- To learn what applied Internet marketing research can do for online marketers
- To explain what primary marketing research methods are used online
- To understand why the Internet is called a marketing research secondary source *gold mine*
- To identify issues that should concern Internet marketing researchers

## Chandra Needs To Know

Chandra is the marketing director for a hundred-year-old company that manufactures power, distribution, and instrument transformers. The company is known industrywide for reliable customer service, excellent engineering support, and superior product quality. For more than a decade, it held a steady market share. Sales in the past two years, however, have been on a slow decline despite a rise in transformer demand. Chandra has to find out why sales are falling, then develop strategies to reverse the trend. She has already determined the magnitude of her company's sales decline compared with its direct competitors, whose sales are not falling. She has evaluated their web sites and found they are far more interactive than her company's stale information-only site with its online version of the company's hard-copy product catalog. All their competitors are members of web B2B electric exchanges like ElectricNet (*http://www.electricnet.com*) or Enporion (*http://www.enporion.com*) and offer customers secure online product ordering. Chandra suspects that

these factors by themselves may explain what is happening to her company's sales, but she must present hard data or her boss will not be convinced. He barely uses his computer, is skeptical that Internet marketing can do anything for the company, and has refused Chandra's repeated requests for support to upgrade the company's web site and make it interactive. Chandra decides the best approach is to survey the company's existing customers by email to solicit their opinions about how the company can better serve them. She writes a brief survey, then randomly selects 10 percent of the company's customers to pretest it. Survey questions are refined using comments from the pretest results. The next Monday morning Chandra emails the final version of the survey to the remaining customers and by Thursday has a 65 percent return. She analyzes the results and one week after the survey was mailed out, meets with her boss to present her report. Chandra's use of the Internet and web email greatly shortened the time required to create, administer, and complete a marketing survey and increased the survey return rate.

Chandra is a marketing professional with some expertise and experience in survey research. Otherwise, she might have hired a consultant to construct, administer, and evaluate the survey for her. Marketing research is not Chandra's primary professional responsibility. It *is* the primary responsibility of other professionals who conduct marketing research online for their own or client's businesses on a full-time basis. Marketing researchers and others use the Internet to administer marketing surveys and conduct focus groups, interviews, experiments, and observations, as well as to collect secondary research. **Internet marketing research** is marketing research conducted on and/or about the Internet, the World Wide Web, or other Internet sectors.

**Internet marketing research**
Marketing research conducted on and/or about the Internet or any of its sectors.

The importance of research to the marketing profession began emerging after World War II, when the expanding postwar consumer market created a need for a more substantive understanding of buyers, competitors, and the marketplace. Marketing researchers developed new methods to apply the research process to areas of marketing interest and attempted to create predictive models. The development of personal computers and software for the more rapid and complex analysis of data propelled marketing research in new directions. Now the Internet is providing an inviting environment for conducting marketing research on a grand scale while realizing great benefits associated with its unique characteristics. At the same time, marketers are also beginning to use new operational data tools that track individual online behaviors and mine vast databases for relationships that can refine and extend marketing offers. Marketing research (Chapter 7) and operational data tools (Chapter 8) make important contributions to marketing knowledge and are directly applicable to solving contemporary marketing problems.

# *Research Basics*

**Marketing research**
Research conducted to solve marketing problems or expand marketing knowledge.

**Marketing research** is the systematic and objectively planned collection and analysis of data that are transformed into information communicated to decision makers for use in solving marketing problems, answering marketing questions, and writing effective marketing plans. Research *describes, predicts*, and *prescribes*. *Descriptive* research identifies and portrays a product, buyers, competitors, behavioral intentions, market situations, or related factors. *Predictive* research assesses and forecasts trends, demand, actions, or events. *Prescriptive* research recommends a course of action.

## APPLIED RESEARCH

Most marketing research is *applied research* dealing directly with contemporary marketing problems experienced by enterprises, as opposed to *basic research* that expands the boundaries of marketing knowledge. Applied marketing research is designed to better understand the interactions of the marketing mix variables: the 4Ps of product, price, place (distribution), and promotion, or buyers (consumers and enterprises), competitors, product markets, or the marketing environment. The focus varies and may include industries, company groups, markets, single firms, or brands. Large consumer companies like Procter & Gamble (P&G at *http://www.pg.com*) spend up to hundreds of millions of dollars each year on marketing research aimed at better understanding consumer preferences, purchase intentions, responses to promotions, and how buyers use P&G products. Small and midsize businesses spend far less on marketing research, and many spend nothing at all.

A considerable amount of research is directed at what is happening on the Internet and the Web. For example, marketing researchers recently examined the current Internet situation in Poland and found that 83 percent of businesses have Internet access, 13 percent sell products online, and 12 percent purchase online. Their study predicted that 81 percent of Polish businesses will have web sites by 2002, up from 56 percent in 2001, and prescribed the need to promote the benefits of Internet marketing among businesses there.[1] In another study, research firms surveyed Internet users online to describe their interest in electronic books. About two-thirds of those surveyed had heard of digital books, almost 50 percent were interested, and only 3 percent were very likely to purchase, indicating a product ahead of its time.[2]

Results from both these studies are immediately applicable. In the Polish study, local business groups might schedule workshops for their members with local ISPs and Internet marketers who can share their Internet knowledge and experiences. In the second study, online publishers might use these results and initiate promotion campaigns targeting the 50 percent of consumers interested in digital books, raising their awareness and pushing them toward trial by offering discounts and special offers for the purchase of these products.

Procter & Gamble has been conducting marketing research online since 1998 and is a strong advocate for using the Internet for marketing research. It conducts over 40 percent of its six thousand product tests and other marketing research activities on the Internet, and that number is growing. The company spends around US$140 million annually on marketing research and hopes to cut that amount in half by shifting more of its research online, a clear indication of cost savings online, as well as other benefits including time savings and expanded subject pools.

Whitestrips is an example of P&G's online marketing research. P&G initiated a highly successful online test market in August 2000 for a new product, Crest Whitestrips, for home tooth whitening. The product's retail price was set at US$44, and consumer acceptance was questionable. Rather than test market the product in the traditional way offline, which is very expensive and time-consuming, P&G marketing researchers went online, offering the strips only at P&G's Whitestrips.com (*http://www.whitestrips.com*) web site. Supporting television and print advertising from August to May 2000 drove traffic to the web site. Customers who requested a product sample from the web site and gave permission to receive product updates by email were recontacted regularly. In the eight-month test market period, P&G sold 144,000 whitening kits from the web site. It recorded a 12 percent conversion rate of site visitors making an online purchase. Confident of the product and its price, Whitestrips were introduced to stores in May 2000 and by late July recorded sales of nearly US$50 million.[3]

A significant amount of Internet marketing research concerns online advertising because of its importance to accomplishing marketing goals, the size of advertising expenditures, visibility of advertising messages, and its susceptibility to criticism. Online advertising currently is a very small part of the total US$7.9 billion advertising market (2001), which is expected to grow to US$18.8 billion by 2005. However, it is an important part that will become more so as Internet commercialization expands and the need for online advertising intensifies.

Internet advertising research takes many forms. It is used to examine trends in the advertising market, report on increases or decreases in advertising spending, develop usage rates for particular advertising forms, or prepare agency report cards. Other studies focus on such topics as the following:

- Advertising effectiveness—how well advertisements accomplish goals set for them
- Click through rates—percentage of visitors viewing an interactive advertisement and clicking on it to reach the advertiser's home page
- Conversion rates—percentage of viewers who make a purchase and convert from viewers to buyers
- Returns on advertiser's investment (ROI)—benefit advertiser receives from the advertisement(s) compared with the advertising investment
- Consumer opinions about advertising—consumer opinions, beliefs, likes, and dislikes about advertising and effectiveness in raising their awareness, interest, and/or intention to purchase as a result of encountering Internet advertising
- How consumers feel about obtrusive pop-up or pop-under advertisements, or floating ads—consumer response to more intrusive, interactive advertisements
- Whether or not consumers use ad-cutting software—if consumers use software that blocks Internet advertisements[4]

Branding is another popular online marketing research topic. As more traditional retailers set up shop online, marketing research is used to study if dominant offline brands are successfully driving traffic to their online web storefronts and how consumers respond to branded web sites. Other research investigates the effect online advertising has on brand building. Contrary to popular opinion, results indicate that online banner advertisements are building and maintaining brands. Recent research reveals that while branded sites are effective at delivering the information consumers want, they waste money when they offer services and frills that consumers do not want.[5]

## RESEARCH METHODS

Why conduct marketing research? Good research collects data that can provide valuable information for better marketing decisions, including personalizing product offers to individual consumers and buyer groups. Results can be used for many purposes, including to

- segment online target markets,
- develop effective Internet marketing communications campaigns,
- expose opportunities and risks,
- forecast trends,
- test market new products,
- set benchmarks for achieving revenue goals,
- obtain feedback on marketing campaigns,
- track competitors' online offers,
- measure marketing plan progress, and
- design products more effectively.

Good research sometimes delivers results that decision makers ignore, which can have serious repercussions. Bad research poorly conceived, executed, and evaluated produces seriously flawed information that compromises decision making and misleads decision makers. In other cases, marketing research is not feasible because of cost, people, time, or methods constraints. Even if research is not used, marketers can

**Primary research**
Original research designed to answer a specific marketing question or solve a particular marketing problem.

**Qualitative primary research**
Original research using in-depth methods such as focus groups, brainstorming, and interviews that require relatively small numbers of participants (subjects, respondents).

**Quantitative primary research**
Original research that is empirical and generates projectable numerical data, sometimes called hard data.

**Secondary research**
Research conducted among existing in-house or external research reported by others; collects *secondary data*.

still gain useful information through careful, continuous, systematic observations of web site visitors, customers, competitors' web sites and product offers, and the market, along with building an in-depth knowledge of their own product category and online competitive strategies.

**Primary research** is original research designed to answer a specific marketing question or solve a marketing problem (figure 7-1). It requires the collection of *primary (original) data* that directly relate to the question or problem and uses qualitative or quantitative methods. **Qualitative primary research** produces *qualitative data* from participants' opinions, behavioral intentions, and beliefs. Popular methods include focus groups, brainstorming, interviews, and chat analysis. It is often labeled exploratory research because it is frequently performed to explore an array of issues or area of interest to identify aspects that can be studied with quantitative methods. Because it uncovers subjective opinions and beliefs, qualitative data are sometimes called *soft data*. **Quantitative primary research** is empirical and generates projectable (generalizable to a population) numerical data, sometimes called *hard data*. Surveys (questionnaires), experiments, and observations are popular quantitative research methods.

**Secondary research** utilizes published qualitative or quantitative studies conducted by others, or reports and data generated in-house for other purposes. If it compares the results of large numbers of secondary studies, it is called metaresearch. Secondary research usually is less expensive than primary research, but sometimes is not totally applicable because it was originally designed for other purposes, samples, or times. Secondary research collects *secondary data*.

Researchers sometimes use multiple methods in the same study. Multiple methods increase costs, but frequently produce more substantive, well-rounded results that provide an internal check on the methods used. For example, to find out why web site visitors are abandoning their shopping basket orders before completing the transaction, researchers can use (1) a *pop-up survey* administered to every nth site visitor to

**Figure 7-1  Marketing Research Methods**

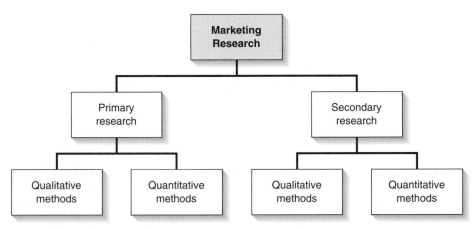

Internet marketers use a variety of marketing research methods online and offline.

the site's home page, (2) *click stream analysis* (an ope
at what point most consumers abandon their baske
every *n*th person who abandons a shopping basket t
take to get them to complete their purchase. Result
converge and clearly identify problems whose sol
rates and increase web site sales.

Marketing research is conducted online by
nesses, governments, universities, private nonpic
nongovernmental organizations (NGOs). Some enterprise
search by hiring consultants or research firms to perform the resea
ers do it in-house. Research is conducted on a regular basis or episodically as in
to solve a particular problem or cope with an emerging marketing crisis or challenge.

**Consumer Insight**
An in-depth understanding of consumers.

Consumer marketing research should contribute to the development of **consumer insight,** an in-depth understanding of what consumers need and want, their product preferences and perceptions, past market behaviors, and possible future actions. Likewise, B2B marketers use research to develop insights about business buyers and markets. One obvious difference between research on consumer and business buyers lies in the numbers, since there are far more consumers than businesses. Whereas an online consumer survey may require a thousand or more respondents (subjects) to satisfy research standards, a business survey may involve several hundred or less. The online consumer research industry is far more visible than its business equivalent, which is more likely to produce proprietary results that are rarely if ever published. Many research consultants and companies have both consumer and enterprise clients while others focus entirely on one client type.

## THE RESEARCH PROCESS

Online and offline applied marketing research require the same careful, systematic process (figure 7-2). The first step *(a),* clearly stating the problem or question, is often the most difficult. For Chandra in the chapter opening vignette, the problem involves an unexpected decline in sales. She will use marketing research to find an answer to the questions *Why are our customers ordering less than last year? What can we do to increase sales?* Based on her professional knowledge and observations, she can offer an educated guess. Systematic, objective research is still needed to develop an explanation that can be substantiated and used with confidence in making decisions about how to do a better job satisfying consumer needs and increasing sales.

Once the problem is stated clearly and concisely to everyone's satisfaction, a plan *(b)* is developed for answering the research question(s). The plan is a blueprint for how the research will be conducted. It states *who* is responsible, *when* it takes place, *what*

**Figure 7-2  The Research Process**

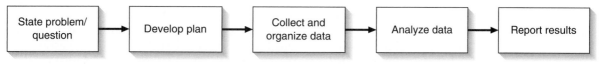

Marketing research is a systematic process.

methods will be used, *how* the data will be collected, *how much* is budgeted, *what timetable* will be followed, and *who* (departments, individuals) will receive the results. The plan directs data collection *(c)*. The Internet has made data collection far easier, faster, and cheaper than offline methods. Data can be collected online in real time through pop-up web surveys or web focus groups, with results input directly into data sets that can be grouped and analyzed electronically. The development of highly sophisticated operational Internet data tools (Chapter 8) has created rich new data sources and complex data mining methods. Data are analyzed *(d)* and transformed into usable information. Information is evaluated and transformed into knowledge for generating a report *(e)* that states the problem, addresses the research question, presents information, and provides recommendations. At this point, it is up to decision makers, marketing managers and others, to take the recommendations and implement appropriate responses. High-quality research produces results that can be used with confidence; poor-quality research is rarely worth the effort.

## ADVANTAGES AND DISADVANTAGES

Advantages of conducting online marketing research relate to sample size, speed, convenience, cost, and technology. The Internet's unique structure means researchers can dramatically increase sample sizes cheaply and quickly. Text-only email surveys can reach all online customers of a small business, if customer email addresses are known. They can also access hundreds of thousands or even millions of consumer members of research panels. Samples of these magnitudes wash out extreme deviations from the norm. Researchers use the Internet to recontact respondents, something that is exorbitantly expensive offline. Multiple contacts can verify responses and form the basis for longitudinal (long-term) studies that retest the same people or others like them repeatedly over long periods of time.

Speed is a significant online research advantage. Surveys can be emailed anytime, received almost immediately, and replied to within minutes. It is not uncommon to have results available within less than twenty-four hours. Convenience is another advantage. Focus group members can participate from home, work, or public facilities like airport or hotel cyperports, or by wireless Internet connections. They do not have to travel to a physical focus group venue. Costs are reduced if venues do not have to be provided or travel reimbursed.

Technology is also an advantage. Web surveys can be tabulated continuously as respondents submit them. Web and email survey returns are faster and response rates are higher than traditional offline methods. Focus group responses can immediately enter databases mechanically, which reduces data entry error, and can be analyzed by sophisticated software. The Internet's electronic reach means that consumers worldwide can participate in research activities while traditional methods are far more place-bound.

Online research also has drawbacks. One obvious drawback is that online samples typically are not representative of the general population. However, this is changing as online and offline populations become almost mirror images of each other. Another disadvantage is cost, since online and offline focus groups are both expensive. While travel and venue costs disappear online, technology costs must be added. Email surveys often require the rental of email address lists and a list broker or permission marketing company to distribute the surveys and collect returns. Email surveys may be confused with spam and trashed. Networks can go offline or software can freeze, which can prematurely terminate online sessions. Online focus group participants or survey respondents may get bored with all the typing required or the stress of keeping up with a typed conversation and *walk away* by clicking off the site. It is far easier to leave an online focus group than walk out of the room where a focus group is taking place. Online anonymity may encourage participants to take on personas and make responses that are dishonest or misleading. Even with these disadvantages, online marketing research is a growth industry, where the benefits outweigh the costs for most marketing research in most situations.

## ✔ CONCEPT CHECK

1. Why is *applied* marketing research so important to Internet marketers?
2. Describe the research process.
3. What are some advantages and disadvantages of online marketing research?

# *Primary Marketing Research*

Marketing is an information-intensive process. Marketers regularly gather information to monitor what is happening to their product offers, customers, competitors, and the environment. They conduct primary research using qualitative and/or quantitative methods.

## QUALITATIVE METHODS

Qualitative methods, particularly focus groups, brainstorming, interviews, and chat analysis, help marketers learn in-depth what consumers think, their perceptions of product offers, their reactions to proposed new products or changes in existing offers, and their responses to competitors' offers. Most popular traditional qualitative marketing research methods have been adapted for Internet use. Other methods are being developed for it.

**Focus groups**

Qualitative marketing research that uses small numbers of subjects for directed discussions of a marketing topic; also known online as cyber groups, egoups, virtual groups, or focus chats.

**ONLINE FOCUS GROUPS** **Focus groups** are the most popular primary qualitative research method. Online they are also called cyber groups, egroups, virtual groups, or focus chats. The first online groups in 1994 used chat room technology. A small number of consumers, usually seven to fourteen, assembled online and chatted about marketing topics in real time with one another and a moderator. Responses were typed and appeared onscreen identified by the contributor's name or alias. Text-only focus groups are still used, but focus group technology has advanced and now may include text, sound, and images. Images are pushed to participants' browser screens by the focus group moderator.

Focus groups are used for every imaginable topic, from how participants store a product to what they do/do not like about banner advertising or a competitor's web site, a new product concept, or product pricing alternatives. It is very risky to rely on only one focus group because the results represent subjective opinions from a small number of people. Results from multiple groups provide a better perspective, but it is still a small sample only representative of the Internet-using population at that time.

Online focus group participants are recruited through email announcements and pop-up online intercepts and are selected from prescreened pools of volunteers who usually are given small incentives for participating. Volunteers complete online registration forms and provide demographic (age, marital status, household income, education), lifestyle (products used, hobbies, vacation preferences), and transaction (product preferences, brand preferences, purchase situation) information. The largest online marketing research companies maintain large pools of prescreened subjects from which they draw focus group participants. The NPD Group, Inc. (*http://www.npd.com*) has online panels with over 2.7 million members. Greenfield Online (*http://www.greenfield.com*) can access 1.2 million panelists. Subjects are selected for a group because they share characteristics relevant to the topic being researched such as age, gender, purchasing habits, attitudes, lifestyles, or product usage. Even though participants are screened, results can still be skewed because the individuals are volunteers and drawn from a pool that excludes anyone not online

Focus group members log on from their homes, work, or other locations and go directly to a web site secured from unwanted visitors. They are given a valid password to enter the firewall-protected chat room. Once logged into the virtual facility, they see either a screen that is an online chat discussion board for text-only focus groups (see the screen shot below) or a screen that is split for text and video. Split screens display product pictures, product concept drawings, print or video advertisements, or even animated 3-D images. The other half screen is where the typed discussion occurs. Group sessions typically last 60 to 120 minutes and cover thirty to forty-five prepared questions. A trained moderator directs the discussion, begins new threads, and maintains the focus. The moderator elicits comments about what consumers think of a client's products or web storefront, their attitudes toward new product concepts or marketing promotions, or how they perceive the client's product offer compared with its competitors. One clear advantage of online focus groups is that researchers can *talk* to the moderator at any time to interject questions or change direction. This cannot be done in traditional offline focus groups.

Traditional offline focus groups follow the same directed discussion format, with some differences. Participants in offline focus groups must travel to a selected facility. Sessions are held in comfortable surroundings where participants sit around a large conference table or relax in a living room setting. Refreshments are served. The focus group organizer provides product samples, when appropriate. An observation room (back room or viewing room) is connected to the facility by a one-way mirror so clients can observe the session in real time. Sessions are videotaped and/or tape recorded. Several focus group sessions can easily cost US$100,000 or more.

A recent study by the Qualitative Research Consultants Association (QRCA) concluded that many companies are al-

**Online Focus Groups**

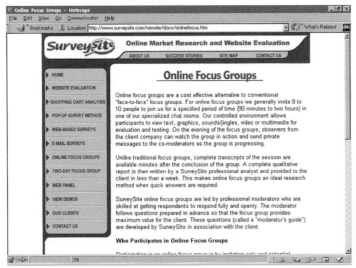

SurveySite hosts focus groups for many different types of clients. *Source:* Reprinted by permission of SurveySite Market Research. *http://www.surveysite.com/newsite/docs/onlinefocus.html.*

ready using online focus groups, and their numbers are growing. QRCA researchers compiled a list of online advantages that include the following:

- A more widespread market for obtaining subjects regardless of geographic location
- Greater access to difficult-to-reach groups (gays and lesbians, college students, mothers with babies, and others)
- Anonymity, which encourages more candid, honest responses
- Less grandstanding by participants trying to dominate sessions
- Greater cost-effectiveness from the elimination of travel and facility rentals
- Faster reporting of results, with clients receiving full transcripts of a session almost immediately after it ends

Some disadvantages of online focus groups are the lack of nonverbal communication cues (body language and other visual and auditory responses), shallowness of responses, difficulty in following the discussion with subjects talking (typing) over one another, lack of representativeness since Internet access is not universal, and the flip side of anonymity as it can breed dishonesty. A person whose real identity is not known may feel no reservation about inventing one and giving dishonest responses.[6] Live video cameras (cams) will eventually allow observation of nonverbal communication, overcoming this problem, and voice commands will eventually replace typing. As the Internet population mirrors the offline population, nonrepresentativeness will be less of an issue. Videocams may also reduce the false identity problem, but dishonest focus group responses can never be eliminated completely online or offline. Larger numbers of participants can minimize the effects of discrepant responses.

Still other shortcomings were not mentioned in the QRCA study. With the current state of technology, whenever an online focus group is conducted, a technician must be available to resolve technical problems. Online group moderators must have both technical and moderator skills, and when they are lacking, group outcomes are likely to be flawed. Responses are typed, which excludes some disabled consumers and the typing challenged. Even people who can type reasonably well may tire if the session is too long, which can lead to premature departure from the group.

The low cost of online focus group sessions, as little as US$3,500 per session, makes them highly attractive. However, it is unlikely that online focus groups will ever completely replace offline groups, despite the cost savings and other advantages, because sometimes it is extremely important to see focus group participants' facial expressions and body language as they make comments or listen to others' comments. Some topics are better suited to either offline or online sessions, so a complementarity between on- and offline methods will continue.

**Brainstorming**
A marketing research method that uses participants to generate ideas about issues or problems.

**ONLINE BRAINSTORMING** Brainstorming, ideation, or idea generation encourages participants to share opinions and generate creative responses to issues or problems. This technique was developed in the 1930s by Alex Osborn, long before the discovery or commercialization of the Internet.[7] Online brainstorming uses the same technique as its offline equivalent but allows more time for the development of ideas over several hours, days, weeks, and sometimes months. Participants are invited to join a brainstorming session generally following the same selection process used for focus groups. Participants are given a password that admits them to a private firewall-protected web site. A trained facilitator begins a discussion thread to focus participant ideas and postings. For example, the facilitator might type *Describe the perfect home entertainment center, one that suits your every home entertainment need.* Participants begin typing their ideas as rapidly as they can. They are identified by self-selected nicknames. For example, Big Momma types *It's got to be big enough for a really, really big TV.* Billy Boy types *It takes up a wall in my family room, floor to ceiling.* Daddy O types *It has a special shelf to store movies so you can see the title on the end of the box.* Tiny types *It has an Internet connection so I can watch TV and surf the Net at the same time.*

The facilitator monitors the session and can enter the idea generation stream at any point to guide ideas or ask new questions (start a new thread). For example, the facilitator may interject *Where exactly do you store movies in your home entertainment center? How tall is the center? Where does the TV sit? Where is it in your house? How does it make you feel when you're using it? What slogan would you use in advertising the entertainment center in television and print advertisements?* Each participant adds a thought or opinion to the threads at his or her leisure. Contributions are visible to all participants and they are encouraged to build on previous ideas. Contributions can be monitored by others without participant knowledge. Responses are identified by participants' nicknames (pseudonyms), a first and last name, nickname, initials, or alias developed specifically for the brainstorming session.

Greenfield Online has an interactive real-time brainstorming system called Mind-Storm–the Online Think Tank. It is a sophisticated program that can expose participants to graphics, videos, audio, and links to competitors' web sites for competitive marketing intelligence activities, for example, to compare shopping basket or navigation systems or conduct long term acquisition studies. Marketers, advertisers, and product developers can probe consumer ideas about product usage, product positioning, and new product ideas, as well as competitor's online market offers. Mind-Storm has been used to create product slogans, advertising headlines and tag lines, catch phrases, product line extensions, and new product concepts. Participants are drawn from subsets of Greenfield's proprietary online panel of prequalified consumers or the marketer's own customers. Panel members are profiled on demographic and behavioral criteria that can be linked to their contributions to create a consumer profile type.[8]

Online brainstorming has been used to get consumers to generate ideas for new products and brand direction for a major beverage maker. More than a thousand ideas were contributed by three hundred consumers over a four- to five-day period. Their brainstorming ideas helped the company decide on product names, descriptions, and how to market the products.[9]

Online brainstorming has many of the same problems as online focus groups. The researcher is still dealing with a small group, typically numbering in the low teens, and it can be costly to run multiple sessions. The ideas may be useful, or not. Interpretation is highly subjective. Some screening is required to keep the group in line and avoid negative comments that can stop the session dead in its tracks. The facilitator must be trained to be firm in handling or even disconnecting overly raucous participants. Technical problems can derail a session and nothing stops a member from clicking out before a session ends.

**ONLINE INTERVIEWS**  The video online interview (VOI) is a fairly recent tool used by executive recruiters and for online chats with business executives. Interviews can be simultaneously broadcast (multicast) to different locations as well as taped for play-back. If bandwidth capacity is not high enough, images are warped and jerky, and sounds are distorted by a several-second delay. These problems will be resolved as bandwidth increases and video online systems improve.

Because most consumers do not have broadband, online real-time web interviews are not yet practical, but a variant technique exists. cPulse, recently acquired by Gartner-Group, Inc. (*http://www4.gartner.com*), offers a proprietary real-time online customer satisfaction interview system (cPulse Network System), which is used by such clients as Procter & Gamble, AT&T (*http://www.att.com*), Compaq (*http://www.compaq.com*), and General Electric. More than seven thousand online interviews have been conducted. For one survey, about 1 percent of a client's site visitors were asked to participate in a sixty-second interview, a short customer satisfaction questionnaire. Interview pop-up boxes were integrated visually into the client's site and participants never left the site, which maintained shopping continuity. Participants also had an opportunity to ask questions while taking the survey. This was the interview component.[10] cPulse and other similar systems use a site intercept method similar to traditional offline mall intercepts. Customers respond to various questions, typically about site security, how easy it is to locate products, and their general satisfaction shopping the site. Results are aggregated, and clients have access to report results in real time. Results provide direction for site redesigns as well as benchmarking with competitors. Since participants self-select whether or not to participate, the representativeness of the convenience sample is questionable. Because participants are shoppers intercepted in the act of shopping, a large enough sample should provide valuable consumer insights while lessening the effects of extreme comments.

**CHAT ANALYSIS**   Communication is the top activity of most consumers once they go online. Many spend considerable time in chat rooms that are active 24/7/365 addressing a myriad of topics, from Barbie dolls to religion. Some marketing researchers analyze discussions in online chat groups to identify opinion leaders and track their contributions in the expectation of spotting emerging trends. Conversations are analyzed in Usenet groups, Yahoo! chat rooms, and other forums. A considerable advantage of collecting comments in these groups is the unobtrusive nature of the research. Participants do not realize they are being observed and recorded, so the assumption is their comments will be more valuable because they are speaking freely. However, the anonymity of these forums can lead some participants to assume personas unlike their real selves and make statements that they would never make using their real names. Although these chats are public forums, performing this type of research without participants' knowledge has serious privacy and ethical implications. While marketing research companies doing chat analysis claim they do not use high-tech tracking to identify participants by their real identities, unscrupulous researchers have no reservations about doing so. Another problem is that participants self-select to be part of these discussion forums, which may make them more passionate about the subject but not necessarily more knowledgeable. They are not representative of the entire online population.

Chat room researchers seek out opinion leaders and monitor their comments because opinion leaders have a powerful influence on others. An opinion leader can sway many times more people than an ordinary discussion participant. Sophisticated mathematical models are used to identify opinion leaders by the quantity and content of their postings. Chat analysis has been used extensively in online financial discussion groups to measure consumer interest in various companies and their stocks. It has been used to analyze consumer comments about automobiles at Edmunds.com's Town Hall (*http://townhall.edmunds.com/TH/townhall*) to learn what brands consumers cross-shop and the features they most value (see the screen shot below). Conversation tracking software identifies the most relevant conversation threads and develops consumer profiles from the content.[11]

Chat analysis seemingly is an Internet marketing research method. However, when it is used to mine for data, it becomes more of an operational data tool, the focus of Chapter 8. The distinction between research method and operational data tool is clear in most cases, but blurred in others.

## QUANTITATIVE METHODS

Methods used in quantitative research include surveys, which are administered to individuals, enterprises, or consumer panels; consumer reviews; simulations; and experiments. Surveys are the most popular primary quantitative research method.

**ONLINE SURVEYS**  A **survey** (or questionnaire) is a set of questions designed to collect specific information from site visitors, buyers, businesses, institutions, or organizations. The first recorded U.S. survey was the 1790 U.S. Census. Although census surveys have been conducted every ten years since, survey research did not become popular, particularly in marketing, until after World War II.[12] The growth of the mass

**Survey**
Primary quantitative marketing research that uses a set of questions designed to collect specific information from consumers or enterprises.

**Car Advice and Auto Talk at Edmund's Town Hall**

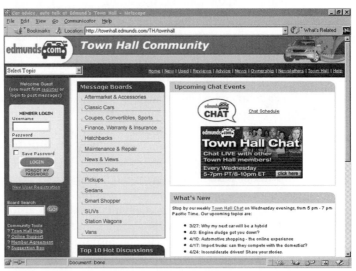

Edmund's offers car advice and a community where car enthusiasts can share experiences and information. *Source:* Copyright © 2002 Edmunds.com, Inc. Reprinted by permission. Screen shot downloaded April 8, 2002. *http://townhall. edmunds.com/TH/townhall.*

market and the need to understand consumer behavior spurred the development of more sophisticated survey forms and statistical methods to analyze results. Today surveys are ubiquitous, and consumers are hard-pressed to escape them, particularly when they unexpectedly pop up on their browser screen. Responses to survey questions can be numerical or written. Questions are closed-ended (preprogrammed responses) or open-ended (unrestrained written comments). Surveys are administered via the Internet's World Wide Web and email, which includes web mail, as well as on intranets and extranets.

Surveys are not to be confused with email feedback on a web site. Email feedback collects qualitative data from consumers who happen to visit a web site and are motivated to post comments or send email. It is difficult to compile these data or have much confidence using them because people who make comments often represent extreme views, particularly negative ones. Important information can be culled from the comments if they address web site functionality, for example, comments like *Your back navigation button isn't working* or *The link to the home page from the shopping basket page is broken.*

Online surveys take two forms, via email or on the Web (Web-centric). Electronic mail surveys are sent in an email message, which is returned to the sender also by email. Alternately, email recipients are directed to a web site where they complete the survey. Many web surveys are pop-ups that appear on the visitor's computer screen in a separate minipage. Others are embedded within a web page, and sometimes the visitor must answer the survey questions to gain access to the site. The latter type of survey, which demands information as the price of entry, is irritating and can elicit retaliatory trash answers rather than useful data.

Online standardized form surveys are constructed using HTML. They are simple to take, code, and analyze. Survey software can be programmed to intercept every *n*th site visitor to draw a random sample of a predefined population. For example, while writing this chapter I was intercepted by an online pop-up survey at weather site intellicast.com (*http://www.intellicast.com*). The survey contained two categories of questions. The first had seventeen questions relating to how the visitor used the site in planning activities or hobbies; the second (thirteen questions) asked how the visitor used the site in business applications. Each question had a five-point Likert-type scale with responses for using the site that ranged from *Never*, to *Several Times a Year*, *Several Times a Month*, *Several Times a Week*, and *Almost Daily*. The survey took less than a minute to complete and when it was submitted, a *thank you* screen popped up and stated that the survey information would be used to help Intellicast "prioritize and focus its effort on new products, content, and applications that meet your interests." Closing the survey page returned me to the weather forecast page; thus, survey respondents never leave the mother site.

**WEB UPDATE**

Online Surveys

Response rates for online surveys are higher than for other survey types, reaching as high as 60+ percent returns versus an average 5 to 15 percent for mail surveys and about 14 percent for telephone surveys.[13] The cost of administering an online survey is significantly lower than traditional surveys. Harris Interactive (*http://www. harrisinteractive.com*) reports that while a traditional telephone survey can easily cost US$300,000, an online survey costs as little as US$50,000. The U.S. Small Business Administration (*http://www.sba.gov*) estimates that small businesses can conduct telephone surveys for anywhere from US$5,000 to US$25,000.[14] An online survey costs far less. A typical mail survey costs an average US$1.56 per survey; a fax survey US$0.56, and both email and web surveys cost around US$0.01 per participant. Email and web surveys eliminate the envelopes that some consumers grew to fear during the late 2001 anthrax scare. At that time, consumers were warned to trash envelopes from senders they did not recognize. This included mail surveys.

Online surveys produce fast results. For example, Harris surveyed one thousand consumers for an advertising client and returned results in twenty-four hours, a response time almost impossible to match using traditional survey methods.[15] An online survey can be transmitted to participants in real time, almost instantaneously when using an existing email distribution list. Mail surveys by comparison may take a month or more to send the initial surveys, collect the first wave of returns, send out reminder postcards (or a second mailing), then wait for the second wave of returns. With email surveys, reminders are sent easily and quickly. Online surveys are flexible and can be modified for different population subsets. Survey data can be entered automatically into a database without input errors, and computations are continuously updated.

Experience has shown that online product-specific survey results are more trustworthy than opinion surveys, which can attract participants with radical views. Although there were initial concerns about reliability and validity, recent research indicates offline and online are comparable.

It is estimated that by 2003, 50 percent or more of all marketing surveys administered will be conducted online. Despite this enthusiasm, some cautions are advised. The hardware and software can be costly, at least initially. Since online surveys are self-administered, confusion over instructions can result in incomplete or inaccurate data collection. Because many web surveys use convenience samples, self-selection bias can skew results. Participants must be online, which eliminates those who are not; therefore, results can be generalized only to current online populations. Consumers often break off from overlong surveys. Multiple surveys can be taken by the same person unless stringent admission controls are in place.

Web surveys must be designed without graphically intense formats that slow download times and discourage respondents from completing them. Surveys that require linking to multiple pages should be avoided as they can frustrate respondents using slow modem connections. To ensure privacy, a *clear form* or *reset* button should remove input data after the completed survey is sent. Encryption should be used for the secure transmission of responses. Surveys sent using Netscape browser are encrypted using Hypertext Transfer Protocol over Secure Socket Layer (HTTPS). Surveys returned using Netscape will also be encrypted by HTTPS.

Like offline surveys, there is the question of whether or not to offer incentives. Some surveys offer respondents money, prizes, tee shirts, or other small incentives to participate. It is unclear if consumers who participate in online surveys without incentives differ from those who participate only if incentives are offered.

SRI Consulting (*http://future.sri.com/VALS/presurvey.shtml*) has been collecting Values and Lifestyles Survey (VALS) data online since the mid-1990s and offline since 1978, when the first VALS survey was introduced. VALS2, released in 1989, is the model for online VALS. VALS data are used to identify adult consumer target markets, position products, match consumer types with media preferences, and develop marketing strategies and new products. Adult participants are typed by their resources (demographics) and lifestyles (psychographics) into mutually exclusive groups that provide insight into factors that motivate purchases. Participants self-select to take the VALS online survey. Their only reward is learning their VALS type—actualizer, fulfilled, achiever, experiencer, believer, striver, maker, or struggler. Meanwhile, SRI is collecting an enormous amount of data on online consumers that is highly attractive to consumer product marketers.

Survey results are also sold by commercial research firms. Syndicated online research is jointly sponsored by businesses in the same industry with similar research interests. Multisponsored research shares the cost of what is often a highly expensive activity. The level of analysis typically is industrywide. Although participants share the data, reports are tailored to the specific needs of each sponsor. Maritz, Inc. (*http://www.maritz.com*), Forrester Research (*http://www.forrester.com*), and Jupiter Media Metric (*http://www.jmm.com*), a division of comScore Networks, perform syndicated research.

**ONLINE PANELS** Online panels, or epanels, take several forms. Sometimes panels are called group interviews or even focus groups, but this is misleading. Many online panels use surveys to generate reviews; thus, an online panel is a quantitative research method. However, panels may also use other methods to collect consumer opinions, including monitoring chat room and online discussions, and asking visitors to post open-ended opinions to research questions, which are qualitative methods. Online panels are something of a hybrid quantitative method, but they are considered here because their principal research method is the survey.

Most online panels are opt-in. Individuals are recruited by email, intercepted when they visit a web site, or click through from a pop-up advertisement. Most panels use a *convenience sample*, selecting participants because they are available. Some research firms maintain large pools of willing prescreened participants, often hundreds of thousands or even millions of consumers. Because demographic and behavioral information is collected for these panel members, a *purposive sample* can be drawn. A purposive sample is a group with characteristics that are found in the population being studied. For example, a panel may require that participants be housewives, twenty-five to forty-five years old, college educated, with two children living at home. A different panel might require college students, males and females, eighteen to twenty-two years old, not living in a dormitory or with parents. Companies with large numbers of panel members can select a stratified random sample of panelists from their member pools. Only consumers with characteristics appropriate to the research topic are allowed to complete the surveys. For example, Greenfield's Health & Wellness panel of more than forty thousand members is used to survey consumers with chronic illnesses in forty-four different medical conditions that require specific medications. A stratified random sample of these preidentified sufferers can be quickly recruited to participate in marketing studies for pharmaceutical companies, health care groups, or wellness organizations.

America Online, Inc. (*http://www.aol.com*) hosts its own online survey and marketing research area through the DMS OpinionPlace (*http://www.opinionplace.com*). AOL members can sign up to take surveys and earn frequent flyer miles for purchasing electronics, books, software, and videos. Surveys last five to twenty-five minutes, and longer surveys earn more miles. Participants are assigned to surveys if their demographic, lifestyle, and/or purchase history match the profile needed. AOL has more than 34 million subscribers in addition to 3 million CompuServe members, 120 million ICQ users, and over 48 million registered Netscape users.

**ONLINE REVIEWS** Online reviews, a far less rigorous, nonscientific variant of the panel, can offer insights into what consumers are thinking and doing. Consumers self-select to provide written opinions of products using a variety of responses. They can be as simple as a yes/no response to the question *Would you recommend this product to others?* Responses can be in the form of stars, from five or more stars (*****), an exceptional rating, to a zero or no stars. Alternately, reviews can be extended written summaries of product use. Comments are often aggregated, analyzed, and results sent to client companies. Representative comments are posted on the host web site. Epinions (*http://www.Epinions.com*) has collected over one million consumer reviews of over two million products in more than thirty product categories, from books and movies to cellular telephones and ski resorts. It provides both monetary and non-monetary incentives for consumers if their reviews are read by site visitors.

ConsumerReview (*http://www.consumerreview.com*) is a metasite for communities of consumers that share *passionate product interests* (company description). These interests include mountain biking, gardening, music, PC games, and photography. In addition to providing product reviews, participants can join site-sponsored chat rooms and use message boards. It is not clear whether or not the chat rooms and message boards are monitored as part of the process of collecting consumer opinions. Having near-experts offer their product opinions is obviously valuable to businesses. However, like all review sites, it can be risky trying to apply results from an analysis of subjective opinions provided in an anonymous setting. These groups may attract extreme views and not reflect the greater majority of product users who tend to remain silent.

My Gómez (*http://www.mygomez.com/indexCom.asp*) uses panels to obtain consumer ratings and reviews for six thousand companies in seventy-five industries. It posts industry specific advice about which online storefronts are best sites. Gómez Proprietary Internet Scorecards are a unique tool for measuring consumer responses. Scorecards have 120 criteria points that panel members use to evaluate sites and product quality. Points on a scale of zero to ten are awarded for ease of use, customer confidence, on-site resources, and relationship services. Gómez emphasizes consumer education and claims to be "the online quality measurement firm for consumers and e-businesses."[16] Although scorecards with criteria points are an attempt to quantify opinions, unless raters are trained to have the same scoring criteria, one person's ten can easily be another's six. Interrater reliability is a problem when untrained raters are used. However, if reviewer numbers are large enough, outliers (extreme responses) should be washed out.

**CONJOINT ANALYSIS** In conjoint or tradeoff analysis, subjects are exposed to a situation where they have to make choices, trading off factors to reach a desired end. This method can help determine what people value in different product features or service attributes. It is often used in automobile feature testing to find the features consumers are willing to give up in order to get something they value more, perhaps forgoing a car compact disc player for side panel air bags. Outcomes help guide new product design or old product redesign or repositioning decisions. Conjoint analysis is used in the travel industry to determine how much consumers are willing to pay for a ticket in order to get more leg room on an airplane. It is used in pharmaceuticals to determine if consumers prefer aspirin or acetaminophen, gel caps or uncoated tablets, for pain relief or to reduce inflammation.

Sample sizes for online conjoint analysis studies can be relatively small, from two hundred to three hundred participants. ConjointOnline (*http://www.conjointonline.com*), a unit of Kingsley Research, Inc., has been conducting online conjoint analysis interviews since 1992. Online conjoint analysis matches midlevel career changers to job types. Like other online primary research methods, these methods claim to be better, faster, and cheaper than their offline equivalents.

Lands' End (*http://www.landsend.com*) uses conjoint analysis in its *My Personal Shopper* feature (see the screen shot below). Consumers call up the web page and are immediately asked to create their own personal profile of apparel preferences. The Personal Shopper database uses this information to make decisions about what apparel choices should be pushed to the consumer's browser screen. The first question asked is about *size*, regular or tall; next is *occasion*, work or leisure. The next screen begins the tradeoff by asking the consumer to select options. Two alternative apparel choices, A and B, are shown on the screen. The consumer selects one from among a choice set by selecting one of the following alternatives:

- I like A, I would not wear B
- I like A somewhat more than B
- No preference
- I like B somewhat more than A
- I like B, I would not wear A

The next screen shows a different pair of outfits for A and B, with the same choice sets. After progressing through six choice screens, the consumer is asked to select from among sets of *Special Considerations*. These include types of fabric preferred, colors, and styling. Finally, the *Personal Shopper*, pushes some suggestions to the consumer's screen. Of course, *My Personal Shopper* is not a real person. It is a sophisticated software program that trades off the consumer's choices to arrive at optimal product alternatives. Data collected from large numbers of conjoint choices can be used in product development and promotion.

**Conjoint Analysis at Lands' End**

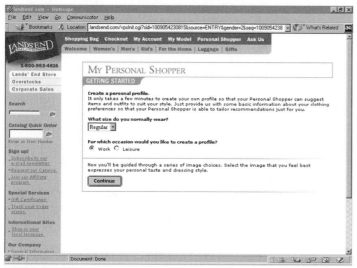

Lands' End's *Personal Shopper* uses conjoint analysis to help a consumer make apparel choices. *Source:* Copyright © Lands' End, Inc. Used with permission. *http://www.landsend.com/vpsInit.cgi?sid=1009054230815&source= ENTRY&gender=2&seq=1009054238.*

**SIMULATIONS** Simulations are another primary quantitative method. They are used in sales tests where participants simulate product trial and use, and as alternatives to test marketing new products, which is very expensive, time-consuming, and alerts the competition to new offers. Most people are familiar with simulations from video or online games like *Combat Flight Simulator 2*. As in other interactive game simulations, sound effects, graphics, and an adjustable realistic setting mirror, to an extent, the reality of an actual air battle. Many undergraduates have used strategic marketing simulations Industrat, MARKSTRAT3, BRANDS, or Compete in class.

e-SIM Ltd. (*http://www.esim.com*), an Israeli company, has been offering virtual product simulations and virtual learning online since 1990. Simulation technology is used in product development, online manuals, and training. Online simulations are not widely used yet because of the complexity of simulation systems and high bandwidth requirements.

## ✔ CONCEPT CHECK

1. Why are qualitative research results more challenging to analyze than quantitative results?
2. Explain the difference between an offline and an online focus group.
3. Why is survey research such a popular online marketing research method?

# *Secondary Marketing Research*

The Internet makes so much secondary data available that it is a virtual gold mine of information for marketing research. At the same time, there is far too much information for most people to sort through, so it is a challenge to find what is needed. Small and midsize businesses can perform secondary research online, although paying someone else to do it (i.e., outsourcing) is a frequently used option. Since most secondary research involves previously published studies, care must be taken to avoid copyright infringement.

### SECONDARY RESEARCH BASICS

Secondary research uses internal information as well as external research published by others, public data sources, and various directories, rankings, and periodicals. It can save time and money, but it can also be unusable if the research is old, inaccurate, at the wrong level of analysis, or uses a different subject group than what is needed. Secondary research results often provide direction for the development of primary research.

The research process is the same for both primary and secondary research. Once the problem is identified and the research question posed, a plan is developed to obtain data from secondary sources. This plan is explicit in identifying types of information to gather and sources, as well as who will perform the research, the amount budgeted for it, time frames, and who evaluates the results, writes a report, and receives it.

Whether secondary research is conducted by one person in a small business, a marketing professional with research expertise, a marketing research department in a corporation, or an outsourced marketing research consultant or company, anyone conducting online secondary research must carefully check sources. Appendix B on the textbook web site considers source accuracy at length, so only a few cautions will be offered here. With any data downloaded from the Web, it is a challenge to determine reliability and value, and whether or not the information can be used with confidence. Anyone can publish almost anything on the Web with relatively little effort. Currently, there are no standards or fact editors, so evaluating information reliability is essential to avoid drawing bad conclusions from bad information. The Web is information rich, yet not all web-based information is worth having or using.

The quantity of information online also presents a problem. There is a vast and growing information glut with several billion unique publicly accessible web pages and an estimated over five billion pages in the invisible or **deep Web**. Even the best search engine can access less than 1 percent of the accessible pages. Deep web sites are inaccessible to most search engines and the general public, many are on intranets or extranets. Some deep web sites use technology that search engines cannot penetrate while others are blocked because a subscription or registration is required to access protected pages.[17] Quality and quantity issues force many companies to turn to professional data librarians, whose efforts still must be guided by a marketing research plan.

**Deep Web**
Invisible or deep web sites inaccessible to most search engines.

## SECONDARY METHODS

Secondary research results are available in a variety of forms. They are published in academic journals; released by governments, universities, foundations, or think tanks; archived by professional associations; or disseminated by organizations. Traditionally, a researcher identifies useful secondary sources, contacts the sources or accesses them in an online library or other facility, and evaluates the contents for applicability to the research problem. This is a *pull* method that is also popular online. The online researcher goes directly to the secondary source because the source's address is bookmarked or the source is identified and linked through a search engine or other intermediary.

A second method takes advantage of the Internet's unique interactivity. For example, research companies like ActivMedia Research LLC (*http://www.ActivMediaResearch.com*), McKinsey (*http://www.mckinseyquarterly.com*), Nua (*http://www.nua.net/surveys*), and CyberAtlas (*http://cyberatlas.internet.com*) *push* opt-in emails or newsletters with announcements about current research to interested users. Pushed content is designed to motivate the receiver to click through to the web site and buy the report and/or establish a relationship with the research company that may someday result in a transaction. Most research newsletters are sent on a monthly or bi-weekly schedule.

## SECONDARY SOURCES

Despite obvious shortcomings, online secondary research can uncover studies, reports, and databases that provide valuable information for use in making marketing decisions. Marketers have a broad array of online secondary sources to use, including governments, private companies, professional groups, and organizations.

**GOVERNMENT** The U.S. government, the largest data collector in the world, hosts a vast number of web pages with free information and some that require a subscription and nominal fee. FirstGov (*http://www.firstgov.gov*), the U.S. government web portal, has links on the home page to business statistics, trade information, patents, copyrights, and government resources. It hosts gateways (portals) for citizens, businesses, and governments.

State and local governments often provide useful information from their web sites. The Library of Congress has a metaindex for state and local government information (*http://www.lcweb.loc.gov/global/state*) as well as state links.

The European Union's web site (*http://www.europa.eu.int*) offers news, activities, and official documents. The United Kingdom's open.gov.uk (*http://www.open.gov.uk*) is a portal to all its government sites and "The easy way to government information and services online." It promises citizens that they will be able to do all their business with government online by 2005. Parliament Online (*http://www.publications.parliament.uk*) has news of the chambers of the British Parliament. The Australian government portal (*http://www.fed.gov.au*) is a massive site with links to all aspects of Australian business and society, and Australian Commonwealth government information. Industry Canada's Strategis business and consumer site (*http://strategis.ic.gc.ca*) was launched in 1996 by the federal government. It offers interactive applications, including filing a patent application online, customizable benchmarking tools, cost calculators, and online business planning tools. All industrialized countries have government sites and most offer valuable information for marketers, although not always in English.

**ORGANIZATIONS** Most international organizations offer data and documents online as well as links to other resources. Notable among this group are the United Nations (*http://www.un.org*), Organization for Economic Cooperation and Development (*http://www.oecd.org*), World Trade Organization (*http://www.wto.org*), World Bank (*http://www.worldbank.org*), and International Monetary Fund (*http://www.imf.org*).

Other web sites provide information for public sector, nongovernmental organizations (NGOs), and nonprofit marketers. The Low Income Networking and Communications Project or Linc Project (*http://www.lincproject.org/Organizations.htm*) is a portal for organizations serving special groups and, particularly people with low-incomes in the United States and other countries. Environmental Organizations Online (EOO at *http://www.envorgs.com*) is a portal for environmental organizations and resources.

**PERIODICALS** Although some online periodicals require subscriptions, many still offer free data at the entry level of their web site. Advertising Age Dataplace (*http://www.adage.com/datacenter.cms*) is hosted by *Advertising Age*. It provides industry data including leading national and international advertisers with advertising spending estimates, a weekly report on web traffic and advertising, advertising spending by the top one hundred brands, interactive market data, and links to top research companies. *Brandweek* (*http://www.brandweek.com*) has media news, directories, and links to other marketing publications. Some information is free; access to other pages requires a paid subscription.

**EDUCATIONAL INSTITUTIONS** Many universities host data-rich research center sites. Purdue University (*http://ciber.centers.purdue.edu*) hosts a portal with links to U.S. Centers for International Business Education and Research (CIBER). The CIBER Network includes the Michigan State CIBER (*http://ciber.bus.msu.edu*), a source for international marketing news and information. Many universities store working papers online. Vanderbilt University's Owen Graduate School of Management has eLab (*http://www2000.ogsm.vanderbilt.edu*), founded in 1994 to study the marketing implications of web commercialization. It is a particularly rich site for marketers. The University of Texas hosts Advertising World (*http://advertising.utexas.edu/world*), the ultimate marketing communication directory, sponsored by a gift from Leo Burnett Worldwide (*http://www.leoburnett.com/splash.html*).

**PROFESSIONAL ASSOCIATIONS** A portal for online marketing professional associations is maintained at Tilburg University in the Netherlands (*http://marketing.kub.nl/ journal1.htm*) with both U.S. and international links. Some associations offer reports and publications; others sponsor meetings and seminars. Many have links to related marketing sites and job listings.

**BUSINESS SOURCES** Many businesses offer free information online as an incentive designed to pull visitors deeper into their site. Dun & Bradstreet (*http://www.dnb.com*) has a resource center with timely information as well as the list of D&B D-U-N-S number holders. The Wall Street Research Net (*http://www.wsrn.com/index.html*) offers market and historical data, research reports, and company data. Internet.com (*http://www.internet.com*) has Internet and IT information. Mediamark Research, Inc. (*http://www.mediamark.com*) offers demographic, lifestyle, product usage, and advertising exposure data. Arbitron (*http://www.arbitron.com*) provides radio ratings and media research information.

## ✔ CONCEPT CHECK

1. Who benefits from the secondary research push method?
2. Is the Internet a secondary source gold mine or information quagmire? Explain.
3. Why must secondary research be guided by a research plan?

# Research Issues

Internet marketing research activities are not risk free, the first issue discussed in this section. Ethics is another issue that should concern anyone involved with Internet marketing research, particularly since consumers are worried about their privacy online and some marketers have no reservation about invading it. Several methods-related concerns should be considered by marketing research professionals as well as novices. Finally, from the perspective of the Internet business considering outsourcing research, there is the question of how to go about hiring a marketing research consultant.

## RISKS

Internet marketing research outsourced to research companies or conducted in-house by marketing professionals generally is less risky than research performed by those without training, experience, or assistance. Even trained professionals make mistakes, but they are less likely to do so than people with absolutely no training or research knowledge who suddenly decide to write and administer a survey. Marketing research novices face risks involving samples, content, methods, bias, and results. If these risks are not avoided, the consequences can be research results that are worthless and potentially seriously misleading.

**SAMPLE** The risk of collecting information from the wrong consumers or customers, people who do not represent the market or have extreme views, or not collecting information from a sufficient number of people so results are skewed or collecting information from too large a sample and being overwhelmed by the quantity of responses. Marketing research conducted on samples of Internet users automatically runs the risk of being unrepresentative of the entire population because non-Internet users are excluded. Using convenience samples can be risky if they are not representative of the population being studied.

**CONTENT**    The risk of asking the wrong questions or too many questions so participants drop out or asking too few questions that do not cover the topic adequately.

**METHODS**    The risk of using an inappropriate research method or using the right method incorrectly.

**BIAS**    The risk of mishandling the data so that it is no longer reliable. Bias can be minimized by using very large, appropriate samples.

**RESULTS**    The risk of collecting a large amount of information and not being able to make sense of it, trying to analyze it statistically but using the wrong test or using the right test and misinterpreting the results, or conveying the results to the wrong decision maker.

Even with the risks, small or midsize Internet marketers may have no choice but to perform their own online research. If so, they can often obtain assistance from a local small business development center (SBDC) or the marketing department in a nearby comprehensive university. SBDCs typically have staff members who can advise about acceptable research methods. Marketing majors may be able to help develop and administer an online survey, run an online focus group or brainstorming session, evaluate complaints collected in a *suggestion box* located on the owner's web site, or conduct secondary research. Another alternative is to go online and look for research tutorials (see "Online Marketing Research Tutorials" below) or books on Internet marketing research at an online bookseller.

## ETHICS

As discussed in Chapter 5, ethics is a set of moral principles or values, principles of conduct that govern individual and group behaviors. Internet marketing research ethics refer to behaviors associated with conducting marketing research online. The principal concerns are about protecting the privacy of participants, using data responsibly and securely, complying with laws that restrict research involving children and young people, and using sound scientific methods so results can be used and reported with confidence.

Several professional research organizations are sufficiently concerned about enforcing ethical research behaviors that they have codified rules of ethical conduct for

### *Online Marketing Research Tutorials*

Many web sites offer useful information about marketing research for the nonprofessional. Listing these sites does not represent an endorsement of their services.

- Web Monkey has pages on qualitative and quantitative research methods at *http://hotwired.lycos.com/webmonkey/e-business/marketing/tutorials/tutorial4.html*
- StatPac has a free tutorial on questionnaires, survey design, and marketing research at *http://www.statpac.com/surveys*
- SurveySite offers online demonstrations of various marketing research methods at *http://www.surveysite.com*
- Quirk's Marketing Research Review includes a Glossary of Marketing at *http://www.quirks.com*

their members. The Marketing Research Association (MRA) was formed in 1954 and currently has around three thousand U.S. members. They include companies and professionals in marketing and opinion research, providers of marketing research, research users, and businesses that support marketing research activities. MRA members have developed codes of conduct that members must honor. Complaints of ethical misbehavior against members can result in censure, membership suspension, or expulsion from the organization.

## MRA Code of Data Collection Standards

MRA expects members to comply with the following data collection standards.

- Conduct research in an honest and ethical manner.
- Instill confidence in research and encourage public cooperation.
- Instill confidence in the business community that research is done in a professional and fair manner.
- Carry out every research project in accordance with the Code.
- Respect the general public.

Two MRA codes of ethics are particularly relevant, the MRA Code of Data Collection Standards (*http://www.mra-net.org/docs/industry/code_dcs.cfm*) and the Internet Ethics Guidelines (*http://www.mra-net.org/docs/industry/internet_ethics_guidelines.cfm*). Online marketing research must comply with the same standard rules and ethical principles of data collection as traditional marketing research and also with online marketing research standards (see "MRA Code of Data Collection Standards" and "MRA Internet Ethics Guidelines" on this page).

The Council of American Survey Research Organizations (CASRO at *http://www.casro.org*), founded in 1975, is the national trade association for commercial survey research firms. Over 170 companies are members and must adhere to the organization's *Code of Standards and Ethics for Survey Research*. Like MRA and ESOMAR, the World Association of Opinion and Marketing Research Professionals, CASRO requires that members respect respondent confidentiality and privacy, avoid harassment, not use unsolicited emails or subterfuge to obtain survey participants, and adhere to the Code in their dealings with survey participants and clients.

## MRA Internet Ethics Guidelines

MRA members must comply with the following ethical guidelines for conducting marketing research online.

- Respondent cooperation should be voluntary.
- Researcher's identity should be disclosed to respondents.
- Respondents' rights to anonymity should be safeguarded.
- Privacy policy statements should be posted online.
- Data security should be maintained.
- Reliability and validity of findings should be disclosed to the public.
- Researchers interviewing minors should adhere to Children's Online Privacy Protection Act.
- Unsolicited email should not be sent to those requesting not to receive any further email.

In-house researchers should adhere to the same principles even if they are not members of an association for research professionals. The small business owner sending an email customer survey should respect customer privacy, guarantee anonymity, not use the survey as a selling tool, and never survey children without the permission of their parents. Unfortunately, it is unrealistic to expect universal compliance with ethical Internet marketing research guidelines. For those who behave in an unethical manner, the burden is on offended consumers and enterprises to report such practices and file complaints with the Federal Trade Commission (FTC at *https://rn.ftc.gov/dod/wsolcq$.startup?Z_ORG_CODE=PU01*), Better Business Bureau Online (*http://*

*bbbonline.org/consumer/complaint.asp*), or TRUSTe's Watchdog (*http://truste.org/users/users_watchdog_intro.html*).

## RELIABILITY, VALIDITY, PROJECTABILITY, AND SAMPLING

Evidence is growing that Internet marketing research can be equivalent to traditional research when it is conducted rigorously and with attention to reliability, validity, sample size, and projectability. This was a serious concern when Internet marketing research was in its infancy and its methodological rigor was unproven. After countless studies, it is far less of a concern now.

**Reliability** is a measure of measurement precision. Used in survey research, it is the extent that independent, comparable measures are the same from one administration of the survey or test to the next. The extent of a method's reliability depends on how much variance is due to random, chance errors and how much is due to imprecision in the survey itself. Reliability tends to increase as more items are added to a survey or scale. This is a problem online as too many items may result in participant burnout and exit. Too few and the survey will not provide the information needed.

**Validity** is a measure of how accurately what was proposed to be measured actually was measured. A valid measure shows differences in observed scores that are true differences and nothing else. A valid measure is also reliable. A reliable measure is not necessarily valid.

Measures that are valid and reliable, assuming that the sample is properly drawn, are **projectable**. This allows marketing research results to be generalized or projected to the population under study. It relies on the assumption that the sample used in the study is representative of the universe and reliability and validity are high.

A *population* is every member of a particular group. If the subject of a marketing research study is Internet users in the United States and Canada, the population is over 180 million. Obviously, it is neither desirable nor feasible to survey all these users. Therefore, researchers select a subset of the population called a **sample**. A sample will be far smaller than the original population. Samples are estimates of the opinions or behaviors of a far larger population. Thus, to ensure that the sample is representative of the population, it is essential to be very careful in selecting it.

*Representativeness* is the key to having a sample from which inferences can be drawn about the population. The way a sample is drawn determines representativeness more than its size. However, as sample size increases, generally the margin of error decreases and the sample becomes more representative of the population. That is why samples of fewer than two thousand can be used to make predictions about the entire U.S. population of over 285 million, with a plus or minus 3 or 4 percent margin of error. While a sample of Internet users today is not representative of the entire U.S. population, as Internet users mirror the entire population more closely, an online random sample eventually will be generalizable to the entire U.S. population. When that happens, even more marketing research will move online.

*Random samples* are representative when they are drawn using equal probability of selection for all members of the target market. Most Internet samples are not random. Instead they are *convenience samples*, that is, individuals selected because they are conveniently available. The exception is random samples drawn from panel member subsets at Greenfield and other research companies. Because their panels are pre-

**Reliability**
A measure of precision of measurement used in survey research.

**Validity**
A measure of how accurately what was supposed to be measured by a survey actually was measured.

**Projectable**
If marketing research is valid, reliable, and used an appropriate sample, then results can be generalized or projected to the population under study.

**Sample**
A subset of a population under study in marketing research.

screened, a large pool of representative participants can be formed. Greenfield can select random samples for surveys from this representative pool.

*Sample size* relates to the number of responses needed to obtain repeatability. Samples that are too large inflate research expenses. Samples that are too small distort and undermine confidence in results. Some samples can be as low as several hundred people. Sample sizes of a thousand or more are often used online to provide repeatability. Since the cost of adding participants is low online, sample sizes can be larger and that increases confidence. Sample size calculators are widely available online.

## IN-HOUSE OR OUTSOURCED?

Some businesses and enterprises are large enough that they have full-time staff researchers, so marketing research is planned and implemented *in-house*. Others need to *outsource*, hiring marketing research consultants or companies that offer a limited or a full range of research services. Marketing research in the United States currently is an over US$6 to $7 billion industry involving more than two thousand firms. Online marketing research revenues grew steadily from US$3.5 million in 1996 to around US$300 million in 2000. Spending in 2001 was estimated at US$1.49 billion. By 2005, online marketing research is expected to represent 50 percent of all marketing research revenues, or about US$4 billion.[18]

Decision rules can help indicate if marketing research should be conducted and if so, by whom. Generally, Internet marketing research should be conducted when the benefits from the research are greater than the costs of conducting the research, or

$$R = BR > CR$$

Where,

$R$ = Conduct Internet marketing research

$BR$ = Benefits of doing the research

$CR$ = Costs of doing the research

The difficulty lies in trying to calculate the benefits and costs. This is one reason why a surprisingly large number of companies marketing online do not have active marketing research programs. Factors affecting the decision to perform online marketing research include the following:

**MARKET SIZE**    Typically, the larger the market size, the more likely marketing research will be conducted. Internet marketers with very small markets are far less likely to either run extensive research in-house or outsource. Small business owner/operators rarely have the money, expertise, or time to conduct marketing research. What they can do is listen carefully to customer feedback, respond quickly to customer email, and visit competitors' web sites to see what they are doing.

**COSTS**    The costs of conducting Internet marketing research will typically be greater than the benefits for businesses with very small markets and small profit margins. The cost of running an Internet survey is far less than a traditional survey; however, hiring a marketing research consultant can still be a very expensive proposition. Marketing research consultants provide estimates, which can be helpful in trying to decide if the research costs are justified.

**BENEFITS**    The greater the estimated benefits that research will deliver, the more likely marketing research will be conducted. Unfortunately, it is often extremely difficult to attempt to calculate expected benefits. This makes the benefit half of the cost/benefit equation far less precise than the cost side.

**COMPETITION**    The more competitive the market, the more likely marketing research will be needed. If competitors are performing Internet marketing research, it exerts a pressure to conform and do the same.

**CUSTOMERS**    If the business is losing customers, experiencing a high rate of shopping basket abandonment, receiving a growing number of customer complaints, experiencing a growing rate of product returns, or otherwise experiencing customer problems, marketing research is needed. It is also needed if a decision has been made to enlarge the customer base or attract new customers.

If the decision is made to outsource Internet marketing research, the next step is to hire a marketing research consultant or full-service marketing research company. Consultants and companies provide advice about doing research online or actually plan, implement, and evaluate the research. They should be hired when their expertise is needed, there is not sufficient time or resources to do the work in-house, an outside objective perspective is needed, there is disagreement in-house about the type or extent of research that is needed, or an expert is needed to give credibility to the research.

Finding the right research consultant or company can be a challenge. So many of them are available both online and offline that it is easy to become overwhelmed trying to sort out the choices. Places to start include local SBDCs, universities, local associations of marketing professionals, marketing research associations like MRA and CASRO that have online directories of their members, and referrals from other businesspeople. Marketing research suppliers are online in large numbers. Their web sites can be extremely helpful if they provide examples of the type of research performed and case studies of client work. Past clients can be useful in recommending the consultant, or not. Once a list of possible consultants or companies is compiled, each should be contacted to initiate a discussion of the following issues:

**OBJECTIVES**    The problem or question the research should answer, what should be achieved by the research

**TIME FRAME**    Deadlines for conducting and completing the research

**OUTCOMES**    Expectations for the type of information presented in the final report

**COSTS**    Itemized estimates of how much the research will cost

**RESPONSIBILITIES**    Who will do what, including provide information and access

**REFERENCES**    Obtain references for recent clients, learn about their experiences with the consultant or firm

**TERMS**    Includes deadlines for specific parts of the work, payment schedules, reporting schedules, other conditions

When a hiring decision is made, a contract typically is written specifying the terms and conditions of the research. It should be signed by those with the authority to do so. Work should be monitored. Specifications for delivery of the final report should be among the terms negotiated.

## ✔ CONCEPT CHECK

1. What are some of the risks that face Internet marketing researchers?
2. What ethical issues should concern Internet marketing researchers?
3. Explain: $R = BR > CR$.

# *Summary*

### *Research Basics*

Marketing research is the systematic, objectively planned collection and analysis of information that is communicated to decision makers for use in solving marketing problems, answering marketing questions, and writing effective marketing plans. Research *describes, predicts*, and *prescribes*. Most marketing research is *applied research* dealing directly with real-world current marketing problems, as opposed to *basic research* that expands the boundaries of marketing knowledge. Marketing research results can be used to segment target markets, develop effective marketing communications campaigns, expose opportunities and risks, forecast trends, test market products, set benchmarks, obtain feedback, track competitors, measure marketing plan progress, and market products more effectively. Primary research is original research designed to answer a specific marketing question or solve a marketing problem. Marketing research is conducted by businesses, governments, universities, private nonprofit research centers, individuals, and organizations. Some businesses outsource, that is, hire consultants or research firms to perform research for them, while others conduct research in-house. Consumer marketing research should contribute to the development of consumer insight, an in-depth understanding of what consumers need and want, their product preferences and perceptions, past market behaviors, and possible future actions. Online and offline research requires the same careful, systematic process—state the problem/question, develop a plan, collect and organize data, analyze data, and report results. The power of online marketing research is that it creates efficiencies and new opportunities. Its advantages are associated with sample size, speed, convenience, cost, and technology. Disadvantages include samples that are not generalizable to the offline population, technology costs and instability, and the ease with which respondents can break off from an online research session. Even with these disadvantages, online marketing research is a growth industry, where the benefits outweigh the costs for most research in most situations.

### *Primary Marketing Research*

Qualitative primary research produces *qualitative data* from participants' opinions, behavioral intentions, and beliefs. Popular methods include focus groups, brainstorming, interviews, and chat analysis. Quantitative primary research is empirical and generates projectable numerical data, sometimes called *hard data*. Surveys (questionnaires), experiments, and observations are popular quantitative research methods. Focus groups are the most popular primary qualitative research method. A recent study concluded that many companies are already using online focus groups, and their numbers are growing. Some disadvantages of online focus groups are the lack of nonverbal communication cues, shallowness of responses, difficulty in following the discussion with subjects typing over one another, lack of representativeness since Internet access is not universal, and the flip side of anonymity as it can breed dishonesty. Brainstorming gets consumers to share their opinions and generate creative responses. The video online interview is a fairly recent method. Some marketing researchers analyze discussions in online chat groups to identify opinion leaders and track their contributions in the expectation of spotting emerging trends. Surveys are the most popular primary quantitative research method. A survey is a set of questions designed to collect specific information from site visitors, buyers, businesses, institutions, or organizations. Online surveys take two forms, email or Web-centric. Response rates for online surveys are higher than for other survey types and produce fast results. Online panels use surveys as a research method. Online reviews, a far less rigorous, nonscientific variant of the panel, can offer insights into what consumers are thinking and doing. Consumers self-select to provide written opinions of products as simple yes/no responses about product quality or extended written summaries of product use. Simulations are another primary quantitative method.

### Secondary Marketing Research

Secondary research utilizes published qualitative or quantitative studies conducted by others, or reports and data generated in-house for other purposes. It is usually less expensive than primary research, but sometimes is not totally applicable because it was originally designed for other purposes, samples, or times. Secondary research collects *secondary data*. The Internet makes so much secondary data available that it is a virtual gold mine of information for marketing research. At the same time, there is far too much for most people to sort through, and readily finding what is needed is a challenge. Secondary research uses internal information as well as external research published by others, public data sources, and various directories, rankings, and periodicals. It can save time and money, but it can also be unfulfilling if the research is old, inaccurate, at the wrong level of analysis, or uses a different subject group than what is needed. Secondary research results often provide direction for the development of primary research. Marketers have a broad array of external secondary sources from which to choose, including governments, private companies, professional groups, and organizations.

### Research Issues

Internet marketing research outsourced to research companies or conducted in-house by marketing professionals is less risky than research performed by those without training, experience, or assistance. Risk can be related to the sample, content, methods, bias, and results. Another alternative is to go online and look for research tutorials or books on Internet marketing research at an online bookseller. The principal concerns are about protecting the privacy of participants, using data responsibly and securely, complying with laws restricting research involving children and young people, and using sound scientific methods so results can be used and reported with confidence. In-house researchers should adhere to the same principles even if they are not members of an association for research professionals. Evidence is growing that Internet marketing research can be equivalent to traditional research when it is conducted rigorously and with attention to reliability, validity, sample size, and projectability. Some businesses and enterprises are large enough that they have full-time researchers on staff. Others need to outsource, hiring marketing research consultants or companies that offer a full range of research services. Generally, Internet marketing research should be conducted when the benefits from the research are greater than the costs of conducting the research, or $R = BR > CR$.

## Internet Marketing Application

Web surveys are more visually attractive than plain-text email surveys. The survey creator has greater flexibility in arranging the questions and response fields, and using color and animation. However, if the design becomes too elaborate, it can confuse respondents and cause them to leave the survey uncompleted.

Visit several of the following sites and look at the surveys. Study but do not take or submit the surveys. Based on your observations, develop a list of *Dos* and *Don'ts* for web survey developers. Include recommendations that should make it easier for respondents to complete a survey. Consider such issues as type of questions asked, question complexity, survey length, type size, type font, colors, question and answer formats, visual design, and navigation from one page to the next. How does the SRI VALS survey compare with these surveys? What are some major differences and similarities?

- Web site evaluation survey from Perseus Development Corporation at *http://www. surveysolutions.com/prs/samplewebfeedback.htm*
- Web purchase satisfaction from Inquisite at *http://www.inquisite.com/cgi-bin/ qweb3.cgi?4HM37D*
- Web site visit from Inquisite at *http://www. inquisite.com/cgi-bin/qweb3.cgi?4HMHZA*

- A variety of sample surveys from SurveySaid Airline Passenger Survey at *http://www. surveysaid.com/survey-software/surveys/ airline.htm*
- Automotive Customer Survey at *http://www. surveysaid.com/survey-software/surveys/ auto.htm*
- Smitty's Grocery Store Survey at *http://www. surveysaid.com/survey-software/surveys/ grocery.htm*
- Web Visitor Feedback Form at *http://www. surveysaid.com/survey-software/surveys/ feedback.htm*

## *Chapter Review Questions*

1. What is Internet marketing research?
2. Why do Internet marketers need applied research?
3. Why are data collected from qualitative research sometimes called *soft data*?
4. Why do marketers need both qualitative and quantitative research?
5. Can all marketing research be performed online?
6. Describe how an online focus group is conducted.
7. If a web storefront operator wants to know how consumers like his/her web site, what type of research might be used to find answers?
8. What are some cautions marketers should exercise in using online surveys?
9. Go to SRI (*http://www.sric-bi.com/VALS/*) and take the VALS survey. What value might VALS data have for Internet marketers?

10. Should incentives be offered to consumers taking an online survey? If so, what form should they take (i.e., money, products, discount coupons for a future purchase)?
11. If a small web storefront owner cannot afford marketing research, where can he/she go for assistance?
12. What type of secondary sources are available to marketers online?
13. How might a web marketer find a marketing research consultant?
14. What types of Internet businesses are more likely to need Internet marketing research?
15. What professional research associations have ethical guidelines for their members?

## Case Study

### Greenfield Online, Inc.

Online marketing research is an important part of Internet marketing and Greenfield Online, Inc. (*http:// www.greenfield.com*) is a highly visible member of the online marketing research industry. Incorpo-

rated in 1994, Greenfield's headquarters is in Connecticut, with an office in San Francisco and regional representatives in five other cities and Mexico City. Annual revenues top US$14.9 million. Greenfield is recognized as one of the top fifty research companies in the United States. Since its inception, the company has performed more than forty-five hundred online research projects.

Greenfield has registered well over a million people who are used for online focus groups, brainstorming sessions, panels, surveys, and concept testing, and it has access to another three million plus respondents. Greenfield is a member of TRUSTe, BBB Online Reliability Program, the Advertising Research Foundation, American Marketing Association, and the Council of American Survey Research Organizations (CASRO). Recent research results reported by Greenfield indicate the breadth of its research efforts. According to the company

- Surveys find that the level of comfort with online gambling would increase if well-known casinos ran the sites.
- Airline tickets consistently rank among most purchased items on the Net.
- Net-savvy job seekers would rather search online than use newspaper help-wanted ads.
- Online teens prefer to buy at traditional stores online.
- More women than men are buying online.
- Online apparel shoppers are more concerned with price than brand.
- Online consumers rate Landsend.com tops for price.
- Internet retailing is taking traffic away from traditional bricks-and-mortar stores.
- Web surfing is a top spare-time activity of gays and lesbians; privacy is a big concern.
- The Internet is winning the price battle over catalogs and bricks-and-mortar stores.
- Over 90 percent of online seniors (≥ 55 years) have shopped online.
- Over 30 percent of college students describe themselves as "Internet dependent."[19]

### CHECK IT OUT

DougStreet.com (*http://dougstreet.com*) has a different approach to online surveys. It is a survey portal with links to sixteen survey companies that actively seek participants. Visit DougStreet.com to see the types of incentives offered survey takers. Click through to visit some of the survey companies that partner with DougStreet. Are any of the names familiar? With all the interest in getting consumers to participate in online surveys, is there a risk that some will become survey junkies? Will they make it their life's work to go from one survey company to the next completing survey after survey? How can companies control online survey junkies? Should they? Why?

### A GLOBAL PERSPECTIVE

Greenfield is a new Internet marketing research company, just over a decade old. NPD (*http://www. npdor.com/About.asp*) has been around since 1953, before the Internet was created. It is one of the ten largest marketing research companies in the United States and has offices and affiliations in thirty-three countries. In 1995 it created NPD Online and began doing market research online.

Visit the NPD Group (*http://www.npd.com*) in the United Kingdom. Click on *Global Reach* and look for the countries served by NPD Group researchers. Explore some of the *Industries and Markets* where NPD performs market research. For example, under *Footwear*, NPD Group has *Sports Tracking Europe*, which offers country-by-country market information in athletic footwear, apparel, and sports equipment purchases. Both retailers and consumers are surveyed to compile a richer market perspective. Retail tracking is for all channels, including online. Online consumer tracking is for toys, interactive entertainment, information technology, fragrances/cosmetics, consumer electronics, and food. NPD operates consumer panels in France, Germany, Italy, Spain, and the United Kingdom. It has international operations in many more countries through NPD Intelect (U.S., Canada, Mexico, Brazil) and the GfK Group (Europe, Asia, and Australia).

## CHAPTER EIGHT

# Operational Data Tools

## LEARNING OBJECTIVES

- To learn database basics and how databases benefit Internet marketing
- To understand how data warehouses and data mining are operational marketing tools
- To describe privacy-sensitive techniques used to develop consumer profiles
- To recognize the importance of the marketing intelligence process and how it is conducted online

## Morgan Cuts Cookies

Morgan has heard enough about cookies to realize they are both good and bad. Cookies are small text files that some web sites clandestinely and automatically store on a user's browser. They contain information about the user and his or her behaviors on the cookie owner's site. Whenever the user returns to the site, the web site's server retrieves information from the cookie and uses it to customize and personalize marketing offers pushed to the user's computer. Cookies also can track the user's *digital footprints,* or clickstreams, the electronic tracks left as he or she moves from page to page and web site to web site. A user's

Internet browser can be programmed to ask for permission to accept a cookie whenever a web site tries to place one. That is what Morgan's browser does with increasing frequency. Cookie placement warnings pop up on his browser screen at almost every web site he visits. Morgan decides it is time to close the cookie jar. He boots up his browser, goes to *Preferences, Receiving Files,* clicks on *Cookies,* and at the prompt directs the browser to *Never Accept* cookies in the future. He selects all the cookies in the file and deletes all but one. Out of curiosity, he opens the one remaining cookie to see what is inside. The text looks harmless enough (table 8-1). Morgan wonders if he has overreacted.

Morgan's adverse reaction to cookies and other data collection tools is shared by others. At the same time, these tools are essential to many Internet marketers seeking to better understand buyers and more effectively target market offers. This chapter examines issues related to operational data tools used in Internet marketing. Some of the same topics are also considered in later chapters as they relate specifically to online price, product, distribution, promotion, and action plans. Since these topics are more commonly associated with information technology (IT), why include them? IT focuses on the specifics of how data tools work, are managed, and can be improved. Internet marketing uses operational data tools specifically to solve marketing problems and

## Table 8-1 Inside a Cookie Viewer

Cookie Viewer

### Cookie Properties

| | |
|---|---|
| Name: | id |
| Server: | doubleclick.net |
| Path: | / |
| Value: | 8000000fghi7467 |
| Expires: | Tue, Dec 31, 2030 11:59 PM GMT |
| Secure: | No |
| Status: | Enabled |

A cookie file has a unique anonymous user number that is accessed whenever the user visits the cookie owner's web site. Cookies can ensure that the user does not see the same advertisements twice at that same site, get entered into an online contest more than once, or be counted more than once in an online survey. Cookies are used for advertising reporting, to tailor advertisements and offers, and to enhance a site for the user.

**Clickstreams**
Electronic tracks or *digital footprints* left as a visitor moves from page to page and web site to web site.

improve customer relations, emphasizing real-world marketing applications. Increasingly IT and Internet marketing professionals collaborate in applying the tools in databases and warehouses, tracking consumer web site behaviors and their digital footprints or **clickstreams,** creating and maintaining web sites, and mining data to develop predictive models. Marketing professionals with data skills are in demand, hinting at the emergence of an exciting career path. More small and midsize businesses, prime employers, are considering utilizing operational data tools that only two to three years ago were overly large, too complex, and extremely expensive. Finally, the issue of privacy is a serious concern and data tools are at the center of the debate. They are exposing consumers and enterprises to a level of privacy intrusions that previously were not possible. If self-regulation is not effective and government intervenes, Internet marketing data collection and information management practices, and the use of operational data tools, will be impacted and perhaps radically curtailed.

# *Operational Data Tools and Databases*

**Operational data tools**
Techniques and methods (databases, data warehouses, cookies, server log files, web analytics, etc.) that marketers and others use to learn more about their own online operations, their competitors, and current and prospective customers.

**Operational data tools** are computer-based techniques that marketers and others use to learn more about their own online operations, their competitors, and most critically, customers, current and prospective. Privacy advocates are incensed that marketers collect masses of data about consumers without their knowledge or consent, and do not give them the opportunity to see or edit it, or stop its collection. They are worried that new tools are being used surreptitiously to collect increasingly broader and more sensitive consumer data. They warn against letting marketers link personal, identifiable data with nonpersonal, anonymous web tracking data, as it will make online consumers more vulnerable to marketers' information advantage. They advocate making the Internet an *opt-in* environment where no data can be collected and used unless the consumer *opts in*, that is, agrees to it. This would be a radical change from the present environment that is overwhelmingly *opt-out*, where the burden is on consumers to request to be left out of data collection activities.

Concerned web users can opt out at most web sites or several designated central web locations, *if* they can find instructions and sites for doing so. They can exercise some control from their own computer by refusing to accept new cookies and purging old ones. They cannot control all the data collected about them from web sites they have visited and some they have not. Nor can they control how data are stored, manipulated, or sold. The Internet is an information-rich environment. Data collection is fast and easy; making sense of it and using it to improve marketing decisions is far more difficult, but that certainly does not deter its collection in immense quantities.

Many Internet marketers believe operational data tools are essential to achieving and maintaining an online competitive information advantage. The tools promise to help them sharpen their targeting and more effectively direct the right offer to the right customers at the right times. Superior targeting based on knowledge gained by using operational data tools increases the probability of purchase, reduces the waste of making offers to the wrong targets (or the wrong offers to the right targets), and drives down marketing costs. This can increase profitability and achieve savings for company and customers. Alternately, instead of being a solution, data tools can cause frustration, drown decision makers in masses of information they do not have the time or expertise to process effectively, and ultimately sour them on data tools in general. Some companies complain the existing technology does not target narrowly enough, failing to drill down far enough to provide the one-to-one detail that marketers need.[1]

Large amounts of data are collected anonymously and aggregated to gain a better understanding of markets as a whole, segments, or groups of consumers. Other data are customer-specific. B2B marketers are not drawing as much criticism for collecting data about their customers, suppliers, and competitors since B2B data are not personal and involve much smaller numbers. However, B2C data collection activities are widespread, invasive, and have many outspoken critics.

The entire subject of operational data tools is contentious, murky, and in a state of seemingly continuous flux. Some practitioners disagree about the tools themselves and how they should be defined and applied. Less complex tools like cookies and server log file analysis are widely used and their benefits and limitations are well known. Other tools that rely on sophisticated data warehousing and data mining are far more complex and costly, and only the largest businesses, governments, and other enterprises are likely to use them. They are more difficult to implement and their advantages and disadvantages are still emerging. At the same time, considerable effort is being directed toward developing newer and more powerful operational data tools, which adds to consumer fears.

## DATABASES

Reference was made in an earlier chapter to the local shopkeeper of a hundred or more years ago who knew what a customer wanted as soon as he or she entered his shop. From years of living in the same community and serving the same customers, he knew their names and family members, ages and genders, what they did for a living, where they lived, what they purchased, how much and often, and whether they paid cash or asked to be carried on the books until payday. He had a lifelong relationship with these people. Marketing was one-to-one, up close, and personal. Customer knowledge directed the shopkeeper's marketing efforts. He was collecting *data* and applying *customer relationship management* long before the terms were invented.

While some shopkeepers stored customer data in a notebook, others kept it in their heads. Their customers probably numbered in the hundreds, thus record keeping and information management were relatively simple. They kept purchase and credit records, along with inventories, consumer product and delivery preferences, and knowledge of customer demographics, lifestyles, and product opinions. Stored data were transformed into information and knowledge that gave the shopkeeper the ability to communicate with his customers in their language, effectively serving their needs and wants. Customer knowledge was a powerful tool that helped him retain their loyalty and when appropriate, *up-sell* (encourage the purchase of more expensive, higher value products) or *cross-sell* (encourage the purchase of related products). Since he probably did not have much competition, attracting new customers was not as much of an issue as it is today. Had he faced competition, intimate knowledge of his current customers might have given him insight into how to identify and attract new customers.

Times certainly have changed and data collection, knowledge development, and customer relationship management (CRM) have become far more complex and costly. Large etailers like Amazon.com (*http://www.amazon.com*), Wal-Mart (*http://www. walmart.com*), and Travelocity (*http://www.travelocity.com*) store millions, billions, and even trillions of data in customer files. **Data** (plural) are distinct sets of text, numbers, sounds, images, or other elements translated into a form, typically binary digital machine-readable, that can be stored and processed by a computer. **Marketing data** are collected from and about markets, segments, competitors, suppliers, partners, consumers, and other marketing areas of interest. Consumer data may be

**DEMOGRAPHIC**    Age, gender, income, occupation, education level data

**TRANSACTION**    Purchase history, credit card use, email and feedback comments, delivery preferences

**LIFESTYLE**    Activities, opinions, lifestyle, panel data

**BEHAVIORAL**    Time spent on a web page, pages visited, links, clickstreams

**TECHNICAL**    Browser type, computer operating system, screen size

Marketers who use computers, software, and operational data tools to manage data and apply the results to marketing problems have adopted a *database approach*. An electronic **database** is a collection of data structured so computer software can quickly find and retrieve select pieces for analysis and application. Internet marketers apply data tools to data in databases in order to extract information that will make them more knowledgeable and improve their decisions. They believe a database approach will provide the knowledge they need to:

**Data**
Distinct sets of information such as text, numbers, sounds, images, or other elements translated into a form, typically binary digital machine-readable, that can be processed on a computer.

**Marketing data**
Data collected from and about markets, segments, customers, suppliers, partners, competitors, and in-house that has marketing applicability.

**Database**
Large tables of related data gathered and organized to make quick retrieval possible and stored in an electronic data warehouse.

- Identify their best and least productive customers.

- Target promotions to customers based on their interests, behaviors, and receptiveness.

- Help customers quickly find what they need on a web site.

- Identify products that customers want/need.

- Establish two-way personal communication with customers and prospects.

- Integrate data collection and management across business divisions to facilitate customer retention and value enhancement.

- Track competitors' market moves.

United Kingdom grocer Tesco (*http://tesco.com*), the world's largest online grocer, is a leader in database management. It began Internet operations in 1996 and currently delivers products purchased online from over 300 of Tesco's 680 UK stores. The company collects detailed customer information from online shoppers, mines it, and uses the results to guide the company's marketing strategy, including decisions about what products are sold in its stores. Its in-store selection model requires that online orders be filled from the customer's nearest Tesco, which eliminates costly additional warehouses. Products available for online purchase are limited to in-store inventory.

Every quarter Tesco sends its ten million Clubcard members a newsletter with a statement of the points they have earned from purchasing at Tesco, along with product coupons targeted to their purchase preferences. Only one in every one hundred customers receives the same offer. Tesco mails a hundred thousand different variations of its newsletter based on customer data, past purchase history, and predicted purchases. Database information is also used to cross-reference what customers purchase and to identify associated new items they might like. The success of this targeting effort has resulted in a steep reduction of in-store promotions from seven hundred per store to two hundred, and profits of over of £1 billion in 2001.

Tesco includes its employees in data collection and dissemination efforts. Every customer touch point, from sales receipts, web site visits, and orders, to customer surveys produces data that are input into the company's massive databases. Tesco has over 900 supermarkets in the United Kingdom, Ireland, Central Europe, and Asia. Total sales increased nearly 12 percent in 2001 to £22.8 billion. The company reported profits of £1.07 billion, but Tesco.com had a loss of £9 million on sales of £237 million.[2]

## SOME BASICS

Data typically are organized into files, records, and fields, then stored in databases. Databases are edited, refined, transformed, cleansed, stored, retrieved, sorted, and transported electronically within a computer, client/server, or network, by parallel processors, on the Internet, intranets, extranets, wirelessly and conventionally. New database technologies link systems with the Internet's unique interactivity and speed to improve data input accuracy, increase data input quantity and retrieval speeds, add predictive value, and drive down information management costs. A **marketing database** is used for many marketing purposes including, but not limited to, the following:

**Marketing database**
Marketing data collected and stored electronically in a database.

- Creating customer contact and inventory lists and directories
- Identifying receptive target customers for special offers
- Matching customers and products for up-sell and cross-sell
- Tailoring marketing messages and offers
- Adjusting distribution schedules
- Predicting purchase probability

A database is an instrument of change. Knowledge derived from successful database management can significantly change the way marketing is conducted, affecting marketing strategy and day-to-day tactics. Because change often is threatening, adopting a database approach indicates willingness on the part of Internet marketers to accept change and be flexible in accommodating its demands. One great change they face is a challenge to the principle that all customers should be treated equally. Operational data tools can identify a company's most productive customers, as well as its least productive ones. Treating the best customers the same as the least productive ones is shortsighted and may jeopardize best customer loyalty. All customers should be treated fairly, but not necessarily equally. This principle is illustrated by airlines that cater to their highest mileage passengers, offering them access to private airport boarding areas, early boarding, and other privileges. Anyone can become a high mileage customer and receive the same preferential treatment, relatively few do.

Chico's FAS (*http://www.chicos.com*) is another example. It sells exclusive private-label, sophisticated casual women's clothing and accessories through a chain of over 320 stores in forty U.S. states, the District of Columbia, and on the web. Every customer is invited to enroll in Chico's Passport Club, which rewards Chico's best customers. Once they earn their way into the Club by spending US$500, members receive a 5 percent discount on every subsequent Chico's purchase along with invitations to special parties and events, private discounts, promotional offers, and free shipping on web purchases. Passport Club members shopping Chico's online sign in and their numbers are accessed automatically from Chico's database. The company makes sure Passport Club members receive the same rewards whether they are shopping online or offline. It also does not charge shipping and handling for online orders.[3]

**Database management system (DBMS)**
The software that stores and processes data from databases in a systematic, orderly way.

A **database management system** (**DBMS**) gives a marketer access to data in databases and tools for converting data to information. The file saving system on a personal computer is a primitive DBMS, invisibly saving digital data, retrieving it on command, and allowing changes in real time. Oracle (*http://www.oracle.com*), IBM (*http://www.ibm.com*), and other companies sell popular database management software, ranging from very expensive custom products to less expensive off-the-shelf packages.

Database management software promises speedier operations, data keeping accuracy, and easy access even by nontechnically oriented employees. It does not always deliver what it promises. Disadvantages are that it has to be installed, data must be entered, it takes time to train users, it can produce more information than can be evaluated and used, and often costs are more than most small and many midsize businesses can afford. For a growing number of businesses, however, the benefits outweigh the costs.

Computer-based data collection and database analysis have evolved over almost a half century. Some milestones include the following.

**1960s**   Data collection and delivery in the 1960s was static, allowing the retrieval of information but not complex queries or extractions. Systems in the 1960s were mostly electronic spreadsheets. Databases could be asked simple questions like *What did our company spend on marketing from 1962 to 1966?*

**1980s**   By the 1980s, relational databases were widely used. They allowed more specific, finely tuned queries like *What did our company spend on marketing in New Mexico and Arizona from June to July 1984?* Data could be extracted to separate discrete markets from total company data. A prime concern was establishing database infrastructures.

**1990s**   Data warehouses and decision support systems in the 1990s facilitated drill downs to even finer questions like *What did our company spend on marketing in Santa Fe, NM, and Phoenix, AZ, from November to January 1993?* A prime concern was automating business processes.

**2000s**   Data mining in the 2000s uses more variables and larger samples, highly sophisticated mathematical formulae and statistical methods to ask predictive questions like *What is our company* likely *to spend on marketing in Santa Fe and Phoenix six months from now? How will this spending affect sales? How will online sales affect in-store revenues?* This predictive capacity represents a quantum leap from the 1960s. A prime concern is simplifying tools so they can be used by any marketing employee and not just IT departments or experts.[4]

## DATABASE PLANNING AND CONSTRUCTION

A marketing database is both an electronic file cabinet and a process that is susceptible to system incompatibility problems, computer glitches, human error, and poor design. Although marketing databases are popular and highly publicized, they are often underutilized. Large companies can easily spend millions of dollars setting up and maintaining databases. Some spend millions to collect and store data but never retrieve and use it. Others retrieve it but do not use it in a meaningful way. Some trash historical data without realizing its value if properly managed. While large corporations can afford to hire experts to construct unique proprietary legacy database systems, smaller companies are more likely to outsource the process or use off-the-shelf software.

Some databases are dedicated solely to customer transaction record keeping. Others are broader and integrate transaction data with behavioral tracking, customer demographic and lifestyle data, and financial records. To advance from having masses of data in incompatible databases to creating an integrated cross-functional operational DBMS requires managers willing to commit sufficient resources to make it happen, professionals who can develop and operate the systems, access to custom-built systems, off-the-shelf software packages, and/or consultants and employees who embrace the database approach and are flexible. A company adopting a DBMS should be customer-centric, able to implement strategic database planning integrated with business and marketing strategy, and willing to form and support cross-functional database teams when appropriate.[5]

Planning is essential to database construction and management. It should begin by identifying current business and marketing strategies, tactics, and resources related to data collection, storage, and application. This includes taking an inventory of what database systems are currently running throughout the company and the historical data already stored. Planning determines what the integrated database will do for marketing and other areas like finance. A plan specifies what data are to be collected, from whom, and how. It explains how data will be organized, formatted, stored, maintained, updated, and deleted, and what reports get generated for whom. It also identifies what employees will have access. Consumer databases are subject to considerable *churn*, that is, changes in address, marital status, family size, or life stage, as well as transaction behaviors. Business databases are far less volatile. Good databases are updated on a regular basis to merge new data with old and purge stale, outdated entries.

Database construction is a multistep process. Working from the database plan, data are collected from numerous designated sources that may include primary and secondary research, online customer transaction records, behavioral tracking, syndicated research, marketing intelligence, and purchases from vendors. For example, DoubleClick, Inc. (*http://www.doubleclick.com*), a highly visible digital marketing company, is responsible for placing most Internet banner advertisements. It sells data collected from click throughs on its online advertisements. DoubleClick's Abacus Division (*http://www.abacus-direct.com*) has a database of 3.5 billion transactions from more than ninety million U.S. households. It is the largest proprietary buyer behavior database in the country with consumer, retail, B2B, publishing, and online transactions markets.[6]

The massive amounts of data collected must be organized and refined. This requires transforming data into a format, usually digital tables, that can be quickly located and accessed. Using a flat file format, each unique consumer can have up to several hundred fields of information associated with his or her unique identification (ID) number. This can include credit card information, transaction records, mailing addresses, purchase characteristics (gift, return, etc.), response to sales and advertising, and the like.

Data files are stored and cleansed, updated, or purged to maintain timeliness and accuracy. Hygiene is essential in all databases, particularly where significant amounts of churn are experienced. Storage includes file transportation and maintenance.

When commanded, computer software sorts the files, aggregating and disaggregating data. Sorting tools can be operated from a desktop computer, client/server, parallel processors, or on the web. Information produced by a sort is retrieved, analyzed, and converted to knowledge applied to a particular marketing problem. Feedback is collected throughout the process to determine how well everything is working. It feeds back into plan updates and revisions.

Although database construction is typically the responsibility of IT specialists, Internet marketers should understand construction basics as well as database applications and shortcomings. This increases their value in making decisions about what data must be collected and formulating database queries. They should be prepared to work on IT/marketing teams. The UCLA Bookstore is an example of how this is being done. With nine locations plus a web site (*http://www.uclaestore.com/uclagm*), it is one of the largest university bookstore and food service operations in the United States. The web site markets products to current students, alumni, and nonstudents, particularly Bruin fans. The sité is a collaborative effort with IT responsible for dynamic elements, particularly security, navigation, and database integration. Marketing and advertising are responsible for the site's static elements of web page content, web site atmospherics (look and feel), product descriptions, and features that make the site distinctively UCLA's. Working together, both groups maintain an inviting, functional, customer-centric web site.[7]

## DATABASE DESIGN

Many types of databases are running on and off the Web. They including bibliographies, catalogs, full text, numeric, medical, and research databases operated by businesses, governments, universities, scientific organizations, hospitals, and others. Each database is designed on an underlying mathematical theory. Most contemporary databases are relational (table 8-2) with data *relating* to each other in tables. All data are stored inside tables and all operations are performed on the tables, which often results in the creation of a new table. Adding data is simplified because each table is arranged

### Table 8-2  A Relational Customer Database

Table A: Customer Data

| Data Field | Customer Number | Customer Name | e-Mail Address | State |
|---|---|---|---|---|
| | 001 | Sonny B. Smith | SBS@aol.com | KY |
| | 002 | Ann B. Short | AnnB3@hotmail.com | IL |
| | 003 | Tim I. Nygof | Tiny@iglou.com | TN |
| | ... | ... | ... | ... |

Table B: Online Transaction Data

| Data Field | Order Number | Customer Number | Billing Date | Invoice Amount |
|---|---|---|---|---|
| | 101 | 001 | 1/4/02 | $   505.68 |
| | 102 | 002 | 1/4/02 | $   497.32 |
| | 103 | 003 | 1/5/02 | $1,989.34 |
| | ... | ... | ... | ... |

Table C: Tracking Data

| Data Field | Browser | Computer OS | Screen Size | Customer Number |
|---|---|---|---|---|
| | Netscape | Win 95 | 400x600 pixels | 001 |
| | Explorer | Mac 9.2 | 400x600 pixels | 002 |
| | Explorer | Mac OSX | 780x480 pixels | 003 |
| | ... | ... | ... | ... |

A relational database is like an extremely large electronic filing cabinet. Each drawer in the cabinet contains files that relate to one another through common elements or data fields. The common data fields allow tables to be linked in a relationship. Relational databases greatly reduce redundancy and allow quick, easy data retrieval. For example, Table A contains customer data. Table B is an order table of online transaction data. Table C is a table tracking customer operating systems and browsers. The common data field or element that allows data retrieval across the tables is Customer Number. This is the unique customer identification number that forms the axis connecting data requests.

in a uniform structure. Extremely powerful relational databases are used for such diverse tasks as analyzing election results by demographic characteristics of voters, maintaining medical records, tracking online grocery shoppers and their purchases, and developing email opt-in permission marketing lists.

## IN-HOUSE AND COMPILED DATABASES

**In-house database**
Databases built from own company data.

**Compiled database**
Data collected by others and if proprietary, sold.

Businesses can operate **in-house databases,** built from their own data, and/or **compiled databases,** data collected by others and purchased, if the data are proprietary. For most marketing purposes, an in-house database has advantages over a compiled database. In-house data include records for buyers who already have a purchase history with the company, buyers who have not purchased recently, and prospects who have visited the web site but not yet purchased. Considerable effort is required to transform in-house data into a usable form. In-house data have greater immediate potential for use in retention, up-selling, and cross-selling based on the belief that past purchase behavior is a good predictor of future purchase behavior. This obviously is not the case for all customers all the time, but it is more often the case than not. A company has greater control over the quality of its own data, and if it has good hygiene, data should be more accurate and current than most compiled lists. Another in-house advantage is familiarity with customers and purchase situations, which adds a valuable perspective.

Compiled databases also have advantages. They provide new targets for businesses seeking to expand customer reach. They are already compiled, and regular updates can be purchased. It often costs less to purchase than compile in-house data. Compiled databases often use multiple data sources that include public records, private sources, and overlays of customer response data. They may contain predictive scores based on data mining or survey data.

Online databases are found on government and organization web sites, and at proprietary sources. Free databases have many of the same problems as secondary data in general. Proprietary databases can be leased from their owners or purchased. They may house niche and/or mass market data. SK&A Information Services (*http://www.skainfo.com*) leases for a year or more databases of key health care decision makers for direct marketing to hospitals, pharmacies, group practices, nursing homes, and other facilities. YesMail.com (*http://www.yesmail.com*) leases lists for email permission marketing campaigns. It gathers databases with names and email addresses of individuals and businesses that opt in to receive mailings on subjects that interest them in over 750 different categories. Popular YesMail opt-in databases include automotive lists with over 2.5 million names, computer software lists with over 3 million names, and a music database with over 5.4 million names. YesMail delivers more than 100 million email marketing messages each month for its clients.

Any Internet marketer considering purchasing proprietary databases should carefully evaluate the seller's reputation and check client references. The database broker's salespeople should be able to provide complete information about advantages or disadvantages of the databases, data sources, database hygiene records, accuracy, costs, and terms of use. They can often provide predictive scores for customer response rates. Compiled databases are frequently used in financial services and by retailers seeking to drive traffic to a web site.

### ✔ CONCEPT CHECK

1. What do a shopkeeper from the early twentieth century and a twenty-first-century customer database have in common?
2. For what purposes are marketing databases used?
3. Do databases and data management always work as expected? Explain.

# Data Warehousing and Mining

A data warehouse is a huge electronic storage bin with finely detailed historical data organized in databases stored in computer tables or files. Data mining is a series of methods for analyzing data in databases and warehouses. Both are praised for their value in cutting through masses of data and extracting information that can be used for more effective marketing. They are also criticized for failing to meet expectations, delivering unusable marketing information, and overwhelming decision makers with too much information.

## DATA WAREHOUSING

**Data warehouse**

Both a storehouse for massive amounts of data in databases and a system for extracting and managing large quantities of data.

A **data warehouse** is both an electronic storage place for massive amounts of data housed in databases and a system that allows the extraction and management of large quantities of data. It is actually a generic term for a single integrated repository for databases obtained from many sources, in-house records and compiled data, from marketing, finance, and other functional areas. It must have a flexible structure to accommodate multiple users and different methods for slicing through the data. A production data warehouse frequently is separate from an operational data warehouse used for nonproduction purposes.

Warehouse queries start with a hypothesis (H); for example, *H1: Customers 45 to 65 years who purchased baby gifts from our web site last holiday season are most likely to respond to email offers of toddler products for this holiday season*. The task is to identify customers from last year who fit the profile. The query to the warehouse is to produce a list of customers forty-five to sixty-five years old with the requisite transaction history. The generated list is used for a promotional email offer sent to those customers who gave permission (opt-in) for the company to contact them. The offer refers directly to last year's purchase, has links to products that make great toddler gifts, offers a discount if a purchase is made before a deadline, and free shipping for orders above a certain amount.

Data warehouses typically are built in three phases. First, databases are gathered from multiple sources throughout the company and compiled by database aggregators. Second, the databases are transformed to a common platform. Inconsistencies in data formats and coding are removed. Databases are loaded (populated) in the warehouse. Third, user interfaces are installed that allow marketers to query the data and request answers to hypotheses.

Enterprises of all types have data warehouses. The National Center for Health Statistics web site (*http://www.cdc.gov/nchs/datawh.htm*) lists the databases in its data warehouse (see the screen shot on p. 200). They include tabulated national health, tabulated state data, microdata for research, database searches and queries, and others. The

College Football Data Warehouse (*http://www.cfbdatawarehouse.com*) is loaded with historical data on NCAA games. The State of Ohio Department of Health (*http://dwhouse.odh.ohio.gov/*) has an information warehouse with Births, Deaths, Marriage & Divorce, and Cancer Incidence databases.

**A List of Databases in a Warehouse**

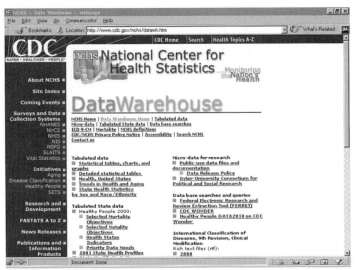

The National Center for Health Statistics web site lists the databases in its data warehouse. *Source: http://www.cdc.gov/nchs/datawh.htm.*

Selected areas in corporate data warehouses are often opened to the company's suppliers, partners, and customers via extranets. Sharing data can help the company and its partners work out solutions to product or production problems. Corporate customers access warehouses to make better informed purchase decisions, obtain detailed product specifications, and check delivery schedules.

Data warehouses are used for collaborative online/offline strategic marketing. Jiffy Lube began its data warehouse project in 1998. Three people made up the planning team—the head of strategic marketing, a senior IT analyst, and an enterprise data administrator. It took seven months to plan the warehouse and longer to load thirty-five million vehicle records. During the process, Jiffy Lube's parent company, Pennzoil, purchased Quaker State and the warehouse had to be expanded to fold in Quaker State's records. The data warehouse's fifty million plus records are used to profile Jiffy Lube's most profitable customers. Service centers use the Jiffy Lube web site (*http://www.jiffylube.com*) to send direct mail to prospects in their service districts who match best customer profiles.[8] Web site visitors are invited to provide their email addresses so they can receive the latest news and maintenance tips.

## DATA MINING

**Data mining**

Software that systematically sifts through databases looking for statistically significant patterns and correlations from previously unrecognized relationships, and predictive relationships.

**Data mining,** also called machine learning or knowledge discovery, is a class of machine-driven methods that look for hidden patterns and relationships in databases and warehouses. Artificial intelligence (AI) neural networks, association rules, and genetic algorithm software systematically sift through databases looking for statistically significant patterns and correlations from previously unrecognized relationships, and predictive relationships. Data mining can substantiate an educated guess about a marketing relationship or, using automated discovery, search for hidden relationships. It is both a descriptive and predictive tool.

The process creates its own theory about why a relationship exists. For example, an etailer wants to reduce online credit card fraud. One alternative is to develop a profile of credit card users most likely to use fake or stolen cards, then use this profile to stop fraud by denying service to any customer who fits the fraud profile. The predictive profile is created from credit card purchase patterns of known credit card fraudsters. Data mining techniques compile the profile, then apply these characteristics to identify others who share them and therefore have a higher probability of committing online credit card fraud.

Data mining is used to answer questions like the following:

- What is the probability that a particular type of customer will purchase at least $500 in apparel from our online spring catalog?
- What is the probability that a particular type of customer will respond to our emailed promotion for US$25 off an online purchase of US$100 or more?
- What customers are most likely to click through to a game site from a banner advertisement?
- What type of credit card applicant is most likely to commit online credit card fraud?
- Which kinds of prospects are most likely to respond to a free shipping offer for a US$100 or more online purchase?
- Which types of customers are most likely to return online purchases?
- Which products are most likely to be purchased in association (bundled) with one another?
- What are the characteristics of customers most likely to have the greatest lifetime monetary value at a web storefront?

Mining requires drilling down through multiple layers of data. Customer transaction data are searched to create profiles of customer purchase behaviors, including lapsed customers who have not recently made a purchase, and those least likely to purchase. Mining creates models for segmenting customers and forecasting attrition and retention rates. It can indicate on what web sites to purchase advertising space in order to reach prime customer types, identify pricing opportunities, suggest cross- and up-selling potential, and describe how to effectively personalize offers. By separating prime customers from those who are not, marketers are able to offer different levels of service based on predicted buying potential, thus operationalizing the 80-20 rule. Vilfredo Pareto (1848-1923), an Italian economist, observed in 1906 that in Italy 80 percent of the land was owned by 20 percent of the population. This ratio was later applied to business in a number of ways, including that 20 percent of a business's customers produce 80 percent of its revenues. The 80-20 ratio also has been applied to gardening and scientific discoveries, among other applications.

Data mining is far more complex than *collaborative filtering,* which produces personal recommendations by comparing a present preference with those of others with the same or similar preferences.[9] Amazon.com (*http://www.amazon.com*) uses collaborative filtering to cross-sell, suggesting to a purchaser of C. S. Forester's *Mr. Midshipman Hornblower* that he or she will also enjoy *Master and Commander* by Patrick O'Brian. This is based on *n* other customers who purchased both books and those who reported enjoying them.

Until recently, highly trained statisticians were needed to operate mostly large-scale Unix-based database mining software. Much of it was proprietary, customized, and costly to create. Now, cheaper off-the-shelf software integrated into database software lets decision makers use English language queries to mine data from their desktop computers.[10] Thus, customer service representatives, telemarketers, and salespeople in large companies can access company databases and mine them, often in real time while still on the telephone with customers or interacting with them by email or on the Web using live chat or instant messaging.[11] This is why less profitable callers wait for a customer service operator, while the most profitable customers receive immediate service. On the Web, it can determine how long it takes before an email question is answered or a personal shopper comes online.

Companies that already had massive consumer databases, particularly large retailers Wal-Mart, Sears, and First Union Bank, are leaders in data mining. Wal-Mart has a data warehouse with over 101 terabytes (trillions of data characters), second only to the Pentagon's, that allows Wal-Mart to tailor its merchandise mix to customer preferences.[12]

J. Crew uses data mining to track visitor movements (clickstreams or virtual tracks) on its web site and predict product recommendations in real time to up-sell and cross-sell customers. J. Crew's data mining also provides recommendations for making its web storefront design more effective, as well as improving marketing and merchandising strategies. Site marketing managers receive daily reports on web site traffic patterns, customer demographics, transactions, and responses to marketing campaigns. J. Crew operates 143 retail stores, a catalog, and forty-one outlet stores in addition to Jcrew.com (*http://www.jcrew.com*). Internet sales increased to US$25.3 million for the thirteen weeks that ended May 5, 2001, over US$19.4 million in the same period in 2000. Internet sales in 2001 continued positive and were greater than in-store sales. The company states it is acquiring lots of new customers at its web site, where it costs less to service them than through catalog sales.[13]

The masses of data generated by Internet commerce coupled with software availability has made some companies believe data mining is all they need to establish a competitive advantage and personal, long-term relationships with their customers. Others fear greater privacy loss. DoubleClick ran afoul of privacy advocates when it announced a plan (later delayed) to merge cookie-derived data with direct-mail consumer databases, then mine these data to personalize online marketing offers. The Federal Trade Commission (FTC) investigated and determined that DoubleClick did not violate its privacy policy; however, negative press reports and rising consumer concern were enough to force DoubleClick to back off the proposal. Data mining is more appropriate for high-volume Internet marketers, not small businesses with customer bases in the hundreds or thousands, or even most midsize businesses, or most smaller B2B marketers. Although it is expensive, complex, and does not always work as expected, it is the best predictive technology currently available for consumer markets.[14]

**WEB UPDATE**

Data Mining Used in Internet Marketing

### ✔ CONCEPT CHECK

1. What is stopping many businesses from creating their own data warehouses?
2. Are businesses the only enterprises using data warehouses?
3. What can data mining tell a marketer?

# Collect and Apply

Cookies, bugs, and web analytics are privacy-sensitive tools. Each is defended for the value it creates for improving web site experiences and online marketing efficiency. At the same time they are highly visible targets for privacy advocates. Internet marketers should exercise sensitivity when using these tools because they have a high potential for privacy invasion. Electronic Customer Relationship Management (eCRM) takes the information generated by the tools and applies it.

## COOKIES AND BUGS

**Cookies**
Small data files placed automatically and surreptitiously on a user's browser by a web site's server and used for information gathering and tracking.

This chapter's opening vignette focused on **cookies,** small data files placed on a user's browser by a web site's server. Cookies are delivered firsthand from a site's web server to the user's computer. When the user revisits the site, the site's web server determines whether or not a site cookie is on the user's computer. The cookie stores *direct* and *indirect data*. Direct data include information the user provides, which is recorded automatically without his or her knowledge. If the user makes a purchase, the cookie records any data provided to complete the transaction. Indirect data include clickstream records of where the user went on the site, how much time was spent at each click, and the user's computer information. These data are collected and stored in databases. Of course, if the user's hard drive does not have a cookie from the site, the server attempts to place one.

How does a user know a cookie has been placed? If the user returns to a site and the page says, *Welcome back,___* and calls the user by name, that is because the cookie file on his or her computer passed information back to the site's web server. The server asked the user's browser, *Do you have any cookies for me?* If the answer was yes, the server retrieved the information and used it to personalize a welcome. Some users find these personalized welcomes very upsetting, others ignore them, and the remainder appear to appreciate the effort at one-to-one marketing.

Many consumers love cookies that save passwords, registrations, and subscription codes, which releases them from having to write down or memorize a long series of numbers and type them in when asked. Cookies can capture a surprising amount of information. Amazon.com is very open about the information collected from its users on cookies and other analytic tools. It includes the IP address that connects the user to the Internet, the user's email address and Amazon password, computer and connection information, browser type and version, computer operating system and platform, user's Amazon purchase history and full URL clickstream path getting to and through Amazon, cookie number, products viewed or searched for at Amazon and zShops visited, Amazon auction history, and the user's telephone number if it was used to call 1-800![15]

**Web beacons (bugs)**
Single-pixel electronic GIF images placed by third-party media and research companies.

**Web beacons** (**bugs**) are single-pixel electronic GIF images placed by third-party media and research companies. They greatly increase the number of web sites where data can be collected. The cookie on a user's hard drive is read whenever the user clicks on advertisements or views pages where advertisements are placed by a third-party like DoubleClick. That is where the beacons appear. Web beacons collect Non-Personally Identifiable Information (NP-II); for example, a user's cookie number, the time and date when a page was viewed, and a description of the page where the web beacon is placed.

What sets web beacons or bugs apart from standard cookies is the ability to track cookies on more than one site. The original web site that placed the cookie may partner with hundreds of other web sites. As the user links to other web sites, the beacons record the visits and send cookie information to the third party.

Yahoo! (*http://www.yahoo.com*) plants web bugs to report aggregate information about users including demographic and usage data, and unique visitor counts. The bugs are on pages within the Yahoo! site as well as on sites owned by Yahoo! partners. Data from the bugs affects the offers Yahoo! delivers. It also lets Yahoo! tailor its web content and advertisements. Yahoo! does not share personal information about users with its partners. It also stipulates that partners must disclose in their privacy policies that Yahoo! bugs are placed on their site. Users can opt out of Yahoo!'s web bug program.[16]

Network advertisers claim the information collected by web beacons allows them to make offers that are more relevant to visitors. Beacons are also useful tools for measuring online promotion effectiveness. However, advertisers also acknowledge significant privacy concerns, which is why the Network Advertising Initiative (NAI at *http://www.networkadvertising.org*) was formed. Member companies are Avenue A, Inc. (*http://www.avenueainc.com*), DoubleClick (*http://www.doubleclick.net*), L90 (*http://www.l90.com*), and 24/7 Media (*http://www.247media.com*). Through the NAI they are addressing privacy issues associated with tools like web beacons. NAI also offers consumers opt-outs from cookies and web beacons placed by its member companies.[17]

## SERVER LOGS

**Server log files**

Plain-text files not really readable by humans that gather web site traffic data.

Most web servers log (record) every request they receive in **server log files.** These files are not really readable by humans but must be read by third party parsing/reporting programs that decipher the mess of lines and code. The files (numbers and letters) usually end in .log. One file requesting data from a web server might look something like

eku.edu/webadmin/home/pub.p/marketing/public_html - [12January/2002:05:47:52 -0800] "GET /~marketing/text/if HTTP/1.0" 200 193847 "http://www.bizcommkt. com:88/~marketing/" "Mozilla/1.12I (X11; I; NEWS-OS 6.1.1 news5000) via proxy gateway CERN-HTTPD/3.0pre5 libwww/2.16pre"

The reporting program pulls out

- the user's name or machine identification number,
- the web file or place requested,
- whether the request for information was successfully filled or a 404 error message was sent,
- the size of the file transferred,
- the browser used,
- the date and time when the request was logged, and
- whether a proxy server was used, which indicates the presence of a firewall.

Server logs are traffic counters that record traffic, or hits. They can be misleading, however, because they cannot distinguish if a visit is unique or a repeat, and they do not record any traffic from files that are cached (stored). Nevertheless, they are useful in tracking what users do while they are on a site, and they can compare site visit trends over time. For example, if page views increased from thirty-three thousand in January to fifty-six thousand in April, it is a significant trend even if the actual number of page views is disputed. Log files can identify if a visitor's browser can support frames or Java or has a sound card installed. Log file records can be obtained from a system administrator or ISP.[18]

## WEB ANALYTICS AND ECRM

With all the data collected and information being generated, something is needed to bring it all together in a form that marketing decision makers can understand. This is a job for people who can see the big picture and are familiar with operational data tools, statistical analysis, and marketing. Professionals trained in **web analytics** analyze results and evaluate changes in channel strategy based on web analytic measures. Web analytics is both the software that runs sophisticated analysis programs and the people who organize, manage, interpret, and apply the results.

Web analysis can involve collecting a huge amount of data, an estimated terabyte (TB—a thousand billion bytes or a thousand gigabytes) of data per year per client. Web analytics takes results from the analysis of these data, decides what is applicable and usable, transforms it into a deeper understanding of customer behavior, develops and implements the right marketing response, then evaluates results and makes necessary changes. Gartner research predicts that by 2005, businesses will need three times as many data analytic employees as they have today. Demand for people who can interpret and use analytics is at least two times greater than the supply.[19]

Web analytics requires people who can connect analysis to marketing solutions and web site improvements. They must be able to identify what needs to be tracked, how to measure it, how to interpret results, and how to apply these results to specific improvements. It requires working with IT people and across departments to integrate marketing, finance, accounting, purchasing, and other databases.

Web analytics consultants and software packages are responding to growing demand. The web analytics industry grew from revenues of US$141 million in 2000 to US$425 million in 2001. It is expected to reach US$4 billion in 2004. This indicates the level of enthusiasm for adopting this technology and approach.[20]

**Electronic customer relationship management (eCRM)** is a broad overall strategy that uses a web analytical approach to anticipate, understand, and respond to current and potential customer needs. It is sometimes referred to as analytical CRM. eCRM is the application of the tools used to operationalize data, primarily from the web.[21]

eCRM has been widely promoted but not widely adopted, thus far. Companies using it typically are very large, with annual revenues well over several hundred million dollars. It is used most often in financial services, computer software, and telecommunications. Spending on CRM, including eCRM, in 2001 was around US$61 billion. This is expected to rise to US$148 billion in 2005.[22]

Like all sophisticated and complex systems, eCRM has problems. Any company that wants to implement eCRM cannot go to one vendor and purchase everything that is needed. Analytical approaches are complex, tools are expensive, and most companies do not have enough employees trained to use them. Many eCRM vendors are expected to fail, which will consolidate the industry and may result in higher prices.

At the same time, some CRM approaches are being widely used, particularly dynamic web pages. Most web pages are static, remaining the same for each visitor. **Dynamic web pages** use databases to provide personalized content for customers, content that changes with each visitor and reflects his or her reason for visiting the

**Web analytics**
The process of collecting, organizing, and analyzing the huge amount of data needed, as much as one terabyte of data per year per client, for data analysis and other marketing applications.

**Electronic customer relationship management (eCRM)**
A broad strategy that uses a web analytical approach to anticipate, understand, and respond to current and potential customer needs.

**Dynamic web pages**
Web pages that are personalized so content changes with each visitor. Content is provided by databases. Sometimes called dynamic content.

site. For example, a visitor arrives at All The Web (*http://www.alltheweb.com*) and begins a search for the keyword descriptor phrase *marketing research*. The search engine uses middleware software to connect to backend databases where content is stored. A search begins for titles and metatags containing the keywords. Middleware is a common communication substrate, a glue that allows different applications to communicate. Links that satisfy the descriptor requirements appear on the visitor's screen. At the same time, however, on each page the All The Web header, footer, and navigation bar remain static; only the content is dynamic and changes with each search. Dynamic databases are often used with sites where content changes frequently. They are found at Amazon.com to retrieve requested books or videos, Charles Schwab (*http://www.charlesschwab.com*) to retrieve customer data and stock reports, FedEx (*http://www.fedex.com*) to track orders, and Lands' End (*http://www.landsend.com*) to display products from the catalog.

## ✔ CONCEPT CHECK

1. Why are cookies, web beacons, web analytics, and eCRM called privacy-sensitive tools?
2. What is the advantage of using web beacons rather than standard cookies?
3. How can marketers benefit from the information provided by web analytics?

# *Marketing Intelligence*

Over twenty years ago it was observed that "A strategic plan can be no better than the information [intelligence] on which it is based."[23] Even before that, ethical, legal business intelligence activities were practiced by domestic and international businesses and organizations. Today, the increased commitment to intelligence gathering and use reflects several forces, some general and others specific to Internet commercialization. Greatly increased global competition, which emerged in the 1970s and accelerated during the late 1980s and 1990s, provides a compelling reason to collect information about international markets and competitors. Shortened product cycles, business deregulation, rapid technology changes, increased competition, and converging technologies contribute to increasingly more volatile environments that require close monitoring.[24]

**Marketing intelligence**
A *process*, a system for collecting and transforming data, and *content*, knowledge for marketing decisions, particularly to track competitors' marketing tactics.

The web's unique interactivity and the ease of collecting information means marketing intelligence gathering can be faster, cheaper, and easier than ever before. **Marketing intelligence** requires collecting and transforming data into information, knowledge, and intelligence about markets, competitors, the environment, customers, and other marketing areas of concern. Intelligence is used to adjust market offers and the process of making them. A growing number of marketing intelligence activities are web based, particularly focusing on competitors and their online market offers.

Competitors require constant monitoring because they can change their offers, prices, promotions, delivery options, shopping carts, and web storefronts at the click of a mouse. Customers require constant monitoring because they can quickly take their business elsewhere if they are not satisfied. Data analytic techniques facilitate the intelligence process to an extent unimaginable just a few years ago.

Although some complain that more intelligence is needed, there is already almost too much information to sift through. Many marketers are falling victim to a web information glut. It is so easy to find information sources and collect data online that marketers can easily overload, and the information excess can cloud their judgment and compromise rather than improve their decisions.

Marketing intelligence has many dimensions. Intelligence activities can be focused in-house, externally, or both. Data can be collected, processed, and reported in the traditional manner by people, totally by automatic computer searches, and a combination of both processes. It is typically machine and labor intensive, and when done right, time-consuming.

Regardless of focus or collection method, marketers have always needed to gather timely, relevant, and accurate information from diverse sources. Once obtained, they analyze and synthesize it to produce intelligence for the development of targeted, predictable marketing activities. The Internet and the Web have greatly expanded the pool of information available, shortened the time needed to retrieve it, and made it easier to retrieve. At the same time companies have become more vulnerable to decisions based on inaccurate or unsubstantiated information because so much is being collected. Companies have also become exposed to increased levels of counterintelligence, espionage, and thievery since others have the same access to analytical tools and the Web.

## THE INTELLIGENCE PROCESS

Intelligence is a *process*, a system for collecting and transforming data, and *content*, knowledge for marketing decisions. In most large businesses, the intelligence process (figure 8-1) is a continuous cycle. The first step is to identify a goal or the reason for

**Figure 8-1  The Marketing Intelligence Process**

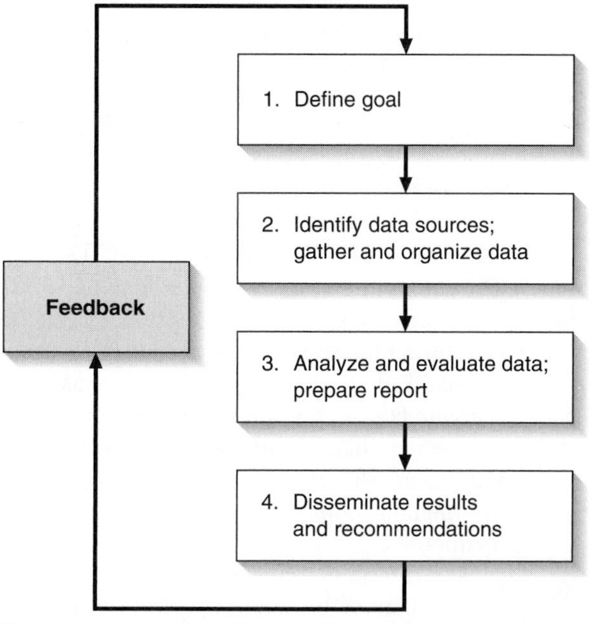

The marketing intelligence process begins with goal definition, then moves through a standard sequence of steps to recommendations and feedback.

initiating the process and define the requirements for reaching that goal. Del Monte Foods (*http://www.delmonte.com*) needed a process to provide real-time marketing and sales intelligence electronically to its field sales force. Salespeople were spread out over twenty-four groups based on location, strategic business unit, and responsibility. In this case, the goal required the development of an internal intelligence process to make data available on twenty-four different proprietary intranet web sites, one for each group.[25] The company did not develop the intelligence process in-house; it hired a consultant to create and implement the system.

The second step is to identify relevant data sources, then gather and organize the data so they can be analyzed. This often means organizing data into a database, as discussed in the previous sections. In the Del Monte Foods case, the sales force needed sales data, demand projections, and customer activity reports. Sources for these types of data typically are in-house from existing sales records, salesperson reports, and customer feedback. Often they are reported in numerical form. Raw data that have not been organized or formatted must be analyzed and evaluated, formatted for the system, then synthesized into easy-to-read reports, with recommendations. The intelligence is disseminated to those needing it, in this case the field sales force, so they can track changes in the marketplace, make decisions on which customer groups to target, and better manage their marketing campaigns and resources. The intelligence process itself should be evaluated and adjusted on a regular basis to ensure that it is providing the quality and quantity of intelligence needed.

## INTELLIGENCE FOR INTERNAL CONTROL

Del Monte Foods is an example of an intelligence process initiated to improve internal controls, in this case, provide intelligence electronically in real time so sales and marketing personnel could make better decisions. The United States Postal Service (USPS) recognized it needed customized marketing intelligence to make it more competitive. It called on a consultant to construct an ebusiness network for its more than three thousand sales and marketing professionals nationwide. This intelligence system provides strategic reports, marketing analysis, and customer data in real time. It is expected to cut costs and allow better customer service while also tracking the competition.[26]

## INTELLIGENCE ABOUT THE COMPETITION AND ENVIRONMENT

The competition plays a large role in any marketer's environment. Information about what one's rivals are doing is often a prime factor in developing marketing offers or countering them. Direct competitors Amazon.com and Barnes & Noble (*http://www.bn.com*) keep track of the marketplace as well as each other, national competitors like Random House, Inc. (*http://www.randomhouse.com*), and strong independent regional competitors like Joseph-Beth Booksellers (*http://www.josephbeth.com*). Competitive intelligence for them is a systematic process of regularly gathering and analyzing information about their competition to find new opportunities, avoid threats, and stay competitive.

The Internet has made competitive intelligence (CI) processes significantly easier. Although many businesses perform it themselves with in-house CI units, others hire professionals for the job. The competitive intelligence industry generates around US$100 billion in annual revenues.[27]

CI data can be gathered in a variety of ways. A panel of buyers or company personnel can visit rivals' web sites and systematically analyze all aspects of the site's marketing activities from the buyer's perspective. Special software directs their site visits. Web site analysis can test online ordering processes, check site navigation and downloads, and learn what it costs to have products delivered and how returns are handled. Site visits may be conducted on a daily basis since web marketing practices can be changed rapidly.

Chat rooms and message boards are fertile grounds for collecting consumer comments about the competition. Heated discussions can be monitored for customer experiences. Collecting the data is easy compared with the challenge of trying to determine what it means, then using the intelligence to effectively adjust marketing strategy and tactics in response.

## KEEPING IT LEGAL AND ETHICAL

Much of the information that any business needs to conduct competitive intelligence is available from open public records, from competitors' public web sites, and from other public sources.[28] The U.S. government regularly files business regulatory documents on the Internet with data that can be analyzed to reveal business strategies to competitors.[29] Web storefronts are rich in information, from press releases to product prices, that can be accessed freely and openly.

Even with the wealth of legal online data, some individuals and organizations still cross the line of acceptable, legal practices to engage in economic (industrial) espionage. Espionage, an attempt by one company to discover another's secrets, is illegal as well as unethical. The 1996 Economic Espionage Act (PL104-294 Title 18 U.S.C.) makes it a federal offense to steal trade secrets or obtain them through fraud. Penalties range from US$500,000 and fifteen years in prison for individual offenders up to US$10 million for businesses. Economic espionage includes the theft of marketing plans, price lists, product specifications, customer lists, trade secrets, and other company documents, as well as breaking into corporate intranets and web sites, bribing company employees to obtain information, and other illegal acts.

## ✔ CONCEPT CHECK

1. What is information overload and how can it affect marketers?
2. What are the dual meanings of intelligence?
3. Outline the intelligence process.

# *Summary*

### *Operational Data Tools and Databases*

Operational data tools are computer-based techniques that marketers and others use to learn more about their own online operations, their competitors, and most critically, customers, current and prospective. Large amounts of data are collected anonymously and aggregated to gain a better understanding of markets as a whole, segments, or even individuals. Marketing professionals with data skills are in demand, hinting at an exciting new career path. The issue of privacy is a serious concern and data tools are at the center of the debate. Data (plural) are distinct sets of text, numbers, sounds, images, or other elements translated into a form, typically binary digital machine-readable, that can be stored and processed by a computer. Marketers who use computers, software, and operational data tools to manage data and apply the results to marketing problems have adopted a database approach. A database is an instrument of change. A database management system (DBMS) gives a marketer access to data in databases and tools for converting data to information. Database construction is a multistep process. Many types of databases are running on and off the Web. Most contemporary databases are relational with data arrayed in tables. Businesses can operate in-house databases, built from their own data, and/or compiled databases, data collected by others and purchased, if they are proprietary.

## Data Warehousing and Mining

A data warehouse is both an electronic storage place for massive amounts of data housed in databases and a system that allows the extraction and management of large quantities of data. Enterprises of all types have data warehouses. Selected areas in corporate data warehouses are often opened to the company's suppliers, partners, and customers. Building a data warehouse is a complex, expensive, and often risky undertaking. Data warehouses are used for collaborative online/offline strategic marketing. Data mining, also called machine learning or knowledge discovery, is a class of machine-driven methods that look for hidden patterns and relationships in databases and warehouses. Artificial intelligence (AI) neural networks, association rules, and genetic algorithm software systematically sift through databases looking for statistically significant patterns and correlations from previously unrecognized relationships and predictive relationships. Data mining can substantiate an educated guess about a marketing relationship or, using automated discovery, search for hidden relationships. It is both a descriptive and predictive tool. Data mining is far more complex than collaborative filtering, which produces personal recommendations by comparing a present preference with those of others with the same or similar preferences.

## Collect and Apply

Cookies, bugs, and web analytics are privacy-sensitive tools. Each is defended for the value it creates for improving web site experiences and online marketing efficiency. At the same time they are highly visible targets for privacy advocates. Cookies, small data files placed on a user's browser by a web site's server, are delivered firsthand from a site's web server to the user's hard drive. Web beacons or bugs are single-pixel electronic GIF images placed by third-party media and research companies. They greatly increase the number of web sites where data can be collected. Network advertisers claim the information collected by web beacons allows them to make offers that are more relevant to visitors. Most web servers log (record) every request they receive in server log files. Server logs are traffic counters. Web analytics is both the software that runs sophisticated analysis programs and the people who organize, manage, interpret, and apply the results. Professionals trained in web analytics analyze results and evaluate changes in channel strategy based on web analytic measures. Electronic customer relationship management (eCRM) is a broad overall strategy that uses a web analytical approach to anticipate, understand, and respond to current and potential customer needs. Sometimes referred to as analytical CRM, eCRM is the application of the tools used to operationalize data, primarily from the Web.

## Marketing Intelligence

The Web's unique interactivity and the ease of collecting information means marketing intelligence gathering can be faster, cheaper, and easier than ever before. Intelligence is a *process*, a system for collecting and transforming data, and *content*, knowledge for marketing decisions. Marketing intelligence requires collecting and transforming data into information, knowledge, and intelligence about markets, competitors, the environment, customers, and other marketing areas of concern. Intelligence is used to adjust market offers and the process of making them. Intelligence activities can be focused in-house, outside, or both. Marketing intelligence can be collected, processed, and reported in the traditional manner by people, totally by automatic computer searches, or by a combination of both processes. A growing number of marketing intelligence activities are web based, particularly those focusing on competitors and their online market offers. Most of the information that any business needs to conduct competitive intelligence is available from open public records. Even with the wealth of legal online data, some individuals and organizations still cross the line of acceptable, legal practices to engage in economic (industrial) espionage. Espionage, an attempt by one company to discover another's secrets, is illegal as well as unethical.

## Internet Marketing Application

Monster.com (*http://www.monster.com*) is the leading worldwide career network. It has web sites in the United States, Canada, the United Kingdom, the Netherlands, Belgium, France, Germany, Italy, and eight other countries. Monster relies on monster databases and warehouses to keep data organized and powerful search tools that retrieve requested information. It has two target markets, job seekers and job providers (employers). Monster offers resume management help, a personal job search agent, networking and discussion boards, and expert advice. Monster.com uses monsterTRAK (*http://www.monstertrak.com/about.html*) to collect data and create databases targeted to more than twelve hundred university and college career centers, and MBA programs. In 2001, its job listing database had over 340,000 files; the student resume databases contained over 750,000 files.

Go to the Monster.com job search (*http://jobsearch.monster.com*) and search for a job in Advertising/Marketing/Public Relations in a location where you would like to live. When the results appear, do a sort by date. Then try a sort by relevance. Explain what you have done in database terms. Using the diagram in figure 8-2, explain the process of matching student and job through Monster's databases. How does information flow into and out of Monster's databases?

**Figure 8-2  Information Flow at Monster.com**

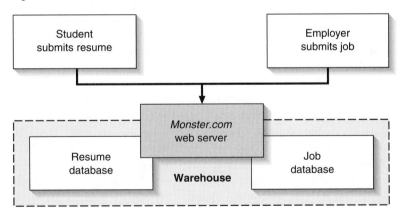

# Chapter Review Questions

1. What is a digital footprint and why would a marketer care about them?
2. Explain the privacy implications of opt-in and opt-out processes.
3. What are the benefits and costs of the web being so information rich?
4. What is the advantage of IT/marketing collaborations?
5. What is a database?
6. What is a database approach?
7. Should all customers be treated equally?
8. Why must databases be cleaned regularly?
9. What are some sources for in-house data?
10. Contrast standard cookies and web beacons or bugs.
11. What types of direct data can cookies store?
12. How does a user know a cookie has been placed on his or her computer?
13. Why can't a marketer just read a server log?
14. Why are people with web analytics skills in demand?
15. Do all marketers need competitive intelligence?

## DoubleClick Clicks On

# Case Study

DoubleClick (*http://www.doubleclick.net/us*), like other net advertisers and advertising placement services, places cookies for targeting user interests, tracking their movements, and directing customized banner ads to their browsers. A recent study revealed that though U.S. consumers are not happy with the many assaults on their privacy, personalized marketing does not bother them, and 60 percent approve of it because the information can help marketers better serve their needs.

Cookies are not well liked by most consumer privacy advocates, but they are tolerated because they are not directly linked to user identity. This changed dramatically in June 1999 when DoubleClick made public its plans to acquire Abacus Direct Corp. This gave DoubleClick access to a huge data warehouse and the opportunity to connect identities, names, ages, and shopping habits. A complaint was filed with the Federal Trade Commission (FTC) that DoubleClick engaged in unfair and deceptive trade practices. DoubleClick was also cited by the Attorney General of Michigan for misleading opt-out practices. The media, privacy advocates, and the public roundly criticized DoubleClick and, by association, the entire online advertising industry for deceptive and intrusive

practices. DoubleClick responded by hiring a chief privacy officer and recruiting a blue ribbon privacy panel to advise the company on its practices. It also agreed to delay the merging of the databases.

Certainly DoubleClick let itself in for a deluge of criticism, but the company's critics also may have overreacted. The privacy of personal financial and medical records should be protected at all costs. However, marketers believe collecting personal consumer data is defensible because it can be used to refine targeting and reduce misdirected promotion, which can also remove some of the online advertising clutter. This illustrates that different types of data require different levels of privacy.

In January 2002, DoubleClick announced it had dropped its Intelligent Targeting service that targeted individuals with customized web advertising. This service tracked where users had been on the web. Based on the type of site they visited, an associated advertisement was directed at them. For example, if a user had just visited a gardening site, then the next time he or she clicked on a site with a DoubleClick beacon, an ad for gardening tools appeared on the page to stimulate the user's interest in visiting the site that sponsored the advertisement. DoubleClick maintained that dropping Intelligent Targeting was not related to privacy concerns. Its Dynamic Advertising Reporting Targeting (DART) service will continue operating, directing ads to DoubleClick sites based on twenty-two targeting criteria, including the user's geographic location and the time of day when he or she reached the site.[30]

## CHECK IT OUT

DoubleClick goes to great lengths to explain its privacy policy (*http://www.doubleclick.net/us/corporate/ privacy/privacy/default.asp?asp_object_1=↺*). It even has an *Ad-Cookie Opt-Out* link prominently positioned at the top of its privacy page. Visit DoubleClick and check out its privacy policies. Considering DoubleClick's affiliation with TRUSTe and the Network Advertising Initiative, what else can the company do to reassure privacy advocates? Has it done enough? Will the "average" visitor be able to read and understand DoubleClick's privacy policies? Will they have the patience to read them?

## A GLOBAL PERSPECTIVE

In Europe, DoubleClick and other U.S. online companies must comply with the Safe Harbor agreement with the European Union (EU). Safe Harbor is a form of geographic privacy wall thrown up around members of the EU but covering U.S. businesses marketing to EU consumers. Signed in 2000 by the U.S. Department of Commerce and the EU, Safe Harbor is an international privacy accord that clearly delineates privacy differences between the United States and the EU. Personal privacy has always been more stringently protected in Europe, far less so in the United States.

The law covers all industry sectors and practically all types of personal information. It places significant limitations on the type of data collected and the flow of data, online and off. Companies that collect consumer data and sign on to the agreement must satisfy the much stricter standards of the European directive. Safe Harbor promises European consumers control over how their personal data are collected and used. One advantage of Safe Harbor is that privacy restrictions are standardized for all fifteen member states. Failure to comply could result in legal action as well as negative publicity.

TRUSTe has begun a special program offering TRUSTe EU Safe Harbor certification (*http://truste. com/programs/pub_harbor.html*). Companies that meet TRUSTe Safe Harbor standards are issued a special stamp to place on their web site front page indicating compliance. A TRUSTe spokesperson said, "Companies that want to compete globally will be strongly motivated to comply with the law." The idea is that if a U.S. company is certified, it will satisfy EU officials that acceptable privacy protection is in place.

Many U.S. companies are concerned about the cost of complying with the voluntary standards. They are also worried that signing on to the EU standards will mean extending those same protections to their U.S. customers. They also do not believe the EU can really enforce the standards. Even privacy advocates in Europe and the United States believe the Safe Harbor agreements are weak and unenforceable.

Check out the following U.S. multinationals. Are they Safe? Can you tell from their front pages? How far into the site does a user have to drill down until it becomes clear that the site is/is not Safe? Is there a marketing advantage to declaring that a web site is Safe Harbor certified? If so, are these sites using it?

- Intel Corp. (*http://www.intel.com*)
- Bell South (*http://www.bellsouth.com*)
- eBay (*http://www.ebay.com*)
- DoubleClick (*http://www.doubleclick.net/us*)
- Hewlett Packard (*http://www.hp.com*)
- Amazon.com (*http://www.amazon.com*)
- IBM (*http://www.ibm.com*)

# Module III
## *The Internet Marketing Mix*

The marketing mix, or 4Ps, of product, price, place (distribution), and promotion are known to anyone who has ever taken an introductory marketing class. Although many attempts have been made to replace or expand the Ps, they have endured as an effective method for organizing the major tactical tools marketers can deploy in a competitive marketplace. Just as the 4Ps have an enduring place offline, their importance online is equally compelling. Many dot-com failures can be attributed to weak or nonexistent attention to the planning, implementation, and control of the marketing mix, and the essential details that mean the difference between profitability and bankruptcy.

Module III begins with Chapter 9, Products and Brands. The next three chapters focus on the remaining 4Ps, their fundamentals and Internet applications. Although the field is still very young and highly dynamic, successful Internet marketing mix models are emerging and providing lessons for others trying to find marketing success online.

# Products and Brands

## Shawn's Soccer Haus

Shawn has been intimately involved with soccer (*football* outside the United States) for almost thirty years. He began playing at five, became a high school and competitive team member in his teens, and was voted All State his senior year. He went to college on a full soccer scholarship and after graduation coached, refereed, and played on local adult teams. Twelve years ago he realized a lifelong dream and opened *Shawn's Soccer Haus* on the first floor of an old two-story house in his hometown. He lived above the store. Shawn has been extremely successful developing his business, marketing high-quality soccer uniforms, bags, shoes, and other soccer equipment to youth and adult teams. It did not take long before he had twenty-three *Shawn's Soccer Haus* stores in a tristate region and on the Web. Three years ago he started a manufacturing operation that customizes team uniforms made of the best moisture management nylons, polyesters, and satins, using imported sublimation dyes. His wife designs unique team logos that are extremely popular with players and coaches. The customization end of his business has prospered, and Shawn is expanding it to his web site to reach customers outside the retail area he currently serves. His IT consultant is developing a user-friendly online ordering system where customers are guided through a menu of options for colors, fabrics, stitching, and styles, culminating with the design of a unique team logo. Shawn traces his success to high-quality customized products, attentive personal service, customer satisfaction, and positive word of mouth. Since most teams he works with travel to tournaments throughout the United States and Canada, Shawn's products have wide exposure. Each team brings extra logo patches to exchange with their opponents after each tournament match. Every player wearing a *Shawn's* uniform and trading *Shawn's Soccer Haus* logo patches promotes his brand name. Shawn's branded web site reflects his deep involvement with his products and sport, and his commitment to establishing long-term relationships with customers. In addition to marketing products from the site, he also has a web page with links to soccer skill training lessons, a soccer video game area, scores for high school and competitive team matches, FIFA (Federation Internationale de Football Association) and World Cup links, and free web space on his server for any team wearing *Shawn's Soccer Haus* brand uniforms. These soccer communities provide feedback and endorsements for his products. They are also Shawn's way of giving back something to his loyal customers and the sport he loves.

Shawn's understanding of soccer and soccer players, and his commitment to high-quality products and long-term customer relationships, are the foundations for his marketing success. He knows an effective web site can extend his offer to markets that would otherwise be difficult if not impossible to reach. It can also help him better serve current customers.

Shawn's customers are consumers purchasing products (branded apparel and equipment) for personal and team use, and schools and universities purchasing products for their soccer teams. His web site offer includes *goods*, a *service* (helping teams design a unique logo patch), digital *information* (score updates, soccer skill lessons), and *entertainment* (soccer video games). Products and brands are the subjects of this chapter. The Internet is creating unique opportunities for marketing products to consumers and enterprises, encouraging the development of complementary strategies with offline products and brands, and creating new online products and brands.

# *Product Fundamentals*

**Product**
The market offer of a good, service, idea, information, or other item or activity offered in exchange for something of value from the buyer, usually cash or credit.

**Product** is the marketing mix variable that determines to a significant extent how strategies are developed for the other Ps—price, place (distribution), and promotion. A product can be a good, service, idea, place, person, information, entertainment, organization, or other object or act offered in exchange for something of value, usually cash or credit. It is the offer made to a market, a bundle of benefits that creates value for buyers. Some benefits derive from what the product does while others are perceptual, relating to the status of owning and using the product. Marketing mix decisions are product-specific, yet marketers rarely have exclusive authority to make all product decisions. Most are made collaboratively by teams of people from marketing and sales, production and manufacturing, finance, and other departments. Marketers contribute essential information to product decisions, particularly knowledge about buyers' responses to product offers, their product preferences, and demand forecasts.

## BUYERS AND PRODUCT USE

Two key criteria in understanding product are *buyer* and *use*. Key questions are *who is the buyer* and *how will the product be used?* Consumers use products to fill needs and wants, satisfy their desire to take possession and own something of value, and send signals about their preferences, buying power, and social standing. Products solve problems for businesses and other enterprises.

Consumer and enterprise buyers sometimes purchase the same products; for example, computer disks and software, light bulbs and fixtures, trucks, and office products. Other times they buy radically different products. Even when they purchase the same products, there are significant differences in the quantities they purchase, purchase and repurchase schedules, purchase processes, price paid per unit, and delivery terms.

Enterprise buyers often are purchasing professionals, trained in making product purchases that satisfy specifications for functionality, quality, price, delivery, and post-purchase service. They establish long-term relationships with suppliers, working with them and negotiating to obtain products customized to meet their business needs. Consumers are not trained buyers and make their own decisions individually, as families, or as groups. Their purchases are more prone to be influenced by emotions and are sometimes inconsistent and even erratic.

## PRODUCT STATE

Products are also differentiated by their state. They can be *goods* (tangible products like a candle), *services* (intangible products like a haircut, a performed service), *digitals* (electronic products like digital cash and digital music in byte form), or a mixture.

**GOODS**    Goods are tangible physical products that can be felt, stored, inventoried, mass-produced or produced in quantity, transported, tested in advance of purchase, and quality controlled. Examples include: pencils, automobiles, potatoes, shoes. Consumer and enterprise goods are offered online, but the transfer of the tangible product to the buyer adds cost (shipping and handling) and lengthens the time between purchase and possession. A significant problem with offering goods online is how they are presented to potential buyers. Consumer goods are commonly shown in thumbnail pictures, presented several to a web page. One-dimensional images are not a good substitute for being able to see, touch, smell, or taste goods in a bricks-and-mortar store. Pictures of goods can be enlarged and rotated online, which makes their presentation on a web page superior to flat static pictures in a hard-copy catalog. For example, at an apparel web site, articles of clothing can be fitted to the consumer's virtual model, colors changed, and the model rotated so the consumer sees how he or she will look wearing the item.

**SERVICES**    Services are performances that cannot be stored, inventoried, mass-produced, transported, tested in advance, or controlled through standardized quality control methods. Services typically are inseparable from their performance; service consumption often cannot be delayed from its delivery. The customer is more or less a participant in the service performance and does not have ownership of it. Examples include: a haircut, marriage counseling, automobile tune-up, computer maintenance. Although some services are delivered online, the majority are delivered offline, and many are a mixture of online/offline delivery. A haircut cannot be delivered online, but a hairdresser appointment can be scheduled online. A customer can evaluate an assortment of haircut styles online, select one, and print it for his/her stylist to copy. Industrial equipment maintenance can be scheduled online, but servicing the equipment must be performed offline. Some computer repairs can be completed online; for example, new printer drivers can be downloaded and installed in the user's computer. Counseling services are offered online, from marriage and divorce to medical.

**Digital (electronic) products**

Products that are created, transmitted, and/or stored electronically in bytes (binary digits) and includes digital cash, digital music, and information.

**DIGITALS**    **Digital (electronic) products** are created, transmitted, and/or stored electronically in bytes (binary digits). Examples include: digital cash, digital music, electronic airline tickets, travel itinerary scheduling. Most digitals are not unique to the Internet but are particularly well suited to Internet purchase and delivery.

**MIXED**    Mixed products are combinations, a mixture of forms. Examples include: an oil change (good and service), a computer operating system upgrade pushed from a software vendor's site (digital and service), video training lessons that accompany an exercise machine (service and good), restaurant dinner (good and service).

Consumers relate better to tangible goods that are readily observed, touched, and easier to define. As a result, marketers frequently associate intangible services and digital products with a readily recognized image to make them more tangible. Met-Life (*http://www.metlife.com*) anchors its life insurance products to the cartoon figure

Snoopy as a metaphor for a friendly product and company. Snoopy is heavily licensed and reproduced as stuffed toys, action figures, on lunch boxes, T-shirts, calendars, and other products. He is featured throughout the MetLife web site. Characters from Peanuts are the property of United Feature Syndicate, Inc. MetLife licenses the characters for use in its promotions and web site, and is very conscientious about providing a copyright disclaimer on each of its web pages.

MetLife has successfully branded its intangible product through association with a readily-identified, highly-popular cartoon figure. Snoopy is a positive symbol of a brand that cares about its customers. Although spokestoons (cartoon *spokes "people"*) are more commonly used with products targeted to kids, Snoopy has a high rating among adults, MetLife's target audience. He is also inoffensive and safe.

MetLife has a *oneline* strategy, using Snoopy offline and continuing the practice online. Other companies also use a oneline strategy. For example, Allstate.com (*http://www.allstate.com*) has its welcoming hands embedded within the company logo and slogan "You're in good hands." Hands also appear in multiple shots on its front page, both as line drawings and in pictures of satisfied customers. Hands in various poses, along with the statement "The right hands make all the difference," appear in a heading that begins each page.

With relatively few exceptions, most goods sold offline are also sold online. This includes durables, nondurables, disposables, and perishables (table 9-1). For those that are not, the offline sale can be facilitated online with a web site that displays the product, provides useful information about it, and drives buyers to contact a salesperson for more information or to visit an offline store. This is certainly the case with large, custom-made industrial and defense products like aircraft or naval vessels that require negotiations over the specifications of their construction. It is also the case with customized enterprise computer systems, computers and other equipment that must be adapted to the unique needs of the business. In both cases, products presented on a web site are designed to drive customers or prospective customers to contact the offline sales force.

## Table 9.1 Goods Purchasable Online

| | |
|---|---|
| *Durables* | Durable goods have relatively long life spans and can be used over and over. A clothes washer is a consumer durable that can last several decades depending on its maintenance and use. Sears sells durable Kenmore washing machines online at *http://www.sears.com* with delivery scheduled from a Sears warehouse via UPS, the USPS, or Sears Home Delivery. |
| *Non-durables* | A shampoo is used up within weeks of purchase and has to be replaced on a regular basis. Shampoo can be ordered online from Drugstore.com at *http://www.drugstore.com*. |
| *Disposables* | A paper cup is a *disposable* (expendable) non-durable used once, then discarded. Drugstore.com also has a full line of paper cups from its Dixie Store. |
| *Perishables* | A *perishable* is a non-durable with a short life span. This includes frozen foods like ice cream. Schwan's has been home delivering frozen food since 1952 and now has online ordering (*http://www.schwans.com*) for direct-to-home delivery. |

DotComGuy proved the point that just about all products needed for human survival are available online. Bachelor Mitch Maddox, a twenty-six-year-old Dallas, Texas, resident, former computing systems manager for UPS, officially changed his name to DotComGuy and moved into an empty two-bedroom house January 1, 2000, with nothing but a laptop computer, a credit card, and an Internet connection. During the following twelve months he completely furnished the house, and purchased food, entertainment, clothing, and even a dog online. Naturally, the pooch was named DotComDog. His activities were broadcast live on the DotComGuy web site, recorded by twenty video cameras. Almost one million people worldwide logged onto the site in one twelve-hour period. He also hosted live chats. The DotComGuy experiment was sponsored and the web site heavily promoted the sponsors' products. DotComGuy emerged January 1, 2001, and promptly proposed marriage to a woman he met online in his chat room.

Was DotComGuy, as he said, trying to *help people realize the possibilities of ecommerce,* or was this a case of uncurbed product placement? Some critics contend he was an example of everything that is wrong with Internet commercialization. Everything he did and almost every product he used was sponsored. Whatever it was, DotComGuy, now returned to his original name, demonstrated the breadth of products available online, the convenience of shopping there, and the commercial potential of the Internet for business and society.[1]

## PRODUCT LAYERS

Products can be thought of in terms of multiple layers. Each layer adds value and an opportunity for marketers to connect with buyers. The layers are the *core product* (functional elements, design, benefits offered, needs satisfied, patent protection), *packaging* (brand name, style, quality, product features, package, packing, trademark, trade dress, price, and image), *support* (delivery, credit, warranty, guarantee, installation, post sale service, repairs, spare parts, and training), and *product potential* (proposed product extensions, modifications, improvements, repositioning, and rebranding).

Consider the example of perfume where the *core product* is a tangible good, a liquid blend of plant and animal products, delicate oils, and various chemicals. Perfumes were used initially to mask unpleasant odors associated with people who did not bathe often, use deodorants, or change their clothing regularly. Today, perfumes are used for pleasure, to appeal to others, as gifts, and as a social statement related to the product's cost, image, and availability. The product formula is legally protected. Branding is extremely important to perfume sales. Consumers can select from among more than thirty-five hundred perfume brands at FragranceNet.com (*http://www. fragrancenet.com/html*) or make their own signature fragrance at Reflect.com (*http:// www.reflect.com*). FragranceNet.com is an example of a web site complementing the offline marketing of the same branded products. Reflect.com is an example of a web site with a unique product offer, products mass-customized to consumer preferences with no widely available offline equivalent.

Perfume is a highly personal product. Most women want to smell a perfume before making an initial purchase unless the purchase is a rebuy. The perfume's fragrance has to satisfy them, yet if asked, most buyers can explain their preferences only in very general terms. As of yet, products cannot be smelled online, although researchers are developing systems that will mimic smells. FragranceNet.com overcomes this sensory limitation by selling known brands. The assumption is that a buyer comes to the

site with a brand already picked out from past experi~~ ~~
Reflect.com, where the buyer creates her own perfume
analysis-based series of choices.

Much of a perfume's allure and considerable expen~~ ~~
most cases, the package costs more than the colorless~~ ~~
fumes are collector's items valued for their distinctive~~ ~~
elaborate embellishments. Consumers interested only~~ ~~
fume, can find what they want at eBay.com. The repu~~ ~~
ated with a brand name, particularly if it is a respected designer s, auus caua ...... ..
the perfume, and supports a higher price.

In addition to the container holding the liquid, additional packing is needed to
safely transport the bottle, display it on a store shelf, and protect it from tampering or
spillage. Product pictures on FragranceNet.com accurately display perfume containers. Spillage is obviously not a concern when perfume is displayed on a web page.
Tampering with a web page and product images are possible, but for most sites, not
likely. Packaging for delivery from a web site is no different than a purchase from a
store, catalog, or telephone sale.

Unlike computers or automobiles, few *support* services are bundled with perfume.
Since perfume is a tangible good, shipping and handling (S&H) are added to the delivery cost, unless the site offers free S&H for sales above a preset amount. Customer-
centric retailers offer product satisfaction guarantees and instructions for product
returns. Support services with other products can be extremely important. Computers, a very popular online product, are often differentiated by the level of support that
comes with the product. Some support can be delivered directly from a web site.
Printer drivers, software, and training videos can be downloaded. Most computer
sites offer pages of *Frequently Asked Questions* (FAQs) that can be used to minimize
expensive telephone service calls.

*Product potential* is where consumers can provide valuable input into product
modifications, extensions, and repositioning. Reflect.com is an example where customers can make their own fragrance and other beauty products, and in the process
provide the company with valuable information about their product preferences. Customer product feedback is evaluated and transformed into information that affects future product decisions. Many sites use onsite pop-up surveys to obtain product
feedback from customers. Others hire marketing research firms to conduct online focus groups that recruit customers to answer product-specific questions.

## MASS CUSTOMIZATION

**Mass marketing
strategy**
Assumes a homogeneous
market, with undifferentiated buyers who will
accept standardized
products and have the
same general preferences
for price, and place/distri-
bution, and can be
reached by the same types
of promotion.

Custom manufacturing, where goods were manufactured on demand and exclusively
for the buyer, was the norm until around the beginning of the twentieth century. That
is when assembly lines and modern mechanization facilitated the development of
mass manufacturing processes and, later, mass marketing. **A mass marketing strategy**
assumes the market is relatively homogeneous, composed of buyers who generally
share preferences for products, price, place/distribution, and promotion alternatives.
The assumption is that these buyers are satisfied with and purchase standardized,
one-size-fits-all mass marketed products and do not demand customized products.
Even within mass markets some differentiation may occur. Cheerios cereal (*http://
www.cheerios.com*), an over sixty-year-old brand, originally came in only one formu-
lation, *The 1 and Only Cheerios* as proclaimed on its web site. Today, the Cheerios

Family of Cereals includes, in addition to original Cheerios, Multi Grain, Frosted, Apple Cinnamon, Honey Nut, and Team & Cheerios. Thus, this is a standardized product with several variants appealing to different tastes.

*Standardized products* are mass-produced uniform products with no direct buyer input about product variations. Examples are canned foods and printer paper. Variations of a product are often produced so buyers have limited choice; for example, Procter & Gamble produces several alternate Tide laundry detergent formulations, including powder and liquid, with and without bleach. Many standardized products are sold online. For example, Walmart.com (*http://www.walmart.com*) offers printer paper while Sam's Club (*http://www.samsclub.com*) sells non-perishable foods and cleaning supplies.

*Mass-customized products* give buyers options, within limits set by the manufacturer. Buyers are involved in the manufacturing process as they provide input to product design. Semimade products are completed with input from buyers. Examples include Reflect.com cosmetics and fragrances, and Dell (*http://www.dell.com*) computers.

*Customized products* are unique. The manufacturer works directly with the buyer to produce an original, unduplicated product. Examples include a hand-tailored shirt, landscaping, home addition. Tailors, garden centers, and building contractors are all online, but to deliver customized products, many typically must still meet the client face to face. In the case of hand tailoring, once the tailor has the client's measurements, subsequent orders can be taken online.

A customized product is made especially for the buyer. ToyBuilders.com (*http://www.toybuilders.com*) turns imagination into reality by letting customers design their own board pieces for Monopoly, Clue, Chess, Checkers, various role-playing games, and even their own toys. Some game pieces incorporate photographs of the customer's family members. Rapid prototyping machines are used to capture customers' designs and translate them into finished, custom-made products. Prospective customers can see product samples to help them create designs. Design ideas can be developed using site interactivity. Customers can then see a model of their order in three dimensions before they give final approval for its manufacture. Online advantages are convenience, timeliness, and availability. Disadvantages are not being able to physically touch or otherwise interact with a tangible product until the completed product is received.

**Mass customization**

Allowing consumers to customize a product online within limited preset options.

**Mass customization** produces a large quantity of *customized* products very quickly because buyer options are limited and products are semiproduced in advance of the final customization. Producers have the flexibility to offer mass customization online backed by modular product design, flexible manufacturing processes, intelligent manufacturing systems, computerized order management, information systems and databases, and delayed assembly.[2]

Mass customization is particularly well suited to Internet marketing, with its worldwide reach and facility for collecting information interactively and quickly. A mass-customized product is often developed from visitor responses to preprogrammed closed-ended questions. Visual images can be used to add greater depth to the choices. Touch and smell limitations online currently restrict using these senses in customizing consumer products but careful choice of keyword descriptors give buyers verbal cues to touch and smell features.

Consider Reflect.com, the site that allows customers to design their own perfume (see the accompanying screen shot). The site was launched in September 1999 as a separate and privately owned Procter & Gamble (P&G) spinoff. P&G retains a 65 percent ownership. A visitor is guided through a series of questions that builds a profile for when the perfume will be worn (occasion) and preferences for top, middle, and bottom notes (fragrance shades). Visitors have a limited number of choices to make, which ensures a manageable number of different perfume formulations. Once purchased and named by the customer, the customized perfume is elaborately packed, shipped without charge, and unconditionally guaranteed. Rather than deal with costly returns, a customer who is not satisfied gets to keep the fragrance and try again. Marketing research has shown that the site has the highest conversion rate (browser to buyer) of any online beauty site and a lower shopping basket abandonment rate than similar sites. The industry's abandonment rate average is from 65 to 85 percent.[3] This suggests that Reflect.com has found a winning formula for satisfying customers with mass-customized products.

**Customization Delivered**

Reflect.com lets women design their own products, within limits. It offers *One-of-a-kind beauty for a one-of-a-kind you. Source:* Reprinted by permission of Reflect.com. *http://www.reflect.com.*

Consumers designing their own fragrances at Reflect.com pose less of a threat to cannibalize offline retailer sales than if P&G offered its existing perfume product line directly to consumers from its web site. There is a powerful incentive for manufacturers to adopt a mass customization approach online and avoid confrontations with their offline distributors. At the same time, Reflect.com's customized, Internet-only perfume is a high margin product because the process eliminates traditional intermediaries from the distribution channel, and the products move quickly out of inventory, reducing inventory holding costs.[4]

General Mills, another mass marketer, test marketed cereal customization at MyCereal.com. Choices were limited, and fresh fruits not allowed. Access to the beta-site was restricted to select visitors while the concept was tested. Customized cereals sold at premium prices (US$1.19 for each 3.3 ounce serving) and buyers could name their cereal, which was boxed and labeled with contents, nutritional values, and the buyer's name. Orders were constrained to between seven and forty-two servings, in seven-serving units. Shipping was extra for two-day Federal Express. Visitors were asked to create a profile based on age, gender, and food allergies. They checked off their preferences for cereal flakes, puffs, other formulations, fruits (dried), nuts, and clusters including banana, shaped, and marshmallow bits. They answered questions about their nutritional and diet requirements, and health issues. The specially formulated cereal contained health and diet information. In mid-2002, the site disappeared and its URL redirected to the General Mills corporate web site. Analysis of the test market results will help determine if it will be relaunched for the general public.[5]

Many, but not all, consumers willingly accept premium or vanity prices for products they customize. Marketers recognize the profit in this strategy and offer online mass customization for a wide variety of products including soccer uniforms (CustomJersey.com at *http://www.customjersey.com/soccer.html*), bicycles (HubBub Custom Bicycles, fitting, and refitting at *http://www.hubbub.com*), and watches (eWatch Factory at *http://www.ewatchfactory.com/retail/en/index.htm*), among others.

Personalization, or one-to-one marketing, is not mass customization. It uses technology, particularly cookies, collaborative filtering, and databases with customer information (stored or collected in real time) to familiarize electronic commerce interactions between a marketer and each customer (see Chapter 8). It appears as a line on the front page welcoming a customer back to the site by greeting him or her by name or in products suggested to the customer because they are like or associated with products already purchased or selected for purchase.

## BUYING PRODUCTS ONLINE: ADVANTAGES AND DISADVANTAGES

Communication and information seeking are still the primary reasons consumers go online. However, online shopping's popularity is growing. Increasing numbers of consumers are going online to purchase products or research them, then make their purchase in stores, catalogs, or by telephone or fax. U.S. online retail sales are conservatively forecast to reach US$104 billion by 2005, up from US$27 billion in 2000, with 63 percent of the Internet-using population expected to be shopping online by 2006.[6]

Online shopping has many advantages but also drawbacks (table 9-2). As more well known bricks-and-mortar retailers establish themselves online, consumers are responding positively to **multichannel retailing,** that is, being able to purchase products through any of several different channels. Consumers like the convenience and expanded choices of buying products online as well as in offline stores, through catalogs, in kiosks, and so on. Retailers have observed that customers who shop multiple channels generate up to eight times the revenue of shoppers who use only one channel.[7]

**Multichannel retailing**
Offering more than one way for consumers to purchase the same product; for example, online, by catalog, and in retail stores.

Consumers want the same products online they can purchase offline, particularly tangible goods. They want the same assortment, quality, brands, and general shopping experience. By 2005, up to 10 to 12 percent of *all* sales of apparel, accessories, health and beauty, and toys will be made online, along with as much as 25 percent of all sales of books, music, software, videos, and consumer electronics.[8]

A greater variety of products are being purchased online than ever before and sales of some old standards are dramatically increasing. Travel services in particular are highly popular both in North America and Europe. Estimated online monthly revenue for travel service sales in Q3 2001 was US$4.258 billion, an increase of 53 percent from Q3 2000 sales of US$2.788 billion. Clothing and apparel sales online increased 77 percent from US$839 million in Q3 2000 to US$1.482 billion in Q3 2001. Computer hardware/peripheral sales increased 22 percent from US$928 million in Q3 2000 to US$1.137 billion in Q3 2001. Book sales grew 79 percent from US$447 million in Q3 2000 to US$798 million in Q3 2001. Sales of music, health/beauty, and home and garden were all approaching US$100 million annually. Gaining ground are sales of vitamins, food and beverages, perishables, and frozen foods. Online purchases also reflect seasonality effects. Online sales of toys and games increased 123 percent from before the start of the holiday buying season in 2001, while consumer electronics jumped 97 percent and apparel rose 67 percent in the same period.[9]

## Table 9-2  Online Product-Related Shopping Advantages and Disadvantages

**Advantages**

Greater product assortment than in stores

Products can be found online that cannot be found in stores

Large number of sellers for product comparison shopping

Rapid product comparisons can be made

Direct delivery of products to local address

Greater access to product information, specifications

Product sales are (currently) mostly untaxed

Provides access to products for shoppers living in remote areas

**Disadvantages**

Security and privacy risk associated with online product purchases

Purchasing process breakdowns

Delivery risk, particularly with expensive products left at consumer's front door

Can't touch, feel, smell, taste products

Product pictures are often small and static

Product colors can be distorted by computer monitors

Quality is difficult to assess

Added costs of product shipping and handling

Product returns and redress can be complicated and frustrating

Lengthy search time for products and prices

Too much product information can overload and frustrate shoppers

Selling goods online also has disadvantages. For example, the perfume example at the beginning of this chapter illustrates the disadvantage of not being able to smell a product where smell is an important selling point. Apparel cannot be felt or tried on, although virtual models help consumers form an image of how apparel will fit their body type. Sensors embedded in a mouse and linked to coded online product pictures will eventually solve the touch disadvantage for some products sold online. Lands' End is tackling the fit problem with its feature *My Virtual Model* that allows a visitor to construct a body model to fit with apparel choices. The model is built by the visitor's answers to a series of questions about his or her body size and shape. If the visitor is honest, the model should be fairly representative of his or her body, but it is not the same as actually pulling on a pair of slacks and making sure the seat has enough room. Products whose size and dimensions are important to consumers should be presented with sufficiently detailed information so customers do not have to guess. This can also help avoid mistakes and costly returns. Pushing a lawn mower, slamming a car door, tasting a piece of cake, and walking in a pair of shoes are certainly out of the question online, at least for now.

Product picture quality is a serious problem online. Colors are notoriously difficult to accurately display and transmit. The problem is usually in the visitor's monitor and how well it is tuned to web-safe colors. Most do not display web-ready colors accurately.

A polo shirt that is tomato red on the web storefront's server may appear as an unappetizing, washed out dirty red-brown on the visitor's monitor. Few buyers are interested in purchasing a dirty red-brown polo.

Another problem is the number of product pictures shown on each page, their size, and how quickly new product pages load. Product pictures that are too small are difficult to see on small monitors. Too many pictures or overly large ones slow download time. Picture enlargements, rotations, and new views all can slow download times. Visitors using slow modems may find online window shopping more trouble than it is worth. This is a serious problem that needs immediate solutions and not waiting for wide-scale consumer adoption of faster connections (DSL, cable, etc.).

All retailers face product returns, overstocks, closeouts, and remainders. Many bricks-and-clicks retailers allow store returns of products purchased online, an advantage for the buyer. Otherwise returns are sent back by delivery carrier. Generally, it is too costly to restock returns, so they are sent to the retailer's own outlet stores or sold to companies like It'sGottaGo.com (*http://www.itsgottago.com*), an ecommerce marketplace that sells closeouts at auction. Overstock.com (*http://www.overstock.com*) sells name brands at clearance prices, sometimes as much as 70 percent off list.

Another problem relates to the nature of services. Services like dry cleaning, shoe repair, child care, oil changes, window cleaning, and dental work do not lend themselves to online performance. However, a dry cleaner can have a web site with prices, delivery times, environmental information about cleaning solutions, and tips on stain removal. A child care center can have a web site with information about the center and its personnel, schedules of special programs, and pictures of kids' art work. Many centers give parents access to private web pages with live video cameras (cams) trained on the classrooms so they can check on their children throughout the day. Service providers can use web sites in highly creative ways to make a positive connection with their customers and prospects.

Online product sales are still only a small fraction of total retail sales, slightly over 1 percent, yet marketers remain optimistic about the future, particularly as more bricks and clicks report profits from online sales. Children and teens who have grown up playing online games and using instant messaging are expected to fuel online sales as they enter their prime buying years. Aging convenience-seeking baby boomers also will contribute more to online sales growth. Wider adoption of broadband and the development of processes that eliminate some key online shopping drawbacks are critical to convincing more consumers to shop online. For the 31 percent of U.S. Internet users with broadband access either at home, work, or school, shopping online is faster and more enticing.[10] As consumers become more familiar with purchasing online, they will do so more often and in larger volumes. As online shopping becomes easier and faster, it will encourage more consumers to try it. The challenge for Internet marketers is to carefully analyze the advantages and disadvantages of offering company products online, then make the necessary adjustments and accommodations.

## ✔ CONCEPT CHECK

1. How can online marketers use the multilayer product concept to differentiate their offer?
2. Why is the Internet an inviting environment for mass customization?
3. What are some disadvantages associated with online product sales?

# *Consumer Products*

U.S. consumers obviously spend considerable time, effort, and money shopping. Their personal high debt load attests to their commitment. Consumer spending (primary demand) is an essential contributor to the nation's economy, accounting for two-thirds of U.S. GDP, and stimulates derived demand for industrial production.

Melvin Copeland recognized the importance of consumer shopping in 1923. In a *Harvard Business Review* article he proposed a classification system for merchandise sold in retail stores. This system is still used today with some modifications, principally of products that were not available in the 1920s.[11] The definition of product was limited solely to tangible goods when Copeland developed his classification system. Today, that definition has expanded dramatically. Copeland's classification is based on buyer habits, the consumer's view of the purchase of convenience, shopping, specialty, and unsought products. These product types form the framework for the examination of online consumer product offers.

## CONVENIENCE PRODUCTS

Convenience products are staples, emergency, and/or impulse products. Many convenience products, particularly staples, have thin profit margins. To be profitable, marketers must have high-volume sales and maintain tight cost controls. High shipping and handling costs, and the eventual collection of sales tax, are working against their online profitability. However, consumers value convenience and this is the foundation of optimistic forecasts for the growth of convenience product sales online.

**STAPLES**   These products are purchased frequently, are readily available in many different locations, and often are disposable, low cost, and require minimal purchase effort, search, or product comparisons. They include *packaged and nonpackaged staples* repurchased on a regular basis like milk, coffee, and paper towels that shoppers buy at a supermarket each week. Nonpackaged staples are products like gasoline or cantaloupe. Consumers are fickle about buying staples, price is important, and branding far less so. Less than 11 percent of consumers purchasing convenience products are totally committed to any one brand.[12] Most convenience staples are necessities; others are more frill than need fulfilling.

At first glance, convenience grocery products do not appear particularly well suited to online marketing, yet they are sold online to a limited extent in the United States and more successfully in the United Kingdom and the Netherlands. Residents of Southern Connecticut; Long Island, New York; the Greater Washington, DC, area; Boston, Massachusetts; or Chicago, Illinois, can shop online for convenience products at Peapod (*http://peapod.com*). Peapod offers packaged food staples, household items, health and beauty aids, along with fresh meat and deli items, produce, and bakery goods for local delivery in the markets served. Buyers select and pay for products online and register for a delivery time. The store has competitive prices and weekly specials and accepts manufacturers' coupons. Its trained shoppers handpick items from the customer's list at free-standing central distribution warehouses maintained by partner supermarkets also owned by Royal Ahold. Drivers deliver the order directly to the customer's door during the requested delivery time. The shopper's list can be saved on the Peapod server and modified until it is ready for checkout. A very modest delivery charge is added to each order. Washington, DC, area delivery charges are

US$5 for orders over US$75, US$9.95 for orders less than US$75, with a minimum order of US$50. Peapod's lists the advantages of using its service as top-quality products, saving money, convenience, first-rate customer service, and shopping from work or home, day or night.

Other traditional grocers are also beginning to recognize profit potential for grocery products online. UK grocery giant Tesco PLC (*http://www.tesco.com*), which calls itself *The World's Largest Online Grocer*, has purchased a 35 percent share in Safeway's online operation (*http://shop. safeway.com*). After the purchase, Safeway, the third-largest chain in the United States, immediately began a web site overhaul and adopted the Tesco in-store distribution strategy. As of the beginning of 2002, Tesco was the only profitable online grocer. It has around one million online customers in the United Kingdom and processes more than seventy thousand orders weekly.

While Kroger, the nation's number one chain, is still deliberating about starting its own branded online storefront selling products with home delivery, it is using the Web to interact with customers from *www.kroger.com*. It is also serving the Denver metropolitan area with online grocery sales and delivery through its King Soopers stores (*http:// www.KingSoopers.com*).[13] The Kroger web site offers weekly store ads online from cities in Louisiana, North Carolina, Ohio, Tennessee, Texas, Virginia, and West Virginia that are keyed to the customer's location by zip code. The online ads are scanned from printed inserts circulated weekly in these locations. For price conscious consumers, online ads can provide an incentive for them to return to the web site. They may also be drawn to Kroger's online store coupons. Kroger has teamed with U-Pons (*http://kroger.upons.com*) to provide free coupons that can be added directly to the customer's KrogerPlus card. The next time they shop at their local Kroger store, they swipe their KrogerPlus card and automatically receive a discount on the products purchased.

Bricks and clicks have a clear advantage over clicks-only convenience goods retailers. They bring established brand names online, like Safeway and Giant Foods, reassuring consumers that they are purchasing from a reliable and familiar store. Grocery businesses with extensive networks of local stores and warehouses do not have to build more warehouses and new logistics system to support the online storefront. By coupling online ordering and payment with an existing logistics system, they effectively use both channels, which benefits customers seeking release from the repetitive drudgery of grocery shopping. Large chains like Ahold, Tesco, and Kroger have buying power that forces prices down on the products they buy, which helps lower inventory holding and overhead costs. Online ordering and delivery of convenience products *is* a considerable convenience for many customers. The disabled, elderly, ill, and busy professionals are prime targets. The biggest problems will continue to be low margins on most convenience products and high delivery costs, which cannot be passed along to customers. Maintaining quality will be a continuous challenge. Having a stranger pick standardized and often branded canned goods or milk off a shelf is not a problem because there is little product variability. It can be a liability, however, when the products are not standardized, for example, as with fresh produce, meat, or other perishables. The customer must rely on the selection skill of his or her shopping surrogate, the availability of top-quality products, and delivery without spoilage.

Datamonitor projects online grocery sales of up to US$26.8 billion by 2005. Consumer motivations for shopping online in addition to convenience are frustration with store checkout line waits, inadequate store staffing, and unfriendly service. Price and greater online assortment are not key motivating factors. Lack of consumer awareness is an obstacle. Only 11 percent of current Internet users are grocery shopping online, another 11 percent have bought but not in the last three months, and 78 percent have never purchased groceries online, mostly because they are not aware this service exists in their local area.[14]

Online grocery sales in the United States will become popular in larger cities, but the high cost of suburban and rural delivery will discourage expansion into lightly populated and remote areas, and at least for the immediate future, smaller urban areas. After a very rocky start that saw the demise of most clicks-only online grocers, online grocery shopping is beginning to find a niche, particularly among busy, affluent consumers in urban areas.

**EMERGENCY PRODUCTS** Products in this category are purchased infrequently and in response to an unusual situation. A hurricane approaching an Atlantic beach community sends consumers rushing to the nearest hardware store to purchase plywood sheets to board up windows. This is a crisis emergency with delivery urgency. Products must be obtained without delay, which means consumers do not have the time to go online, order plywood sheets, and wait two weeks for delivery.

It is also possible to purchase noncrisis emergency products, precautionary products appropriate for regular delivery. A resident of San Francisco, California, can go to EarthquakeStore.com (*http://www.earthquakestore.com*) and purchase emergency earthquake supplies and a personal survival kit for the next big one. Hand-crank emergency AM/FM radios that play on spring power for thirty minutes are sold online as are emergency power generators and solar-powered flashlights. Although the Internet may not be useful for buyers seeking crisis emergency products for immediate delivery, it can provide many noncrisis emergency products. Convenience and availability are two clear advantages of purchasing these products online.

**IMPULSE** Other convenience products are spur-of-the-moment, or *impulse*, purchases of candy, gum, or magazines at the grocery checkout lane, a soft drink from an icy tub next to the counter in a gas station, or an ice cream cone from a street cart on a hot summer day. An impulse purchase requires little thought, search, or buyer involvement.

Marketers are finding ways to tempt consumers with online impulse products. Amazon.com (*http://www.amazon.com*) uses collaborative filtering techniques (see Chapter 8) to push products to a visitor's screen and cross-sell them. These products are either based on data about the visitor's previous Amazon purchases or associated with a current request. A visitor searching for Theodore Levitt's *The Marketing Imagination* is tempted by an announcement for a related book that pops up directly below the Levitt listing. Williams-Sonoma's (*http://www.williams-sonoma.com*) online recipes include sidebars listing related products used in the recipes. Will consumers respond? Some will, particularly if the offer includes free shipping with purchase of the impulse product.

### SHOPPING PRODUCTS

When consumers spend more time, effort, and money searching for, comparing, and selecting, they are searching for *shopping products*. These products include high-ticket items like washing machines, apparel, and furniture, as well as airline tickets, compact music discs, videodiscs, and computer games. Consumers are more involved with these products than convenience products, principally because they cost more, they are not as readily available, and there is greater risk in making a poor choice.

*Homogeneous shopping products* are very similar to one another, but still have some characteristics that justify search and comparison, particularly price, design, content, functional features, and availability. Small television sets are *commodity products;* there is not much to distinguish one thirteen-inch color television set from another. When faced with homogeneous commodities, consumers look for points of differentiation and price often is the key. A price-conscious consumer might compare prices on thirteen-inch televisions at Sears.com, BestBuy.com (*http://www.bestbuy.com*), and CircuitCity.com (*http://www.circuitcity.com*), looking for the lowest price and/or free shipping and handling. This is easy to do using any of the popular price comparison shopping robots (shop bots). The ease of making price comparisons (see Chapter 10) is one of the clear advantages offered by Internet shopping for homogeneous shopping products.

*Heterogeneous shopping products* have features that are important enough for price to be somewhat less important. Consumers will shop around to find a product with the desired features. When shopping for an expensive large-screen projection television set, consumers may want to compare sharpness and number of lines of horizontal resolution, color reproduction, screen size, front or rear projection, analog or digital, front-to-back size, sound system, and more. A shopper may visit many sites seeking product descriptions, detailed product specifications, complete ordering and shipping information, and return instructions. The consumer can compare product attributes and make an informed decision. The Internet excels at offering product information far beyond what is typically available offline in most stores. An added advantage is when the online retailer also has a personal shopper at a 1-800 telephone number waiting to answer questions. Contrast this with what often happens offline where untrained, uninformed, and often disinterested salespeople know less about a product than the consumer trying to purchase it.

Maytag (*http://www.maytag.com*) sells washing machines online, but the orders are filled by independent Maytag dealers and local retailers nearest the buyer. This is a **B2B2C model** where the online business sells to a consumer who takes delivery of the product from another business. After-hours ordering is a big advantage to buying a washing machine online. Maytag reports that 43 percent of its online orders are made after regular working hours.[15] This model is also used in automobile sales; orders may be taken online, but automobiles are delivered and serviced by local dealers.

Some online shopping products are under attack. Cigarettes and other tobacco products are readily available online, to the anguish of smoking foes. Offline tobacco is heavily taxed; online it is a different story. The Ojibwas Trading Post (*http://www.ojibwas.com*), operated by the Ojibwas Indian Tribe, is located (as stated on the web site), "on Sovereign Indian Territory. All transactions are initiated and concluded on Indian Territory and governed by Indian Law and applicable Indian Treaties. [Furthermore] Ojibwas.com DOES NOT report to ANY state taxation or tobacco department!" Even if Internet sales are taxed, sales from Ojibwas.com and other Native American web sites will continue to be tax free. The site's front page also contains the Surgeon General's health warning and a pop-up screen asks visitors to certify they are

**B2B2C model**
Businesses that allow consumers to place orders online but the purchased product is delivered offline by local affiliates, which avoids antagonizing dealers and local retailers.

eighteen years or older. Critics complain this type of filter is ineffective in stopping underage buyers.

Web site tobacco sales are booming. Although some states have passed laws or sued sites for selling tobacco to minors, courts are overturning prohibitions. In New York State, a U.S. court ruled that a recently passed state law prohibiting mail order, Internet, and telephone cigarette sales was unconstitutionally placing an unfair burden on interstate trade. Maryland, Texas, Michigan, and New York are aggressively trying to prohibit or restrict online tobacco sales. As a result, some sites will not ship tobacco products to them, which is accomplishing the intended goal.[16] At the same time, international web sites like Yesmoke.com (*http://www.yesmoke.com/eng/index.asp*) from Switzerland are picking up the slack. They offer both foreign and premium U.S. brands to U.S. consumers, often at prices far lower than what can be purchased locally. YesSmoke also offers free delivery everywhere except to the European Union. As a bonded warehouse, YesSmoke exports its products with a *duty-free sales only* stamp. Each carton is shipped individually, which reduces the product value and the chance it will be taxed in the receiving country. It also raises delivery costs.

Wine is sold online, although post-Prohibition laws ban direct sales to consumers in twenty-seven U.S. states, and it is a felony to do so in seven states. Consumers and wineries are battling these laws in at least fifteen states. In states where the bans have been lifted, they have often been replaced by complex requirements that include having wine shipped to an authorized local distributor, where the consumer can pick it up.[17] This is another example of the B2B2C model. Trying to set up a national distribution network for these products under current laws is next to impossible as long as states determine whether or not spirits can be sold directly to their citizens. Intrastate sales are also complex in states with dry communities, where care must be taken not to send alcohol products to a dry area in a wet state. Unless the laws are changed, it is doubtful if the online wine market will ever justify the cost of establishing a web site.[18] Wine.com by eVineyard.com (*http://www.evineyard.com*) is one of the few businesses trying to establish a national wine distribution network despite the complex laws discouraging such an effort. It sells wine in 27 states, reaching over 75 percent of the wine drinking U.S. off-premise market.

While the spirits industry, with annual sales in excess of US$106 billion, is tightly controlled by state and federal laws restricting the actions of suppliers, distributors, and retailers selling to consumers, there is more latitude in B2B exchanges. BevAccess.com (*http://www.BevAccess.com*) created an online global exchange and procurement system for trade members from wineries, breweries, distilleries, retailers, and wholesalers worldwide.

Many X-rated videos and adult content sites are profitable, despite a vocal segment of the public objecting to the products offered. Yahoo's announcement in Spring 2001 that it was expanding its DVD and video selection to include X-rated products was met by enormous public protest. Responding to the negative reaction, Yahoo! stopped offering X-rated products and banned adult items from its classified advertisements and auction listings.[19]

Some pharmaceutical products are far too easy to purchase online. Viagra, a male potency drug, can be purchased online without a prescription or medical evaluation. Ciprofloxacin (Cipro), an antibiotic used in the treatment of anthrax, is readily available from foreign-based web sites. The Federal Drug Administration warned consumers in

November 2001 against purchasing Cipro from these sites because it could be missing the active ingredient, contain the wrong dose, or be made of potentially harmful substances. It also warned foreign-based web site owners not to sell the drug to U.S. citizens.

Airline tickets and travel services are shopping products particularly well suited to online marketing. Airline tickets are a high-cost, perishable service product. Online sales cut ticket printing and distribution costs, as well as eliminate travel agent commissions. Southwest Airlines (*http://www.southwest.com*) was the first airline to host a web site. In 2000, approximately 30 percent of the carrier's total sales, about US$1.7 billion, were booked online through southwest.com. Its booking cost per ticket is only US$1.00, compared with US$10 if booked through a travel agent. Southwest identifies itself on its web site as *a Symbol of e-freedom.*

Airline tickets and services are also sold by airline-affiliated sites like Travelocity (*http://www.travelocity.com*), a Sabre Company subsidiary of American Airlines AMR, and Orbitz, owned by American, United, Continental, Delta, and Northwest. Travel products are also offered by agencies known as *bucket shops* that purchase blocks of spare seats from airlines, then resell them. Priceline (*http://www.priceline.com*) is an independent agency that operates this way. Online sales work well for simple itineraries, easily scheduled point-to-point flights. Complex travel plans may require a travel agent's help. Booking flights online can be a hassle, with too many confusing screens and pages for the average buyer, consumer or enterprise purchaser, to negotiate. Computer crashes in the middle of ordering can leave the buyer frustrated and unsure whether or not the purchase registered. Unless buyers are convinced it saves them money, the effort and frustration of completing arrangements online can easily lead to shopping basket abandonment.

Despite the tragedies of September 11, 2001, the immediate closure of U.S. airports for the next several days, the imposition of stricter airport security measures, and subsequent security failures, U.S. air travel began to slowly rebound within months. Delta.com (*http://www.delta.com*) registered a record year in 2001 with US$1 billion in online ticket sales, about 10 percent of Delta's total ticket sales for the year. Delta expects online sales in 2002 to rise 50 percent and represent more than half its total ticket sales. All online airline ticket sales are expected to rise 28 percent in 2002, about 32 percent of total sales.[20]

Some digital shopping products are selling well, others are not. For example, although two-thirds of online shoppers have heard of ebooks, only 3 percent report they are *very likely* to purchase one. Drawbacks are their price, roughly the same as hardcopy books, and delivery, having to read the book online or download and print it.[21] Despite these problems, some established authors are creating them. Stephen King's sixty-six-page solely digital novella *Riding the Bullet* was released online in March 2000. More than five hundred thousand people downloaded copies at US$2.50 each. Other publishers are releasing ebooks before hard-copy versions are available as a means of stimulating word of mouth and sales. Andersen Consulting and the Association of American Publishers estimate a US$3.5 billion market for online books by 2005.[22] While ebook publishers are counting on new readers from among children and teen online game players and instant message users, they will have to lower ebook prices to attract these buyers. It is doubtful that older consumers will risk eye strain to read large amounts of text online. Slow modems and old computers make downloading a large ebook a chore and often a sure-fire invitation to crash. In addition, printing ebooks on a home printer is slow and tedious and adds cost to the purchase. At least for the immediate future or until the technology improves, Amazon's model, selling hard- or soft-copy books online with home delivery, works better.

Online banking offers great advantages for consumers. It eliminates long teller lines and the inconvenience of banker's hours and makes it easier to transfer funds, review accounts, and pay bills. Growth in electronic billing is increasing at a steady 2.5 to 2.8 percent per month. This is attributed to an increase in targeted consumer promotions by online financial institutions. Consumers are beginning to adopt this digital service and the forecast is for continued rapid growth, from 18.6 million households in 2001 to 49 million in 2006. Sweden leads the world in online banking services. About a third of its population uses online banking. Its online banks offer a full range of competitive services, which is forcing their traditional banks to improve services offline.[23]

Many consumers still find that opening an account at many online banks is a complex, highly frustrating process. Some online banks have better interest rates for loans than bricks-and-mortar banks, but finding posted rates requires the skills of an Indiana Jones. Most online banks do not have ATM networks, and when questions arise, it can be next to impossible to connect with a customer service representative at clicks-only online banks. Generally, it is much easier to find help when the online bank is a subsidiary of an established bricks-and-mortar bank.[24] This is another product where bricks and clicks have the advantage. Established banks with trusted brand names convey a security and quality image that can convince apprehensive consumers to give online banking a try. However, the online banking process must improve significantly before this product is simple enough for the majority of consumers.

Online brokerages were popular before the dot-com crash of 2001 and will revive along with the nation's economy, but slowly. They offer the advantages of *speed*, letting investors monitor their portfolios in real time as the market changes and make fast trades, and *information*, providing up-to-date data on companies and markets. However, speed and information are not advantages for consumers who trade only occasionally and are easily overwhelmed by the amount of information available for financial products. They may be fine for day traders, if any still exist, but the 2001 downturn emphasized how risky investing can be and probably scared off many consumers who might have tried it.

Education is a digital online shopping product. The Massachusetts Institute of Technology (MIT at *http://web.mit.edu/ocw*) was the first higher education institution to put all its more than two thousand courses online, from lecture notes to problem sets, and give the public free access. MIT has taken a huge leap into elearning with its OpenCourseWare (OCW) project. Most other higher education institutions with elearning products have standard courses online, where students must register and pay per credit hour or course.[25] Online classes and degrees are not effective for every student or professor, but they are invaluable for nontraditional students who cannot afford the time to attend classes in a distant university. They are not an effective delivery system for students who lack the discipline needed to maintain contact with the class and contribute to online interactions. Their success also depends on the teacher's ability to effectively use technology for course delivery. Teaching is a performance that cannot be standardized, and quality control is difficult if not impossible to implement. While hundreds of educational institutions have developed elearning courses and degree programs, many will find they cannot compete for distance learners with more prestigious universities. They will also realize that online courses cannot replace face-to-face instruction for large section and advanced classes.

Elearning is also happening with online training. Web-based training is forecast to grow to US$11 billion by 2003, up from US$2.2 billion in 2001. InfoWorld.com (*http://www.infoworld.com*) offers courses in business and technical skill development. Enrollment in their self-paced courses is by subscription.[26] Elearning can be highly effective, particularly when the lessons integrate audio, video, text, animation, and interactive discussions. It is cost-effective because it eliminates expensive travel and time spent away from the job. Mass customization allows employers and employees to select courses on subjects appropriate to specific job descriptions.[27] However, some employees still learn far better face to face and elearning can be a failure when hands-on experience is required.

Many people go online seeking information, which is also a product. Most content sites, however, have not figured out how to profit from the popularity of their products. It does not help that competitors often offer the same content free. Sites that are likely to succeed at charging are those with unique content, just-in-time delivery of time-sensitive information, and industry trade content.[28]

Online games, gambling, and adult content are all highly profitable products. Online games are by far the least controversial of the three. Gambling and adult content products are market leaders for paid online content. These products are well suited to the Internet's anonymity, rapid interactivity, ease of use, and global reach. They are expected to continue dominating the content product category for paid subscriptions and memberships.

Shopping products are well suited to Internet marketing activities. Consumers benefit from the Internet's capacity for rapid interaction, comparison shopping, and rapid information retrieval. Growth in shopping product sales should continue to rise far more rapidly than sales in other consumer product categories, particularly as established retailers go online bringing current customers with them and attracting new customers to their web sites.

## SPECIALTY PRODUCTS

Consumers are highly involved with specialty products and trying to locate them. They are more difficult to find than shopping products so search is an important component of the purchase process. These are often unique products, available in very limited numbers, or found at only a few retailers. Consumers are often so happy to find them that price is not an issue; their relative scarcity adds to their value. Because they are more costly and riskier, they often convey messages about the social status of the buyer. Examples include high-fashion designer clothing and jewelry, luxury automobiles, and handcrafted furniture.

Most specialty product and luxury storefronts have not done very well online. Ashford.com (*http://www.ashford.com*) targets up-scale consumers and corporate clients, offering luxury and premium-quality jewelry, handbags, women's scarves and men's ties, watches, and fragrances from more than four hundred luxury brands and fifteen thousand products. High-resolution product pictures are used throughout the site. Most products carry an extended Ashford warranty and thirty-day return policy.

Same-day shipping is offered for in-stock products ordered before 3:00 P.M. Central Time. Orders of US$100 or more receive free shipping.

Ashford was losing money before the terrorist attacks on September 11, 2001. The company posted a net loss of US$14.4 million for Q2 2001 and faced Nasdaq delisting. Amazon.com had bought a 13 percent stake in Ashford in 2000 for US$90 million. By 2001, that stake was worth about US$1.7 million. Ashford announced in September 2001 that it had agreed to be purchased by Global Sports. Other luxury goods storefronts closed their doors or were acquired by other companies.[29]

Bricks-and-mortar specialty retailers often are shopping destinations. Shoppers will travel considerable distances to purchase a certain type of professional photography equipment, jewelry, or a designer handbag from a specific retailer. Tiffany.com (*http://www.tiffany.com*) is a destination upscale jewelry retailer online and off. Because it accepts orders online, it reaches consumers who might find it difficult or impossible to visit a bricks-and-mortar location. Tiffany has stores in North America, Europe, and Asia; however, unless a buyer lives in a large urban or affluent area, there will not be a store nearby.

Affluent consumers (assets ≥US$1 million) make up a relatively small proportion of online shoppers, but they shop online more often, spend more time looking for products, and purchase an average US$1,466 online annually, about 56 percent more than other consumers. Convenience is the main reason they shop online, followed by service and speed.[30] Serious problems will continue to plague specialty online marketers. Luxury shoppers expect special treatment in upscale surroundings offline. They want personal attention commensurate with the high prices they are paying. They also do not want to worry about the security of their purchase in transit or the possibility of purchasing counterfeit products. Online high-end sites must provide convenience, speed, personal service through an online shopping assistant or telephone help line, security, and appropriate site atmospherics.

Music123.com (*http://www.music123.com*) is a specialty product category that should not work well online, but does. Music123.com went online in early 1997 selling musical instruments, accessories, software, and sheet music and offering products from manufacturers that typically are highly restrictive in awarding franchises. Generally, musicians want to test an expensive instrument before purchasing it. In this case, they are willing to forgo testing in exchange for product selection, the key to this site's success. International buyers shop Music123.com to purchase instruments not readily available in their home countries and obtain brand names known for quality and performance consistency.[31]

## UNSOUGHT PRODUCTS

The final category of consumer products are *unsought*—products consumers avoid, search for out of necessity, or are unaware of because the products are new to the market or simply unknown. For example, funeral caskets (see the screen shot on p. 236) are an unsought product readily available online from such retailers as The Casket Store (*http://www.thecasketstores.com*), Funeral Depot (*http://www.funeraldepot.com*), and Direct Casket (*http://www.directcasket.com*). Most offer next-day or two-day delivery.

Casket shopping online has benefits. It avoids having to visit a funeral home, which many people find upsetting. Buying a casket online in a nonemotional, impersonal environment should encourage a more objective purchase decision. It avoids the up-selling attempts of a salesperson trying to lay a guilt trip on the buyer for selecting a cheaper model. It is unlikely that a large price advantage exists from online product sales because it is so difficult to make price comparisons when product features differ so widely. Whether consumers seek such products online is another story, particularly since most do not shop for a casket offline before it is actually needed.

Legacy.com (*http://legacy.com/legacyhome.asp*) performs a digital service that most consumers are unaware of. The company, founded in 1998, is backed by investors including the Tribune Company and Gannett Co., Inc., the largest newspaper group in the United States. This web site's mission is to provide space for the recently bereaved to celebrate the life of their loved one, posting tributes, eulogies, photographs, and memorials. For under US$200, a Legacy Life Story will be posted online permanently; temporary listings cost less. Potential customers can learn about the service from newspaper obituary writers, funeral directors, and word of mouth. If family and friends cannot attend a funeral, an online memorial tribute to the deceased lets them share their emotions. Each listing also includes directions to the funeral service and charities designated by the family.

## Unsought Products

Most consumers do not like to consider buying a funeral casket for themselves or anyone else. One way to avoid a trip to a bricks-and-mortar funeral home is to buy a casket online. *Source:* Reprinted by permission of CasketXpress.com. *http://www.CasketXpress.com.*

Although unsought consumer products are the least well suited to web shopping, some will be profitable. Product avoidance offline is probably a good predictor that online offers will be equally unpopular unless there is a clear online advantage. Legacy.com's advantage is offering a service that could only exist online. There is no offline equivalent. Online funeral casket sellers have an advantage in eliminating a funeral home visit and avoiding up-selling attempts. Some casket sellers claim they offer cut-rate prices, but this is an area where the seller has a tremendous information advantage over the buyer. Most consumers do not have information about casket prices, and if they need one in a hurry, price may not be the deciding factor. A low price may be avoided because it implies disrespect for the recently departed. Finding unsought products online is not as much of a problem as it was in the past because of vastly improved search engines.

### ✔ CONCEPT CHECK

1. Are all convenience products equally well suited to online sales? Explain your answer.
2. Why are travel services and airline tickets selling so well online?
3. What are the drawbacks of offering specialty products online?

# *Enterprise and New Products*

An enterprise is a group of similar entities producing, supplying, purchasing, and/or servicing products. Enterprises can be businesses, governments, hospitals, universities, and other organizations that purchase products for the enterprise and not personal use. Multiple types of entities exist within each enterprise group. These entities purchase a wide array of products used to make other products, to run their operations, or to resell.

More businesses than ever before are purchasing and selling products via electronic marketplaces on the Internet's public World Wide Web, corporate and supplier web sites, extranets, corporate intranets, and one-to-one supplier electronic data interchanges (EDI). They cite customer service, ease of use, cost savings, and reliability as prime reasons to buy or sell in electronic marketplaces. Price, product quality, order accuracy, and product availability are key criteria for selecting product vendors. Products most frequently purchased online are raw materials and industrial equipment, stationery/office supplies, office equipment (including computers), and software.[32]

Many corporations have not yet gone online to buy or sell, some because they are satisfied with their present product procurement processes, others because online procurement is still too complicated for them, they do not believe they have the time to do so, or they fear online transactions are not secure. Larger companies increasingly require their suppliers to be online, but for many small suppliers it means connecting electronically to their prime or sole buyer's extranet. Midsize businesses are intensifying their eprocurement efforts. As many as 40 percent are purchasing online. The top benefits they experience are faster order time, convenience, cost savings, and time savings. They also appreciate receiving more product information online.[33]

Online B2B buying is understandably more focused on goods than services. Even though many companies currently are disappointed in their experiences with online product procurement, they realize they will be using electronic methods far more in the future. Most anticipate cost savings not from lower product prices, but from streamlining ordering processes. In addition to procuring products online, businesses anticipate collaborating with partners online to develop new products, outsource product manufacturing, plan and forecast product demand, direct logistics, and manage customer relationships. Worldwide, the total value of B2B products (primarily goods but also services) purchased electronically is forecast to be US$4.3 trillion by 2005, an annual compound growth rate of 73 percent from US$282 billion in 2000.[34]

## ENTERPRISE PRODUCTS

Rather than classifying products by shopping behaviors, enterprise products are typed by how they solve problems. For these buyers, products include the following:

### *GOODS*

**RAW MATERIALS AND PARTS**    Products used as inputs in a production process. For example, iron ore and scrap are raw materials needed for steel production; windshields inserted into automobiles.

**EQUIPMENT AND SUPPLIES**    Products to run the business or organization. A metal stamping machine is equipment used to stamp out automobile body frames; paper and printer cartridges are expendable office supplies that must be replaced on a regular basis.

**FINISHED GOODS, SERVICES, OR DIGITAL PRODUCTS**    Products manufactured or purchased for resale by wholesales and retailers, and/or destined for eventual purchase by personal use consumers.

***SERVICES***    Products that are performances including equipment repairs and maintenance, training, assembly line redesign, and other activities that contribute to production and operations.

***INFORMATION***    Information products are found in abundance online, and many businesses, as well as other enterprises, purchase information from various vendors. These products include competitive marketing intelligence, research reports, economic forecasts, and trend analysis.

Raw materials include *soft goods* (agricultural commodities) such as raw wheat, barley, and oats essential to the production of cereals like Kellogg's Corn Flakes, chemicals used in the production of pharmaceuticals, or fabric used to make apparel. Raw materials are also *hard goods* used in the production of machines, instruments, and consumer durables, like steel used in producing automobiles or polymers for plastics. Most raw materials are sold in long-term contracts lasting a year or more; thus, buyers shop for these products infrequently.

Some raw materials are sold directly from corporate web sites, many are sold through online exchanges. Exchanges typically are private, independent public exchanges, or a consortia public exchange. The complexity of managing an exchange and the difficulty of finding sufficient numbers of buyers and sellers to make them functional has resulted in many failures. One survivor is RawMart.com (*http://www.rawmart.com*), a commodity exchange matching buyers and sellers for raw materials used in agribusiness, chemicals, energy, metals, minerals, plastics, pulp and paper. RawMart is a global exchange that operates in English, Chinese, Russian, Japanese, Spanish, Portuguese, and Korean. It facilitates buyer/seller exchanges in more than six hundred industrial raw materials and commodities groups, meeting materials and logistics needs through market exchanges.

Partially or completely finished parts are used in production. Examples are picture tubes used in television sets and computer chips inserted into computers. Electronics parts buyers and sellers are linked on electronic portals like Electrosupport Online (*http://www.electrosupport.com*), a member of PartsLogistics.com (*http://www.partslogistics.com*). Electrosupport Online provides direct access to wholesalers, distributors, and manufacturers of a wide variety of electronics parts. PartsLogistics.com does the same with multiple industry parts, products, and services. These exchanges make finding an outsourcing partner for product manufacturing anywhere in the world much easier than in the past.

Capital equipment products include tools and equipment used in production, and the buildings where production occurs. GE Healthcare (*http://www.gehealthcare.com*), which offers health care facilities and products for sale and lease, customizes products to suit buyer's needs.

Expendable supplies are purchased to run the enterprise and include operating supplies and maintenance supplies. Consumers and enterprises can go online to purchase home office supplies from Office Depot (*http://www.officedepot.com*), which also provides small businesses services in marketing, communication, management, and human resources.

Finished products for resale are what wholesalers and retailers purchase to sell to consumers and other businesses. These products were covered extensively at the beginning of this chapter.

It is far easier and faster to conduct product searches online than off. This includes visiting online trade shows where products are displayed. Some trade shows also have salespeople standing by to answer visitor questions. Acteva (*http://www.acteva.com*) and NetShows (*http://www.netshows.com*) both arrange and host online trade shows. The popularity of these shows is growing as they are far less costly than traditional trade shows and have the potential to reach more buyers in less time. They also eliminate travel and display costs.

## GOVERNMENT AND ORGANIZATION PRODUCTS

The U.S. government is the largest retailer on the Internet, outselling even Amazon.com. The government operates over 160 different web sites that generated US$3.6 billion in 2000.[35] However, these figures can be misleading as most of these sales were by one agency. The top seller is Treasury Direct (*http://www.publicdebt.treas.gov/td/tdstorefront.htm*) operated by the U.S. Treasury Department, which reported Year 2000 revenues of US$3.3 billion from the sale of U.S. savings bonds, T-bills, and treasury notes. Other government products for sale include gravesite flowers at U.S. military cemeteries overseas from the American Battle Monuments Commission (*http://www.abmc.gov*), property from the General Services Administration's Office of Property Disposal (*http://www.gsa.gov/pr/prhome.htm*), and luxury goods confiscated from drug dealers by the U.S. Marshals Service (*http://www.bid4assets.com*).

The extent of U.S. government online marketing is beginning to be debated. Critics believe the government is violating federal law that prohibits it from competing with the private sector in selling products directly to consumers. Some government products, like surplus U.S. Coast Guard Cruisers, are not found in civilian stores. Their sale could be considered for the common good as it is better to sell them, returning the profits to the treasury, than have them rust away. Other products compete directly with businesses, however, and this causes concern. One very large target is the federal-government-owned, self-supporting postal corporation. The U.S. Postal Service (*http://usps.com*), which recently changed its domain name from .gov to .com, directly competes with UPS (*http://www.ups.com*), Federal Express (*http://www.fedex.com*) and others. Critics believe it has an unfair advantage since the federal government is there to bail out the USPS if needed.

Government procurement online is a multibillion-dollar business involving purchases of almost every type of good and many services. The U.S. and most state governments are establishing processes where vendors can bid for state purchasing contracts online. The National Association of State Procurement Officials (*http://www.naspo.org*), a nonprofit organization of the central purchasing officers in all fifty U.S. states, DC, and U.S. territories, publishes a vendor guide for small businesses to help them bid on state purchasing contracts. Products are purchased to solve such problems as feeding federal prisoners at institutions nationwide or keeping government printers stocked with paper. The federal government has established FedBizOpps (*http://www.fedbizopps.gov*), the point of entry for government procurement information, to streamline the bidding process and encourage small and midsize businesses to participate in bidding for contracts over US$25,000.

The State of Virginia is moving toward a fully electronic procurement system. By mid-2002, the eVA site (*http://www.eva.state.va.us*) already had 5,598 registered vendors and 503 e-Mall vendor catalogs. As the site proclaims, EVA is *Virginia's Total e-Procurement Solution*. Recently it needed a vendor to install a Lucent telephone system in two middle schools in Fauquier Country, a roof replacement in the state Department of Transportation, and janitorial supplies at the University of Virginia.

Organizations purchase many of the same products as governments. Expendable medical supplies and equipment can be purchased online from individual sellers and through global medical portals like InviMed, Inc. (*http://www.advantmed.com*). Universities purchase products directly from retailers like OfficeDepot.com or on state contracts if they are public institutions and the orders are large. OfficeDepot.com illustrates the blending of products for use by consumers and enterprises.

## NEW PRODUCTS

New products are the lifeblood of an enterprise and the Internet offers a platform where consumers and enterprises can collaborate in their development. The new product development process is a series of steps that progress from scanning the market for product gaps to commercialization, bringing a new product to market. New products are expensive, time-consuming, and risky to develop. It is not unusual for a new product to cost a large or midsize business from US$20 million to over US$100 million or more to commercialize. The new product failure rate is extremely high; three out of every four new products fail. Close to 50 percent of the cost of developing and commercializing new products is never recouped.

Marketing activities already occurring online can lessen costs and risks, and shorten the time to commercialization. For example, online commercial intelligence chat rooms and consumer panels can be used for opportunity scanning, determining what the competition is offering and listening to what consumers are saying about existing products (see Chapters 7 and 8). Online focus groups are used for idea generation and screening. Online concept testing and test markets can be conducted on restricted web sites, like General Mill's MyCereal.com. Commercialization and new product launch can be announced online, supported with online promotions, and tracked to evaluate results.

Most new products are modifications of existing products or *continuous innovations,* that is, tweaking some product feature and calling it *new and improved*. Many web sites use this ploy as they upgrade their processes or redesign pages. Some new products are *product line extensions,* like the addition of the *Wall Street Journal Online* to the Dow Jones stable of print publications. Others are *repositioned products,* products that have changed their features, functions, target markets, or marketing strategies. For example, AOL (*http://www.aol.com*) repositioned itself as an entertainment company after its purchase of Time Warner. Very few new products are so radically different and unique that they can be labeled *discontinuous innovations*. Email is such a unique product. People had to learn a new way of communicating, and for many, initially it was a very frustrating process.

*How different are online products from offline products?* A close look at most consumer and enterprise products reveals they are the same online and offline. Lands' End (*http://www.landsend.com*) drifter sweaters sold online are exactly the same as drifter sweaters sold in a Lands' End catalog or one of its stores.

*Are there products whose existence is inextricably linked to the electronic global marketplace?* Without the Internet it is highly questionable whether there would be internet service providers (ISPs); routers, servers, and related hardware and software; modems, DSL, WebTV; web directories, search engines, spiders, and bots; web browsers; flash and related products; HTML editors; animated gifs, jpgs, and buttons; streaming audio and video; ecards, ebooks, elearning, emagazines, etickets, ecash; and so on. The Internet and the Web have stimulated the production of many products whose existence depends on a global electronic marketplace teeming with buyers and sellers.

*Have some old products been modified because of the Internet and the Web?* Absolutely! This is readily apparent when on-screen announcements pop up during a television program encouraging viewers to visit the channel's web site to learn more about the topic being presented. Stories in the *Wall Street Journal* print edition refer readers to the *Journal* web site. It is evident in the replacement of hard-copy airline tickets by electronic tickets and paper checks by online bill payment. Many university libraries are dropping subscriptions to traditional hard-copy journals and instead subscribing online to their electronic versions.

## ✔ CONCEPT CHECK

1. How do enterprise products differ from consumer products?
2. Why is the federal government criticized for selling products online?
3. How can the Web be used to gather ideas for product changes or new products?

# *Branding*

As Internet space becomes more crowded, branding becomes more vital to online marketing success. A well-known branded Internet company like an Amazon.com or eBay (*http://www.ebay.com*) is a beacon drawing buyers to its web site. Experience with the branded site provides reassurance that the business is reliable, safe, and trustworthy. It also saves buyers time because they know what to expect at the site and can avoid having to shop around for an alternative. Branded products can provide the same benefits.

For many companies, their brand name is the company name. Where would Starbucks (*http://www.starbucks.com*), Lexus (*http://www.lexus.com*), Amazon.com, or Yahoo! be without their distinctive, instantly recognized brand names? The company brand extends to its products, as in Starbucks flavored or bottled coffees.

While branding is commonly associated with consumer products, it is also important to enterprises, Boeing (*http://www.boeing.com*) and John Deere (*http://www.deere.com*) are examples. A quality brand is more important than price in many enterprise transactions.

Brands are not built overnight and they cannot be created with a massive one-time advertising expenditure. Brand building requires careful planning and the following:

- Knowledge of the entity to be branded, company, product, etc.
- Knowledge of the target market—their needs, wants, and problems
- A clear understanding of how the brand will benefit the target market
- Knowledge of the competition—their brand(s) and the promise(s) they make
- Monitoring brand perceptions to know when brands lose their luster and brand aid is needed

**Brand**
A name, symbol, design, or other element that differentiates one product or entity from another, identifies ownership, and provides tangible and intangible meaning.

**Brand name**
The spoken part of the brand; for example, when a person says *Amazon, Sears,* or *eBay.*

**Brand mark**
The unspoken part of a brand; for example, the apple on a Macintosh computer that identifies it as an Apple (*http://www. apple.com*) product.

**Service mark**
Trademarked brand identification for services.

**Cyberbrands**
Brand names created from scratch, for example, Amazon.com, e*Trade, and Yahoo!; most first movers were pure cyberbrands.

A **brand** identifies ownership and represents tangible and intangible associations. It is a promise, feeling, unique name, symbol, design, reputation, or other element that differentiates one product or entity from another. A **brand name** is the spoken part of the brand, when a person says eBay or Yahoo! A **brand mark** is the unspoken part, the apple on a Macintosh Computer (*http://www.apple.com*) or the red target of Target.com (*http://www.target.com*). A **service mark** is the trademarked brand identification for services. Branding is considered such a vital part of product marketing that an over US$2 trillion industry has developed for brand creation and maintenance.

In an electronic environment where there is often a high degree of uncertainty, a brand name is a cognitive anchor, a point of recognition. When buyers need a product, store, information, or entertainment, they often seek a brand they know and trust. A brand name guides them to a web site. Loyal Wal-Mart customers offline are drawn to Wal-Mart.com (*http://www.walmart.com*); loyal Target customers seek out Target.com.

Registered brands are legal protection of product assets, a key communication tool, and a way to differentiate products and companies from competitors. Brands are huge investments for many enterprises, and their management is a key marketing responsibility. Brands must be built and maintained; if they are not, they can easily fade away or be overtaken by aggressive competitors. When buyers are loyal to a brand, perceive its quality, and repurchase, it increases the brand's equity. *Brand equity* is a measure of a brand's extra financial worth and market power created by buyer loyalty.

## BRAND NAMES

Most of the first movers online were pure **cyberbrands,** brands that existed only on the Internet's World Wide Web. Clicks-only companies like Yahoo!, eBay, and Amazon.com built online brands from nothing. Because they existed only online, they could not rely on existing brand names, awareness, and previously formed associations with buyers.

Most early cyberbrands were *company brands,* branding companies that marketed Internet access (AOL), directory assistance (Yahoo!), or books (Amazon). They spent hundreds of millions of dollars on advertising and promotions and used press releases, media interviews, and virtually any promotion device that would raise the public's initial awareness of their new online businesses. AOL aggressively marketed its name through direct mail, sending its software to consumers on floppy disks and later on CDs. It continues this practice today. Yahoo! was everywhere initially, in television commercials, magazine advertisements, and print articles. The success of these efforts is reflected in their rank in the initial e-Branding Index. The Index is a benchmark study of top Internet brands. Not surprisingly the top five brands in 2000 were AOL, Yahoo!, Amazon.com, Netscape, and eBay.[36]

Bricks and clicks faced a different challenge when they initially went online. They had to decide if they would use the same brand name offline and online in an *inte-*

*grated, one-brand name strategy*. AT&T, IBM, Dell, and others created web sites with immediately identifiable name brand URLs. Wal-Mart and Target followed them with integrated online/offline brand names. Most bricks and clicks with well-established, highly regarded offline brand names rely on them to build online web site awareness.

Other bricks and clicks, like Procter & Gamble, have a *mixed brand name strategy*. There is a P&G corporate site and other sites named for products (Reflect.com) or product brands like Tide (*http://www.tide.com*). Cobranding came later. For example, Amazon.com and Toys R Us formed a ten-year alliance in August 2000 that expanded Amazon's product offer into toys without adding the expense of building inventory. Toys R Us benefited from being on a high traffic site and escaping the expense of maintaining its independent web site. Cobranding is mutually beneficial for both.

Offline brand popularity does not always translate into site popularity. For example, Levi's (*http://www.us.levi.com*), a top youth brand, fails to attract young consumers to its site because it does not offer what they want. It does not sell products online and the type of entertainment it offers can be found elsewhere. Coca-Cola makes the same mistake by cramming its site with games, advertisements, and content that will not bring consumers back, despite the power of its brand name.

## THE DOMAIN NAME

Brand building online begins with a first step, selecting a domain name. The name should be meaningful, short, descriptive, and associated with characteristics of the product or company, or be the name of the business. Domain names identify brands online. They create awareness as well as addresses. Yahoo!, eBay, and Amazon are businesses with .com domains that identify them as commercial enterprises. They are coined names that were created and built, with no initial meaning in the marketplace. Short company names are integral parts of their complete domain names.

Bricks and clicks with highly regarded, well-known brand names wisely obtained identical domain names. IBM, AT&T, Dell, and others were able to do so. Some companies had to pay off cybersquatters to claim appropriate domain names. This is less of a problem today with the enforcement of anticybersquatter legislation.

Having the right domain name is not enough to guarantee web marketing success; having the wrong name can be overcome with smart marketing. Pets.com, a great name for a pet supply storefront is highly descriptive, easy to remember, and short. Unfortunately, the name alone could not keep the company solvent. Boo.com (*http://www.boo.com*) is not descriptive and sounds more like a Halloween than an apparel site. It failed once and has been reopened under new management, Fashionmall.com. On the other hand, eLuxury.com (*http://www.eluxury.com*) is a web site with a highly descriptive domain name that immediately creates an image of the products and lifestyle it sells. Because eLuxury.com is so descriptive, it also helps establish a brand personality, the face presented to site visitors. Unfortunately, e-Luxury.com and the other ebrands run the risk of overloading consumers with the *e* word.

Similar-sounding brand names and URLs make it difficult for buyers to cut through the online clutter and find what they need. Word repetitions make it hard to differentiate between SmartShip.com, GoShip.com, Accuship.com, ShipNet.com, ShipChem.com, Shipper.com, and ShippingAuction.com.[37]

A brand needs a great name. Most large and midsize companies, and many small ones as well, turn to professional naming experts to develop an appropriate brand or company name. The same holds for domain names. Brand naming and management is a multi-billion-dollar business that now includes many domain name consultants. As might be expected, many domain naming businesses are online, offering their services to startups as well as established enterprises.

## BUILDING BRAND AWARENESS

A brand needs awareness. If you name it, buyers still will not come unless they are aware the brand exists. Brand awareness is often built through online and offline promotions working together. Initial awareness can be developed through advertising, direct marketing, sales promotions, and email marketing. Awareness is also built by listing brands in search engines. A recent study reports better brand recall from search engine listings than seeing button or banner ads.[38] Awareness is built through press releases, events, appearances on talk chat shows, community involvement, and encouraging positive word of mouth. Some online marketers use *viral marketing* to build awareness. They enter chat rooms, discussion boards, list serves, and other areas where they can build positive buzz about a brand. An increasing number of web sites post *Tell a Friend* suggestions in the hope that a satisfied customer will email a friend with the site's address.

Advertising is very important to online brand building. Researchers have found that greater brand awareness is related to multiple exposures to banner advertisements, sparing use of animation, longer exposure to the advertisement, larger advertisements, and uncluttered banners. Slow-loading online advertisements lessen brand impact.[39] These results confirm that online advertising can play a key role in brand building despite rising consumer frustration with their numbers and intrusiveness, and growing online advertising clutter.

Awareness is not the only goal in brand building. It is important to associate the message with the brand, make an attractive and meaningful brand promise, and move the consumer toward interest in the brand. Interest should lead to a belief that the brand is the right one to satisfy a need or solve a problem. Purchase intention and, it is hoped, purchase should follow. Online advertising is used throughout this process, reinforcing the brand message and reiterating the brand promise.

## CREATING AND MAINTAINING THE BRAND

Positive brand images are built through positive experiences and impressions. Customer relationship management is important to brand building. Providing a good experience and product satisfies consumers, adds to brand equity, and gets buyers to return. It also stimulates positive word of mouth, which can be far more powerful in building a brand than any advertising campaign. On a web site this means taking the following actions:

- Creating an inviting home page
- Keeping content fresh, useful, and helpful
- Providing clear navigation links that work
- Using interactivity where appropriate and not where it is inappropriate
- Offering user-friendly shopping baskets and ordering forms
- Answering customer email promptly
- Avoiding the use of senseless animation that slows download time

- Offering easy, convenient product returns
- Handling customer complaints carefully and sensitively
- Listening to customer feedback and following through on useful suggestions
- Building trust through honest transactions
- Avoiding 404 error messages that appear to blame the customer for reaching the wrong page
- Not overpromising
- Delivering quality products, as promised
- Using every point of contact with customers and prospects as an opportunity to promote a positive image of the brand

Brands can be built and maintained through online communities, groups of people who share interests and meet online to discuss them. Positive word of mouth among people sharing common interests builds brand awareness. Opinion leaders in these groups can be effective brand advocates if they share positive brand experiences.

## BRAND RISKS

Unfortunately, the more well known the brand, the more likely that it will become a target for hackers, complaints, and theft. High-visibility brands are tempting targets for hackers and those who would steal images, content, and designs. An entire site can be stolen or defaced in several minutes. Intellectual property theft is a significant problem because it is so easy online. The threat is that images, design, and content associated with one brand can turn up on an imposter's site. Visitors to the imposter's site can be deceived, have a bad experience, then tell others about it as negative word of mouth, which can be highly destructive to the legitimate brand.

Another risk is from cobranding. A bad match in a cobranded product or company can be a disaster. At the least, any cobranding effort must be thoroughly evaluated for the possible effects it will have on both brands. For every good cobranding experience, like Amazon.com and Toys R Us, there are other bad matches.

Brands are vulnerable to complaints, derogatory comments, and even defamation at suck sites and from comments in chat rooms, discussion boards, and other public forums. Whether or not comments are inaccurate does not matter. If they are widely disseminated, they can undermine the brand's value.

While web marketers should constantly monitor the Web to see if their brand is being threatened, there are far too many sites and pages for most to do it effectively. Brand risks can be reduced through the use of security software and solutions to uncover piracy, copyright infringement, libelous postings in discussion groups, and similar problems. Companies like Cyveillance (*http://www.cyveillance.com*) and Cobion (*http://www.Cobion.com*), and others, are active in this field. Cyveillance lists Merrill Lynch, Goodyear, Nintendo, the *Washington Post,* and Dow Jones among its online clients. It uses automated intelligence gathering and human analysis to protect its client's brands by locating stolen content and monitoring discussion groups. Cobion also deals in content security and brand and copyright protection. It uses visual content search, content analysis, and intelligent content processing to safeguard intranets, gateways, and web sites. It specializes in detecting brand infringements on the Web. Clients include Bayer, Adidas, Daimler Chrysler, and Dow Chemical. VeriSign (*http://www.verisign.com*) offers an online brand management and protection service for large companies. This service includes domain name protection, online monitoring of brand misuse, and brand promotion.[40]

## ✔ CONCEPT CHECK

1. Why is branding online even more important today than it was in the mid-1990s?
2. What does branding do for consumers? For enterprises?
3. What are brand risks and how can they be confronted?

# *Summary*

## *Product Fundamentals*

A product can be a good, service, idea, place, person, information, organization, or anything offered in exchange for something of value. It is the offer made to a market, a bundle of benefits that creates value for buyers. Buyer and product use are two key criteria in understanding product. Consumers use products to fill needs and wants, satisfying their desire to take possession and own something of value. Products solve problems for enterprises. Products sold online can be tangible goods, intangible services, digital, or a mixture of these forms. Durable and nondurable goods, and even perishables, are sold online. Most products are composed of multiple layers, each providing value and an opportunity for marketers to connect with customers. Mass customization allows a large quantity of products to be produced quickly because buyer options are limited and products often are semiproduced in advance of final customization. Personalization, or one-to-one marketing, is different from mass customization. It uses technology to personalize electronic commerce interactions between a marketer and each customer. Advantages of selling products online include greater availability and assortment, convenience, expanded choice, and rapid product comparisons. Disadvantages include purchase process breakdowns, inability to engage the senses in product evaluation, lengthy search process, excess information, and problems in returns.

## *Consumer Products*

The popularity of online shopping is growing, as are sales. Convenience, shopping, specialty, and unsought products are available online. Convenience products are purchased frequently, readily available in many different locations, and often are disposable, low cost,

and require minimal purchase effort, search, or product comparisons. To be profitable, convenience product marketers must sell high volumes and maintain tight cost controls. Grocery products are sold online but thus far with only limited success in the United States. Bricks and clicks have an advantage selling convenience products online because of their established brand names, functioning logistics processes, and in-store returns. Shopping and specialty products require more effort to find and purchase. Shopping products include books, airline tickets, consumer durables, and education. Shopping products are the best suited to online sales. Consumers are highly involved with specialty products and trying to locate them. Specialty products are unique or hard to find. Unsought products consumers avoid, search for out of necessity, or are unaware of because the products are new to the market or simply unknown.

## *Enterprise and New Products*

An enterprise is a group of similar entities producing, supplying, purchasing, and/or servicing products. Enterprises include businesses, organizations, hospitals, and governments. Enterprise products are typed by how they solve problems. They include raw materials and parts, equipment and supplies, finished goods, services, or information products. The U.S. government is the largest retailer on the Internet, outselling even Amazon.com. The extent of U.S. government online marketing and whether it competes with businesses online is debated. Organizations purchase many of the same products as governments. The new product development process is a series of steps that progress from scanning the market for product gaps to commercialization, bringing a new product to market. New products are very expensive, time-consuming, and risky to develop. Most new products are modifications of existing products. Some new products are product line extensions. Very few new products are so radically different and unique that they are discontinuous innovations. Feedback and ideas for new products or extensions can be obtained from chat groups and other discussion areas. Many new products have been created specifically for the Internet environment.

## Branding

As Internet space becomes more crowded, branding becomes more vital to online marketing success. Not all products need branding; some could not exist without the cachet associated with their brand. A brand identifies ownership and provides tangible and intangible meaning. Brands are important to both consumers and enterprises. A brand name is the first contact many consumers have with a product or entity,

and the impression it makes is lasting. Brands are legal protection of product assets, a key communication tool, and a way to differentiate from competitors. Brands are large investments for many enterprises and their management is a key marketing responsibility. Cyberbrands exist only online. Some companies integrate their offline and online brands. Others use a mixed branding strategy. Domain names identify brands online. The proliferation of similar-sounding brand names and URLs makes it difficult for buyers to cut through the online clutter and find what they need. Most of the first movers online were pure cyberbrands that had to create their brand names from scratch. A brand needs awareness. Brands are built through positive experiences. Brands can be built and maintained through online communities, advertising, and other means. Risks associated with high-visibility brands are being attractive hacker targets, targets for complaints particularly at suck sites, and content theft.

## Internet Marketing Application

The Internet is particularly well suited to product mass customization. At the same time, there is a big difference in how web sites implement the process and even define the term. Visit any two of the following sites and test their customization options. Evaluate each from the consumer's perspective for the criteria listed in the following table. Add criteria that you believe are relevant to the process.

### Evaluation of Mass Customization at Two Web Sites

| Criteria | Web Site 1: | Web Site 2: |
|---|---|---|
| Visibility of customization option | | |
| Clarity of instructions | | |
| Examples shown | | |
| Number of options available | | |
| Online ordering available | | |

Some sites that might be visited include

- Soccer uniforms (CustomJersey.com at *http://www.customjersey.com/soccer.html*)
- Bicycles (HubBub Custom Bicycles at *http://www.hubbub.com*)

- Custom-made shirts and suits (New International Boutique House at *http://www.nibh.com*)
- Watches (eWatch Factory at *http://www.ewatchfactory.com/retail/en/index.htm*)
- Perfume (Reflect.com at *http://www.reflect.com*)

# Chapter Review Questions

1. What are the 4Ps? What P comes first and why?
2. How do enterprise buyers differ from consumer buyers?
3. Explain the different product states. Which are sold online?
4. How can nonpackaged nondurables be sold online?
5. How can consumers contribute to product potential online?
6. Are niche products sold online? Explain.
7. Why do you think P&G did not give its company name to Reflect.com?
8. What are the greatest advantages of shopping for products online?
9. Contrast the types of consumer products by how involved consumers are with their purchase.
10. Should tobacco and alcohol be sold online?
11. What enterprise products are sold online?
12. What is keeping some businesses from trying eprocurement?
13. What can the online environment contribute to the new product development process?
14. How have some products been modified for the online environment?
15. Why is brand such an important consideration in Internet marketing?

## Nike's iD

# Case Study

"Choose it. Build it. Buy it." That is what Nike (*http://www.nike.com*) is inviting consumers to do with its Nike iD custom shoe-building feature. Are consumers willing to pay a little more (US$10) and wait two to three weeks for a mass-customized shoe? Nike is sure they will, particularly since it has iD experts online to answer their questions and offers an attractive return policy.

Nike can sell its branded products online because it has sufficient marketing clout to counter channel member complaints. It is by far the dominant player with about a 40 percent share of the U.S. athletic footwear market. Nike is restricting sales of its brand by other online marketers in order to retain control of the product and avoid any possibility of the brand being sold at discount, which Nike CEO Phil Knight believes "would be the death of the brand."

Nike iD can take a thousand orders a day and offers a variety of color patterns and designs. It plans to extend the brand into apparel. Nike iD shoes are not achieving the *brand of one* idealization of custom marketing. Its mass customization process limits feature combinations to a reasonable number so its factories can keep up with orders.

Nike iD is not without risks. Naming shoes can be a problem, as Nike found out when it rejected a buyer's request for shoes to be named *Sweatshop*. Nike was not amused by the request. Surprisingly, the negative publicity about the incident spurred interest in Nike iD and spiked sales on the site. There is also the problem of customers who design and wear shoes with hideous color or pattern combinations that also sport the Nike logo. This can be damaging to Nike's reputation.

Returns are also a problem. That is where online remainder retailers may be used to sell returned customized shoes that Nike has no way of selling on its site. Companies like Wal-Mart and Target have an advantage when it comes to product returns. They let customers return products purchased online to any of their offline stores, no questions asked.[41]

### CHECK IT OUT

Have you customized products for yourself or others online? Is this an attractive way to satisfy consumer desires to express individuality? Does it mean the end of brands if everyone *does their own thing*? What, if anything, should Nike do about customers who design hideous shoes through Nike iD? Had you heard of Nike iD before reading about it in this chapter?

Go to the Nike U.S. home page (*http://www.nike.com/usa/index.html*). How difficult is it to locate Nike iD? Go to Nike iD and design your own shoe. Evaluate the process using the same criteria used for the *Internet Marketing Application* exercise. How does Nike stack up? Would you buy the shoe you made? If so, how long will it take to deliver? Are you willing to wait that long? What about returning them if you are not satisfied? Overall, is this a good way to bring customers back to the Nike site? Is it a good way to maintain Nike's brand image?

## A GLOBAL PERSPECTIVE

Over the years, Nike has been criticized for outsourcing product manufacturing to parts of the world where labor is cheap and working conditions in sweatshops are far below acceptable standards in the United States. College students have protested and forced some of their universities to sell Nike stock and stop using Nike products in collegiate athletics. Anti-Nike sites attack Nike for its labor practices.

Check out a resource page for anti-Nike sites (*http://www.geocities.com/Athens/Acropolis/5232/links.html*), then see how Nike responds to these charges on its web site (*http://www.nikebiz.com/labor/kudong_updates.shtml*). When it comes to disputing the charges made by the anti-Nike sites, is Nike's response effective? What else should it do to protect its brand name? Should college students be involved in these labor issues? Should U.S. labor standards be applied to outsourced manufacturing locations in other countries?

## CHAPTER TEN

# Price

## LEARNING OBJECTIVES

- To identify factors that affect how Internet prices are set
- To learn about online price issues that concern consumers and enterprises
- To identify alternate Internet pricing models and understand why some price strategies are successful and others are not
- To examine Internet payment alternatives and determine how buyers can pay for products online

## Nadia Seeks A Price Advantage

Nadia is a purchasing officer for a large group medical clinic. The clinic has 140 doctors in thirty specialties from allergy to urology. It operates seventeen centers in six adjacent counties, in addition to its main campus. Nadia is responsible for consolidating orders from all centers and obtaining the best deals possible for price, quality, quantity, and delivery on disposable (wipes, needles, syringes, sharps) and nondisposable products (examination robes, uniforms, scissors, and surgical accessories). In the past, Nadia purchased many products as straight rebuys, standing orders with vendors she had been purchasing from for years. Other products were modified and new task buys that required contacting vendors and asking them to submit specifications and bids. This lengthy process involved lots of paperwork, lengthy telephone calls, and many emails and fax messages. This is about to change because Nadia will be using a new purchasing process for the next buying cycle. She will be placing requests for quotes (RFQs) on a web health care exchange. Online exchanges (electronic marketplaces) simplify the ordering process and increase purchasing efficiency. Nadia expects to receive more price quotes from different vendors than ever before and be able to quickly compare their offers. Exchange ordering reduces paperwork and the time needed to request, receive, and analyze price quotes and make purchase decisions. Vendors like exchanges because it gives them access to a greater number of buyers and promises to even out variations in demand. Nadia has buying clout on the exchange because her clinic orders are large, tens of million of dollars annually. Exchange prices are from 4 to 10 percent less than what she paid for the same products last year.

Marketing is the functional business activity directly responsible for generating revenue and price is a key marketing mix tool used to achieve revenue goals. Most consumers use price as a determining or contributing factor in deciding whether or not to purchase a product. Most businesses use price as a revenue-generating tool and to compete strategically with other businesses. They also want a reasonable price for the products they purchase. Some organizations and governments constrain price and require lowest-bid purchasing. Others regard product quality as the prime concern, followed by price. When quality is not clearly evident, price frequently becomes a surrogate cue for quality.

Price is often a lightning rod for complaints. Consumers complain because they believe prices are unfair and too high (rarely are they too low). Businesses complain because competitors undercut their prices or they believe they are paying too much for their own purchases. Government wants to encourage competition and ensure that prices respond legitimately to market demand. Marketers complain about the difficulty of setting the right price, one that is low enough to attract buyers, yet high enough to hit revenue and profit targets. Price is a flexible variable; it can be changed quickly to respond to changes in demand, seasons, competitors, the economy, government regulations, and societal tastes. It can be changed in real time online to respond to competitors' price changes. Price is also complex and often misunderstood.

## Price Fundamentals

**Price**

How much buyers must give up of something they value in order to take possession of or use a product.

**Price** determines how much buyers must give up to take possession of or use a product. It is a measure of the *value* buyers associate with a product and their demand for it. Once buyers accept a price, sellers take payment in the form of something that both they and buyers value. In the United States, credit cards are the preferred payment mechanism along with debit cards, and cash. Almost 88 percent of online sales by consumers are made directly or indirectly with credit cards.[1]

Price allocates products, determining who can buy, possess, and use them. Price also clears markets following the law of supply and demand. When demand increases and more products are sold, existing product inventory is reduced. When existing inventory falls to a designated point, it is typically replaced through increased production. Thus, marketing has a market clearing role.

### PRICE AND DEMAND

Most buyers will not make a purchase if they think a price is not honest or fair. Likelihood of purchase depends on how badly they need and/or want the product, their perception of price fairness, the availability of alternatives, and whether they have the means to complete the purchase. Most consumers are highly *price sensitive* with convenience and shopping products, unwilling to pay above what they think is a fair price and suspicious of product quality if the price is too low. Since convenience and many shopping products are widely available online, consumers can shop around fairly easily, seeking the best price. Sometimes consumers do not shop around and will pay a higher price in return for something they value more, like convenience. Tesco (*http://www.tesco.com*), the world's largest and thus far only profitable online grocer, reaches 91 percent of Britain's population with its online ordering and offline delivery services. Experts warned Tesco managers before the service was launched that consumers would not pay extra to have their groceries delivered. They were wrong. Every week Tesco's more than seventy thousand online customers willingly pay £5 (about US$7.19) per delivery, which means the company collects more than US$27 million annually in delivery fees. Obviously, Tesco's customers are willing to pay more for the convenience of online grocery shopping. They feel safe purchasing from a trusted brand, a local company that has long been a familiar part of their everyday lives. Shoppers pay the same price in-store and online. Payment is by laser (sic) or credit card from Visa, Mastercard, and American Express. Secure Server Software encripts all credit card information. Tesco.com's in-store pickers pick more than 4.5 million items each week for home delivery.[2]

Many consumers are conditioned to be *price conscious* by retailers that regularly have sales and quickly mark down prices from their original highs. This makes many consumers unwilling to pay full price because they know if they wait, the product will soon be reduced. Price conscious consumers are attracted to price comparison web sites where sale or shopping robots (shop bots) make *price comparisons* easy and fast. This helps reduce *price information asymmetry,* the price information advantage previously enjoyed by sellers. *Status-conscious consumers* use price as an indicator of prestige, and, for them, a lower price product may be unattractive. They may be attracted to sellers like Ashford.com and eLuxury.com.

Businesses closely monitor consumer *primary demand* because it generates *derived demand* for enterprise products. As consumers buy more, products are moved through channels, inventories are reduced, and production increases. Consumer spending fuels the U.S. economy. Consumer purchasing sentiments are monitored through two major monthly surveys, the Conference Board's *Consumer Confidence Index* (*http://www.conference-board.org*) and the University of Michigan's *Consumer Sentiment Index* (*http://www.isr.umich.edu*). Evidence suggests consumer spending is positively associated with consumers' confidence about their own jobs and income. It also has a positive relationship with the movement of single family house prices, the greatest single investment most consumers will ever make.[3]

Elasticity is a measure of consumer sensitivity to price changes. Although a reduction in price typically results in an increase in demand, the *amount* of the change in demand varies. Essential products, necessities, addictive products, products whose purchase cannot be delayed, and those with few substitutes are *inelastic.* Demand is relatively *price insensitive* and a 1 percent change in price has a less than 1 percent change in demand; thus, the slope of the demand curve is flatter. For example, if a salesperson must fly to Chicago unexpectedly and immediately to make sure a sale does not come apart, he or she typically will pay whatever is necessary to get on the earliest flight out. The airfare is US$920 for a ticket purchased one day in advance. Had the ticket been purchased thirty days in advance, it would have been only US$255. Under the circumstances, paying the higher price is understandable. Demand insensitivity also suggests the salesperson will avoid online ticket auctions that require bidding for airline tickets over a several day or week period and instead go straight to Orbitz (*http://www.orbitz.com*) or another site to purchase the electronic ticket (eticket) that expeditiously delivers him or her to Chicago.

Products that are not essential, can be delayed, are expensive, or have many substitutes are *elastic* and demand is relatively *price sensitive* for them. A 1 percent change in price will have a greater than 1 percent change in demand for elastic products. For example, Ford, General Motors (GM), and DaimlerChrysler offered interest-free or very low financing after the September 11, 2001, terrorist attacks and into early 2002 to stimulate sales. This hood money resulted in a buying frenzy. GM and Ford both saw over 30 percent sales gains in October 2001. For GM, this was the highest sales spike in fifteen years. It broke a thirty-four-year-old sales record at Ford.[4]

Understanding the demand curve for different types of products and consumer sensitivity to price changes gives Internet marketers extremely useful information for setting and changing prices. At the same time, consumers can get price comparisons for many online competitors, so they can find alternatives to a price change designed to get them to increase their purchases.

## CUSTOMER VALUE

All buyers do not contribute equally to the bottom line. The Pareto Principle, or 80-20 rule, observes that some customers are more valuable than others and about 80 percent of revenues are contributed by only about 20 percent of buyers. While 80-20 may not be an exact proportion for all businesses, it suggests the fallacy of treating all buyers equally when it comes to pricing. Delta Air Lines (*http://www.delta.com*) differentiates service levels by passenger value. Delta's BusinessElite frequent business flyers are a high-margin, preferred-buyer segment. They receive enhanced service on the ground and in the air, their seats have more legroom, they eat five-course meals, and they drink good wines. Compare this with what happens to passengers in cheap coach seats on the exact same plane. Delta and other airlines complicate the issue immensely by selling tickets on the same flight at many different prices. Price becomes a function of how far in advance the tickets were purchased, the time and day of the flight, its passenger load factor (filled seats), and other factors. Before web sites like Priceline.com (*http://tickets.priceline.com*), Travelocity (*http://www.travelocity.com*), CheapTickets (*http://web.cheaptickets.com*), and Orbitz (*http://www.orbitz.com*) appeared, airline companies could hide prices from buyers. Now, determined buyers can hunt down bargains and expose, to a certain extent, airfare price discrepancies.

Marketers can identify their preferred customers using operational data tools, by data mining and query techniques. They can also determine which customers are most likely to be receptive to inducements that will move them from being profitable to preferred. Ultimately, the best customers are those with high lifetime value. Over the life of their relationship with the business, they contribute more to profits than others.

Lifetime value is not always easy to calculate or project. An enterprise with extensive customer sales records can calculate the profit contributed by a specific customer over a several year period, then compare it to the average profit per sale over the same period. Average profit per sale is total sales revenue minus costs of the sales (product costs, marketing expenses including web site costs, fulfillment expenses) divided by the total number of sales. Obviously, the effective use of price can be a powerful factor moving some customers toward more frequent purchases, increased quantities, and more expensive products. New customers can be compared to profiles of existing customers to facilitate forecasting their potential lifetime value. If a new customer fits the best customer profile, then the enterprise may consider making attractive initial offers, including significant discounts, on the assumption that their future revenue contributions will more than compensate for the discounts.

## INFLUENCING FACTORS

In a completely rational market in economic terms, price should be used for only one purpose, to accumulate revenue (and profit) for the business and its shareholders. In

| Table 10-1 Factors Influencing Price | |
|---|---|
| *Internal objectives* | What goals does the business set for price? Gain market share? Increase revenues? Build brand equity? |
| *Buyer segments* | What segments will be served? What do they want from the product? |
| *Demand* | Is buyer demand elastic or inelastic? |
| *Cost* | What will it cost to produce and market the product? |
| *Economy* | What is the state of the economy? Boom or bust? |
| *Consumer confidence* | Is consumer confidence supporting product purchases? |
| *Competitors* | What are competitors' prices for comparable products? |
| *Free alternatives* | For content sites, is anyone giving away the same content free? |
| *Channel members* | What markups do channel members add? |
| *Government* | What constraints does government place on prices? |
| *Special events* | Are the products to be sold at special events? |
| *Seasons* | If the product is seasonal, where in the cycle is it? |
| *Promotions* | Will promotions be run to stimulate demand? |
| *Weather* | If weather is a factor, what weather is expected? |

reality, other goals are often set for price, and it can be influenced by a variety of factors (table 10-1). Whatever the goal, it must be clearly identified so the right price is set and appropriate tactics are developed to support it. For example, if the goal is to build web site traffic, move inventory, gain market share for a new product, or spike sales of an existing product, a *bargain price* may be needed. If the goal is to attract and sustain the interest of high-end shoppers, then a *prestige (premium) price* is more appropriate.

Many clicks-only businesses rushed online in the late 1990s believing the hyperbole about first mover advantage and the imperative need to attract buyers and crowd out potential competitors. Taking this as their goal, they set prices ridiculously low and piled on free shipping and handling (S&H), product freebies (free products), and special discounts. This strategy attracted extremely price conscious bargain hunters, who are notoriously fickle about paying above a discount price. As the first movers burned through their cash reserves and investors began withdrawing support, the pricing environment shifted and pricing started becoming more rational. For many businesses, it was too late.[5]

Now that so many bricks-and-clicks businesses are competing online, they need to maintain consistency between online and offline price goals to avoid compromising them, confusing buyers, and potentially damaging their brands. Neiman Marcus (*http://neimanmarcus.com*) uses a prestige pricing strategy to support its brand image online and in its bricks-and-mortar stores and catalogs. Wal-Mart (*http://www.walmart.com*) boasts *Always low prices!* online and off. Thus, both are consistent in their online and offline channels. Price consistency is also an issue with individual products. Prices for identical products in multiple channels—online, in a store, or by catalog or other channel—should be identical unless clearly stated otherwise to avoid confusing and antagonizing buyers.

Some factors that influence price must be considered on a regular basis, like competitors' actions, channel member markups, and consumer demand. Other factors exert infrequent or sometimes unique influences. The 2002 Winter Olympics in Salt Lake City (*http://www.saltlake2002.com*) and the FIFA 2002 World Cup (*Federation Internationale de Football Association* at *http://www.fifaworldcup.com*) in South Korea and Japan occur infrequently, every four years, and are unique events for the host cities. Products targeted to buyers at Olympics or World Cup matches will be priced commensurate with the added value of their association with very special events.

Product life cycle stage also influences price setting. Price can be set high when innovators and early majority buyers are eager to purchase the product, then reduced later to attract the late majority and laggards. Products on the market for a long time and nearing termination, and seasonal products near the end of the season, may require a *discount price*. Government regulations can constrain price setting, particularly in utilities. Geography can influence price setting. Shipping products to distant locations, big city retail stores, or stores in expensive malls can add to the price. Products that are overstocks, end-of-season remainders, or from liquidated companies are sold at bargain prices.

## PRICE SETTING

Prices typically are set within a range. The *ceiling price* is the highest buyers can or are willing to pay for a product. It is also the price set by direct competitors for identical products. The *price floor* is the lowest price that a business can afford or is willing to accept. It may be the breakeven point or below breakeven when price is deliberately set low at a *penetration price* level to quickly develop market share in a new market. It may even be below breakeven if the product is used as a *loss leader* designed to attract traffic to a web site.

The range of *acceptable prices* lies between the ceiling and floor. When given a choice of similar products within a range, consumers tend to buy the midpriced product. Therefore, Internet marketers should try to set the top price close to the ceiling in order to ensure that the midpriced product's price is also higher and boosts profit margins. A recent study showed that as long as online products are priced within their acceptable range, customer response is not affected. This supports the strategy of pricing up to the ceiling. But competitors' and buyers' probable responses also must be considered. If competitors probably will price *below* the ceiling and buyers will probably seek price alternatives online, products priced up to the ceiling will be punished. Ironically, a large number of online shoppers do not compare prices although they have ample opportunity to do so. Almost 90 percent of book shoppers and 84 percent of toy shoppers purchase at the first site they reach and do not shop around.[6]

**Price testing**

Using dynamic online pricing processes, price can be tested by offering different prices to different customers in real time, then tracking their responses.

The Internet lends itself to **price testing,** making price changes in real time to determine buyer receptiveness to different prices. These tests are run on different types or segments of buyers. Cookies can be used to identify consumer characteristics, their purchase history, or newness to a web storefront. Product prices can then be set to vary according to preselected variables; for example, a lower price is set for buyers making their first visit to the site or for buyers from a particular part of the country. An alternate decision rule might be to offer a different price to every *n*th visitor. In both cases, consumer responses (purchases) are tracked in real time and used to adjust prices based on buyer price tolerance. For example, if price testing shows that consumers will purchase at a higher price, then it can be used. However, if testing shows consumers are price sensitive, then a lower price is set.

Consumer responses to peak-time prices can also be tested. The Weather Underground (*http://www.weatherunderground.com*) tested visitor receptiveness to its pay-per-page view subscription service before rolling it out. Access to the site is for members only from 8:00 A.M. until 6:00 P.M. Eastern Standard Time. Subscriptions are only US$5 per year, a small price for most consumers to pay for access to high-value, timely content (see the screen shot below), and to access the site without encountering irritating advertisements.

**Paying for a Page View**

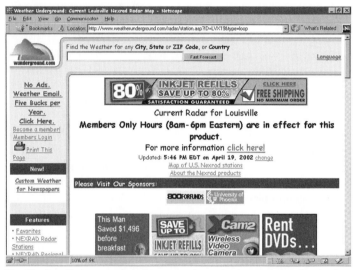

The Weather Underground charges a very low price for a subscription to view the site during prime-time daylight hours. An added membership advantage is that the screen has no advertisements. *Source:* Reprinted by permission of The Weather Underground, www.wunderground.com. *http://www.weatherunderground. com/radar/station.asp?ID=LVX19&type=loop.*

Before the Internet, setting a price in most businesses was arguably more art than science. Today, businesses with large databases full of buyer behavioral data and intelligence software that tracks competitors' prices can claim that, at least for them, setting a price is more science than art. Others fall somewhere between art and science and many prices are still set using seat-of-the-pants decisions. Some businesses let others set prices for their products when they use a *parity price*, adopting the price used by direct competitors with substitute products, or a *follow-the-leader price*, where a market leader sets a price and everyone else more or less follows it.

Setting a price should be a carefully considered, systematic process. For too many businesses it is not, and price setting is neglected or expedient. Few products remain priced at the same level for any appreciable time. Price volatility, particularly in consumer products, is more likely than long-term price stability, which is more characteristic of many enterprise products, particularly some raw materials. Price volatility online is even greater than offline because price transparency motivates competitors to respond with price adjustments in real time.

Consumers are not usually thought of as product sellers offline, but they are a growing presence online. For example, they are active sellers in C2C exchanges, primarily auctions where they sell to other consumers with the aid of a facilitator like eBay.com (*http://www.ebay.com*) or sometimes directly, without an intermediary. By mid-2001, 64 percent of all online auction sales were generated at eBay. By mid-2002, eBay had 46.1 million registered users, a 55 percent increase from mid-2001.[7] Consumers sell new and used products on eBay, from closet clutter to valuable antiques and even real estate. Top auction categories are automobiles, computers, consumer electronics, books/music/movies, and collectibles. The seller sets the opening bid price in a classic forward auction. Factors influencing the opening bid price are product state (new, used), condition, price (original, list), comparative price (price of identical or comparable products), recent sale price (if a comparable item was recently sold at auction), and auction fee (paid by seller).

Half.com (*http://www.half.com*), eBay.com's fixed-price marketplace, gives sellers advice about pricing their products and judging quality. Consumers and enterprises offer new, overstocks, remainders, or used products for sale at Half.com. The price floor is a minimum asking price of US$0.75. The ceiling is 50 percent of the best online retail price if the product is *like new*. Prices slide down from there with 45 percent of the best online retail price suggested for *very good* condition products, 40 percent for *good*, and 35 percent for *acceptable*.

## PRICE AND SUSTAINABLE COMPETITIVE ADVANTAGE

Survival is an overriding goal for businesses, whether they are global corporate giants like General Electric (GE at *http://www.ge.com*), which competes in more than a hundred countries, or a local small business. Price is important to GE and contributes to the company's competitive advantages. But price can be changed, matched, or bettered almost instantly, particularly online and even for GE. Relying on it as the only point of differentiation is very risky. It undermines the value of brands and customer loyalty and can lead to price wars and margin erosion. GE offers competitive prices, but it pairs price with an outstanding reputation, stability, innovations, and customer-centric marketing. Price must be used strategically with the other marketing mix tools to deliver what buyers need and want, sometimes even before they know they have a need or want.

Retailers identified with prestige pricing, like Neiman Marcus and Tiffany (*http://www.tiffany.com*), sustain their advantage by offering unique high-quality products, superb online service, flawless delivery and return policies, and a clear focus on customer satisfaction. eBay.com is not primarily about price; it offers entertainment and the allure of finding or selling treasure, even though what sells may be flea market jumble to some. Discounters like Wal-Mart attract price-conscious and bargain shoppers and those who want the convenience of in-store returns for products purchased online. Targeting bargain hunters increases a web storefront's vulnerability to price transparency and downward price pressures. Price obviously cannot be ignored, but online transparency can make it less effective in building a competitive advantage.

## ✔ CONCEPT CHECK

1. Explain how marketing helps clear the marketplace.
2. What factors influence price setting?
3. A consumer wants to sell a good condition copy of a book at Half.com. The book's original retail price was US$50. What opening bid price should the seller ask?

# *Price Issues*

Price touches most aspects of Internet marketing, from access price to what consumers must pay to read articles from the *Wall Street Journal Online* (*http://www.wsj.com*). Price issues are complex, and some are quite sensitive. Other price-related issues help explain why many dot-coms have failed to meet expectations.

## DOWNWARD PRESSURE OR NOT?

Initially the Internet was expected to be a price utopia, where free and complete knowledge of prices forced them down toward marginal costs. Sellers would experience a price squeeze, forcing them to compete on other factors. Enterprise buyers would be able to readily identify price discrepancies, then enter B2B exchanges (emarketplaces) and, through their informed buying power, force prices lower. Marketers could easily and rapidly monitor competitors' price changes, then respond and communicate price change information to their customers by email or on their web sites. Offline **price information asymmetry,** where buyers (particularly consumers) are at a disadvantage because they lack comparative price information, would disappear online, and **price information symmetry** (all parties can access the same price information) would prevail.

A decade after the start of commercialization, one part of this scenario has happened as forecast. Price information and comparisons are available to anyone with the time, skill, and motivation to find them. They include insurance premium quotes (*http://Insurance.com*) and gasoline prices at local service stations identified by zip code proximity (*http://www.gaspricewatch.com*), price comparisons for electronics (*http://shopper.cnet.com*) and computer components (*http://www.pricewatch.com*), book search and prices (*http://www.addall.com*), prices and products from around the Web (*http://www.mysimon.com*), and many others.

Initially, buyers had to be educated about price comparison web sites, primarily through advertisements and onsite instructions, because no direct offline equivalent exists. To make price comparisons offline, buyers would have to contact each potential seller directly, visit stores, or search *Consumers Reports* (*http://www.consumerreports.org*) or other hard-copy sources for information on the sought product. Now, price comparison sites are more familiar, but there are still drawbacks. The amount of price information returned from a search can be overwhelming. It takes time to initiate and wait for a search to be completed. Some price search sites *top list* merchants that sponsor the site or buy onsite advertising, so price listings can be misleading and are not objective. Product model differences can make direct price comparisons difficult. Consumers are advised to perform multiple price searches, using at least three search sites, and if possible, to sort lists by price with the lowest price listed first.[8]

Price search sites like MySimon.com and DealTime.com (*http://www.dealtime.com*) are having an impact. They are directing buyers to the lowest-price online retailers. This may drive prices down if retailers begin to court the search sites, recognizing that this is a more effective way to build site traffic than online advertisements. It may also contribute to the erosion of brand value.

Internet commercial activity currently represents a small part of total U.S. economic activity, slightly more than 1 percent of both B2B and B2C sales. For commercial activity to continue to grow, online prices must at least be comparable to offline prices and lower in some product categories, or other benefits like convenience and wider product choice must compensate for higher prices. Thus far results are mixed. Some B2B exchanges are reporting downward price pressures, but it is unclear how much is due to price information and auction efficiencies, reduced paperwork, or to lower interest rates that reduce inventory holding costs. Some savings from online business process efficiencies and eprocurement are passed along as price reductions or price stabilizations.

**Price information asymmetry**

One party to the buyer-seller exchange has more information about price than the other.

**Price information symmetry**

Both buyers and sellers have the same price information.

Downward pressure is far less apparent in U.S. consumer prices, and in some cases prices are rising. The dot-com bust and renewed emphasis on profitability has resulted in the discontinuation of many price discounts and free S&H. More sites are charging for content that previously was free. Consolidations and bankruptcies have reduced the number of online retailers and competitors, which reduces price competition and contributes to pressure to increase prices and generate greater revenue.

A lower price by itself is not always enough to persuade consumers to buy. For example, Amazon.com 's (*http://www.amazon.com*) books are not always priced less than its rivals, but consumers are willing to pay more at Amazon because brand awareness and trust make it a preferred seller. It also saves consumers search time wasted in comparison shopping. Books.com consistently underpriced Amazon but still could not attract enough customers to stay in business. It was bought and absorbed by Barnes & Noble (*http://www.bn.com*).

## TRANSPARENCY AND SEARCH SITES

**Price transparency**
When prices for competing products are clearly visible and easily obtainable by all interested market members—buyers, sellers, competitors, and regulators.

**Price transparency** means making prices for competing products visible and easily obtainable so buyers and competitors can readily make price comparisons. Transparency highlights price discrepancies. Buyers with this information are better equipped to make more effective price decisions. If price transparency exists, all things being equal, competitive pressure should drive prices down. It should also reduce profit margins on transparently priced products and impede sellers from making different price offers for the same product in different markets. Price transparency may change some parity products to commodities. It may also erode customer loyalty and brand value. Transparency coupled with data mining on competitors' web sites allows sellers to quickly determine competitors' prices and adjust their own prices accordingly. Sellers that signal price changes this way and collude in setting prices are breaking the law.

Buyers are beneficiaries of price transparency and the Internet's anonymity. For example, women and minorities typically pay more for automobiles than white males, from US$45 to US$500 per car. However, when women and minorities purchase online, that difference disappears. The Internet is an *equalizer* for price disparities that occur in offline car dealerships. These differences are related to price haggling (negotiating) skills and having less information with which to negotiate.[9]

**Search sites**
Web sites that collect and compare product information for visitors.

**Search sites** like MySimon and DealTime use intelligent agents, search software, and/or human monitors to search online stores, collecting price, product, store, and product availability information. Because online prices can be changed quickly, continuous sweeps of the Web are required to capture the most current price and shipping information. Search site prices are far more current than static offline published prices, but it is still advisable to also check the seller's site for the most current information. Most search sites offer click throughs to seller sites along with merchant reviews. Buyers should use price information cautiously and carefully compare prices for add-ons, particularly S&H, and state sales tax.

A model is emerging of online/offline price complementarity. Consumers frequently search online for product and price information. Armed with the information, they go offline to complete the purchase in a store or catalog to avoid perceived Internet shopping risks, to eliminate S&H costs, or because the retailer does not sell online. This is an online information search and offline purchase model.

Online price transparency could be a solution to some *price gouging* situations, where prices are perceived to be artificially inflated to increase seller profits. This is a frequent complaint levied against oil companies when gasoline prices rise sharply. In a move against price gouging, the Australian Competition and Consumer Commission (ACCC) is considering proposals to list all petrol (gasoline) station fuel prices online in a public web site. The goal is for online price transparency to drive down or stabilize offline prices. Any price increase would have to be posted on the site before implementation.[10] U.S. and Canadian gasoline and home heating oil prices can be compared at Gaspricewatch.com, another example of online/offline complementarity. Over thirteen human spotters report on gasoline prices in their neighborhoods. Site users enter their zip code to get a list of stations and current prices within a zero to twenty-mile radius of the zip.

All industries are not equally enthusiastic about price transparency. GemConnect (*http://www.gemconnect.com*) is a neutral platform for buyers and sellers in the gem industry. It hosts an independent B2B marketplace for gemstone and jewelry exchanges and claims to solve information asymmetry in an industry with too few trading partners, suboptimal pricing, and inadequate management practices.[11] Obviously, asymmetry and opaque pricing has worked to the advantage of some sellers, particularly those that can exert market control.

FreeMarkets, Inc. (*http://www.freemarkets.com*), founded in 1995, is an independent and neutral worldwide exchange whose members include Owens Corning, Smith Kline Beecham PLC, and Visteon Corp. Its sourcing market, the largest in the world, illustrates how price transparency has obvious benefits for B2B exchange members. FreeMarkets has brokered over US$ 35 billion in sales and realized a US$7 billion cost savings for its members, with auction prices averaging 19 percent lower than what businesses paid previously for the same products.[12] It serves over 21,000 suppliers and 111 companies in more than 200 supply categories. Exchanges are conducted in thirty different languages. Emerson, a global diversified manufacturer, used the exchange to consolidate purchases of printed circuit boards in its fourteen global divisions. Using a *downward auction*, where the buyer lists the top price it is willing to pay and suppliers compete for the contract by bidding the price down, Emerson received 755 bids from forty-three ISO10000-certified suppliers and consolidated its supply base to nine vendors. The company saved approximately US$10 million from its previous US$36.1 million supply cost.

## ACCESS

Before commercialization, Internet users idealized it as an unrestrained environment characterized by free and open access for all. However, even then users had to pay a price to be part of it. The **Internet access price** is what consumers and enterprises without direct Internet access pay a service provider to connect to the service and Internet. Initially, U.S. access pricing was metered, and users paid per hour online. Today, it is almost universally a flat rate price, a monthly fee that guarantees unlimited access. AOL (*http://www.aol.com*) has five consumer price plans that allow buyers to connect to AOL and the Internet. They range from a low price for light use to the highest-priced premium services.

Dial-up, DSL, ISDN, and cable prices vary between vendors, plans, and buyer groups, and by special temporary price promotions. They also differ for consumers

**Internet access price**
The price consumers and some enterprises pay to a service provider to connect to the service and Internet.

and enterprises. DSL consumer rates from Verizon (*http://verizon.com*) in early 2002 varied in a range from a low US$49.95 per month for Package 1 to US$79.95 per month for Package 4. Each price point adds benefits in faster upload and download data rate/speed.

Access prices vary worldwide. In many countries, access is still metered and very expensive, which is detrimental to the growth of Internet use. This is clearly a factor in the relatively low Internet adoption rate in Eastern Europe and Latin America where access rates are very high. By comparison, the Scandinavian countries have low access rates and high Internet use. The price of forty hours of Internet use per month at peak traffic times is US$173 in the Czech Republic, US$144 in Poland, US$150 in Hungary, US$87.20 per month in Luxembourg, and less than US$24 in the United States. Prices reflect purchasing power parity.[13]

**Content pricing**
Charging a price for access to information content on a web site.

Access price also refers to **content pricing,** charging for access to content on a web site. Some sites offer content free, trying to generate revenue from other sources, like on-site paid advertising or not considering the site as a revenue generator, instead using it as a content driver, pushing visitors to offline stores or salespeople. Others offer limited free public content, then charge by subscription or per unit for private, premium content. A third type is members-only with no free public content and access restricted to paid members.

Web sites that charge for content must have something that buyers really value, otherwise price will reduce or destroy site traffic. *Consumer Reports Online* (*http://www.consumerreports.org*) is a profitable content site. Some content is free. Product recalls is a valuable free area where visitors can check the latest recalls in a long list of products from appliances to vehicle accessories. A subscription includes access to the magazine's archives with reports on product tests and prices. Consumer Reports brings its objective reports and valuable brand name to its web site. Because its reports save buyers money and search time, many consumers believe content value justifies paying the site's nominal price.[14]

Internet marketers should be cautious about access pricing. Some sites clearly are not candidates for it, including storefronts selling products like apparel, toys, books, automobiles, appliances, computers, and software. Information content sites are more promising candidates. The *Wall Street Journal Online* and *Consumer Reports Online* show it can be done profitably. Other sites are having great difficulty charging for content because comparable content is free. Some adult content sites are profitable, but because most are privately held, accurate revenue figures are not available. Content sites trying to charge an access fee have to contend with the Internet's free and open history. As more new users go online, this historical memory will fade and a greater number of sites will try to develop revenue streams through access pricing, with varying degrees of success.

## FAIRNESS

A fair price is hard to define, but consumers know it when they see it. A fair price is one that is equitable, where the product is worth what is being asked for it. Fairness typically is perceived as not being taken advantage of. It is the opposite of price gouging, grossly overcharging. Generally, the perception is the lower the price, the greater the fairness, all things being equal. However, a low price has negative connotations for prestige products and, for convenience and shopping products, can signal low quality.

Of course, a fair price to one buyer may be a swindle to another. Price fairness is a highly subjective judgment unless unbiased evidence can be found to substantiate fairness and buyers accept it.

The Internet has leveled the price fairness playing field to a considerable extent and with time, patience, and skill, consumers and enterprises can obtain timely comparative price information and make fairness judgments. This even extends to works of art, which are notoriously difficult to price and are often involved in price gouging. AskArt.com (*http://askart.com*) offers comparative price information and lists recent sale prices for the top hundred selling artists, topped by prices near US$30 million. It also has information and price lists for regional artists, different art styles like cartoonists and sculptors, and art books. Although online art price information may help an experienced buyer, a consumer purchasing for his or her own collection is still vulnerable to price asymmetry when purchasing paintings, sculpture, and other unique art works online.

Price fairness at auction sites verges on being an oxymoron. Auction participants tend to display a herd instinct, rushing to heavily bid auctions where product value and price fairness are secondary to bidding frenzy. The herd's bidding enthusiasm overwhelms thoughts of price fairness, at least until auction passions cool. Some information about auctions and product prices can be found in social communities like ezboard.com (*http://www.ezboard.com*), with over one million communities and eight million registered users. Although this is the largest community online, like all communities, information is subjective and should be used with caution when making a purchase decision. Most consumers do not have the time or patience to browse through auction bulletin boards, reading subjective perceptions of auction and price fairness.

StrongNumbers.com's (*http://www.strongnumbers.com*) Blue Book for Everything is a product and price reference guide for fair market value of hundreds of thousands of popular consumer products. It furnishes fair market values and market trends for enterprises as well. StrongNumbers calculates values for products on sale at over 250 auction sites and over 2,000 retailers daily. It provides a range of final sale prices along with its own StrongNumbers of fair market value, a regression line drawn through a sale price scatter plot. It includes sale details including product specifics, item condition, and type. This site appears to be a valuable asset in trying to determine price fairness for many popular products sold at auction. It is also a useful reference for calculating fair market value for charitable donations. A limitation is that most buyers probably have never heard of StrongNumbers.com.

Price fairness has yet another dimension. Consumers want to know the full price they will have to pay for purchases. This includes showing S&H costs early in the buying process so it will not come as a shock later and cause shopping basket abandonment. Applicable taxes should also be identified. The problem is determining when to provide the information. S&H and taxes typically are not calculated until the buyer is ready to check out and provides purchase information.

## SHIPPING AND HANDLING

Shipping and handling, the cost of order fulfillment and product delivery, is a contentious issue. Initially, free S&H was an inducement for consumers to purchase online. It was part of an attractive price reduction duo—no sales tax, no S&H. With the dot-come meltdown and heightened emphasis on profitability and building revenue streams, companies moved away from free S&H and began charging consumers. By mid-2001, the fifty most visited web sites all charged S&H.[15]

S&H pricing methods vary. The most common is a graduated scale, adding a fixed amount calibrated to the purchase price. Lands' End's (*http://www.landsend.com*) standard shipping begins at US$3.95 for orders up to US$25 and tops out at US$11.95 for orders above US$150.01. A flat shipping rate is less common. Bluefly.com (*http://www.bluefly.com*) charges US$5.95 per order for standard shipping in the continental United States and Canada. Some sites still offer free S&H for purchases over a preset amount. Tiffany.com has free ground shipping to one address for orders over US$1,000.

The demise of free shipping raises a serious question. Do Internet marketers really want bargain shoppers who are so price sensitive they abandon a site when they have to pay S&H? Remember the 80-20 rule. A better profit margin can be achieved with a smaller, more select customer base that is less price sensitive. It is unlikely that a small S&H charge will deter most buyers, particularly if it is perceived as fair and they avoid state sales tax and the added time and travel costs of shopping for the product offline.

Price information can spread online like wildfire. Amazon.com got itself into hot water with consumers over a free shipping promotion in mid-June 2001. It offered buyers free shipping for orders of two or more books, music CDs, or videos. At the same time Amazon increased some product prices and reduced others. To illustrate the power of price transparency, buyers checked Amazon's new prices against others at ISBN.nu (*http://ISBN.nu*), which lists comparative prices with and without shipping. Consumers cried foul, calling Amazon's free shipping a price increase in disguise. They quickly spread the word through online communities that buyers could "game the system" by ordering *The Book of Hope* at US$0.49 (used, US$0.02) as their second purchase to qualify for free shipping. To illustrate the importance of shipping costs, an estimated 63 percent of customers abandon their online transaction when they learn how much shipping adds to the price. Within twenty-four hours of Amazon's free shipping offer, *The Book of Hope* climbed from number 995 to 75 on Amazon's Top 100 Sellers list. A week later it was number 31. Of course, Barnes&Noble.com immediately matched Amazon's free shipping offer, without similar negative press. Within two weeks, Amazon abandoned what it called a *price test* to see if consumers preferred to have S&H costs rolled into the purchase price.[16] This is also an example of how closely direct competitors monitor price on each other's sites. Book prices at Amazon.com and Barnes&Noble.com tend to be the same or only pennies different. Even small and midsize businesses can perform regular online price benchmarking.

Sellers can gain a competitive advantage by offering free shipping on a regular or short-term basis. In particular, price discounters attract price-sensitive buyers for whom S&H costs are important. Buy.com (*http://www.us.buy.com*), which advertises *Lowest Prices on Earth*, has used free shipping as an inducement for its specials, specially designated offers of products the store is trying to move. However, it also reserves the right to end free shipping at any time, which can catch consumers off guard.

## CROSS-BORDER

Prices published on public access World Wide Web sites obviously cross borders. Worldwide price transparency exposes price discrepancies that were not obvious before the Internet. This makes it easier to compare prices for the same products in different country or regional markets. For example, a consumer in the Netherlands visits a French web site and finds the same model bicycle for 20 percent less than its retail price in Utrecht, NL. She might purchase it online or drive several hours south to purchase the bike in France. If price transparency becomes widespread, it will put downward pressure on regional prices and reduce their differences. This may become a considerable problem in some product categories since price discrepancies often reflect real differences in the cost of doing business in different countries or regions.[17] Although the Internet and Web are worldwide, some sellers will not sell internationally because they do not want to deal with converting prices to country currencies, calculating tariffs, posting measurement differences, and dealing with international shipping. For them, cross-border pricing issues are an impediment to going international online.

## ILLEGAL PRACTICES

In a perfect world, all prices would be fair and price fraud would not exist. This is not the case offline or on. Bait and switch, credit card fraud, investment fraud, loan fraud, discriminatory pricing, and other illegal practices that haunt offline transactions are online as well. Online auctions, which are extremely popular, are an enticing target. Even so, online fraud is no more prevalent than offline, just more exposed.[18] Fraud also differs in reach, as the Internet has the potential to reach far more victims faster, and anonymity, where it is difficult if not impossible to check an online buyer or seller's authenticity and honesty. It is more difficult for online buyers to confront a storefront they believe overcharged them. Sometimes when they try, the storefront ignores their complaints or has disappeared. Buyers using credit cards with dispute-protection clauses have more protection against fraud. Online sellers face their own hazards. All buyers are not authentic or honest. When an online seller encounters fraud, he or she typically absorbs 100 percent of any fraudulent transaction costs.

Online retailers accepting credit card charges face a *card not present* situation with almost every transaction. A standard address verification search is not sufficient to guard against unauthorized charges. Etailers with high fraud rates may end up paying higher expense fees for their merchant accounts. Because the sale of digital products leaves a particularly thin paper trail, these sales are often the most vulnerable to *spoofing*, illegally using someone else's identity for a purchase. Sellers also lose when a buyer claims a fraudulent credit card charge and demands restitution. The charge-back to cover the original charge is a cost to the seller and if the processing bank levies penalties, the final cost may be greater than the cost of goods sold (COGS). Fraud rules and screening software are helping large sites screen buyers (consumers and enterprises) to ensure they fit an authenticity profile. These processes are currently too expensive for most small and midsize enterprises.[19]

Auction fraud is the biggest source of online fraud. It includes nondelivery of goods, misrepresentation of goods auctioned, fee stacking (adding hidden charges postsale), and various bidding misrepresentations. In 2001, the Internet Fraud Complaint Center (IFCC at *http://www1.ifccfbi.gov*) received almost fifty thousand complaints from consumers, 43 percent about auction fraud. Most complaints (76 percent) are against individuals. Only 1 percent of auction transactions result in reported fraud; the amount of unreported fraud is unknown but probably much higher.[20] Although online auction fraud was again the top Internet fraud complaint in 2002, the overall incidence is on the decline. This reflects greater consumer caution as well as actions taken by auction sites to combat fraud and protect their customers.

Auction leader eBay aggressively combats fraud on its web sites. In May 2000, eBay discovered a seller and his associates bidding up an oil painting price. The company investigated, canceled the auction, and suspended the seller and fourteen others from doing business on eBay. Three men were indicted in March 2001 for this episode. eBay monitors its auctions closely, looking for evidence of shill bidding. It has fought infractions and has a page (*http://pages.ebay.icq.com/help/community/shillBidding.html*) that defines shill bidding and explains why it is not allowed.

Gangs of shill bidders sometimes work together and engage in *cross-bidding* to drive up online auction prices. They post highly positive comments about the seller on auction site feedback areas. These fraudulent postings are designed to encourage bidders to trust the seller and enter the auction. Online auctions currently generate over US$6 billion in sales annually, with eBay taking a 64 percent share.[21]

Another fraud is *price fixing* or *signaling*. Because online sellers can constantly monitor competitors' price changes, price collusion can occur without the sellers actually planning it in advance. The consolidation of B2B exchanges and their reduced numbers provides greater opportunity for price collusion, an antitrust infraction. Open bidding in exchanges means price information is shared by the participants, some of whom may work together to fix the price. This noncompetitive behavior is illegal.[22]

The Federal Trade Commission delayed approval for the launch of Covisint (*http://covisint.com*), the automobile suppliers and OEMs (original equipment manufacturers) exchange created by GM, Ford, and Daimler Chrysler, to determine if it encouraged noncompetitive pricing. The case was dismissed in September 2000, which cleared the way for the site going online.[23]

**WEB UPDATE**

Auction Fraud

### ✔ CONCEPT CHECK

1. Why should price transparency exert a downward pressure on prices?
2. Why do some consumers collect price and product information online, then go offline to purchase the product?
3. Why does it appear that price fraud is more prevalent online than offline?

# *Alternative Price Models*

Highly creative alternative Internet price models sprang up like weeds in the late 1990s, and many disappeared just as quickly. Most failed models defied all business common sense; others may still succeed in another form with a new owner. Although some pricing models were transferred unchanged from offline, others were modified to better suit the virtual environment.

### FIXED PRICES

**Fixed price**
A price posted by the seller that the buyer can take or leave, no haggling.

When the seller sets a price and buyers can take it or leave it, it is a **fixed price** (posted price) at a particular point in time, no haggling, negotiating, or bargaining, and no reduction for large purchases. Amazon.com uses fixed prices for new books, Lands' End for nonclearance apparel, AOL for Internet access, and the *Wall Street Journal Online* for subscriptions. Fixed or standardized prices have been the norm in retail since

1890, when Fred Kohnle invented a machine that quickly printed price tags and attached them to individual product items.[24] Sears & Roebuck Co. was among the first to offer a fixed price on products sold nationwide in its stores and catalogs. Fixed price tags replaced *haggling*, or price negotiation. Negotiation and variable pricing, that is, reduced prices for large purchases or purchases made before a deadline, are still more likely to occur with enterprise products, although fixed prices are also common.

Fixed prices predominate online, even at eBay.com's Half.com. Half.com fills a need for people who do not like auctions and want the product now. It avoids fraud by billing the buyer and paying the seller, and it has a buyer-protection guarantee on all sales.[25]

Offline fixed prices are far more static than online fixed prices, which can be extremely dynamic. There is a high labor cost involved in price changes offline and almost no labor cost to changing them online. Although a price is fixed, it can be and often is changed almost instantly online. A site that uses sophisticated data analysis techniques to determine real-time demand can use that information to change price as demand shifts, particularly by lowering price to stimulate demand often during nonpeak use times. Fixed prices also change at clearance or when a sales promotion is offered.

In other cultures, a fixed price means nothing more than the starting point for bargaining. Americans traditionally have found bargaining somewhat undignified and uncomfortable. However, that is changing, and it is becoming more common to hear about bargain prices being negotiated from hotels as an *educator's rate, government rate*, or *military rate*. It is also the basis for eBay's success, where consumers haggle over prices during auctions.

Fixed pricing simplifies the pricing process for small and midsize businesses that do not have the time, money, expertise, or need to negotiate or use dynamic pricing. It makes price comparisons easier and more accurate if prices are stable and thus facilitates price transparency. However, sellers with the tools and expertise to use dynamic pricing have an advantage by tailoring price to the target market, which should make it more attractive to online buyers, and, as a result, creating less transparent prices that competitors have a harder time tracking and matching.

## NEGOTIATED PRICES

**Negotiated prices**
Buyer and seller bargain, haggle over price.

**Negotiated prices** require bargaining between seller(s) and buyer(s). The process is as old as human history. Today it occurs at auctions and on price search web sites for products of all types. The negotiation opens with a proposed price, then participants counter back and forth until a mutually satisfactory price seals the sale. Participants can be traditional buyers and sellers, buyers haggling with other buyers, or sellers negotiating with other sellers. Negotiated pricing is the strategy behind online auctions and exchanges and occurs in all markets—business, consumer, and enterprise. Negotiations are particularly common among channel members, and bargaining is traditional with agricultural products.

Although the Internet's interactive and dynamic characteristics appear ideally suited to negotiated price models, it is unrealistic to think that negotiating appeals to all consumer or enterprise buyers. Many prefer fixed prices because they do not want to deal with the stress and uncertainty of negotiations or lack of information about quality or price fairness. Others enjoy the thrill of negotiating and the prospect of winning a bargain.

**AUCTIONS** Online auctions are extremely popular. Auctions certainly exist offline, but online they reach millions more participants who can follow the bidding at their leisure. Over 6.2 million U.S. Internet users bought products at online auctions in May 2001, spending US$556 million, an increase of 1.1 million buyers and US$223 million from May 2000. Auctions are the third most popular spending category online. They occur at exchange marketplaces like eBay and on single company sites. House auctions were tested by retailer JCPenney.com (*http://www.jcpenney.com*), which test marketed auctions of its own clearance products. Person-to-person auctions, operated by intermediaries like eBay.com, host a large number of auctions for a broad assortment of products. eBay is the most popular online auction site and ranks highest in consumer satisfaction and conversion rates.[26]

*General auctions* accept items from many different product categories. eBay is a general auction and while it accepts just about any item imaginable, it also prohibits sales of animals, human parts and remains, stocks and other securities, guns, and many other illegal or objectionable items. Other auctions are *product-specific*, like DanceAuction.com (*http://danceauction.com*) and PotteryAuction.com (*http://www. potteryauction.com*).

Classic *forward auctions*, where participants bid up a price and the highest bidder wins, are the most common. They are vulnerable to price fraud, particularly shill and cross-bidding. *Reverse auctions*, where the lowest bid wins, also are common. Other types of auctions include pooled, private, reserve price, and Dutch (multiple product).

**DEMAND COLLECTION OR NAME YOUR OWN PRICE** Priceline.com (*http://www. priceline.com*) pioneered the method where buyers name their own price in an anonymous reverse auction. Buyers lock in their bid price for a particular product and guarantee it with their credit card. Conditions are restrictive and consumers cannot pick brands, sellers, and/or product features. Priceline.com contacts suppliers that bid to close the deal from their excess inventory. Sellers generate incremental revenue without affecting their existing distribution network or retail price structure. Buyers learn the details of their purchase only after the deal is closed because buyers do not know the identity of the sellers bidding for their business; that is, the seller's brand is shielded.[27]

**THE FALLING PRICE GAME** In 2001, JC Penney's clearance section operated a classic forward auction on sale items and an automatic markdown auction, Falling Price prices began at full retail price, then fell at preset increments once or twice daily. Buyers could place a bid at any incremental price point. Bids were tallied and winners notified after the sale closed. Consumers were warned in advance that the item they were bidding on could be sold before their bid was reached. However, if the bid price fell to their bid before all the products were sold, they got the product. Although there is some entertainment value in this approach, its value in moving inventory remains to be seen.[28] By early 2002, Falling Price was no longer on the JC Penney web site.

**Barter**
A nonmonetary exchange of something of value between two or more parties who trade goods, labor, or other products, item for item.

**BARTER** **Barter** is a nonmonetary exchange of something of value between two or more parties who trade goods, labor, travel, or other products, item for item. Barter is widely used offline in media promotions, where radio or television advertising time is exchanged for products being advertised. Barter is growing in popularity online, although it is small when compared with straight auctions.

Barter can take at least two forms, *direct barter* and *network pool barter*. In direct barter, items are traded one for one. In a network pool, members do not trade directly but work through barter dollars (trade credits, tokens) credited to their accounts and used to make a purchase. Most sites offer free memberships and some have small transactions fees for products traded.

Barter sites can be brand-specific. The SwapZone (*http://www.swapzone.net*) operates a swap shop for classic automobiles, trucks, and motorcycles, including Harley Davidsons. Sites can also be product-specific like the Game Swap Shop (*http://www.gameswapshop.com*) that facilitates swaps, trades, and exchanges of used games, software, CDs, and DVDs. Members list what they have to swap, and the data are input into a searchable database. If a member bargains for an item and a deal is made, it is entered into the system and both members must surrender a SwapToken to demonstrate their seriousness. Tokens are £1 each, about US$1.44. This is the price paid to the eshop for managing swaps.

Some barter sites are experience-specific as in the Sporting Swap Shop (*http://www.less-stress.com/swap*), a free barter-listing for men and women who want to swap hunting, shooting, or fishing trips. Recent offerings included *Good goose shooting in Scotland; Fishing for king mackerel, tuna, dolphin and marlin, SE USA;* and *Fly fishing for salmon or trout in UK or Ireland*. The site is very careful to post a disclaimer, *The publishers of Sporting Swap Shop cannot accept any responsibility for any consequences arising from the use of the facilities of this web site which is provided on a goodwill basis only.*

One site no longer trading is Beanieswap.com (*http://www.beanieswap.com*), an apparent victim when the bottom fell out of the Beanie Babies collector market. Other collectibles are still popular swap sites. The marketing viability of online barter is small when compared with the traffic at an eBay. However, since they target relatively small but very loyal niche markets, large traffic counts are not as vital to their success if customers return and regularly swap.

## SINGLE CHANNEL, MULTICHANNEL, AND MULTITIER PRICES

Clicks-only sellers use only one channel of distribution, so they do not have to worry about the consistency of their prices in other channels. Bricks-and-clicks sellers operate through multiple channels, so multichannel pricing is a concern. Price transparency has forced many companies to adopt **uniform cross-channel pricing,** using the same price across all channels. Others do it because it fits their marketing strategy. Lands' End, Williams Sonoma (*http://www.williams-sonoma.com*), and Oracle (*http://www.oracle.com*) charge the same product price in all channels—catalogs, stores, and online. This model assumes that the same price is justified across all channels. It is also far easier to administer and runs less of a risk of arousing customer anger because prices vary across channels.

An alternative model is **variable channel pricing,** where product prices are not the same in all channels. This model proposes that channels and markets are sufficiently different to justify different prices. This was the most widely used model in the late 1990s. It is based on an idealized pricing strategy of first-degree price discrimination, where sellers should charge exactly what the market will bear.[29]

**Uniform cross-channel pricing**

Using the same price for a product across all channels in which it is sold.

**Variable channel pricing**

Prices differ in different channels.

**Multitier pricing**
Charging different prices for different levels of service or product types at a web site.

**Multitier pricing** requires charging different prices for different levels of service or product types. Content sites often use multitier pricing. Content in the entry or public level is free. However, content on the next level is by subscription or a per unit price. Content sites like the *Wall Street Journal Online* use subscriptions to control access. Internet search engine Northern Light (*http://www.northernlight.com*) provides some free links and articles but charges for articles in its Special Collection, an extensive online business library that charges for each article downloaded.

## DYNAMIC AND TEST PRICES

**Dynamic pricing**
When a potential buyer visits a web site, he or she may be offered a product at a higher or lower price depending on demand and inventory level, or buyer characteristics.

**Dynamic pricing** occurs when price adjustments are made online in real time based on demand and product inventory level. The adjustment can be made as visitors shop the site. They can be mass-customized when inventory levels trigger a price change. Visitors are offered a lower price on a product that is not selling as expected, a higher price on one where demand is great and inventory is low. Dynamic pricing runs on highly sophisticated software. It also has the potential to lead to individualized or one-to-one pricing in real time, which raises privacy concerns. When a customer who previously purchased from a site returns, his or her past purchase behavior data is mined to determine if a price change will encourage a new purchase; thus, price is customized for each customer in real time.

Traditional bricks-and-mortar stores have used various forms of dynamic or customized pricing for years. Geographic pricing varies price according to zip code demographics. Consumers in affluent zip codes receive catalogs with higher prices; less affluent zip codes receive the same catalog with lower prices. Victoria's Secret (*http://www.victoriassecret.com*) has used this strategy quite successfully.[30] Buyers rarely realize differential pricing occurs offline because they cannot easily perform price comparisons; thus, price nontransparency (opacity) occurs. This is not the case online. Price transparency reveals price discrepancies, which leaves dynamic pricing open to a consumer backlash. The key is whether buyers perceive that price differences are fair.

Customized pricing is common in credit cards, apparel, and airline tickets. Customers are differentiated by their preferences or characteristics and their willingness to pay. Bargain hunters are offered lower prices and reduced services. Service hunters are offered more services and a higher price. In many clothing lines, large sizes pay more. Magazines have preferred subscription rates for educators. IBM (*http://www.ibm.com*) is testing dynamic pricing on its server lines. Hewlett Packard (*http://www.hp.com*) is using it in a strategy it calls *contextual pricing*, where prices change as customers add multiple items to a specified promotion. These companies look on it as a way to reduce inventories and optimize profits.[31] Customized or differential pricing is rational under the Paerto (80-20) Principle, where distinctions are made between customers based on the revenue stream they generate, the cost to serve them, and the profit they produce.

In September 2000, Amazon.com got slapped for price testing online. It offered different prices on DVD players to randomly selected customers. Some learned of the price differences and complained in online communities. Amazon quickly stopped the test and made refunds. Amazon was not using dynamic pricing, it was randomly testing the effect of price on demand.[32]

Despite problems and concerns, dynamic pricing is here to stay and becoming more popular. It is risky because changing prices almost instantaneously, if not done right, can alienate buyers and undermine the bottom line. Forrester Research estimates that by 2004, 50 percent of all B2B trade in marketplaces will use dynamic pricing. Customers and the competition will force many sellers into some form of either dynamic pricing or reverse auction.[33]

## BARGAIN PRICES: DISCOUNTS, LIQUIDATIONS, FREE-AFTER-REBATE

The Internet is filled with bargain hunters looking for discounts. Some shop discounts at *house clearances* like Lands' End's, where first-quality Lands' End branded products are sold at up to 80 percent off. Overstock.com (*http://www.overstock.com*) is a *discount consolidator* that purchases first-quality excess inventory from such brands as Sony, Toshiba, Kodak, Remington, Samsonite, and Waterford, then sells it online at 40 to 70 percent off. Brand names sell excess inventory to a consolidator to avoid having sale items on their own sites at the same time they are trying to sell regular-price merchandise.

Another type of discounter is the *remainder liquidator* that takes merchandise from bankruptcies, receiverships, freight claims, and other distress situations to sell at extremely reduced prices. LiquidationWorld.com (http://www.liquidationworld.com/) is a liquidator that expanded its offline business to the Web where it offers liquidated, clearance, closed out, and distressed merchandise.

CyberRebate.com pioneered a failed *free-after-rebate* discount model. Up to 100 percent of the purchase price of books, toys, housewares, and other products was rebated to the buyer. About 30 percent of the site's inventory was offered at a whopping 100 percent rebate. Highly price sensitive customers paid for their purchase, took delivery, and then had to apply for the rebate. As many as 10 percent never collected rebates, and because the markup prices were high, CyberRebate profited from their loss. It also used the float, collecting interest on the purchase price before rebates were delivered. This was not enough to keep the company afloat. CyberRebate.com, Inc. filed for Chapter 11 bankruptcy May 16, 2001.[34]

IDerive.com is another failed discount model. Its motto was *Save or get paid.* The buyer named the price, which was locked in. iDerive.com agreed to find a seller at that price by a certain date or pay the buyer a predetermined amount of cash. This was a put option where suppliers had until the delivery date to sell the merchandise for more than the bid price. It was a complicated model that most buyers were not willing to endure, particularly when price bots could find the same product at a comparable or lower price.[35]

LastMinute.com (*http://www.lastminute.com*) is *The Best Place to Look at the Last Minute*. It is the perfect site for procrastinators, buyers faced with a last-minute trip, and the romantically inclined looking for spontaneous adventure. Products include hotels, restaurants, flights, holiday travel, car hires, vacation rentals, and skiing. Its prices are sometimes far lower, but travel times are often off-peak and subject to availability. This is a bucket shop for tour companies trying to fill seats on already arranged trips.

## ESTIMATORS

Home improvements are highly popular yet prone to escalating costs, as most people who have survived a remodeling can confirm. Interactive estimators or price wizards help consumers calculate the probable price of a remodeling job. Price wizard software lets consumers pick design options, then make tradeoffs between options and what they can afford. Parameters can be changed to get new estimates. Kitchens and bathrooms are the most frequent remodeling jobs, with more spent on them than other home improvements.[36] Estimate prices are locally adjusted and include labor, materials, and installations. An example is ImproveNet's bathroom estimator (*http:// www.improvenet.com/projecttools/estimators/bathroom*) that estimates costs based on the type of job, size, and budget available localized to the owner's zip code.

Another type of estimator works on home and personal loans and insurance. On-line loan estimation, application, and processing eliminates sales pressure and human error, but not paperwork. HomeAdvisor.com (*http://homeadvisor.msn.com*), part of the MSN Network, offers a Loan Finder search and a Home Value Estimator that estimates present value of an existing home. Loan Finder determines whether the consumer qualifies for a loan, then calculates the cost of the best price loans to match his or her financial situation. Home loans is an over US$20 billion industry, and about one hundred mortgage lenders currently work online.[37]

Generally, loan prices are comparable online and off, although some online lenders claim lower rates. Online lenders are beginning to profit. Housing sales are strong, and refinancing is up despite the weak economy beginning in 2001. The number of online loans increased fivefold between 2000 and 2001.[38]

## EXTRANET PRICING

Extranets (Chapter 2) selectively allow approved visitors access to a company's intranet or a specially constructed multicompany web site firewall protected from unauthorized users. Companies use extranets extensively to identify their supply needs and post RFQs. Suppliers post price changes for their strategically important customers on extranet web pages, which allows 24/7/365 access. Visitors can use internal price search engines to locate current price information. As prices change, real-time responses can be initiated. Before extranets, price and product updates were sent by email or fax during working hours, which varied by time zone. Extranet pricing is far more dynamic and accessible.[39]

## DEMAND AGGREGATORS

**Demand aggregators**
Technology or intermediaries that bring buyers together to form a group with the intent of gaining price discounts through bulk purchases.

The rationale behind **demand aggregators** is that groups of buyers purchasing together will force prices down because a group gets bulk rate prices. Demand aggregators are intermediaries that bring buyers together to form a group and organize a reverse auction for the products they want to purchase. Dynamic group buying online for consumers has not worked. Promised deep discounts did not materialize, products got stale while waiting for more buyers to join the group, and groups often could not get sufficient numbers of buyers to sign up.

The two top consumer demand aggregators were Mercata and MobShop. Mercata went out of business in January 2001 when additional financing could not be found. It could not get the deep discounts that customers wanted, had a limited number of products in some categories, and its prices were often higher than what shop bots could find.[40]

MobShop took a slightly different path. It closed its B2C operation, also in mid-January 2001, and began selling its demand aggregation technology B2B and to enterprises, including the U.S. General Services Administration (GSA), which uses it for online government volume purchasing in the eFAST sector of its site.[41]

### ✔ CONCEPT CHECK

1. Why would sellers and buyers prefer fixed rate pricing online?
2. Explain how a name-your-own-price auction works.
3. Why might variable channel pricing upset consumers?

# Payment Strategies

Purchases must be paid for whether they are tangible goods, services, entertainment, or web site content. Credit cards are used more in the United States than in other parts of the world. Most web sites that require payment do so by offering a variety of credit cards, house (a site's own card) and bank cards. Consumers have expressed concern about using their credit cards online since they began shopping there. Doubts about privacy, safety, and security persist, but their constraint on shopping appears to be lessening as more consumers have positive experiences online. In the meantime, overall online credit card use is declining somewhat as alternate payment mechanisms are adopted.

## CREDIT AND SMART CARDS

Credit cards have been around almost three decades. They began as a way to speed customers through retail checkout lanes, and they are still one of the easiest ways to complete store, online, and cross-border payments. People who use them regularly, and most U.S. consumers do, are reluctant to abandon them unless something considerably better comes along.

**Smart cards**
Stored value credit cards that have more memory and are capable of performing additional operations like security encryption and decryption, data management, and authentication.

Credit card authorizations are made over telephone lines, a relatively inexpensive data transfer method in the United States. European telephone charges have always been much higher than in the States, so U.S.-style credit cards are less popular. This contributed to the rapid adoption of **smart cards,** or smart credit cards, an advanced form of the credit-ATM-cash debit-ID card. A smart card, or stored value card, is an intelligent credit card. It is the same size as a standard plastic credit card but has an integrated circuit embedded in it. The typical plastic credit card can hold only about a hundred bytes of read only memory (ROM). A smart card can store as much as 8K of information and perform operations like security encryption and decryption, data management, and authentication. Smart cards are also called chip cards, IC cards, and memory cards. Although they have become popular in Europe, they are slow to catch on in the United States.

American Express (*http://www.americanexpress.com*) offers the Blue card, a credit card with a computer smart chip for online transaction security. Blue comes with a Smart Card Reader that generates temporary transaction numbers for online shopping. Credit card dominance will drop as newer technologies make online payments easier and more secure.[42]

## ALTERNATE PAYMENT SYSTEMS AND MICROPAYMENTS

Although smart cards may find a market in the United States, others are looking to alternate systems for safety and convenience. Yahoo! offers Yahoo! Wallet (*http://wallet.yahoo.com*), a free service that securely stores a user's credit card number and billing information but does not actually use them to make purchases. Instead, users

pay Yahoo! merchants with the Wallet instead of their credit card. The Wallet is accepted for all Yahoo! features. A Security Key, like an ATM pin number, is the identifying number that allows users to access secured areas. It is actually a secure cookie that cannot be traced to the user's credit card number. Yahoo! Wallet is not accepted by nonparticipating merchants.

PayPal.com (*http://www.paypal.com*), with over sixteen million users in thirty-eight countries, is by far the most popular ecurrency and appears to be in the best position to replace many consumers' credit cards online. Launched in 1999, initially it was free for individuals and merchants. Since June 2000 vendors taking in more than US$100 in PayPal transactions must pay from 0.07 to 2.9 percent of each transaction, plus 30 cents for use of the PayPal process. This is still 2 percent less than what most credit card companies charge merchant accounts. Soon even small merchant transactions will be charged, which will anger some customers.

Paypal.com filed for an US$80.5 million IPO in October 2001 despite never reporting a profit. It is the most popular method of payment on eBay. As of mid-2002, PayPal had over 2.2 million business accounts and was reporting profits. Like the other virtual cash systems, PayPal can only be used with another member of the system. New members receive US$5 for joining and another US$5 for persuading someone else to join. In July 2002, eBay announced plans to buy PayPal for US$1.4 billion in stock. This move makes eBay the market leader in Internet payments. About sixty percent of PayPal's business is from eBay transactions.[43]

**Micropayments**

Online virtual cash systems that allow consumers to make extremely small payments, US$5 or less.

Unlike virtual currency designed for moderate to large price products, **micropayments** are extremely small payments, US$5 or less. They have been the promised salvation of online content providers since the mid-1990s, but their promise has largely gone unfulfilled. Content providers want to charge a small amount for the content users access. However, using a credit card for a small purchase will drive consumers away, which is why the concept of micropayments is so appealing.

Only Japan's NTT DoCoMo is having any success with them. Each time a customer accesses a wireless DoCoMo service, from cell phones to games, maps or photo sharing, a small charge is placed on their monthly subscriber bill. The changes range from US$0.85 to US$2.50. Wireless is the key, because PC users tend to think in terms of larger purchases and do not want more hassle in paying for them. Micropayments do not simplify the payment process. They also are not as secure as other forms of payment, so the fraud potential is increased.[44]

**Honor system**

Processes whereby visitors can donate small amounts to their favorite web sites.

PayPal and Amazon.com have devised **honor systems** for sites that have trouble generating revenue and do not want to hassle customers with credit card transactions for small amounts. Growing numbers of web sites are asking visitors to *donate* to their continued operation. The premise is that a visitor gaining value from the site should want it to survive, so dropping a few dollars into a paybox icon is fast and relatively painless. Amazon's cookie activates on any cooperating web site, addressing the visitor by name, which many find quite disconcerting. An Internet marketer signs up for the program at Amazon and follows directions to get registered and have a paybox installed on the marketer's front page. Each web site can personalize its message in the paybox. When one of Amazon's over twenty-nine million customers visits the site, the Amazon cookie is activated and the paybox addresses the cookie holder by name with a personal invitation to contribute. Amazon customers can turn off the use of their name at Amazon but cannot turn off the cookie unless they do so in their browser's cookie file. Featured members include National Public Radio's *Lost and Found Sound* initiative, the BannerAdMuseum, JunkScience.com, TrekWeb, RecipeSource, and others. The paypage at Amazon records the contribution with Amazon's one-click payment. The site sends a customized thank-you to the customer.

Non-Amazon visitors who see a paybox and do not have an Amazon cookie can still click through to Amazon and contribute with a credit card. Amazon's fee is 15 percent and 15 cents per donation. Only Amazon knows the donor's identity. Contributions can be as low as one cent up to US$1,000. More than that requires bank verification. Most contributors pay what the site recommends. Amazon's Honor System gives small web storefronts and content sites access to a revenue stream that can help them stay in business.[45]

## ONLINE BILL MANAGEMENT

A big obstacle that online bill paying must overcome is the reluctance of many consumers to change their banking habits. Bill-paying alternatives exist, but most consumers do not know about them. For example, PayMyBills.com (*http://paymybills. com*), PayTrust.com (*http://www.paytrust.com*), and StatusFactory.com (*http://www. statusfactory.com*) compete for bill payers, but thus far there are relatively few takers.

This service has significant potential, as more than 210 billion bills are mailed each year, at a cost of about US$0.10 per bill. Online payments significantly reduce the cost of processing bills, along with eliminating the need for the payee to stamp a return envelope. The United States Postal Service (*http://www.usps.com/paymentservices/ welcome.htm*) anticipated the revenue potential and the effect on stamp sales if online payments catch on. It has initiated its own online bill-paying system with the reassuring slogan, "Secure? Of course. It's the Postal Service."

Online banks and portals are competing for bill-paying customers, as are Yahoo! and General Electric. It is a small sector now but is expected to grow. About 6.3 million bills were paid online in 2000, up from 2.6 million in 1999. By 2005, an estimated 14 percent of all bills issued will be paid online. Bill-paying companies charge consumers and businesses a set monthly fee. Prices are decreasing, with the average currently just under US$6.00 per month.[46]

## ✔ CONCEPT CHECK

1. What is the advantage of a smart card over a credit card?
2. Why have micropayments failed to achieve their expected potential in the United States?
3. What are the advantages of paying bills online?

# *Summary*

## *Price Fundamentals*

Price, which determines how much buyers must give up to take possession of or use a product, is a measure of value. It allocates products, determining who can buy, possess, and use them, and clears markets following the law of supply and demand. Consumer primary demand generates derived demand for enterprise products. The 80-20 rule observes that some buyers are more valuable than others and about 80 percent of revenues are contributed by only about 20 percent. Price is influenced by many factors, including its objective, target markets, demand, costs, the economy, and competitors. A bricks-and-clicks business should set its online price objective to be compatible with and support its offline price objective. Some factors that influence price must be considered on a regular basis, like competitors' actions, channel member markups, and consumer demand. Consumers are a growing presence in C2C exchanges, primarily through auctions where consumers sell to other consumers with the aid of a facilitator. Prices typically are set within a range, where acceptable prices are between a ceiling and floor. For too many businesses, setting a price is not a carefully considered, systematic process. Consumers also set prices when they sell through C2C online auctions or fixed price sales. With few exceptions, price alone cannot provide a sustainable competitive advantage.

## *Price Issues*

Price information is readily available online, and price search sites are having an impact, directing consumers to low-price retailers. This may drive prices down if retailers begin to court the search sites, recognizing that this is a more effective way to build site traffic than online advertisements. This may also erode brand value in the long term. For commercial activity to grow, online prices must at least be comparable to offline prices and, in some product categories, lower. Price transparency makes prices for competing products clearly visible and easily obtainable so buyers and competitors can make price comparisons, identify price discrepancies, and use this information to make effective price decisions. If price transparency exists, all things being equal, competitive pressure should drive prices down. Many consumers search for information online but purchase offline. An Internet access price must be paid to connect to a service provider and the Internet. Access price also refers to content pricing. Price fairness is a highly subjective judgment unless unbiased evidence can be found to substantiate fairness and the buyer accepts it. Initially, free S&H was an inducement for consumers to purchase, as part of an attractive price reduction duo—no sales tax, no S&H. Now, sellers can gain a competitive advantage by offering free shipping on a regular or short-term basis. Prices published on public access web sites cross borders. Online auctions are an enticing target for fraud. Even so, online fraud is no more prevalent than offline, just more exposed.

## *Alternative Price Models*

Highly creative alternative online price models sprang up like weeds in the late 1990s, and many quickly disappeared. When the seller sets a price and the buyer can take it or leave it, it is a fixed or posted price. Fixed pricing online can be extremely dynamic. Negotiated prices involve bargaining over price. Online auctions are extremely popular. General auctions accept items from many different product categories. Other auctions are product-specific. Demand collection or name your own price is a strategy where consumers lock in their bid and sellers participate in an anonymous reverse auction for their business. Barter is a nonmonetary exchange of something of value between two or more parties who trade goods, labor, or other products, item for item. Bricks-and-clicks sellers operate through multiple channels, so multichannel pricing is a concern. Price transparency has forced many companies to adopt uniform cross-channel pricing, using the same price across all channels. Variable channel pricing, where product prices are not the same in all channels, proposes that channels and markets are sufficiently different to justify different prices. Multitier pricing is charging different prices for different levels of service or product types. Dynamic prices are price adjustments made online in real time based on demand and product inventory level. The Internet is filled with bargain hunters looking for discounts. Some shop discounts at house clearances while others visit discount consolidators or liquidators. Interactive estimators help consumers calculate the probable cost of a remodeling job. Other estimators are used for home mortgages and insurance. In extranet pricing, buyers and sellers share price information on restricted web sites. Demand aggregators get groups of buyers together so they can purchase as a group and take advantage of group discounts.

### Payment Strategies

Consumers have expressed concern about using their credit cards online since they began shopping there. Credit cards have been around almost three decades. People who use them regularly are reluctant to abandon them unless something considerably better comes along. Smart cards are an advanced form of the credit-ATM-cash debit-ID card. A smart card, or stored value card, is an intelligent credit card that can perform operations like security encryption and decryption, data management, and authentication. Smart cards are far more popular in Europe than the United States, where consumers still use credit cards but are receptive to alternate systems offering greater safety and convenience. Unlike virtual currency designed for moderate to large price products, micropayments are extremely small payments, US$5 or less. Growing numbers of web sites are asking visitors to *donate* to their continued operation through an honor system operated by Amazon.com. A big obstacle that online bill paying must overcome is the reluctance of many consumers to change their banking habits. Online payments significantly reduce the cost of processing bills, along with eliminating the need for the payee to stamp a return envelope.

## Internet Marketing Application

Most American drivers have automobile insurance, and all should have it. Before the Internet, if a buyer wanted to compare rates (prices) and coverage from ten insurers, he or she had to telephone or visit ten insurers. This has changed dramatically, thanks to the Web's interactive environment. Although only about 1 percent of insurance policies of all kinds are actually sold online, it is quite easy to get price and coverage comparisons. The Web's facility for price comparisons has already had a powerful impact. Rates for term life insurance fell as much as 15 percent between 1995 and 1997 because greater price transparency heightened competition.[47]

See if you can find a better rate for your automobile insurance online. Try any two of the following multiquote sites. Follow the directions for getting automobile insurance quotes.

- Insweb.com at *http://Insweb.com*
- Insurance.com at *http://Insurance.com*
- Youdecide.com at *http:// youdecide.com*
- Quotesmith at *http://quotesmith.com*

### Insurance Quote Site Analysis

| | Site 1 | Site 2 |
|---|---|---|
| Do both sites use the same companies? How many companies were used for the quotes? | | |
| How thorough are the questions asked in compiling a driver's history? | | |
| Is there a 1-800 toll-free number available to call if help is needed? | | |
| Is there a calculator for determining the level of coverage needed? | | |
| How do the quotes compare with your current auto insurance rates? | | |
| What is the process for purchasing a policy? | | |
| Would you recommend this site to other buyers? Why/why not? | | |
| How could the site be improved? | | |

What are the advantages of shopping for insurance online? What are the disadvantages?

# *Chapter Review Questions*

1. Why is price often a lightning rod for consumer complaints?
2. Explain how consumer primary demand affects derived demand.
3. Explain why a prestige price retailer should also adopt a prestige strategy online.
4. Why do marketers try to set a price near the ceiling?
5. What is price information asymmetry? What is price information symmetry?
6. How do search sites drive consumers to retailers?
7. What initial conclusions can be drawn about the Internet driving down prices?
8. Explain the reason for search online and purchase offline behavior.
9. Explain the practice of content access pricing.
10. Who determines if a price is fair?
11. How does a falling price auction work? What type of auction is it?
12. What are the benefits of barter?
13. Why is dynamic pricing online vulnerable to consumer backlash?
14. Why didn't consumer demand aggregation work?
15. How do micropayments differ from virtual currency?

## Let's Auction! Ebay.Com Leads the Way

# Case Study

There was no online C2C online auction market before eBay went into business in 1995. Today, it is the world's largest online auction with a 64.3 percent market share. Its closest competitor is uBid.com (*http://www.ubid.com*) with a 14.7 percent share. Yahoo! Auctions and Amazon Auctions trail with about a 2 percent market share each. eBay steadily build its customer base, and by 2002 had over 46.1 million registered users and in 2000 transacted over US$5 billion in merchandise sales and registered 264 million items listed for sale. When measured by total user minutes, it is the most popular shopping site on the Internet. It is also one of the very few clicks-only sites that has been profitable almost from its launch.

While it may have started as the nation's online flea market, eBay has gone international and upscale. It has country-specific sites in Argentina, Australia, Austria, Brazil, Canada, France, Germany, Ireland, Italy, Japan, Korea, Mexico, New Zealand, Singapore, Switzerland, Taiwan, and the United Kingdom. It has expanded into premium art, antiques, and rare collectibles at eBay Premier (*http://*

*www.ebaypremier.com*). The specialty site realizes the goal of making eBay Premier the preferred destination for buying or selling works of art online. It also offers Half.com with fixed price trading, eBay Motors buying and selling all things automotive, Buy It Now fixed price auctions, eBay Professional Services for small businesses, eBay Live Auctions where users can participate in real time at more than three hundred auction houses around the world, and now, PayPal.

One of the company's smartest moves was creating The Feedback Forum, where users register comments about other users, buyers and sellers. It is a way that users can help the company build a rating format that is public and cumulative. In May 2001 the auction giant launched eBay Seller Classifieds, classified ads in local papers where loyal eBay users can search for items listed online. Management projects the company will hit US$3 billion in net revenues by 2005—an annual growth rate of almost 50 percent without manufacturing anything. eBay does not hold inventory or move goods, but it does a remarkable job of satisfying its customers. It is expanding direct involvement with customers by taking eBay University on the road. This popular two-day workshop teaches people how to buy and sell online. Topics include Browsing & Buying, Basic Selling, and Improve Listings with Photos and HTML.

Businesses have also discovered eBay. Manufacturers, liquidators, and retailers are using eBay as a sales channel. They are selling returns, refurbished products, and season remainders. Smaller sellers are being crowded out of the eBay marketplace, which is very risky for the company. Rising discontent among small sellers could lead to mass bailouts for other auctions.[48]

## CHECK IT OUT

Is there anything that eBay does not sell? Check the following product categories. Do a search and see what turns up. After you have searched for these items, try to find eBay's rules where a long list of *Prohibited, Questionable*, and *Potentially Infringing* products are listed.

- Guns
- Alcohol
- Tobacco
- Animals
- Plants and seeds

Are children allowed to participate in eBay auctions? If they do participate, how can they get around the problem of not having a credit card? Should kids be allowed on eBay?

## A GLOBAL PERSPECTIVE

Visit the other English-speaking eBays. Does eBay adapt the sites to the countries? If so, how? Is this an effective way to customize a web site? Select several products from the U.S. Prohibited list. Are they also prohibited at international eBays? If they are, does this imply that eBay is exporting U.S. values or are these values already shared?

## CHAPTER ELEVEN

# Place

## LEARNING OBJECTIVES

- To classify online distribution (place) activities and learn how they are influenced by the Internet environment
- To identify online place issues that concern Internet marketers
- To characterize successful online consumer channel strategies and understand the reasons for their success
- To see how CRM can be used to meet buyer expectations and establish long-term relationships

## Gerard Hears About Gazoo

Gerard 's family has owned and operated a Toyota dealership in Canada for twenty-seven years. His dad was the first Toyota dealer in the province. Today, there are twenty-one dealerships. Each dealership has its own clientele, and customers typically buy a car or truck at the nearest dealer, where they return for repairs, service, and parts. Each dealer also carries a large inventory of pre-owned vehicles of all brands. Profit margins on new car sales are getting thinner because customers are better prepared to negotiate price, which reduces dealers' price-setting flexibility. Well over 70 percent of prospective buyers come to a dealership with invoice price information downloaded from the Internet. This has shifted revenue growth to service, parts, and repairs, particularly since today's cars can easily last one or even two hundred thousand miles. Gerard recently heard from another Toyota dealer about Gazoo (*http://gazoo.com*), Toyota Motor Corporation's B2C site in Japan that also includes an English language portal (*http://www.gazoo.com/eng*). Gazoo.com was established in 1998 and is now one of the largest web portals in Japan with more than 1.1 million members. Members can buy almost anything at Gazoo's online malls, including automotive parts, CDs, bicycles, and travel packages. Gazoo also brokers automobile auctions. Toyota sells used cars more quickly from Gazoo than from its dealerships. Every month between five and seven thousand customers use Gazoo to request quotes from dealers and add data to Toyota's database of prospects. Around 14 percent of site users purchase an automobile within six months of their initial visit to Gazoo. Gazoo.com does not sell Toyota cars online, which avoids angering its network of Japanese neighborhood dealers and door-to-door sales force. Toyota has placed thirty-two hundred standalone Gazoo terminals (kiosks) throughout Japan in Toyota dealerships and convenience stores (*konbini*), where buyers go to pick up their online purchases. Gerard began thinking about the effect on his dealership if Toyota opened a Gazoo portal for North America. His used car sales are already feeling the effect of the growing popularity of eBay Motors Canada (*http://pages.ca.ebay.com/ebaymotors*). Would Gazoo hurt his sales or might he gain customers by linking the dealership's web site to Gazoo? The only thing Gerard knows for sure is that selling automobiles is changing, and the future will be even more challenging.[1]

Gerard is right about changes in automobile distribution. In the United States, Ford Motor Company (Ford at *http://www.ford.com*) and General Motors (GM at *http://www.gm.com*) are expanding their online distribution channels. Ford selected Auto-Trader.com (*http://www.autotrader.com*), which bills itself as *The biggest and best used car site on the planet,* to power FordDirect.com's (*http://www.forddirect.com*) local dealer inventory and used vehicle search. This alliance doubles the volume of Ford products offered online. Buyers can locate and select new cars and trucks from participating Ford dealers' inventories by going to AutoTrader's new car marketplace, but online sales are finalized offline at the buyer's local Ford dealer. According to J.D. Power and Associates, AutoTrader.com is the top online source for used car sales.

GM and Autobytel.com (*http://www.autobytel.com*) are targeting new car buyers. Autobytel, launched in 1995, is credited with inventing Internet automobile marketing sales and service. It is responsible for about 4 percent of total U.S. auto sales, US$17 billion in 2001 for dealers using its marketing services. Customers go to the Chevrolet Showroom at Autobytel to choose a vehicle type, interior, and color. They select a local dealer and payment method and can place a down payment on the vehicle from the web site. The transaction must be completed by a local GM dealer. GM is registering around a thousand new online sales leads per week for its dealers.[2] Autobytel software and databases are also used by BMW, DaimlerChrysler, Ford, General Motors, Honda, and Toyota.

Online auto sites are mostly *lead generators* for new cars. They provide information, allow the user to select options online and negotiate price, but sales are completed offline at local dealers. Some refer the prospective buyer directly to their nearest dealer, others bid the purchase out to a nationwide network of qualified dealers. This is the approach taken by CarPoint.com (*http://carpoint.msn.com*) and others. While few *direct sellers* are online for new cars, used cars are readily available through dealers, automobile web sites, and eBay Motors (*http://pages.ebay.com*).

Auto manufacturers include their dealers in online sales, at least for now. Although they initially hoped to reduce marketing and distribution costs as much as 31 percent by selling new cars directly from their web sites, the states have blocked them. In 1970, laws in only two U.S. states prohibited everyone but franchised car dealers from selling to consumers. By 2001, forty-seven states had such laws. Selling new cars online will be dealer referrals unless the laws are changed.[3] Even if the laws are changed, cars purchased directly from manufacturers will still need dealers for test drives, product delivery, and service. Dealers will carry far less inventory on their lots, which will reduce their operating costs.

What is happening in automobile distribution illustrates the Internet's influence on *place*, the third marketing mix variable. **Place,** also called distribution, concerns how buyers purchase products and take possession, and how products get where they are needed and when, in appropriate amounts and assortments. Marketing channels supply production processes and distribute finished products to buyers. They also operate in product returns. A considerable part of Internet marketing is about place. This chapter examines how the Internet affects place fundamentals and related place issues. Place strategies are considered along with customer relationship management (CRM).

**WEB UPDATE**

Automobile Marketing Online

**Place**
Refers to Marketing channels that supply what is needed for production and move finished products to buyers.

# *Place Fundamentals*

When asked to define marketing, rarely if ever do people mention marketing channels or distribution. Yet without channels, production would grind to a halt, store shelves would empty, automobiles would not get made or delivered, and the distribution of content and other products via the Internet would cease. Most consumers are unaware of channel activities except for the retail stores where they shop and the delivery trucks that bring goods to their doors. Although many channel processes do not directly involve consumers, they are the ultimate focus of all place activities.[4]

## MARKETING CHANNELS

**Marketing channels**

The place or distribution variable in the marketing mix composed of supply channels at the front end and distribution channels at the back end.

**Supply channels**

Supply channels provide *upstream value* by bringing raw materials, supplies, and parts directly into production, and furnishing equipment and materials to maintain and operate the enterprise.

**Distribution channels**

Marketing channels that move finished products to buyers provide *downstream value*.

**Marketing channels** (figure 11-1) are *supply channels* at the front end and *distribution channels* at the back end. **Supply channels** provide *upstream value* by bringing raw materials, supplies, and parts directly into production, and furnishing equipment and materials to maintain and operate the enterprise. **Distribution channels** provide *downstream value* by bringing finished products to end users. Channel members (intermediaries) contribute value added services at each transfer (touch) point in the channel through their specialized knowledge, skills, experience, and contacts.

Channels are expensive to create and maintain. Large corporations spend hundreds of millions, even billions, of dollars for equipment, buildings, land, raw materials, employees, parts, and expendable supplies. Distribution is one of the last areas left where businesses can wring out inefficiencies, automate, and reduce costs. That is why so many businesses were excited about the potential of the Internet to facilitate considerable distribution cost reductions and savings. Online ordering, or eprocurement, was seen as the way to reduce or eliminate purchase paperwork, increase the number of suppliers and buyers, lower supply and materials costs, increase fulfillment efficiency, speed delivery times, reduce inventory and inventory holding costs, close costly warehouses, and even eliminate some intermediaries.

The industrial revolutions and rise of mass production and marketing increased the distance between producers and consumers and created a need for specialized intermediaries. Today, intermediaries perform valuable functions, smoothing out discrepancies between supply and demand. They add value or *utility* by meeting or exceeding

## Figure 11-1  Marketing Channels

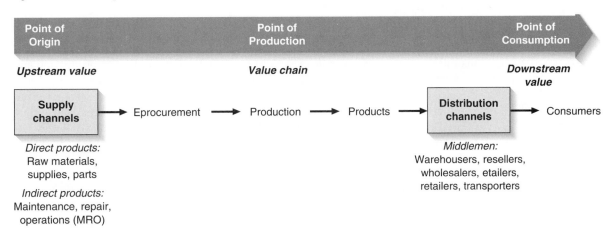

Marketing channels include supply and distribution channels. Supply channels provide inputs to production, while distribution channels facilitate exchanges with consumers.

buyer expectations. The following place-related utilities are associated with Internet marketing:

**TIME UTILITY**     Products are available *when* buyers want them to be 24/7/365 on etailer and other marketing web sites. Buyers can quickly access web sites and download pages, transactions are fast, order confirmation is received almost immediately by email, and questions about orders can be sent by email and answered in real time; digital products ordered online are delivered directly to the purchaser's computer without delay.

**PLACE UTILITY**     Products are available *where* buyers want them, on a corporate web site, at an etailer's web site, in an online shopping mall, linked to a portal, or on an extranet. Web shopping eliminates travel time and expense, avoids crowded and sometimes dangerous parking lots, and the need for the purchaser to personally transport purchases. Bricks-and-clicks etailers like Walmart.com (*http://www. walmart.com*) simplify returns by accepting them in local Wal-Mart stores. Others provide return envelopes for front-door pickups by UPS, FedEx, or the USPS.

**FORM UTILITY**     Products come in the *type* buyers want. Tangible goods are in the desired size, color, technical specification, and appearance. Operating systems and browsers are compatible, document sharing is seamless, and digital products can be accessed and downloaded.

**POSSESSION UTILITY**     Buyers exchange something of value (purchase order, digital cash or check, credit, epayment alternative) for a product and take *ownership* of it. It may be rented (short-term possession) or owned.

The Internet adds another very important utility, *interactivity*. Buyers and sellers in the Internet environment can interact one-to-one in real time regardless of their geographical location. In a sense, it is a step back to the days before mass production and mass marketing when buyers and sellers interacted directly and personally. Interactivity also promotes visibility. It is more difficult to hide product prices, specifications, or buyers' (dis)satisfaction with them. This tends to reduce the information advantage previously enjoyed by sellers and increases fairness.

## SUPPLY CHANNELS

**Suppliers**
Individuals or businesses that make up a supply channel and furnish enterprises with direct and indirect products.

**Suppliers** are individuals and businesses that make up a supply channel providing manufacturers and other enterprises *direct products* that are used in production and *indirect products* needed for enterprise operations. Supply channels are usually very direct with few if any intermediaries. Traditional supply channels are characterized by long-term commitments, personal relationships, negotiations, customized selling efforts, and extended supply contracts. It may take years to develop a completely satisfactory supply channel whose members fill supply needs, are reliable, can modify orders and products on demand, and sustain efficient and generally harmonious channel relationships. This traditional way of doing business on a personal level has worked against online marketplaces trying to get supply chain buyers and sellers together through eprocurement. Emartketplaces have not been accepted by many businesses that fear becoming involved with suppliers or buyers they do not know and whose reliability and honesty are unproven. They also fear using public marketplaces or exchanges that may not be secure, where proprietary information can be exposed. As many as 45 percent of B2B buyers say they will not go online because they do not trust suppliers in online exchanges. They also complain about slow online ordering, unresponsive technology that cannot accommodate unusual orders, and technical problems that hinder order completion.

Supply channels often are led by powerful manufacturers, channel leaders like a Ford or General Electric (GE at *http://www.ge.com*), or dominant retailers like Wal-Mart (*http://www.walmartstores.com*), which in 2002 for the first time topped the Fortune 500 list as the world's largest company.[5] Channel leaders or captains can issue orders to their suppliers and buyers, but they usually find that guidance, cooperation, and negotiation work best in getting members to adopt new business methods. GEPolymerland.com (*http://www.gepolymerland.com*) is an example. It was one outcome of GE's Internet initiative designed to improve efficiency and cut costs. GEPolymerland went online in 1996 as the GE resins distribution site targeting engineers, designers, and specifiers using plastics. By 2000, it was the industry's leading B2B web site with data on over thirty thousand resins, easy online ordering and order tracking, and active industry discussion groups. It began 2000 with online sales of US$5 million and, by the end of the year, was generating US$50 million in weekly sales. GEPolymerland generated 25 percent of the company's total resin sales, had over US$1.5 billion in online orders in 2000, and served as a model for the digitization of other GE SBUs.

GE worked with channel members in planning the site, which eased their transition to online ordering (eprocurement) and removed some of their reluctance to adopt the technology needed to use the site. The site cuts GE's transaction and inventory costs, eliminates paperwork, speeds up ordering time, and expands customer service options. Customer questions are answered online, at a cost of about US$0.50 each, considerably less than a personal service call, which can cost as much as US$80 per call. In 2000, GE saved US$1.6 million through Internet-enabled efficiencies, including saving US$600 million through eprocurement at its online auctions. Another US$1 billion was saved through eproduction efficiencies in its twenty major SBUs. Internet sales were about 5 percent of GE's total 2000 US$130 billion revenue, considerably short of the 30 percent corporate goal but a promising step in the right direction.[6] Online GE Plastics sales in 2001 set a record, US$2.5 billion.

Other companies are also using the Internet for internal (targeted to dealers and employees) and external (targeted to customers) marketing. High-end office furniture manufacturer Herman Miller (*http://hermanmiller.com*) uses the Web to link to its four hundred dealers. It gives dealers access by extranet to instant ordering and shipment tracking. DuPont chemicals (*http://dupont.com*) moved its purchasing online and cut procurement costs US$200 million in 2001, about 5 percent of its total procurement costs.[7]

Goods, services, and digital products can all be bought and sold online by supply channel members in private and public web marketplaces or exchanges. Between 1995 and 2000, around seven hundred exchanges went online; by 2002 the majority had folded. Those that failed could not achieve a significant mass of businesses willing to participate. Their operating costs far exceeded any profits. Survivors should learn from the mistakes of others and be in a prime position to capture new business when more companies adopt eprocurement.

Some exchanges are public, operated by neutral independent dot-com businesses; others are private and run by large corporations or joint venture business partners. They generate revenue by charging sellers a percentage of each sale, selling on-site advertising, licensing their proprietary software, and/or charging subscriber fees to access their online auctions.

Some exchanges are *horizontal*, general exchanges for products of different types, from airline tickets to office supplies. They need large numbers of participants to be profitable. Commerce One.net's Global Trading Web (*http://CommerceOne.com*) is an example. Commerce One.net's global online trading community partner list includes Boeing, GM, Daimler/Chrysler, GE, and De Beers, among others. Other exchanges are *vertical*, industry-specific exchanges specializing in products for specific industries like power, health care, automobiles, or apparel. Metal Site (*http://metalsite. com*) is a global metals marketplace dedicated to helping its members streamline, automate, and optimize their supply chains. Use of Metal Site and Scrap Site are free for buyers while sellers pay a small transaction fee. Deals are arranged through online sealed-bid and open auctions, and negotiated sales. ChemConnect (*http://www.chemconnect.com*) is a worldwide exchange for chemicals and plastics. It has more than seventy-five hundred member companies in 135 countries worldwide in plastics, chemicals, pharmaceuticals, pulp and paper, textiles, food additives, oil and gas, and other industries. Transaction volume in 2001 was over US$4 billion.

Traditional supply channels are almost always linear, with a straight path from supplier to producer and little information shared between channel members. Pre-Internet, companies used electronic data interchange (EDI) to speed supply chain transactions. EDI can process applications, inquiries, acknowledgments, purchasing, and other transactions electronically, but is far less flexible than the Internet. EDI systems are often proprietary and incompatible with any firms not part of the system. They are limited in their capacity, not interactive, and asynchronous with potentially lengthy delays between a call and a response. The Internet and the Web are replacing EDI in many companies, and channel management is changing. Interactive information flows are making channel members more efficient, increasing real-time information exchange, and encouraging more transparent operations, which should encourage price transparency.

Covisint, LLC (*http://www.covisint.com*), a global, independent B2B supply exchange for OEMs (original equipment manufacturers) and suppliers developed by Ford, GM, DaimlerChrysler, CommerceOne, Oracle, and Renault, is an effort to provide the automobile industry with collaborative product development, eprocurement, and technologically enhanced supply chain tools. Its goals are to shorten the vehicle product development cycle, compress order-to-delivery cycles, achieve greater asset efficiency and utilization, reduce business process variability, and promote integrated supply chain planning. It promises to cut paperwork and procurement costs, reduce delivery times, facilitate build-to-order manufacturing, and reduce showroom and lot inventory. The site went online in 2001 after the FTC ruled that it did not violate antitrust rules. It sells maintenance, repair, and operating (MRO) supplies and auto components and handles purchasing for direct and indirect products. Multiple vendors participate in the exchange, and small businesses are encouraged to participate. Some suppliers still have reservations about the exchange, but online parts buying grew rapidly from US$1 billion from January to March 2001, to US$36 billion through June. More than seventeen hundred companies joined the exchange in its first year of operation. As for the manufactured name, *Co* stands for connectivity, collaboration, communication, and cooperation; *vis* is visibility on the Internet and Web; *int* is the integration of the automotive supply chain.[8]

Despite the 2000–2001 dot-com meltdown and recession, companies continue developing and participating in eprocurement and web-based supply systems. Forrester Research surveyed the one thousand largest U.S. companies and found that while the crash is making them more realistic about the difficulty of making eprocurement and collaborative production work smoothly, 84 percent are sticking to their Internet business expansion plans and commitment to online supply and distribution chain processes. While 35 percent are already selling online to enterprises and consumers, 30 percent more are rolling out storefronts, and 16 percent are considering them. Only 21 percent have moved customer service online, but 34 percent more are poised to do so. According to a National Association of Purchasing Management (NAPM) study, over 20 percent of both manufacturing and nonmanufacturing companies purchased products online at B2B auctions in 2001, a 5 percent increase from 2000.[9]

Corporations could save from 8 to 10 percent of their procurement costs through eprocurement. By 2003, 80 to 90 percent of the country's largest five thousand companies are expected to use eprocurement, which could result in aggregated savings of US$2.3 trillion. Online supply auctions are also growing in popularity. At least 40 percent of U.S. midsize businesses use eprocurement. Most still use multiple channels, including traditional channels, EDI, and the Internet.[10]

As more companies convert to online automated supply procurement, the need for industrial marketing and numbers of industrial salespeople will not decline dramatically; however, their roles will change. They will become more like consultants than salespeople, advising customers rather than haggling with them over prices and terms. Whereas some industries and companies will move rapidly toward the online sales consulting model, others will move more slowly because of the expense and complexity of converting to an online consulting system, products that require face-to-face contact, or highly conservative industries. The US$13 billion pharmaceutical marketing industry is an example. In-field pharmaceutical company representatives (PCRs) will continue making expensive personal sales calls on physicians, pharmacists, hospitals, and clinics to provide information and product samples. Face time is a hallowed tradition, yet Internet marketing is making inroads even here through edetailing, real-time video-on-demand interaction with PCRs where customers can receive information between regularly scheduled meetings. This transfer of contact with the salesperson-consultant online has been a subject of heated debate for over five years. Some pharmaceutical companies, Eli Lilly in particular, are testing online detailing triggered by physician request. When edetailing becomes widely accepted, it will augment, not replace, traditional detail pharmaceutical marketing.[11]

Some channel members will continue to resist change, even when others in their industries report considerable savings by going online. Large companies will be the first to transition; many small and midsize enterprises will lag behind, and some will never become fully committed online participants. Enterprises with call centers are likely to continue staffing them and delivering personal service to suppliers and producers for the immediate future. Preferred customers will receive the best service, online and offline. At some point in the near future, entirely online sales support and service will be the norm in many industries and for many businesses.

## DISTRIBUTION CHANNELS

Enterprise and consumer products have different distribution channels, although this is blurring as more of the same products are sold to both. Distribution channels deliver downstream value and products to end users.

Enterprise distribution channels move finished products from the producer to businesses, governments, educational institutions, health care facilities, or other enterprises. Like supply channels, enterprise distribution channels are direct, with few or even no intermediaries. A manufacturer may sell directly to businesses from its web site. Dell Computer (*http://www.dell.com*) has always used a direct channel for enterprises, initially by telephone and now online. Dell lets enterprise buyers configure and price systems online, order, and track orders. It also shares information via extranet with its suppliers at *https://valuechain.dell.com*. Dell reports that approximately 113,000 enterprises worldwide use its extranet business pages.

Consumer channels typically have more intermediaries than enterprise channels. Some producers distribute products directly to consumers or have a vertically integrated distribution system and control all channel members. Otherwise, independent channel members must be recruited to perform one or more highly specialized distribution tasks. Ideally, in an efficient, smoothly operating distribution channel, channel members should be an interdependent team of independent businesses performing exchange, physical distribution, and/or service tasks cooperatively.

**DIRECT DISTRIBUTION CHANNELS, PRODUCER TO BUYER**  Even in today's complex marketplace, many exchanges are still direct, seller to buyer without intermediaries. Buyers purchasing online from Dell Computer make their exchange directly with the manufacturer by telephone or online. Their computers are made to order and delivered within one to two weeks. The speed of order taking, manufacturing, and delivery, low inventory stockpile costs, no intermediaries or capital tied up in retail stores, and aggressive pricing give Dell a competitive advantage. Finished computers are shipped from one of Dell's manufacturing plants to a home or business by FedEx (*http://www.fedex.com*) or United Postal Service (UPS at *http://www.ups.com*). In 2001–2002, Dell expanded into direct mail brochures and selling on QVC television home shopping. Low interest rates, falling computer prices, and aggressive online marketing solidified Dell's position as the PC market share leader. Dell is a success story for multichannel marketing that is increasingly dependent on Internet sales.

Dell embraced the Web early, establishing a storefront in 1993. By 1999, it was selling US$40 million worth of computers daily from the site. About half its technical support and three-quarters of order-status transactions happen online. It is moving toward getting its suppliers online. Electronic order taking reduces paperwork significantly. Dell maintains an industrial sales force that works with enterprises to design computer systems for their unique needs. These salespeople are key to maintaining Dell's price advantage. Customer support delivered online reduces costs and often is more satisfying to buyers because they do not have to hold while waiting for service by phone. Dell's use of Internet marketing is a model for other products that can be mass-customized and sold directly to buyers. In 2002, Dell announced that it was extending its direct sales reach to multimedia web kiosks in select retail malls. Its first kiosk opened in the Highland Mall, Austin, Texas with 20 more kiosks due in other

U.S. malls. Customers can try Dell's latest computers and accessories, then place orders directly from the kiosk to www.dell.com.[12]

**DIGITAL DIRECT DISTRIBUTION**  Some products—like music, airline tickets, hotel reservations, video games, magazines, newspapers, radio and television programs, information, entertainment tickets, and financial services—are digital products that can be distributed directly to end users via electronic channels. Speed and convenience are two great advantages of digital distribution; security, privacy, and legality are drawbacks. Music distribution is perhaps the classic case, which also illustrates problems of copyright, royalties, and controlled distribution. Most music is distributed through a tight band of major labels, including Universal Music Group, Sony Music Entertainment, EMI Group, BMG Entertainment, and AOL-Time Warner, that failed to realize the great opportunity and threat of online music distribution. Instead, it fell to file-sharing sites, Napster.com (*http://www.napster.com*) in particular, to take the lead in distributing music online. Napster.com facilitated the spread of peer-to-peer music sharing that initially ignored copyrights and royalties, allowing individuals to freely share music over the Internet. Napster proved demand exists for downloaded digital music. Music sites now are trying to keep music flowing while also honoring copyrights and paying royalties. Subscriptions are one possible answer. Online music will be a US$5.4 billion industry in the United States by 2005.

**Multichannel distribution**

A strategy that uses more than one channel to reach consumers, trying to reach them wherever they are willing to buy.

**MULTICHANNEL DISTRIBUTION**  A **multichannel distribution** strategy uses more than one channel to reach consumers, providing products wherever they are willing to buy. It can be two channels, as in dual distribution, or up to five or more. Gateway (*http://www.gateway.com*) uses three channels to distribute its computers, all under its complete control. It was among the first major computer makers to sell products online. Gateway's web site was launched in 1996. It accepts orders by telephone, with sales handled by five thousand salespeople worldwide. It also has online ordering, as well as service and tech support, and online downloads that simplify repairs and upgrades. Gateway eSupport has system information, tutorials, and video help, service, and chat. Customers can test drive and purchase its computers at 275 retail Gateway Country stores in the United States, where it also offers service and training. Gateway's advantage is in service and returns directly to its stores. It is repositioning to increase its information technology services through online bill paying, in-store technical centers, and small business services.[13]

Compaq Computer (*http://www.compaq.com*) uses multiple distribution, some not under its control. It sells online at its web site, in a retail channel at Sears stores offline and the Sears web site (*http://www.sears.com*), and PCWarehouse.com (*http://www. pcwarehouse.com*) online and catalog. This channel structure is more complex than a direct or dual channel. It has more intermediaries and opportunities for markups and channel conflict. Whereas Compaq offers flexible configurations (mass customization) online, computers purchased from Sears and PCWarehouse have fixed configurations. Prices vary according to inventory levels, retailer markups, and other factors. Online customers can compare prices and models, but the information can be very confusing. Buying a computer has become more frustrating than purchasing an automobile. Compaq is competing against its own products offered at Sears and PCWarehouse. It loses control of its products when they are sold through retailers, but it also expands its customer reach. If buyers go to the Compaq web site for after-sale service, the company can use this opportunity to build a relationship with them. Is Compaq cannibalizing its sales by having so many distribution channels? Perhaps, but it is also dramatically extending its reach. Of the three computer box makers, Dell, Gateway, and Compaq, Dell is by far the most profitable. The simplicity of its distribution strategy and the close integration of its online/offline sales effort that reduces expensive in-face and by-phone contact, and eliminates retail stores contributes to its success.

**CHANNEL AGREEMENTS** Channel contracts are regularly formed and broken. For example, Tupperware is expanding its channel structure to include sixty-two Super-Target stores nationwide and Target's web site (*http://www.target.com*) in addition to its own online Tupperware Shop (*http://www.tupperware.com*). In-store selling by a Tupperware employee or independent sales agent and online at Target.com adds to its traditional in-house party selling, mall kiosks, and Home Shopping Network channels. Within five years, Tupperware expects retail, television, Internet, and mall kiosks to represent 40 percent of its revenues from sales of storage and serving containers.

**TYPES OF INTERMEDIARIES** Intermediaries have different names and relationships with producers. *Agents* have legal authority to act in the name of a manufacturer, thus they are manufacturers' agents. An agent's sales force may handle similar products for different manufacturers, selling them in different territories. *Brokers* bring buyer and seller together, directly and often face to face, to negotiate a sale. Real estate brokers are intermediaries facilitating the sale of real estate, travel agents are brokers for travel services, and financial services brokers transact stock and bond exchanges. Of all the intermediaries threatened by the Internet, brokers are the most vulnerable, because their work can be duplicated by electronic exchanges. Travel agents that only sell tickets can easily be replaced by Internet travel sites, particularly for point-to-point trips. Travel agents that add value with tangible cost savings and complex trip scheduling will survive. This is an industry where multichannel distribution has always been standard.[14]

**CHANNEL STRUCTURE** Channel structure is the form a channel takes, its length, arrangement and size, which is a function of company attributes, product type, customer characteristics and expectations, competitors, custom, and the marketing environment. Digital music is often distributed through a music site to consumers who share it peer to peer. Consumers are part of the music distribution channel and its end users. eBay is a virtual intermediary providing a platform where buyers and sellers can interact. It has no physical product, no inventory, and no channel members, yet is a virtual touch point for transactions. Services are distributed through online financial services brokers and Internet kiosks.

### LOGISTICS/PHYSICAL DISTRIBUTION

Logistics/physical distribution (PD) intermediaries store, handle, and move products through channels and ultimately to end users. *Supply distribution* moves raw materials and parts into production, and *physical distribution* moves products from producer to consumer. *Logistics* stores, handles, and moves. It is distribution from point of supply to point of production to point of sale.

United Parcel Service provides logistics and physical distribution services for enterprises and consumers in more than two hundred countries. It delivers 55 percent of all online purchases made and receives more than five million tracking requests online daily. Over 152,000 ubiquitous brown trucks deliver to almost every U.S. address, 13.2 million packages each day. UPS moves products from manufacturers to warehouses, shipping docks to trucks and planes, and trucks to end users. Electronic tags embedded in delivery packages allow tracking with an accuracy of up to three feet. UPS offers customers choices: faster air delivery or slower ground delivery; simple delivery services or storage, tracking, repair, and shipping. U.S. packages are all routed through one massive central warehouse in Louisville, Kentucky, USA.[15]

UPS and other carriers work with etailers to help them prepare for peak delivery periods, particularly around Christmas. Many also do order fulfillment for etailers. UPS e-Logistics operates warehouses, filling and shipping orders for a number of etailers. Ryder (*http://www.ryder.com*), formerly only a trucking company, has also entered the efulfillment business. Some established bricks-and-clicks etailers with established fulfillment systems are doing online fulfillment in-house.[16]

The importance of logistics cannot be overstated. Offline, most purchases leave the store with the buyer. Internet sales require physical delivery, unless the product is digital. Understandably, the role of the chief logistics officer (CLO) in bricks-and-clicks companies is becoming more prominent. CLOExpress.com (*http://www.cloexpress.com*) is a web portal for CLOs. Like CLOs, the portal concentrates on transportation, warehousing, and related logistics activities. Its content is designed to help CLOs coordinate their activities with marketing, purchasing, operations, finance, and information systems. In large companies, a CLO's job is highly complex and can have a direct and immediate impact on costs, revenues, and customer satisfaction.

### ✔ CONCEPT CHECK

1. How is the Internet changing automobile sales?
2. How does the Internet affect supply channels?
3. What consumer products other than computers lend themselves to online direct distribution?

## *Place Issues*

The Internet is changing many place traditions and introducing new channels of supply and distribution. Some changes have been radical, others just fine-tunings, and many have initiated process changes whose effects will not be felt for years. Place changes eventually will directly or indirectly affect all enterprises, from the largest global corporations to the smallest owner-operated businesses. The largest companies receive the most attention because their place issues involve millions or even billions of dollars and thousands of jobs, and they are at the forefront of channel changes. Some place issues are controversial. Others show that some facets of Internet marketing are traditional marketing in a new channel environment.

## DISINTERMEDIATION AND REINTERMEDIATION

**Disintermediation**

The collapsing of channels, removing intermediaries from supply and/or distribution channels to reduce costs, increase efficiency, and better serve customer needs.

Disintermediation was initially associated with households removing their savings from low-paying bank accounts and investing in money market and mutual funds, where their money could earn higher interest rates.[17] **Disintermediation** online is the collapsing of channels; that is, removing intermediaries from supply and/or distribution channels in order to reduce costs, increase efficiency, and better serve customer needs. It reduces the number of touch points that can slow distribution, add costs, and increase errors. Financial services remain particularly vulnerable to disintermediation, because consumers can perform tasks online that brokers previously performed. They can obtain information, pay bills, trade stocks, and make investment decisions. Financial services companies are very concerned about this threat and the loss of business it could represent. Many have responded by rushing to offer the same services online and aggressively marketing these services to current and prospective customers.

Travel agents are another group threatened with disintermediation by such travel sites as Travelocity (*http://www.travelocity.com*), Expedia (*http://www.expedia.com*), Priceline.com (*http://www.priceline.com*), Orbitz (*http://www.orbitz.com*), and others. The loss of commissions from ticket sales is driving many limited-service travel agents out of business, which pleases air carriers that have embarked on ambitious programs to sell tickets directly to buyers online and bypass travel agents and their commissions entirely. In 2001, travelers spent US$19.4 billion purchasing tickets online, a significant channel shift. Delta Airlines sold 13 percent of its tickets online in 2000 and saved US$45 million in commissions and fees.[18] Despite the growing popularity of online ticket sales, travel agents will continue to plan complex travel arrangements and help non-Internet-using consumers. There will just be far fewer of them providing these services.

Disintermediation is having some success in flowers. Flowers are a US$16 billion industry consisting of 11,500 growers supplying the industry, over 1,000 U.S. wholesalers, 16,400 plant nurseries and garden centers, 26,200 retail florists, and 23,000 supermarket floral shops. About 70 percent of the flowers sold in the United States are imports, almost 60 percent from Colombian growers. Because flowers are a perishable good, and fast delivery is essential, the goal is to get them from grower to end user as rapidly as possible. It takes about ten days using traditional channels to go from farms to exporters (if grown outside the United States), importers, wholesalers, retailers, and, finally, end users.

Flowergrower.com (*http://www.flowergrower.com*) is a web intermediary linking retailers directly with growers. Growers enter their production schedules on the web site where retailers access the lists to select products. Retailers pay for their purchases by credit card. Growers deliver their flowers to Flowergrower.com and receive payment. Flowergrower.com breaks bulk, then sends the smaller assortments to retailers to fill their orders. The site handles logistics and financial transactions. It outsources transportation to FedEx and Airborne Express, promising a seventy-two-hour transport cycle from farm to retailer. Fresher flowers means higher quality, less waste, and extended vase life. Flowergrower.com also has an automated standing order system that automatically resupplies retailers when restock trigger points are reached.

Flowergrower.com disintermediates by cutting out exporters, importers, and wholesalers. Proflowers.com (*http://WWW1.proflowers.com*) takes disintermediation one step further by eliminating retailers. It ships directly to end users, twenty-four to forty-eight hours after flowers are cut. Proflowers delivers by FedEx in the United States, Puerto Rico, and the Virgin Islands.[19]

Not all flower intermediaries are trying to disintermediate. Some see the Internet as just another marketing channel to augment existing channels. Florists' Telegraph Delivery (FTD) is an example. FTD was founded in 1910 when fifteen U.S. retail florists agreed to exchange telegraphed out-of-town orders. Thus, it was the first electronic flower distribution network. In 1965, the company was renamed Florists Transworld Delivery in recognition of its growing international reach. Today, FTD (*http://www.ftd.com*) has approximately 20,000 retail florists in the United States and Canada, and twenty eight thousand florists in 152 countries outside North America. It has been profitable online since 2000. The company self-branded its web site because it has 95 percent name recognition among consumers. It has controlled overhead by setting up its Internet marketing operations inside the FTD headquarters and using the parent company's established distribution network.[20]

Both FTD.com and 1-800-flowers.com (*http://www.1800flowers.com*) complement their offline distribution channels with web sites. Their highly recognized brand names instill trust, reduce the time it takes for consumers to search for a flower site, and are a proxy for quality. 1-800-flowers.com has approximately thirty thousand on-line affiliate marketing and distribution partners and around fifteen hundred partner florists, including 120 company-owned or franchised stores that fill orders. It also distributes through Plow & Hearth catalogs. The complementarity shown by FTD.com and 1-800-flowers.com is quite different from the disintermediated models of Flowergrower.com and Proflowers.com. Both models will continue to draw buyers looking for different things from a flower marketer. When freshness and cost are priorities, Flowergrower.com and Proflowers.com have an advantage. When brand name and search time are priorities, FTD.com and 1-800-flowers.com have an advantage.

**Reintermediate**

When a previously direct marketer creates a new distribution channel.

Amazon.com (*http://www.amazon.com*) is an example of what happens when a clicks-only retailer realizes the need to **reintermediate,** that is, create a distribution channel. Amazon's went online in July 1995. Its original model as a virtual bookseller did not involve holding inventory. Orders were taken at the Amazon.com web site, then outsourced for fulfillment by book wholesalers that also arranged delivery. As Amazon grew to become a one-stop shop for almost every imaginable product type— movies, health and beauty, electronics, tools, and automobiles—it added channel partners and distribution centers. Amazon reintermediated, adding channel members in order to continue serving customer needs as it expanded its product offers.[21]

## CHANNEL CANNIBALS

**Channel cannibalization**

The loss of sales in an existing channel when a new channel is introduced to sell the same products.

**Channel cannibalization** is the loss of sales in an existing channel when a new channel is introduced to sell the same product(s). Sometimes cannibalization is planned. For example, a business may start a competing channel even though it anticipates the loss of sales in an existing channel because it wants to block sales by a competitor or, in the case of Internet channels, it is imperative to establish a web presence. Unplanned cannibalization is an unexpected loss in sales when a new channel is implemented. P&G avoided cannibalizing existing channels and angering its retail distributors by restricting sales of Reflect.com (*http://www.reflect.com*) products to the online channel and not using the company name on the web site. Ford and GM redirect online buyers to their dealers and avoid cannibalizing dealer sales and undermining their dealer networks.

Levi's (*http://www.levis.com*) initially sold its jeans online from a site launched in November 1998 and ordered its retailers not to sell Levi's online. However, by January 2000 the company reversed its strategy and now does not sell jeans online. Although Levi's company officials will not admit that retailer pressure caused the reversal, they do say a "little bit of tension" existed. Visitors to the Levi's site are advised to go to one of Levi's online retail partner's web sites to make a purchase. This includes JC Penney.com (*http://www1.jcpenney.com*), Kohl's (*http://www.kohls.com*), Urban Outfitters (*http://www.urbn.com*), or Macys.com (*http://www.macys.com*).[22] This is a good example of why it will be very difficult to get rid of intermediaries.

Staples, Inc. (*http://www.staples.com*) is a US$11 billion retailer that reported US$1 billion in online revenues in 2001, up from US$512 million in 2000 and US$94 million in 1999. Online sales are projected to rise twenty-five percent in 2002 and 2003. The company sells office supplies, business services, furniture, and technology in the United States, Canada, the United Kingdom, Germany, the Netherlands, and Portugal. It has had a web storefront since 1998, in addition to more than fourteen hundred stores, a mail-order catalog business, and web kiosks in over a thousand of its stores. Staples has found that rather than cannibalizing offline sales, its web site increases sales. The average yearly spending of small business customers increased from US$600 to US$2,800 when they shopped online. When buyers shop all three of Staples's channels their purchases are 4.5 times greater than if they shop only one channel. Staples's experience is confirmed by Spiegel Inc.'s Eddie Bauer Unit (*http://www.eddiebauer.com*) distributing through catalogs, retail stores, and online. The retailer reports that a consumer shopping in only one channel spends US$100 to $200 annually. Shopping in two channels, sales increase to US$300 to $500 a year. A customer shopping in all three channels averages US$1,000 a year. Most sales still come from retail stores (70 to 75 percent), 25 percent from catalogs, and 5 percent online. A multichannel approach gives consumers the choice of when, where, and how they want to shop Eddie Bauer. Evidence also suggests that a shift is under way, from catalogs to online sales as a result of increased web site security and growing consumer preference for the convenience of shopping online.[23]

## METAMEDIARIES

**Metamarkets**

Clusters of activities and vendors that consumers perceive to be related and complementary.

**Metamarkets** are web site clusters of related and complementary activities and vendors. They provide advice and links for users seeking their services. TheWeddingChannel.com (*http://weddingchannel.com*), launched in 1997, is a **metamarket intermediary (metamediary)** for a wedding metamarket where visitors can find everything they might possibly want for a wedding. A metamediary is a virtual intermediary that aggregates metamarket members, helps them find appropriate sellers, and offers advice and web space for community-related activities. TheWeddingChannel.com links to retailers offering bridal registry services, travel services, gowns, and everything associated with getting married. It has become a virtual one-stop shop for all things wedding.

**Metamarket intermediary (metamediary)**

A virtual intermediary that aggregates metamarket members for easy access.

Metamediaries are unique communities of buyers voluntarily joining together to share information and links and provide evaluations of products. That does not mean metamediaries have no commercial involvement. Many either sell products directly on site or have links to sites that do. It is very tricky trying to determine if a site is a true metamediary or simply a customer-centric portal. At least four types of B2C metamediaries have been identified.

**AFFINITY**    Metamarkets organized around characteristics of its members. The National Alliance for the Mentally Ill (NAMI at *http://www.nami.org*) is a resource site for information, support, education, and research with links for the mentally ill and their caregivers.

**INSTRUCTION**    Metamarkets for avocations, enthusiasts who want to learn more about their hobbies, share information, and purchase products. Orchid enthusiasts can visit the North of England Orchid Society's *All About Orchids and How to Grow Them* web site (*http://www.orchid.org.uk*) maintained by the world's oldest orchid society.

**TIME/EVENT**    Griefnet.org (*http://griefnet.org*) is for people dealing with death and dying. In addition to support groups and memorials, the site also has a library with links to Amazon.com.

**ASPIRATIONS**    People who aspire to be adventure travelers can get unbiased information from iExplore.com (*http://IExplore.com*), a site associated with the National Geographic Society. The site is rich in content and links for the armchair traveler seeking adventure.[24]

## AUTOMATIC REPLENISHMENT

**Automatic replenishment (AR)**

In enterprises, automatic replenishment is an automatic rebuy, a standing order to restock supplies on a regular basis by prearrangement between buyer and seller.

A magazine subscription is a prepaid agreement for **automatic replenishment (AR)** of magazines each month. Enterprise AR is an automatic *rebuy*, a standing order to restock supplies on a regular basis by prearrangement between buyer and seller that can be activated over an extranet. PETsMART.com (*http://www.petsmart.com*) offers consumers Frequent Fetcher Repeat Home Delivery (*http://www.petsmart.com/misc/regular_delivery.shtml*), a subscription service for pet supplies. Participants can change, add, delete, or cancel their standing order on the web site at any time. Their credit card is billed when a delivery is initiated. The Repeat Home Delivery service is free and covers any products offered by PETsMART.com. The question is how much consumers are willing to pay for shipping that twenty-pound bag of dog kibble purchased at PETsMART.com.

Consumers need to replenish pet supplies on a regular basis. What about milk, printer paper, ink jet cartridges, pharmaceutical products, or bread? The AR distribution model can be applied to many regularly consumed commodity products. Consumers control the flow of products and delivery times. The storefront can assist with email reminders that restocking is due. Alternately, the consumer and storefront can arrange for replenishment with no notice in a passive form of distribution.[25]

## MULTILEVEL MARKETING

**Multilevel marketing (MLM)**

Also known as network marketing, a form of direct selling involving many levels of distributors.

Considerable controversy surrounds multilevel marketing. Also known as network marketing, **multilevel marketing (MLM)** is a form of direct selling involving many levels of distributors that bring in new distributors to purchase products, sell to consumers, and recruit others who will also become distributors. It is both a distribution system and personal selling.

The concern comes from its resemblance to pyramid schemes, which are illegal. Legitimate MLM distributors sell a product that fills a need and satisfies buyers. Distributors do not profit *solely* from recruiting others to become distributors. They sell products that work and are priced at fair market value. A pyramid scheme draws in naive people who believe they will get rich quick by recruiting other sellers. Profits derive from getting paid for recruiting new distributors and the distributors they recruit. The people at the top of the pyramid make money; most others do not.

The Internet's interactivity is a natural attractant for MLM activities because it is easy to build customer relationships online, and that is the foundation for MLM. Amway (*http://www.amway.com*) is the best-known MLM. Founded in 1959, it currently has over three million distributors selling Amway products in eighty countries. Sales are about US$5 billion annually through its global distribution network. Amway does not sell its products or directly recruit distributors from its web site. Quixtar.com (*http://www.quixtar.com*), owned by Amway's founders, sells products online. To purchase any product from the site, consumers must contact an independent business owner (IBO) who gives them a referral number (IBO identification number) by email. Launched September 1999, Quixtar is a member of the Alticor group of companies that includes Amway. IBOs refer clients and members to the site to make purchases and sponsor others who want to become IBOs. By not using the Amway name, Quixtar may attract customers who have negative impressions of Amway.

### ✔ CONCEPT CHECK

1. Explain the attraction of a disintermediation strategy.
2. What types of buying situations might be used to form a metamarket?
3. Why is the Internet such an attractive place for MLM?

# *Consumer Channel Strategies*

Many online channel strategies are evolutionary, not revolutionary, but this does not lessen their impact. In addition, most are in their infancy, so it is difficult to predict how they will change in the next five or ten years of Internet marketing activity. Enterprise and consumer channel strategy similarities will persist. Both use web sites and marketplaces (exchanges, auctions) to buy and sell products, reduce surplus inventory, and arrange product delivery and return. Enterprises and consumers rely on information content channels to deliver product information. While enterprises are usually thought of as sellers, they are also buyers. The Internet also allows consumers who are typically cast in the role of buyers to be sellers.

Since there are far more consumers than businesses offline and on, it is not surprising that B2C sites report more visitors than B2B sites, an average fifty-four thousand each week versus twenty thousand at B2B sites. At the same time, total B2B sales revenues are higher. Storefront profit center sites draw much more traffic than content, customer support, or public relations sites. Sites that have been on the Internet longer and are more experienced at Internet marketing have higher conversion rates (visitor to buyer), averaging 12 percent (one in eight). All web storefronts are more than just end points in the distribution chain. They are also sites where data about customers and prospects can be collected. They are service centers and can be drivers to offline stores. Some Internet marketers realize that not all web sites are profitable, but some have value as loss leaders to attract buyers. Thus, they have value to their owners far beyond just revenue generation.

Total U.S. online retail sales in 2001 were over US$33 billion, up 19.3 percent from 2000. Total retail sales increased only 3.3 percent in the same period. Online sales are particularly popular during the Christmas buying season, when convenience draws shoppers online.[26]

## WHAT CONSUMERS WANT FROM ONLINE STOREFRONTS

Understanding what consumers want from an etailer is just as difficult as determining what they want from a traditional store retailer. Consumers are fickle; their needs and wants can change in a flash. They often do not know what they want, or, sometimes, they do know and are not truthful about it. Failing to try to understand them, however, can be a fatal marketing mistake.

**CONVENIENCE** Consumers want convenience. Dataquest Inc. reports that convenience is the reason almost 75 percent of shoppers go online and the number one factor behind their online store choice. Online banking is finally catching on to the convenience advantage and giving customers 24/7/365 access to their accounts. They can look up checking account balances, pay bills, and transfer money between accounts. As of mid-2001, 22 percent of Internet users were doing some banking online.

Consumers also want convenience in product returns. This gives store-based retailers like Target and BestBuy an advantage over clicks-only and bricks-and-clicks retailers that do not accept returns from online sales in their stores. Others like Nordstrom (*http://www.nordstrom.com*) have front-door delivery service pickups for returns. This is an important issue for etailers since returns will increase along with online sales, particularly as purchases increase for products that are more risky than books, airline tickets, and computers. Store returns for women's apparel, a high-risk product category, average 20 percent. Catalog return rates for women's apparel average around 33 percent, while online returns are nearly 40 percent. This is a serious problem since returns cost four to five times more than initial delivery. Many etailers do not bother restocking returned items because of the cost. They add them to clearance sales, remainder them to liquidators, or sell them on eBay. Others turn to web outlet malls that specialize in discounted first-quality merchandise like SmartBargains (*http://www.smartbargains.com*). Some companies outsource returns. Catalog companies with long histories of handling returns are in the best position to constrain online return costs.[27]

**INFORMATION** Consumers want information. Product information is extremely important, particularly information about product availability and price. Consumers need better information about products, including accurate product pictures, close-ups, and multiangle views. They want to know if the web site has the same products as in-store. They want complete information about shipping and handling, including costs. Price information obtained online can drive traffic to the etailer's offline stores. Sears estimates that 10 percent of its store appliance sales are influenced by information downloaded from Sears.com.

Consumers want information about store policies. This is a challenge for multi-channel retailers that should explain any differences in their policies between channels. For example, if a product ordered online is returned to one of the retailer's stores and there is a difference between the product's online and offline price, which is the refund price? What price is right when there is a discrepancy between a catalog and online price? Are online markdowns and clearance sales on the same schedule as offline sales? Can gift certificates be redeemed online only?

Consumers expect brand manufacturer's sites to provide product and contact information, particularly toll-free telephone numbers and email. They are far less interested in games, activities, and features that try to build communities. Consumers are willing to share product satisfaction information with the manufacturer, but they are not being asked to do so by most manufacturers.[28]

Some web storefronts whose products are not particularly well suited to online sales use their sites to provide information that directs consumers to their retail stores. Home Depot (*http://www.homedepot.com*) sells more than twenty thousand items online, but that is only a small part of the forty thousand to fifty thousand products available in offline stores. Few consumers, however, are willing to pay shipping for lumber or wait for delivery of an immediately needed kerosene heater. Instead, consumers can visit the *Home Improvement Projects Index* where they learn how to *Fix It, Build It, Grow It, Decorate It, and Install It.* Tools to complete the projects are recommended and can be purchased either online or in a Home Depot Store. The site provides free storage space where consumers can compile Personal Project Files for the how-to projects they are most interested in. The site also has *Learn Abouts*, featured tips about such topics as lighting controls, drip irrigation, and clothes washers/dryers. Home Depot uses a dual channel strategy designed to build synergy between online and offline sales.

**SPEED**  Some consumers want speed. Rather than wait three or four days for a purchase to arrive, they want same-day delivery. Kepler's Books and Magazines (*http://www.keplers.com/index.html*) partners with Ensenda to offer free same-day delivery on in-stock books to thirteen cities in the San Francisco Bay area for orders of US$50 or more. Even Amazon.com cannot deliver that fast. Other consumers are willing to pay extra for two-day delivery. Most are content to pay as little as possible and receive their purchases in around a week. Consumers trading online also want rapid access to exchange data and their accounts. They want trades to be instantaneous.

**PRIVACY AND SECURITY**  Consumers want guarantees that information they provide is not shared without their permission. They need reassurance that sites are safe and secure. A Brigham Young University (BYU) study confirmed that consumers remain apprehensive about credit card security. Consumers expect security statements on manufacturers' web sites, but only 59 percent actually post them. Trust is a very important marketing tool at online storefronts. That is why retailers that have already earned consumers' trust offline have an advantage when that trust is transferred online.[29]

**SERVICE**  Consumers want service, real people answering their e-mail and providing assistance when requested. Lands' End (*http://www.landsend.com*) understands the value of live customer service representatives. It offers consumers live text chat or telephone assistance while online. It also has interactive finders, search engines that return clothing suggestions based on information provided by the consumer. Consumers can create their own virtual models, representing their body shapes, and select clothing styles to try on the model. Timely responses to inquiries, informative content, and communication with a real person contribute to customer satisfaction. The payback is that 90 percent of satisfied customers say they will return; 87 percent recommend the etailer to others.[30] Like speed, however, consumers want varying levels of service. Some are willing to pay more for it; others are willing to do more for themselves if they can pay less.

**SIMPLICITY** Consumers want simple site technology that makes navigation easy. They need better functioning in-site search engines. Most consumers are not technology sophisticates, so overly complex sites richly endowed with high-end bandwidth features can drive them off.

**CONVERGENCE** Consumers want etailer sites that look and feel like their offline counterparts.[31] A unified look is reassuring. Joseph-Beth Booksellers' web site (*http:// www.josephbeth.com*) captures its store ambience, including the fireplace and easy chairs where patrons can relax and take a book on a test read. Consumers want to duplicate the offline shopping experience while also taking advantage of interactivity that allows sites to provide feedback from other consumers and comparisons.

## ETAILING

Internet retailing (etailing) has been called the third significant transformation of the retail industry. The first began in the 1950s with the introduction of shopping centers and malls. In the 1970s it was the arrival of large discount stores and nationwide chains. In the mid-1990s, it was the Internet. The Internet transformation is not just the number of etail storefronts that have gone online since 1993 but also changes in retail stores. For example, over 151,000 Internet kiosks with touch screen menus are in use worldwide. By 2004, that number is expected to increase to over five hundred thousand. Consumers use kiosks to check product availability, access and place orders from online gift registries, and order products that are out of stock in the store. Since kiosks are self-service, they hold the promise of allowing stores to further reduce staffing.[32]

For most clicks-only etailers, the first mover advantage was myth, not reality. Later arrivals like traditional retailers Sears.com, Target.com, and Nordstrom.com learned from earlier dot-com mistakes. They have the advantage of brand name recognition, familiarity and trust, stores where products can be picked up or returned, and established distribution centers and delivery systems.[33] Both clicks-only and bricks-and-clicks etailers can generate multiple revenue streams. In addition to selling products online, they can also sell on-site advertising space, generate revenue from affiliate networks, host honor system payboxes, sell customer data (although this is not advised), and sell services like order fulfillment to other storefronts as well as proprietary software.

Online customer acquisition costs are falling and currently average around US$18 per customer. Conversion rates are increasing, from an average 1.5 percent in Q1 2000 to 2.3 percent in Q1 2001. Landsend.com has a conversion rate of 9 percent, JCPenney.com has 8.9 percent, Gap.com is 5.2 percent, and luxury product storefront Ashford.com has 0.7 percent.[34] These trends are welcome news to many struggling etailers and represent profit for others.

Almost 70 percent of online retailers are bricks and clicks. In 2000, one-third of total bricks-and-clicks revenue came from their Internet sales. ActivMedia estimates that by 2003, this will rise to 55 percent. Online etail is only slightly more than 1 percent of total retail sales, but about 50 percent of etailers are profitable.[35]

Bricks-and-clicks retailers like Circuit City (*http://www.circuitcity.com*) are creating new ways to simplify online shopping and make it more convenient and less costly. It offers *Express Pickup* where consumers select a product online, select the nearest local Circuit City store from a pulldown menu, and at the online checkout select the store where they want to pick up the product. On large products like computers, *Express Pickup* can be a significant money-saver. JCPenney.com promotes cooperation between its online and offline stores, taking online returns at its 1,074 JC Penney stores or catalog desks in its 2,643 Eckerd's Drugstores. If customers prefer, online and catalog orders can be processed as *will calls* for pickup in the stores.[36]

Catalog retailers are more likely to be profiting online than other types of retailers. More than 70 percent of catalogers with online storefronts are profitable. Lands' End has been profitable at least since 1998. Spiegel (*http://www.spiegel.com*) and LL Bean (*http://www.llbean.com*) also report profits online. Catalogers have many advantages, including experience in the postsale channel, dealing with returns, exchanges, and adjustments, and providing customer service. Returns average about 8 percent of online purchases, compared with 5 to 6 percent for catalogs. Some product types have higher return rates than others, particularly apparel.[37]

**ETAILER DECISIONS** Going online forces retailers to make a large number of key decisions (table 11-1). Staying online means these decisions must be continuously evaluated and adjusted to ensure they continue to serve the etailer's goals and satisfy

### Table 11-1  Etailer Decisions

| | |
|---|---|
| *Service level* | Service provided by the etailer (full, limited) and extent of self-service consumer will perform. Includes credit, delivery options, order tracking, packaging, gift registry, shopping assistance, returns. |
| *Products* | Full product line (identical to catalog and/or store) or limited. Some products are not appropriate because of their bulk, low margins, and high delivery costs. High inventory turn products are preferred to those with low turns. |
| *Product assortment* | Width (different types of products) and depth (different alternatives within a product type) offered; convenience, specialty, discount, brand, prestige, etc. |
| *Inventory turns* | How often to change online products, same as offline or less/more frequently. |
| *Prices* | Discount, prestige, off-price, or other mixture of prices; same or different from retail stores. |
| *Returns* | By independent distribution company (UPS, FedEx), or USPS to an outsourced return intermediary processor, to the seller, to a return reseller. |
| *Trust* | Join TRUSTe, VeriSign, BBBOnline, or other enterprise that reassures consumers about seller trustworthiness. |
| *Facilitation* | Accept payment by credit card, easy installment payments, PayPal, or other payment system. |
| *Aftermarket service* | Postsales channel, service and support in-house, through an intermediary like AfterMind.com (*http://www.aftermind.com*). |

customers. Why do retailers go online? They certainly should clearly identify their reasons. Fear of being left out is one. Others are stores that stay open 24/7/365, expanded customer reach, low rent on server space compared with opening high-cost bricks-and-mortar stores, possibility of international sales, collecting customer data, using the web site as a driver for offline sales, testing new merchandise lines and categories, and generating additional revenue. These potential benefits must be weighed against the costs of going online, which include initial and continuing web maintenance costs, vulnerability to comparison shoppers, high product return rates, security breaches, consumer privacy complaints, and high customer service costs.

**ETAILER TYPES** With the mass migration of bricks-and-mortar retailers online, there are few if any retail types that are not online. Some are well suited to the virtual environment, offering products that lend themselves to the Internet and interactivity. Others are ill suited, offering large, bulky, low-price items whose shipping and handling costs exceed product value. Even these retailers are online providing information that directs traffic to their offline stores. Apparel, travel, books, and computer etailers are posting profits; many others are not. Forecasts vary greatly on when profitability will become more widespread.

**TOP ETAILERS** Half of all U.S. Internet users were shopping online as of mid-2001. More than US$3.5 billion was spent in shopping online in March 2001. Top shopping categories in that month were travel (US$1 billion) and apparel (US$360 million). Bricks and clicks continue to solidify their positions online. Amazon.com was the audience and sales leader, with a 15.1 percent purchaser share. eBay was next at a 14.5 percent share, but if its customers and sales are combined with its subsidiary Half.com, it has more online customers than Amazon. Rounding out the top ten were BMG Entertainment, Barnes & Noble, Columbia House Music, Half.com, JCPenney.com, Travelocity, CDnow.com, and Southwest.com.[38]

**WEB UPDATE**

Etailers and Their Market Offers

**Shopping basket**
Software that lets customers make selections from throughout the site, compiling the data while they continue shopping, then completing the order.

**Shopping basket abandonment**
Leaving a shopping basket before purchase.

**SHOPPING BASKET ABANDONMENT** A **shopping basket** is software that lets customers make selections from throughout the site, compiles the order while they continue shopping, then completes the order of all products selected. Etailers are concerned about the high rate of **shopping basket abandonment,** since as many as 65 percent of consumers leave their basket before the sale is completed. Top reasons are sticker shock at the total cost of their order and/or shipping costs. Over 40 percent experience technical problems at checkout. Others complain about overly complex ordering forms or forms that take too long to download. Consumers often do not find out a product is not in stock until they are ready to pay for the order. Computers crash, the site will not accept their credit card, or they just decide at the last minute they really do not want the product(s).[39]

Fear of abandoned shopping baskets is getting in the way of etailers realizing that browsing consumers can also result in sales. Browsing is what many consumers find most pleasurable about retail shopping offline. Web sites are short-circuiting browsing by sending consumers targeted emails with hot links to special offers that bypass the rest of the storefront. More than a third of consumers searching for gifts online purchase products they happen to see while web browsing.[40] PotteryBarn.com (*http://www. potterybarn.com*) encourages consumers to browse their *Home Tour* that highlights products for every room in the house. The tour is laid out with a floor plan that encourages consumers to travel from room to room at their leisure.

**CONTENT SITES**  Content is offered through online newspapers and magazines, television and radio sites, game sites, and other entertainment storefronts. Most content sites are struggling and not profitable, principally because they have not figured out how to charge for the content they provide. Micropayments eventually may be the answer, but many content sites will not survive the wait until some type of near-universal micropayment system is accepted by buyers.

## AUCTIONS

Consumers have shown how much they like online auctions, the primary mechanism for consumers to become online sellers. Historically, traditional auctions have not been a big factor in balancing supply and demand, or in consumer purchasing. They have been a factor in agriculture, other commodity markets, fine art, and antiques, markets most average consumers never approach.

According to Harris Interactive, thirty-five million Americans participate in online auctions. eBay.com is by far the most popular and trusted public auction, offering its auction platform to consumers and enterprises. It performs a quality control function that reduces the risk of auctioning on its site.[41]

Consumers like auctions because they can clean out their closets, garages, and attics at a profit. Many find them entertaining and exciting; some are addicted to them. The Internet opens online auctions to millions of people and sophisticated software allows multiple interactions between large numbers of buyers and sellers. Online auctions are far faster and more convenient than visiting traditional auctions. However, they do not always result in lower or even fair prices. Online auctions attract buyers and sellers from all sectors—consumers, businesses, governments, and other enterprises. As mentioned in Chapter 10, there is more than one type of auction engaging consumers online, including forward, reverse, Dutch, pooled, and private.

Auction fraud continues to be a serious problem, but there are signs that it is beginning to abate. Problems arise because of legitimate differences of opinion about the value of products. More serious problems are deliberate misrepresentations or fraud. A number of online businesses offer services to make auctions less risky. Escrow companies like Escrow.com (*http://Escrow.com*) act as intermediaries in online B2B, B2C, and other auctions. As a third-party intermediary, it collects payment from the buyer and retains it until either the buyer accepts the purchase or returns it to the seller. Square-Trade (*http://www.squaretrade.com*) offers neutral third-party online dispute resolution for eBay disputes, real estate, and other parties. The company handles over twelve thousand resolution cases each month with a worldwide network of more than 250 professional mediators and arbitrators. Ask the Appraiser at the CollectingChannel.com (*http://www.collectingchannel.com/cMart/cesATEIndex.asp*) takes a different approach, offering appraisals for auctions. Sellers submit a digital photo and short description of their auctionable item, pay US$19.95 per item, and receive a professional appraisal within three working days. Buyers and sellers both use BiddersEdge.com (*http://BiddersEdge.com*) searches of more than five hundred online auctions. It can be used for side-by-side price and product comparisons. These sites provide valuable services but most consumers are unaware that they exist.

Some manufacturers and etailers are using eBay and other auctions to clear their surplus inventories. eBay, which was profitable from its launch, has developed a model that is copied across the Web. It does not hold inventory and acts only as an intermediary, never handling merchandise, but providing a platform for its sale. It is by far the most successful electronic exchange venue. The model has even been extended to patent auctions. For example, Yet2.com (*http://www.yet2.com/app/about/home*) is a technology transfer marketplace for scientists and researchers that auctions patents, intellectual property, and licenses.

A distinguishing feature of successful auctions, etailers, and content sites is a powerful internal search engine. eBay's buyers and sellers initiate thirty million searches daily, looking for products to bid on or to check bids. To keep transactions current, it needs search engine technology that continuously updates auction postings and bids. Lands' End uses data mining search engine technology that pushes products to users that fit or are associated with the search term. Efficient search engines compensate for common misspellings and use dynamic technology to broaden searches beyond the initial request.[42]

**WEB UPDATE**

Search Engines

### ✔ CONCEPT CHECK

1. What do consumers want online?
2. What is there about etailing that consumers like?
3. Explain the eBay auction model.

## *Customer Relationship Management*

A top priority of supply and distribution channel marketers should be solving customer problems, satisfying their needs and wants. The customer-centered approach is called by different names, including customer relationship management (CRM), one-to-one marketing, real-time marketing, technology-enabled marketing, relationship marketing, and learning relationships. Whatever the name, it is an advance over previous marketing approaches that cast marketers and customers as adversaries, emphasized short-term sales over *lifetime value*, the value of a customer over his or her purchasing lifetime, and treated all customers the same. The Internet's interactivity, computers, databases, and data mining technology give marketers the tools to differentiate preferred customers from the rest, personalize marketing offers, customize (or mass-customize) products, communicate directly with customers, and convert first-time buyers into lifelong customers. In the Internet marketing environment, where transparent prices undermine price competition, eCRM can deliver a competitive advantage to businesses that successfully implement and sustain it.

### THE BASICS

eCRM is a five-stage process of (a) *identifying* customers, (b) *segmenting* them by their needs and value to the business, (c) *interacting* with them effectively, (d) *customizing* the marketing offer made to them, and (e) *updating* information about them and their changing needs so marketing offers can be updated. This approach means that all customers are not treated the same. It does not mean low-value customers should be ignored. Because they have purchased in the past, a baseline relationship exists and it could become more active in the future. Higher-spending customers receive better treatment because they have higher lifetime value or **customer share,** the

**Customer share**
The relative share of revenue a customer produces and projects over his or her purchasing lifetime.

relative share of revenue produced by a customer and projected over his or her purchasing lifetime. The highest-value customers visit more often, spend more at each visit, communicate more frequently with the enterprise, and have lasting loyalty.

A long-term relationship locks in high-value customers who incur high costs if they take their business elsewhere. For example, an experienced, longtime LandsEnd.com customer knows the company has high product quality control. Their products are proprietary; that is, no brands are sold by them other than Lands' End, which gives them greater control over suppliers. This means slacks in woman's size 10 that fit the customer in the past have a very high probability of fitting her in the future, assuming she does not gain weight. Buying slacks at another etailer carries a high risk that size 10 is more variable, slacks purchased there will not fit, and she has to initiate the return process. Lands' End provides free hemming, a self-created virtual model on which she can fit clothes, a personal shopper to assist her in selecting matching outfits, and an unbeatable customer satisfaction guarantee, which makes it even more difficult for her to leave.

A key to eCRM is its long-term perspective that acknowledges the high cost of customer acquisition and the necessity of retaining valued customers. It is considerably less expensive to retain a customer than acquire a new one. A Jupiter Communications study reports that a business can increase its profits almost 100 percent by retaining 5 percent more of their valued customers. Etailers are focusing more on retaining customers, and almost half their revenues come from repeat customers. eCRM at its most fundamental level is about customer acquisition, loyalty, conversion of high potential customers, and retention.

Three technologies make eCRM possible. Databases, data warehouses, and the technology to mine them form the basis for the information used to develop customer profiles (see Chapter 8). Internet interactivity expands the contact points where customer data can be collected, from web sites, emails, call centers, and order forms. Mass customization gives businesses the flexibility to design individualized products in response to real-time customer demands.

Why implement eCRM? Beside delivering customer satisfaction and locking in valuable customers, it has the potential to reduce operating costs, increase revenues and profits, and wring inefficiencies from marketing channels. By improving customer contact and establishing long-term relationships, it offers opportunities for increasing customer sales, cross-selling, and up-selling. These should be smart choices for consumers, not just adding more choices to confuse them. Well-deployed eCRM can deliver sustainable competitive advantage for the company that does it right.

## ECRM IMPLEMENTED

eCRM is personalizing and customizing. Personalizing is relatively simple, greeting a customer by name each time he or she revisits a site. Customizing requires modifying a product or adding products specifically tailored to the customer's preferences and past purchasing behaviors. Some products are not appropriately customized; others are highly differentiated and lend themselves to customization and eCRM. For example, Dell Computer achieves a competitive advantage by offering mass customization in its products for consumers and true customization for enterprise customers. Which customer is more valuable to Dell? Obviously the business ordering five hundred computer workstations is more valuable than a consumer ordering one of Dell's least expensive computers for home use. Dell's enterprise customers deserve far more customer support based on their lifetime value to the company. However, consumers also vary in their value. Some consumers purchase a high-end computer every two years. These consumers have a higher value to the company than consumers purchasing the lowest-priced computer every five years. Real-time access to databases and interactivity allow Dell to make the distinction between online customers and focus sales efforts on the highest-value customers.

Other businesses suited to eCRM approaches include online supermarkets, apparel etailers, financial services, telecommunications, and business travel. These businesses interactively communicate with customers on a regular basis and have products that can be customized and repurchased. Consider this hypothetical example. A business traveler who needs to fly from Chicago (ORD) to New York (JFK) links to Orbitz, a partnership of thirty-five airlines, four large hotel chains, and seven car rental agencies. This is her first visit to the site, so no past purchase information exists in its database. This is where the eCRM process begins. She types in her flight needs on the site's front page, and the search returns five alternatives. She selects the one that fits her appointment schedule and budget constraints. To book the flight, she has to become an Orbitz member, which requires completing a short online information form. Once registered, she proceeds to book the flight and pay for it with a company credit card. An eticket is issued, which saves the airline US$5 to $10 compared to the cost of a paper ticket. She logs off Orbitz and checks her email. The first message waiting for her is from Orbitz Traveler Care welcoming her to Orbitz and thanking her for registering. The message reassures her that her information will be kept private and confidential. The message ends with *We look forward to assisting you with your future travel plans. Visit Planet Earth at Orbitz.* This is the first link in the relationship that Orbitz intends to establish with this customer, assuming that the flight goes well and she returns (figure 11-2).

The flight to New York is uneventful. Two weeks later, she returns to Orbitz to book a flight to St. Louis. This time she enters Orbitz using her member password. When she makes her reservation, her name comes up automatically in the *Traveler's Name* window. Orbitz began a file on her with her first visit, then accessed that file on her second visit, and with each revisit, adds to her file. Since she is a business traveler and travels more frequently than consumers on holiday, Orbitz treats her like a highly valued customer. Soon a pattern emerges. Every three months, she makes two-day trips to New York, St. Louis, Dallas, and San Diego. Orbitz responds with marketing offers keyed to

**Figure 11-2  Data for an eCRM**

| Visit 1 | Register for Orbitz | Book Flight | Pay with Credit Card |
|---|---|---|---|
| | Title | Departure city | Card vendor |
| | First name, last name | Arrival city | Card type |
| | Email address | Preferred times | (company, own) |
| | Password | Non-stop, one stop | Number |
| | Security question/answer | | Expiration date |
| | Zip code | | |
| | Preferred home city airport | | |

Registering with Orbitz requires providing information. Booking a flight gives up more information. It is all entered into a database, along with credit card information.

her business schedule, low fares, special car rentals, and hotel discounts. It sets up a special travel account for her so all she has to do is enter the account, type in new travel dates, and Orbitz does the rest, including charging her corporate credit card. Orbitz pampers her, makes travel scheduling easy, and locks her in as a loyal customer who does not have the time or inclination to change to another site and start all over again.

Think ahead to how this process might evolve. Perhaps at some time in the future, Orbitz makes an alliance with Amazon.com. They link their customer databases and Orbitz cross-matches its customers with Amazon's. The next time our business traveler books a flight with Orbitz, she gets a book recommendation for good reading on the plane and a hot link to the book at Amazon.com. The recommendation is based on what she has purchased from Amazon in the past. That is fine as long as she was buying books for her own reading pleasure and not as gifts. Jump ahead even further and perhaps along with the book recommendation from Amazon, she also receives a clothing recommendation from Travelsmith (*http://www.travelsmith.com/home.jsp*) for new travel boots designed to stimulate blood flow to the legs during long flights. Perhaps she receives healthy flying tips and a recommendation for Melatonin (a sleep aid) from Drugstore.com (*http://www.drugstore.com*). Each visit to Orbitz or any site committed to eCRM results in more information and products designed to serve her needs and make her life easier, happier, and less stressful. Although this all sounds wonderful to some consumers, to others it is a horrifying specter of privacy invasion at its worst. One solution is to require consumers to opt in to any eCRM process. This avoids offending consumers with low tolerance for personal data collection while also concentrating the list of consumers that are more susceptible to cross-selling.

### IT'S HARDER THAN IT LOOKS

eCRM should be intuitively appealing to all marketers that believe in a customer-centered approach. It uses current technology to provide customer satisfaction. However, it is not an easy process to get right, nor is it feasible for all businesses. It requires integrating direct customer contact activities at etailer and other web storefronts with databases and data warehouses, and mining them. It means the entire marketing channel is part of the system. The advantages are obvious; getting it to work smoothly and efficiently is harder than it looks.

From the customer's perspective, eCRM works when he or she has a seamless experience across the multiple channels used to interact with the company. It is far more than just being greeted by name when entering a web storefront. It means being able to easily return a web-purchased product without a hassle, getting product questions answered by a person, being told immediately when there is a problem with a recently purchased product, and having a returned credit card purchase refunded without delay. Customers want their problems solved or better yet, not to have problems at all. Even businesses that find the eCRM approach beyond their present capacities should learn the basic lesson of eCRM. Satisfying customers, as difficult as it may sometimes appear, is the best investment any business can make.[43]

### ✔ CONCEPT CHECK

1. Why might eCRM create privacy concerns?
2. Who benefits from a well-executed eCRM process?
3. Should eCRM be a total channel approach?

# Summary

## Place Fundamentals

Place is where buyers purchase products and how products get there. Marketing channels are supply channels at the front end and distribution channels at the back end. Supply channels provide *upstream value* by bringing raw materials, supplies, and parts directly into production and furnishing equipment and materials to maintain and operate the enterprise. Many intermediaries and marketplaces have gone online buying and selling supply channel products. Distribution channels provide *downstream value* by bringing finished products to end users. Although many channel processes do not directly involve consumers, they are the ultimate focus of all place activities. Channel members (intermediaries) contribute value-added services at each touch point in the channel. Intermediaries help even out discrepancies between supply and demand. Suppliers are individuals or businesses that make up a supply channel. Supply channels often are led by powerful manufacturers or retailers. This is also true online, where powerful bricks-and-clicks retailers are beginning to dominate etailing. Online supply channels exist for goods, services, and digital products. They usually are very direct with few intermediaries. Supply exchanges are horizontal or vertical. Enterprise and consumer products for the most part have different distribution channels. Distribution channels can be direct, dual, or multichannel. Although some direct clicks-only channels still exist, most web storefronts and content sites are dual or multichannel. Agents, brokers, wholesalers, resellers, transporters, and retailers are some distribution channel members that are all represented online. Logistics/physical distribution (PD) intermediaries store, handle, and move products through channels and ultimately to end users.

## Place Issues

Place changes eventually will directly and/or indirectly affect all enterprises, from the largest global corporations to the smallest businesses. Disintermediation is the collapsing of channels; that is, removing intermediaries from supply and/or distribution channels to reduce costs, increase efficiency, and better serve customer needs. The initial assumption was that online distribution would result in an overwhelming amount of disintermediation, but this has not been the case. Reintermediation is creating a distribution channel. Many of the original clicks-only sites are finding that they must have more than one channel. Channel cannibalization is the loss of sales in an existing channel when a new channel is introduced to sell the same products. It is a serious problem online since bricks-and-clicks that sell online may undermine their retail partners offline. Internet metamarkets are clusters of activities and vendors that consumers perceive to be related and complementary. Automatic replenishment in enterprises is a straight rebuy. With consumers it is a strategy with great potential and is beginning to be offered at some web sites. Multilevel marketing (MLM) is a form of direct selling involving many levels of distributors who bring in new distributors to purchase products, sell to consumers, and recruit others who will also become distributors. It is both a distribution practice and personal selling. The Internet's interactivity is a natural attractant for MLM activities because it is easy to build customers relationships online.

## Consumer Channel Strategies

Many online channel strategies are evolutionary, not revolutionary. Online consumers want convenience, information, speed, privacy and security, service, simplicity, and convergence with offline stores. Internet retailing (etailing) has been called the third significant transformation of the retail industry. Almost 70 percent of online retailers are bricks and clicks. Catalog retailers are more likely to be profiting online. With the mass migration of bricks-and-clicks retailers online, there are few if any retail types that are not online. Etailers are concerned about the high rate of shopping basket abandonment. Browsing consumers can also result in sales online. Consumers have shown how much they like online auctions, the primary mechanism for consumers to become online sellers.

## Customer Relationship Management

Customer relationship management is an advance over previous marketing approaches, which cast marketers and customers as adversaries, emphasized short-term sales over lifetime value, and tended to treat all customers the same. eCRM is a five-stage process that is particularly well suited to the Internet environment and its unique interactivity. This approach means that all customers are not be treated the same. Higher-spending customers receive better treatment because they have higher lifetime value or customer share, the relative share of revenue a customer produces and projects over his or her purchasing lifetime. A long-term relationship locks in high-value customers that incur high costs if they take their business elsewhere. Databases, data warehouses, and the technology to mine them form the basis for the process used to develop customer profiles. eCRM is not an easy process to get right, nor is it feasible for all businesses. Even those that find the eCRM approach beyond their present capacities should learn the basic lesson of eCRM. Satisfying customers, as difficult as it may sometimes appear, is the best investment any business can make.

## Internet Marketing Application

The eighth-largest retailer in the United States is online. No, it is not Target, Kroger, or Sears. It is the AAFES Exchange Store (*http://www.aafes.com*). AAFES is the Army and Air Force Exchange Service, which has been serving military personnel for over 106 years and today has 7.3 million customers at military bases in the United States, Europe, and the Pacific. AAFES is a profit center that returns 100 percent of its earnings back to customers for programs that improve their quality of life. Since 1990 over US$2 billion has been contributed to army and air force libraries, sports programs, swimming pools, youth activities, hobby shops, and similar activities. It employs more than fifty thousand people, many of whom are military family members. The site has an extensive suppliers handbook online (*http://www.aafes.com/pa/selling/index.html*) with specific instructions for selling to the exchange. Military customers have many of the same concerns as their civilian counterparts. How does AAFES deal with security issues? Does it allow the resale of products purchased on the site? Who can shop the site? Who cannot? Look at the drop-down menu in the Customer Information options. What topics are not unique to military consumers? Look at the page About AAFES (*http://www.aafes.com/pa/default.asp*) and see if the site uses email permission marketing. How different is this retailer from its civilian equivalents?

## Chapter Review Questions

1. Why do you think people do not associate place/distribution with marketing?
2. What is a value chain? Why should marketers be concerned about them?
3. Why are supply channel functions sometimes outsourced?
4. Explain how disintermediation is being tried in flowers.
5. Why would a business cannibalize its own channels?
6. Why is automatic replenishment considered a potentially valuable consumer strategy?
7. Is speed important to all consumers?
8. What are Internet kiosks? How are they used?
9. Is shopping basket abandonment really a problem?
10. What can an etailer do to avoid shopping basket abandonment?
11. What evidence can you offer that consumers like online auctions?
12. Explain the importance of the lifetime value of a customer.
13. How might a business estimate the lifetime value of a customer?
14. Explain the stages of establishing eCRM.
15. What is customer share and why is it important in eCRM?

## Ford and E-automobility

Henry Ford, a machinist and engineer with the Edison Company, built his first experimental car in a workshop behind his house in 1892. In 1903 he founded the Ford Motor Company and began building the first Ford cars by hand in a small assembly plant in Detroit, Michigan, USA. The Model T was introduced in 1908. In 1913, Ford built the first moving mass production automobile assembly line. Ford's revolutionary business mission was to build a motorcar for the great multitudes, creating mass personal *automobility*. Prior to the Model T, motorcars were built by hand for wealthy status symbol seeking consumers. A Model T in 1909 cost just US$825, was reliable, and easy to drive. It had four cylinders and a semiautomatic transmission and ran on a twenty-horsepower engine. Ford could mass-produce cars so cheaply because he cut production costs and controlled raw materials and distribution. He paid skilled labor enough to reduce turnover, and raw materials were cheap and abundant.

Within ten years, Ford produced more than half the automobiles sold in the United States and operated over twenty assembly plants around the world. Ford Motor Company was the largest automobile producer in the world. The company relied on suppliers to keep its assembly lines operating and dealerships to distribute its cars and trucks to buyers. Dealers were signed up and facilities built to show cars, store parts, and house repair services. Ford introduced installment sales to automobiles during the 1920s, establishing the practice of purchasing expensive consumer goods on credit.

Mass automobility changed America. The steel and petroleum industries were direct beneficiaries. It allowed people to move to the suburbs. Automobiles needed better roads, so highways were built. It stimulated travel and tourism, and led to the largest public works program in history, the Interstate Highway Act of 1956. A hundred years ago, Henry Ford dealt with a linear channel process. He negotiated contracts face to face with suppliers to provide steel, paint, rubber, and other raw materials and parts to operate his assembly plants. Automobiles were mass-produced in those plants,

then assortments were transported to Ford dealers in the United States, Canada, and around the world. Each intermediary did his own specialized job, and most were independent owner/operators. Consumers visited Ford dealerships, drove the cars, kicked the tires, negotiated prices and terms, placed an order, and after a wait of varying lengths, returned to the dealership to pick up the new car and drive away, only to return when the automobile needed service, repairs, or parts.[44]

Henry Ford would be amazed to see how the automotive industry has changed. His emphasis on mechanization and mass production has been transformed and the company he founded is now into digitization and mass customization. Perhaps someday in the near future, customers will truly be able to customize their new automobile, order and pay for it online, purchase insurance online, then have the car delivered to their home by a common carrier. This vision will transform the automobile industry and radically change the nature of automobile dealerships turning them into primarily service and repair centers.

### CHECK IT OUT

Are there advantages to the traditional U.S. way of automobile distribution for the consumer? For the dealer? What should be retained of the traditional process and how can it be integrated into Internet-based automobile distribution? What advantages should there be from purchasing an automobile directly online from the manufacture? Visit the Ford Motor Company web site (*http://ford.com*) and check out the *Shopping Guide*. Is this a feature customers want? How efficiently does it work? Is it better than visiting a dealer's showroom?

### A GLOBAL PERSPECTIVE

Ford is truly an international company as illustrated by its branded lines—Volvo, Mazda, Jaguar, Aston Martin, and Land Rover in addition to traditional U.S. brands. Can buyers purchase Ford automobiles online in other countries or does Ford use its international sites as lead generators? Begin with Australia (*http://www2.ford.com.au/buyonlinev2/buyFrameset.asp*) and see what Ford sells online.

# CHAPTER TWELVE

## *The Promotion Mix*

### LEARNING OBJECTIVES

- To identify how marketing promotion is affected by the Internet
- To learn what online promotion issues concern Internet marketers and why
- To understand why some online advertising strategies are successful while others are not
- To analyze how sales promotions and permission marketing can be used effectively online

### Fiona Cans Spam

When Fiona checked her email this morning she found ten new unsolicited commercial email (UCE) messages. She quickly deleted each one without reading it. Every day more unwanted email messages clog her in box. Sometimes she finds them frightening; other times they are embarrassing or just irritating. She is particularly offended by messages with subject lines that read *Make zillions at home* or *Increase your sexual potency*. She is also irritated by streaming video emails she receives from etailers whose sites she has no intention of visiting. Spam email is bad enough, but every time she goes to her favorite weather site, up pops a persistent *pop-under* half-screen advertisement (ad) that opens behind the browser. When she leaves the site, the spawned ad remains open and she has to click on it to clear the screen. Whatever happened to the late 1990s Internet where easily ignored banner ads were the primary form of online promotion? Is this the price of commercialization, to be hounded by ads wherever she goes on the Web and hostage to spam cluttering her email box?

Unfortunately, Fiona is not alone in feeling overwhelmed and angered by spam email and annoying web ads. This is a growing problem for Internet marketers because it threatens the effectiveness of their online promotions and their ability to reach receptive target audiences and generate revenue. Marketers are faced with a deepening dilemma—how to successfully cut through the growing clutter, that is, the increasing numbers of sites, pages, and promotions, to reach buyers without antagonizing them and risking a backlash. The challenge is to make marketing promotions more effective and meaningful to target audiences, both online and off, increasing their value in alerting buyers to important information about new products, special offers, new web sites, and events. At the same time, marketers must accept reasonable limits on promotion, be more aggressive in protecting the privacy of target audiences, and continue searching for effective promotion tactics that accomplish their marketing goals.

**Promotion**

Marketing communication that is planned, persuasive, targeted, and designed to build awareness and brands, persuade, inform, remind, and entertain.

**Promotion** is planned, persuasive, targeted, goal-driven marketing communication. Primary online promotion goals are to build awareness, brand and rebrand, position and reposition products, increase traffic to sponsors' web sites and/or offline stores, and sell products. Effectively executed and targeted promotion can stimulate demand, differentiate a product from its competitors, and make a sale. This chapter examines promotion fundamentals and issues that concern marketers. It concludes with a closer examination of advertising, sales promotions, and permission marketing.

# Promotion Fundamentals

All promotions are advertising, right? Actually, that is not the case. Traditional marketing promotion is attention-grabbing advertising (electronic, print, outdoor, etc.), sales promotions, personal selling, publicity/public relations, and direct marketing. The average person is bombarded with hundreds if not thousands of commercial messages each day in his or her morning newspaper, on television, through telephone sales calls, and on clothing and store signs, highway billboards, bus signs, sides of trucks, and the Internet. This barrage of information has made everyone an expert on marketing promotion and, frequently, its vocal critics.

**Message**

The contents of communication used by marketers to promote products.

Internet promotion, like Internet commercialization, is in its infancy and currently represents only a fraction of total promotion revenue production. Many approaches are being tried; some have already been found lacking, and others are very promising.

**Feedback**

Audience comments and actions associated with the marketing communication that may be used to refine the message and/or change the channel or product.

## THE PROMOTION PROCESS

Marketers use promotion to send a **message,** a set of words, images, and symbols *encoded* by a sender, conveyed through a channel to a receiver, *decoded* by the receiver, and either acted on immediately or stored in the receiver's memory for later use. Audience responses provide **feedback,** comments and actions related to the message, channel, or product that may be used to refine the message and/or change the channel or product. **Noise,** which can distort or block the message at any point, can result when the sender or receiver's computer crashes, the receiver's computer takes forever to download rich media ads, the receiver is distracted while viewing an animated banner ad, or a consumer like Fiona deletes commercial email messages before reading them.

**Noise**

Anything that distorts or blocks the message at any point during the marketing communication process.

Promotion can also be an **incentive,** an online cents-off coupon, product sample, two-for-one special, sweepstake, or other short-term inducement to immediately move a target audience toward an exchange, typically to make a purchase or, in the case of the sales force, to motivate them to increase their productivity. Senders (marketing communicators) create and convey a message that is typically paid for by an identified sponsor (advertiser). Ideally, the promotion delivery channel (media) distributes the message and/or incentive where and when it is most relevant to the audience (receivers). This does not always occur as planned.

**Incentive**

A promotion such as a cents-off coupon, product sample, sweepstake, or other short-term inducement to immediately move a target audience toward an exchange.

Traditional mass market promotion is a *one-to-many* distribution process. The same message or incentive is delivered simultaneously to a mass audience, perhaps as they watch the Super Bowl or World Cup matches, or repeated multiple times to catch the audience at different times over a week, month, or longer. The designation *mass market* is somewhat misleading. Even though advertisers at the World Cup may reach over a billion viewers, the audience is targeted by a shared interest in soccer.

Internet promotion has the potential to be *one-to-one*, although most businesses are not prepared to achieve this goal because it is costly and requires sophisticated software. Many web sites already mass-customize online promotion messages and incentives to deliver personally relevant messages to site visitors or email list members who fit specific criteria. Web site visitors identified by cookies can be matched to their purchase history and other personal data. This allows personal promotion messages and/or incentives to be sent to them one-to-one. Customization is a desirable advantage of Internet promotion; however, in addition to raising costs and requiring sophisticated software applications, it also raises serious privacy concerns (see Chapters 5 and 7). These processes are most likely to be used by the largest enterprises that can afford the technology and staffing costs. Even many international corporations are gathering data but not yet using it to personalize or customize promotions.

The Internet is primarily a *pull environment* where users link to a web site and pull content back to their computer or wireless device. It can also be a *push environment*, where content is pushed to the user's computer from a web site. For example, when a user signs up for financial news updates or customized weather reports, the content is pushed to his or her computer along with embedded promotions. A weather site may include embedded travel ads along with the weather report, while a travel site may include a weather button ad. When the user subscribes to an online email newsletter, the contents are pushed to his/her email box. Netscape.com (*http://my.netscape.com*) invites viewers to make the Netscape home page their *start page* and personalize the page settings, content, and layout by creating *My Netscape*. If they do, each time they boot up and go online, their personalized *My Netscape* page is the default page and appears first as the portal or gateway to the Web, along with associated ads. Content and promotions are pushed to their computer, but if they want detailed information, they must click through on the hypertext link. This is a *push-pull hybrid* that combines elements of both models. Getting a user to accept a site as his or her default page gives the site owner an opportunity to initiate a long-term relationship.

## PROMOTION GOALS

If marketing communications ceased, how would users know that new web sites are online and offering special services, content, or information, or that a web site has a new URL, name, or owner? How would they learn about special offers, discounts, coupons, sales, contests, or free samples? How would interested buyers find out about new and improved products, product line extensions, or new movies and CDs? Promotion communicates important marketing information to target audiences. Target market audience members may include consumers and/or enterprises that need/want a product and have the authority to make a purchase as well as the cash or credit to complete the exchange. It also reaches noninterested and sometimes hostile audiences that are uninterested in the message and irritated by its delivery. This is promotion *waste*. Reaching the wrong audience with the wrong message is far less costly online than offline, but it can still result in hard feelings and, possibly, negative word of mouth.

Ideally, promotion is supported by all marketing mix variables working together.

The best promotion is a good *product* sold at a fair *price* in a readily accessible *place* that benefits the buyer. Satisfied customers talk about good products in chat rooms, through email to friends, and via other electronic and nonelectronic channels. Their positive word of mouth is a priceless form of online promotion. An outstanding promotion, however, cannot deliver repurchases for a bad product, an unfairly priced product, or a good product that is unavailable. The quickest way to kill a bad product is with good promotion that moves an audience to product trial, then dissatisfaction, and negative comments to friends, family, and/or millions of strangers at Internet complaint (suck sites) sites.

Marketing promotions also remind buyers about products they have not purchased recently. Promotions can build goodwill and add value, position and reposition products, brand, rebrand, and entertain. New online promotion forms such as cybercinema minifilm ads, streaming web advercasts, floating animated ad overlays, and **advergaming** (embedding a brand in a custom-designed interactive game) can be highly entertaining. Their effectiveness is still being debated.

## THE PROMOTION MIX

The marketing mix is a conceptual framework for understanding the strategic use of the 4Ps. The **promotion mix** is a conceptual framework for understanding the strategic use of traditional promotion for communicating marketing messages and/or delivering incentives to target audiences. Marketing promotion is funded by a *promotion budget,* an amount allocated for planning, implementing, and evaluating promotion. A typical large-scale promotion campaign includes many forms implemented concurrently or sequentially, often online and offline in a complementary and *synergistic* effort. Synergistic promotion requires that all promotions deliver the same consistent, integrated message, design, and feel. This is not always easy to accomplish, but when it works, the impact on the audience is far greater than if promotions deliver uncoordinated, conflicting messages and images.

Offline ads are often effective at directing consumers to web sites and raising awareness of web companies and their products. Amazon.com (*http://www.amazon.com*), eBay (*http://www.ebay.com*), and AOL (*http://www.aol.com*) could not have become household words without massive offline promotion campaigns. AOL has mailed millions of floppy and CD-ROM disks with its software and offered the short-term incentive of free online time. e*TRADE rebranded itself E*TRADE Financial (*http://us.etrade.com/e/t/home*) during Super Bowl XXXVI in 2002 through ads and sponsorship of the halftime show. Its musical monkey ads and sponsorship built awareness of the rebranded company and drove traffic to its web site and associated offline services. e*TRADE also had considerable success with its 2001 Super Bowl monkey ads that raised top-of-mind awareness of the company's brand name 64 percent.

Other **promotion points of contact,** where an audience gains knowledge and forms a perception of a brand or product, are not directly included in a promotion budget or considered traditional promotion mix forms. They include such nontraditional promotion forms as the distinctive design of a perfume bottle, the visual appearance of a web storefront, product guarantees, or product delivery conditions. The Longaberger Company (*http://www.Longaberger.com*), which makes handwoven wood baskets, is an example. Its corporate headquarters building looks like one of the company's distinctive woven baskets, a seven-story, US$30 million basket with two handles, each

**Advergaming**
A promotion hybrid exclusively found online that uses custom-designed web site games to promote a brand.

**Promotion mix**
The promotion forms that include advertising, personal selling, direct marketing, sales promotion, and publicity/public relations.

**Promotion points of contact**
Where an audience forms a perception of a brand by coming into contact with some element that communicates an image or message about the brand.

weighing seventy-five tons.[1] The basket building is displayed on its web home page. All promotion points of contact are not as eye-catching as the Longaberger basket building, but points of contact are important instruments for communicating marketing messages, particularly building web site awareness, building brands, and driving traffic. They should be considered in the planning and management of promotion programs but rarely are.

Internet promotion is new and rapidly evolving. The stakes are high to find promotion that works well, capitalizes on the Internet's unique characteristics, and creates a satisfactory return on the promotion investment (p-ROI). Although all promotion mix forms are used online, some exploit the Internet's unique interactivity, immediacy, 24/7/365 availability, and reach far more effectively than others. Some are identical to offline promotion forms, others are adapted to the virtual environment, some are immediate and intimate, and others, like **search engine promotion** (promotion on search engines), are unique with no direct offline equivalent. The following section briefly introduces each of the promotion forms and illustrates their online use. Advertising, sales promotion, and email marketing are discussed at greater length later in the chapter.

**Search engine promotion**
Using search engines to promote a site.

**ADVERTISING** **Internet advertising** is the most visible promotion form and includes banner ads, sponsorships, interstitials and other rich media ads, pop-ups, pop-unders, onscreen floating overlays, classified ads, in-stream and gateway webcast ads, mini-movies, advergames, and other forms. Internet ads are commercial and sometimes noncommercial messages distributed on the Internet, intranets, and/or extranets, paid for by an identified sponsor and designed to build awareness, brand and rebrand, drive traffic, make a sale, remind, position and reposition products, and entertain. The sponsor's message is distributed to hosting web pages exactly as created and is clearly recognized as a paid-for message by an identified advertiser. Hypertext links directly deliver audience members to the advertiser's site *if* they click through. Target audiences rarely distinguish between marketing promotion forms and usually call all promotion advertising whether it is online or off.

**Internet advertising**
The most visible promotion form, which includes banner ads, advergames, sponsorships, interstitials and other rich media ads, pop-ups, pop-unders, classified ads, Yellow Pages, in-stream and gateway webcast ads, and other forms.

**SALES PROMOTIONS** **Internet sales promotions** are temporary inducements to stimulate demand, increase storefront traffic and/or sales, and/or encourage distribution channel members to distribute, stock, or purchase a product. Sales promotions are found on about 93 percent of commercial web sites.[2] Web sites run contests or sweepstakes or offer downloadable discount coupons for purchases made at offline retailers. They provide games, free product samples, or memberships in product clubs. Offline print catalogs increasingly include dollars-off coupons for purchases made from the company's web site in an effort to drive customers online and reduce offline call center costs. Incentives can quickly stimulate sales, unlike most advertising that often has a delayed effect.

**Internet sales promotion**
Temporary inducements to stimulate demand, increase storefront traffic and/or sales, or encourage distribution channel members to distribute, stock, or purchase a product.

**PERSONAL SELLING** Personal selling occurs when a salesperson interacts with potential or current customers face to face, door-to-door, by telephone, fax, or on the Internet, the Web, intranets, or extranets by email, instant messaging, live chat, or telephony. Salespeople are trained to provide information, answer questions, make offers, counter objections, overcome resistance, complete the sale, and provide postsale service. Personal selling plays a key role in enterprise promotion, although the cost per contact is very high and rising. Personal selling electronically from an extranet or web site is far less expensive than offline and can be as effective as traditional methods, particularly with relatively uncomplicated purchases. Some salespeople use email to make sales pitches directly to enterprise end users in an effort to bypass purchasing departments. Commercial email can be personalized, one-to-one. It can also be sent in bulk, one-to-many, as part of a large-scale email marketing campaign to a permission list or, less attractively, as unsolicited commercial email (UCE), spam or junk email. Many web sites provide sales service by email. IBM (*http://www.ibm.com*) combines online information with offline sales negotiations for its high-end enterprise computer systems.

**PUBLIC RELATIONS (PR)/PUBLICITY** Like advertising, public relations (PR) also has an identified sponsor that pays for the development and implementation of PR programs to create and maintain a favorable image and goodwill, persuade an audience, and/or generate traffic, which is often referred to as *identity building*. PR includes community-based events, open house plant tours, and other activities that generate a favorable impression. Many enterprises host live chats with company officials or schedule online events to launch new products or embellish the company's image. Some sites host virtual plant tours like those accessed through Superfactory (*http://www.superfactory.com/general_resources/tours.htm*).

Volvo North America (*http://volvocars.com*) held the first solely digital automobile launch in September 2000. Its S60 model was introduced online with no national television or national print support. Deals were made with AOL (*http://www.aol.com*) for banner and column ads placed on general and special interest pages in AOL's auto and men's areas and on MapQuest. AOL subscribers received special free-option offers up to US$2,100 on the S60, and giveaways occupied prime space on AOL's home page. More than five hundred thousand promotional CD-ROMs showcasing the car were mailed to current Volvo owners and top prospects. Targeted print advertising appeared in *Motor Trend* and *Car & Driver*. Volvo initiated the launch online because 89 percent of its Model 2000 owners are Internet users and a past purchase is a good predictor of a future purchase. Being the first to have an online automobile launch generated interest and considerable free media coverage, and it was also far cheaper than a traditional offline launch. The elaunch did not sit well with some Volvo dealers that felt prospective buyers should have been directed to their showrooms and not the Web. Undeterred, Volvo next used three new media channels—personal digital assistants (PDAs), Internet handheld wireless devices, and WebTV—to determine which media pulled best results for Volvo ads shown during 2001 NCAA basketball games. All messages directed receivers to *http://www.revolvolution.com* where they could enter a contest to win a Volvo S60. Cost of the two-week campaign was estimated at US$400,000 to US$600,000. Volvo, a division of Ford Motor Company, is aggressively testing new media channels, anticipating their importance will grow. At the time of the campaign, personal computer users far outnumbered other receivers in the United States, over 122 million to fewer than 9 million with PDAs, slightly over 29 million Internet handheld device users, and around 1.7 million with WebTV access.[3]

Pillsbury (*http://www.pillsbury.com*) began as a flour milling company in 1869. Today, its brands are marketed in more than seventy countries. Pillsbury has embraced online PR with its Pillsbury Bake-Off (*http://www.bakeoff.com*), an event with an over-fifty-year history. The Bake-Off, cosponsored by GE Appliances and Pillsbury,

**Viral marketing**
Directed word of mouth; getting customers and visitors to spread word about the site, product, and/or brand.

**WEB UPDATE**

Viral Marketing

has its own web site. The grand prize is US$1 million and over half its tens of thousands of entry registrations are received online, which fattens the Pillsbury database of mineable names for future email contact. The site offers Bake-Off recipes and encourages copying and distribution, a form of **viral marketing** or directed word of mouth that has customers spreading its brand name without additional cost to the company. The concept, drawn from biology, is analogous to the spread of a virus. Delicious Bake-Off recipes give customers a good reason to spread the word. Many sites encourage visitors to tell a friend by sharing a page or information. A positive recommendation, site endorsement, or web page sent from a friend or family member carries more weight than other promotions. Are friends spamming friends on behalf of companies? If the friends did not ask to receive the commercial message, then it is spam even if it did not come directly from the company. Having a friend deliver the message makes it far more palatable but raises troubling issues about fairness and taking advantage of customers.

Publicity is promotion that provides information to the media for use in a hard or soft news story, or editorial. When a press release is distributed to third parties, reporters receiving it can use all, some, or none of the information provided. The message may gain credibility and believability if it is not directly paid for by an identified sponsor, but the sponsor loses control over the message, and media distortions or misreporting can produce unwanted and sometimes unexpected results. The press release may even be totally ignored. Most corporate web sites have pressrooms with archived press releases for publicity purposes. Others send press releases by email to media targets—newspapers, magazines, radio, and television. Online pressrooms like Forrester Research's (*http://www.forrester.com/ER/Press/0,1772,0,00.html*) post press releases that describe what the company is doing and contain information about current marketing research that students may find valuable in their classes. They also email press releases to media in the expectation that greater exposure will lead to increased sales of their proprietary reports. PR Newswire (*http://www.prnewswire.com*) is a business that posts and emails targeted press releases to interested audiences. Its PRN Press Room (*http://media.prnewswire.com/en/jsp/main.jsp*) is a free resource for journalists looking for stories. It is also a useful channel for businesses disseminating information. The caveat with all press releases is their objectivity. Enterprises put positive spin on press releases even when the news is bad, so they must be read with caution. As a means of raising awareness and disseminating information, they play a useful promotion role.

**Internet direct marketing**
Marketing that includes click through advertising, interactive commercial email, web catalogs and brochureware, and online shopping networks.

**DIRECT MARKETING** Some marketers consider all Internet promotion direct marketing since it is interactive, creates personal contact with audience members, and encourages an immediate direct response. **Internet direct marketing** includes click through advertising, interactive commercial email, interactive web catalogs and brochureware, and online shopping networks like iQVC.com (*http://www.qvc.com*) or Home Shopping Network (*http://www.hsn.com*). Traditional direct marketing forms include catalog sales, direct mail letters, bill stuffers, direct response television ads, and telemarketing.

Something of a reversal is happening as clicks-only businesses adopt traditional direct marketing approaches to reach their target markets. For example, clicks-only web storefront EZiba (*http://www.eziba.com*) sells exotic handmade crafts and art objects from its web site but recently added ten hard-copy catalogs mailed to a highly target customer list. Amazon.com mailed Christmas and Father's Day catalogs for the first time in 2001 and, later, garden and home products catalogs with orders taken online or by toll-free telephone numbers. A glossy catalog can cost from US$0.50 to over US$1 per receiver if millions are mailed at low bulk mail rates. However, eZiba, Amazon, and others are learning that hard-copy catalogs drive buyers to web sites, just like web ads can drive customers offline to make a purchase. Interactive online marketing is a natural extension of offline traditional direct marketing.[4]

## PROMOTION DELIVERY CHANNELS

**Promotion delivery channels**

Methods used to deliver promotions both online (the Internet and the Web) and offline, including web-enabled elevators, taxi tops, and gasoline pumps.

Before the Internet's commercialization, promotion typically was delivered through such traditional **promotion delivery channels** as face-to-face personal selling, electronic mass media (television, radio), print media (magazines, newspapers), outdoor (billboards, kiosks), and direct mail. Recent channel additions include computer disks, facsimile (fax) machines, bill stuffers, automobile and bus wraps, grocery store floors, and even print ads placed on public toilet stall doors. Some of the same delivery channels are used online in electronic form, others are different, and a number are impossible to use in an electronic environment. Some channels link the offline and online, as in net-ready ad-flashing gasoline pumps that allow customers to view interactive Internet ads while filling up. Another form is Vert Intelligent Displays (VID at *http://www.vert.net*), a web server that displays ads from taxi-top electronic billboards. The small billboards are mounted on taxi hoods and continuously display eye-catching ads. They represent the integration of wireless Internet, Global Positioning System (GPS) technology, and video. The advertising message changes as the taxi moves from one city block, neighborhood, or zip code to another. In a financial district, the billboards deliver streaming stock quotes, passing through an Hispanic neighborhood an advertising message is delivered in Spanish, and near a medical center the message is health-related. Messages are in color and displayed on high-resolution, bright screens.[5]

Companies like Pillsbury are using the Internet to create *buzz*, encouraging word-of-mouth communications where consumers communicate among themselves about products. Yahoo! (*http://buzz.yahoo.com*) measures online buzz, identifying buzz *movers* and *leaders* of the moment on Yahoo! Identifying what is *hot* can help others decide what movie to see, DVD to buy, or television program to watch. Buzz can also be dangerous. Boo.com (*http://boo.com*), a clicks-only trendy apparel site, became a victim of its own buzz. It was initially scheduled to become an interactive selling site in early 1999. The launch failed to happen as delays set in. The promotion campaign was re-worked and finally implemented for a July launch of the site. An enormous amount of buzz was generated about the site before the storefront opened. Then technical problems delayed the site launch again until November. In the meantime, the promotion campaign was generating great interest in a nonoperational web site. Heavily front-loading the promotion campaign to create buzz without first determining what buyers liked about the site built up expectations that Boo could not deliver; thus, Boo created buzz but disappointed customers. Boo is estimated to have burned through £100 million (around US$141.5 million). It went bankrupt, and later its technology and name were sold for £340,000 (around US$481,000). Boo has since reappeared as Fashionmall.com. Clearly, front-loading promotion prior to a product's introduction or site launch can be a very risky strategy, particularly on the Internet where buyer patience is short.[6]

## PROMOTION TARGETS

Promotion sponsors do not want to waste their money sending messages to disinterested or inappropriate targets, so they attempt to select audiences receptive to their market offers. Targets can be defined broadly—for example, U.S. men ages thirty to fifty-five years—or narrowly—for example, male college graduates, ages forty-five to fifty-five, white-collar professionals living in urban areas of one million or more population, married with two children under the age of fifteen, avid golfers who recently purchased US$200 or more of golf equipment online. The narrow, or *niche,* definition relies on purchase history, and demographic and psychographic (lifestyle) data to identify targets for email commercial messages or customized online ads.

Targets can also be part of a mass online market, just like mass marketing offline. An example is the campaign for the X10 wireless video camera. Ads (*http://ads.x10.com/ yahoo3/yahoo18_neleh.htm*) were online everywhere throughout 2001 and 2002 as half-screen persistent pop-unders that spawned their own window underneath the viewer's browser screen. The low cost of online advertising compared with traditional offline allowed the delivery of virtually unlimited numbers of ads to an increasingly irritated mass market of receivers. However, the mass market approach was effective, and the X10 gained awareness and click throughs. X10.com (*http://www.X10.com*) was fourteenth on the list of most popular web destinations in April 2001, just three places below eBay.[7]

Consumers are the principal targets of most web advertising and sales promotions. However, commercial email is targeted to both consumers and enterprises, and the amount of enterprise B2B email is growing rapidly. Its ability to reach receivers at work is unsurpassed. Some web advertising is targeted to both audiences on sites where both consumers and enterprises shop or info-search for travel information (Orbitz.com at *http://www.orbitz.com*), maps (Mapquest.com at *http://www.mapquest.com*), or office supplies (Office Depot at *http://www.officedepot.com*). Enterprise intranets are used for promotions targeted to a company's employees, motivating them to sell more, urging compliance with safety rules, or encouraging enrollment in training classes. Promotions are targeted on extranets to select channel members. B2B ads have a powerful advantage online as they reach workers during work hours when they are online and able to take immediate action. B2B ads can be personalized based on cookie tracking information stored on the worker's hard drive.

Marketing promotion is performed by nonprofit organizations, governments, causes and individuals as well as businesses. Not-for-profit organizations such as the American Red Cross (*http://www.redcross.org*) use online promotions to increase awareness about their activities, collect relief donations, arrange gifts or planned giving, recruit volunteers, and generate goodwill. After the terrorist attacks on September 11, 2001, many web sites began displaying Red Cross click through boxes on their front pages, urging visitors to donate to the Red Cross Relief Fund for victims in New York and Washington, D.C. Hundreds of millions of U.S. dollars were raised this way, and the sites did not charge for the space.

The Advertising Council (*http://www.adcouncil.org*) targets individuals and enterprises with public service announcements (PSAs) on television, radio, newspapers, magazines, out-of-home, and the World Wide Web (see the screen shot on p. 317). Online banner PSAs are created pro bono by some of the country's top advertising agencies and placed on donated web space. Recent PSAs were developed for child abuse, domestic violence prevention, colon cancer detection and prevention, crime prevention, drunk driving prevention, and fire safety on space donated by various web page owners.

**Online PSAs**

The Advertising Council promotes its public service ad campaigns on the Web.
*Source: Reprinted by permission of The Advertising Council. http://www.adcouncil.org.*

## PROMOTION DIRECTS BEHAVIOR

Promotion decisions are often based on the assumptions of a hierarchy-of-effects model first proposed in the 1960s. The model proposes that promotion, particularly advertising, helps move some target audience members through steps that climax in purchase and repurchase. Promotion makes an audience *aware* of a brand or product. After awareness they develop product *knowledge* through repeated exposures to product messages. Hopefully, the audience develops *liking*, a *preference* for the brand, and *conviction* that it is the best one for them, which leads to a *behavioral intention*. All things being equal, intention should lead to *purchase* and *repurchase*, although this certainly does not always happen. This is a rational model based on high audience involvement with the product. Some target audience members will not respond to promotion or move through the steps, regardless of the effectiveness of the campaign. Others will start moving through the steps but break off before they purchase. Repurchase is what most marketers strive for, as customer retention is far less costly than new customer acquisition.

Most products are not involving and represent a casual choice between comparable (parity) products. Rather than a rational stepwise approach to purchase, these product decisions rely on emotions and feelings. Since the Internet is a low- or no-emotion environment, generating emotional content in online promotions is not easy. Some online promotion is exciting like the dynamic flash-based banner ads used for gambling sites. Persistent pop-unders for the X10 *Amazing Video Camera* add a human touch by devoting a third or more of the large rectangular banner to an engaging, smiling face. Classmates (*http://www.classmates.com*) makes an appeal to aging baby boomers to *Rediscover Your Past* by registering and locating classmates from high school. The site and its banner ads show pictures of 1960s and 1970s high school students.

Advertising can be effective in raising consumer awareness as illustrated by the online promotion campaign for Bristol-Myers Squibb's Vaniqa (*http://www.vaniqa.com*), the first and only prescription cream that slows unwanted facial hair growth in women. When the online advertising campaign began, the product had only 23 percent awareness in the target audience. After one exposure to a skyscraper ad, awareness rose to 30 percent (a 30 percent increase); one exposure to a large rectangle raised awareness to 33 percent (a 43 percent gain).[8]

Coca-Cola, a brand with almost 100 percent consumer awareness, wanted online advertising to increase interest and purchase intention among teens and twenty-somethings. The company ran very large banners, skyscrapers, and large rectangular ads on the Snowball.com (*http://www.snowball.com*) Network's IGN.com, which calls itself the leading network for Generation i-Internet. Skyscrapers increased purchase intention from 58 to 63 percent, and large rectangulars increased it from 58 percent to 65 percent. The conclusion is that ad size can increase awareness.[9]

Involvement is another indicator of whether an ad will register with receivers. If receivers are involved with a product or buying situation, or feel emotional about the sender, they tend to be more engaged with an associated ad. However, this also applies to web site content. If a receiver is highly involved with compelling web site content, it reduces the probability that he or she will break off contact with the site and react to an ad or click through. To increase awareness, ads should be associated with site content. For example, ads for food and food preparation equipment on recipe, health, and nutrition sites. Ideally, visitors should be able to access the ads without leaving the content site.

## PROMOTION PLANNING

Effective promotion requires planning by in-house marketers, outside promotion agency specialists, or both working together. Promotion planners must consider the target audience, their characteristics, preferences, and how and where to reach them. Cost is a major consideration, as online promotion can be expensive to create, implement, and evaluate, although it is often less so than offline promotion. Another factor is the economy, as a downturn often results in sharp reductions in promotion budgets at a time when promotion is most needed. Planners should evaluate how the competition is promoting its products, whether government or industry self-regulation will affect or restrict a promotion form, if cultural or legal constraints exist, and the availability of promotion distribution channels. Planning should include strategies for developing synergy by integrating online and offline efforts.

### ✔ CONCEPT CHECK

1. What are the goals of marketing promotion?
2. What traditional promotion forms are used online?
3. Why is promotion planning important?

# Promotion Issues

The Internet has the potential to intensify the promotion message, achieving one-to-one intimacy that is rare offline, and to improve accountability. At the same time, the Internet has limitations that can weaken some promotion forms. Three problems are its lack of emotion, which leaves email messages open to misinterpretation and makes banner ads flat and unengaging, clutter, which is even greater than what is found offline, and irritation quotient, persistent on-screen promotions and spam that can be exceedingly irritating.

## CONSUMERS IN CONTROL?

Consumers have always had the power to ignore marketing promotion, throw away junk mail, or turn off the radio or television. They can opt out of direct marketing lists by registering with the Direct Marketing Association (*http://www.the-dma.org/cgi/*

*offmailinglistdave*), the national trade association of direct marketers. This will not stop all direct marketing contacts, but it should reduce their numbers. Consumers can control telemarketing calls by using caller identification technology that screens out unknown, unwanted callers. Television viewers use remote controls to channel surf or tape programs and avoid commercials entirely.

At the same time that consumers try to exert control, marketers try to counter it. When there were only three national television networks, advertisers could set up *roadblocks*, showing the same commercial on all three networks at the same time to capture channel changing consumers. Today, cable and television channel proliferation makes a roadblock extremely expensive and difficult or impossible to implement. It can be accomplished online. **Web page roadblocks** occur where one advertiser purchases all available advertising space on a page or a site owner serves house ads only. Pepsi and Yahoo! collaborated to organize an online roadblock on Yahoo! for the launch of a new Pepsi television commercial starring pop music star Britney Spears. Two hours before the commercial was to be aired at the 2001 Academic Awards, it was broadcast on Yahoo!, then archived by Pepsi (*http://www.pepsi.com/current/index.html*). Yahoo! also ran current Pepsi ads with Britney Spears. The Pepsi roadblock was the first Internet premier for a broadcast television commercial. Pepsi purchased every available advertising unit on Yahoo! for the forty-eight hours prior to the commercial's debut. During this period, twenty to twenty-five different banner ads rotated throughout Yahoo! pages. They included large rectangle flash ads that recorded a 10 percent click through rate. Skyscraper banners registered a 1.5 percent click through, while traditional banners had a 1 percent rate. Pepsi also delivered one million commercial emails announcing the event, primarily to an in-house collected list where 68 percent were in the company's prime target audience, ages thirteen to thirty-four. By early 2002, the commercial had been viewed over two million times.[10]

Consumers and enterprises can avoid roadblocks or any online ads by clicking past the page or installing ad-blocking software like AdSubtract.com (*http://www.adsubtract.com*) or WebWasher.com (*http://www.webwasher.com*). AOL subscribers can access their Marketing Preferences commands to block pop-ups. For those who see the ads, a roadblock can raise their awareness and their irritation by viewing repetitions.

More web sites are resorting to aggressive tactics to corral visitors. In addition to spawning ads like pop-ups and persistent pop-unders that launch an ad on entering, exiting, or triggering a command, some sites mouse-trap. A mouse-trapped visitor is forced to stay on the site, unable to go forward or backward or to exit. Often the only resort is to reboot. Fear of an audience backlash has convinced some advertisers to back off host-initiated instant streaming audio technology. In this technology, an endless audio loop begins broadcasting in rich audio as soon as a visitor downloads a hosting page. Visitors may have to reboot their computers to stop the loop. Advertisers also are using less irritating opt-in audio ads, where the visitor must initiate contact for audio to play. Audio ads increase click throughs up to 7 percent, so they are not likely to disappear.[11]

Consumers are increasingly exposed to large, intrusive ads that slow page downloads. For example, it's not unusual to find a 39K web home page loaded with a 17K skyscraper, 14K big box, 9K banner, 3K button, and 7K house ad. The ads take up more space than page content. While ad-blocking software can solve the problem, there is a downside. Ad blocking denies site owners the opportunity to *monetize* their web space. If ad blocking catches on, advertising revenue will fall and more site owners

**Web page roadblocks**
Refers to when one advertiser purchases all available advertising space on a page or a site owner serves house ads only.

may be forced to charge for content, find other ways of generating revenue, or join the ranks of dead dot-coms.[12] This is where accommodation is needed; advertisers should have access to consumers but avoid needlessly irritating them.

## PROMOTION INTEGRATION

**Promotion synergy**
The result that occurs when promotion forms work together in an integrated, coordinated way, communicating the same relevant, consistent message.

Promotion forms online and offline must work together so the overall effect is consistent and greater than if only one form or environment had been used. An Internet *integrated marketing promotion* approach avoids sending conflicting messages about a product that may confuse the audience. When promotion forms work together in an integrated, coordinated way, communicating the same relevant, consistent message, the effect is magnified and results in **promotion synergy,** where the whole promotion effect is greater than its individual parts. This occurs in both directions: Online promotions can drive traffic to offline stores or events, and offline promotions can drive traffic to web sites. In a recent study, a majority of respondents (70 percent) said television ads, word of mouth, and newspaper sources were the reason they went online to visit a particular web site. Web and magazine ads were less motivating, and the least helpful were radio ads, direct mail, and out-of-home ads like billboards.[13]

**WEB UPDATE**

*Online-Offline Promotion Synergy*

## CLUTTER AND SEARCH ENGINE PROMOTION

**Web advertising clutter**
A multidimensional problem of glut created by growing numbers of ads, email messages, and web sites and pages.

**Email clutter**
A glut of ads, sales promotions, and email spam.

Clutter is created by growing numbers of online ads, email messages, sales promotions, web sites, and pages. **Web advertising clutter** makes it difficult for marketers' messages to be received because the large number of ads, including those on the same page, tend to block the view. It is growing because more owners are trying to monetize their sites by selling advertising space on their pages, ads are getting bigger and more intrusive, more ads are loaded on pages, and more sites are going online. New commercial sites often host their own *house ads,* sell space to advertisers, and advertise on other sites. **Email clutter** is growing because more commercial email is being sent to growing numbers of receivers, and messages are changing from text-only to high-bandwidth streaming media (audio and video). The average buyer must sift through an almost overwhelming amount of clutter to locate personally meaningful and useful marketing communications.

Web clutter also makes it more difficult for promotion to drive traffic. Hundreds if not thousands of new web sites go online each day worldwide. As the clutter grows, marketers are beginning to recognize the effectiveness of search engines as clutter cutters. Nine out of ten Internet users visit a search engine or use a search engine on a portal or community site. They also revisit at least five times monthly. Fifty-seven percent of Internet users search the Web daily, the second most frequent Internet activity after email (81 percent). Consumers are more likely to initiate product searches by typing the product name at a search engine (28 percent) than linking directly to a store URL (23 percent), typing in the brand (9 percent) or store (5 percent) name in the search engine, using a search engine's shopping area (5 percent), or clicking on a banner ad (4 percent). Search engine listings are low-cost, highly relevant, consumer-initiated actions when interest is high. Search engines beat standard banner or button advertising in creating favorable brand impressions and leading visitors to web sites. Search listings are more effective than ads in brand recall, favorable opinion, and purchase intention. Brand recall was three times better with search listings than ads.[14]

**Bid search engines**
When web site owners bid for placement to have their site listing appear first or at the top of a search list.

A growing number of web site owners use **bid search engines** to make sure their site comes up near the top of the list when a keyword search is conducted. Owners bid against one another to have their listing placed at the top of the search queue. Each time a visitor clicks on their link, the site owner has to pay the amount of the accepted bid. The average price is US$0.19 per click. Advertisers pay only for qualified lead traffic by click through. If a site owner bids US$0.05 per click and receives a hundred clicks in a week, the cost is US$5. Since bids change frequently, a top listing that sold for US$0.05 will likely be higher next week. For some search engines, bid search payments generate as much as 50 percent of their revenue.

Bid search placements are attacked by organizations that believe special bid fees undermine the validity of Internet searches and violate federal laws against deceptive advertising. Little if any screening is performed on the top-listed sites. Commercial Alert, a consumer activist watchdog group, says search engines are abandoning their objectivity without letting users know how concealed fees affect rankings.[15]

Another search engine promotion tactic is to identify the most popular search terms, then insert the terms in web page source code as metatags (see "Metatags" below). A growing number of sites track search term requests and sell the information. BestKey-Words (*http://www.bestkeywords.asmartbiz.com*) compiles reports from web search engines on the most used search terms and how many sites are using them in their source code. Most search engines also list top search terms, although the information can be difficult to find. Many have hidden pages with unfiltered search terms. These pages typically have disclaimers and block underage visitors or those who do not agree to site terms, because the lists are heavy on keywords related to *sex* and *porn*. Analysis of key word usage provides insights into the development of effective metatag coding.

## *Metatags*

A metatag is two or more lines of Hypertext Markup Language (HTML) code describing web page contents. Information in a metatag is used by search engines to index a page so someone searching for that information can find it. The metatag is placed in the heading at the top of the HTML in a web page. Most important metatags for search engine indexing are *keywords* and *description* metatags. Keywords list the words or phrases that best describe page contents. Description is a one- or two-sentence description of the page. Both the keywords and the description are used by search engines in indexing the page. Most search engines also use page contents as a way of determining how to index it. Skillfully written metatags can help the page rank higher in search results. Metatags for an interactive advertising agency might appear as

<META NAME="description" CONTENT="A full-service interactive advertising, Internet marketing communications, online advertising agency with offices in Chicago, Illinois, Madison, Wisconsin, Philadelphia, Pennsylvania, and Cincinnati, Ohio">

<META NAME="keywords" CONTENT="advertising, interactive, Internet, marketing, communications, online, chicago, illinois, madison, wisconsin, philadelphia, pennsylvania, cincinnati, ohio, agency, agencies, banners, pop-ups, overlays, animations">

Most search engines and portals are loaded with ads. Of the major search engines, only Google.com accepts no advertising on its front page. Google reports performing more than 150 million searches per day and searches over two billion web pages. Its AdWords Select program offers cost-per-click (CPC) pricing that charges the advertiser only when a visitor clicks through on the ad. Ads can be changed as often as the advertiser wants and targeted by keywords, country, and language.

All businesses do not have an equal need to use search engine promotion. An IBM, Dell, Wal-Mart, or other well-known brand with a short, easy-to-remember URL is less likely to need help directing Internet users to its web site than a far smaller national or regional brand. A local brand with a very restricted geographical service area has even less need as its customer base and reach are exceedingly small by Internet standards. Small local businesses can drive local traffic to their web sites by other means, including the following:

- Placing their site URL on register tapes, packaging, and store signage
- Training salespeople to remind customers to visit the site for special offers
- Including their site URL on print and online classified ads
- Using reciprocal banner ads, web rings, and product-related communities where sites with similar content place links for one another on their sites
- Developing a house email distribution list for special offers and a periodic store newsletter
- Asking online customers to email a friend about the site
- Creating descriptive metatags in their web page source code

## CRITICISMS

Internet marketing promotion is highly visible and intrusive, often blocking a user's view of page content, clogging an email box, slowing download time, or even mouse-trapping, which helps explain why it is so often criticized. Longtime Internet users complain that promotion is excessive, clogs the Internet, and has accelerated commercialization. Promotion is criticized for targeting children, teens, compulsive gamblers, and other vulnerable audiences. Criticisms are mainly directed at advertising but complaints from consumers, enterprises, and regulators about commercial email are growing. Complaints about advertising include scams (deceptive promotions), promotions that target vulnerable audiences like children and the elderly, visual blight from ads cluttering web sites, tasteless advertising that some find offensive, and privacy issues associated with customizing ads and sales promotions.

Despite its criticisms, promotion is defended for its key role in letting buyers know about marketing offers. It provides information that increases competition, which exerts downward pressure on prices. Advertising revenues subsidize content sites and help keep most content free or nominally priced. Web PSAs are a public service, although they are not widely distributed. Promotion also provides employment for hundreds of thousands of people in the United States and worldwide.

Internet promotion is monitored and controlled by government at the federal, state, and local levels. The Federal Trade Commission (FTC at *http://www.ftc.gov*) hears complaints, investigates, and can mandate change, levy fines, or close sites. The FTC is particularly alert to email scams and supports legislation to limit junk email. Consumer protection laws extend to the prohibition of unfair advertising practices online and off. Promotion is regulated by state attorney generals and trade associations, the American Association of Advertising Agencies (*http://www.aaaa.org*), the Interactive Direct Marketing Association (*http://www.the-dma.org*), Better Business Bureau (*http://www.bbb.org*), and others.

## ✔ CONCEPT CHECK

1. Are Internet consumers in control of online promotion? Explain.
2. What is the advantage of online and offline promotion integration?
3. Are criticisms of Internet promotion justified?

# *Advertising Applications*

Internet promotion is still in its infancy; slightly over a decade's worth of results have accumulated. Lots of trial and error is happening online as marketers, site owners, agencies, and media try to figure out what works best and how to measure it.

## ADVERTISING OVERVIEW

Online advertising spending, around US$ 7.3 billion in 2001, is about 3 percent of total U.S. advertising spending. It is forecast to rise to almost US$9.3 billion by 2003 and US$20 billion by 2005, still far below total advertising spending, but a significant number when judged against US$0 spent online in 1994. More is spent advertising online than on outdoor advertising (US$1.8 billion) and almost as much as cable television advertising (US$11.2 billion).[16]

Internet advertising takes many forms, including banners, floating ads, interstitials, sponsorships, rich media, classifieds, referrals, keyword search, minimovies, advergames, and interactive ads in commercial email. Revenues from banner ads and sponsorships declined in 2001 but increased in 2002, while classifieds and keyword searches continued to generate increasing revenue. Traditional advertisers are moving more of their advertising budgets online. The largest spenders are in consumer brands (retail, music, automotive), computing, media, and financial services.

Most but not all Internet advertising is *direct response,* soliciting an immediate response from a target audience encouraged to click a hypertext link in a web page ad or commercial email. Repetitions build awareness, remind, and encourage audience members to store the promotion message for future use. They also irritate. Most online ads (63 percent) are directed toward branding, awareness, positioning, and informing an audience about features and benefits.

## ADVERTISING FORMS

**Banner ads**
Online interactive billboard-style marketing communication messages on or linked to web pages designed to raise awareness, build a brand, rebrand, and remind about a product, brand, and/or web site.

Internet advertising comes in different forms, but banner ads are still the most widely used although they declined from almost 60 percent of total Internet ad revenues in 1997 to 35 percent in Q3 2001. Other forms are being created as dissatisfaction with plain banners grows.

**BANNER ADS** Online **banner ads** are interactive billboard-style messages on or linked to web pages designed to raise awareness, build a brand, and remind about a product, brand, and/or web site. They can also be used as a directed path to a purchase.

The first web banner ads were placed by IBM on travel site Hotwire (*http://www. hotwire.com*) in 1994 and generated a 30 percent click through rate. By 2002, average banner click through rates had declined to between 0.3 and 0.75 percent. Although click through rates obviously are decreasing, that does not mean banners are ineffective, as they appear to be useful in branding and raising awareness, and their low cost and broad reach make them highly attractive for those purposes. Cost per thousand (CPM) in 2002 was a low US$6 to $60 depending on host site traffic.[17]

Banners come in many sizes and shapes. Although attempts at standardization are under way, ad sizes vary and are dictated by site property owners. If standardized banner ad sizes become widely accepted, advertisers will be able to place the same banner on multiple sites without resizing. The Interactive Advertising Bureau's (IAB at *http://www.iab.net*) Ad Unit Task Force has issued voluntary guidelines for **interactive marketing unit** (**IMU**) ad formats used by web publishers. The guidelines (*http:// www.iab.net/iab_banner_standards/bannersource.html*) are optional, and publishers can alter or disregard them. The Task Force is a committee made up of IAB members AOL, CNET Networks, Inc., DoubleClick, Excite@Home, MSB, New York Times, Walt Disney Internet Group, Yahoo!, and other top media companies. It meets biannually to review ad effectiveness and propose IMU format changes.

Some banners are getting larger in an effort to capture viewers' attention and make a more lasting impression. Viewers are increasingly finding skyscrapers, large rectangles, and big boxes on web pages. Big, aggressive, flashy ads build awareness, and larger ads with greater visual exposure are more likely to increase branding effectiveness. Studies have found that skyscraper and large rectangles can increase branding awareness for a single exposure by as much as 40 percent. Flash and DHTML (Dynamic HTML) lift branding metrics 19 percent. Large rectangles are even more effective than page pop-ups by 55 to 52 percent. Interstitials increase brand metrics over 194 percent. With more Internet users on fast connections, larger and more media-rich ads will be less irritating to download, which increases the probability that advertisers will use them. An exception is persistent pop-unders. While they get attention and may drive a mass audience to a web site, the gains in traffic do not convert to purchases. Relevance is more important than format in the case of pop-unders.[18]

These and other results must be viewed with caution. So many factors determine advertising effectiveness that size alone cannot be relied on as the deciding factor. However, it does appear that all things being equal, size is important and bigger is better, at least until consumers get bored and tune out or block online advertising entirely.

Banners are placed at various locations on a page. Initially, they were mostly at the top or bottom. Today they are positioned on all four sides, as well as in the middle with wraparound text and even as floating ad overlays that pop up somewhere on the page, then float to another area. While on screen, they block content. Preliminary evidence suggests that a top placement may draw more viewers, but this is not certain. Expandable banners allow the viewer to get more information or even make a purchase without leaving the original site through the use of pop-up minisites. Banner ads can pop up or pop under a page. Both types are persistent and must be removed with a click.

No universally applicable banner ad rules can possibly apply to all situations and products. However, some attributes can make banners more effective. Banner content

**Interactive marketing unit (IMU)**

Advertising size formats used by web publishers to standardize ads.

should be simple if branding is the objective. Banners should be surrounded by white or blank space to highlight the ad and focus on its contents. Since the Internet is an information-intense medium, high information content is appropriate in many product categories and particularly in B2B banner advertising. Banners should be unexpected, placed where receivers least expect them. Excessive use of animation or distracting creative elements can undermine awareness and branding effectiveness. The company or brand logo should be prominent. Repetition works, and at least five impressions per banner may be optimal for awareness, although this varies by industry. While the Internet is emotionless, a human face in banners increases interest and conveys an otherwise missing emotional link. Likewise, attention is drawn to branding characters, cartoons, or clever action figures whose dimensions, colors, or actions can be changed with a click. While many offline ads strive for humor, humor can be risky online, particularly if ads are directed toward an international audience. Banner ads should send users to the right place if they click through. Far too often, click throughs land users far from where they can make a purchase.[19]

**House ads**

Ads on a web site placed there by the site's owner to promote the site or a product sold on the site.

**HOUSE ADS**   All advertising is self-promoting, and **house ads** are self-promotions on an owner's own web site. AOL frequently uses persistent pop-up house ads, along with other advertisers' ads. In Q4 2000, house ads took up approximately 28 percent of advertising space on the top web sites. This was up from 15 percent earlier in the year. Up to 30 percent of ads on entertainment and societal sites are house ads, up to 22 percent on news and information sites. This self-promotion can dilute other advertisers' messages and reduce the rate they are willing to pay for ad space. Their effectiveness is also diluted by the clutter which is expected to grow from 620 marketing impressions per day per user to 950 in 2005.[20]

**Sponsorships**

Web page ads, usually the size of a small button banner ad, placed adjacent to content related to the sponsor's product.

**SPONSORSHIPS**   **Sponsorships** are web page ads, usually the size of a small button banner ad, placed adjacent to content related to the sponsor's product. For example, Nestlé Carnation Infant Nutrition sponsors YourBabyToday.com (*http://www. yourbabytoday.com/afronet*). The sponsorship announcement reads *We would like to thank our sponsor[Nestlé] for enabling us to produce this independent editorial program*. The tie-in between company and web content is obvious. The company helped prepare this special web editorial but is not mentioned in the contents. The sponsored content was offered without charge to site owners with related content and ran for twenty-six consecutive weeks on Baby Place, Mommy Place, Whole Family, and portals and ISPs. Site owners' benefit in two ways by hosting sponsored content. It encourages their viewers to stay on the site longer to read the content, and advertising space on the page(s) can be sold by the site owner. Sponsorships are also used for games and interactive tools like currency, size, and mortgage calculators.

Most sponsorship button ads are interactive, but not intrusive. They are not rich media, so they can be viewed by anyone with a graphical browser. They capitalize on the goodwill viewers express for sponsors providing useful content. They are particularly attractive to large corporations that use them for public relations purposes. Even so, sponsorship are declining in popularity. In 1998 they generated 40 percent of all advertising revenue; by Q3 2001, its share of revenue had fallen to 25 percent. It is generally agreed that sponsorships increase awareness and are more cost-effective than banner ads. However, there are no standards for sponsorship deals and therefore, each has to be negotiated between the sponsor and site property owners that host the content.[21]

**Interstitials**
Rich media ads that closely resemble slimmed-down television commercials or print ads in a magazine.

**INTERSTITIALS** Interstitials are rich media ads that closely resemble slimmed-down television commercials. They are flashy, intrusive audio, animation, and video ads that last five to thirty seconds. More than five to ten seconds on the Internet is a very long time, so interstitials must be scheduled sparingly. They can be extremely annoying to people trying to use the Web as an information source because they block content. They also require fast connections, so it is important to run them on pages likely to attract viewers using the latest browsers and high bandwidth connections on DSL, cable, or a T-1 at work. Interstitials play between web pages, much like print ads in a magazine. Viewers complain that interstitials block the screen and slow their access to a site.

**Superstitials**
Precached interstitials that are less intrusive than interstitials.

**SUPERSTITIALS** Unicast (*http://www.Unicast.com*) offers precached interstitials that the company calls **superstitials**, *The Internet's Commercials*. A visitor goes to a web site and the front page downloads. When the download is finished, the visitor views the page and his or her modem goes idle. That is when the superstitial invisibly downloads into the visitor's browser's temporary memory. If the visitor moves to another page, superstitial download stops, then continues the next time the modem is idled. The visitor does not know what is happening and his or her progress is not slowed, so it is a *polite delivery* of ad content. When the commercial is fully downloaded, intact, and ready to play, as the visitor clicks to another page the superstitial begins playing with CD-ROM quality while the new page loads behind the superstitial. The company records all plays of the commercial, compiles the data, and reports it to the superstitial's sponsor. Because superstitials load in the background and do not play until fully loaded, it alleviates browser and bandwidth deficiencies. However, the way they are loaded invisibly is bound to raise privacy concerns. The appearance of impropriety may make advertisers reluctant to use superstitials even though the technology is appealing and having the ad fully loaded before playing is an advantage.

**Minimovies**
Very short cinema-like ads filmed specifically for Internet showing.

**MINIMOVIES** Although they are very expensive to produce, **minimovies** are beginning to appear online. They are very short cinema-like ads filmed specifically for Internet showing. Automobile company BMW North America's short cinema ads (*http://www.bmwfilms.com/site_layout/index.asp*) took far longer to create than any web site banner ad and were much more expensive to produce. The five- to six-minute short DVD-like films, *The Hire Film Series*, were filmed by top international directors, John Frankenheimer and Ang Lee among others, for the Internet and show the BMWs in exciting situations. The standalone minifilms are short on plot but long on car chases. The minimovies were launched with a promotion campaign of television, print, and web ads, viral marketing, and public relations. Each film stars a different BMW automobile. The cinema ads also ran on the Independent Film Channel (IFC) and Bravo as paid media buys. The media fed on this launch, loading it with coverage in the entertainment and business presses. The web strategy was driven by studies that indicated 85 percent of BMW buyers researched their car purchase online before visiting a dealer's showroom. BMW and their agency, Fallon Worldwide (*http://www.fallon.com*), found that BMW drivers spent more time in contact with BMW promotions online than were reached by BMW television ads. Unlike traditional advertising, where more is spent on media than creative, this web advertising spent more on creative than media. The minifilms are estimated to have cost around US$15 million. The films are not interactive. Between April 2001, when the films were launched, and July 2001, they were downloaded over six million times. Visitors stayed an average of sixteen minutes on the site in June 2001.[22]

**YELLOW PAGES ADVERTISING**  Yellow Pages are directional advertising. People go to local print directories when they are actively seeking information and ready to purchase. The same is true online, where the click through rate for online Yellow Pages directories is 1.5 percent, almost five times higher than for plain banner rates. Online U.S. Yellow Pages produced revenues of around US$306 million in 2000, compared with US$13.6 billion in revenue for traditional print Yellow Pages. The Kelsey Group predicts that online Yellow Pages will generate around US$1.5 billion in 2006. Traditional Yellow Pages purchases are sometimes bundled, so when an advertiser purchases a print line listing or a display ad offline, an online listing is bundled with the print purchase, at no extra charge.

Leading online directories are YellowOnline.com (*http://www.yellowonline.com*), Verizon SuperPages (*http://www.superpages.com*), Yahoo! Yellow Pages (*http://yp.yahoo. com*), SBN.com (Superior Business Network at *http://SBN.com*), and AOL (*http://yp.aol. com*). They are all localized; users access listings by zip code and/or city and state, and business category. Directories typically provide address information, telephone number, web site link (if available), driving instructions, maps, and sometimes coupons. Most pages have localized display, banner, and/or pop-up ads. A considerable advantage of online directory listings is they can be modified or corrected in real time. Hardcopy directory listing changes are often delayed several months to a year until the next year's directory is printed.

**CLASSIFIED ADS**  Most newspaper sites run online classified ads. The *Lexington Herald-Leader* (*http://www.kentucky.com/mld/kentucky/classifieds*) accepts local individual and business ads. The *New York Times* (*http://www.nytimes.com/classified*) runs local ads and banner ads specific to the classified category. *USAToday* (*http:// www.usatoday.com/shop/classified.htm*) also runs classified ads, both line listings and display ads, and connects to partners that list rentals nationwide, automobiles, homes, and singles.

Some classified ads are included as features on large sites or portals. Yahoo! (*http:// classifieds.yahoo.com*) has classified ads in such categories as real estate, pets and animals, business opportunities, services, and personals. The search can be local or nationwide. Others are run on sites dedicated to classified ads C2C, B2B, and/or B2C. There are hundreds of small sites online, but it is unknown whether they are generating any revenues or many visitors.

**WEBCAST ADS**  Webcasts are audio, video, or audio/video streaming broadcasts on the World Wide Web. Some are live, others are rebroadcasts, many are archived, and a large number are streaming audio from traditional radio stations like the BBC (British Broadcasting Company at *http://www.bbc.co.uk/radio*) and NPR (National Public Radio at *http://www.npr.org*).

Real.com (*http://www.real.com*) sells RealPlayer Plus with links to more than two thousand online radio stations. Copyright problems have forced many radio stations to stop broadcasting online. Until copyright payment issues can be resolved, growth in webcasts will be limited.

Webcasters generate revenue by selling in-stream ads within the streamed content and gateway ads that appear on the page that links to the webcast. Most webcasters sell a combination of forms, including sponsorships, in-stream, and gateway ads. Many advertisers are wary of webcast ads, and particularly in-stream ads, because they are so new and lack measurement and rate standardization information. Top webcast advertisers are automotive companies, entertainment, music, and alcoholic beverages. Webcasting is also used by Wall Street analysts to broadcast information exclusively to larger institution clients. Merrill Lynch, Lehman Brothers, and Morgan Stanley were among the first to launch audio/video webcasts. About 34 percent of Internet users, 19 percent of the U.S. population, are also web radio listeners. It is unclear if streaming audio will be an effective advertising channel since radio availability is already extremely broad. Lack of audience measures is a considerable problem that will be difficult to overcome. Dayparts are meaningless when it comes to the Internet, so using drivetimes and other metrics makes no sense in a virtual venue.[23]

**MOBILE ADS**  Although personal computers are by far the most popular way to access the Internet in the United States, wireless access is growing. Wireless PDAs or mobile Internet sets have smaller screens and slower downloads than computers, so advertising has to be modified in size and content to accommodate the screen and download time. DoubleClick.com (*http://www.doubleclick.com*) is leading a group trying to develop a model for wireless advertising. This includes ad formats, serving standards, and privacy protection, as wireless is more vulnerable to privacy invasions. Measurement problems remain to be solved, particularly how results will be measured, by click through, ad views, conversions, or some other measurement.[24]

### PLACING ADVERTISING

An advertiser that wants to place its ads somewhere other than its own web site has several options. It can go to a well-known, heavily trafficked site like AOL (*http://mediaspace.aol.com*) or Yahoo! (*http://docs.yahoo.com/info/advertising*) and purchase advertising space directly from the site owner. It can purchase space on the web site of a complementary product or category. For example, BusinessWeek Online (*http://www.businessweek.com*) has house ads along with button ads for AOL Time Warner and AOL, its preferred ISP, and various brokers that sponsor its market information. Nonprofits and government agencies may qualify for free banner ads and placements through the AdCouncil's online PSA program.

Most host sites have highly specific instructions for advertisers. AOL's (*http://mediaspace.aol.com/index.adp?fname=art*) instructions run for several pages and address issues of file formats, maximum file sizes, color palette, animation, and sponsorship buttons. Advertising rates are often posted on the host's site or can be obtained from a placement service or a third party like Bankrate.com (*http://www.bankrate.com/brm/news/biz/tcb/20000221a.asp*).

Less costly alternatives are available for small and midsize businesses. **Reciprocal advertising links** or co-op links are free ad banners and links swapped among cooperating host sites. A host site offers space for reciprocal hypertext linking. Advertisers placing ads on the host's site reciprocate. Reciprocal space is also available in some

**Reciprocal advertising links**

Free ad links swapped between cooperating host sites.

online magazines. MS-Links Exchange (*http://ms-links.com*) hosts a banner exchange where potential advertisers can link up. The problem with reciprocal advertising is lack of traffic. Although common interests may encourage receivers to visit reciprocally linked sites, low numbers limit their effectiveness.

Affiliate marketing is another way to place banner ads. Affiliate or associate programs are offered by most major sites including Amazon.com, AOL, Yahoo!, and eBay. Affiliate advertising works to the advantage of the sponsor. Affiliate members receive a small fee for each of their site visitors who clicks through and buys something from the network sponsor. Of course, visitors leave the affiliate's site to make the purchase, which can rob the affiliate of a sale. The affiliate may gain a small revenue stream, but it is the sponsor that benefits from increased traffic. Some sites have adopted newer software that allows the visitor to link to the affiliate network owner and make a purchase without leaving the affiliate member's site.

Most small businesses have little budgeted for online promotions. Surprisingly, 38 percent of the small business owners who responded to a marketing survey said they used online advertising to reach a national audience; 35 percent targeted local customers only; and 9 percent targeted an international audience. Over 50 percent of these respondents spent less than US$250 a month on online promotions; more than a third spent more than US$250 a month on offline promotions. These small businesses reach target audiences using direct email (29 percent), reciprocal links (20 percent), affiliate networks (9 percent), community chat groups (8 percent), bulletin boards (8 percent), free banner ads (11 percent), and paid banner ads (2 percent).[25]

## ADVERTISING METRICS

Measuring advertising effectiveness online should be relatively easy because almost all of it is direct advertising, where the audience sees (or hears) the ad and immediately can click through to make a purchase. The problem involves developing accepted standardized measures for determining what is really happening. Thus far, advertising measures (metrics) have been an area of intense debate complicated by the difficulty in monitoring when and where ads appear online.

**Web advertising metrics**

How online advertising is measured including CPMs, impressions, conversion rates, and click throughs.

**Web advertising metrics** are measurements used in determining what is happening when ads are used on the Web. Metrics measure audience size and reach, brand building, audience contact with ads and recall, and effectiveness in leading to a behavior (visit to a web site, a purchase), stimulating recall, or raising awareness. Site owners, advertisers, agencies, media, and others want widely accepted, standardized measurements because they lend credibility to reports of audience size and characteristics, contacts, and ad effectiveness, which are all important in setting rates. Standardized measurements allow meaningful comparisons between web advertising forms, media, and offline advertising. They are needed to demonstrate that advertising is effective and efficient and justifies the price paid for it. The Internet and the Web are unique in their capacity to allow marketers to gather more information than other channels and at a remarkable depth and specificity. The challenge is to make the information worthwhile.

From about 1994 through 1999, demand for ad space was greater than supply, and host sites selling valuable space had the upper hand in setting rates. In market conditions where sellers had the advantage, they did not have to provide much information about audiences or effectiveness. With the dot-com meltdown at the turn of the century and the decline in advertising spending, power shifted to advertisers (ad space buyers) that could negotiate rates downward and demand more information from a site owner about numbers of visitors served, how long they stayed, and their characteristics (demographics, spending, preferences). More information, however, is not necessarily better information. Measurement inconsistencies and, in some cases, deliberate overcounting resulted in erroneous measurements, particularly impression miscounts.[26] Rates are still highly negotiable on most sites, and the listed or placed rate is not necessarily final. Quantity discounts are often given depending on space availability.

Web advertising measurements are in a state of flux. At the beginning of web advertising, a **hit** (table 12-1) was the metric used to describe advertising effectiveness. It soon became evident that the gross number of times a page was seen (served) did not provide sufficient information about uniqueness or conversion rate, that is, the percentage of people who click through and actually make a purchase (convert from visitor to buyer). Many critics contend that hits and click throughs have become meaningless, but they are still widely used. *Stickiness* is another term that was highly popular and is now rarely heard. This measure assumes that the longer visitors stay on a site, the more likely they are to purchase. There is little proof that stickiness directly relates to conversions.

**Hit**

The metric initially used to describe advertising effectiveness; the number of ads on a page served to a visitor requesting it.

## Table 12-1  Advertising Terms

| | |
|---|---|
| *Click through* | When a visitor clicks on a banner ad, activates the hypertext link, and is linked to the advertiser's site. Also called ad clicks or transfers. Click through does not report whether or not a purchase resulted. |
| *Click rate* | Click through rate is the percentage of times an ad is clicked divided by the number of times it is served. Example: A banner ad on Yahoo! is served (placed in front of a visitor) five hundred times. In that five hundred times, the ad is clicked on ten times. The click rate is 10/500, or 2 percent. Prices are set by US$/number of click throughs or US$ times click rate. |
| *Clickstream* | An early method of determining effectiveness that used hits, pages, visits, users, and identified users. It is prone to exaggerate numbers. |
| *Conversion rate* | Rate of audience members who respond to an ad and become buyers. Calculated as buyers/viewers. |
| *CPM* | Cost per thousand, where M is the Roman numeral for one thousand; the cost of one thousand ad impressions. CPMs vary according to the value of the host site. The average CPM in 2001 was US$33.00/1,000 impressions. |
| *Eyeballs* | The number of site visitors (actually, their eyeballs) that see an ad. |
| *Frequency* | The number of times a visitor is exposed (served) an ad during the period of the campaign. |
| *Hits* | The number of files served from a page. When a visitor requests a web page and it is served, the hits are the number of ads in the page. If a page has three banner ads, one graphic image, and one sponsorship, it counts as five hits on the assumption that the visitor actually sees all five. This is a discredited metric because it fails to identify any contact between the ad and the visitor, and it makes no attempt at tracking what happens after viewing. |

## Table 12-1  Advertising Terms (*continued*)

| | |
|---|---|
| *Impression* | An impression is an opportunity to see an ad, the number of times it is available for viewing; also called page impressions or page views. Priced on US$/number of page views guaranteed. Front (home) pages are the entry point to most web sites and receive the most page views, which is why so many advertisers want to purchase space on front pages. |
| *Pages* | The number of pages downloaded from a site. The visitor may not actually view each page or its ads. |
| *Page views* | See *Impression*. |
| *Rate* | The amount charged for placing an ad on a page; list prices are also called rate cards. Rates are posted and many can be negotiated. They vary by site and are set by the site owner. For example, in Q1/Q2 2000, health and fitness sites averaged CPMs of US$42.50, game sites averaged US$24.13, general news sites averaged US$37.47. The American Society of Health-System Pharmacists (*http://www.ashp.org/public/marketing/web-ads.html*) publishes its vertical banner ad rates onsite. It charges US$2,000 per month for a small banner (126 X 60 pixels), US$3,600/month for a medium banner (125 x 120 pixels), and US$5,000 per month for a large banner (125 X 80 pixels). It gives no guarantee on the number of exposures or click throughs but states the site gets one million visitors each month from a highly targeted audience, mostly its members. |
| *Reach* | The percentage of users visiting a site and exposed to an ad at least once during the period of the campaign. |
| *Run* | The amount of time an ad is scheduled to appear on a site. An advertiser pays to run an ad for a specified length of time. |
| *Stickiness* | Total page views/month divided by unique visitors per month. An indicator of attractiveness that has fallen into disuse. |
| *Unique visitor* | The unduplicated number of people visiting a web site in a period of time. Even if someone visits multiple times, he or she is only counted once. Identified by cookies or IP number. |
| *Visitor* | The total number of people who visit a web site in a period of time. If someone visits multiple times, each time is counted. This is a duplicated measure. |

Advertising rates generally are set by the web owner selling the space, but local custom and competitive pressure, as well as economics, also influence rate setting. Sites that add value, have more attractive audience statistics, or whose space is highly sought after charge higher rates. Space owners post their rates on their sites or provide a contact number for rate cards. Space brokers, advertising, and promotion agencies also provide rates.

The debate over click through continues. It averaged 8 percent in 1996, by 2001 was down to less than 0.5 percent, and in 2002 averaged around 0.3 percent. This decline has led critics to recommend using alternative audience measures, including campaign reach, postimpression analysis, and brand awareness.[27] Although click through rates are disappointing, banner ads still provide valuable information for window-shopping consumers who do not purchase online but use web-based information to guide their offline purchases. Marketers should consider window-shopping consumers when planning ad campaigns and use integrated, consistent messages in all delivery channels with the expectation that for some buyers, online views will drive offline sales. Research also supports the observation that viewing ads even without clicking can drive conversions postview. If clicked, 61 percent convert within thirty minutes. A surprising 32 percent of all conversions are made without a click, eight to thirty days after exposure to the ad.[28]

Higher frequency means a greater chance of reaching potential customers. Advertising continuously to reach consumers as they are ready to act can increase sales. Reach is equally important as ads must reach enough people enough times without causing banner burnout. For example, a new P&G snack food brand was heavily advertised in a sixteen-week test period that tracked fifty-five thousand shoppers. Branding was the number one goal. Online ads increased sales volume 19 percent with only a 0.27 percent click through rate. Four or more impressions over three weeks increased ad recall 10.4 percent. One impression increased recall 5.6 percent. The goal was one or two online ad impressions per week to raise awareness.[29]

### ✔ CONCEPT CHECK

1. What is the value of standardizing web ad sizes? Who benefits?
2. Will minimovies become a widespread online advertising form? Explain.
3. Why is it so important to standardize ad metrics?

# Sales Promotions and Permission Email Marketing

Sales promotions are designed to move an audience quickly toward a desired action, principally a purchase. Permission email marketing directs marketing messages and incentives toward audiences that are interested enough to allow their names to be included on a commercial email distribution list. Initial indications are that the former is still a very small factor online, and the latter is being overused to the point of burning out its desirable audiences.

## SALES PROMOTIONS

Coupons are among the most visible sales promotion form. Between 248 and 330 billion coupons are distributed yearly in the United States with a redemption rate of only 1.3 to 1.8 percent. Newspaper freestanding inserts (FSIs) are the dominant distribution channel (over 80 percent), with point-of-purchase displays a distant second (8 percent). Coupon distribution online is about 0.5 percent, but it is growing as more women and lower-income consumers go online. These groups are the most loyal coupon clippers. Online coupons are highly attractive because their redemption rate (around 57 percent) is so much higher than offline coupons. Once coupon receptive target audiences have been identified, a relationship can be established based on interest in the product and nurtured by continued contact. The risk is being too generous with coupons. Fraud is also a concern as home-printed coupons are far harder to control than those printed on special high-gloss multicolor paper.

Coupons made their way online in 1995. Now, more than twenty-five thousand retailers participate in various online coupon programs. Coupons are particularly attractive to stores with private labels because their margins average 40 percent higher than manufacturer brand coupons. Coupons are distributed in several ways. Coupon sites like ValPak.com (*http://valpak.com/index.jsp*) offer coupons in many categories to a variety of local stores. ValPak is also the largest offline coupon distributor, mailing print coupons in distinctive bright blue envelopes. ValPak went online in late 1998. In addition to grocery coupons ValPak has rebates, online deals, and free samples. H.O.T.! Coupons (*http://Hotcoupons.com*), like ValPak, has consumers type in their zip code or geographic area. Coupons for that location are then shown onscreen. Localized screens also carry local retailers' banner ads in a stacked vertical banner. Popular coupon categories are groceries, books, health and beauty, music, fast food, apparel, and toys.[30]

Contests are a popular sales promotion. General Mills (the sponsor) used an external promotion company Promotions.com (*http://www.Promotions.com*) to create and implement an Internet promotion for Pop.Secret Microwave Popcorn (*http://popsecret. com*) as part of a national campaign with NASCAR legend Richard Petty called "Guess Richard Petty's Favorite Paint Scheme" Sweepstakes (*http://www.Promotions.com/ promo/case03.html*). Participants had to guess which of three color combinations Petty preferred for his NASCAR Winston Cup car driven by John Andretti in the Pop Secret Microwave Popcorn 400 race. The grand prize winner received a four-night, five-day trip for two to the race and $25,000. The web site had games, instant prizes, and information about the drivers. Support for the Internet sweepstakes included store point-of-purchase (POP) displays, coupons in FSIs, promotions on eight million packages of Pop Secret Microwave Popcorn, and events at State Fairs nationwide.[31]

Many Internet users like giveaway sites where they can win cash or merchandise without making a purchase or buying a lotto ticket. Marketers like the sites because they offer the opportunity for one-to-one marketing, assembling house email lists, and collecting customer data. A recent Jupiter Communication study revealed that about 93 percent of all commercial sites offer a promotion using discounts, sweepstakes, giveaways, or other freebies. Marketers spent US$0.9 billion on Internet sales promotions in 1999 and US$1.8 billion in 2000 and are expected to spend US$14.4 billion by 2005. They report that promotions drive traffic, increase email contacts, build brand awareness, create customer relationships, and lead to purchase.

## PERMISSION EMAIL MARKETING

Sales promotions are a short-term strategy designed to create an immediate inducement to purchase. Permission marketing by email is a long-term strategy designed to establish a meaningful relationship with customers unlike spam which is a short-term strategy and does not ask permission.

Most Internet users have email accounts where they send and receive personal messages and receive commercial email. Personal messages are one of the great Internet success stories and the single most widely used Internet service. **Commercial email** is marketing promotion messages and incentives conveyed by electronic mail. It is direct marketing, an interactive method for making an offer and initiating an exchange. It is widely praised by marketers who use it because it can reach a highly segmented target market almost instantaneously at a far lower cost than other direct marketing forms. It is denounced by consumers and businesses whose email in-boxes are clogged by unsolicited email messages they did not request and resent receiving.

**Commercial email**
Promotion messages sent by email to enterprises and/or consumers with or without their permission.

Some commercial email is less odious than others, particularly when the receiver has given permission (opted in) to the sender to deliver a promotion message or incentive. Opt-in is more expensive for the marketer than opt-out, but far more desirable, because it keeps the receiver in control and reduces the waste of sending messages or incentives to totally disinterested receivers.

Any company engaged in traditional direct marketing should find it relatively easy to use email marketing, which is actually much cheaper than the offline method. House lists can be used with email addresses collected through buyer information, online product registrations, web site registrations, newsletter subscriptions, on-site contests, and other inducements. The challenge for most businesses is implementing the email marketing campaign. Many run their own email campaigns. The advantages are complete control over the list, message, timing, follow-up, and customization. Disadvantages are the time and technology required to do so, and the limited scope of house lists. That is why many companies, large and small, turn to outside vendors for their email campaigns.

Many businesses offer email services, including YesMail.Com (*http://YesMail.Com*), NetCreations.com (*http://w3.netcreations.com*), and PostMasterDirect.com (*http://rentals.postmasterdirect.com*). Most target U.S. and sometimes Canadian, but usually not international, audiences. E@symail Interactive (*http://www.easymailinteractive.com*) is the oldest independent email list broker in the United States. It represents over 1,500 unique domestic and international B2C and B2B lists, with more than 276 million opt-in email consumer addresses, 35 million B2B addresses, and 105 million international addresses. E@symail has select lists of opt-in audiences in such categories as *adventure outdoors, animals, antiques, shopping/online, real estate, sports, wedding, wireless, and weekend trips.* It only offers opt-in lists.

A client contracts with a list broker to rent a specified number of email addresses in a category and then creates the email piece exactly as it will be distributed, text-only, HTML, or rich media. The email piece is sent to the list broker and distributed to the designated opt-in audience. Tracking is performed in real time and/or within a prespecified time frame. Lists cost around US$0.10 to $0.50 cents a name, US$100 to $500 CPM. Charges usually include list rental, email distribution, tracking, and final reporting. The obvious advantages of permission email marketing are greater reach, at a cheaper price, faster with real-time tracking of results, and more privacy for the audience. Costs can be reduced by sharing a list and sending a group mailing with other vendors. Traditional postal direct mail has about a 1 to 2 percent response rate. Permission email response rates have been as high as 30 to 40 percent.

Tracking the results of an email campaign is easier and more efficient than tracking an advertising campaign. When interactive messages are distributed, an identifier code number is placed in the email. When receivers click through, the code number tracks that they reached the site from the distributed email. Millions of email messages can be distributed simultaneously. The message sponsor can tell when the messages are received and acted on as site traffic will increase accordingly. Tracking is in real time and highly accurate, providing both a unique visitor rate and conversion rate.

Small and midsize businesses are particularly drawn to permission email for its low cost. This is a promotion form they can use effectively because it is affordable and fast. However, if a majority of the millions of small businesses in the United States begin sending commercial email, the impact could be overwhelming. The number of corporate email messages received jumped 50 percent between 2000 and 2001, and it is predicted to grow another 35 to 50 percent in 2002. It has been suggested that if every employee spent an average five minutes reading each email, it would take four hours every workday to clear his or her email in box.[32]

**OPT-OUT** The majority of sites take advantage of visitors by automatically capturing their email address when they enter the site, adding them without their permission to an email distribution list. Somewhere, hidden in their site, there is a place where visitors can choose an **opt-out,** that is, tell the site they do not wish to receive mailings. Depending on message quantity and content, unsolicited email can be a minor nuisance or a major annoyance. For businesses it can be extremely costly, as bulk email sent to many of their employees at once can crash their servers and waste employee time purging email in-boxes of spam.

**Opt-out**
When visitors command a site to drop their names from an email list.

**OPT-IN** By far the better alternative is **opt-in,** which asks permission for the marketer to make future contact. The address owner's consent is needed before he or she is added to an email distribution list. It is less intrusive than opt-out, but it also carries a higher risk. The relationship can be broken if email messages come too frequently, are too long, or fail to engage the visitor's interest. If this happens, unsubscribe rates rise. Even when permission is given, sometimes people forget and when they receive the opt-in mail, believe it is spam. This can poison a relationship.

**Opt-in**
When visitors request that their names be added to an email distribution list.

**DOUBLE OPT-IN** This form of permission marketing requires agreement twice. The first is the standard opt-in permission. This is followed up with a confirmation opt-in to ensure that the holder of the email address is the same person who gave the original permission. It also serves as a reminder and avoids the misperception of spam when the email arrives.

**MAILING LISTS** The best possible list is an opt-in (or double opt-in) compiled from a house list, the customers and/or visitors who have already interacted with the business. Compiled lists can be obtained from list brokers and email companies that specialize in providing lists of email addresses for people or enterprises that fit the purchaser's specifications. Lists can also be compiled from memberships, directories, and other sources with large numbers of addresses.

*WEB UPDATE*

Current Status of Email Marketing— What's Hot and What's Not

Businesses considering using permission email marketing should adhere to some fundamental rules. They should send email only to those who have given their permission to receive it, keep the email short and to the point, and should not send email too often. Probably the most important rule is *Don't spam!*

## ✔ CONCEPT CHECK

1. Do you think ecoupons will have higher redemption rates than print coupons?
2. What is wrong with the opt-out method?
3. Explain why double opt-in is a better method than opt-in.

# *Summary*

### *Promotion Fundamentals*

Promotion is planned, persuasive, targeted, goal-driven marketing communication. Primary online promotion goals are to build awareness and brands, increase traffic to a sponsors' web site, and generate sales. Traditional marketing promotion is advertising, sales promotions, personal selling, publicity/public relations, and direct marketing. Marketers use promotion to send a message and deliver an incentive. Most traditional promotion is a one-to-many distribution process. Internet promotion has the potential to be one-to-one. The Internet is primarily a pull environment but can also be a push environment. Promotion communicates important marketing information to receptive target audiences that need/want a product and have the authority to make a purchase as well as the payment mechanism to complete the exchange. Multiple promotion goals may operate concurrently. The best promotion is a good product sold at a fair price in a readily accessible place. In addition to building awareness, marketing promotion can inform, persuade, and remind buyers about products, build goodwill and value, brand and rebrand, position and reposition products, and entertain. Marketing promotion is funded by a promotion budget. Internet advertising is the most visible promotion form and includes banner ads, sponsorships, interstitials and other rich media ads, pop-ups, pop-unders, classified ads, advergames, Yellow Pages, in-stream and gateway webcast ads, and other forms. Internet sales promotions are temporary inducements to stimulate demand, increase storefront traffic and/or sales, or encourage distribution channel members to distribute, stock, or purchase a product. Personal selling is where a salesperson interacts with potential or current customers. Public relations (PR) has an identified sponsor that pays for the development and implementation of PR programs to create and maintain a favorable image and goodwill, persuade an audience, and/or generate traffic. Publicity is promotion that provides information to the media so it can be used in a hard or soft news story, or editorial. Some marketers consider all Internet promotion direct marketing since it is interactive, creates personal contact with audience members, and encourages an immediate response and purchase. Internet direct marketing includes click through advertising, interactive commercial email, web catalogs and brochureware, and online shopping networks. Promotion can be designed to stimulate word-of-mouth communications or buzz. Promotion targets can be narrowly or broadly defined or be a mass market. Promotion decisions are often based on the assumptions of a hierarchy-of-effects model. Effective promotion requires planning by in-house marketers or outside promotion agency specialists.

### *Promotion Issues*

Two singular problems of Internet promotion are its lack of emotion and clutter. Consumers have always had the power to ignore marketing promotion. Consumers are increasingly exposed to large, intrusive ads that slow page downloads. Ad blocking denies site owners the opportunity to monetize their web space. Fear of audience backlash has convinced some advertisers to back off host-initiated instant streaming audio technology. Promotion forms online and offline must work together so the overall effect is consistent and greater than if only one form or environment had been used. Clutter is a multidimensional problem created by growing numbers of ads, email messages, and web sites and pages. Marketers can increase the odds of having their target audiences find them by registering on search engines, directories, and portals. Criticisms are mainly directed at advertising, but complaints about commercial email are growing. Promotion is defended for its critical role in letting buyers know about marketing offers. Advertising revenues subsidize content sites and also help keep content free. Web PSAs are public service ads.

### *Advertising Applications*

Internet advertising takes many forms. Online banner ads are interactive billboard-style messages on or linked to web pages designed to raise awareness and remind about a product, brand, and/or web site. Some banners are getting larger in an effort to capture viewer's attention and make a more lasting impression. All advertising is self-promoting and house ads are self-promotions on an owner's web site. Sponsorships are web page ads, usually the size of a small button banner ad, placed adjacent to content related to the sponsor's product. Interstitials are rich media ads that closely resemble slimmed-down television commercials. Superstitials are precached interstitials. Yellow Pages are directional advertising. Webcasters generate revenue by selling in-stream ads within the streamed content and gateway ads that appear on the page that links to the webcast. Advertising has to be modified for wireless in size and content to accommodate the screen and download time. Reciprocal advertising links or co-op links are free ad links swapped among cooperating host sites. Web advertising metrics refers to how advertising is measured. A debate is currently raging over the accuracy of advertising effectiveness measurements; few are satisfied with current practices. Advertising rates generally are set by the host selling the space, but local custom and competitive pressure, as well as economics, also influence rate setting. While click through rates are disappointing, banner ads still provide valuable information for window-shopping consumers who do not purchase online but use web-based information to guide their offline purchases.

### Sales Promotions and Permission Email Marketing

Sales promotions are designed to move an audience quickly toward a desired action, principally a purchase. Permission marketing directs marketing messages and incentives toward audiences that are interested enough to allow their names to be included on a commercial email distribution list. Coupon distribution online is growing as more women and lower-income consumers go online. Contests are another popular sales promotion. Many sites have free offers, two-for-one specials, and other short-term incentives for products sold from their storefront. Many Internet users like giveaway sites where they can win cash or merchandise without making a purchase or buying a lotto ticket. Most Internet users have email accounts where they send and receive personal messages, and receive commercial email. Commercial email is marketing promotion messages and incentives conveyed by electronic mail. Tracking the results of an email campaign is easier and more efficient than tracking an advertising campaign. Small and midsize businesses are particularly drawn to permission email for its low cost. The majority of sites take advantage of visitors by automatically capturing their email address when they access a site and adding them to an email distribution list. By far the better alternative is opt-in, which asks permission for the marketer to make future contact. Double opt-in requires getting permission confirmed.

## Internet Marketing Application

Clutter has been cited as a major problem online, interfering with the effective delivery of promotion to intended receivers, but what exactly is it? Try your hand at defining clutter. What constitutes clutter (a) on a web page, (b) in email, and (c) on the Web? Apply your definition of web page clutter to the following home pages. How must the definition change to accommodate content, product, and business differences? How *cluttered* are each of the following pages?

- Yahoo! at *http://www.yahoo.com*
- Google at *http://google.com*
- Apple at *http://www.apple.com*
- Dell at *http://www.dell.com*
- Wall Street Journal Online at *http://online.wsj.com*

## Chapter Review Questions

1. Why are consumers and enterprises so angry about spam?
2. Explain what happens during the marketing communication process.
3. Explain how traditional promotion forms and promotion points of contact work together.
4. Can word of mouth really be effective promotion online?

5. How can promotion direct behavior?

6. How can emotion be added to online promotions?

7. What types of promotion are particularly well suited to the Internet and Web?

8. What is promotion synergy?

9. Why should online and offline promotions be complementary?

10. What are metatags and how are they used in promotion?

11. Why might top-of-page banner ads be better placed than those at the bottom of the page?

12. Are minimovies an effective online promotion?

13. Will webcasting ads be effective in the future? Explain.

14. Why do consumers like sales promotions?

15. Why are marketers drawn to permission marketing?

## Marketing Movies Online

# Case Study

Harry Potter is a phenom! J. K. Rowling's books about the precocious Harry have sold more than a hundred million copies worldwide. Children, teens, and adults all enjoy the books and rushed to movie theaters to see *Harry Potter and the Sorcerer's Stone,* which grossed over US$186 in its first two weeks in theaters. Warner Brothers, an AOL Time Warner company, paid US$1.4 million in 1998 for the rights to transform the first two books in the series into movies. Having the vast entertainment conglomerate backing the films means they will get extensive cross-promotional marketing in all AOL Time Warner channels. Cross-promotions will increase anticipation for the movies and drive traffic to related web sites, stores, and theaters.

Marketing Harry Potter is a job for integrated marketing promotions. AOL Time Warner divisions are synchronizing their activities to ensure integration and coordination. Advance ticket sales from AOL's moviephone.com (*http://www.moviefone.com*) topped one million before the film opened. Movie merchandising includes almost five hundred toys along with a wide variety of other products including toothpaste, hair gel, and chocolates. Trailers from the film were shown in theaters and online months before the movie's debut. Harry Potter minisites sell merchandise and build buzz. At Timeforkids (*http://www.timeforkids.com*), Harry Potter is a prime topic for the site's kid reporters and viral marketing. The Internet is a strategic channel for reaching key movie goers, particularly the hot tar-

get markets for the Potter films—fans twelve to twenty-four years old. By 2004, over thirty million twelve year olds will have access to the Internet at home or school. This will play a significant role in building awareness, audiences, and long-term relationships for future Potter films.

Hosting an official film web site is by now an established form of movie promotion. Harry Potter's site (*http://harrypotter.warnerbros.com/?fromtout= homepage_b2*) is elaborate and exciting and captures the mood of the film. It also sells related products. Its community area offers space for fans to share their observations and feelings.

There are risks to frenetic movie marketing online. It is one thing to build buzz for a successful film, but building it in advance of a failure could chill future efforts. Sponsors are another issue. Coca-Cola purchased exclusive global marketing rights for £110 million (around US$150 million) but is restricted in the use of Harry's image on Coke products. Some health advocates are very sour about Coke's sponsorship, claiming it is unhealthy and Harry should not be associated with a drink that is sugar rich. The controversy resulted in an anti-Coke email campaign urging the author to kill the deal in order to protect children's health.[33]

### CHECK IT OUT

Go to the *Save Harry* web site (*http://www. SaveHarry.com*) and read the email petition for Ms. Rowling. Who sponsors the site? Is this anti-marketing in general or something else? Read about the *Save Harry* campaign. Do you believe the campaign will achieve its desired results? Is this an example of viral marketing online?

## A GLOBAL PERSPECTIVE

Next to Hollywood, the most active, vibrant film community in the world is in India, often called *Bollywood*. In terms of film production, it is the world's largest producer, almost doubling Hollywood's annual production. Film came to India in 1896, and the first Indian-made film was released in 1913. American films have always been enjoyed there by a relatively small audience, but Indian-made films became extremely popular with the introduction of sound in the 1930s and the creation of the uniquely Indian song-movie. The song tradi-

tion continues in Indian films, and while there are many social and art films made there, mass marketing promotes a steady stream of highly popular song films. Indians love films and fourteen million Indians attend movies each day. Of the Indian population of more than one billion, only about 0.5 percent is online. Those who are online can participate in chat rooms about Indian film stars, download pictures of their favorite actors, and see film clips. As more Indians go online, particularly educated younger people in major cities, online film marketing will become multichannel and more aggressive. Experience Indian films online at *http://filmfare.indiatimes.com/cms.dll/default.*

# Module IV

# Internet Marketing Action Plans

There is a big difference between knowing what successful Internet marketing requires and actually doing it. Effective planning, implementation, and control can contribute significantly to online success. Planning, the subject of Chapter 13, requires constructing a blueprint for action, that is, identifying what it will take to be an online marketing success. Implementation, operationalizing marketing plans, includes decisions about content, design, and construction—substance, look and feel, and functionality, the subject of Chapter 14. Control is measuring actual performance against expected performance, analyzing the results, and adjusting plans to correct shortcomings, respond to environmental changes, and amplify what is successful.

The Web's turbulent commercial environment increases the importance of planning, implementation, and control. Marketing products in this environment demands attention to emerging trends, changing customer preferences, and new technologies.

## CHAPTER THIRTEEN

# *The Web Marketing Plan*

## LEARNING OBJECTIVES

- To identify the value of marketing planning and writing a web marketing plan
- To describe what should be included in a web marketing plan and why
- To examine how web marketing plans are implemented and controlled
- To understand the role of a web marketing budget

## Kim Plans A Web Marketing Site

Kim and several friends have been operating a small business from her basement for the past two years. They custom assemble gift baskets for special occasions like birthdays, graduations, anniversaries, adoptions, births, and even divorces. The business began after friends and family urged Kim to turn her beautiful baskets into a home business. What makes her baskets unique are personalized designs painted on the exterior surfaces and their handcrafted contents. Her baby baskets are highly prized. They contain knit caps and booties, crocheted crib blankets, embroidered bibs, and a woodcut mobile to suspend over a crib. The business has grown primarily through positive word of mouth from satisfied customers. Kim is ready to take a giant step and launch a web site to showcase her baskets, increase sales, expand her customer base, and reduce costs. From the beginning of her business, she has received assistance from the local Small Business Administration's (*http://www.sba.gov*) small business development center (SBDC) and intends to use their resources in developing a web marketing plan. Kim is confident that her web marketing site will bring her business to a new and more profitable level.

Kim is an entrepreneur who runs a very small business out of her home. There are only two part-time employees and the owner. Annual revenue is under US$150,000. Other small businesses have millions of dollars of annual receipts, many more employees, and operate out of home in office buildings, retail stores, warehouses, manufacturing complexes, and other sites. Small businesses vary greatly. According to the Small Business Administration, a small business is independently owned and operated and not dominant in its field of operation. Most have far fewer than five hundred employees and many are owner operated. Small businesses can also be agricultural.[1]

Many small home businesses like Kim's are a silent, almost hidden part of the U.S.

economy, yet represent over 50 percent of all businesses, generate 10 percent of U.S. GDP, and employ over 3.5 million people. The second information revolution has amplified the importance of the home-based business and made it an attractive although risky option for many people.[2] The Web has given small businesses unprecedented opportunities for worldwide exposure. The low cost of creating, hosting, and maintaining a web site has encouraged many small businesspeople to try their hand at web marketing. They can perform marketing intelligence online and assess their competition, as well as find gaps in the market that their offers might fill. Since the Web is a vast library, they can find resources that were previously inaccessible. They can also locate suppliers and partners and new products. At the same time, if they do not have sound plans and good execution and cannot find a sufficiently large market, they can also quickly fail.

This is an exciting opportunity for Kim and her friends. By combining their unique product offer with cutting-edge Internet technology, they will be able to reach customers nationwide and worldwide, if they decide to accept international orders. Expanding this home business to a web storefront could greatly increase demand for its products. However, it is a risky venture. The site may get lost in web clutter, or at the other extreme, the partners could be overwhelmed by orders they cannot fill. To increase the probability of success, they need a well-designed marketing plan, carefully implemented, with controls that indicate how well the plan is meeting performance goals, and a realistic budget. They need to maintain their focus, find their online niche and stick with it. These are the topics considered in this chapter.

# Planning Fundamentals

Plans are blueprints for the future, road maps designed to move an enterprise from its current position to a desired prospective state. They are partly visionary and mostly practical, with specific instructions for what should happen and when.

Planning in large corporations is often left to professional planners trained to write comprehensive, complex, multifunctional plans. Although marketers usually contribute to business plans, they have full responsibility for writing marketing plans. Not all the marketers in an enterprise, particularly large corporations, directly participate in writing marketing plans. However, even if they are not directly involved in plan construction, salespeople, brand and product managers, advertising and public relations managers, and others contribute information used for planning purposes. Marketing plans are more common in larger enterprises than smaller ones, but size alone is no guarantee that a plan will be written and implemented, or that it will be successful.

Marketing planning should be conducted by enterprises of all sizes in all industries. It is not. Far too often marketing activities are conducted on an ad hoc basis, guided by an idea crystallizing in someone's mind propelled by a lack of understanding of market volatility or customer fickleness. Planning is something many people shy away from, claiming they do not have the time, information, expertise, or need to do it. But planning is not as intimidating as it sounds, and good plans effectively implemented can reduce costs, increase receipts, and protect the enterprise against marketplace disruptions. Effective marketing planning is a key to competitiveness.[3]

**Figure 13-1  A Nest of Plans**

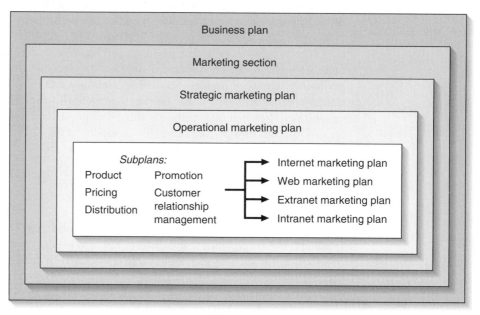

Marketing plans are nested within other plans, particularly the business plan.

## A NEST OF PLANS

Any business seeking funds from a bank or other lender must present a business plan that clearly and systematically documents how the business intends to operate. The lender wants evidence the business can create a profitable revenue stream and repay the loan within a prescribed time. The dot-com crash and 2000–2001 economic downturn dried up funding for many Internet ventures, but money is still available to support well-conceived, carefully planned Internet ventures.

A marketing section within the business plan generally addresses how marketing will be conducted to meet business plan goals. This is not a marketing plan. An operational **marketing plan** is a detailed, comprehensive, exhaustive blueprint for how marketing mix strategies and tactics will satisfy customers and meet business goals within a short period of time, usually one year. Figure 13-1 illustrates how a marketing plan is nested within a business plan.

A **strategic marketing plan** presents a blueprint for marketing activities to be conducted over a longer period of time, often three to five years or more. It provides a vision for what marketing can accomplish during that period, though it lacks the details of an operational marketing plan. An **operational marketing plan** is a detailed, month-to-month and sometimes week-to-week or even day-to-day tactical blueprint for marketing goals and performances within a short period of time, usually one year. It should be revisited on a regular basis, at least every quarter, for revision and updating. Some plans are updated far more frequently than that.

The operational marketing plan is highly functional, directing performances in the marketplace and establishing how those performances are evaluated. It contains sub-

**Marketing plan**
A detailed, comprehensive blueprint for how marketing mix strategies and tactics will be implemented to satisfy customer needs and meet business goals typically over a period of one year.

**Strategic marketing plan**
A plan for a longer period of time, often three to five years or more.

**Operational marketing plan**
See *marketing plan*.

plans for product management, pricing, distribution, and promotion, and customer relationship management that are highly detailed and provide specific tactical guidance.

**Web marketing plan**
A detailed set of instructions for how web marketing will be conducted.

A **web marketing plan** moves marketing planning from the traditional to the Internet environment. The web plan is either freestanding, particularly for clicks-only businesses that market only on the Web, or integrated into a traditional marketing plan or Internet marketing plan that also includes plans for marketing on other Internet sectors. This discussion focuses on public web marketing planning because that is the area of greatest activity. A web marketing plan is a detailed set of instructions and an operational plan for how web marketing will be conducted. It identifies goals and objectives, strategies and tactics, along with expected performances and outcomes. A web marketing plan also serves business plan goals and the mission statement. Ideally, all plans should be integrated, coordinated, and complementary. Sometimes they are not, which causes significant problems for the business and its managers.

## PLAN RESPONSIBILITIES

In large corporations, marketing managers simultaneously run multiple operational marketing plans. Plans are written for brands, product lines, product categories, target markets, or served geographical areas. They are written for Internet, intranet, extranet, and web marketing. Many corporate marketing managers run sophisticated computer programs and data warehouses that allow them to create highly detailed, numerically rich plans that can be tracked electronically in real time. They can forecast demand and sales receipts, simulate the effects of price changes, and develop cost projections. They can use data mining to develop descriptive and predictive models.

People with small businesses may lack the resources and time to write extremely detailed, highly sophisticated formal marketing plans, but this does not mean they should not plan. Lack of planning is one of the principal reasons so many dot-coms failed in 2000–2001. Planning requires the business to confront key issues that affect its success and survival. The process of writing the plan requires organization and an objective assessment of the business's readiness to engage in Internet and web marketing.

Because they lack time to prepare web marketing plans and expertise, small businesses are more susceptible to engaging offers from online firms that make extravagant claims for their ability to construct and implement *fantastically successful* web marketing plans. These firms promise access to vast numbers of new customers and revenue streams, all for a ridiculously low fee. Legitimate consultants are online, but it is difficult to separate them from the hucksters. Small businesses should exercise great care in selecting marketing plan consultants.

In large corporations, marketing managers writing operational web marketing plans frequently are isolated from customers and the marketplace, and specialists designing and implementing web sites and pages. In small businesses, the same people writing the web marketing plan are probably also interacting directly with customers. They answer questions and correspond with customers by email, so they are personally familiar with customer questions, complaints, purchases, and suggestions. They may be updating web content themselves or working directly with information system technicians to refresh pages. Web marketing by small businesses can be more personal and immediate than in large corporations, which can be a considerable advantage when plans are being developed in a volatile Internet environment that requires nimble responses to rapid changes.

Small business marketers have other advantages. Since their businesses have few management levels, they can revise a web marketing plan or site without seeking multiple approvals at successively higher management levels. Because they are closer to the customer and marketplace, they can personally monitor the environment and their competitors and make quick changes to a web site and market offer in response to emerging trends. Speed can be a considerable competitive advantage online, even more so than offline. Finally, because in many small businesses, people multitask, that is, perform multiple business functions, they avoid the turf conflicts that can arise in large corporations where functional area managers must compete for resources. They also avoid interdepartmental friction that arises from resistance to web marketing or conflicting goals for a web marketing site.

## ANSWERING KEY QUESTIONS

Marketers should address several key questions whose answers set plan boundaries. The questions will differ depending on the size of the enterprise, its industry, and the environment it faces. Forcing managers to consider these questions should lead to the identification of primary objectives for the web marketing site.

The first question is fundamental as it relates to the mission. *Why is this business going online?* What goals will the web site accomplish? Effective goals are hard but reasonable, specific, measurable, relevant, and stated with benchmarks and time limits. Goals can be to gain awareness, sell products, build brands, position or reposition products, increase profits, drive customer traffic to an offline storefront or salespeople, clear stale inventory, provide information, entertain, service customers, reduce costs, create goodwill, spread a message, maintain parity with the competition, or collect customer data.

*Who is responsible for web site marketing?* If the business is a small owner-operated business, the owner may take responsibility or work closely with a web management consultant, perhaps a local ISP, to create, host, and refresh the site on a regular basis. In larger enterprises, it can be done in-house, outsourced to external service consultants, or done by a combination of the two. Even companies as large as Texas Instruments (TI at *http://www.ti.com*) use a combination of in-house experts and outside service consultants. Outside talent can sometimes add a needed fresh perspective and expertise.[4]

Web site marketing may be solely a marketing responsibility or a team effort that includes members from other functional areas of the business. Collaboration is preferred, where all departments with a stake in the success of the web site work together. Depending on the enterprise, this may include advertising, public relations, sales, computing services, human resources, corporate management, finance, production, information technology, and others.[5] Alternately, each department or brand may support its own web site, and marketers with finance, human resources, or other departments focus on running an in-department effort.

A related question concerns personnel within the marketing department who will work with the information systems specialists. Will their web responsibilities be added to their regular marketing duties or will they be shifted totally to the Web? If so, can their vacated position be filled? If it is not possible to use existing personnel to run the web site, will permission be given to hire new people or will current personnel be retrained? Launching and maintaining a web site creates a series of sometimes thorny human resource problems. These problems are exacerbated when there is a recession on and hiring is frozen and/or needed skills are in great demand while people with needed skills are in short supply.

*How difficult will it be to gain cooperation for the web marketing effort?* In a very small business, it is assumed that the owner/operator supports the concept of web marketing or it would not be attempted. In any business with more than one employee, it should be a top priority to gain the cooperation of anyone directly involved with the web marketing effort who can benefit from it or imperil it. In a larger business, it is important to gain the support of other departments that may not directly help or benefit from the web marketing effort but that could block resources and its success. If the web marketing effort is not viewed as important to corporate goals, it may require powerful persuasion to get doubters to cooperate.

A final question deals with financing. *How will the web site be financed?* Will the costs be carved out of the existing marketing budget? Will the enterprise have to seek additional internal funds or external loans to launch and maintain the site until it is self-sufficient or will the site be a loss leader, run without profit because it makes other contributions to business operations? If it is a loss leader, run for public relations or other reasons, whose budget covers the costs? Web grocers have historically operated at a loss; however, the survivors are realizing that a losing money online service can be a powerful competitive advantage for its offline retail business. Many customers like online ordering and home delivery. It increases their loyalty to the grocer, online and off. This service may grow in importance as baby boomers age. It may even become profitable if larger numbers of loyal users use online ordering, so it is an investment in the future.

## MARKETING PLAN FORMATS

Most marketing students are familiar with the components of a traditional marketing plan and realize there is no single standardized universally used plan format. Most plans cover the same topics but vary in naming the different parts. Formats vary by enterprise, type, size, and industry. Marketing plan formats and examples of completed marketing plans are online at such sites as The Small Business Start-Up Center (*http://www.bplans.com*) and BizPlans.com (*http://www.bizplans.com*). Other web sites have software to guide marketing plan development. For example, Marketing Plan Pro (http://www.paloalto.com/ps/mp) provides an online guided tour that outlines the steps in marketing planning and a company example.

**Internet marketing plan**

Marketing plans that expand coverage to include all Internet marketing activities, the Web, intranets, and extranets, and other Internet services.

**Internet marketing plans** expand coverage to include all Internet marketing. If an enterprise has an intranet and/or extranet, then marketing plans are designed for them. Marketing plans may be written solely for an intranet or extranet if sufficient marketing activities occur there. Intranet marketing may target employees or stakeholders like investors. Extranet marketing targets suppliers, distributors, and customers who are part of the company's extranet. Internet marketing plans should also complement offline marketing. Marketing plans for clicks-only web enterprises *are* Internet/web marketing plans.

## ✔ CONCEPT CHECK

1. Explain the statement "Plans are blueprints for the future."
2. How does the web marketing plan fit into the nest of plans?
3. What key questions should be asked/answered by those writing web marketing plans?

# The Web Marketing Plan

Web marketing plans focus on how marketing will be accomplished on the business's web site and if there is a bricks component, how the two will work together. The parts are much like those of a traditional marketing plan, but the focus is specifically on web marketing.

**WEB UPDATE**

Web Marketing Plans

Every web marketing plan is unique. Format and detail depend on enterprise characteristics, the environment in which it operates, resources available for developing the plan, and reason(s) for going online and/or maintaining a web presence. Regardless of format, each plan should include

1. a company and market analysis that evaluates the company, market, customers, competitors, and relevant online/offline environments,
2. marketing mix analysis,
3. an action plan that implements (operationalizes) the marketing mix,
4. financials that project expected costs, revenues, and profits, and
5. control and feedback processes that determine how well the site and plan are performing and provide guidance for how plan and site should be revisited and revised (see "Web Marketing Plan Elements" below).

## Web Marketing Plan Elements

Formats for web marketing plans vary, but have these parts.

**Internet Marketing Plan**
1. Company and Market Analysis
   a. Company and Industry Overview
   b. Market Analysis
   c. Online Environmental Analysis
   d. General Environmental Analysis
2. Marketing Mix Analysis
   a. Goals and Objectives
   b. Strategies and Tactics
3. Action Plan
4. Financials
5. Controls and Feedback

## COMPANY, MARKET, AND ENVIRONMENTAL ANALYSIS

The company analysis considers (a) what unique benefits and value it can offer its target market, (b) how it expects to benefit from web marketing, and (c) its readiness to do so. The market offer is the foundation for web marketing. It is how the company web site adds value (utility) and benefits customers. For example, an office supply web site adds *convenience value* by selling reasonably priced home office supplies delivered directly to the home office. A bank's web site adds *time value* by letting customers access their checking accounts online 24/7/365 and pay bills online, thus avoiding postage. An auction site provides *entertainment value* and possibly, but not always, *price value*.

Web marketing benefits must be stated for the enterprise as well as its customers. Some businesses want their web sites to generate additional revenues by attracting new customers, by penetrating an existing market, or entering a new one. Others want the site to better service existing customers and strengthen their loyalty. The site's principal benefit may be to cross-sell or up-sell current customers. Alternately, the web site's principal purpose may be to drive traffic to an offline store. Benefits should be clearly stated and quantified, if possible.

Readiness is examined from management, cost, and human resource perspectives. Ideally, web marketing should be supported by all parts of the enterprise and not become a magnet for conflict. It is important to determine if managers in other functional areas support web marketing and whether web marketing requires that funds be taken from their budgets. Few managers surrender resources willingly. If web marketing clearly benefits all parts of the company, this is a powerful message that can help build support for the web marketing effort companywide.

Costs are a key consideration, particularly since poor planning and high start-up and maintenance costs drove many first movers off the Web. Cost projections are needed to compare with expected benefits through a cost/benefit analysis. The business must determine if it has sufficient resources to initiate and maintain the web effort short term or must seek outside funds. If outside funds are sought, does the company have the stability and track record to support its application and get funded?

From a human resource perspective, the web effort requires web-savvy marketers and technology system specialists working together. Some technology responsibilities can be outsourced. If it is an in-house effort, resources should be dedicated to it, which often requires reallocating and retraining people and filling vacancies caused by their reassignment.

The industry overview examines how other companies are using the Internet in their marketing efforts and industry trends, including growth of Internet use by companies in the industry. Many industries have trade associations with web sites that may have case studies of other company's experiences with Internet marketing. DMOZ The Open Directory (*http://dmoz.org/Business/Industries/Retail/Associations*) lists many trade associations with links to their web sites, including toy retailers, warehouse clubs, retail hardware stores, home furnishing retailers, etailers, store planners, picture framers, and many others including the Association of Professional Gift Basket Designers (APGBD at *http://www.apgbd.com*).

Market analysis also examines the present state of the company's specific market, including its size and numbers of buyers, customer demographics and purchasing characteristics, numbers of competitors and their distribution (clicks only, bricks and clicks, bricks and mortar), and identification of principal online direct and indirect competitors. Marketing intelligence should be gathered about main competitors, which includes information about their strengths and weaknesses. Their web sites should be visited and evaluated, and their market offers studied. Products and prices should be analyzed, along with shopping baskets (if it is a selling site), return policies, site navigation, feedback options, and use of new technology. The analysis should specify the extent of the direct and indirect online competition, and if the market is saturated or there is a gap to be filled. Do competitors have a synergistic online/offline marketing effort? Do they have a competitive advantage? Answers to these questions should indicate positioning opportunities.

Market analysis is of served and prospective target markets. If the business has an offline presence, offline customers should be considered, particularly if they can be moved online. Marketing research can answer questions about how difficult it will be to persuade target markets to become Internet users, if they are not already, or what customers want on a web site. What promotions appeal to this market? How price sensitive are they? Will they be willing to pay shipping and handling for products purchased from the web site? Web site marketing requires getting inside customers' heads and trying to understand what motivates them and how to appeal to them and build long-term relationships. While marketing research is recommended, it can be costly, time consuming, and beyond the capacities of some very small businesses.

A SWOT analysis (strengths, weaknesses, opportunities, threats) is commonly used in marketing planning and can help assess web readiness. Strengths and weaknesses analyses directly address the business's resources, including managers' determination to commit to developing a successful web marketing site. Opportunities and threats assessments evaluate environmental factors. These include the economy, technology, and competition that can jeopardize the web marketing effort or present opportunities for growth and expansion. An opportunity analysis should identify gaps in the web market that the business can fill with its market offer and resources.

Some marketing academics question the value of a SWOT analysis. They consider the time and effort needed to conduct one a drain on company resources, and evidence is lacking that a SWOT directly affects profitability. However, the *process* of conducting a SWOT is valuable. It causes planners to focus on issues that require attention and to identify issues that are not as important. Systematically addressing issues that underlie the SWOT categories may not be *directly* traceable to increased profits, but to ignore them without an adequate substitute could be shortsighted and ultimately, costly.

## MARKETING MIX ANALYSIS

Marketers manage the marketing mix (4Ps) variables and use them to make offers that target markets find attractive, if not irresistible. Early in the planning process, goals and objectives are established for what the web site is to accomplish for the firm. A goal is broader than an objective and sometimes may overlap several marketing plans, each covering a one-year period. A web site marketing goal may concern profitability. Specific objectives are stated for details of how the goal will be achieved. Several objectives may be stated for each goal. In the case of the profitability goal, objectives include instituting stringent cost controls for web site operations and getting customers to buy more at the site. Objectives should be stated in measurable terms as performance outcomes. Performances and outcomes objectives include sales objectives, site traffic objectives, customer service objectives, cost reduction objectives, and personnel reduction objectives.

Objectives stated numerically with time limits provide performance benchmarks that can be monitored to see if they are being achieved. Multiple objectives can be operationalized simultaneously. Whatever the objectives, they should be stated simply, clearly, measurably, and with time limits. Large corporations can have hundreds of marketing plans, each with multiple objectives, operating concurrently. Kim, from the opening vignette, and other home-based small business owners may state only one or two web site objectives. Her sales objective is to increase sales receipts by 10 percent in the next three months. A cost reduction objective is to get 5 percent of her offline customers to order online within the next three months. This will reduce the amount of time she and her friends have to spend on the telephone taking orders and the time cost of diverting their attention from making gift baskets. These objectives are clear, simple, achievable, measurable, and time based.

Strategies are approaches that will be used to achieve the web marketing objectives. Strategies are broadly stated activities and performances for the marketing mix variables (4Ps), customer relationship management, and web site content, design, and technology (figure 13-2). Marketing mix and technology strategies must be customer-centric, designed to make the web experience positive for customers and to satisfy their needs/wants with the company's product offer.

**Figure 13-2  Web Marketing Strategies**

Strategies are approaches designed to accomplish objectives. Strategies should be developed for the marketing mix variables, customer relationship management, and the web site.

   Before Kim or any Internet marketer can develop strategies, they must figuratively get inside their customers' heads. Strategies should flow from customer insight based on an analysis of customer characteristics, buying preferences, and interaction history. Kim believes in the marketing concept and makes customer satisfaction the central premise for her web marketing effort. To design web marketing strategies that will satisfy them, she needs to know the following about her customers:

**WHO THEY ARE**    What are their demographics and psychographics, and what are the identities of the heavy-user 20 percent? How many of their purchases are new buys or rebuys? Kim needs to know if she has made any progress in attracting corporate gift basket buyers. If she has, she can build on experiences with these customers to attract others like them. If she has no corporate customers, she might want to consider moving into this lucrative market and targeting it with a permission email marketing campaign. Small businesses are well advised to target concentrated markets, groups (niches) with specialized needs that their market offer can satisfy.

**WHY THEY BUY**    Kim needs to look closely at her sales records over the past two years to identify the most popular occasions for basket purchases. Are customers purchasing baskets for themselves and family members, for friends? Why are they purchasing her gift baskets? What unique features and benefits attract customers?

**WHEN THEY BUY**    Are purchases concentrated around religious or secular holidays, or events like graduations? If so, promotions should be heavied up prior to when customers make their decisions. Permission email campaigns should be timed to hit just before purchase decisions are made. If purchases are made for family events, email reminders can be sent prior to the events.

**WHAT THEY BUY**    What types of baskets by contents and price are most popular? What custom designs are most often ordered?

**HOW THEY BUY**    What payment forms are preferred? Do most customers use credit cards? If so, what cards? Popularly used credit cards must be accepted online as a customer service.

**HOW THEY FOUND HER**    Kim advertises in the local hardcopy Yellow Pages and pays for small display ads in the local newspapers around Christmas. However, most of her customers find her business through word of mouth from friends. Kim needs to know what proportion of customers find her from each contact point.

Once Kim has systematically evaluated her current customers and developed consumer insight, she needs to consider strategies to meet her objectives. Her sales objective is to increase sales receipts by 10 percent in the first three months after the web site is launched. Based on her currently monthly offline sales receipts, Kim must generate US$3,249.99 in sales in order to achieve this objective. Considering the average price of her baskets, that is around a total of forty to forty-five baskets sold from the web site in three months. Kim's strategies must focus on traffic, products, pricing, order fulfillment, promotions, CRM, and the web site. Tactics are the details, the short-term tasks that accomplish the strategies. They include the following:

**TRAFFIC**   *Tactics:* Kim must develop tactics for getting customers to her site. Offline, she will send mailers to current customers offering a 10 percent one-time only one-basket discount for web purchases. She will add an additional 10 percent discount for any current customer who gets a friend to make a purchase from the web site. The discount will eat into her profits, but added traffic will increase sales. Online, she will register with search engines, join web rings and gift communities, add reciprocal links, and use email permission marketing to announce her web site launch to consumers and corporate buyers. She will hire a web site positioning company for search engine optimization or use Web Site Traffic Builder (*http://www.intelliquis.com*), which can register her domain name with more than nine hundred search engines.

**PRODUCTS**   *Tactics:* She needs to showcase her products in the best possible light. This means displaying her entire product line in clear, high-definition, enlargeable, multiview pictures accompanied by descriptive text and testimonials from satisfied customers. Free gift wrap and cards will be offered with purchases over US$75 because her offline customers always want them.

**PRICING**   *Tactics:* To stimulate corporate sales, Kim will offer multipurchase corporate discounts for web purchases. She will post the price of each product in U.S.dollars. Initially, she will not sell her products to other countries, which eliminates the need for currency converters and dealing with currency fluctuations. She will provide clear explanations of shipping and handling costs, and transportation options. Free shipping will be offered for purchases of US$200 or more to the same address in the continental United States. She will contract with major U.S. credit card vendors for payment fulfillment.

**FULFILLMENT**   *Tactics:* Order fulfillment will be in-house and shipping will be handled by UPS. UPS package tracking is a popular service that customers appreciate.

**PROMOTION**   *Tactics:* Her promotion strategy is to use as many free or reciprocal promotion devices as possible. She will pay several highly popular bid search engines to get top listed and hire her current local ISP to create the site, host, and maintain it. The site will be interactive with email going from customers directly to Kim's home computer. She plans to contract with a permission marketing company to send email announcements of her online business to corporate executives who opt in to receive promotions about corporate gift offers by email.

**CUSTOMER RELATIONSHIP MANAGEMENT**    *Tactics:* Because her customers value privacy, Kim will have a clear, concise, simple privacy statement on the web site front page that states no information will be sold to third parties. All ordering information will be encrypted. Data collected from customers will be used to contact them in the future, with their permission. She will offer an email reminder service for customers. With their permission, Kim will contact them by email with a reminder of an approaching date when they have purchased gift baskets in the past.

**WEB SITE**    *Tactics:* Kim has found that her customers are not interested in games or other distractions when they are shopping online. Therefore, she will not clutter her web site with anything that detracts from the shopping experience. She will make sure shoppers can find what they want quickly, order it securely, and track package delivery. She also knows they are interested in how the gifts are crafted, so several pages of information will be linked to the web site front page showing Kim and her friends painting baskets and making the contents. Kim will work with her ISP technology service consultant to ensure the site design is clean, bright, uncluttered, and easy to navigate and has shopping basket software that works quickly, simply, and accurately.

## THE ACTION PLAN

**Action plan**

A step-by-step blueprint for implementing tactics that will achieve marketing strategies.

An **action plan** is a step-by-step blueprint for implementing tactics that will achieve the strategies. Tactics are highly detailed tasks with deadlines. They identify responsibilities and who will fill them. For example, under product tactics Kim will take digital pictures of each type of basket she sells and write detailed descriptions of their contents and the images that can be painted on the wooden slats. Her ISP consultant will convert the digital pictures into web images for product page displays. Kim will contact current customers and ask them for short testimonials that state their satisfaction with her gift baskets. Their statements will be displayed on a *Satisfied Customers* web page along with pictures of the baskets they purchased. She will get signed releases from them for the use of their statements and initials on the web site. With the assistance of her SBDC consultant, Kim will select an email list broker for a permission email mailing to announce the launch of the site and an online marketing firm to register her site with the most popular U.S. search engines and reregister it every thirty days. She will contact VeriSign's Network Solutions (*http://www.networksolutions.com*) and register an appropriate domain name for her site.

An action plan should be sufficiently detailed so a stranger can pick it up and immediately know what has to be done, within what time frame, and by whom. It should not be cluttered with documentary materials that belong in an appendix. It should be realistic about what can be achieved with the number of people and resources available. Action plans should be revisited and revised as the plan is implemented.

## FINANCIALS

By now the marketer should be able to forecast what it will cost to create, launch, and maintain the web site. Expected revenues, profits, and losses should be projected. Several scenarios should be developed for different levels of demand. If demand is higher than expected, what are the implications for fulfillment, receipts, costs, and profits? If demand is lower than expected, how will losses be covered? What sales levels trigger alarms that require revisions to the plan?

Creating and maintaining a web site, even if it is a static, information-only site, carries a cost. Most businesses tend to underestimate costs, and when they are selling online, they overestimate revenues. It is a function of the relative youth of the online environment coupled with a lack of experience on the Web. As the Web matures and more businesses reach profitability, case histories of financial successes will become models for others to follow.

## CONTROLS

**Control**

The process of identifying and implementing measures that will be used to compare actual marketing performance and outcomes to projected performance and outcomes.

Marketers use controls to track the progress of marketing plan implementation. **Control** is the process of identifying measures that will be used to compare actual marketing performance and outcomes to projected performance and outcomes. The purpose is to evaluate whether or not web marketing objectives have been met and if not, why. Control, like planning and implementation, is a systematic process. Controls should be in place to measure the performance of each tactic.

Performance must be monitored continuously because of web, environment, competitor, and customer volatility. Depending on the results, alterations should be made to the plan in order to bring actual performance in line with the ideal (projected performance). Controls must be developed along with the plan and implemented beginning with site launch.

Control tracking systems apply yardsticks to collected data. As mentioned, Kim's sales objective is an increase in sales by 10 percent in three months and her cost reduction objective is to get 5 percent of her offline customers to order online during the same time period. These objectives are measurable benchmarks. The control mechanism in this case is to take actual sales and costs in three months and determine how they compare with the objectives. If both exceed the objectives, Kim is doing something right. Missing the objectives is a clear signal that some adjustments might be needed.

Some controls run continuously, particularly those tracking site traffic and sales. They can be reported daily, or summary statements can be prepared weekly. With the Web's volatility, monthly or quarterly reports are too infrequent to be of real value. Large, highly active web sites report data in real time, which is far beyond what a small business needs or can digest.

Web marketers must decide when and how much control information is needed in order to control marketing activities without causing information overload. With the technology available, the volume of information generated and distributed can easily overwhelm the ability of any marketer to analyze and use it.

**WEB UPDATE**

*Small Business Web Marketing Plans*

## ✔ CONCEPT CHECK

1. Explain the relationship between goals, objectives, strategies, and tactics.
2. What is an action plan?
3. Why are controls needed?

# Implementing the Plan

**Implementation**
The process of activating or operationalizing marketing plans.

Web marketing plans are meaningless until they are activated. This process is known as **implementation,** where resources (people and money), technology, and materials are brought together in an organized way to execute plan tactics and achieve web marketing strategies, objectives, and goals. Planning and implementation, followed by control, are the three interrelated, unified marketing management processes that occur in all enterprises. They are managed formally in large corporations. Small businesses also use the processes, although they may not be identified by name.

## TIMELINE

Launching and maintaining a web marketing site in large corporations involves many people, functional specialists who work full-time on narrowly defined tasks. Web marketers in small or midsize businesses typically multitask, tending to other responsibilities while overseeing the total web marketing effort. Regardless of enterprise size or resources, time has a tendency to slip away, which makes a timeline important to successful plan implementation. A timeline should have dated deadlines by which specific tasks are to be accomplished. For example, Kim sets a deadline of six weeks from the start of implementation to receive testimonials and signed releases from satisfied customers. When the time has passed, she can check this task off the list. Within that period of time, she will be performing other tasks, which also have deadlines. Timelines should be maintained on charts or computer spreadsheets so tasks can be checked off as they are completed and deadlines noted so work can be planned to meet them.

## SITE CONSTRUCTION AND MANAGEMENT

An important part of plan implementation concerns web site construction and management. While the technical work can be performed in-house, small businesses are more likely to outsource. Selecting, hiring, and working with a technical system consultant or firm requires collaboration and the constant exchange of information. Arrangements vary, but technical consultants can help create web marketing plans or concentrate solely on web site design, construction, hosting, and management. Decisions about content, design, site navigation, and other site-specific issues should not be left solely in the hands of any consultant. If the site is to capitalize on customer insight developed in the process of web marketing planning, then plan developers must collaborate to ensure that the site accomplishes its customer relationship marketing purposes. Alternately, construction and maintenance can be in-house. Some web sites offer assistance for the do-it-yourselfer. For example, Staples Business Center (*http://www.staples.com/BizServices*) offers sales and marketing help that includes many facets of web site planning, implementation, and maintenance

Once a site is constructed and launched, the real marketing work begins. It is not enough to launch it, then ignore it. A web marketing site is a constant *work in progress*. Content must be refreshed on a regular basis. Prices must be changed, as needed. Design standards change and nothing is worse than a stale, old-fashioned web site design. If external links are used, they must be checked regularly to ensure they are still active. Site management is an issue that must be resolved before the site is launched.

## PLAN REVISION

Control data can flag problems early so changes can be made in time to avert disaster. They can also show what is effective so resources can be redirected to support successful offers. A web site without controls leaves the marketer in the dark. Haphazardly implemented controls give untrustworthy, unusable results. Excessive control data can cause an information glut. If results are good, the response may be to maintain the status quo. If results are bad, action must be taken or the situation will get worse. This often means revising web marketing action plans and/or reconstructing all or parts of the web site.

### ✔ CONCEPT CHECK

1. What does it mean to implement a web marketing plan?
2. Why should marketers establish an implementation timeline?
3. Why should web marketing plans be revised?

# *The Web Marketing Budget*

**Web marketing budget**
A blueprint for how funds are allocated to various web marketing activities.

A **web marketing budget** is a blueprint for how funds are allocated to various web marketing activities. As a policy statement, it is a detailed plan that identifies priority spending areas and how marketing will be conducted to achieve its performance goals. It is a projected profit and loss statement for the year, linked to financial reporting periods. In large businesses, it is also an evaluation tool for measuring a manager's performance.[6]

In large businesses and corporations, marketing managers receive a marketing allocation, then distribute it through a marketing budget. Many small businesses do not budget for marketing, let alone web marketing. They get trapped in a race to survive week to week, month to month, moving funds from one account to another, paying bills as they collect receipts, always worried about covering their costs and making margins. Funds for marketing activities are provided on an ad hoc basis and are often what is left over after bills are paid. Others write budgets but never follow them. Even those businesses that follow budgets rarely have enough money to do everything they want to do. Instead, they have to choose between alternatives based on costs, estimated benefits, projected revenue, and available funds. Regardless of business size, all marketers should create a reasonable web budget tied to performance outcomes that serve web marketing goals. They should stick to a marketing budget, yet be flexible enough to revise it when necessary.

### THE WEB BUDGET IN THE MARKETING BUDGET

A marketing budget is a component part of the business's operating budget. A web marketing budget may be part of the marketing budget or a separate entity. It may be carved out of other budgets, which can generate conflict if other departments do not support the web marketing effort. A budget should state expenses (fixed and variable costs), sales, and projected net profit.

### EXPENSES, REVENUE, AND PROJECTED NET PROFIT

Web marketing expenses include both web site and related offline fixed and variable costs. A comprehensive expense estimate includes initial web site development and launch costs, as well as site maintenance and upkeep, marketing and promotion cost estimates. Costs should be kept in line through the use of controls that monitor actual expenditures compared with projected expenditures and activate triggers that signal cost overruns.

Some costs are fixed and recurring, others are variable. Initial creation and launch costs are associated with content, design, technology, and promotion activities. Some costs continue after launch, as the site is maintained. Others will appear again when the site is refreshed or relaunched. Most sites can take advantage of multiple revenue streams. Even if the site is not a web storefront, affiliate marketing and selling on-site advertising can generate revenue. Some sites add revenue by selling their email lists, which results in customers getting unwanted email. Obviously, online sales are a prime revenue source for many sites. What is less clear is how to account for offline sales by customers who first use the web site for information and direction offline. Revenue streams may include advertising, affiliate marketing, product sales, paid subscriptions, and selling customer lists.

The budget is incomplete without the final calculation of projected net profit. Profit is total sales (minus cost of sales) minus total expenses. The web site generates profit if sales are greater than expenses; it operates at a loss if they are not. Some sites are not meant to be profit centers. Whether they are designed to run at a loss is another issue.

## ✔ CONCEPT CHECK

1. Why is the budget considered a policy document?
2. How are total web costs calculated?
3. Explain why some web sites may not be run as profit centers.

# *Summary*

### *Planning Fundamentals*

Plans are blueprints for the future, road maps designed to move an enterprise from its current position to a desired state in the future. They are partly visionary and mostly practical, with specific instructions for what should happen and when. Businesses of all sizes in all industries should conduct marketing planning. The marketing section within a business plan is not a marketing plan. A marketing plan is a detailed, comprehensive, exhaustive blueprint for how marketing will be conducted. A strategic marketing plan presents a blueprint for a longer period of time, often three to five years or more. An operational marketing plan is a detailed, month-to-month and sometimes week-to-week or even day-to-day tactical blueprint for marketing performances within a short period of time, usually one year. It should be revisited on a regular basis, at least every quarter, for revision and updating. A web marketing plan is either freestanding or integrated into a traditional marketing plan or an Internet marketing plan. It is a detailed set of instructions for how web marketing will be conducted, with expected performances and outcomes. Plans are written for brands, product lines, product categories, target markets, or even served markets. They are written for Internet, intranet, extranet, and web marketing. In small businesses, the same people writing the marketing plan are probably also interacting directly with customers. Even before the planning process begins, marketers must address some key questions whose answers set plan boundaries. There is no single standardized universally used marketing plan format.

### *The Web Marketing Plan*

Every web marketing plan is unique. Format and details depend on the enterprise, its environment, and its reason(s) for going online and/or maintaining a web presence. Each plan must consider the company, market, and environment, set goals for the web site, and present strategies to achieve them. An action plan operationalizes strategies with highly detailed tactics. Financials project expected costs, revenues, and profits. Feedback and control processes determine how well the site is performing and provide insights into how the plan and site should be revised. The company analysis considers (a) what unique benefits and value it can offer its target market, (b) how it expects to benefit from web marketing, and (c) its readiness to do so. Benefits can be stated for both the enterprise and its customers. Readiness should be examined from management, cost, and human resource perspectives. A SWOT analysis (strengths, weaknesses, opportunities, threats) is commonly used in marketing planning and can be valuable in assessing web readiness. The costs of web marketing are a key consideration, particularly since poor planning and high start-up and maintenance costs drove many first movers off the Web. Market analysis examines the present state of the market, including what competitors, present and future, are doing and demand for the market offer. Objectives are what the web site is to accomplish for the enterprise. Some frequently used objectives are for sales, traffic, service, cost reduction, and personnel reduction. Objectives stated numerically with time limits provide performance benchmarks that can be monitored to see if they are achieved. Strategies are approaches that will be used to achieve the web marketing objectives. They integrate the mission and its policies and actions into a cohesive whole. Web marketers should know their customers before trying to develop strategies to satisfy them. They need to know who they are, why they buy, when they buy, what they buy, how they buy, and how they found the web site. An action plan is a step-by-step blueprint for implementing tactics that will achieve the stated strategies. Tactics are highly detailed with deadlines. The marketer should be able to forecast what it will cost to create, launch, and maintain the web site. Expected revenues, profits, and losses should be projected. Marketers use controls to track the progress of marketing plan implementation.

## Implementing the Plan

Web marketing plans are meaningless until they are activated, which is the process of implementation. Planning and implementation, followed by control, are the three interrelated, unified marketing management processes. A timeline should be constructed with dated deadlines by which specific tasks are accomplished. An important part of plan implementation concerns web site construction and management. Once a site is constructed and launched, the real marketing work begins. A web marketing site is a constant work in progress. Control data can flag problems early so changes can be made in time to avert disaster. They can also show what is effective so resources can be redirected to support successful offers. Control tracking systems apply yardsticks to collected data. Controls can run continuously, particularly those that are tracking site traffic and sales.

## The Web Marketing Budget

A web marketing budget is a blueprint for how funds are allocated to various web marketing activities. As a policy statement, it is a detailed plan that identifies priority spending areas and how marketing will be conducted to achieve performance goals. It is a projected profit and loss statement for the year, linked to financial reporting periods. In large businesses it is also an evaluation tool for measuring managers' performance. A marketing budget is a component part of the business's operating budget. Some costs are fixed and recurring; others are variable. Initial creation and launch costs are associated with content, design, technology, and promotion activities. Multiple revenue streams, including advertising, affiliate marketing, product sales, and subscriptions, can generate receipts for the site. The budget is incomplete without the final calculation of projected net profit. Profit is total sales (minus cost of sales) minus total expenses.

# Internet Marketing Application

While marketing is most often associated with for-profit businesses, a considerable amount of marketing takes place in nonprofit enterprises. Nonprofit marketing is conducted by organizations that, along with governments, contribute over 20 percent of U.S. GDP. Over one million registered nonprofit organizations employ over ten million people, about 7 percent of the U.S. workforce.

Careers in nonprofits give marketers an opportunity to make a difference in society, as well as apply their marketing skills very early in their career. Many nonprofits are small, and even large ones may not have more than a handful of marketers on staff. As a result, marketers frequently make broad decisions about many aspects of marketing. Rarely are they pigeonholed into only one or two decision areas.

Many web sites promote specific nonprofit groups or act as portals to information about nonprofits with links to their sites. GuideStar, the National Directory of Nonprofits (*http://www.guidestar.org*), has detailed

analyses of individual public charities. The Nonprofit Gateway (*http://www.nonprofit.gov*) is a network of links to federal information and nonprofit services.

Visit any two of the following web sites. Evaluate the contents of the site, then compare them on the marketing plan criteria listed in the table below.

- American Association of Retired Persons (AARP at *http://www.aarp.org*)
- American Diabetes Association (*http://www.diabetes.org*)
- American Humane Association (*http://www.americanhumane.org*)
- American Red Cross (*http://redcross.org*)
- Hospice Foundation of America (*http://www.hospicefoundation.org*)
- Oxfam International (*http://www.oxfam.org*)
- United Way of America (*http://national.unitedway.org/index.cfm*)

## Nonprofit Web Marketing Site Analysis

| Marketing Plan Criteria | Site 1 | Site 2 |
|---|---|---|
| What is the site's marketing goal? | | |
| What are the site's marketing objectives? | | |
| What strategies and tactics are used? | | |
| Are any controls evident? | | |
| Is feedback collected? | | |
| How effectively does the site market the nonprofit? Explain. | | |

# Chapter Review Questions

1. Why are small businesses so important to the U.S. economy?
2. Explain why all businesses should have a marketing plan.
3. Contrast a strategic and an operational marketing plan.
4. Why is it important to assign responsibilities in a web marketing plan?
5. Is the marketing section in a business plan the same as a marketing plan? Explain.
6. How can a marketing plan help a dot-com get financing?
7. What are the parts of a traditional marketing plan?
8. Why is an environmental analysis conducted during marketing plan development?

9.  What does web marketing readiness mean?
10. How detailed should strategies be in a web marketing plan?
11. What financials should be included in a web marketing plan?
12. Timelines are useful tools. Why?

13. Is a web site ever finished? Explain.
14. What costs should be included in a web site expense statement?
15. Why are some web sites deliberately constructed not to be profit centers?

# Case Study

## A Plan for Monster.com

Monster.com (*http://www.monster.com*) is making a move. As of the end of June 2001, it became the world's largest online recruitment company. At that time, it acquired HotJobs.com (*http://www.hotjobs.com*) for about US$460 million, which combined with its own 60 percent market share in the United States will give it a 71 percent share. It is the number one career site and fifty-third most visited web property.

Monster is one of the few pure play dot-coms benefiting from the 2000–2001 economic downturn. As jobs get harder to find and layoffs increase, more people turn to online career management companies. Unique visitors to the site jumped from 1.8 million in July 2000 to 6.3 million in July 2001, 7.2 million in September 2001, and almost 8.9 million by the end of December 2001.

Monster's advantage over offline recruiting sites is more targeted information available quicker. Monster measures its success by customer satisfaction and loyalty. Monster was one of the first movers in online recruitment. It focused on brand building and creating a sustainable brand. The good news for Monster is that U.S. college students are almost 100 percent online and very career oriented. This should guarantee Monster a large pool of applicants to serve to companies as demand grows.[7]

### CHECK IT OUT

Monster.com has been adding extra services lately. Among them are a new resume product designed to help job seekers raise their awareness of their skills and showcase them more effectively, and a learning center. Monster also has MonsterTRAK (*http://www.monstertrak.com*) career resource and MonsterLearning (*http://www.monsterlearning.com*), a learning site related to career management. Check out what Monster has to offer. It might be to your advantage to look for information about nonprofit marketing careers. Monster has a comprehensive area dedicated to nonprofits and provides valuable information about career opportunities with these employers.

### A GLOBAL PERSPECTIVE

Monster's gone global! Its Global Gateway lists jobs in countries where Monster now has affiliates. The Monster Network reaches Australia, Canada, several European countries and the United Kingdom, New Zealand, Hong Kong, Singapore, and India. Its international network of twenty-one countries is growing. International sites are local content and local language. Monster recently completed a strategic alliance with AOL Europe to bring Monster's career resources to AOL's European online subscribers. Monster will be featured prominently on AOL Europe and promoted by AOL in its European markets. Visit Monster (*http://www.monster.com*) and link to some international sites to evaluate how Monster localizes content. What is Monster's goal in going global? What are its objectives, strategies, and tactics? How many web marketing plans might Monster be running at any point in time? Is Monster hiring?

## CHAPTER FOURTEEN

# Marketing Site Development: Content, Design, and Construction

## LEARNING OBJECTIVES

- To examine issues that must be considered prior to web site development
- To identify content issues that affect site development decisions
- To understand how web site design can advance site marketing goals
- To explain the impact of construction issues on web site effectiveness

## Toby Becomes The Web Site Project Director

Toby is Vice President for Marketing Communications of his company's pet care products division. The company has decided that each product division should develop its own standalone branded web site to sell its products. In response to this directive, Toby's boss asked him to be project director for the development of the pet care division's web site. Toby will be working with brand managers, the company's graphic and interface designers, information system architects, programmers, usability experts, and others to create and maintain the site. His top priority is to make sure the site serves the needs of pet owners who care deeply about their pets and are willing to spend more to make sure their cats and dogs are well cared for and healthy. He wants the site to appeal to owners' emotional attachments to the animals that share their lives. As part of his preparation, Toby plans to meet with each pet care brand manager to hear his or her ideas for the site and determine what content each can provide. Toby's overriding concern is to extend the division's custom care concept to the web, making sure loyal customers get the same excellent service online they have grown to expect from the company's traditional store and catalog sales offline. The division is developing its web site in-house because its employees have the expertise to do so. They also want to make certain the web site clearly reflects their customer-centric philosophy of marketing.

Marketers must learn the *reason why* visitors come to their web sites. Reason why should be a prime directive in site content, design, and construction (CDC) decisions. Customer-centric sites are designed to satisfy customer needs and solve their problems. They also must achieve company goals. In Toby's case, his division's goal is to extend customer service and sales online, make the web marketing site a seamless, integral part of the company's retail store and catalog sales, and attract new customers.

Although Toby's company is large enough to tackle web site construction in-house with a multidisciplinary, cross-functional team, smaller companies often must hire consultants and outsource all or some tasks. Some small and midsize enterprises (SMEs) do it themselves, using online tutorials and site design and construction software. Others receive help from their local small business development center (*http://www.sba.gov/sbdc*) or university students with web site design and construction expertise. CDC issues are the subject of this chapter.

# Site Fundamentals

An enterprise shows its face to the public through its web site, which makes each web site unique. A site should reflect the enterprise's goals and image in a clear, positive way. Sites should not promise more than they can deliver, yet they must be rich enough to attract, service, and bring customers back. Sites are developed through a series of interrelated, coordinated decisions about CDC. Some decisions are guided by past best practices. Others are guided by the results of marketing research, data mining, and marketing intelligence. An unknown number are guided by what competitors do. Because the Web is an evolving commercial environment, opportunities exist for highly creative marketing along with the risk of failure.

Although this chapter discusses marketing sites on the public Web, private intranets and extranets also have marketing pages and sites that use web protocols and are developed through CDC decisions. Marketing occurs on many of these secure sites without the majority of Internet users being aware of their existence. Just like public sites, they also must be goal-driven and customer-friendly. Intranet web sites focus internally and are often used for employee marketing. They provide information and incentives to the sales force, distribute corporate information, and host newsletters and documents. Extranets focus both internally and externally. These web sites have a select audience of joint venture partners, suppliers, preferred clients and customers, and other stakeholders. Some extranet web sites allow one company's employees to make corporate purchases from another company's web marketing site. Businesses like Lands' End (*http://www.landsend.com*) create web marketing sites specifically for corporate partners. These sites are tailored to a company's special apparel needs, offering only company-approved products and logos.

**Transaction web site**
A highly interactive marketing web site where products are sold.

**Information web site**
A marketing web site that provides information without interactions or selling.

## SITES EVOLVE

Observers of the Internet's first decade of commercialization have seen a pattern emerge as many corporate and other enterprise web sites evolved through three developmental stages—information only, interactive, and transaction. Initially, web sites were static, information-only sites. Later most were redesigned and some interactive elements like email, surveys, or search functions were added. Many sites progressed no further. However, sites that did begin selling products online faced substantial web site redesigns, overhauls, and often entire relaunches. Although Toby's division currently is developing a **transaction web site,** a highly interactive site where products will be sold, the company's first site went online in 1995 as an **information web site,**

**Interactive web site**
A marketing web site where customers interact with the enterprise but cannot purchase products online.

**Web site content**
The substance of the site, information and products, special features, market offers, and services that customers want to access and the company needs to provide.

**Web site design**
The layout of the site, a pattern of text, graphics, and other elements.

providing information about the company and its products without interactions or selling. The site went through a massive redesign in 1997, emerging as an **interactive web site** where customers could send the company email, comment on products, search online catalogs, and participate in online surveys, but not purchase products online. As the company's goals for the web site changed and new, improved, and less costly technology became widely available, the site was updated from information-only to selling. Not all sites evolve this way. For those that do, the teams of people working on site development change along with site goals. Teams tend to become more interdisciplinary and cross-functional as they move toward online selling and developing the complex infrastructure needed to fulfill online orders.[1]

Customer-centric web marketing sites typically result from similarly oriented web marketing plans (figure 14-1). They focus on satisfying customer and enterprise goals through effective integration of Web site CDC. **Web site content** is the substance of the site, that is, the information and products, special features, market offers, and services that customers want to access and the company needs to provide. **Web site design** is the layout of the site—its style or pattern of text, graphics, and other elements constructed to function in a manner that is compatible with content and target market needs and serves the web marketing plan and enterprise goals. Design should reflect target market preferences and characteristics and be compatible with content.

**Figure 14-1  Developing Web Marketing Sites**

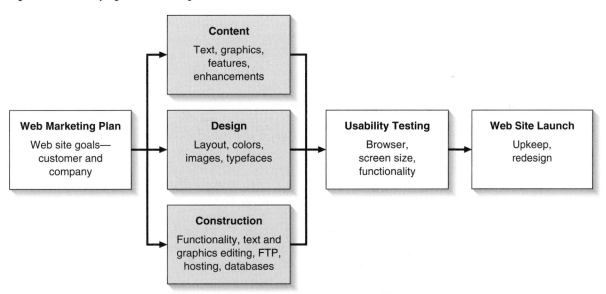

Web marketing plans direct the development of web marketing sites. Web site development includes decisions about content, design, and construction that reflect enterprise goals and target markets needs. Usability testing is an integral part of the process and should be conducted prior to launching a site, during regular operations, and when upkeep and maintenance changes are made. Although design and technology are dependent on and must be compatible with content, they should be developed concurrently to facilitate integration and coordination.

**Web site construction**
The technical processes that make the site accessible and functioning as planned, including service center operations, order processing, and customer relationship management.

**Web site construction** is functionality—web technology, page coding, links that work, navigation and searches that get customers where they want to go, shopping carts that are efficient, the incorporation of multimedia, file transfer of pages to web servers, server storage, server hosting, and the integration of backend databases and warehouse with content and design processes.

## SITE DEVELOPMENT DECISIONS

The same types of questions about CDC must be answered however the site is developed, in-house or outsourced. These decisions should be made concurrently since CDC decisions are interrelated. Content decisions are about what content is needed, who provides it initially and from where, and who maintains and refreshes it. Content responsibilities should be primarily in-house, where product and consumer knowledge are greatest. Designers, site architects, and database system managers should be included in the decision-making process since their responsibilities are content related. Design and technology responsibilities are frequently outsourced to individuals and businesses with the expertise and resources to construct or redesign sites quickly.

## WEB SITE UPFRONT AND BACKEND

**Upfront**
What the site visitor sees and experiences at the web site.

Web marketing sites are composed of two linked sectors, upfront and backend. **Upfront** is what the site visitor sees and directly experiences at the web site. It is determined by site goals and resources available for content acquisition, design, site construction, and maintenance. Some upfronts are very small scale, essentially static product brochures (brochureware) that require little backend support. Often they are no more than collateral materials, brochures, or product catalogs scanned and converted to HTML, then made into web pages and transferred to a server for visitors to scroll through page by page. Large-scale interactive and transaction site upfronts are rich in media, content, interactivity, and features that can make a site visit a happening. However, there is high risk in creating an overdone site with excessive, superfluous interactivity. Highly enhanced interactive, media-rich sites are slow to download, cause confusion because so much is happening at once, overload and crash older browsers, and frustrate visitors who want information or products quickly. It is all too easy for web designers to become infatuated with animated .gifs, flash, or other enhancements. Unless the web site is a designers' site, it is wise to avoid giving customers more than they want or need of animated design elements. This also applies to unwanted text.

The interface is where upfront and back interact. It is a seamless and invisible link between what the customer sees and experiences on the web site frontend and order fulfillment, data collection, and relationship management activities that are managed through the backend. Both are essential to smooth operations and delivering customer value.

**Backend**
The technology that supports content and design, including navigation, product and information searches, order processing, and fulfillment.

While upfront is important in initiating and sustaining customer contact, getting customers to return and repurchase (from storefronts) relies on backend efficiency. Customers do not see **backend** operations, but it is what makes the site function. Backend, the functional technology that supports content and design, includes navigation, product and information searches, order processing and fulfillment, dynamic content, data gathering, and databases that run shopping baskets, service centers, and other customer-centric operations. Initially, backend software was custom coded, took a lengthy time to create, and was very expensive. Today, the widespread availability of relatively inexpensive backend software means that backend coding is often off the shelf and less expensive. As a result, it is now cost-effective for sites that initially were solely information providers to become interactive and/or transaction storefronts or data collectors gathering customer information for in-house use or selling it to other companies.

## DEVELOPMENT COSTS

Web site development costs vary according to site content, size, features, and complexity. Costs can be low for an SME whose three-page static information-only site is constructed in-house with some technical tasks outsourced to a local ISP or ASP. Restaurant sites with two to three pages for their menus, contact information, and a map are examples. Costs rise as sites add goals, target markets, content, time-sensitive material, pages, features, interactivity, and complexity. Some sites, particularly those developed by global corporations like Microsoft (*http://www.microsoft.com*) and IBM (*http://www.ibm.com*) cost hundreds of millions of dollars to develop and maintain.

Factors that affect development costs include the following:

**GOALS**   What the enterprise wants from the site and visitors expect. Multiple goals increase the number of pages as well as their size, complexity, and costs. Sites will disappoint visitors if the enterprise ignores the reasons why visitors access the site. Too many enterprise web sites are designed for the organization (or site designers) and not the customer.

**TARGET(S)**   What targets the site is designed to reach (i.e., enterprises, consumers, or both). Enterprise sites typically are more expensive to construct and maintain than most consumer sites. Targeting multiple buyer segments increases costs.

**CONTENT**   Whether the site is text or media-rich, or both. Text is cheaper than media-rich formats. Graphics, animations, interactivity, transactivity, and other enhancements add complexity and cost.

**SIZE**   The number of pages planned for the site and page size. More pages and larger file sizes increase costs.

**TIMING**   Frequency of upkeep. Static information sites need maintenance and redesign far less frequently than interactive and transaction sites. News, sports, weather, and financial services are examples of sites that require constant updating. Weather radar feeds and stock tickers may be updated in real time. More frequent maintenance, redesign, and updating increase costs.

**BUDGET**   How much is allocated for site development, maintenance, and redesign. While commitment to web site development may be strong, efforts will be hampered unless sufficient resources are allocated to support it. A constrained budget can force decision makers to contain costs and reduce or eliminate features customers want. Budget decisions also include whether advertising or other revenue generating features will be used on the site.

**BACKEND**   The extent of backend operations. Greater backend development increases costs. Proprietary backend software is more costly than off-the-shelf software.

**TASKS**    Whether the site will be designed, implemented, and maintained in-house or outsourced. In some cases, outsourcing reduces costs because expertise does not exist in-house and do-it-yourself web site development can lead to costly mistakes and/or longer development time. In other cases, outsourcing can increase costs, particularly if decisions about consultants and contracts are not made wisely.

Almost any SME can develop a simple, small site in-house using inexpensive or even free HTML editors or by hiring a university student or free-lance consultant with HTML and graphical editing skills. Netscape (*http://www.netscape.com*) Composer (see Appendix E on the textbook web site.) is bundled with the Netscape browser, which can be downloaded free. It is a simple-to-master and effective hypertext editor. Obviously any site constructed with Composer will not have the latest, most sophisticated design elements or interactivity.

Small-scale, no-frills, three- to four-page B2C sites can be constructed for as little as US$20 to US$300 per text-only page. An online survey of web site developers revealed estimates for full-scale development of B2B sites ranging from US$65,000 for a small site, US$125,000 for a medium site, and up to US$250,000 and more for large sites.[2] Web sites for major international corporations may cost in the millions or hundreds of millions to create and maintain. Online web site cost calculators like those at Easybiz Business Web Services (*http://www.easybiz.com.au/Calculators/Web%20Site%20Cost%20Calculator.htm*) or Gentek Solutions Corp. (*http://www.gentek.net/gentek/webcalc.html*) estimate development costs for sites with various combinations of pages, images, and features. All require site setup and domain registration fees.

One of the few bright spots in the collapse of the dot-com bubble in 2000–2001 was a drop in web site development costs as consultants cut their prices to attract clients from a shrinking pool. Another contributor to cost containment is that less code has to be custom-written because cheaper, off-the-shelf backend code is now available. A slowdown in the introduction of technology innovations and the growing savvy of web site developers also has helped contain costs.[3]

Like development costs, maintenance costs also vary. Some sites need relatively little maintenance because they offer static information that does not require frequent updating. Sites with time-sensitive content and interactive and transaction sites require more costly maintenance. Sites maintained in-house should be less expensive than outsourced maintenance. Estimates for monthly maintenance of complex sites vary from as much as US$2,500 for simple, small sites to US$5,000 for medium-size sites, and US$14,000 and more for large sites.[4] Maintenance of large-scale corporate sites can easily rise into the millions.

## IMPLEMENTING PRIVACY AND SECURITY

Privacy and security are prime concerns of consumer and enterprise buyers alike. Some sites post short privacy statements on their front page; most have links from the front page to privacy statement pages within the site. Although these statements will not drive traffic to a site, they can potentially drive customers *from* a site if privacy assurance is absent or misleading. Two-thirds of active web users state that they leave a site if they are asked for personal information. Equally worrisome are the 21 percent who enter false information to gain access. Consumers are far more likely to stay on a site and surrender some personal information if prominent privacy and security statements are displayed.[5]

Because Internet users are sensitive to the collection of information about themselves and their site visits, all sites should have a clear, understandable privacy statement and adhere to it. Content of the privacy statement is site-specific. A growing number of site owners post TRUSTe (*http://www.truste.org*) privacy seals on their front pages as further evidence of their privacy commitment and to reassure visitors that an impartial third party has certified their truthfulness. Far too many sites have lengthy, obscure privacy statements that most buyers will not read or cannot decipher. Sites take this route at their own peril as it may cost them the very visitors they are trying to convert to buyers. Some relief may be found in the Platform for Privacy Preferences (P3P) Project developed by the World Wide Web Consortium (W3). If it becomes widely adopted, it will become a standard for how users can gain greater control over the information collected about them when they visit a web site. Sites participating in P3P will have an advantage with privacy-sensitive visitors.

Security has multiple meanings. For consumers, it is the safety of their online transactions. An Ipsos-Reid *Face of the Web* study confirms that consumer fear of credit card fraud is keeping some people from shopping online. Credit card fraud against enterprises is a far greater threat than fraud against consumers. Transaction site developers must determine before site launch how backend processes can offer protection. Onsite fraud protection can be outsourced to companies like VisualWare (*http://visualware.com/authentishield/index.html*) whose AuthentiShield provides fraud-detection profiling that integrates with standard credit card processing. Credit card security should be in place before any site is activated, monitored closely to make sure it is working, and replaced if it is not.

Another security concern involves hackers and crackers. Site defacement, denial of service attacks, theft of data with credit card information, and other illegal acts should concern all site owners and administrators. Strong hardware firewalls carefully checked and maintained are a security necessity for transaction sites to protect stored customer data. Like credit card security, firewalls must be in place before a site is activated. Most ISP hosts offer firewall protection on their servers. Web administrators should determine whether this protection is available and, if so, whether it is sufficient.

## USABILITY

**Usable site**
A site that is easy for visitors to learn to use, is suitably constructed for its purpose, and employs appropriate technology.

Most enterprises want a user-friendly, customer-centric site. Having said that, designing and implementing a usable site is far more difficult than it might appear. A **usable site** is one that is easy for visitors to learn to use, has content customers want and need, is suitably designed for its purpose, and employs appropriate, efficient, and sufficient technology. A usable site must be designed from the start with knowledge of customers' needs, preferences, limitations, and reasons for going to the site. This is why so many large enterprise sites use focus groups to develop and test their sites. This helps avoid the *self-reference* problem where a site is designed for the developer(s) and not the user(s).

Usable sites offer familiar features and design elements. If a site has an internal search process, then a standard small rectangular search box should be placed onscreen in a highly visible place. It makes no sense to change the style and force visitors to search for the search box. Other familiar features are a logo in the masthead at the top of the page and navigation bars in the footer at the bottom of the page or vertically on the left side of the page in a table or frame.[6]

Consistency, another usability factor, requires uniformity of elements throughout a site. If a left-hand vertical navigation bar is used on the front page, it should be used throughout the site on the left-hand side of the screen. In the past, frames were not recommended because most browsers could not read them. That has changed, however; today's browsers can read frames, and the antiframe bias is fading. Typeface and font size, colors and page width, and image types and sizes should remain the same on each page or be complementary. Consistency makes it easier for visitors to use the site, reinforces the site's visual identity, and reassures them that they are still on the site even when they have traveled several pages deep within the site. This is also why page titles are recommended as page markers.

**Usability testing**

A process in which testers actually use and report on site functions to ensure that a site is usable and all features work as planned.

Although usability consultants are readily available, usually offering expensive testing alternatives, usability testing can be performed inexpensively in-house. **Usability testing,** in house or outsourced, requires using the site, testing features, and making sure the site operates as expected. Current site visitors and customers can help with usability testing, systematically using site features to ensure that everything works as planned. After all, who is better able to determine if a site is easy to use than the people who are already customers or visitors? The Motley Fool's (*http://www.MotleyFool.com*) usability manager brings in a group of site users every two weeks to observe how they move through the site and interact with its financial service features. With their help, problems are quickly pinpointed and resolved. The key to effective testing is to do it often with the right subjects while the site is under development, when it is launched, and throughout its use and eventual redesign. In-house testing can be highly cost-effective, often less than US$1,000.[7]

**Drill down**

Moving from the front page through successive pages in the site to the page where the task is completed.

Testing can be *free-form,* asking individuals to surf the site without a specific task to complete. It can also be *directed,* or *task based,* where people are given specific tasks to perform, then are monitored as they perform them. For example, testers of a women's apparel site might be directed to search for a woman's long sleeve pink cotton turtleneck sweater in size large. Their keystrokes and movements through the site are observed as they search for the product, use the shopping basket, and complete the order. Individuals testing a financial services site might be directed to set up a portfolio and purchase selected quantities of several stocks. These processes require significant **drill down,** where the user has to move from the front page through successive pages to the page(s) where the task is completed. The *three-click rule,* which suggests that a visitor should be able to reach his or her destination page in only three clicks, is often used as a measure of design efficiency. Realistically, it often takes far more drilling. Testing can determine whether drill down is excessive, and analysis can identify click-reduction strategies. Excessive drill down can drive off prospective customers.

Selecting the right participants for a usability test is critical. Usability testing of existing or relaunched sites should be conducted with current customers. For prelaunch testing, a visitor relationship management company like WebTrends (*http://www.WebTrends.com/sbMarketer.htm*) or an online marketing research and web site evaluation company like SurveySite (*http://www.surveysite.com*) can assemble testers. Once a site is launched, server logs record what pages and features visitors click on and help identify problem areas. The points at which shopping baskets are abandoned can be exposed through server log file analysis, but further study is needed to determine *why* buyers break off before completing the transaction. Usability testing is an ongoing process at large sites.

Alternately, a web development team can identify the site's target markets and run simulations of their site usage. This requires personifying representative users, developing scenarios for how they use the site, and testing the site by assuming visitor characteristics and using the site as users would. This technique is called a *pluralistic walkthrough*. It can be helpful in identifying problem areas, particularly prelaunch.[8] It can also give misleading results since it relies heavily on the ability of developers to second-guess buyers.

The 80-20 rule also applies to usability. Eighty percent of the time only 20 percent of the pages in a site are heavily used. Server log files can identify these pages. They are the core content pages, the ones that must be the most user-friendly and freshest.[9]

## SITE REDESIGN

Why redesign a site? The simple answer is *because it is needed*. Initially, the web was such a new environment that few early sites were anything more than just rough sketches or visions in developer's heads of how pages might be linked together. New pages were added without regard to a master plan, which in many cases did not exist. Sites grew like Topsy, sprouting in all directions with pages that displayed irritating *Under Construction* signs and others that deadended. Within a relatively short time, particularly as sites evolved, disorganization became more glaring and irritating to visitors. Some site administrators realized sooner, others later, that site redesign was necessary. Customer feedback, focus group results, and server log files that track site use can indicate when redesign is required. Web marketing intelligence can show when competitors have redesigned their sites, which often triggers redesign. However, reactive redesign is less desirable than proactive redesign initiated because the site needs it. Widespread adoption of larger monitors, faster modems, updated graphical browsers, new applications software, and changes in competitor's sites also are reason to consider site redesign.

Site redesign varies from a simple touchup of several pages to a complete site overhaul and relaunch. Touchups or simple maintenance may be nothing more than changing product or price lists, contact information (phone, fax, address), or reducing typeface size. Static billboards may need no more than a rollover of the copyright date. Overhauls involve content, site architecture, design, and backend operations. Transaction sites typically change products, prices, and information on a regular basis. Some products are seasonal, so updates occur when seasons change or sales are held. Other sites offer information that is changed daily and even multiple times each day. News sites in particular require continuous upkeep, as do financial sites with real-time updates of stock market actions, and weather sites that broadcast *weather maps in motion*.

As sites evolve they usually need an overhaul and integration between online and offline operations, upfront and backend. Although a large-scale redesign may be necessary, customers will not necessarily like it. Some will resist relearning how to navigate a redesigned site and resent having to do so. Sometimes an incremental redesign rolled out over several months is less disturbing than an immediate radical makeover that changes an old friend into a complete stranger.

Some sites undergo continuous design modification. For example, InfoWorld (*http://www.infoworld.com*) went online in late 1999 and had hundreds of design adjustments within its first months of operation. They were driven by visitor email comments, survey and online focus group results, and customer tracking. Market research showed

InfoWorld served at least three diverse markets—hard-core tech-savvy programmers, high-level strategic nontech managers, and a large middle-ground audience seeking technology news. Site redesign efforts for this user-centric business began with developing scenarios for each key target market. They were personified as *Mike the Mad Manager, Pete the Powerful Programmer,* and *Ned the (Tech) Newshound.* The challenge was to create a site that served the needs of all three markets. Site developers also realized that even when the site was redesigned, they could not let it get stale, so redesign was built into the budget and corporate culture.[10]

Rapid site redesigns sometimes occur because of unexpected events and emergencies. This happened at news sites on Tuesday, September 11, 2001, when terrorists flew passenger aircraft into the World Trade Center buildings in New York City and the Pentagon in Washington, D.C. Record site traffic levels were recorded at CNN.com (*http://www.cnn.com*), MSNBC (*http://www.msnbc.com*), and ABC (*http://www.abcnews.com*) after the attacks. MSNBC counted over 12.5 million unique visitors in the next twenty-four hours. MSNBC stripped its home page of all graphics and contracted with third parties to increase server space in order to shorten download times and allow more visitors access to the site. CNN did the same. It normally serves fourteen million visitors but on the day of the attacks was receiving about nine million visitors *an hour,* which rose to nineteen million an hour by Wednesday. *USAToday* (*http://www.usatoday.com*) took a different approach. It did not strip its pages but instead created an entirely new home page just for the unfolding tragedy. These sites removed advertising entirely or greatly reduced it. The *Wall Street Journal Online* (*http://interactive.wsj.com*), which normally restricts access to many of its pages to subscribers, opened its entire site to all visitors from 10 P.M. Tuesday through 6 P.M. Wednesday in response to the emergency, as did the *New York Times Online* (*http://www.nytimes.com*).[11] Many visitors used Internet news sites as their primary or secondary sources for current information.

#### ✔ CONCEPT CHECK

1. Explain the statement "An enterprise shows its face to the public through its web site."
2. Why should usability testing be conducted?
3. Why is customer input an important part of site redesign?

## *Web Site Content*

On the Web, content is king. Content is what visitors seek at a site, and fresh content keeps them coming back. Content online refers to both verbal (text) and nonverbal elements. Verbal content includes newspaper stories, product descriptions, magazine articles, dictionaries, travel schedules, and the like. Nonverbal content includes images and graphics, and such interactive devices as insurance and mortgage calculators, news, weather, sports tickers, and electronic slot machines. A site's market offer is made through its content. Some offers are heavily text based. Others use multimedia, text, and nontext elements. Content decisions both drive and must be integrated with design and construction decisions.

Content shelf life varies. Reference materials that rarely need updating, like topographical maps and dictionaries, have a long shelf life. Content on financial, weather, or news sites has an extremely short shelf life that requires dynamic updating several times a day or, in the case of stock market tickers, real-time streaming content. Content with a medium shelf life is updated weekly, monthly, or within a six-month period. The challenge is to keep content fresh enough to satisfy customers without overwhelming content providers and web administrators, and precipitously increasing costs.

Although the Web is a multimedia environment, many sites are still heavily text based. Web writing is not the same as writing for print newspapers or magazines. Web text should be shorter, more concise, useful, and where appropriate, interactive, but not gratuitously so. Information should be *chunked,* broken into small, related, more easily digested segments separated by headings and subheadings. Teasers are used to link headlines to full articles. Content sites use teasers extensively, but teasers are also found on etailer sites and other storefronts.

- The Wall Street Journal Online (*http://online.wsj.com/home/us*) front page has a prominent box with large type that reads "What's News." The font size and box draw the visitor's eye to a section of news headline teasers with links to longer articles on pages within the site.
- Wal-Mart (*http://www.walmart.com*) prominently displays a box on its front page at a similar location as The Wall Street Journal Online's "What's News" box. In this case, the box is titled "Low Prices" and encourages visitors to click through to product descriptions.
- Yahoo! (*http://www.yahoo.com*) uses the word "New!" in a bright orange teaser for new products.
- Google (*http://www.google.com*) uses "New!" in a bright red teaser for new services.

KISS (*Keep It Simple Stupid*) is advised for most but not all web writing. This is not meant to imply that visitors are stupid, only that many find reading online tiring, so they tend to scan rather than concentrate. As a result, web text should be scannable, which saves the reader time. In most cases, web text should be objective, not puffery or hype, and use approachable language, not technical jargon.[12]

The Web's interactivity and browser support of colors, sound, visual images, animation, and other features makes nonverbal content prominent on many web sites. The tendency with animation is overkill, wretched excess that overwhelms the visitor and clutters the screen, moving images that distract rather than entertain. Images should be used sparingly and for a clear purpose that serves site and page goals. Original photographs or drawings are preferred to overused clip art. Streaming audio and video should be used sparingly and only if target markets are using browsers that can read the files. Far too often they cause significant download delays and computer crashes. Server log files can determine what browser most visitors and, more important, preferred customers are using, which should carry significant weight in decisions about using streaming files. Streaming video is still a problem for many people operating slow modems. The images are likely to be jerky, with sounds not synchronized with action. KISS is also advised for nonverbal content. The major exceptions are gambling and game sites where animation, blinking images, loud colors, and blaring sound excite the visitor and stimulate greater interaction with the site. Sites targeted to children are also more likely to be rich in graphics, colors, and animation.

**WEB UPDATE**

Effective and Ineffective Web Marketing Sites

## FINDING CONTENT

Content decisions are about what to offer on a site, where to find it, and who will provide it. Content depends on the goal of the site and the *reason why* customers are there. A small pet grooming business with an information-only site has an extremely simple, limited content requirement. The purpose is to have an online presence as a driver to its offline location. The site is no more than one or two pages with a description of services offered, hours of operation, a price list, contact information, and a map to the business. It has a relatively long shelf life and will not need redesign until something changes. Content at other sites is far more complex and spread over multiple pages, sometimes hundreds or even thousands nested in directories and subdirectories.

Most marketing departments in larger enterprises regularly generate content for advertising copy, sales promotions, collateral materials, direct marketing, public relations, events, publicity, and sales manuals. Content may be taken without alteration from these sources or produced uniquely for a site or may be a combination of the two. Hard-copy brochures scanned and converted to HTML then uploaded to a web server are still used on brochureware sites. In this case, little or no content is unique to the site. Brochureware content is two-dimensional and static. It fails to take advantage of the Internet and the Web's unique capacities to engage visitors and establish relationships through interactive exchanges.

Some sites have onsite catalogs for easy reference and ordering. For example, the apparel company Coldwater Creek (*http://www.coldwatercreek.com*) has a catalog quick order search where the customer can order just about anything from one of the company's currently circulating mail catalogs. Hard-copy catalogs are presented online with few if any alterations. Customers enter the catalog item number and are sent directly to an order form. Alternately, a customer can also search an interactive online catalog for products.

Other sites have content that is completely original, without an offline equivalent. In some cases, content that originates online is later reproduced in an offline catalog. Eziba (*http://www.eziba.com/StoreFront*) offers handcrafted products sourced worldwide. Originally, it was a clicks-only site with completely original content. Today, it also has a mail catalog that reproduces some online content in hard copy.

Far too often, content is stolen from other sites. Copying online content is so easy that it encourages theft. Even bold copyright statements posted on web site front pages will not stop a committed thief. Relatively few sites follow up and prosecute; most site owners do not have the resources to track down and sue offenders. Images are the most tempting targets, but lines of text and sometimes entire pages and sites also are stolen.

Content can be legally obtained from content providers, and sometimes it is free. A site owner or web administrator can link to a weather ticker without charge by joining Weather.com's (*http://www.weather.com*) *Weather on Your Site* affiliate program. Dynamically generated content (*Weather Magnet* or *Weather Viewer*) is inserted on a page with just a few lines of cut and paste HTML code. Tickertech.com (*http://www. javaticker.com/home.mpl*) offers stock and sports tickers, charts, news, and other content. Other sites have graphics, cartoons, and tips. Moreover.com (*http://www. moreover.com*) offers more than three hundred content categories including news and professional content portals. It delivers content to The Economist Showcase, Time/AOL, and Worldcom. As its name implies, Cartoonlink.com (*http://www.cartoonlink.com*) has email cartoons as well as cartoons for web pages and an affiliate program. Dr. Wilson's weekly syndicated marketing tips (*http://www.doctorebiz.com*) appear on over 350 subscribing sites.

Content can be purchased from freelancers and professional service providers. EffectiveContent.com (*http://www.effectivecontent.com*) has real estate, automotive, finance, and travel content. In the real estate area, it lists over five hundred separate pages of information on a wide variety of topics. A site can select specific topics or purchase entire packages. Under the heading *Buying a Home,* pages are available for *Financial Preparation, Finding a Home, Building a Home, Home Inspections,* and related topics. This type of service may be too expensive for most SMEs, but the benefits are obvious for those sites that can afford it. The problem with syndicated content is keeping it fresh. When too many sites in the same industry use identical syndicated content, duplication conveys a negative impression.

## MANAGING CONTENT

**Content management**
An organized system for identifying what content is needed, procuring it, determining when and how content should be changed, and implementing the changes.

All sites need some form of **content management,** an organized system for identifying what content is needed, procuring it, determining when and how content should be changed, and implementing the changes. Small sites, particularly static information-only sites, can manage content manually in-house through **content audits,** monitoring the site and its pages on a regular basis to remove and replace outdated content. Customer comments can be extremely helpful in identifying new content that should be added or pinpointing problem spots.

**Content audits**
Monitoring the site and its pages on a regular basis to identify, remove, and replace outdated content.

As sites evolve, grow, and add pages, content management can become overwhelming. Links get broken and users begin to complain about receiving 404 error messages. Dynamic content makes the task even more daunting. Large numbers of pages and/or site complexity make it impossible to manage manually. Site owners and web administrators often turn to automated processes or outsourcing content management when it no longer is possible to visualize the entire site. This also occurs when a site evolves to a transaction stage, when it is personalized, has many different types of content, and/or requires frequent design changes.

## ORGANIZING CONTENT

**Web storyboarding**
A process that identifies what will be contained on web pages, both text and visual content, and how the pages will be linked.

SMEs developing or refreshing web site content may use a marketing communication technique known as **Web storyboarding.** Storyboarding identifies what will be contained on web pages, both text and nontext content, design elements, enhancements, and how the pages will be linked. Storyboarding can be conducted manually or with the help of storyboarding software like BoardMaster (*http://www.boardmastersoftware.com*) or electronic presentation software like PowerPoint (*http://www.powerpoint.com*).

Small site developers may use a far simpler approach and storyboard using three-by-five Post-it Notes or card stock, with each card representing one web page. This process begins with brainstorming what content is needed for the site starting with the front page and creating cards for each page nonsequentially. Once content has been placed on separate cards, the cards are sorted, laid on a flat surface, and moved around to represent relationships and hypertext links.

Another approach to storyboarding is to create PowerPoint slides, each slide representing a different web page. The slides are printed, separated, then sorted into the appropriate order. This can also be accomplished electronically using the PowerPoint program and shuffling slides in the slide editor. However, this is more difficult to visualize than shuffling hard copy.

Although storyboarding may add to development time, it offers important advantages for those developing a site or involved in its upkeep. It forces developers to concentrate on content and to identify key information that must be included, along with a path to the pages. Omissions should become evident by close observation of a laid-out storyboard. Designers and technical people can contribute their expertise at this point with suggestions that unify page content and avoid problems later in the development process. Ideally, storyboarding should lead to the development of **template pages,** pages that are models for consistent use of text, graphics, and layout. By duplicating the basic elements of each page, site developers maintain consistency.

Storyboard pages typically include detailed information that guides HTML coding. Each page should be identified with a descriptive title that will become the web page title. Text elements, image captions, links, and other relevant information is on the cards or attached to notes. An important note for each page should be to add a copyright statement, typically of the form (© date), and a disclaimer that the site owner is not responsible for the content of external sites linked from the owner's site.

**Template pages**
Pages that are models for consistent use of text, graphics, and layout.

## THE POWER OF THE FRONT PAGE

As soon as visitors reach a site, the front page, also called a splash, home, or entry page, should clearly let them know what the site is about. Highly stylized, ambiguous front pages frustrate and confuse visitors, often speeding their departure from a site. Therefore, it is important to get to the point and make it easy for visitors to move from the front page to their destination with as few clicks as possible. Ideally, but often not realistically, visitors should be able to get to the reason why they came to the site within three clicks, known as the *three-clicks rule*.

The front page should be customized with a logo, contact information (address, phone, fax, etc.), navigation bar, and an appealing image that reflects the enterprise and its goals. It should be a single screen with no scroll down or scroll across. The most important content should be displayed within the top 350 pixels of the screen, where visitors look first and often make a split-second decision about whether to stay or go.

## ✔ CONCEPT CHECK

1. Why is content king on the Web?
2. Does all content have to be original?
3. What is web storyboarding and how does it contribute to the web development process?

# *Web Site Design*

Design is the way a site looks and feels; that is its structure and organization and visual and, increasingly, aural appeal. It is a plan for how content will be organized and presented on the front and subsequent pages with text, graphics, animation, and other features. Web site design is a combination of aesthetics and usability. Good design reflects attention to detail, functionality, and creativity.

Unlike books, magazines, and other traditional hard-copy materials, web sites are *nonlinear*. Visitors can to jump within a page from one place to another, from one page within a site to another, or from one server to another. A visitor can easily become disoriented and, after several jumps, be unsure of his or her present location. This discontinuity shows the importance of design consistency. The same look and feel on the front and subsequent pages provides a visual anchor that orients a visitor and helps clarify his or her location. It also illustrates the importance of always using page titles.

Most pages should be designed for skimming unless the site is educational, contains reference material, or is used for training. Lengthy text that scrolls on for multiple screen lengths stands an excellent chance of never being read. The sound-bite generation, weaned on Sesame Street and MTV delivery speeds, is less receptive to text-intense pages. Seniors, who are more likely to be readers, often need larger text that makes pages appear longer. Although the user can change font size, page designers cannot rely on the visitor making the adjustment.

Navigation is a design as well as a construction issue. Navigation includes the visual interface that visitors access and the actual linking. Functional navigation icons are essential and must be readily identified as *hot* or hypertext linked. The standard for identifying hot icons is a blue frame around a graphic, underlined blue text font, and a hand that appears when the mouse moves across either. These visual cues are the default on most browsers and should be adhered to for the sake of consistency and to avoid confusing visitors.

Unlike print, television, and radio, users have control over web site design. They can adjust the size of their screen using browser preference menus. They can influence colors by not calibrating their screens to show web-safe colors. If they copy a page, it typically loses all its formatting. Some people turn graphics off to speed download times and see the site as text only. Others turn off sound cards.

## WEB SITE ATMOSPHERICS AND FLOW AESTHETICS

A retail store establishes a mood and sustains its image through such features as color schemes, product displays, floor layouts, dressing room fixtures, music, flooring, salesperson uniforms and attentiveness, products, promotions, and pricing. Differences in store atmospherics are readily apparent from the front door. An upscale department store like Neiman Marcus (*http://neimanmarcus.com/index.jhtml*) is obviously very different from a Target (*http://www.target.com*). Although the same customers may shop both, their expectations for experiences at each store differ sharply. Their expectations are often confirmed from web site atmospherics, design elements used sitewide to establish a mood and consistent image. A site can be visualized as a landscape on the Web, or a *webscape*.

**WEB UPDATE**

Site Atmospherics and Flow

Consistency is achieved by adopting a page model and replicating it for each page in the site. This template specifies primary, secondary, and complementary colors; font type and size; graphics; navigation bars, buttons, marks, and icons; and other elements standardized sitewide, although page content will vary. Consistency also requires the use of only one logo on all pages. Screen size should be set either at no more than 590 pixels for a 640-pixel-wide screen or 760 pixels for an 800-pixel-wide wide screen. The navigation icons, buttons, bars, or lines should appear at the same place on each page. Ideally, navigation will include *breadcrumbs*, a tracer that shows where the visitor is and how he or she got there. They take the form: Home > Research > Web Content > [Title of onscreen page].

Feng Shui, or the Chinese art of arranging things, offers many insights for site designers. It suggests that there should be a flow to each page, an energy that comes from the compatible arrangement of elements. In the virtual environment of the web page, visitors should be able to easily move from one feature to the next as their right brain processes graphics images and their left brain absorbs alphanumeric text, merging the two to provide an intuitive understanding of the site.[13]

Flow occurs in bricks-and-mortar stores where customers are so familiar with the store layout and the location of frequently purchased products that they can navigate the space easily without conscious effort. Web sites should be designed so customers can do the same online, that is, navigate the space at a low level of cognitive processing because of its familiarity and flow.

## LAYOUT ISSUES

Layout is a plan for how design features relate to one another on a page and the arrangement of the pages in a web site. Layouts differ, as expected, according to site goals, target audiences, and resources. Sites in the same product or industry category often can share some layout characteristics, but a quick look at their site maps shows how pages differ. For example, web site front pages of print broadsheet newspapers typically have a masthead with the same logo used on the hard-copy version and three- to four-column-wide text blocks with organization similar to the print version. Little if any animation appears in stories, although some may be used in advertising, often within vertical skyscrapers. Text is black on a white background, and pictures are relatively small. On the other hand, gambling sites use a generous amount of flashy animation, reverse type (white on a black background, gold on a dark purple background), and bold colors, and try to convey the excitement of casino gambling with large titles and headings. Government sites are very conservative, use black text on white backgrounds, are text-intensive and not very colorful, and generally emphasize functionality over creativity.

Layout and design tips can be found at a number of web sites including Webmonkey (*http://hotwired.lycos.com/webmonkey*); the Web Developer's Resource, The Yale Style Manual (*http://info.med.yale.edu/caim/manual/contents.html*); and Useit.com, Jakob Nielsen's site (*http://www.useit.com*). Some recommendations include the following:

**HEADING**   A front page should begin with a heading (masthead), typically a logo and other identifying information. Key information should be top loaded, placed within the first 350 pixels so it can be seen without scrolling down.

**TYPEFACE**   Typography refers to electronic type composition measured in pixels. It is the design of letters, numbers, and symbols. Choices for online typeface are far more limited than for mechanical type. Certain type families are recommended because they are read unchanged by the majority of graphical browsers. Popular typefaces or fonts used online are Verdana (also Arial), Chicago, Courier, Times New Roman (also Times), and Geneva. Although a site may be constructed in one of these typefaces, a browser will not read them as such unless it stores that typeface. Instead, the site will appear in the browser's default font, usually Times or Times New Roman. Typefaces can be read unchanged by browsers if they are created as a graphic in a design program like Adobe Photoshop. Typefaces should not be mixed on a page or in a site. Microsoft offers free downloads of TrueType fonts that allow visitors to view sites as their designers created them. Different languages require language fonts. There are at least 124 available language fonts. Overly large and overly small fonts should be avoided. Capital letters should be used sparingly and only where appropriate. Words totally in capitals, other than company logos, scream at visitors and are more difficult to read than a mixture of upper- and lowercase. A text-only option should be available for visitors without graphical browsers, people with visual disabilities using digital readers, and those who want to speed downloads. The availability of a text-only option should appear in the header or at the beginning of the body on the front page.

**ALIGNMENT**    Text should be left justified. Avoid center-aligned and right-justified text layouts, which are harder to read. The exception is the navigation bar that is often centered at the bottom of a page and a logo centered at the top of a page.

**TEXT BLOCKS**    Text blocks should be broken into smaller segments that are easier to read. They can be used as design elements separating information and layout sectors. Lengthy text should be separated into pages linked from a table of contents or introductory page. Chunk information into segments that appeal to visitors and allow them to select what they want to read. Visitors typically will not tolerate more than a ten-second download time, which is a strong incentive to avoid overly long and graphics-rich pages.

**TABLES**    Tables are often used as design elements and arranged to anchor text and graphics on a screen. Avoid lengthy tables that can spread across two or more typed pages. They are difficult to read, particularly as table headers disappear with scrolling down. It is better to use several smaller tables than one extremely large table or use cells within a table to set off content.

**FRAMES**    Although frames are more acceptable with newer browser versions, many browsers still cannot read them. Therefore, it is better to use tables to anchor layout elements than frames, at least for the immediate future.

**SITE MAP**    A site map should be used for sites with twenty or more pages. It is a road map or interactive overview of the pages in a site and their organization.

**COLORS**    Color, a design element that conveys messages, creates contrasts, and stimulates emotions, is a powerful tool for the web site designer. Color schemes involve the selection of primary, secondary, and accent colors. Primary colors are darker and bolder than secondary colors. Accent colors are darker and bolder than either primary or secondary colors. Overly rich, bold background colors and designs increase download times and detract from the text. Since type should contrast with background color, the darker the background color, the lighter the type. However, reverse type (light type on a dark background) is harder to read, particularly when it is very small. Some color combinations are extremely difficult to read including yellow type on a blue background, red type on a green background, or green type on a red background.

**LINKS**    All pages should link back to the home page. No page should deadend. Pages should have bidirectional links that go backward, perhaps to the home page, and forward to another page. Links should be checked on a regular basis to ensure they still work. Link checks can be performed manually or automatically with link checking software.

**SEARCH**    Search boxes typically are in the top part of a web page. They should be simple, load quickly, and provide instructions for simple and advanced searches.

**ORGANIZATION**    Pages are arranged in hierarchical, radial tree, or other form. The first page is the home, splash, or entry page. This page provides the first impression a visitor has of a site. It links to content pages. Sites should avoid being too shallow, with too many top-level content pages, or too deep with top-level content pages that lead to large numbers of second-level pages.

**MENUS**    A menu is a list of links or submenus for other pages in the site. It can be pull-down, rollover, or another form. Menus should function as categorized minisite maps.

**FAQS**    Where appropriate, sites should include a Frequently Asked Questions (FAQ) page. Visitor comments and questions can be used as FAQ content.

**VISUAL AXIS**    If the target audience is Western, they read from top to bottom and upper left to bottom right. Page layout should reflect this preference. The top of the screen is dominant for Western readers.

**FEEDBACK**    Feedback options, particularly email, are typically offered on a separate content page. They include response forms, guest books, requests for information, and surveys.

## GRAPHICS AND ANIMATION

Some of the flashiest sites are targeted to gamblers and children. Filled with bold colors, bright contrasts, and lots of movement, they are designed to catch attention, not for lengthy reading. They break the generally accepted rule of limiting animated graphics to one or two per page.

Some sites still display far too many horizontal rules, bullets, flashing icons, pulsating text, buttons, and other embellishments. Page fade-ins and Java script text scrolling have also been overdone. While they were used extensively in the early days of web commercialization, now they look outdated and unprofessional. Contemporary web design emphasizes the use of small, appropriate graphics. Randomized graphics are a useful method for displaying an array of images without cluttering a page. The images appear in a box and change at regular intervals to give the site a fresh appearance. This technique is often used on university home pages to show a montage of campus life scenes.

Many web site owners cannot afford custom graphics. Instead they rely on far cheaper off-the-shelf images. Digital camera costs have fallen dramatically, which has also reduced the cost of custom images. Royalty-free web-ready photo sites include GettyImages's Photodisc (*http://creative.gettyimages.com/photodisc*) and Picturequest (*http://www.picturequest.com*).

Simple is best for most graphics decisions. What is interesting when new and fresh becomes irritating when old and overdone. For that reason, it is best to avoid using hit counters on a site front page. They are meaningless additions, since gross duplicated hits are highly inaccurate traffic counts. If they show a very low count, it implies the site is an unvisited backwater. If a hit counter must be used, it should be invisible to visitors.

Web users are notoriously short on patience. A widely used rule of thumb for how long visitors are willing to wait for a page to download is ten seconds. To apply the ten-second rule, a front page should be no larger than 100 kilobytes so the page can download in several seconds. For the same reason, large numbers of large file-size graphics should be avoided. Since most browsers can read no more than 72 pixels per inch (PPI), higher resolution graphics are a waste of space and unnecessarily slow downloads.

Other irritants are *Under Construction* warnings or animated .gifs showing construction workers in hard hats. It is not necessary to show these signs, and, fortunately, their use is diminishing. Another irritant is overly large accusatory 404 error messages that stridently blame the visitor for making an address mistake. It is better to custom design an error message that clearly states the error is not the visitor's fault and provide explanations for why it occurred and the alternatives for finding the requested page.

The last several years have seen the introduction of streaming audio and video, flash animation, video clips, and other new forms. These files cannot be opened by all browsers. Often they require downloading a plug-in, which some visitors will not or cannot do, so the impact is lost. In the case of Portable Network Graphics (PNG), which was designed to replace older graphic formats, most older browsers cannot read PNG-8 or PNG-24, so a broken icon appears on the browser screen. At this time, PNG is probably not a desirable option unless the site's target audience is highly likely to be operating up-to-date browsers.

## SPECIAL CONSIDERATIONS

Some target markets and visitors need special consideration. For example, the numbers of online non-English speakers are increasing. If a site's target audience includes non-English readers, consideration should be given to providing translations or mirror sites in their language.

The disabled are another frequently overlooked audience. They include the visually impaired, the deaf, and people with motor skill limitations. People who are colorblind cannot process color images and therefore cannot distinguish colored icons from a colored background. Because colors appear gray to them, icons should include text descriptors to avoid leaving the colorblind stranded on a page. For example, rather than a color icon of a house to indicate a *Home* link, the icon should have *Home* written in text on or near it. The hearing impaired may need visual readers to interpret streaming audio.[14] The alt tags in HTML can be used to provide explanations for how graphics function so print disabled or blind users using digitized speech software will hear the contents of a web page. This illustrates the importance of using text captions for all pictures and images.

If seniors are a site's target market, they may also need special attention. Since older people frequently have some visual impairment, readability can be improved by using sans serif typeface and at least 12- or 14-point type. Text should not be written completely in capital letters but instead, in both upper- and lowercase. As already mentioned, text is easier to read when it is left justified; center alignment is more difficult to read. The colors yellow, blue, and green should be separated because older people often cannot discriminate between them. Patterned backgrounds and reverse type (white on dark backgrounds) are particularly difficult to read and should be avoided.[15]

## ✔ CONCEPT CHECK

1. What messages can web site atmospherics send?
2. Why should key information be placed in the top third of a web screen?
3. What target markets need special consideration and why?

# Web Site Construction

Construction requires using technology, software, and databases to create web pages and sites, and install them on web servers. The early years of web commercialization were marked by a tidal wave of new technologies, which made web site development more difficult because it required constantly learning new software and mastering new techniques. The learning curve was very steep, and development time and costs were high for sites striving to be on the cutting edge. Today, the technology is even more complex, but developers are more experienced and better trained, which is a partial explanation for decreasing web site development costs.

It is beyond the scope of this book to explore web construction in depth or deal with such issues as which platform to use, Windows NT, Macintosh, or Linux. Realistically, few corporate marketing or brand managers, salespeople, advertising or sales promotion professionals have more than a cursory knowledge of such issues and leave construction to the experts. SME marketers are more likely to be personally involved with web site development and technical professionals who do the construction that makes content and design work as planned.

## PREPARING CONTENT

Content must be coded before pages can be transferred and stored on a web server. Web site developers who spend their professional lives constructing pages and sites typically write HTML code. Large, complex sites have teams of programmers constructing pages. SMEs that create sites in-house are far less likely to have developers writing HTML. Their alternative is to use image editing software like the professional graphics standard Adobe PhotoShop (*http://www.adobe.com*) or Macromedia Fireworks (*http://www.macromedia.com*), and Web page editors like Adobe's GoLive or Macromedia's DreamWeaver. Adobe Systems, Inc. was a leader in imaging products long before web commercialization.

Web pages carefully coded or created by popular page editors can still be a problem for some browsers. Not all browsers interpret code the same way, which can lead to broken links, missing graphics, and unreadable text. Anyone creating pages should check them on all current browsers. Each page should be closely examined both in Netscape and Microsoft Explorer and, at the least, on Windows and Macintosh operating systems, before being transferred to a server. Pages should be viewed with a text-only browser or a graphical browser with images and sound turned off. Most developers do not transfer pages directly to a server without first checking them in a staging area, a place on the server that is not open to the public.

## BACKEND CONSTRUCTION

Marketers typically are not directly responsible for constructing or installing backend systems that manage data, but they do contribute to determining what data will be collected and used. They also manipulate databases once they are established. Marketers have pushed for the use of personalization as a customer retention tool and that requires establishing a comprehensive database, warehouse, and mining rules. Using the Internet to sell, up-sell, and cross-sell means establishing dynamic databases that can be entered and manipulated.

Dynamic web pages, customer relationship management, interactive searching, and communication require constant management and upkeep of databases and data warehouses. Large corporations have information technology or information systems specialists to capture, scrub, store, manipulate, retrieve, and use data. SMEs with interactive sites are more likely to outsource these tasks. Many small businesses are moving toward becoming transaction sites. As they do so, they need well-designed, dependable, simple shopping baskets that simplify and speed up transaction processing. Shopping baskets are currently used in around 72 percent of B2C sites.[16]

Web marketers must be assured that transactions and sites are secure. This is a construction, technology, and policy issue. It requires a total commitment to firewalls, encryption, credit card verification, and related processes for ensuring privacy and online safety. Sufficient resources must be committed to ensure that customers can interact and transact on the site with confidence, and site owners are protected as much as possible against customer fraud. Likewise, electronic payment mechanisms must be available for online ordering. These processes must be acceptable and usable, flexible enough to accommodate multiple options, and available nonstop.

A web site is not online until page files have been transferred to a web server for storage. Servers may be owned and maintained in-house or outsourced to an ISP or other web hosting business. Each site has dedicated space assigned to it on its host web server. This space is identified with the site's unique URL. Most files are electronically transferred to the server and stored in the addressed space using a File Transfer Protocol (FTP). Various versions of FTP can be downloaded free. The FTP program allows the user to delete, modify, and put files on the server.

## ✔ CONCEPT CHECK

1. How is construction related to content and design?
2. What is the purpose of using a product like GoLive or DreamWeaver?
3. Once pages are made, why should they be viewed in different browsers and platforms?

# Summary

### Site Fundamentals

Many web sites evolve through three stages, information-only, interactive, and transaction. This process requires site design and redesign. Customer-centric web marketing sites focus on satisfying customer and enterprise goals through effective integration of web site content, design, and construction (CDC). Private intranets and extranets also have marketing pages and sites that use web protocols and are developed through CDC decisions. The best web marketing sites evolve from a clear vision of what they are designed to accomplish for the enterprise and its customers. Web marketing sites are composed of two linked sectors, upfront and backend. Web site development costs vary according to site content, size, features, and complexity. Maintenance costs also vary. Consumer and enterprise sites should contain relevant, appropriate privacy and security statements and adhere to them. A usable site is one that is easy for visitors to learn to use, is suitably constructed for its purpose, and employs appropriate technology. Usability testing, in house or outsourced, involves actually using the site, testing features, and making sure the site operates as expected. Consistency requires uniformity of elements throughout a site. Site redesigns are needed for a variety of reasons. They vary from a simple touchup of several pages to a complete site overhaul and relaunch.

## Web Site Content

Content is what visitors seek at a site; fresh content keeps them coming back. Content shelf life varies. Although the web is a multimedia environment, most sites are still heavily text based. Web text should be scannable, which saves the reader time. Content decisions include what to offer on a site, where to find it, and who will provide it. Content depends on the goal of the site and customer needs. Web content may be taken without alteration from in-house marketing materials prepared for other purposes. Many sites have content that is completely original. Content is sometimes stolen from other sites. Content can be legally obtained from content providers, sometimes without charge. All sites need some form of content management, an organized system for identifying what content is needed, procuring it, determining when and how content should be changed, and implementing the changes. Web storyboarding is used to describe web page content, both text and nontext, design elements, enhancements, and how the pages will be linked. The web site front page, also called a splash, home, or entry page, should clearly let visitors know what the site is about.

## Web Site Design

Design is the way a site looks and feels—its structure and organization and its visual and, increasingly, aural appeal. It is a plan for how content will be organized and presented on the front and subsequent pages with text, graphics, animation, and other features. Web site design is a combination of aesthetics and usability. Web sites are nonlinear. Most pages should be designed for skimming. Navigation is a design as well as a construction issue. Users have control over web site design. Web site atmospherics are design elements that are used sitewide to establish a mood and consistent image. A site can be visualized as a landscape on the Web or a webscape. There should be a flow to each page, an energy that comes from the compatible arrangement of elements. Layout is a plan for how design features relate to one another on a page and the arrangement of the pages in a web site. Simple is best for most graphics decisions. Some target markets and visitors need special design consideration.

## Web Site Construction

Construction requires using technology, software, and databases to create web pages and sites and install them on web servers. Content must be coded before pages can be transferred and stored on a server. Web pages carefully coded or created by popular page editors can still be a problem for some browsers that are unable to read them. Marketers typically are not directly responsible for constructing or installing backend systems that manage data, but they do contribute to determining what data will be collected and used. Web marketers must be assured that transactions and sites are secure. A web site is not online until page files have been transferred to a web server for storage. Most files are electronically transferred to the server and stored in the addressed space using a File Transfer Protocol (FTP).

# Internet Marketing Application

Web storyboarding is a useful technique for small and midsize businesses developing and redesigning their web sites. To illustrate how easy it is to apply this technique, create six storyboard cards for a small business going online for the first time. Block out what will appear on the front page and the five additional pages that will constitute the site. Three-by-five-inch Post-it Notes are large enough to contain necessary content information and can be moved around easily. Once the notes are complete, lay them out on a flat surface on top of two pieces of paper laid side-to-side (figure 14-2) and draw links between pages.

The hypothetical business is *CJ's By Design*. Conveniently, it is located in your city, so you can create a realistic address, phone number, fax number, and email address. CJ has been making personalized pottery for more than twenty years from her home. Her logo is the name of her company written in Comic Sans MS typeface placed within an oval. She works out of a studio attached to her garage where she has an electric kiln and supplies. CJ's training is from your university's art department, where she was a star student. She makes large pieces that adorn local banks, retail stores, and office lobbies. Using information provided by the client, she decorates these large pots, vessels, and vases with corporate logos, significant dates, and various objects that represent company icons. Colors are complementary to the areas where the pottery will be displayed. CJ has a two-person sales force that works a three-state region signing up clients and three assistants who follow her designs and help throw, decorate, fire, and deliver the pots. She does not want to sell her work online but does want to interact with potential customers and direct them to her salespeople.

**Figure 14-2  Storyboarding CJ's By Design**

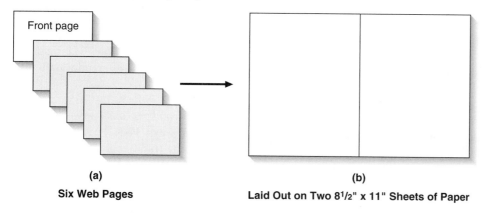

| (a) | (b) |
|---|---|
| **Six Web Pages** | **Laid Out on Two 8¹/₂" x 11" Sheets of Paper** |

# Chapter Review Questions

1. Are transaction sites also interactive? Explain.
2. Should all sites be transaction sites?
3. Why do many SMEs turn to SBDCs for help?
4. Why should CDC decisions be made concurrently?
5. Who should make content decisions?
6. What is the relationship between goals and development costs?
7. What can Netscape Composer do for SMEs?
8. Do information-only sites have the same security concerns as transaction sites?
9. Contrast free form and task-based usability testing.

10. Why is it important to determine the shelf life of a site's content?
11. What is KISS and why is it such good advice for web site developers?
12. Can there be too much dynamic content on a front page? Explain.

13. What is content management and why should all sites do it?
14. Web sites are nonlinear. How does this affect design?
15. Contrast Tiffany.com and Walmart.com for their designs and webscapes.

# Case Study

## Adobe Everywhere

Adobe, the second-largest PC software company in the United States, was a leader in imaging products long before web commercialization. The company was founded by computer scientists John Warnock and Charles Geschke in 1982. Both are former employees of Xerox Corporation's Palo Alto (California) Research Center (PARC). Adobe is known for its printing, publishing, and graphics software. Its graphics software, Adobe PhotoShop, is an industry standard. In 2001, the company published Adobe Atmosphere, the first web authoring and viewing program for interactive web 3-D. This is a considerable advance for the over two million content developers currently working in two dimensions.

Adobe Acrobat PDF files are rapidly becoming the standard for document sharing. The latest Acrobat versions have strong encryption to protect order forms and other interactive enhancements. The company has entered the mobile market with an Acrobat reader for Palm OS. Adobe has created a highly customer-centric web site filled with free downloads and how-to features. Adobe Studios has easy-to-follow tutorials and demonstrations of how professionals have used Adobe products to create some remarkable web effects. Adobe's site demonstrates many customer-centric CDC principles. It is clean, clear, easy to access, and helpful. The type font is black on white backgrounds except where illustrations are used in product demonstrations. Illustrations match products and are used appropriately. It is remarkable for its lack of gratuitous animations. Adobe's web site is an example of what good designers can create with exceptional products and an understanding of the *reason why* visitors come to the site.[17]

### CHECK IT OUT

See for yourself whether or not Adobe has designed a customer-centric web site. Begin at the Adobe home page (*http://www.adobe.com/main.html*). What downloads does it offer without charge? Search for *GoLive*. Was the search quick and accurate? What is *Free Tryout*? Is it product sampling? Is this an effective tactic to convert visitors to buyers? What is going on in *Adobe Studio*? What does Adobe offer visitors in its *Learn* section? Is it accurate to say that Adobe assumes an educational role on the site? Explain the marketing strategy behind this approach. How many different channels does Abobe use to sell its products (*http://www.adobe.com/store/otherplaces/main.html*)? Can Adobe products be purchased online? Is Adobe a transaction site? Is it interactive? Does it offer information?

### A GLOBAL PERSPECTIVE

Adobe's slogan is *Everywhere You Look*. This can be interpreted in two ways. Visually, Adobe products have been creating traditional print materials for over twenty years. Now, Adobe products are used to design some of the web's best sites. So everywhere you look visually online and off, you will find Adobe products hard at work. On the other hand, Adobe products are worldwide, hence the second meaning. Adobe *online stores* are in at least twenty countries (*http://www.adobe.com/store/otherplaces/main.html*). In this case, stores are online. Adobe products can be purchased worldwide offline and, now, online.

Visit Adobe online stores in Austria, Belgium, France, Germany, or Ireland. In what currency are prices quoted? What effect did the changeover to the euro have on Adobe's European online stores?

# Chapter 1

1. Philip Hensher, "A Hard Act to Follow," *The Spectator*, 29 January 2000 review of Nicholas Boyle, *Goethe: The Poet and the Age*, Volume II, *Revolution and Renunciation, 1790–1803*, (Oxford: Oxford University Press, 2000), pp. 44–45.
2. Richard Williamson, "Dot-Com Failures Pass 700," *Interactive Week*, 31 October 2001, http://www.ecruitinginc.com/news/news.asp?ID=107, accessed 6/02; James Surowiecki, "The Financial Page: Let the Bad Times Roll," *The New Yorker*, 3 September 2001, p.34.
3. Avivah Litan, "Anthrax Scare Spikes Interest in Already Surging e-Billing," Gartner Group, 5 November 2001, http://www4.gartner.com/DisplayDocument?doc_cd=102155, accessed 6/02.
4. "History of the Information Revolution and Communications Technology: A Timeline of Technology," San José State University, http://myron.sjsu.edu/caesars/COMM.HTM, accessed 6/02.
5. Special Collections Department, "History of the Written Word," University of South Florida, 17 February 2000, http://www.lib.usf.edu/spccoll/wrtword.html, accessed 1/01.
6. "The Invention of Printing—Gutenberg (1450?)" and "The Gutenberg Press," Printer's Mark, Inc., http://printersmark.com/Pages/Hist2.html#Anchor-The, accessed 6/02 ; "Gutenberg.DE, The Time of Gutenberg," http://www.gutenberg.de/english/zeit.htm; Eva-Maria Hanebutt-Benz, "Gutenberg and Mainz," http://www.gutenberg.de/english/zeitgum.htm, accessed 6/02.
7. Lisa Jardine, "The Future Began in 1455," *The Spectator*, 16 October 1999, pp. 42–43.
8. Peter Drucker, "Beyond the Information Revolution," *The Atlantic Monthly*, October 1999, http://www.theatlantic.com/issues/99oct/9910drucker.htm, accessed 6/02.
9. Phil Shannon, "The Short Inspiring Reign of King Ludd," review of Kirkpatrick Sale, *Rebels Against the Future: The Luddites and Their War on the Industrial Revolution* (Cambridge, MA: Perseus Publishing, 1996), http://jinx.sistm.unsw.edu.au/~greenlft/1996/254/254p28.htm, accessed 6/02; Felix Silverio, "The Luddites," http://www.gober.net/victorian/reports/luddites.html, accessed 6/02; Kirkpatrick Sale, "Lessons from the Luddites," *The Nation*, 5 June 1995, http://www.gn.apc.org/pmhp/dc/activism/sale, accessed 1/01.
10. National Inventors Hall of Fame, http://www.invent.org/hall_of_fame/1_1_search.asp, accessed 6/02; David Crane, "The Great Unsung Victorian Machine-Maker," *The Spectator*, 13 May 2000, p. 32.
11. Mary Bellis, "Herman Holerith—Punch Cards," Inventors, About.com, http://inventors.about.com/library/inventors/blhollerith.htm?terms=Herman+Hollerith+, accessed 10/01.
12. Martin H. Weik, "The ENIAC Story," Ordnance Ballistic Research Laboratories, Aberdeen Proving Ground, January–February 1961, http://ftp.arl.mil/~mike/comphist/eniac-story.html, accessed 6/02; "The Emerging Digital Economy," Chapter One, "The Digital Revolution," U.S. Department of Commerce, April 1998, http://www.esa.doc.gov/508/esa/TheEmergingDigitalEconomy.htm accessed 6/02; Rachel K. Sobel, "Faulty Memory," *U.S. News & World Report*, 11 February 2002, p. 71.
13. United States Bureau of the Census, "World Population Today: World POPClock Projection," 26 June 2000, http://www.census.gov/cgi-bin/ipc/popclockw, accessed 6/02 ; David Levine, "World Population Today," University of North Carolina, http://www.ibiblio.org/lunarbin/worldpop, accessed 6/02; United States Bureau of the Census, "Historical Estimates of World Population," 28 February 1996, http://www.census.gov/ipc/www/worldhis.html, accessed 6/02 .
14. Joyce L. Morris, "The Technology Revolution," in D. Schon, *Beyond the Stable State* (New York: W.W. Norton, 1971), http://www.uvm.edu/~jmorris/comps2.html, accessed 6/02.
15. U.S. Department of Commerce, "The Emerging Digital Economy II: Executive Summary," http://www.esa.doc.gov/508/esa/TheEmergingDigitalEconomyII.htm, accessed 6/02.
16. Bob Schaller, "The Origin, Nature, and Implications of Moore's Law," 26 September 1996, http://www.iso.gmu.edu/~rschalle/moorelaw.html, accessed 6/02 ; Intel Processor Hall of Fame, http://www.intel.com/intel/museum/25anniv/hof/moore.htm, accessed 1/01; Dori Jones Yang, "Leaving Moore's Law in the Dust," *U.S. News & World Report*, 10 July 2000, http://www.usnews.com/usnews/issue/000710/moore.htm, accessed 2/01.
17. Steve Schoenherr, "The Cold War Begins," University of San Diego, 19 May 1999, http://history.acusd.edu/gen/20th/coldwar0.html, accessed 6/02; "Sputnik," The University of Michigan, http://www.windows.umich.edu/space_missions/ sputnik.html, accessed 1/01; Roger D. Launius, "Sputnik and The Dawn of the Space Age," NASA, 11 August 1999, http://www.hq.nasa.gov/office/pao/History/sputnik/, accessed 6/02 ; Sputnik recording at http://www.hq.nasa.gov/office/pao/History/sputnik/sputnik.wav; New York Times on AOL, "The Times Looks Back: Sputnik," *New York Times*, 1997, http://www.nytimes.com/partners/aol/special/sputnik/, accessed 6/02 ; sound file http://www.nytimes.com/partners/aol/special/sputnik/sputnik.rm; Michael Wright, "Beep, Beep, Beep . . . Here Comes Sputnik!," 20 May 2000, http://www.batnet.com/mfwright/sputnik.html, accessed 6/02.
18. Ibid.
19. Charles M. Herzfeld, presentation "On Information Technology: Why Was the ARPAnet Started?" at the Information Technology Summit, Defense Technical Information Center, U.S. Department of Defense, http://www.dtic.mil/summit/ma02%5F1a.html, accessed 1/01.
20. Barry M. Leiner, Vinton G. Cerf, David D. Clark, Robert E. Kahn, Leonard Kleinrock, Daniel C. Lynch, Jon Postel, Larry G. Roberts, Stephen Wolff, "A Brief History of the Internet, Version 3.31," last revised 4 August 2000, http://www.isoc.org/internet/history/brief.shtml, accessed 6/02; Robert H. Zakon, "Hobbes' Internet Timeline v.v.5.6," 1 April 2002, http://www.zakon.org/robert/internet/timeline/, accessed 6/02.

21. Ibid.
22. John Naughton, "The Man Who Wove the Web," *The Spectator*, 16 October 1999, pp. 45–56; Tim Berners-Lee, "Biography," World Wide Web Consortium, http://www.w3.org/People/Berners-Lee/, accessed 6/02; Tim Berners-Lee, "The World Wide Web: A Very Short Personal History," World Wide Web Consortium, 7 May 1998, http://www.w3.org/People/Berners-Lee/ShortHistory.html, accessed 6/02.
23. University of Texas, Austin and Cisco Systems, "January 2001 Internet Economy Indicators," Center for Research in Electronic Commerce, http://www.internetindicators.com/internetindic.html, accessed 6/02; *CyberAtlas*, "Internet Pumps $507 Billion into U.S. Economy," 3 November 1999, http://cyberatlas.internet.com/markets/professional/article/0,1323,5971_227421,00.html, accessed 6/02; The Internet Economy Indicators, "The Internet Economy Supported an Additional 650,000 Jobs During 1999, a 36 Percent Increase Over 1998," 26 June 2000, http://www.internetindicators.com/key_findings_june_00.html, accessed 6/02; The Internet Economy Indicators, "Executive Summary," 26 June 2000, http://www.internetindicators.com/executive_summary_june_00.html, accessed 6/02 ; The Associated Press, "Millions of Web-Slingers," ABCNews.com, accessed 1/01.
24. Ibid.
25. U.S. Department of Commerce, "The Emerging Digital Economy II: Executive Summary," April 1998, http://www.esa.doc.gov/508/esa/TheEmergingDigitalEconomyII.htm, accessed 6/02.
26. See note 23.
27. "Online Shopping Will Grow To $11 Billion This Holiday Season," Forrester Research, 16 October 2001, http://www.forrester.com/ER/Press/Release/0,1769,638,00.html, accessed 6/02.
28. Mortimer B. Zuckerman, "Tensions on the Net," *U.S. News & World Report*, 24 April 2000, pp. 75–76 .
29. Ibid.
30. Gary S. Becker, "How the Web Is Revolutionizing Learning," *Business Week*, 27 December 1999, p. 40; Mary Lord, "Suddenly, E-Commerce Is the Hot New Specialty," *U.S. News & World Report*, 10 April 2000, pp. 62–64.
31. Randall E. Stross, "Digital Divide Hooey," *U.S. News & World Report*, 17 April 2000, p. 45.
32. "Lands' End, Inc. Company Capsule," Hoover's Online, http://www.hoovers.com/co/capsule/3/0,2163,10883,00.html, accessed 6/02; Jenny Price, "Lands' End Comes into Its Own as Major Player in e-Commerce," *Lexington Herald Leader*, Business Monday, 20 December 1999, p. 2; Sara Nathan, "Online Retail Sales Soar, Jobs Rocket," *USA Today*, 27 October 1999, pp. 3B, 1A; Greg Sandoval. "Lands' End Gives Web Shopping the Personal Touch," CNET News.com, http://news.cnet.com/news/0-1007-200-120829.html, 16 September 1999, accessed 6/02; Bloomberg News, "Lands End Looks to Net to Cut Costs," CNET News.com, 11 March 1999, http://news.cnet.com/news/0-1007-202-339822.html, accessed 6/02; Ellen Messmer, "Lands' End Bulks Up Custom-designed Web Sites," Network World, http://www.nwfusion.com/news/2000/0321landsend.html, accessed 6/02; "Customer Profile: Cisco and Lands' End," Cisco Systems, http://www.cisco.com/warp/public/779/ibs/success/landsend_cp_rev2.pdf, accessed 6/02; "Customer Profile: Cisco and Lands' End Customer Profile in the Extreme," http://www.cisco.com/warp/public/cc/pd/cucxsw/profile/lnden_cp.htm, 21 November 2000, accessed 10/01; "Financial Reports," Catalog Age, 7 November 2001, http://www.industryclick.com/magnewsarticle.asp?newsarticleid=251190&siteid=2&magazineid=153, accessed 6/02; Paul Miller, "Lands' End Works to Rev Up Corporate Sales," 1 October 2001, http://www.industryclick.com/magazinearticle.asp?releaseid=9361&magazinearticleid=128707&siteid=2&magazineid=153, accessed 6/02; Adam Lashinsky, "Sears Corrects an Earlier Mistake," Business2.0, 13 May 2002, http://www.business2.co.uk/articles/web/
print/0,1650,40559,FF.html, accessed 5/02; Keith Regan, "Can Lands' End Bring Sears Up to Speed Online?", E-Commerce Times, 20 May 2002, http://www.ecommercetimes.com/perl/printer/17846/, accessed 5/02; Tad Clarke, "Editorial: Sears . . . and Company," DM News, 20 May 2002, http://www.dmnews.com/cgi-bin/artprevbot.cgi?article_id=20455, accessed 5/02.

## Chapter 2

1. Internet World, "Internet World Fall 2001," http://www.internetworld.com/events/fall2001/, accessed 11/01.
2. Staff, "Broadband Use Up in U.S.," Federal Communications Commission, 14 August 2001, http://www.nua.net/surveys/index.cgi?f=VS&art_id=905357082&rel=true, accessed 6/02.
3. Jason Fry, "The Broad Jump," *Wall Street Journal*, 26 June 2000, pp. R22, R24.
4. BBC News, "Internet Takes a Break," BBC Online Network, 23 February 1999, http://news.bbc.co.uk/hi/english/sci/tech/newsid_284000/284702.stm, accessed 6/02.
5. J.J. Ross, "Software and Software Engineering," 30 June 1998, http://www.linfield.edu/~gross/400/lect1.html, accessed 6/02.
6. Amy Cortese, "Here Comes the Intranet," *Business Week*, 16 June 1997, http://www.businessweek.com/1996/09/b34641.htm, accessed 6/02.
7. Heidi Anderson, "The Rise of the Extranet," *PCToday*, 1997, http://www.pctoday.com/editorial/goingonline/970235b.html?guid=Okewm1d0, accessed 6/02.
8. Ellen Messmer, "Lands' End Bulks Up Custom-Designed Web Sites," *Network World*, 21 March 2000, http://www.nwfusion.com/news/2000/0321landsend.html, accessed 6/02.
9. Vinton Cerf, "The Internet Is for Everyone: How Easy to Say – How Hard to Achieve!," 10 May 2000, The Internet Society, http://www.isoc.org/isoc/media/speeches/foreveryone.shtml, accessed 6/02.
10. Thomas E. Weber, "Terrorist Attacks Raise the Issue of How Best to Protect the Internet," *Wall Street Journal E-World*, 8 October 2001, p. A15; Dorothy E. Denning, "Cyberterrorism: Testimony Before the Special Oversight Panel on Terrorism Committee on Armed Services, U.S. House of Representatives," Georgetown University, 23 May 2000, http://www.cs.georgetown.edu/~denning/infosec/cyberterror.html, accessed 6/02; Staff, "Increased Potential for Distributed Denial of Service (DDoS) Attacks," National Infrastructure Protection Center, Advisory 01-026, 2 November 2001, http://www.nipc.gov/warnings/advisories/2001/01-026.htm, accessed 6/02.
11. Harry Hochheiser and Robin Rice, "Who Runs the Internet?" Computer Professionals for Social Responsibility, 3 May 1998, http://www.cpsr.org/onenet/whoruns.html, accessed 1/01.
12. TRUSTe, "Building a Web You Can Believe In," http://www.truste.com/, accessed 6/02; National Association of Boards of Pharmacy, "Verified Internet Pharmacy Practice Sites (VIPPS)," http://vipps.nabp.net/verify.asp, accessed 6/02; BBB Online, "About the Reliability Program," http://www.bbbonline.org/reliability/index.asp, accessed 6/02.
13. CERN, "How the Web Works," European Organization for Nuclear Research, 3 December 1997, http://public.web.cern.ch/Public/ACHIEVEMENTS/WEB/howworks.html, accessed 6/02.
14. Jared Sandberg, "At Thousands of Web Sites, Time Stands Still," *Wall Street Journal*, 11 March 1997, pp. B1, B3.
15. Roger Clarke, "Domains: A Primer on Internet Technology," Australian National University, 15 February 1998, http://www.anu.edu.au/people/Roger.Clarke/II/IPrimer.html, accessed 6/02.
16. Robert H Zakon, "Hobbes' Internet Timeline vol. 5. 6," 2002, http://info.isoc.org/guest/zakon/Internet/History/HIT.html, accessed 6/02.

17. Avery Comarow, "Just What's Dot Next?" *U.S. News & World Report*, 16 October 2000, p. 50.

18. Internet Corporation for Assigned Names and Numbers, "Preliminary Report, Meeting of the ICANN Board in Yokohama," ICANN, 16 July 2000, http://www.icann.org/minutes/prelim-report-16jul00.htm, accessed 6/02.

19. NameEngine, "Master of Their Domains?" NameEngine Inc., *Business Week E.Biz*, 3 April 2000, p. EB14.

20. Paul M. Eng and Marsha Johnston, "Get Your Hands Off My .Com," *Business Week*, 28 July 1997, p. 88.

21. Dow Jones Newswire, "Julia Roberts Wins Control of Domain Name on Web," *Wall Street Journal*, 1 June 2000, p. B12.

22. Electronic Frontier Foundation (EFF), "S. 1255, Anticybersquatting Consumer Protection Act," http://www.eff.org/pub/Intellectual_property/ Internet_address_adisputes/19990801_cybersquat_bill. html, accessed 1/01.

23. Matt Lake, "Get Your Own Domain Name, *PCWorld*, 1 June 2000, http://pcworld.com/heres_how/article/0,1400,16967,00.html, accessed 1/01.

24. Catherine Yang, "Still the Master of Its Domain," *Business Week*, 13 March 2000, pp. 104–105.

25. The Internet Corporation for Assigned Names and Numbers, "List of Accredited and Accreditation-Qualified Registrars, 10 July 2000," ICANN, http://www.icann.org/registrars/accredited-list.html, accessed 6/02.

26. NetValue, "Home Net Use Soars in Hong Kong," *Nua*, 1 August 2001, http://www.nua.net/surveys/index.cgi?f=VS&art_id=905357042 &rel=true, accessed 6/02; eMarketer, "Half of Hong Kong Homes Online," *Nua*, 14 November 2001, http://www.nua.net/surveys/ index.cgi?f=VS&art_id=905357403&rel=true, accessed 6/02; Nielsen NetRatings, "Sixty Percent of Americans Are Online," *Nua*, 15 February 2001, http://www.nua.net/surveys/index.cgi?f= VS&art_id=905356461&rel=true, accessed 6/02.

27. Richard A. Oppel, Jr., "High Speed Internet Access Hot Commodity in Homes," *Lexington Herald-Leader*, 27 May 2000, pp. A3, A11; Staff, "Home Networking Market Hits 'Knee in the Curve': Home Market to Reach $9.2 Billion by 2006," Cahners InStat Group, 1 October 2001, http://www.instat.com/pr/2001/rc0108hn_pr.htm, accessed 6/02.

28. John Gartner, "Buy a TV, Get a Free ISP," *Wired News*, 6 January 2000, http://www.wired.com/news/technology/0,1282,41042,00.html, accessed 6/02; Joe Wilcoz, "Do Gamers Want Web Access?" CNET Gamecenter.com, 1 September 2000, http://games.netscape.com/ News/Item/Textonly/0,78,0-4704,00.html, accessed 1/01; Stephanie Miles, "WebTV Caught Between MSN Deals, Free PCs," Cnet.com, 11 August 1999, http://news.cnet.com/news/0-1006-202-345961.html, accessed 1/01; Catherine Yang, "Turn On, Tune In, Interact," *Business Week*, 29 May 2000, pp. 90–94; Walter Mossberg, "AOL Takes a Bold Step in Linking TV to Web, But It's a Weak Link," *Wall Street Journal*, 12 July 2000, p. B1; Saul Hansell, "America Online to Buy Time Warner for $165 Billion," *New York Times*, 11 January 2000, http://www.nytimes.com/learning/general/featured_articles/ 000113thursday.html, accessed 6/02.

29. Steven Rosenbush and Peter Elstrom, "Internet Phoning Isn't Just Talk Anymore," *Business Week*, 10 April 2000, p. 46; Steve Rosenbush and Bruce Einhorn, "The Talking Internet," *Business Week*, 1 May 2000, pp. 174–188.

30. Eileen Smith, "Can Your Refrigerator Surf?" *PC World*, 6 January 2000, http://www.pcworld.com/news/article.asp?aid=14675, accessed 6/02.

31. Emily Thornton, "Digital Wheels," *Business Week*, 10 April 2000, pp. 114–124.

32. Melissa Goldfine, " Going Up? The Net Hits U.S. Elevators," ZDNN, 15 January 2000, http://www.zdnet.com/filters/printerfriendly/

0,6061,2422987-2,00.html, accessed 6/02; Jennifer Tanaka and Michael E. Ryan, "A World of Web," *Newsweek*, 15 May 2000, p.12.

33. James R. Dukart, "Will Pay Phones Evolve into Internet Kiosks?" Office.com, 12 June 2000, http://www.office.com/global/0,2724,167-18136,FFhtml, accessed 1/01; Simona Chiose, "Web Kiosks Spring Up in Unlikely Places," *The Globe and Mail*, 26 September 2000, http:// www.globetechnology.com/archive/gam/Specials/20000926/ECKIOS. html, accessed 6/02; Bruce Orwall, "AOL Follows You Everywhere, Even on Vacation," *Wall Street Journal*, 12 October 1999, p. A3.

34. P.J. Huffstutter and David Streitfeld, "Suddenly, New Jersey's Not Just a Wall Street Punch Line," *Los Angeles Times*, 30 September 2001, http://www.latimes.com/news/nationworld/ nation/la-093001jersey.story, accessed 11/01.

35. Staff, "84 Million People in the United States Will Plug Into Wireless Internet by 2005," IDC, 17 October 2001, http://www.idc.com/ communications/press/pr/CM101701pr.stm, accessed 11/01; Michael Pastore, "Wireless Looks for a Lift to Clear Adoption Hurdles," *CyberAtlas*, 16 March 2001, http://cyberatlas.internet.com/markets/ wireless/print/0,,10094_715841,00.html, accessed 6/02; William Echikson, "Suddenly PCs are Falling Flat," *Business Week*, 11 December 2000, p. 66.

36. Intermarket Group, "Eighteen-fold Growth for Wireless Net," *Nua*, 26 October 2001, http://www.nua.net/surveys/index.cgi?f=VS&art_ id=905357341&rel=true, accessed 6/02.

37. Peter Hadfield, "I Need I-mode, Do You Need I-mode?" *U.S. News & World Report*, 9 October 2000, pp. 47–48.

38. Ephraim Schwartz and Cathleen Moore, "E-Commerce on the Go," *InfoWorld*, 23 October 2000, pp. 1, 29.

39. Stephen H. Wildstrom, "Wireless Gets Easier and Faster," *Business Week*, 29 May 2000, p. 34.

40. Janet Rae-Dupree, "Bluetooth Lets Gadgets Speak in One Language," *U.S. News & World Report*, 15 May 2000, pp. 58–59; Stephen Baker, "A Revolution Called Bluetooth," *Business Week*, 18 September 2000, pp. 62–64.

41. Jeanette Borzo, "The Wireless Web," *Wall Street Journal*, 17 April 2000, p.R46.

42. Michael Pastore, " Wireless Looks for a Lift to Clear Adoption Hurdles," *CyberAtlas*, 16 March 2001, http://cyberatlas.internet.com/ markets/wireless/print/0,,10094_715841,00.html, accessed 6/02.

43. Erin Bergamo, "Industry Leaders Create Mobile Wireless Internet Forum," Cisco Systems Press Release, 2 February 2000, http://www. cisco.com/warp/public/146/pressroom/2000/feb00/sp_020200.htm, accessed 6/02; Wylie Wong, "Cisco Sets Its Sights on Software," *CNET News*, 23 May 23 2000, http://news.cnet.com/news/0-1004-202-1933855.html, accessed 1/01; Network World Fusion, "Cisco," *NW Fusion*, 1999, http://www.nwfusion.com/power99/power99-cisco.html, accessed 1/01 Nancy Singer, "Cisco Systems and U.S. Small Business Administration E-Learning Program Empowers Growing Companies to Utilize Internet for Business," Cisco Systems Press Release, 19 July 2000, http://www.cisco.com/warp/public/146/ pressroom/2000/jul00/smb_071900.htm, accessed 6/02; David Kirk-patrick, "Cisco Still Bets On the Net," *Fortune*, 15 October 2001, http://www.fortune.com/, accessed 11/01.

## Chapter 3

1. Year of the Rose, "Story of the Rose Named 'Peace'," American Rose Society, 26 August 2001, http://www.rose-2002.org/peace.html, accessed 6/02; Barrie Collins, "Peace," Timeless Roses, 1997, http:// www.timelessroses.com/ Peace.htm, accessed 1/01.

2. U.S. Census Bureau, "Statistics of U.S. Business," Census Bureau, 7 November 2001, http://www.census.gov/epcd/susb/1998/us/US—.HTM, accessed 6/02.

3. Ibid.

4. Patrick O'Rourke, "Number of Businesses by Revenue and Asset Size," 1998, http://www.bizstats.com/bizsize.htm, accessed 6/02; SBA Office of Advocacy, "Small Business Frequently Asked Questions," U.S. Small Business Administration, 16 July 2001, http://www.sba.gov/advo/stats/sbfaq.html#q2, accessed 6/02 ; U.S. Census Bureau, "Statistics About Small Business Size," U.S. Small Business Administration, http://www.census.gov/epcd/www/smallbus.html, accessed 6/02.

5. Dun & Bradstreet, "20th Annual Small Business Survey," March/April 2001, http://www.dnb.com/about/media/press_release/1,,0-223-1012-0-1052.html, accessed 6/02; CyberDialogue, "U.S. Small Firms Take to Wireless Net," Nua, 21 August 2001, http://www.nua.net/surveys/index.cgi?f=VS&art_id=905357103&rel=true, accessed 6/02.

6. eMarketer, "E-Data, B2B Growth Projections," Information Technology Association of America, http://www.itaa.org/isec/pubs/e20007-8.pdf, accessed 6/02.

7. eMarketer,"U.S. Firms Turning to Broadband," Nua, 24 September 2001, http://www.nua.com/surveys/index.cgi?f=VS&art_id=905357224&rel=true, accessed 6/02 .

8. ActivMedia Research, "The Web Is Unfolding As a Powerful Communication Medium and Business Profit Center," ActivMedia Research News, 18 July 2000, researchnews@Activ MediaResearch.com, received 18 July 2000; ActivMedia Research, "B-to-B E-Commerce Revenues Tripling in 2001," ActivMedia Research, 9 January 2001, http://www.activmediaresearch.com/magic/pr010901.html, accessed 6/02.

9. U.S. Census Bureau, "POPClocks," Population Division, 5 January 2001, http://www.census.gov/main/www/popclock.html, accessed 6/02; Nicholas Kulish, "Census 2000: The New Demographics," Wall Street Journal, 15 May 2001, p. B1; Vanessa O'Connell and Jon E. Hilsenrath, "Advertisers Are Cautious as Household Makeup Shifts," Wall Street Journal, 15 May 2001, pp. B1, B4; Rick Cook, "Internet Not Just for Kids Anymore," E-Commerce Times, 4 April 2000, http://www.ecommercetimes.com/news/articles2000/000404-2.shtml, accessed 6/02; Roger O. Crockett, "A Web That Looks Like the World," Business Week e.BIZ, 22 March 1999, pp. EB 46–47.

10. MarketFacts, "Market Facts Study First to Show That Internet Users Mirror Behaviors and Attitudes of Other Americans," Market Facts, Inc., http://www.marketfacts.com/news/980915.shtml, accessed 6/02; eStats, "User Demographics: Introduction/Overview," eMarketer, 14 September 1999, http://www.emarketer.com/estats/demo_intro.html, accessed 1/01; Michelle Nelson, "Who's Going Online?" PCAlmanac Reference Series, December 2000, vol.4, no.4, pp. 24–27; Nielsen Net Ratings, "Average Web Usage," Nielsen Net Ratings, 18 November 2001, http://pm.netratings.com/nnpm/owa/NRpublicreports. usageweekly, accessed 6/02; eBusiness Advisor, "Change in Online Population Will Dictate Changes in eBusiness Marketing Models," IDC, 25 August 2000, http://www.internationaldatacorp.com:8080/eBusiness/press/EBIZ082500pr.stm, accessed 6/02; Kim Allen, "Online Demographics Match U.S. Population," Digitrends, 12 July 2001, http://www.digitrends.net/ebna/index_16546.html, accessed 6/02; Lee Rainie and Dan Packel, "More Online, Doing More," Pew Internet & American Life Project, 18 February 2001, http://www.pewinternet.org/reports/toc.asp?Report=30 accessed 6/02; Michael Pastore, "Internet Remains a Man's Domain," CyberAtlas, 26 July 2001, http://cyberatlas.internet.com/big_picture/demographics/print/0,,5901_809341,00.html, accessed 6/02.

11. Kim Allen, "Online Demographics Match U.S. Population," Digitrends, 12 July 2001, http://www.digitrends.net/ebna/index_16546.html, accessed 6/02.

12. Susannah Fox, "Wired Seniors," Pew Internet & American Life Project, 9 September 2001, http://www.pewinternet.org/reports/toc.asp?Report=40 accessed 6/02.

13. Lee Rainie and Dan Packel, "More Online, Doing More," Pew Internet & American Life Project, 18 February 2001, http://www.pewinternet.org/reports/toc.asp?Report=30 accessed 6/02; Cyber-Atlas, "40 Percent of America's Kids Online," CyberAtlas, 8 June 2000, http://cyberatlas.internet.com/big_picture/demographics/article/0,,5901_390941,00.html, accessed 6/02; NewsBytes, "Internet: Women Use Internet More," Lexington Herald-Leader, 13 August 2000, p. F1.

14. Roger O. Crockett, "Forget the Mall. Kids Shop the Net," Business Week e.BIZ, 26 July 1999, p. EB14; Tony Pugh, "New 'e-wallets' Created to Tap Teens' Online Buying Power," Lexington-Herald Leader, 22 May 2000, pp. A1, A10.

15. Ibid.

16. Harris Interactive, "Soon-to-be Graduates Truly Web Savvy," Nua, 28 May 2001, http://www.nua.net/surveys/index.cgi?f=VS&art_id=905356805&rel=true, accessed 6/02; VirginStudent, "Almost All UK Students Online," Nua, 13 July 2001, http://www.nua.net/surveys/index.cgi?f=VS&art_id=905356977&rel=true, accessed 6/02 ; European Commission, "EU Schools Mostly Online," Nua, 12 October 2001, http://www.nua.net/surveys/index.cgi?f=VS&art_id=905357292&rel=true, accessed 6/02; eMarketer "U.S. Public Schools Are Online," TechSoup.org, 21 May 2001, http://www.techsoup.org/news_article.cfm?newsid=591&btcfile=news_article, accessed 6/02; Michelle Nelson, "Who's Going Online?" PCAlmanac Reference Series, December 2000, vol.4, no.4, pp. 24–27; Michael Pastore, "U.S. College Students Use Net for Shopping," CyberAtlas, 8 August 2000, http://cyberatlas.internet.com/big_picture/demographics/article/0,,5901_432631,00.html, accessed 6/02.

17. Michael Pastore,"Internet Remains a Man's Domain," CyberAtlas, 26 July 2001, http://cyberatlas.internet.com/big_picture/demographics/print/0,,5901_809341,00.html, accessed 6/02; Michelle Nelson, "Who's Going Online?" PCAlmanac Reference Series, December 2000, vol.4, no.4, pp. 24–27; eStats, "Net User Demographics: Gender," emarketer.com, 17 March 1999, http://www.emarketer.com/estats/demo_sex_2html, accessed 1/01; eStats, "Net User Demographics: Gender," emarketer.com, 17 March 1999, http://www.emarketer.com/estats/demo_sex_3html., accessed 1/01; Media Matrix, "Women Use the Web More Than Men," Nua Internet Surveys, 10 August 2000, http://www.nua.ie/surveys/index.cgi?f=VS&art_id=905355965&rel=true, accessed 6/02.

18. Nielsen Net Ratings, "More African Americans Now Online," Nua, 19 September 2001, http://www.nua.net/surveys/index.cgi?f=VS&art_id=905357205&rel=true, accessed 6/02; eMarketer, "Minorities Less Likely to Buy Online," Nua, 22 August 2001, http://www.nua.net/surveys/index.cgi?f=VS&art_id=905357110&rel=true, accessed 6/02; Cyber Dialogue, "Net Use Up Among African-Americans," Nua, 16 August 2001, http://www.nua.net/surveys/index.cgi?f=VS&art_id=905357088&rel=true, accessed 6/02; Forrester Research, "U.S. Hispanics Active Online," Nua, 25 September 2001, http://www.nua.net/surveys/index.cgi?f=VS&art_id=905357228&rel=true, accessed 6/02; Pew Internet & American Life, "Half of U.S. Hispanics Now Online," Nua, 27 July 2001, http://www.nua.net/surveys/index.cgi?f=VS&art_id=905357024&rel=true, accessed 6/02; CyberAtlas, "U.S. Ethnic Groups Increasingly Web-Savvy," Nua, 19 February 2001, http://www.nua.net/surveys/index.cgi?f=VS&art_id=905356468&rel=true, accessed 6/02.

19. Michael Pastore, "West Coast Cities Among Most Wired in U.S.," CyberAtlas, 3 April 2001, http://cyberatlas.internet.com/big_picture/geographics/print/0,,5911_732051,00.html, accessed 6/02; Internet Demographics, "Profile of the Average Internet User," nservices.com, July 2000, http://nservices.com/internet.htm#InternetDemographics, accessed 1/01; Jim Battey, "Most Wired Cities," InfoWorld, 23 October 2000, p.16; CyberAtlas, "Top Five States for Consumer E-Commerce," CyberAtlas, 20 April 2000, http://cyberatlas.internet.

com/big_picture/demographics/print/0,1323,5901_344751,00.htm, accessed 6/02.

20. Karen Petska, "North America Is the Leading Region for Internet Use," Computer Industry Almanac Inc., December 1999, http://www.c-i-a.com/, accessed 6/01; Nua Internet Surveys, "How Many Online?" *Nua*, http://www.nua.net/surveys/how_many_online/index.html, accessed 6/02; Dataquest, "Asia to Become Largest Net Market," *Nua*, 7 August 2001, http://www.nua.net/surveys/index.cgi?f=VS&art_id=905357053&rel=true, accessed 6/02.

21. Staff, "Internet Activities," Pew Internet & American Life Project, December 2000, http://www.pewinternet.org/reports/chart.asp?img=Daily_Internet_Activities.jpg accessed 6/02.

22. Lee Rainie, "How Americans Used the Internet after the Terror Attack," Pew Internet & American Life," 15 September 2001, http://www.pewinternet.org/reports/toc.asp?Report=45 accessed 6/02.

23. Carnegie Mellon University, "Carnegie Mellon Study Reveals Negative Potential of Heavy Internet Use on Emotional Well Being," 1998, http://homenet.hcii.cs.cmu.edu/progress/pressrel.html, accessed 6/02; Susannah Fox, "Wired Seniors," Pew Internet & American Life Project, 9 September 2001, http://www.pewinternet.org/reports/toc.asp?Report=40 accessed 6/02.

24. Al Urbanski, "Campus Web-Watching," PROMO, January 2000, pp. 19–22; CyberAtlas, "Young Consumers Shy Away from E-Commerce," Internet.com, 2 June 2000, http://cyberatlas.internet.com/big_picture/demographics/print/0,1323,5901_386591,00.htm, accessed 6/02; Jennifer M. O'Brien, "God on the Internet—Churches Go Online to Spread the Word," *Computer Dealer News*, 11 February 2000, http://www.findarticles.com/cf_0/m3563/3_16/60904647/print.jhtml, accessed 6/02.

25. Patricia O'Connell, "The Airlines vs. Expedia and Travelocity," *Business Week* Online, 25 October 2001, http://www.businessweek.com/bwdaily/dnflash/oct2001/nf20011025_8474.htm, accessed 6/02.

26. See note 22.

27. Roger O. Crockett, "Netting Those Investors," *Business Week e.BIZ*, 18 September 2000, p.EB26.

28. Al Urbanski, "Campus Web-Watching," *PROMO*, January 2000, pp. 19-22.

29. Michael Pastore, "Gaming and the Internet Maintain Collision Course," *CyberAtlas*, 22 August 2001, http://cyberatlas.internet.com/big_picture/applications/article/0,,1301_871111,00.html, accessed 6/02.

30. Michael Pastore, "Net Users Finding P2P Music Alternatives," *CyberAtlas*, 11 October 2001, http://cyberatlas.internet.com/big_picture/applications/article/0,,1301_901921,00.html, accessed 6/02; Matthew Swibel, "Sweet Sounds or Sour Notes?" *Business Journal*, 28 July 2000, http://www.findarticles.com/cf_0/m5024/14_18/63825923/print.jhtml, accessed 6/02.

31. Chris Trumble, "It's a Wired, Wired World," *PCAlmanac*, December 2000, vol.4. no.4, pp. 4–7; ActivMedia Research LLC, "50% of all E-Commerce Businesses Purchase Online," ActivMedia, 28 November 2000, researchnews@mail.activmediaresearch.com, received 28 November 2000; *The Economist*, "A Thinker's Guide," Economist.com, 1 April 2000, http://economist.com/displaystory.cfm?Story_ID=298218, accessed 6/02

32. Joseph B. White, "What Works?" *Wall Street Journal*, 23 October 2000, p.R4.

33. Michael Pastore, "B2B Projections Remain High Despite Obstacles," *CyberAtlas*, 9 January 2001, http://cyberatlas.internet.com/markets/b2b/article/0,,10091_555291,00.html, accessed 6/02; Marcia Stepanek, "Are You Web Smart?" *Business Week* Online, 18 September 2000, http://www.businessweek.com/2000/00_38/b3699029.htm accessed 6/02; The Economist Survey Business and the Internet, "The Net Imperative," *The Economist*, 26 June 1999, http://www.economist.com/editorial/freeforall/19990626/su9828.html accessed 1/01.

34. Thane Peterson, "E-I-E-I-E-Farming," *Business Week*, 1 May 2000, p. 202.

35. Data Nugget, "Web Training Explodes," *Business Week* Online, 22 May 2000, http://www.businessweek.com/ebiz/0005/dm0522.htm, accessed 6/02.

36. Nick Wingfield, "Dot-Com Liquidator," *Wall Street Journal*, 14 November 2000, pp. A1, A8.

37. Roger O. Crockett, "So the Rich Are Different," *Business Week* e.BIZ, 24 July 2000, p. EB16.

38. Michael Pastore, "US College Students Use Net For Shopping," *CyberAtlas*, 8 August 2000, http://cyberatlas.internet.com/big_picture/demographics/print/0,,5901_432631,00.html, accessed 6/02; Al Urbanski, "Campus Web-Watching," *PROMO*, January 2000, pp. 19-22.

39. Datamonitor, "Teens Tipped for Online Spending Spree," *Nua*, 7 September 2001, http://www.nua.net/surveys/index.cgi?f=VS&art_id=905357170&rel=true, accessed 6/02; Michael Pastore, "New Payment Options Will Open E-Commerce to Teens," *CyberAtlas*, 7 September 2001, http://cyberatlas.internet.com/markets/retailing/article/0,,6061_880271,00.html, accessed 6/02; Amy Barrett, "To Reach the Unreachable Teen," *Business Week*, 18 September 2000, pp. 78–80; Ann Grimes, "Jim Clark Invests in Web Site Aimed at Teenage Girls," *Wall Street Journal*, 28 February 2000, p.B8; CyberAtlas, "Kids and Teens to Spend More Online," Internet.com, 7 July 1999, http://cyberatlas.internet.com/big_picture/demographics/article/0,1323,5901_150331,00.html accessed 6/02.

40. Cyberscope, "Different Appeals," *Newsweek*, 13 March 2000, p.15.

41. Kathy Foley, "Divided States of Europe," *Nua*, 19 November 2001, http://www.nua.ie/surveys/analysis/weekly_editorial.html, accessed 11/01.

42. Barbara Marquand, "Designing for the Disabled Online," Office.com, 8 June 2000, http://www.office.com/global/0,2724,505-18123-18417,FF.html, accessed 1/01; Washington Post, "Better Electronic Access for the Disabled," Nua Internet Surveys, 25 August 2000, http://www.nua.ie/surveys/index.cgi?f=VS&art_id=905355999&rel=true, accessed 6/02.

43. Carnegie Mellon University, "Carnegie Mellon Study Reveals Negative Potential of Heavy Internet Use on Emotional Well Being," 1998, http://homenet.hcii.cs.cmu.edu/progress/pressrel.html, accessed 6/02; Norman H. Nie and Lutz Erbring, "Internet and Society: A Preliminary Report," Stanford Institute for the Quantitative Study of Society (SIQSS), 17 February 2000, http://www.stanford.edu/group/siqss/, accessed 6/02

44. Peter Mitchell, "Internet Addiction: Genuine Diagnosis or Not?" *The Lancet* Interactive, 19 February 2000, http://www.findarticles.com/cf_0/m0833/9204_355/59579155/p1/article.html, accessed 1/01.

45. Tony Pugh, "Online Complaints Empower Consumer," *Lexington Herald-Leader*, 26 April 2000, pp. A3, 11.

46. AsiaPulse/Yonhap, "Disgruntled Consumers Have Giants in Their Sites," *Asia Times* Online, 11 January 2000, http://www.atimes.com/media/BA11Ce02.html, accessed 6/02.

47. Raymon J. Peypoch, "The Case for Electronic Business Communities," Business Horizons, September–October 1991, http://www.findarticles.com/cf_0/m1038/n5_v41/21186692/p1/article.jhtml?term=The+Case+for+Electronic+Business+Communities, accessed 6/02.

48. General Electric, "GE's e-Volution of 2000," e@GE, http://www.ge.com/news/spotlight/evolution.html, accessed 6/02; General Electric, "GE Fast Facts," e@GE, http://www.ge.com/news/spotlight/fast_facts.html, accessed 6/02; Eric Young, "GE to Launch Digital Exchange," *The Standard*, 11 August 2000, http://www.e-businessworld.com/english/crd_ebiz_223162.html, accessed 6/02; Howard Rudinsky, "Changing the Corporate DNA," *Forbes*, http://www.forbes.com/global/2000/0724/0314099a.html, accessed 6/02;

Jon Burke, "Is GE the Last Internet Company?" *Red Herring*, 15 December 2000, http://www.redherring.com/companies/2000/ 1215/com-mag-88-ge121500.html, accessed 6/02.

## Chapter 4

1. Graduate Management Admission Council, "MBA Forums," http://www.gmac.com/mba/maximize_services/mba_forums , accessed 6/02.

2. Richard A. Wright, "A Brief History of the First 100 Years of the Automobile Industry in the United States," Wayne State University Department of Communications, 1996, http://www.theautochannel.com/mania/industry/history/chap1.html accessed 6/02.

3. ActivMedia Research News, "The Web Is Unfolding as a Powerful Communications Medium & Business Profit Center," ActivMedia Research, ActivMedia Research.com, received 18 July 2000.

4. Business Editors, "eZiba.com Reports Record Sales for Holiday Season; E-Tailer of Handcrafted Goods Surpasses Own Aggressive Plan," *Business Wire*, 11 January 2001, http://www.findarticles.com/cf_0/m0EIN/2001_Jan_11/69010479/p1/article.jhtml, accessed 6/02.

5. Megan Barnett, "Getting Real," *The Standard*, 13 November 2000, http://www.thestandard.com/article/display/0,1151,20036,00.html, accessed 6/02.

6. Business Wire, "Lands' End Joins Forces with Quick Dog to Offer Personal Shopper Technology to Other E-Tailers," *Business Wire*, 8 January 2001, http://www.findarticles.com/cf_0/m0EIN/2001_Jan_8/68857313/print.jhtml, accessed 6/02.

7. Laura Hellee, "Quest for Web Success Begins Anew with Dot.Com Venture," DSN Retailing Today, 5 June 2000, http://www.findarticles.com/cf_0/m0FNP/11_39/64694075/p1/article.jhtml, accessed 6/02; Press Release, "Wal-Mart Announces Buyout of Accel Partners' Minority Interest in Walmart.com," Wal-Mart, Inc., 23 July 2001, http://www.walmart.com/cservice/aw_pr_072301_01.gsp?NavMode=9, accessed 6/02.

8. Bernhard Warner, "Starbucks Gives Kozmo a Jolt," *The Standard*, 14 February 2000, http://www.thestandard.com/article/display/0,1151,10144,00.html, accessed 6/02.

9. Spencer E. Ante and Arlene Weintraub, "Why B2B Is a Scary Place to Be," *Business Week Online*, 11 September 2000, http://www.businessweek.com/2000/00_37/b3698100.htm, accessed 6/02.

10. Staff, "Productivity Growth Is Boosted by Moving to Web Technologies," *Wall Street Journal*, 4 December 2001, p.B6.

11. Vital Statistics, "Uncle Sam Wants You To Shop on the Internet," *U.S. News & World Report*, 11 June 2001, p.12.

12. Business/Technology Editors, "Circle.com Turns American University's Business School Web-centric; Over 95% of Prospective Student Applications Submitted via School's Web Site," Business Wire, 25 April 2000, http://www.findarticles.com/cf_0/m0EIN/2000_April_25/61638384/print.jhtml, accessed 6/02.

13. Odvard Egil Dyrli, "Web-Based Virtual Campus Tours," Matrix, June 2000, http://www.findarticles.com/cf_0/m0HJE/1_1/65014396/print.jhtml, accessed 6/02.

14. Rachel Hartigan, "How Students Can Use the Web to Research Colleges," *U.S. News & World Report*, America's Best Colleges 2001, http://www.usnews.com/usnews/edu/college/articles/cosurf.htm, accessed 6/02.

15. Heather O'Mara, "Improve Training, Cut Costs with E-Learning Programs," *Los Angeles Business Journal*, 20 November 2000, http://www.findarticles.com/cf_0/m5072/47_22/67939556/print.jhtml, accessed 6/02.

16. Genia Jones, "Hallelujah, It's the Internet! Religion Is Proving to Be More Popular on the Web Than Online Auctions or Banking, According to a New Study," *The Standard*, 21 December 2000, http://www.thestandard.com/article/display/0,1151,21011,00.html, accessed 6/02.

17. Berta Delgado, "Church Adding Dot.Com to Name As Ministry Tool," *Lexington Herald-Leader*, 3 February 2001, http://www.kentuckyconnect.com/heraldleader/news/020301/faithdocs/dotcom03.htm, accessed 2/01.

18. Judy Sarles, "Internet Marketing Deal Links Church Web Sites with Bookseller," *Nashville Business Journal*, 4 October 1999, http://nashville.bcentral.com/nashville/stories/1999/10/04/story7.html, accessed 6/02.

19. Samuel Flint, "Building Your NonProfit Organization Through the Internet," The Alford Group, May 2000, http://www.donornet.com/general/articles/may00flint.htm, accessed 6/02.

20. Carol Ebbinghouse, "Avoiding Charity Fraud and Misinformation from Non-Profits on the Internet," Searcher, July 2000, http://www.findarticles.com/cf_0/m0DPC/7_8/63993325/print.jhtml, accessed 6/02.

21. Pew Trusts, "Charitable Groups Discover New Revenue in Retailing Goods Via Their Own Web Sites," *The New York Times*, 27 March 2000, http://www.pewtrusts.com/ideas/ideas_item.cfm?content_item_id=85&content_type_id=13&page=13&issue=10&issue_name=Society%20and%20the%20Internet&name=Newspaper/Magazine%20Articles accessed 6/02.

22. Robert Travis, "Shop-for-a-Cause Web Sites: Conclusions and Speculations," NCIB's Wise Giving Guide, Fall 1999, http://www.give.org/guide/index.asp, accessed 6/02.

23. Business Wire Features, "Shopping Online for the Holidays Helps Raise Money for Charities; Commission Junction's Technology Allows Consumers to Donate to Charities Online," *Business Wire*, 14 December 2000, http://www.findarticles.com/cf_0/m0EIN/2000_Dec_14/68013336/print.jhtml accessed 6/02; Beth Kaner, "Exploring Online Fundraising for Nonprofit Arts Organizations," Idealist.org, http://www.idealist.org/beth.html, accessed 6/02.

24. Patricia Berry, "Scams Swiftly Follow Terrorist Attacks: Beware of Cons Tied to Tragedy," AARP, November 2001, http://www.aarp.org/bulletin/departments/2001/consumer/1105_consumer_1.html, accessed 6/02.

25. E-Commerce Times, "Final Whistle Blows for Sports Retailers," *Nua*, 8 February 2001, http://www.nua.net/surveys/index.cgi?f=VS&art_id=905356435&rel=true, accessed 6/02.

26. Jodie T. Allen, "Unconfident Consumers," *U.S. News & World Report*, 12 February 2001, http://www.usnews.com/usnews/issue/010212/econ.htm, accessed 2/01.

27. Eric Palmer, "Computers, Internet Blamed for Higher Gas Prices, Shortage," *Kansas City Star*, 5 February 2001, http://www.kentuckyconnect.com/heraldleader/news/020501/nationaldocs/05Close-up.htm, accessed 2/01.

28. Tom Spring, "Terror, Tragedy of Attacks Ripple to the Net," *PCWorld*.com, 11 September 2001, http://www.pcworld.com/resource/printable/article/0,aid,61604,00.asp, accessed 6/02; Dwight Cass and Matthew Crabbe, "September 11: Dealing with the Aftermath," *Risk Magazine*, October 2001, http://www.riskwaters.com/risk/latest/oct01/cover01.htm, accessed 11/01; Randy Barrett & Interactive Week Staff, "Safety Net," *Interactive Week*, 17 September 2001, http://www.interactiveweek.com/print_article/0,3668,a%253D14477,00.asp, accessed 11/01.

29. Mike Troy, "Better Late Than Never for Traditional Stores," Discount Store News, 13 December 1999, http://www.findarticles.com/cf_0/m3092/23_38/58331767/p1/article.jhtml?term=Wal-Mart.com accessed 6/02; Staff, "A Leader Beyond Bricks and Mortar," *Discount Store News*, October 1999, http://www.findarticles.com/cf_0/m3092/1999_Oct/57578942/p1/article.jhtml?term=Wal-Mart.com, accessed 6/02; Wal-Mart Stores, Inc., Corporate Site Information, http://www.walmart.com, accessed 6/02; Laura Heller, "Making Walmart.com 'the Wal-Mart of the Web'," *Drug Store News*, 12 June 2000, http://www.findarticles.com/cf_0/m3374/8_22/63411741/p1/article.

jhtml?term=Wal-Mart.com, accessed 6/02; Thane Peterson, "Walmart. com's Jeanne Jackson: 'A Foundation-Building Year'," *Business Week Online*, 30 October 2000, http://www.businessweek.com/bwdaily/dnflash/oct2000/nf20001030_321.htm, accessed 6/02; Hoover's Online, "Wal-Mart Stores, Inc. Company Capsule," Hoover's, http://www.hoovers.com/co/capsule/0/0,2163,11600,00.html, accessed 6/02.

# Chapter 5

1. FTC Consumer Alert, "Going Shopping? Go Global! A Guide for E-Consumers," U.S. Federal Trade Commission, March 2000, http://www.ftc.gov/bcp/conline/pubs/alerts/glblalrt.htm, accessed 6/02; FTC and AOL, "Guide to Online Payments," U.S. Federal Trade Commission and America Online, March 1999, http://www.ftc.gov/bcp/conline/pubs/online/payments.htm, accessed 6/02; MasterCard, "More Ways to Shop Smart," MasterCard International, http://www.mastercardintl.com/newtechnology/set/bestpractices.html, accessed 6/02; National Consumers League, "Be E-Wise: How to Shop Safely Online," National Consumers League, http://www.nclnet.org/BeEWISEbroch.html, accessed 6/02.

2. UNCITRAL, "UNCITRAL Model Law on Electronic Commerce with Guide to Enactment," 1996 (additional article 1998), http://www.uncitral.org/english/texts/electcom/ml-ecomm.htm, accessed 6/02.

3. ABA Cyberlaw Press Release, "ABA Group Releases Study on Cyberspace Jurisdiction," 10 July 2000, American Bar Association, http://www.abanet.org/media/jul00/cyberspace.html, accessed 6/02.

4. WTO Briefing Note, "Electronic Commerce: Work Programme Reflects Growing Importance," World Trade Organization, http://www.wto.org/english/tratop_e/ecom_e/ecom_briefnote_e.htm, accessed 6/02.

5. FTC and OECD, "Electronic Commerce: Selling Internationally," Federal Trade Commission, March 2000, http://www.ftc.gov/bcp/conline/pubs/alerts/ecombalrt.htm, accessed 6/02.

6. Lisa M. Bowman, "Global Treaty—Threat to the Net?" ZDNet.com, 22 June 2001, http://news.zdnet.co.uk/story/0,,t269-s2089815,00.html, accessed 6/02; Elizabeth Hurt, "Border Disputes Simmer," 30 April 2001, *Business2.0*, http://www.business2.com/articles/web/print/0,1650,15697,FF.html, accessed 6/02; Peter Griffin, "Global Web Law a Thorny Issue," *New Zealand Herald*, 16 July 2001, http://www.nzherald.co.nz/storydisplay.cfm?storyID=200279, accessed 6/02.

7. Juliet M. Oberding and Terje Norderhaug, "A Separate Jurisdiction for Cyberspace?" *Journal of Computer Mediated Communication 2*, no. 1, June 1996, http://www.ascusc.org/jcmc/vol2/issue1/juris.html, accessed 6/02.

8. United Nations, "Convention on the Law of the Sea," UN Division for Ocean Affairs and the Law of the Sea, 2001, http://www.un.org/Depts/los/convention_agreements/convention_overview_convention.htm, accessed 6/02.

9. Merriam-Webster's Dictionary of Law, "Jurisdiction," Merriam-Webster, 1996, http://www.lawyers.com/lawyers-com/content/glossary/glossary.html, accessed 6/02.

10. Christopher Wolf, "Internet Jurisdiction," FindLaw.com, 1999, http://profs.lp.findlaw.com/netjuris/index.html, accessed 6/02.

11. Matthew Friedman, "There Are Rules for the Internet—But Whose?" *Computing Canada*, 25 June 1999, 25, no.25, pg.23.

12. Robin Peek, "Customizing the World on the Web," *Information Today*, May 2000, http://www.infotoday.com/it/may00/peek.htm, accessed 6/02.

13. Darrel Menthe, "Jurisdiction in Cyberspace: A Theory of International Spaces," *Michigan Telecommunication Technical Legal Review*, 23 April 1998, http://www.mttlr.org/volfour/menthe.html, accessed 6/02.

14. Martin Stone, "Japanese Court Ruling Could Impact Internet Law," *Newsbytes PM*, 23 March 1999, http://www.findarticles.com/cf_0/m0HDN/1999_March_23/54201297/p1/article.jhtml, accessed 6/02.

15. Chris Mugan, "Internet Porn Ruling Could Hit ISPs," *Computer Weekly*, 8 July 1999, http://www.findarticles.com/cf_0/m0COW/1999_July_8/55170364/p1/article.jhtml, accessed 6/02.

16. John Burgess, "Amazon Reverses on Hitler Book," *Newsbytes*, 18 November 1999, http://www.findarticles.com/cf_0/m0NEW/1999_Nov_18/57649504/p1/article.jhtml, accessed 6/02.

17. Stephen Lawson, "Judge Dismisses French Case Against Yahoo," IDG News Service, 9 November 2001, http://www.pcworld.com/resource/printable/article/0,aid,70323,00.asp, accessed 6/02.

18. John Roemer, "Where's the Courthouse in Cyberspace?" The Industry Standard, 18 January 2000, http://www.thestandard.com/newsletters/NLdisplay/0,2936,120-1005,00.html, accessed 2/01.

19. Elizabeth Hurt, "Border Disputes Simmer," 30 April 2001, *Business2.0*, http://www.business2.com/articles/web/print/0,1650,15697,FF.html, accessed 6/02.

20. Rick Perera, "30 Countries Sign Controversial Cybercrime Treaty," PCWorld.com, 26 November 2001, http://www.pcworld.com/news/article/0,aid,72903,00.asp, accessed 6/02; Council of Europe, "Convention on Cybercrime, ETS no. 185," 23 November 2001, http://conventions.coe.int/Treaty/EN/WhatYouWant.asp?NT=185, accessed 6/02.

21. D. Ian Hopper, "New Law Lets U.S. Nab Foreign Hackers," Associated Press, 26 November 2001, http://www.infowar.com/law/01/law_112601b_j.shtml, accessed 6/02; Jessica Reaves, "Antiterrorism Bill Becomes Law," Time.com, 26 October 2001, http://www.time.com/time/nation/printout/0,8816,181437,00.html, accessed 6/02.

22. ETForecasts, "Global Net Population to Hit 1 Billion by 2005," *Nua*, 7 February 2001, http://www.nua.ie/surveys/?f=VS&art_id=905356430&rel=true, accessed 6/02.

23. Bob Sullivan, "Just How Bad Is Online Fraud?" MSNBC, 25 June 2001, http://www.cardcops.com/CC_OLD/msnbc1.htm, accessed 6/02.

24. Patricia Berry, "Scams Swiftly Follow Terrorist Attacks: Beware of Cons Tied to Tragedy," AARP, November 2001, http://www.aarp.org/bulletin/departments/2001/consumer/1105_consumer_1.html, accessed 6/02.

25. emarketer.com, "Online Auction Fraud Tops Cybercrime List," *Nua*, 12 January 2001, http://www.nua.ie/surveys/index.cgi?f=VS&art_id=905356338&rel=true, accessed 6/02; National White Collar Crime Center and the Federal Bureau of Investigation, "Six-Month Data Trends Report," Internet Fraud Complaint Center (IFCC), May–November 2000, http://www1.ifccfbi.gov/strategy/6monthreport.PDF, accessed 6/02.

26. CyberAtlas staff, "Businesses Better Understanding Online Fraud," *CyberAtlas*, 3 December 2001, http://cyberatlas.internet.com/markets/retailing/print/0,,6061_932941,00.html, accessed 6/02; Staff, "New Report Reveals Latest Internet Fraud Trends, Statistics, and Hotbeds," National White Collar Crime Center, http://www.nw3c.org/sixmonth_trendsreport.htm, accessed 6/02; Joanna Glasner, "FBI: Net Fraud Reports Rising," *Wired News*, 13 June 2001, http://www.wired.com/news/politics/0,1283,44452,00.html, accessed 6/02.

27. See note 25.

28. Staff, Wall Street Journal Online, "Judge Dismisses eBay Fraud Case," ZDNet News, 19 January 2001, http://www.zdnet.com/zdnn/stories/news/0,4586,2676115,00.html, accessed 6/02; Margaret Mannix, "Sure It's a Great Deal. But Is It Real?" *U.S. News*, 11 December 2001, http://www.usnews.com, accessed 6/02.

29. Mathew Schwartz, "Busting B2B e-commerce Fraud," *Computerworld*, 19 February 2001, http://www.itworld.com/Tech/2409/CWSTO57770/pfindex.html, accessed 6/02.

30. Joshua Haliford, "B-to-B Buying Picks Up Speed," *The Standard*, 2 October 2000, http://www.thestandard.com/article/display/0,1151,18974,00.html, accessed 6/02.

31. Fraud Protection Network, "New Web Site Helps E-Tailers Combat Online Fraud," Worldwide E-Commerce Fraud Protection Network," 15 January 2001, http://www.merchantfraudsquad.com/pages/release_115.html, accessed 6/02; Sharon Curry, "E-Commerce Fraud," *Internet ScamBusters* Issue #39, 31 August 2000, http://www.scambusters.org/Scambusters39.html, accessed 6/02.

32. Mike France, "Did 'Deep-Linking' Really Get a Green Light?," *Business Week* Online, 31 July 2000, http://www.businessweek.com/ebiz/0007/ep0731.htm, accessed 6/02.

33. Doug Mellgren, "Teen-age Computer Whiz Scares Hollywood, Inspires Hackers," *Lexington Herald-Leader*, 25 February 2001, p.A11.

34. George A. Chidi, "Akamai, Digital Island Will Square Off In Court," *InfoWorld*, 8 February 2001, http://www.infoworld.com/articles/hn/xml/01/02/08/010208hncourt.xml, accessed 6/02; Damien Cave, "Patently Absurd?" Salon, 3 March 2000, http://www.salon.com/tech/feature/2000/03/03/patent/print.html, accessed 6/02; Scott Rosenberg, "Amazon to World: We Control How Many Times You Must Click!" Salon, 21 December 1999, http://www.salon.com/tech/log/1999/12/21/bezos/, accessed 6/02; David Sims, "Amazon.com Patents Enemy-Making Process," *The Standard*, 28 February 2000, http://www.thestandard.com/article/display/0,1151,12377,00.html, accessed 6/02.

35. Saul Hansell, "Surging Number of Patents Engulfs Internet Commerce," *NY Times* Online, 11 December 1999, http://www.nytimes.com/library/tech/99/12/biztech/articles/11web.html, accessed 6/02; Karen Rodriguez, "Dot-coms Scramble for Patent Protection in Record Numbers," *Silicon Valley Business Journal*, 8 September 2000, http://sanjose.bcentral.com/sanjose/stories/2000/09/11/story8.html, accessed 6/02.

36. Maxine Lans Retsky, "Trademark Applications Simplified," *Marketing News*, 14 February 2000, http://www.findarticles.com/cf_0/m4313/4_34/61493365/print.jhtml, accessed 2/01.

37. Jill Priluck, "The Reel.com Deal," *The Industry Standard*, 10 May 2000, http://www.thestandard.com/article/display/0,1151,14946,00.html, accessed 6/02.

38. Doug Isenberg, "The Year in Net Law," *Internet World*, 15 December 2000, http://www.findarticles.com/cf_0/m0DXS/24_6/68155732/p1/article.jhtml, accessed 6/02.

39. "Anheuser-Busch Favorably Settles Cybersquatting Lawsuit," *Business Wire*, 17 November 2000, http://www.findarticles.com/cf_0/m0EIN/2000_Nov_17/67047355/p1/article.jhtml,accessed 6/02.

40. Staci D. Kramer, "Cybersquatters Squat on Rosie's McCall's," *The Standard*, 8 January 2001, http://www.thestandard.com/article/display/0,1151,21347,00.html, accessed 6/02.

41. Lee J. Johnson, "Offering Medical Advice on the Web," *Medical Economics*, 10 July 2000, http://www.findarticles.com/cf_0/m3229/13_77/64997098/p1/article.jhtml, accessed 6/02.

42. Carol Ebbinghouse, "Webmaster Liability: Look Before You Link, and Other Admonitions for Today's Webmaster," Searcher, February 1998, http://www.infotoday.com/searcher/feb98/sidebar.htm, accessed 6/02.

43. Bruce Schneier, "Bad Signs," *The Standard*, 30 October 2000, http://www.thestandard.com/article/display/0,1151,19485,00.html, accessed 6/02.

44. Patty Edfors, "Your John Hancock Goes Digital," *Communications News*, December 2000, http://www.comnews.com/stories/articles/c1200guest.htm, accessed 6/02.

45. Peter Crush, "Out to Get You," *Management Today*, November 2000, http://www.clickmt.com/index.cfm, accessed 6/02.

46. Linda Rosencrance, "Online Sales Continue to Climb," *Computer-world*, 21 February 2002, http://www.pcworld.com/news/article/0,aid,85424,00.asp, accessed 6/02; L.J. Martinez and Jon Weisman, "Bush Signs Off on Extension of Net Tax Ban," E-Commerce Times.

29 November 2001, http://www.ecommercetimes.com/perl/story/15021.html, accessed 6/02.

47. Andrew Caffrey, "States at Odds Over Web Taxes," *Wall Street Journal*, 7 March 2001, p. B3; Jason Anders, "Pressure Grows to Allow Web Sales Taxes," *Wall Street Journal*, 15 March 2001, p. B12.

48. Associated Press, "Bush to Sign Internet Tax Moratorium Bill," *Newsday*, 16 November 2001, http://www.newsday.com/business/ny-biz-itax1116.story, accessed 11/01.

49. Marci McDonald, "Online Gambling Proves Addictive – Even to the Big Casinos," *U.S. News & World Report*, 16 October 2000, pp. 44-46; Beth Cox, "Could Online Gambling Be Banned?", Internet.com, 13 March 2002, http://dc.internet.com/news/article.php/990891, accessed 6/02.

50. Ibid.

51. Melba Newsome, "The Plastic Police Are Cracking Down," *Red Herring*, 1 September 2000, http://www.redherring.com/mag/issue82/mag-pornography-82.html, accessed 6/02; ABC News, "Porn Pullout," ABCNews.com, 7 May 2001, http://abcnews.go.com/sections/business/DailyNews/yahooporn010507.html, accessed 6/02.

52. Edvard Pettersson, "Porn Entrepreneur Gives Inside Look at Profiting Online," *Los Angeles Business Journal*, 27 November 2000, http://www.findarticles.com/cf_0/m5072/48_22/67643185/p1/article.jhtml accessed 6/02; Erik Gruenwedel "Tricks of the Trade," *Brandweek*, 30 October 2000, http://www.findarticles.com/cf_0/m0BDW/42_41/66705311/p1/article.jhtml , accessed 6/02; John Buskin, "The Web's Dirty Little Secret," *Wall Street Journal*, 17 April 2000, p.R54; Keith Regan, "Online Porn Profits Still Lurk in Shadows, Ecommerce Times, 31 January 2002, http://www.newsfactor.com/perl/story/16088.html, accessed 6/02.

53. Stephen Lacey, "Playboy.com IPO Has the Harder Core Eyeing Public Marts," *Investment Dealers' Digest*, 4 October 1999, http://www.findarticles.com/cf_0/m3628/1999_Oct_4/66164381/print.jhtml, accessed 3/01; Playboy Enterprises, 2001 10K SEC Filing, Playboy Enterprises, Inc., 21 March 2002, http://www.corporate-ir.net/ireye/ir_site.zhtml?ticker=PLA&script=700, accessed 6/02.

54. Lisa Shuchman, "Teach Your Children Well," *The Standard*, 13 November 2000, http://www.thestandard.com/article/display/0,1151,20043,00.html, accessed 6/02;

55. Dru Sefton, "Sociologists Lurk on Net to Examine Our Behavior," *USA Today* Tech Report, 7 June 2001, http://www.usatoday.com/life/cyber/tech/cth732.htm, accessed 6/02; Jeffery R. Young, "Committee of Scholars Proposes Ethics Guidelines for Research in Cyberspace," *Chronicle of Higher Education*, 11 October 2001, http://chronicle.merit.edu/free/2001/10/2001101102t.htm, accessed 6/02.

56. American Marketing Association, "Code of Ethics for Internet Marketing," AMA, 2002, http://www.marketingpower.com/index.php? &Session_ID=65fedee52ed844349f5a86d338d964c8, accessed 6/02.

57. Federal Trade Commission, "How to Comply with the Children's Online Privacy Protection Act," FTC, November 1999, http://www.ftc.gov/bcp/conline/pubs/buspubs/coppa.htm, accessed 6/02; Michael Pastore, "Children Likely to Reveal Information Online," *CyberAtlas*, 24 May 2000, http://cyberatlas.internet.com/markets/advertising/article/0,,5941_379511,00.html, accessed 6/02.

58. Martin Stone, "Two Spam-Scanners Sentenced for Web Fraud," *eMarketer*, 3 January 2001, http://www.findarticles.com/cf_0/m0NEW/2001_Jan_3/68713210/p1/article.jhtml, accessed 6/02.

59. Kevin Featherly, "AMA Releases Online Med-ethics Guidelines," *Newsbytes*, 22 March 2000, http://www.findarticles.com/cf_0/m0NEW/2000_March_22/60583455/print.jhtml, accessed 6/02; Margaret A. Winker, Annette Flanagin, Bonnie Chi-Lum, John White, Karen Andrews, Robert L. Kennett, Catherine D. DeAngelis, and

Robert A. Musacchio, "Guidelines for Medical and Health Information Sites on the Internet: Principles Governing AMA Web Sites," *Journal of the American Medical Association 283*, no. 12, 22/29 March 2000, http://jama.ama-assn.org/issues/v283n12/ffull/jsc00054.html, accessed 6/02.

60. Editors, "DoubleClick Appoints Consumer Privacy Advisory Board; To Include Leading Consumer Advocates and Online Privacy Experts," *Business Wire*, 17 May 2000, http://www.findarticles.com/cf_0/m0EIN/2000_May_17/62141718/print.jhtml, accessed 6/02.

61. Declan McCullagh, "Court Says Anti-Smut Law Illegal," *Wired*, 22 June 2000, http://www.wired.com/news/politics/0,1283,37171,00.html, accessed 6/02; Keith Perine, "De-COPA-tated," *The Standard*, 26 June 2000, http://www.thestandard.com/article/article_print/0,1153,16352,00.html, accessed 6/02.

62. Harris Interactive, "Website Privacy Policies Need Plainer English," *Nua*, 4 December 2001, http://www.nua.net/surveys/index.cgi?f=VS&art_id=905357471&rel=true, accessed 6/02.

63. HarrisInteractive, "New Survey Reveals Trust Gap Exists Between Consumers and Businesses About Information Exchange," The Privacy Leadership Initiative, 2 April 2001, http://www.harrisinteractive.com/news/printerfriend.asp?NewsID=260, accessed 6/02.

64. Heather Green, "Your Right to Privacy: Going . . . Going . . . ," *Business Week*, 23 April, 2001, p. 48; Glenn R. Simpson, "The Battle Over Web Privacy," Wall Street Journal, 21 March 2001, pp. B1, B4; Christina Le Beau, "Mountains to Mine," *American Demographics*, 1 August 2001, http://www.americandemographics.com/, accessed 10/01.

65. Pamela Mendels , "The Rise of the Chief Privacy Officer," *Business Week* Online, 14 December 2000, http://www.businessweek.com/careers/content/dec2000/ca20001214_253.htm, accessed 6/02.

66. Thomas E. Weber, "The New Key To Shopping," *Wall Street Journal*, 26 March 2001, p. B1.

67. Dennis Fisher, "Feds Escalate Warning About e-commerce Hacks," PC Week's eWEEK, 8 March 2001, http://www.linuxsecurity.com/articles/government_article-2656.html, accessed 6/02.

68. Bob Trott, "Virus That Hits Word and Excel Discovered," *InfoWorld*, 1 September 1998, http://www.infoworld.com/cgi-bin/displayStory.pl?98091.wnshiver.htm, accessed 6/02.

69. Warren Cohen, "Napster's Rap Sheet," *U.S. News & World Report*, 8 May 2000, p. 45; Staff, "Napster's Musical History," *The Standard*, 12 February 2001, http://www.thestandard.com/article/article_print/0,1153,22139,00.html, accessed 6/02; Dan Goodin, "Can Napster Change Its Tune," *The Standard*, 18 February 2001, http://www.thestandard.com/article/article_print/0,1153,22296,00.html, accessed 6/02; Scott Rosenberg, "The Napster Files," Salon, 4 February 2000, http://www.salon.com/tech/col/rose/2000/02/04/napster_swap/print.html, accessed 6/02.

70. "Music Usage Policy: Copyright Notice," MP3 Australia, 2002, http://www.mp3.com.au/musicuse.asp, accessed 6/02.

## Chapter 6

1. WebSideStory, "55 Percent of All Web Traffic Worldwide Comes from Outside the United States," 23 January 2001, StatMarket, http://statmarket.com/cgi-bin/sm.cgi?sm&press&press, accessed 7/02; Staff, "U.S. Will Lose Global eCommerce Stronghold," eMarketer Stats & eNews, 23 March 2001, http://www. emarketer.com/Feeds/NumbersInTheNews/Story01.html?ref=b2b, accessed 7/02.

2. Theodore Levitt, "The Globalization of Markets," *Harvard Business Review*, 1 May 1983, http://www.hbsp.harvard.edu/hbsp/prod_detail.asp?83308, accessed 7/02.

3. World Bank Group, "Data By Topic," The World Bank, http://www.worldbank.org/data/databytopic/class.htm#Definitions_of_groups, accessed 7/02; Staff, "The UN in Brief," The United Nations, http://www.un.org/Overview/brief.html, accessed 7/02.

4. Ibid.

5. Central Intelligence Agency, "Ethopia," CIA World Factbook 2001, 1 January 2001, http://www.cia.gov/cia/publications/factbook/, accessed 7/02; International Telecommunications Union," Internet Indicators: Hosts, Users and Number of PCs," ITU, December 2000, http://www.itu.int/ITU-D/ict/statistics/at_glance/Internet00.pdf, accessed 7/02.

6. Irwin Arieff, "Click a Mouse for a Sheep: UN Touts E-Commerce," Reuters, 20 November 2001, http://www.reuters.com, accessed 11/01.

7. Central Intelligence Agency, "Bangladesh ," CIA World Factbook, January 2001, http://www.odci.gov/cia/publications/factbook/geos/bg.html, accessed 6/02.

8. Geographic.Org, "GDP Per Capita," CIA World Factbook, http://www.photius.com/wfb1999/rankings/gdp_per_capita_0.html, accessed 7/02; Mick Brady, "Reality Check: The State of E-Commerce, Part II," E-Commerce Times, 12 July 2000, http://www.ecommercetimes.com/news/articles2000/000712-2.shtml, accessed 7/02; Staff, "Risk E-Business: Seizing the Opportunity of Global E-Readiness," McConnell International, August 2000, http://www.mcconnellinternational.com/ereadiness/EReadinessReport.htm, accessed 7/02.

9. Sam Paltridge, "Local Access Pricing and the International Digital Divide," e-OTI: OnTheInternet, October 2000, http://www.isoc.org/oti/printversions/1000paltridge.html, accessed 7/02.

10. Jeffrey D. Sachs, "A New Map of the World," *The Economist*, 22 June 2000, http://www.economist.com/PrinterFriendly.cfm?Story_ID=80730, accessed 7/02.

11. Paulo Rebêlo, "Casting a Wider Net in Brazil," *Wired*, 30 July 2001, http://www.wired.com/news/print/0,1294,45526,00.html, accessed 7/02; Viva Rio, "Viva Rio and Viva Favela: Who Are We?" 2001, http://www.vivafavela.com.br/english.asp, accessed 7/02.

12. See note 10.

13. Mick Brady, "Reality Check: The State of E-Commerce, Part II," E-Commerce Times, 12 July 2000, http://www.ecommercetimes.com/news/articles2000/000712-2.shtml, accessed 7/02.

14. Kathy Foley, "2000: Year in Review," Nua Internet Surveys, 28 December 2000, http://www.nua.ie/surveys/analysis/yearinreview/archives/2000_yearly_review.html, accessed 7/02; *CyberAtlas*, "The World's Online Populations," Internet.com, 6 April 2001, http://cyberatlas.internet.com/big_picture/geographics/article/0,1323,5911_151151,00.html, accessed 7/02; James Ledbetter, "Making a Global Web Audience Count," *The Industry Standard*, 22 March 1999, http://www.thestandard.com/article/0,1902,3785,00.html?printer_friendly=, accessed 7/02.

15. Michael Pastore, "Global Internet Population Moves Away from U.S.," *CyberAtlas*, 11 January 2001, http://www.cyberatlas.internet.com/big_picture/geographics/print/0,,5911_558061,00.html, accessed 7/02.

16. Ipsos-Reid, "U.S. No Longer Dominates Net," Nua Internet Surveys, 17 May 2001, http://www.nua.ie/surveys/?f=VS&art_id=905356771&rel=true, accessed 7/02; U.S. Census Bureau, "Top Ten Countries With Which the U.S. Trades," U.S. Department of Commerce, U.S. Census Bureau, March 2001, http://www.census.gov/foreign-trade/top/dst/current/balance.html, accessed 7/02.

17. Roger Ricklefs, "U.S. E-Tailers Expand Efforts North of the Border," *Wall Street Journal*, 31 January 2000, p. A21; Statistics Canada, "Majority of Canadians Have Net Access," Nua Internet Surveys, 27 March 2001, http://www.nua.net/surveys/index.cgi?f=VS&art_id=905356596&rel=true, accessed 7/02; Ipsos-Reid, "Canada and Taiwan Lead Music Downloads," Nua Internet Surveys, 29 May 2001, http://www.nua.ie/surveys/index.cgi?f=VS&art_id=905356811&rel=true, accessed 7/02; CNEWS, "Good News for Canada's Online Retailers," Nua Internet Surveys, 15 March 2001, http://www.nua.ie/surveys/index.cgi?f=VS&art_id=905356559&rel=true, accessed

7/02; Mo Krochmal, "U.S. Culture Pervades Global E-commerce," TechWeb, 21 January 2000, http://www.techweb.com/printableArticle?doc_id=TWB20000121S0010, accessed 7/02; SES Research, "B2B Growing for Canadian Small Firms," Nua Internet Surveys, 14 May 2001, http://www.nua.ie/surveys/index.cgi?f=VS&art_id=905356759&rel=true, accessed 7/02.

18. eMarketer, "Young Mexicans Get Wired—Not Wireless," Nua Internet Surveys, 5 February 2001, http://www.nua.ie/surveys/index.cgi?f=VS&art_id=905356420&rel=true, accessed 7/02; Wired, "Mexican e-Commerce Market Shows Promise," Nua Internet Surveys, 16 January 2001, http://www.nua.ie/surveys/index.cgi?f=VS&art_id=905356347&rel=true, accessed 7/02.

19. Reuters, "Latin America Will Have 75m Online in 2005," Nua Internet Surveys, 4 April 2001, http://www.nua.ie/surveys/index.cgi?f=VS&art_id=905356630&rel=true, accessed 7/02; Reuters, "AOL Scales New Heights in Latin America," Nua Internet Surveys, 18 May 2001, http://www.nua.ie/surveys/index.cgi?f=VS&art_id=905356778&rel=true, accessed 7/02; Excite News, "Internet Use to Boom in Latin America," Nua Internet Surveys, 15 March 2001, http://www.nua.ie/surveys/index.cgi?f=VS&art_id=905356561&rel=true, accessed 7/02.

20. Ipsos-Reid, "U.S. No Longer Dominates Net," Nua Internet Surveys, 17 May 2001, http://www.nua.ie/surveys/?f=VS&art_id=905356771&rel= true, accessed 7/02; Marc Spiegler, "Glocalization: Easier Said Than Done," The Standard, 9 October 2000, http://www.thestandard.com/article/0,1902,18890,00.html accessed 7/02.

21. Brandon Mitchener, "Businesses, Individuals Push EU Web Use Higher," Wall Street Journal, 29 November 2000, p. B9; Sandra Gittlen, "Global Web Usage," Network World E-commerce Newsletter, 28 August 2000, http://www.nwfusion.com/newsletters/ecomm/2000/0828ecomm1.html, accessed 7/02.

22. Nevin Cohen, "eMarketer: Credit-card Penetration Lags in Europe," ebusinessforum.com, 16 April 2001, http://www.ebusinessforum.com/index.asp?layout=rich_story&doc_id=3089, accessed 5/01.

23. Michael Bartlett, "French Soon Will Embrace The Web," NewsBytes, 10 August 2001, http://www.findarticles.com/cf_0/m0NEW/2001_August_10/77116844/p1/article.jhtml, accessed 7/02.

24. Adam Lincoln, "Localisation Services May Be Key to Crossborder Revenues," The Economist Intelligence Unit, 19 April 2001, http://www.ebusinessforum.com/index.asp?layout=printer_friendly&doc_id=3141, accessed 7/02; Marc Spiegler, "Glocalization: Easier Said Than Done," The Standard, 9 October 2000, http://www.thestandard.com/article/0,1902,18890,00.html, accessed 7/02.

25. Reuters, "China Number Two In Home Net Usage," Nua, 22 April 2002, http://www.nua.net/surveys/index.cgi?f=VS&art_id=905357873&rel=true, accessed 7/02; Kumiko Aoki, "Cultural Differences in E-Commerce: A Comparison Between the U.S. and Japan," First Monday, 1 November 2000, http://firstmonday.org/issues/issue5_11/aoki/index.html, accessed 7/02; Nick Wingfield, "EBay Will Close Japan Auction Site As Sales Rates Remain Below Normal," Wall Street Journal Online, 27 February 2002, http://online.wsj.com/, accessed 7/02.

26. Michael Pastore, "Where in the World is the Best E-Commerce?" CyberAtlas, 15 May 2001, http://cyberatlas.internet.com/big_picture/geographics/print/0,,5911_766411,00.html, accessed 7/02.

27. Mitch Betts, "Taiwan, Estonia Emerge as Good Places for e-Commerce," Computerworld, 22 August 2000, http://www.computerworld.com/managementtopics/ebusiness/story/0,10801,49046,00.html, accessed 7/02.

28. Adam Lincoln, "Localisation Services May Be Key to Crossborder Revenues," The Economist Intelligence Unit, 19 April 2001, http://www.ebusinessforum.com/index.asp?layout=printer_friendly&doc_id=3141, accessed 7/02; Staff, "Global Internet Statistics (By

Language)," Global Reach, March 2001, http://www.glreach.com/globstats/index.php3, accessed 7/02.

29. James Ledbetter, "Making a Global Web Audience Count," The Industry Standard, 22 March 1999, http://www.thestandard.com/article/0,1902,3785,00.html , accessed 7/02; Adam Lincoln, "Localisation Services May Be Key to Crossborder Revenues," The Economist Intelligence Unit, 19 April 2001, http://www.ebusinessforum.com/index.asp?layout=printer_friendly&doc_id=3141, accessed 7/02; Ipsos-Reid, "U.S. No Longer Dominates Net," Nua Internet Surveys, 17 May 2001, http://www.nua.net/surveys/?f=VS&art_id=905356771&rel=true, accessed 7/02.

30. Marc Spiegler, "Glocalization: Easier Said Than Done," The Standard, 9 October 2000, http://www.thestandard.com/article/0,1902,18890,00.html, accessed 7/02.

31. Pamela Druckerman, "Latin Web Firms Venture Out to Markets in Spain, U.S.," Wall Street Journal, 12 April 2000, p. A23.

32. Keith Shipton, "Multilingual Web," Adobe Systems, 2001, http://www.pacific.adobe.com/web/spotlights/multilingual/main.html, accessed 7/02.

33. Suzanne Baran, "A Small, Small World," Internet World Magazine, 1 April 2001, p.18.

34. Canadian Official Languages Act (R.S. 1985, c. 31 (4th Supp. ) ) updated 30 April 2001, http://laws.justice.gc.ca/en/O-3.01/text.html, accessed 7/02; Martin O'Malley and John Bowman, "Language in Quebec," CBC News Online, June 2001, http://www.cbc.ca/news/indepth/language/, accessed 7/02; Tyler Hamilton, "Quebec Language Agency Cracks Down on English-only Web Site," The Globe & Mail, 8 June 1999, http://aix1.uottawa.ca/~geist/globejune899.html, accessed 7/02.

35. Dylan Tweney, "Lost in Translation Software," eCompany Now, 13 February 2001, http://www.ecompany.com/articles/web/print/0,1650,9453,00.html, accessed 7/02.

36. Connie Ling, "Learning a New Language," Wall Street Journal, 12 March 2001, p.R18.

37. Lynda Radosevich, "Going Global Overnight," Info World, 19 April 1999, http://www.express-shopper.com/docs/going_global.html, accessed 7/02; Staff, "Business Protocol: China," Asia Business Today, http://www.asiabusinesstoday.org/2know/china.cfm; Staff, "Business Protocol: India," Asia Business Today, http://www.asiabusinesstoday.org/2know/india.cfm, accessed 7/02; Andrew Marlatt, "Can One Site Appeal to All?" Internet World, 16 November 1998, http://www.findarticles.com/cf_0/m0DXS/1998_Nov_16/53250776/print.jhtml, accessed 7/02.

38. StudentsCount, "Are You Driven by Numbers," Certified General Accountants of Ontario, http://www.studentscount.com/unlucky/scary.shtml, accessed 7/02; Kylie Hsu, "Lucky and Unlucky Numbers," California State University Los Angeles, http://www.calstatela.edu/faculty/khsu2/cartoon3.html, accessed 7/02.

39. "Business Protocol: China," Asia Business Today, http://www.asiabusinesstoday.org/2know/china.cfm, accessed 7/02; Staff, "Business Protocol: India," Asia Business Today, http://www.asiabusinesstoday.org/2know/india.cfm, accessed 7/02.

40. Leo Deegan, "Writing Dates in Chinese," University of California, Berkeley, http://www.stat.berkeley.edu/users/deegan/dates.htm, accessed 7/02.

41. Andrew Marlatt, "Can One Site Appeal to All?" Internet World, 16 November 1998, http://www.findarticles.com/cf_0/m0DXS/1998_Nov_16/53250776/print.jhtml, accessed 7/02.

42. Marc Spiegler, "Glocalization: Easier Said Than Done," The Standard, 9 October 2000, http://www.thestandard.com/article/0,1902,18890,00.html, accessed 7/02.

43. Matt Gallaway, "French (Dis)Connection," eCompany Now, 4 December 2000, http://www.ecompany.com/articles/web/print/

0,1650,8943,00.html, accessed 7/02; Matt Gallaway, "International Jurisdiction Soup," eCompany Now, 27 February 2001, http://www.ecompany.com/articles/web/print/0,1650,9579,00.html, accessed 7/02; Randall E. Stross, "Pardon My French," *U.S. News & World Report,* 12 February 2001, p. 41.

44. Glenn R. Simpson, "U.S. Officials Criticize Rules on EU Privacy," *Wall Street Journal,* 27 March 2001, p. B7; Robyn Weisman, "U.S. Lawmakers Blast EU Internet Privacy Rules," NewsFactor Network, 9 March 2001, http://www.osopinion.com/perl/printer/8079/, accessed 7/02; Brian Krebs, "U.S. Businesses Slow to Adopt EU Safe Harbor Agreement," 4 January 2001, http://www.infowar.com/law/01/law_010501a_j.shtml, accessed 7/02; Brandon Mitchener, "Microsoft Plans to Sign Accord on Data Privacy with the EU," *Wall Street Journal,* 16 May 2001, p. A14; Staff, "TRUSTe Approves First Web Site Under EU Safe Harbor Privacy Program," PR Newswire, 12 February 2001, http://www.findarticles.com/cf_0/m4PRN/2001_Feb_12/70354892/print.jhtml, accessed 7/02.

45. Jason Dean, "China Issues 'Trial' Online Ad Licenses in First Step Toward Regulating Sector," *Wall Street Journal,* 1 June 2000, p. B18.

46. Robert Guy Matthews, "Tariffs Impede Trade Via Web on Global Scale," *Wall Street Journal,* 17 April 2000, p. B1.

47. Thomas Crampton, "Beijing Uses Cyberspace to Widen Control," *International Herald Tribune,* 24 March 2001, http://www.iht.com/articles/14484.html, accessed 7/02

48. Staff, "150 Organizations in 28 Countries Tackle Internet Fraud," U.S. Federal Trade Commission, 23 March 2000, http://www.ftc.gov/opa/2000/03/rich.htm, accessed 7/02.

49. Connie Ling, "Yahoo! Starts First TV Ad Campaign in China Area in Bid for Market Share," *Wall Street Journal,* 8 May 2000, p. A39; Kara Swisher, "Who Has What It Takes To Lead Yahoo?" Wall Street Journal, 2 April 2001, p. B1; Staff, "Yahoo! No. 1 Search Engine in 100 Countries," StatMarket, 27 February 2001, http://statmarket.com/SM?c=stat022701, accessed 5/01; Ken Belson, "Yahoo Japan Wins Hoorays," *Business Week,* 19 June 2000, p. 104; Chen May Yee, "Yahoo! Makes Grass-Roots Push in Asia," *Wall Street Journal,* 1 August 2000, p. B9; Michael Pastore, "International Net Usage Follows U.S. Lead," *CyberAtlas,* 13 June 2000, http://cyberatlas.internet.com/big_picture/geographics/article/0,,5911_393761,00.html, accessed 7/02; Ellen Neuborne, "Pepsi's Aim Is True," *Business Week* e.BIZ, 22 January 2001, p. EB 52; Brandon Mitchener, "What Slowdown? AOL Boosts European Members by 40%," *Wall Street Journal,* 22 March 2001, p. B8.

# Chapter 7

1. Polish Market Review, "B2B on the Rise in Poland," Nua Internet Surveys, 17 August 2001, http://www.nua.ie/surveys/index.cgi?f=VS&art_id=905357095&rel=true, accessed 7/02.

2. Michael Pastore, "Consumers Still Soft to Idea of E-Books," *CyberAtlas,* 5 June 2001, http://cyberatlas.internet.com/markets/retailing/article/0,,6061_778851,00.html, accessed 7/02.

3. John Gaffney, "How Do You Feel About a $44 Tooth-Bleaching Kit?" *Business2.0,* September 2001, http://www.business2.com/articles/mag/print/0,1643,16977,FF.html, accessed 7/02; Crest Dental Resource-Net, "Professional Crest Whitestrips," 2001, http://www.dentalcare.com/soap/cws/pgintro.htm, accessed 7/02; Ron Lieber, "P&G Has Something to Smile About," Fast Company, August 2001, http://www.fastcompany.com/lead/lead_feature/pg2.html, accessed 7/02.

4. Michael Pastore, "It's Diversify or Die for Online Media Firms," *CyberAtlas,* 19 December 2001, http://cyberatlas.internet.com/markets/advertising/print/0,,5941_943041,00.html, accessed 7/02; Christopher Saunders, "Sites Trending Toward Aggressive Web Advertising," *CyberAtlas,* 30 November 2001, http://cyberatlas.

5. Michael Pastore, "Offline Brands Bringing E-Commerce to the Masses," *CyberAtlas,* 1 August 2001, http://cyberatlas.internet.com/markets/retailing/print/0,,6061_858051,00.html, accessed 7/02; Michael Pastore, "Banners Can Brand, Honestly, They Can: Part II," *CyberAtlas,* 19 July 2001, http://cyberatlas.internet.com/markets/advertising/article/0,,5941_804761,00.html, accessed 7/02; Michael Pastore, "Brand Web Sites Come Up Short with Many Consumers," *CyberAtlas,* 24 April 2001, http://cyberatlas.internet.com/markets/advertising/article/0,,5941_751271,00.html, accessed 7/02.

6. Casey Sweet and Jeff Walkowski, "Online Qualitative Research Task Force: Report of Findings," Quirk's Marketing Research Review, December 2000, http://www.quirks.com/articles/article_print.asp?arg_articleid=643, accessed 7/02.

7. Peter Lloyd, " The Basics of Brainlining," Geocreate, 2001, http://www.gocreate.com/articles/abl101.htm, accessed 7/02.

8. Staff, "Greenfield Online Announces Availability of MindStorm-TM Interactive Online Brainstorming Service for Marketing Research," *Business Wire,* 10 September 1998, http://www.findarticles.com/cf_0/m0EIN/1998_Sept_10/21108626/print.jhtml, accessed 7/02.

9. Staff, "Online Brainstorming," Buzzback.com, 2001, http://www.buzzback.com/case_studies.asp, accessed 7/02.

10. Business/Technology Editors, "cPulse Customer Satisfaction Tool Helps Crutchfield.com Prepare for Rush of Online Holiday Shoppers," *Business Wire,* 24 October 2000, http://www.findarticles.com/cf_0/m0EIN/2000_Oct_24/66293713/print.jhtml, accessed 7/02.

11. Dylan Tweney, "Analyzing Chat," *Business2.0,* 20 April 2001, http://www.business2.com/articles/web/print/0,1650,11467,FF.html, accessed 7/02; David Orenstein, "Hidden Treasure," *Business2.0,* July 2001, http://www.business2.com/articles/mag/0,1640,14841,FF.html, accessed 7/02.

12. CASRO, Council of American Survey Research Organizations, http://www.casro.org/survandyou.cfm, accessed 7/02.

13. Maryann Jones Thompson, "Market Researchers Embrace the Web," *The Standard,* 26 January 1999, http://www.thestandard.com/article/display/0,1151,3274,00.html, accessed 7/02; Jon Rubin, "Online Marketing Research Comes of Age," *Brandweek,* 30 October 2000, http://www.findarticles.com/cf_0/m0BDW/42_41/66705290/print.jhtml, accessed 7/02.

14. Small Business Administration, "Marketing Research and the Small Business," SBA, http://www.sba.gov/gopher/Business-Development/Success-Series/Vol3/Mark/mark.txt, accessed 7/02.

15. Peter Coy, "Harris Interactive: A High Opinion of Online Polling," *Business Week* Online, 11 January 2000, http://www.businessweek.com/technology/content/0001/ec0111.htm, accessed 7/02.

16. Staff, "About Gomez," Gomez, Inc., http://www.mygomez.com/, accessed 7/02.

17. Reuters, "Search Engines Grapple With Constant Web Growth," CNN, 27 March 2000, http://www.cnn.com/2001/TECH/internet/03/27/search.engines.reut/index.html, accessed 3/01.

18. Erin White, "Market Research on the Internet Has Its Drawbacks," *Wall Street Journal,* 2 March 2000, p. B4; David Lake, "Online Research Market to Hit $230 Million," 24 January 2000, http://www.thestandard.com/article/0,1902,10101,00.html, accessed 7/02; Dana James, "The Future of Online Research," Marketing News, 3 January 2000, http://www.findarticles.com/cf_0/m4313/1_34/61538777/print.jhtml, accessed 3/01; Larry Gold, "Online Research," ICONOCLAST, 14 September 2000, http://www.iconoclast.com/dotcom/marketing/research.html, accessed 7/02; Staff, "Harris Interactive Announces 40% Increase in its Internet Client Base," Harris Interactive, 13 April 2000, http://www.harrisinteractive.com/news/allnewsbydate.asp?NewsID=81, accessed 7/02; Jon Rubin, "Online Marketing

Research Comes of Age," *Brandweek*, 30 October 2000, http://www.
findarticles.com/cf_0/m0BDW/42_41/66705290/print.jhtml, accessed
7/02; CASRO, "Market Trends: Online Research Growing," Greenfield Online, 2002, http://www.greenfield.com/research_solutions/
rsrch_solns_main.htm, accessed 7/02.

19. Greenfield Online, Inc., http://www.greenfield.com/, accessed 4/01;
Staff, "Greenfield Online Reports Students Active Net Shoppers,"
*DSN Retailing Today*, 18 September 2000, http://www.findarticles.
com/cf_0/m0FNP/18_39/66190252/p1/article.jhtml accessed 7/02;
Lori Enos, "Study: Seniors Top Online Shoppers," E-Commerce
Times, 12 July 2000, http://www.ecommercetimes.com/perl/story/
3753.html, accessed 7/02; Dick Kelsey, "Internet Beats Catalogs,
Stores on Price," *Newsbytes* PM, 27 January 2000, http://www.
findarticles.com/cf_0/m0HDN/2000_Jan_27/59042208/p1/article.jhtml
accessed 7/02; Karen Benezra, "Advertisees Anonymous," *Brandweek*,
13 March 2000, http://www.findarticles.com/cf_0/m0BDW/11_41/
61297858/p1/article.jhtml accessed 7/02; Staff, "Shoppers Staying At
Home," Bobbin, February 2000, http://www.findarticles.com/cf_
0/m3638/6_41/59646892/p1/article.jhtml accessed 7/02; David Lake,
"Another Drop in the IPO Bucket," *The Industry Standard*, 17 March
2000, http://thestandard.com/article/0,1902,13095,00.html?printer_
friendly=, accessed 7/02; Maryann Jones Thompson, "When Market
Research Turns into Marketing," *The Industry Standard*, 23 August
1999, http://thestandard.com/article/0,1902,5995,00.html?printer_
friendly=, accessed 7/02; Susan Meier Roth, " Online Brainstorming:
Today's Hot Qualitative Research Methodology," *Greenfield Online*,
Inc., http://www.greenfield.com/, accessed 3/01.

# Chapter 8

1. Stephanie Miles, "DoubleClick Halts Service That Targets Ads to Web
Surfers," *Wall Street Journal*, 10 January 2002, p. B6.

2. Harriet Marsh, "Dig Deeper Into the Database Goldmine," *Marketing*, January 2001, pp. 29–30; Staff, "Tesco Profits Top £1bn," BBC,
10 April 2001, http://news.bbc.co.uk/hi/english/business/newsid_
1269000/1269918.stm, accessed 7/02.

3. Investor Relations, "Management Slide Presentation," Chico's, 2001,
http://www.chicos.com/frames/investor_relations.asp, accessed 7/02.

4. Kurt Thearling, "An Introduction to Data Mining," Wheelhouse
Corporation, 1996, http://www3.shore.net/~kht/text/dmwhite/
dmwhite.htm, accessed 7/02.

5. Larry Selden and Geoffrey Colvin, "A Measure of Success," *Business2.0*,
October 2001, http://www.business2.com/articles/mag/print/0,1643,
17414,FF.html, accessed 7/02; Alan Weber, "14 No-fail Steps to
Building a Database," Target Marketing, vol. 23, no.10, October 2000,
pp. 153-163.

6. Staff, "DoubleClick Abacus," DoubleClick, 2001, http://www.abacus-
direct.com/, accessed 7/02.

7. Jim Carr, "Commerce Demands Cooperation," *Infoworld*, 6 January
1997, http://www.britannica.com/magazine/print?content_id=11694,
accessed 1/02.

8. Bill Miles, "Slick Move," *Darwin Magazine*, 1 June 2001, http://www.
darwinmag.com/read/060101/headfirst.html, accessed 7/02.

9. Todd Wasserman, "Mining Everyone's Business," *Brandweek*, 28
February 2000, http://www.findarticles.com/cf_0/m0BDW/9_41/
60805315/print.jhtml, accessed 7/02.

10. Joseph McKendrick, "Mining Specification Promises Rich Returns,"
ENT, 12 April 2000, vol.5, no.6, p. 44.

11. Joaquim Menezes, "Database Makers Deepen Mining Capabilities,"
*Computing Canada*, 30 July 1999, http://www.findarticles.com/cf_
0/m0CGC/29_25/55330813/print.jhtml, accessed 7/02.

12. See note 9.

13. Business/High Tech Editors, "J.Crew Deploys digiMine Data
Mining Solutions," *Business Wire*, 13 November 2001, http://www.
findarticles.com/cf_0/m0EIN/2001_Nov_13/80004308/p1/article.
jhtml, accessed 7/02; *Business Editors*, "J. Crew Group Announces
April 2001 Revenue Results," *Business Wire*, 10 May 2001, http://
www.findarticles.com/cf_0/m0EIN/2001_May_10/74415430/p1/
article.jhtml, accessed 7/02; Staff, "J. Crew Group Announces October
2001 Revenue Results," *PR Newswire*, 8 November 2001, http://www.
findarticles.com/cf_0/m4PRN/2001_Nov_8/79852702/print.jhtml,
accessed 7/02.

14. Stefanie Olsen, "FTC Drops Probe Into DoubleClick Privacy Practices," CNET News.com, 22 January 2001, http://news.cnet.com/
news/0-1005-200-4563509.html, accessed 7/02; Clarence Henderson,
"Database Marketing: Digging for Business Gold," Asia Market
Research, April 2001, http://www.asiamarketresearch.com/columns/
datamining.htm, accessed 7/02.

15. Staff, "Amazon.com Privacy Notice," Amazon.com, 2002, http://www.
amazon.com/exec/obidos/tg/browse/-/468496/104-3648062-6041503,
accessed 7/02.

16. Staff, "Yahoo! Web Beacons," Yahoo!, 2001, http://privacy.yahoo.com/
privacy/us/pixels/details.html, accessed 7/02.

17. Staff, "Web Bug Standards to Be Developed, NAI Announces New
Program to Address Important Consumer Privacy Concerns," Network
Advertising Initiative, 4 October 2001, http://www.networkadvertising.
org/aboutnai_news_pr100401.asp, accessed 7/02.

18. Thomas Dowling, "Lies, Damned Lies, and Web Logs," *School
Library Journal*, May 2001, http://www.findarticles.com/cf_0/m1299/
5_47/75090796/print.jhtml, accessed 7/02.

19. Staff, "Gartner Says Analytics Will Be a Hot Career Choice," *Gartner*,
14 May 2001, http://www4.gartner.com/5_about/press_room/
pr20010514a.html, accessed 7/02; Staff, "Got Analytics? You're Hired!"
Advisor.com, 23 May 2001, http://www.advisor.com/Articles.nsf/aid/
SMITT245, accessed 7/02; John Webster, "Staffed for Web Analytics,"
InfoWorld, 15 October 2001, http://www.findarticles.com/cf_0/
m0IFW/42_23/79150090/print.jhtml, accessed 7/02.

20. Jennifer Lewis, "Customers in the Crosshairs: Web Analytics
Promises to Get Advertisers Closer to Consumers," *Red Herring*,
20 March 2001, http://www.redherring.com/mag/issue94/1040018304.
html, accessed 7/02; Business/Technology Editors, "Web Analytics
Market Increases 200% Annually; Projected to Grow to $4 Billion in
2004," Business Wire, 13 December 2000, http://www.findarticles.
com/cf_0/m0EIN/2000_Dec_13/67927066/p1/article.jhtml, accessed
7/02; John Webster, "Staffed for Web Analytics," *InfoWorld*, 15
October 2001, http://www.findarticles.com/cf_0/m0IFW/42_23/
79150090/print.jhtml, accessed 7/02; Keith Ward, "Web Analytics
Can Turn Knowledge into Profits," ENT, 29 January 2001, http://
www.findarticles.com/cf_0/m0FOX/1_6/75645090/print.jhtml,
accessed 7/02.

21. Roger Marsden, "Managing Customer Information from Cradle to
Grave," Customer Inter@Ction Solutions, vol. 20, no. 3, September
2001, pp. 30-33.

22. Michael Pastore, "Most CRM Projects Remain in Planning Phase,"
*CyberAtlas*, 29 May 2001, http://cyberatlas.internet.com/big_picture/
applications/article/0,,1301_774831,00.html, accessed 7/02; Michael
Pastore, "Benefits of CRM Justifying Costs," *CyberAtlas*, 13 June
2001, http://cyberatlas.internet.com/big_picture/applications/article/
0,,1301_783781,00.html, accessed 7/02; Michael Pastore, "CRM to
Lead Market for Analytical Applications," *CyberAtlas*, 24 January
2001, http://cyberatlas.internet.com/big_picture/applications/article/
0,,1301_569511,00.html, accessed 7/02.

23. David B. Montgomery and Charles B. Weinberg, "Toward Strategic
Intelligence Systems," *Journal of Marketing* 43 (Fall 1979): 41–52.

24. Sumantra Ghosbal and Seok Ki Kim, "Building Effective Intelligence Systems for Competitive Advantage," *Sloan Management Review* (Fall 1986): pp. 49–58.

25. Business & Technology Editors, "Del Monte Foods Selects Proscape Technologies—The Most Advanced Marketing Intelligence Solution Available," *Business Wire*, 14 November 2000, http://www.findarticles.com/cf_0/m0EIN/2000_Nov_14/66916421/print.jhtml, accessed 7/02.

26. Marketing Resources,"US Postal Service Selects Epicentric for Nationwide Marketing Intelligence Network," *PR Newswire*, 8 January 2001, http://www.findarticles.com/cf_0/m4PRN/2001_Jan_8/68854600/print.jhtml, accessed 7/02.

27. Mubarak Dahir, "Getting the Dirt," *The Standard*, 26 June 2000, http://www.thestandard.com/article/display/0,1151,16201,00.html, accessed 7/02.

28. Jonathan L. Calof, "What's Your Competitive Intelligence Quotient (CIQ)?" 20 October 1999, http://strategis.ic.gc.ca/SSG/mi04122e.html/, accessed 3/01.

29. Timothy M. Maier, "Corporate Snoops Sharpen Skills," Insight on the News, 31 August 1998, http://www.findarticles.com/cf_0/m1571/n32_v14/21079080/p1/article.jhtml, accessed 7/02.

30. Stephanie Miles, "DoubleClick Halts Service That Targets Ads to Web Surfers," *Wall Street Journal*, 10 January 2002, p. B6; Stefanie Olsen, "DoubleClick Turns Away from Ad Profiles," CNET News.com, 8 January 2002, http://news.com/2100-1023-803593.html?legacy=cnet, accessed 7/02; Kim Gilmour, "Private Sales," *Internet Magazine*, October 2001, http://www.findarticles.com/cf_0/m0CXD/2001_Oct/79056383/print.jhtml, accessed 7/02; Chet Dembeck and Robert Conlin, "Beleaguered DoubleClick Appoints Privacy Board," *E-Commerce Times*, 17 May 2000, http://www.ecommercetimes.com/perl/story/?id=3348, accessed 7/02; Staff, "Interactive Advertising Bureau (IAB), DoubleClick, MSN, and CNET Networks Release Groundbreaking Online Brand Research Findings," DoubleClick.com, 3 August 2001, http://www.doubleclick.net, accessed 8/01; Rob Norton, "Ma! The Internet Keeps Looking at Me!" *Business2.0*, June 2000, http://www.business2.com/articles/mag/0,1640,6588,FF.html, accessed 7/02; Chris Oakes, "Web Enters Privacy 'Safe Harbor'," *Wired*, 2 November 2000, http://www.wired.com/news/politics/0,1283,39909,00.html, accessed 7/02; Juliana Gruenwald, "Stormy Seas Ahead Over 'Safe Harbor'" *Interactive Week*, 30 October 2000, http://www.zdnet.com/zdnn/stories/news/0,4586,2646060,00.html, accessed 1/02; Declan McCullagh, "Safe Harbor Is a Lonely Harbor," *Wired*, 5 January 2001, http://www.wired.com/news/politics/0,1283,41004,00.html, accessed 7/02; Brian Krebs, "Intel Signs Up for EU 'Safe Harbor' Agreement," *Newsbytes*, 2 July 2001, http://www.findarticles.com/cf_0/m0NEW/2001_July_2/76163365/p1/article.jhtml, accessed 7/02.

## Chapter 9

1. Michael Mahoney, "One Year Ago: DotComGuy Emerges from E-Commerce Captivity," *E-Commerce Times*, 3 January 2002, http://www.ecommercetimes.com/perl/printer/15223/, accessed 7/02; Richard Stenger, "Does DotComguy Live in e-utopia or a Publicity Hut?" CNN Interactive, 25 January 2000, http://www.cnn.com/2000/TECH/computing/01/25/dotcomguy/index.html, accessed 7/02; Staff, "DotComGuy to Live Off Net for Year," Editors-Service.com, 2000, http://www.editors-service.com/articlearchive/dotcom2000.html, accessed 7/02; Michelle Delio, "DotComGuy, Gone and Forgotten," *Wired*, 3 January 2001, http://www.wired.com/news/print/0,1294,40940,00.html, accessed 7/02; Janelle Brown, "A Poster Child for

Internet Idiocy," *Salon*, 1 August 2000, http://www.salon.com/tech/feature/2000/08/01/dotcomguy/print.html, accessed 7/02.

2. Toby B. Gooley, "Mass Customization: How Logistics Makes it Happen," Logistics Management & Distribution Report, 1 April 1998, http://www.findarticles.com/cf_0/m0GZB/n4_v37/20877568/p1/article.jhtm, accessed 7/02.

3. Staff, "Reflect.com Broadens Scope," Women's Wear Daily, 2 March 2001, Reflect.com About Us In the Press, http://www.reflect.com/, accessed 7/02; Erik Linden, "Procter & Gamble-backed Dot-com Puts on a Happy Face as It Hires Engineers to Buoy Growth," *Silicon Valley Business Ink*, 4 May 2001, http://www.svbizink.com/headlines/article.asp?aid=1563, accessed 7/02.

4. Joelle Tessler, "Cosmetics Site Offers Mass Customization," *Mercury News*, 19 September 2000, http://www0.mercurycenter.com/svtech/news/indepth/docs/reflec092000.htm, accessed 5/01.

5. Debbie Levitt, "A Review of MyCereal.com," Suite101.com, 3 July 2001, http://www.suite101.com/article.cfm/internet_business/71040, accessed 7/02; Paul Spinrad, "The Gist: Build-to-Order Breakfasts," *Wired*, 9 June 2001, http://www.wired.com/wired/archive/9.06/streetcred.html?pg=6, accessed 7/02; Larry Riggs, "Directions: Cereal Drama Custom Crunch," IndustryClick,15 May 2001, http://industryclick.com/magazinearticle.asp?magazinearticleid=102065&mode=print, accessed 7/02.

6. Michael Pastore, "E-Commerce Trudges Through Current Slowdown," *CyberAtlas*, 22 May 2001, http://cyberatlas.internet.com/markets/retailing/print/0,,6061_770811,00.html, accessed 7/02.

7. Sandra Swanson, "Online Sales Inch Forward," InformationWeek, 28 November 2001, http://www.informationweek.com/story/IWK20011128S0007, accessed 7/02

8. Ernst & Young UK, "Online Sales Set to Grow and Grow," Ernst & Young, 15 January 2001, http://www.ey.com/global/gcr.nsf/UK/Consumer_Products_-_Report_-_Global_Online_Retailing_Survey_2001, accessed 7/02.

9. Ernst & Young UK, "Online Sales Set to Grow and Grow," Ernst & Young, 15 January 2001, http://www.ey.com/global/gcr.nsf/UK/Consumer_Products_-_Report_-_Global_Online_Retailing_Survey_2001, accessed 7/02; Staff, "Government Says e-commerce Sales Stall in Q3," CyberAtlas, 29 November 2001, http://cyberatlas.internet.com/markets/retailing/print/0,,6061_930841,00.html, accessed 7/02; Michael Pastore, "E-Commerce Trudges Through Current Slowdown," *CyberAtlas*, 22 May 2001, http://cyberatlas.internet.com/markets/retailing/print/0,,6061_770811,00.html, accessed 7/02; CyberAtlas, "Toys Continue to Top E-Commerce Lists," *CyberAtlas*, 7 December 2001, http://cyberatlas.internet.com/markets/retailing/print/0,,6061_935841,00.html, accessed 7/02.

10. Arbitron New Media, "A Third of US Net Users Have Broadband," Nua Internet Surveys, 22 June 2001, http://www.nua.ie/surveys/index.cgi?f=VS&art_id=905356900&rel=true, accessed 7/02.

11. Melvin T. Copeland, (1923), "Relation of Consumers' Buying Habits to Marketing Methods," *Harvard Business Review* 1, no.3, April, pp. 282–289.

12. Gil McWilliam, "Building Stronger Brands Through Online Communities," *Sloan Management Review*, Spring 2000, http://www.findarticles.com/cf_0/m4385/3_a41/62280556/print.jhtml, accessed 7/02.

13. Elizabeth Gardner, "With New Leadership and New Owners, Will Peapod 2.0 Have a New Business Plan?" *Internet World Magazine*, 1 February 2001, http://www.internetworld.com/020101/02.01.01fastforward1.jsp, accessed 5/01; Business Editors, "Peapod Positioned for Success in 2001 Record Fourth Quarter Sales Reported; Ahold Partnership Strengthened," *Business Wire*, 21 February 2001, http://www.findarticles.com/cf_0/m0EIN/2001_Feb_21/70703721/

print.jhtml, accessed 7/02; Miguel Helft, "Reality Check, Aisle 5," *The Industry Standard*, 30 April 2001, http://www.thestandard.com/article/0,1902,24035,00.html?printer_friendly=, accessed 7/02.

14. Michael Pastore, "Online Grocery Sector Needs a Little Marketing," *CyberAtlas*, 26 April 2001, http://www.cyberatlas.com/markets/retailing/print/0,,6061_753121.00.html, accessed 7/02.

15. Ken Yamada, "Shop Talk: Big Appliances Sell on the Web," *Red Herring*, 17 April 2001, http://www.redherring.com/industries/2001/0417/210019021.html, accessed 7/02.

16. Lori Enos, "Shakeout Can't Put Out Web Tobacco Sales," E-Commerce Times, 23 February 2001, http://www.ecommercetimes.com/perl/printer/7625, accessed 7/02; Elizabeth Blakey, "U.S. Court Lifts Ban on Web Cigarette Sales," *E-Commerce Times*, 8 June 2001, http://www.ecommercetimes.com/perl/printer/11132, accessed 7/02.

17. Stephanie B. Goldberg, "Fermenting a Wine-Sales Revolution," *Business Week*, 21 March 2001, http://www.businessweek.com/smallbiz/content/mar2001/sb20010321_758.htm, accessed 7/02.

18. Thane Peterson, " Wine Online: It Doesn't Have to Be This Bitter," *Business Week*, 17 April 2001, http://www.businessweek.com/bwdaily/dnflash/apr2001/nf20010417_735.htm, accessed 7/02.

19. Robert Kilborn and Stephanie Cook, "News in Brief: Business & Finance," *Christian Science Monitor*, 16 April 2001, vol.93, no.98, p. 20.

20. David Lewis, "Delta Sees $1 Billion in 2001 Online Sales," *InternetWeek*, 25 November 2001, http://www.internetwk.com/story/INW20011115S0006, accessed 7/02.

21. Barrie Rappaport, "E-books Spawn Yawns," CNNFN, 1 June 2001, http://www.cnn.com/2001/BUSINESS/06/01/ebooks.reut/, accessed 7/02.

22. Matthew Rose, "Simon & Schuster to Release Story by Stephen King on the Web Only," *The Wall Street Journal*, 8 March 2000, p. B8; Tom Lowry, "Will e-Books Be Real Page-Turners?" *Business Week*, 23 October 2000, p.117; Diane Brady, "Story of E," *Business Week e.BIZ*, 24 July 2000, pp. EB 47–50.

23. Staff, "Anthrax Scare Will Not Affect Growth of Online Billing in the US, Reports Jupiter Media Metrix," Jupiter Media Metrix, 12 November 2001, http://www.jmm.com/xp/jmm/press/2001/pr_111201.xml, accessed 7/02; Reuters, "Sweden Turns to Banking Online," ZDNet.com, 2 January 2002, http://www.zdnet.com/filters/printerfriendly/0,6061,5101155-2,00.html, accessed 7/02.

24. Sarah Rose, "The Truth About Online Banking," *Money*, 1 April 2000, vol.29, no. 4, p.114.

25. Mark Sappenfield, "Internet as Portal to Ivory Tower," *Christian Science Monitor*, 6 April 2001, vol.93, no.92, p.1.

26. Laura Wonnacott, "E-xpand Your Mind with the Growing List of Online e-ducators," *InfoWorld*, 15 December 2000, http://www2.infoworld.com/, accessed 4/01.

27. Dylan Tweney, "Want Smarter Employees? Get on the E-train," *eCompany Now*, http://www.business2.com/articles/mag/0,1640,9001,FF.html, accessed 7/02.

28. Alexis Gutzman, "Making Content Profitable," Internet.com, 22 October 2001, http://ecommerce.internet.com/news/insights/ebiz/print/0,,10379_908501,00.html, accessed 7/02; Kim Stewart, "Coming Soon: End of Net's Free Ride," Wall Street Journal Online, 1 November 2001, http://www.zdnet.com/filters/printerfriendly/0,6061,282174-2,00.html, accessed 1/02.

29. Greg Sandoval, "Global Sports Keeps Expansion Going," CNET News.com, 14 September 2001, news.cnet.com/news/0-1007-200-7163697.html?tag=mn_hd, accessed 1/02; Lori Enos, "Luxury Site Ashford.com Warned by Nasdaq," *E-commerce Times*, 20 April 2001, http://www.ecommercetimes.com/perl/story/9109.html, accessed 7/02.

30. Anita Chabria, "Too Gauche for Comfort," *The Industry Standard*, 22 March 2001, http://www.thestandard.com/article/0,1902,23062,00.html, accessed 7/02.

31. Lisa Vickery, "Change of Tune," *The Wall Street Journal*, 17 July 2000, p. R40.

32. Michael Pastore, "Digital Marketplaces Deemed Crucial to Strategy," *CyberAtlas*, 18 December 2000, http://cyberatlas.internet.com/markets/b2b/print/0,,10091_539051,00.html, accessed 7/02; Michael Pastore, "E-Procurement Gaining Converts Among Mid-Sized Businesses," *CyberAtlas*, 6 December 2000, http://cyberatlas.internet.com/markets/b2b/print/0,,10091_528481,00.html, accessed 7/02.

33. Ibid.

34. Staff, "B2B E-Commerce Will Survive Growing Pains," *CyberAtlas*, 28 November 2001, http://cyberatlas.internet.com/markets/b2b/print/0,,10091_930251,00.html, accessed 7/02.

35. Pew Internet & American Life Project, "US Government is Behemoth of Online Retail," *Pew Foundation*, 30 May 2001, http://www.pewinternet.org/releases/release.asp?id=23, accessed 7/02.

36. Wanda Cummings, "Online Branding: Developers and Designers Hold the Key," *WebReference Update Newsletter*, 27 April 2000, http://www.webreference.com/new/branding.html, accessed 7/02; Business Editors & Internet/Online Writers, "e-Branding Index Introduced by Corporate Branding," Business Wire, 14 January 2000, http://www.findarticles.com/cf_0/m0EIN/2000_Jan_14/58578156/print.jhtml, accessed 7/02.

37. Brian Milligan, "Transportation and The Internet: Brand-Name Recognition Problem Raises Its Head," *Purchasing*, 2 November 2000, http://www.findarticles.com/cf_0/m3148/8_129/69241014/p1/article.jhtml, accessed 7/02.

38. Christopher Saunders, "Study: Online Ads Focus on Building Brand, Not Clickthroughs," *Internet News*, 8 November 2000, http://www.internetnews.com/IAR/print/0,,12_506671,00.html, accessed 7/02; Christopher Saunders, "Study: Search Listings Better at Branding, Sales Than Banners," *InternetNews*, 13 February 2001, http://www.internetnews.com/IAR/print/0,,12_587751,00.html, accessed 7/02.

39. Michael Carlon, Marc Ryan, and Risa Weledniger, "The Five Golden Rules of Online Branding," *AdRelevance and 24/7 Advertising*, 23 October 2000, http://www.nyecomm.org/Misc/docs/Five_Golden_Rules.pdf, accessed 7/02.

40. David McGuire, "Addressing Giant VeriSign Launches Online Brand Protection," *Newsbytes*, 6 December 2001, http://www.newsbytes.com/cgi-bin/udt/im.display.printable?client.id=newsbytes&story.id=172756, accessed 1/02.

41. Michelle Goldberg, "Traffic: Trendspotting in the New Economy," *The Industry Standard*, 10 November 2000, http://www.thestandard.com/article/0,1902,19634,00.html?printer_friendly=, accessed 7/02; Sol Tucker, "No Other Shoe Will Be Like It," *ECA Magazine*, 2 April 2001, http://www.ecamagazine.com/010402nikeprestoid.htm, accessed 7/02; Philip Van Munching, "The Devil's Adman," *Brandweek*, 12 March 2001, http://www.findarticles.com/cf_0/m0BDW/11_42/71766839/print.jhtml, accessed 7/02; Staff, "NIKE iD—The 'Running' Mate of the GOP and Democratic Parties," 7 November 2000, PR Newswire, http://www.findarticles.com/cf_0/m4PRN/2000_Nov_7/66650702/print.jhtml, accessed 7/02; Steven M. Zeitchik, "Marketing Muse: The New Brand You," *The Industry Standard*, 14 March 2001, http://www.thestandard.com/article/0,1902,22859,00.html?printer_friendly=, accessed 7/02; Bernhard Warner, "Nike's New Net Religion," The Industry Standard, 29 May 2000, http://www.thestandard.com/article/0,1902,15217,00.html?printer_friendly=, accessed 7/02.

## Chapter 10

1. Darren Allen, "eConsumers: Get Lots of Credit," eMarketer, 20 June 2001, http://www.emarketer.com/analysis/ecommerce_b2c/20010620_b2c.html, accessed 7/02.

2. Andy Reinhardt, "Tesco Bets Small—And Wins Big," *BusinessWeek* e.biz, 1 October 2001, pp. EB25-32; Staff, "Q&A With Tesco.com's John Browett," BusinessWeek e.biz, 1 October 2001, http://www. businessweek.com/magazine/content/01_40/b3751626.htm, accessed 7/02.

3. Charles J. Whalen, "Consumer Confidence No Crystal Ball," *Business Week*, 19 March 2001, p. 65.

4. Staff, "October Auto Sales Soar," *Money*, 1 November 2001, http://money.cnn.com/2001/11/01/companies/carsales, accessed 7/02.

5. Rebecca Quick, "Shoppers Find Blowout Sale on Net is Over," *The Wall Street Journal*, 21 June 2000, pp. B1, B4.

6. Keith Regan, "Harnessing the Power of Online Pricing," *E-Commerce Times*, 22 March 2001, http://www.ecommercetimes.com/perl/printer/ 8370, accessed 7/02.

7. Staff, "Americans Spent a Record 556 Million Dollars in Online Auctions, Jumping 149 Percent in Past Year, According to Nielsen/ NetRatings and Harris Interactive," Nielsen/Net Ratings, 28 June 2001, http://www.nielsen-netratings.com/pr/pr_010628.pdf, accessed 7/02.

8. Roy Furchgott, "Shop Bots Can Save You Money," eCompany.com, October 2000, http://www.ecompany.com/articles/mag/print/0,1643, 7148,FF.html, accessed 7/02.

9. Andrew Quinn, "Minorities Get Better Car Deals on Internet-Study," *Reuters*, 11 December 2001, http://www.reuters.com/news_article. jhtml?type=internetnews&StoryID=446841, accessed 1/02; Ronald Roach, "Study Says Minorities Get Better Auto Deals Online," Black Issues in Higher Education, 3 January 2002, http://www.findarticles. com/cf_0/m0DXK/23_18/82472609/p1/article.jhtml, accessed 7/02.

10. Staff, "Consumers Welcome Internet Pricing Plans," ninemsn, 4 June 2001, http://news.ninemsn.com.au/sci_tech/story_13929.aspLTH, accessed 6/01.

11. Rebecca Smith, "Web Site Aspires to Open Up Gem Trade, But Industry May Resist Transparency," *The Wall Street Journal*, 2 June 2000, p. B7.

12. Douglas A. Blackmon, "Price Buster," *The Wall Street Journal*, 17 July 2000, p.R12.

13. Noah Elkin, "How to Beat the High Cost of Internet Access," *eMarketer*, 19 December 2001, http://www.emarketer.com/, accessed 7/02.

14. Timothy J. Mullaney, "Sites Worth Paying For?" *BusinessWeek e.BIZ*, 14 May 2001, pp. EB10-EB12.

15. Ian Mount, "Best Things in Life . . . Never Mind," eCompany.com, June 2001, http://www.ecompany.com/articles/mag/print/0,1643, 11623,FF.html, accessed 7/02.

16. Nick Wingfield, "Amazon.com's Free-Shipping Promotion Has Customers Crying, 'Price Increase'," *The Wall Street Journal*, 27 June 2001, p. A3; Greg Sandoval, "Amazon Stops Shipping Goods For Free," Cnet News.com, 6 July 2001, http://news.com.com/2100-1017- 269534.html?legacy=cnet accessed 7/02.

17. Don Durfee, "The Transparency of the Web Has Forced Many Companies to Adopt Uniform Cross-Channel Prices," eCFO, originally published on the EIU ebusiness forum, January 2001, http://www. e-cfonet.com/articles/al_online_pricing.html, accessed 6/01.

18. Claudine Thompson, "Online Fraud: Young Dogs, Same Old Tricks?" *eMarketer*, 14 November 2000, http://www.brandera.com/features/00/ 11/20/numbers.html, accessed 7/02.

19. Brian Fonseca, "Keeping Internet-Business Fraud In Check," *InfoWorld*, 13 March 2000, http://www.infoworld.com/articles/hn/xml/ 00/03/13/000313hnetrend.xml, accessed 7/02.

20. IFCC, " 2001 Internet Fraud Report," Internet Fraud Complaint Center, 30 May 2001, http://www1.ifccfbi.gov/strategy/IFCC_2001_ AnnualReport.pdf, accessed 7/02.

21. Judith H. Dobrzynski, "The Bidding Game: A Special Report; In Online Auction World, Hoaxes Aren't Easy To See," *The New York Times*, 2 June 2000, http://www.newyorktimes.com, accessed 7/02.

22. Matt Gallaway, "Internet Exchanges Face Antitrust Scrutiny," eCompany.com, 7 November 2000, http://www.ecompany.com/ articles/web/print/0,1650,8846,00.html, accessed 7/02.

23. Staff, "B2B or Not B2B—That's the Net Question," The Times, 7 May 2000, http://www.frontier-economics.com/news%20and%20 publications/press%20cuttings/articles/ecommerce1.htm, accessed 7/02; Erich Luening and Rachel Konrad, "FTC Green-lights Big Three Net Exchange," cnet.com, 11 September 2000, http://news. cnet.com/news/0-1007-200-2748632.html, accessed 7/02.

24. Owen Thomas, "Amazon.com Tests the Notion of Fixed Prices," eCompany.com, 28 September 2000, http://www.ecompany.com/ articles/web/print/0,1650,8527,00.html, accessed 7/02.

25. Adam Cohen, "Less Hassle, By Half: eBay's Baby," Time.com, 5 February 2001, http://www.time.com/time/magazine/printout/ 0,8816,97077,00.html, accessed 7/02.

26. Nielsen NetRatings, "Auction Sites Ever More Popular," Nua Internet Surveys, 28 June 2001, http://www.nua.ie/surveys/index.cgi?f= VS&art_id=905356927&rel=true, accessed 7/02.

27. Ephraim Schwartz and Brett Mendel, "Auctions Preserve Pricing," *InfoWorld*, 18 October 1999, http://ww1.infoworld.com/cgi-bin/ displayArchive.pl?/99/42/t23-42.12.htm, accessed 7/02.

28. Staff, "JCPenney and FairMarket(SM) Online Auction Site Standing Strong; Site Gains Momentum as More Consumers Bid on Overstocked Merchandise," *PR Newswire*, 30 May 2000, http://www. findarticles.com/cf_0/m4PRN/2000_May_30/62441674/print.jhtml, accessed 7/02; Elizabeth Blakey," Exclusive Interview: JCPenney. com," E-Commerce Times, 6 December 2001, http://www. ecommercetimes.com/success_stories/success-jcpenney.shtml, accessed 7/02.

29. David P. Hamilton, "The Price Isn't Right: Internet Pricing Has Turned Out to Be A Lot Trickier Than Retailers Expected," *The Wall Street Journal*, 12 February 2001, http://update2.wsj.com/public/ current/articles/SB981489999136217335.htm, accessed 7/02.

30. Kevin Featherly, "Personalized Pricing—Online Retail's Next Trend?" BizReport.com, 26 April 2000, http://exn.ca/stories/2000/04/26/03, accessed 7/02.

31. Michael Vizard, "Suppliers Toy with Dynamic Pricing—Users Face Prospect Of Daily Server Pricing Changes As Industry Pursues Profits," *InfoWorld*, 11 May 2001, http://iwsun4.infoworld.com/ articles/hn/xml/01/05/14/010514hndynamic.xml, accessed 7/02.

32. See notes 24 and 29.

33. Sari Kalin, "How Low Can Price Go," *Darwin Magazine*, April 2001, http://www.darwinmag.com/read/040101/low_content.html?printer= no, accessed 7/02.

34. Peter Edmonston, "One Web Retailer's Watchword: 'Free After Rebate'," *The Wall Street Journal*, 5 March 2001, pp. B1, B5.

35. Thomas E. Weber, "Priceline Woes Suggest Novelty Isn't Enough to Succeed on the Web," *The Wall Street Journal*, 16 October 2000, p. B1.

36. Business Editors, "ImproveNet Unveils Lavatory Laboratory: Online Bath Estimator Helps Homeowners Make Most of Powder Rooms," *Business Wire*, 14 January 2000, http://www.findarticles.com/cf_0/ m0EIN/2000_Jan_14/58575345/print.jhtml, accessed 7/02.

37. June Fletcher, "The Great E-Mortgage Bake-Off," *The Wall Street Journal*, 2 June 2000, p. W12.

38. T. Mullaney, "Don't Expect Miracles," *Business Week*, 16 April 2001, pp. EB8, 10.

39. Staff, "NewerRAM Launches Extranet Site for Up-to-Date Pricing and Product Information," *PR Newswire*, 18 May 2000, http://www.

findarticles.com/cf_0/m4PRN/2000_May_18/62438585/p1/article.
jhtml, accessed 7/02.

40. Greg Sandoval and Dawn Kawamoto, "Group-buying Site Mercata
to Shut Its Doors," CNET News.com, 4 January 2001, http://news.
cnet.com/news/0-1007-200-4372403.html?pt.ecompany.srch..ne,
accessed 7/02.

41. Joellen Perry, "Bulk Buying on the Web Rewards Togetherness," *U.S.
News & World Report*, 21 August 2000, p. 62; Dick Kelsey, "Bulk
Buying Site Mercata Heads South," Newsbytes, 4 January 2001,
http://www.findarticles.com/cf_0/m0NEW/2001_Jan_4/68876776/p1/
article.jhtml, accessed 7/02; John Dodge, "Mobs Tended to Avoid
Shopping At Online Demand Aggregators," WSJ.com, 16 January
2001, http://www.mobshop.com/ar011601, accessed 6/01; James
Turner, "'Group Buying': Bogus Bargains?" *Christian Science
Monitor*, 1 May 2000, http://www.csmonitor.com/durable/2000/05/01/
p20s2.htm, accessed 7/02; Bob Liu, "MobShop Discontinues
Consumer Service," 15 January 2001, Internet.com, http://www.
internetnews.com/bus-news/article.php/3_560081, accessed 7/02.

42. Adam Bryant, "Plastic Is Getting Smarter," *Newsweek*, 16 October
2000, p. 80; Tim Selby, "Smart Cards, E-Checks, & ACH Online
Payments Increasing Dramatically," ActivMediaResearch.com,
27 September 2000, e-mail alert, received 9/00.

43. Staff, "Dreams of a Cashless Society," The Economist, 5 May 2001,
vol.360, issue 8220, p.65; Staff, "PayPal Files $80.5M IPO," CNN
Money, 1 October 2001, http://money.cnn.com/2001/10/01/deals/
paypal, accessed 7/02; Nick Wingfield and Jathon Sapsford, "Ebay to
Buy PayPal for $1.4 Billion," *Wall Street Journal*, 9 July 2002, p.A6.

44. Geoffrey Smith, "A Penny-Ante Business Worth Billions,"
*BusinessWeek Online*, 23 April 2001, http://www.businessweek.com/
technology/content/apr2001/tc20010423_871.htm, accessed 7/02;
Joseph Nocera, "Easy Money," *Money*, August 2000, p.71; Julia
Angwin, "And How Will You Be Paying for That?" *The Wall Street
Journal*, 23 October 2000, p.R37.

45. Jane Bryant Quinn, "Web Sites Can't Demand Money, So They Ask
for It," *Lexington Herald Leader*, 15 July 2001, p.H3; Carol King,
"Amazon Honor System Draws Scrutiny," InternetNews,com, 6
February 2001, http://www.internetnews.com/ec-news/article/0,,4_
580621,00.html, accessed 7/02; Troy Wolverton, "Amazon Debuts
Honor System," Cnet.com, 6 February 2001, http://news.cnet.com/
news/0-1007-202-4723935.html?tag=pff, accessed 7/02.

46. Mindy Charski, "Online Bill Paying Is Still Waiting for the Big
Payoff," *U.S. News & World Report*, 6 March 2000, p. 57; Dean Foust,
"The Check Is in the e-Mail," *Business Week*, 30 October 2000,
pp. 120–122.

47. Anne Tergesen, "An Insurance Hunter's Weapon of Choice: The Web,"
*BusinessWeek*, 11 June 2001, pp. 157–158.

48. Nick Wingfield, "Corporate Sellers Put the Online Auctioneer On
Even Faster Track," *Wall Street Journal*, 1 June 2001, pp. A1,6;
Michael Bartlett, "Ebay Leads Surge In Online Auction Spending,"
bizreport.com, 28 June 2001, http://www.bizreport.com/article.
php?id=1639&width=800, accessed 7/02; Staff, "Americans Spent a
Record 556 Million Dollars in Online Auctions, Jumping 149 Percent
in Past Year, According to Nielsen/NetRatings and Harris Interactive,"
Nielsen NetRatings, 28 June 2001, http://www.nielsen-netratings.com/
pr/pr_010628.pdf, accessed 7/02; Barbara Pollack, "Ebay Woos High
Rollers,"Art in America," March 2001, http://www.findarticles.com/cf_
0/m1248/3_89/71558196/p1/article.jhtml, accessed 7/02; Martin Stone,
"Ebay Goes Hard Copy," *Newsbytes*, 4 May 2001, http://www.
findarticles.com/cf_0/m0NEW/2001_May_4/74095943/print.jhtml,
accessed 7/02; Russ Banham, "Sittin' on the Dock of eBay," CFO,
Winter 2000, http://www.findarticles.com/cf_0/m3870/15_16/
68160596/print.jhtml, accessed 7/02.

# Chapter 11

1. Toyota Annual Report 2001,"Gazoo: Unlimited Possibilities," 2001,
http://toyota.irweb.jp/IRweb/invest_rel/annualreport/annual_
report01/features/value01.html, accessed 7/02; David Bicknell,
"E-world Is Round, Not Flat," *Computer Weekly*, 22 June 2000, http://
www.findarticles.com/cf_0/m0COW/2000_June_22/63057304/p1/
article.jhtml, accessed 7/02; Staff, "The Stars of Asia—Managers," 2
July 2001, Business Week, http://www.businessweek.com/magazine/
content/01_27/b3739054.htm, accessed 7/02; Emily Thornton, Larry
Armstrong, and Kathleen Kerwin, "Toyota Unbound," *Business Week
International*, 1 May 2000, http://www.businessweek.com/2000/00_18/
b3679007.htm, accessed 7/02; David Welch, "Car Dealers Say: Follow
That Mouse," *Business Week*, 10 April 2000, pp. 106–110.

2. Jeff Bennett, "GM, Ford See Potential in Sites That Haven't Died,"
*Detroit Free Press*, 11 July 2001, http://www.auto.com/industry/
carcom11_20010711.htm, accessed 7/02; Press Release, "FordDirect,
AutoTrader.com Form Partnership to Expand Listings and Customer
Choices," Ford Motor Company and AutoTrader.com, 10 July 2001,
http://media.ford.com/newsroom/release_display.cfm?article_id=
8853&id=363&art_ids=0&bn=1 and http://www.autotrader.com/
about/press_releases/article.jtmpl?article_id=1012&ac_afflt=none,
accessed 7/02; Steve Hamm, "E-BIZ: Down But Hardly Out,"
*Business Week*, 26 March 2001, pp. 126–130.

3. Eric C. Evarts, "Why You Can't Cut Out the Middleman," *Christian
Science Monitor*, 2 April 2001, http://www.csmonitor.com/durable/
2001/04/02/fp11s1-csm.shtml, accessed 7/02.

4. Peter Coy, "Dark Days Ahead," 14 May 2001, *Business Week*,
pp. 42–44.

5. Business Editors, "Wal-Mart Tops 2002 Ranking of the Fortune
500; Oil Giant Exxon Mobil is No. 2 On List; GM Takes No. 3
Spot," *Business Wire*, 31 March 2002, http://www.findarticles.
com/cf_0/m0EIN/2002_March_31/84292078/p1/article.jhtml,
accessed 7/02.

6. Annual Report 2000, "Business Review: Plastics," General Electric
Co., 2001, http://www.ge.com/annual00/business/plastics.html ,
accessed 7/02; Staff, "B2BWorks Signs Strategic Advertising Alliances
With GE Services Network," *B2BWorks*, 27 March 2001, http://www.
b2bworks.com/corporate/pressrelease.cfm?releasenum=30&year=
2001, accessed 7/02; Bob Tedeschi, "GE Has a Bright Idea," *PC
Computing*, 14 May 2001, http://techupdate.zdnet.com/techupdate/
stories/main/0,14179,2711901,00.00.html, accessed 7/02; Alex Frangos,
"Just One Word: Plastics," *The Wall Street Journal*, 21 May 2001,
p. R20; Staff, "Older, Wiser, Webbier," The Economist, 30 June 2001,
vol.359, no.8228 p.10.

7. Matt Murray and Jathon Sapsford, "GE Reshuffles Its Dot-Com
Strategy to Focus on Internal 'Digitizing'," *The Wall Street Journal*,
4 April 2001, pp. B1,4; David Rocks, "The Web as a Lifeline,"
*Business Week e.BIZ*, 29 October 2001, pp. EB16–23.

8. Susan Carney, "Covisint Clicks Up Customers," *The Detroit News*,
9 September 2001, http://detnews.com/2001/technews/0109/09/b01-
288616.htm, accessed 7/02; Covisint, LLC, "Company Profile,"
Covisint, http://www.covisint.com/about/, accessed 7/02; Carlos
Grande, "Ford Recoups Investment in Covisint Web Exchange,"
FinancialTimes.com, 1 July 2001, http://www.covisint.com/about/
pressroom/news, accessed 7/02; Lisa D. Connell, "Autos' New
Driving Range," Industrial Distribution, October 2000, http://www.
findarticles.com/cf_0/m3263/10_89/66279847/print.jhtml, accessed
7/02; William J. Holstein, "Detroit Reaches into Its Bag of E-tricks,"
*U.S. News & World Report*, 29 January 2001, p. 31.

9. Forrester Research, "More Firms Using Online Procurement," *Nua*,
23 July 2001, http://www.nua.net/surveys/index.cgi?f=VS&art_id=

905357007&rel=true, accessed 7/02; Steve Hamm, "E-Biz: Down But Hardly Out," *Business Week,* 26 March 2001, pp. 126–130.

10. South China Morning Post, "E-Procurement Could Save a Fortune," Nua Net Surveys, 18 December 2001, http://www.nua.net/surveys/index.cgi?f=VS&art_id=905357504&rel=true, accessed 7/02; Keith Regan, "Report: B2B E-Commerce Gaining Strength," E-Commerce Times, 17 January 2002, http://www.ecommercetimes.com/perl/story/?id=15847, accessed 7/02; Staff, "Mid-Sized Companies Are Rapidly Moving to the Internet for Purchasing, Citing Faster Order Time and Convenience, According to a New American Express Study," American Express, 5 December 2000, http://home3.americanexpress.com/corp/latestnews/ept_study.asp, accessed 7/02.

11. Adrian Michaels and Betty Liu, "Online Incentives Sought," *Financial Times,* 26 April 2001, http://specials.ft.com/pharmaceuticals2001/FT3176MN0MC.html, accessed 7/02.

12. Dell Press Room, "New Austin Dell Direct Multimedia Kiosk Gives Consumers First-Hand Experience With Dell Products," *Dell,* 27 June 2002, http://www.dell.com/us/en/gen/corporate/press/pressoffice_us_2002-06-27-aus-000.htm, accessed 7/02; John H. Sheridan, "Dell Courts Customers Online," Industry Week/IW, 3 April 2000, http://www.industryweek.com/CurrentArticles/asp/articles.asp?ArticleID=795, accessed 7/02; David Shook, "The Winner of the PC Price Wars: Dell," *Business Week Online,* 1 May 2001, http://www.businessweek.com/bwdaily/dnflash/may2001/nf2001051_655.htm accessed 7/02; Andrew Park and Peter Burrows, "Dell, the Conqueror," *Business Week,* 24 September 2001, pp. 92-102.

13. Arlene Weintraub, "Can Gateway Survive in a Smaller Pasture?" *Business Week,* 10 September 2001, p. 48.

14. Mark W. Vigoroso, "Online Travel Success Forces Offline Agents to Adapt," *E-Commerce Times,* 10 September 2001, http://www.ecommercetimes.com/perl/printer/13426/, accessed 7/02; Rob Spiegel, "Middlemen Join List of Endangered Species," eCommerce Business, 20 November 2000, http://graffiti.virgin.net/www3.org/newintermediaries.htm, accessed 7/01.

15. Charles Haddad, "Ground Wars," *Business Week,* 21 May 2001, pp. 64–68.

16. Faith Keenan, "Warehouse Trouble," *Business Week,* 20 November 2000, pp. 125–126.

17. Frederic Jallat, "Disintermediation in Question: New Economy, New Networks, New Middlemen." *Business Horizons,* March 2001, http://www.findarticles.com/cf_0/m1038/2_44/73000998/print.jhtml, accessed 7/02.

18. Michael Pastore, "2001: An Online Travel Odyssey," *CyberAtlas,* 16 January 2002, http://cyberatlas.internet.com/markets/travel/print/0,,6071_956051,00.html, accessed 7/02; Saul Hansell, "Web Sales of Airline Tickets Are Making Hefty Advances," *New York Times.com,* 4 July 2001, http://www.nytimes.com/2001/07/04/technology/04FLY.html?searchpv=day03, accessed 7/02.

19. Ken Cottrill, "Taking Root," *Traffic World,* 12 February 2001, http://www.findarticles.com/cf_0/m0VOO/7_265/70461244/p1/article.jhtml, accessed 7/02; Sherri C. Ranta, "Airport Area Businesses Bloom with Flower Power," *Miami Today,* 8 February 2001, http://miamitodaynews.com/news/010208/story4.shtml, accessed 7/02; Howard LaFranchi, "Colombia's Hope: Less Coca, More Carnations," *Christian Science Monitor,* 24 March 2000, http://www.csmonitor.com/durable/2000/03/24/p1s5.htm, accessed 7/02.

20. Calmetta Coleman, "Pruning Costs," *The Wall Street Journal,* 12 February 2001, p.R30.

21. Janis Mara, "Amazon.com: Best E-Commerce Experience," *Brandweek,* 5 June 2000, http://www.findarticles.com/cf_0/m0BDW/23_41/62918981/print.jhtml, accessed 7/02; Emily Thornton, "Can Amazon Make It?" *Business Week,* 10 July 2000, pp. 38–43.

22. Stacy Perman, "Why the Web Can't Kill the Middleman," *Business2.0,* April 2001, http://www.business2.com/articles/mag/0,1640,9600,FF.html, accessed 7/01; Jason Anders, "Sibling Rivalry," *The Wall Street Journal,* 17 July 2000, p. R16.

23. Gene Marcial, "Listening to the Staples' Story," *BusinessWeek Online,* 23 April 2002, http://www.businessweek.com/bwdaily/dnflash/apr2002/nf20020423_9778.htm, accessed 7/02; Sarah L. Roberts-Witt, "Site Design as Business Decision," *PC Magazine,* 25 September 2001, http://www.pcmag.com/print_article/0,3048,a=12672,00.asp, accessed 7/02; Jason Anders, "Sibling Rivalry," *The Wall Street Journal,* 17 July 2000, p. R16; Joellen Perry, "The Best of the Web," *U.S. News & World Report,* 8 October 2001, pp. 59–60; Michael Pastore, "Consumers Shift from Catalogs to the Web," *CyberAtlas,* 10 December 2001, http://www.cyberatlas.com/markets/retailing/print/0,,6061_937191,00.html, accessed 7/02.

24. John Erik Garr, "Secrets of the You-Universe," *Context Magazine,* October/November 2000, http://www.contextmag.com/setFrameRedirect.asp?src=/archives/200010/CEOUsersGuide.asp, accessed 7/02; Mohanbir Sawhney, "Making New Markets," *Business2.0,* March 2000, http://www.business2.com/articles/mag/print/0,1643,13464,FF.html, accessed 7/02.

25. Staff, "The Passive Shopping Network," *Business 2.0,* September 2000, http://www.business2.com/articles/mag/0,1640,14067,FF.html, accessed 7/02.

26. Michael Pastore, "U.S. E-commerce Spikes in Q4 2001," *CyberAtlas,* http://cyberatlas.internet.com/markets/retailing/article/0,,6061_977751,00.html#table, accessed 7/02.

27. Bob Tedeschi, "Online Retailers Grapple with the Age-Old Problem of Handling Returned Merchandise," *New York Times,* 28 May 2001, p. C6.

28. Michael Pastore, "Brand Web Sites Come Up Short with Many Consumers," *CyberAtlas,* 24 April 2001, http://cyberatlas.internet.com/markets/advertising/print/0,,5941_751271,00.html, accessed 7/02; Emily Nelson, "Shoppers Find Web Sites Fail to Satisfy Them," *The Wall Street Journal,* 20 April 2001, p. B8.

29. Michael Pastore, "Online Shopping a Tough Sell for Online Retailers," *CyberAtlas,* 17 July 2001, http://cyberatlas.internet.com/markets/retailing/print/0,,6061_803191,00.html, accessed 7/02; Information Resources, "Security," Shop.org, 23 April 2001, http://www.shop.org/learn/stats_ebizz_security.html, accessed 7/02; Ellen Neuborne, "It's All About Trust," Business Week e.biz, 3 December 2001, p. EB10.

30. Jeanette Brown, "Service, Please," *Business Week e.biz,* 23 October 2000, pp. EB48–50.

31. Ellen Neuborne, "Seamless Shopping," Business Week, 20 November 2000, p. EB18.

32. Ronald J. Bauerly and Paul Thistlewaite, "Retailing 2010: The Potential Impact of the Internet," Marketing Management Association, 2000, pp. 27–32; William M. Bulkeley, "What's Ahead for . . . Retailing," *The Wall Street Journal,* 25 June 2001, p. R16; Stephanie Miles, "Netkey Transforms Kiosks into E-Salespeople," *The Wall Street Journal,* 17 May 2001, p.B6.

33. Brad Stone, "Look Out, Jeff Bezos," *Newsweek,* 27 November 2000, p. 64.

34. Michael Mahoney, "Report: Despite Sales Slump, E-Tailers Turning More Surfers into Buyers," *E-Commerce Times,* 7 June 2001, http://www.ecommercetimes.com/perl/story/11070.html, accessed 7/02; Michael Totty, "Making the Sale," *Wall Street Journal E-Commerce,* 24 September 2001, p. R6.

35. ActivMedia Research, "Traditional Retailers Selling More Online," 20 June 2001, Nua Internet Surveys, http://www.nua.ie/surveys/index.cgi?f=VS&art_id=905356886&rel=true, accessed 7/02; Rebecca

Quick, "Returns to Sender," *The Wall Street Journal*, 17 July 2000, p. R8; Clare Saliba, "Study: Half of E-tailers Are Turning a Profit," E-Commerce Times, 13 March 2001, http://www.ecommercetimes.com/perl/printer/8142/, accessed 7/02.

36. Carolyn Said, "Teaming Internet, Stores, Catalogs Makes Lots of Cents for JC Penney," 27 November 2000, *Lexington Herald Leader*, http://www.kentuckyconnect.com/, accessed 11/00.

37. Rebecca Quick, "Returns to Sender," *The Wall Street Journal*, 17 July 2000, p. R8; Katherine Hobson, "Bucking the E-biz Trend," U.S. News & World Report, 4 June 2001, pp. 36–38; Nick Wingfield, "As Web Sales Grow Mail-Order Sellers Are Benefiting Most," *The Wall Street Journal*, 2 May 2001, p. B8.

38. Michael Pastore, "Half of American Adults Now Shop Online," *CyberAtlas*, 24 April 2001, http://cyberatlas.internet.com/markets/retailing/article/0,,6061_751021,00.htm, accessed 7/02.

39. Allison Stein Wellner, "A New Cure for Shoppus Interruptus," *American Demographics*, 1 August 2000, vol.22, no.8, p.44.

40. Ellen Neuborne, "No Buy? Then Bye-Bye," *Business Week e.biz*, 16 April 2001, p. EB6.

41. Staff, "The Heyday of the Auction," *The Economist*, 24 July 1999, vol. 352, no.8129, p.67; Harris Interactive, "Online Auctions," Shop.org, 31 January 2001, http://www.shop.org/learn/stats_ebizz_auctions.html, accessed 7/02.

42. Robert D. Hof, "Desperately Seeking Search Technology," *Business Week*, 24 September 2001, p. 89.

43. Staff, "A Crash Course in Customer Relationship Management," Harvard Management Update, March 2000, pp. 3–5; B. Joseph Pine II, Don Peppers, and Martha Rogers, "Do You Want to Keep Your Customers Forever," *Harvard Business Review*, March–April 1995, pp. 103–113; Patricia B. Seybold, "Get Inside the Lives of Your Customers," *Harvard Business Review*, May 2001, pp. 81–89; Brian Christie, "Web Services Are Future for Business Services," *Digitrends.net*, 17 May 2001, http://www.digitrends.net/ebiz/13643_15798.html, accessed 7/02; Staff, "Customer Relationship Management," Progressive Dynamics, http://www.progressive-dynamics.com/crm.htm, accessed 7/02; Katherine Bull, "Are Three Channels Better Than One?" *InfoWorld*, 18 December 1999, http://iwsun4.infoworld.com/articles/op/xml/99/12/20/991220opnewsdesk.xml, accessed 6/00; Bob Trott, "Customer Relationship Management Hailed," *InfoWorld*, 25 October 2000, http://iwsun4.infoworld.com/articles/hn/xml/00/10/25/001025hncustomers.xml, accessed 7/02; Jessica Davis, "Who Is Taking Ownership of Your Company's CRM Implementation Strategy?" *InfoWorld*, 18 December 2000, http://www.infoworld.com/articles/op/xml/00/12/18/001218opprophet.xml, accessed 7/02; Martin LaMonica, Getting Customer Service Basics Right," *InfoWorld*, 11 December 2000, http://www.infoworld.com/articles/op/xml/00/12/11/001211opnewsdesk.xml, accessed 7/02; Constance Gustke, "eCRM: Connecting with Customers," *Internet World Magazine*, 1 March 2001, http://www.talisma.com/press/articles/internet_world_001031/index.asp, accessed 7/02; Todd Coopee, "E-CRM Calls Customer King," *InfoWorld*, 26 June 2000, http://www.infoworld.com/articles/es/xml/00/06/26/000626escrm.xml, accessed 7/02; Keith H. Hammonds, "Value Propositions," Fast Company, August 2000, http://www.fastcompany.com/online/37/ideazone.html, accessed 7/02.

44. The History Channel, "Henry Ford," http://www.historychannel.com/, accessed 7/01; Frontenac Motor Company, "The Ford Model T," http://www.modelt.ca/background-fs.html, accessed 7/02; Staff, "EGM Head Pursues Broad e-commerce Plan," InfoWorld, 6 March 2000, http://www.infoworld.com/articles/hn/xml/00/03/06/000306hnhotseat.xml, accessed 7/02.

## Chapter 12

1. Maria Mallory, ". . . A Tasket?" *U.S. News & World Report*, 17 November 1997, p. 65.

2. Karl Greenberg, "Follow the Money," *Brandweek*, 5 June 2000, http://www.findarticles.com/cf_0/m0BDW/23_41/62918975/print.jhtml, accessed 7/02.

3. Karen Lundegaard, "Volvo Plans Online Ad Campaign for Latest Launch," *Wall Street Journal*, 25 September 2000, p. B14; Suzanne Vranica, "Volvo Campaign Tests New Media Waters," *Wall Street Journal*, 16 March 2001, p. B5.

4. Ellen Neuborne, "Coaxing With Catalogs," *BusinessWeek e.Biz*, 6 August 2001, p. EB6.

5. Alexei Barrioneuvo, "Chevron and BP Amoco Test Web Ads at Pumps," *Wall Street Journal*, 12 June 2000, p. B6; Staff, "The Sizzle: What's Up in Digital Marketing and Advertising," *Business2.0*, April 2001, http://www.business2.com/articles/mag/0,1640,14635,FF.html, accessed 7/02.

6. Sarah Ellison, "Boo.com: Buried by Badly Managed Buzz," *Wall Street Journal*, 23 May 2000, p. B10; Jamie Doward, "From Boo to Bust and Back Again," *The Observer*, 26 August 2001, http://www.guardian.co.uk/internetnews/story/0,7369,542632,00.html, accessed 7/02.

7. Thomas E. Weber, "Can You Say 'Cheese'? Intrusive Web Ads Could Drive Us Nuts," *Wall Street Journal*, 21 May 2001, p. B1.

8. Rex Briggs, "Measuring Success," Interactive Advertising Bureau,1, no.3 (July 2001), http://www.iab.net/measuringsuccess/index.html accessed 7/02.

9. Rex Briggs, "Measuring Success," Interactive Advertising Bureau,1, no.2 (June 2001), http://www.iab.net/measuringsuccess/index.html accessed 7/02.

10. Kenneth Hein, "Pepsi on Yahoo!" *MediaWeek*, 11, no. 42, 12 November 2001, p. IQ7.

11. Christopher Saunders, "Sites Trending Toward Aggressive Web Advertising," *CyberAtlas*, 30 November 2001, http://cyberatlas.internet.com/markets/advertising/article/0,1323,5941_931541,00.html, accessed 7/02.

12. Tom Hespos, "The Dilemma of Ad-Blocking Software," ClickZ.com, 19 April 2001, http://www.clickz.com/media/media_buy/article.php/840581, accessed 7/02; Terry Lefton, "Disappearing Act," *The Industry Standard*, 23 April 2001, http://www.thestandard.com/article/0,1902,23640,00.html, accessed 7/02.

13. Lawrence Pintak, "Attack of the Killer Audio Ads," ChannelSeven.com, 22 November 2000, http://www.turboads.com/richmedia_news/2000rmn/rmn20001122.shtml, accessed 7/02.

14. Danny Sullivan, "Search Engine Ratings," 29 April 2002, Jupiter Media Metrix, http://www.searchenginewatch.com/reports/mediametrix.html, accessed 7/02 ; Staff, "Searches Per Day," SearchEngineWatch.com, July 2002, http://www.searchenginewatch.com/reports/perday.html, accessed 7/02; Keen.com, "Consumer Daily Question Study," Keen.com and Lewis, Mobilio & Associates, 12 February 2001, http://www.keen.com/documents/corpinfo/pressstudy.asp, accessed 7/02; Christopher Saunders, "Study: Search Listings Better at Branding, Sales Than Banners," InternetNews—Advertising Report, 13 February 2001, http://www.internetnews.com/IAR/article/0,,12_587751,00.html, accessed 7/02; InternetNews, "Search Engines Beat Banners," Nua Internet Surveys, 14 February 2001, http://www.nua.net/surveys/index.cgi?f=VS&art_id=905356456&rel=true, accessed 7/01.

15. Margaret Mannix, "Search Me, Please," *U.S. News & World Report*, 30 July 2001, p. 37; Alex Salkever, "Search Engines: Leading Us Astray?" *Business Week*, 6 August 2001, p. 8; Bill Koelzer, "The Easy

Way to Be #1 on Many Search Engines," RealtyTimes.com, 24 January 2001, http://realtytimes.com/rtnews/rtapages/20010124_search.htm, accessed 7/02.

16. John Gaffney, "The Online Advertising Comeback," *Business2.0*, June 2002, http://www.business2.com/articles/mag/0,1640,40430,FF.html, accessed 7/02; Mick Brady & Lori Enos, "Experts Echo Net Ad Bureau Findings," *E-Commerce Times*, 20 April 2000, http://www.ecommercetimes.com/perl/printer/3057/, accessed 7/02; Michael Pastore, "It's Diversify or Die for Online Media Firms," *CyberAtlas*, 19 December 2001, http://cyberatlas.internet.com/markets/advertising/print/0,,5941_943041,00.html, accessed 7/02; New Media Group of PricewaterhouseCoopers, "IAB Internet Advertising Revenue Report," Interactive Advertising Bureau, December 2001, http://www.iab.org/, accessed 7/02.

17. Owen Thomas, "Way Beyond the Banner," *Business2.0*, June 2002, http://www.business2.com/articles/mag/0,1643,40552,FF.html, accessed 7/02; Jupiter Media Metrix, "Entertainment Sites Running More Self-Promotional Online Ads Than Any Other Media Companies, Says Jupiter Media Metrix," AdRelevance.com, 28 February 2001, http://www.adrelevance.com/press/press_releases.jsp?pr=010228, accessed 7/02.

18. Staff, "Internet Advertising Bureau (IAB) Finds Growing Usage Of Larger Ad Units," Internet Advertising Bureau (IAB), 3 April 2001, http://www.IAB.net/, accessed 7/02.

19. John Buskin, "Imagine This," *Wall Street Journal*, 14 January 2002, http://online.wsj.com/, accessed 2/02; Jeffery Graham, "Internet Advertising Best Practices," Clickz.com, 23 October 2000, http://clickz.com/print/jsp?article=2651, accessed 7/02; Katherine Hobson, "Ads That Just Don't Click—No, Literally," *U.S. News & World Report*, 12 March 2001, p. 56.

20. Staff, "Entertainment Sites Post Too Many House Ads," *Digitrends.net*, 2 March 2001, http://www.digitrends.net/ena/index_14709.html, accessed 7/02; Jupiter Media Metrix, "Entertainment Sites Running More Self-Promotional Online Ads Than Any Other Media Companies, Says Jupiter Media Metrix," AdRelevance.com, 28 February 2001, http://www.adrelevance.com/press/press_releases.jsp?pr=010228, accessed 7/02.

21. Michael Pastore, "Web Sponsorships Tackle ROI Debate," *Ad Resource*, 9 November 2000, http://adres.internet.com/feature/article/0,1401,8961_507481,00.html, accessed 7/02.

22. Aaron Barnhart, "BMW Car-Chase Ads Raise the Standard for Internet Movies," *Lexington Herald-Leader*, 25 June 2001, p. 19; Anthony Vagnoni, "Action Mini-Movies Feature Top Actors and Cool Cars," AdAge, 23 July 2001, http://www.adage.com/news.cms?newsId=32430, accessed 7/02.

23. Michael Pastore, "Webcasters Spread the Gospel of Webcast Advertising," *CyberAtlas*, 9 May 2001, http://cyberatlas.internet.com/markets/advertising/print/0,,5941_762271,00.html, accessed 7/02; Carol Pickering, "Live! From Merrill Lynch?" *Business2.0*, May 2001, http://www.business2.com/articles/mag/0,1640,14703,FF.html, accessed 7/02.

24. Pamela Parker, "DoubleClick, Vindigo, MoniSky Team for Mobile Ad Tests," InternetNews-Advertising Report, 6 November 2000, http://www.internetnews.com/IAR/article/0,,12_503811,00.html, accessed 7/02.

25. Staff, "Small Business Online Promotions Focus of SmartAge.com-Millward Brown IntelliQuest Survey," *PR Newswire*, 31 October 2000, http://www.findarticles.com/cf_0/m4PRN/2000_Oct_31/66570101/print.jhtml, accessed 7/02.

26. Ronna Abramson, "Little Safety in Ad Numbers," *The Industry Standard*, 26 January 2001, http://www.thestandard.com/article/display/0,1151,21735,00.html, accessed 7/02.

27. Suzanne Vranica, "Web Sites Seek to Turn Data into Dollars," *Wall Street Journal*, 27 July 2001, p. B8.

28. Christopher Saunders, "Seeing Online Ads Seems to Drive Conversions," 13 November 2000, *CyberAtlas*, http://cyberatlas.internet.com/markets/advertising/article/0,,5941_509941,00.html, accessed 7/02.

29. Rex Briggs, "Measuring Success," Internet Advertising Bureau 1, no. 2, June 2001, http://www.iab.net/, accessed 7/02.

30. James P. Santella, "Couponing Expected to Increase in 2001," Santella and Associates, http://www.santella.com/Trends.htm, accessed 7/02; Cecily Fraser, "Sites Direct Consumers to Clipless Coupons," CBS.MarketWatch.com, 26 June 2000, http://aol.marketwatch.com/source/blq/aol/archive/20000626/news/current/consumer.asp, accessed 7/01; Roger O. Crockett, "Penny-Pinchers' Paradize," *BusinessWeek e.Biz*, 22 January 2001, p. EB12.

31. Business Editors, "General Mills Launches Integrated Promotion to Enhance Pop Secret Brand Online; Promotions.com Chosen to Develop Integrated Internet Promotion for Leading Consumer Foods Company," *Business Wire*, 26 June 2000, http://www.findarticles.com/cf_0/m0EIN/2000_June_26/62915915/print.jhtml, accessed 7/02.

32. David Ferris, "Drowning in Email Overload? Ferris Research Forecasts It Will Only Get Worse," Ferris Research, 31 July 2000, http://www.ferris.com/, accessed 7/01; Theresa Forsman, "Are You Serving Spam?" *Business Week*, 29 May 2001, http://www.businessweek.com/smallbiz/content/may2001/sb20010529_737.htm, accessed 7/02; Tom Yager, "Customer, May I? Getting the OK to Sell," *InfoWorld*, 22 January 2001, http://www.itworld.com/Man/2695/IW010122tcpermission, accessed 7/02; Dylan Tweney, "Radically New E-mail Marketing Campaigns," eCompany.com, 30 November 2000, http://www.business2.com/articles/web/0,1653,8925,00.html, accessed 7/02; Jakob Nielsen, "Jakob Nielsen's Alertbox Mailing List Usability," eCompany.com, 20 August 2000, http://www.useit.com/alertbox/20000820.html, accessed 7/02.

33. Claudia Eller, "AOL Time Warner's Marketing Wizardry," Los Angeles Times, 2 December 2001, http://www.latimes.com/business/la-000095782dec02.story, accessed 1/02; Frank Ahrens, "'Lord of the Rings' Employs 2-Prong Marketing Method," *Lexington Herald Leader*, 20 December 2001, pp. C1, C2; Ronald Grover, "Harry Potter and the Marketer's Millstone," *Business Week*, 15 October 2001, pp. 90, 93; Nancy Wong Bryan, "Universal Catches Online Marketing Fever," *Digitrends*, December 2000, http://www.digitrends.net/marketing/13638_14480.html, accessed 7/02; Brad King, "The Force Is With Harry Potter," *Wired*, 16 November 2001, http://www.wired.com/news/print/0,1294,48399,00.html, accessed 7/02; Julia Day, "Harry Potter Fans Oppose Coke Deal," *The Guardian*, 18 October 2001, http://media.guardian.co.uk/marketingandpr/story/0,7494,576422,00.html, accessed 7/02; Becky Anderson, "Harry Potter Casts Marketing Spell," CNN, 4 November 2001, http://www.cnn.com/2001/WORLD/europe/11/02/potter.marketing, accessed 7/02; Martin Lindstrom, "Is Harry Committing Suicide?" Clickz.com, 4 December 2001, http://www.clickz.com/brand/brand_mkt/article.php/932631, accessed 7/02; Christopher Saunders, "Yahoo!, Sony Flesh Out Movie Marketing Details," InternetNews.com, 17 October 2001, http://www.internetnews.com/IAR/article/0,,12_905381,00.html, accessed 7/02; Staff, "Coca-Cola Controversy," ABCNews.com, 8 November 2001, http://abcnews.go.com/sections/GMA/GoodMorningAmerica/GMA011108Harry_potter.htm, accessed 7/02.

## Chapter 13

1. SBA, "Starting Your Business: What Is A Small Business?" SBA, 4 September 2001, http://www.sba.gov/starting/indexwhatis.html, accessed 7/02.

2. Joanne H. Pratt, "Homebased Business: The Hidden Economy," Small Business Research Summary, Number 194, March 2000, US SBA, http://www.sba.gov/ADVO/research/rs194.pdf, accessed 7/02.

3. Roger Brooksbank, "Essential Characteristics for an Effective Marketing Plan," *Marketing Intelligence & Planning,* 9, no. 7, 1991, pp. 17–20.

4. Kim Bayne, "What Now, Webmaster?" American Demographics Marketing Tools, August 1997, p.22.

5. Shelly Reese, "The Very Model of a Modern Marketing Plan," American Demographics, January/February 1996, http://www.americandemographics.com/, accessed 8/01.

6. Russell Abratt, Maria Beffon, and John Ford, "Relationship Between Marketing, Planning, and Annual Budgeting," *Marketing Intelligence & Planning* 12, no. 1, 1994, pp. 22–28.

7. Business & High-Tech Editors, "Monster.com Announces Strategic Alliance With AOL Europe—Extends AOL Relationship," *Business Wire,* 15 November 2001, http://www.findarticles.com/cf_0/m0EIN/2001_Nov_15/80079943/p1/article.jhtml, accessed 7/02; Staff, "Monster.com Site Traffic Soars to Record Heights in Europe; Monster.com Shatters Previous Record Highs in Europe with 1.2 Million Unique Visitors in September," *Business Wire,* 30 October 2001, http://www.findarticles.com/cf_0/m0EIN/2001_Oct_30/79541097/print.jhtml, accessed 7/02; Business/Technology Editors," Site Traffic Numbers Reflective of Monster's Global Brand Leadership," *Business Wire,* 15 October 2001, http://www.findarticles.com/cf_0/m0EIN/2001_Oct_15/79117658/print.jhtml, accessed 7/02; Business/Technology Editors, "Monster.com to Provide Global Online Recruiting Solutions for Ernst & Young," *Business Wire,* 21 August 2001, http://www.findarticles.com/cf_0/m0EIN/2001_August_21/77344653/print.jhtml, accessed 7/02; Staff, "Imanager Profile," *Inter@ctive Week* 8, no. 30 (6 August 2001): 43; Brian Farrey, "Monster.com Hopes for Big Win After Yesterday's Big Game," *Computerworld* 35, no. 5 (29 January 2001): 38–41; Adrienne Mand, "Job Sites Pounding the Web," *Advertising Age* 72, no. 34, 20 August 2001, pp. 37–40; Staff, "The Web-Connected Generation," *Futurist* 35, no. 5, September/October 2001, pp. 9–14; Julekha Dash, "Labor Department Teams with Monster.com," Computerworld 35, no. 26, 25 June 2001, p. 12; David Goetzl, "ESPN and Monster Strike Deal," *Advertising Age* 72, no. 24, 11 June 2001, pp. 50–52; Staff, "Wanted: E-Recruits," *PC Magazine* 20, no. 8, 8 May 2001, p. 72; Anne Fisher, "Surviving the Downturn," *Fortune* 143, no. 7, 2 April 2001, pp. 98–105.

## Chapter 14

1. Kim Guenther, "Creating Cross-Functional Web Teams," *Online,* May/June 2001, pp. 79–81.

2. Matt Carmichael, "2001's Median Prices for Full-site Development," *BtoB: The Magazine for Marketing and e-Commerce Strategists,* 14 May 2001, http://www.netb2b.com/webPriceIndex/, accessed 7/02.

3. Matt Carmichael, "Time to Build: Development Costs Have Dropped, Meaning," *BtoB: The Magazine for Marketing and e-Commerce Strategists,* 14 May 2001, http://www.btobonline.com/cgi-bin/article.pl?id=5972, accessed 7/02.

4. Matt Carmichael, "2001's Median Prices for Full-Site Development," *BtoB: The Magazine for Marketing and e-Commerce Strategists,* 14 May 2001, http://www.btobonline.com/webPriceIndex/, accessed 7/02.

5. Michael Pastore, "Privacy Remains a Concern for Online Consumers," *CyberAtlas,* 11 June 2001, http://cyberatlas.internet.com/markets/advertising/print/0,,5941_781741,00.html, accessed 7/02.

6. Darlene Fichter, "Designing Usable Sites: A State of Mind," *Online,* January 2001, http://www.findarticles.com/cf_0/m1388/1_25/68656987/print.jhtml, accessed 7/02.

7. Alexei Oreskovic, "Testing 1-2-3," *The Industry Standard,* 5 March 2001, http://www.findarticles.com/cf_0/m0HWW/9_4/71561484/print.jhtml, accessed 7/02.

8. Darlene Fichter, "Testing the Web Site Usability Waters," *Online,* March 2001, http://www.findarticles.com/cf_0/m1388/2_25/70910893/print.jhtml, accessed 7/02.

9. Alison J. Head, "DemystiFying Intranet Design: Five Guidelines for Building Usable Sites," *Online,* July 2000, http://www.findarticles.com/cf_0/m1388/4_24/63568431/print.jhtml, accessed 7/02.

10. Laura Wonnacott, "Web Site Design Is a Combination of Both Science and Art That Satisfies Many Users," *InfoWorld,* 31 January 2000, http://www.infoworld.com/articles/op/xml/00/01/31/000131opsavvy.xml, accessed 7/02.

11. Melinda Patterson Grenier, "Traffic to News Web Sites Over Two Days Sets Records," *Wall Street Journal Online,* 13 September 2001, http://interactive.wsj.com/articles/SB100037289444669854.htm, accessed 7/02.

12. Janet Bingham Bernstel and Hollis Thomases, "Writing Words for the Web," *Bank Marketing* 33, no. 2, March 2001, pp. 16–21.

13. Michael Heim, "The Feng Shui of Virtual Worlds," Computer Graphics World, January 2001, http://cgw.pennnet.com/Articles/Article_Display.cfm?Section=Archives&Subsection=Display&ARTICLE_ID=89345&KEYWORD=The%20Feng%20Shui%20of%20Virtual%20Worlds, accessed 7/02.

14. Anne Clyde, "Bobby Approves—Web Accessibility for the Print Disabled," *Teacher Librarian* 28, no. 4, April 2001, pp. 52–54.

15. Staff, "Tips for Creating a Senior-Friendly Web Site," *Geriatrics* 56, no. 6, June 2001, p. 17.

16. ActivMedia, "Website Technical Sophistication Succeeds; Smoke & Mirror Sites Fail," Research LLC, 7 August 2001, http://www.activmediaresearch.com/magic/pr080701.html accessed 7/02.

17. Jenny Donelan, "Adobe Goes 3D," Computer Graphics World, July 2001, http://www.findarticles.com/cf_0/m0CGW/7_24/76895873/print.jhtml, accessed 8/01; Julie James, "Adobe Acrobat 5.0," *School Library Journal,* July 2001, http://www.findarticles.com/cf_0/m1299/7_47/76654461/print.jhtml, accessed 7/02; Test Center Analysis, "Streaming Media for the Enterprise," *InfoWorld,* 14 February 2000, http://www.britannica.com/magazine/print?content_id=161252, accessed 8/01.

# Index

*Key terms appear in boldface type.*

Has the internet ~~changed~~ made the way marketing more unethical markets Do Business